The Life of Sarmiento

The Life of Sarmiento

BY

ALLISON WILLIAMS BUNKLEY

GREENWOOD PRESS, PUBLISHERS
NEW YORK

Reprinted by arrangement
with Princeton University Press

First Greenwood Reprinting 1969

Library of Congress Catalogue Card Number 77-90475

SBN 8371-2392-5

PRINTED IN UNITED STATES OF AMERICA

IN MEMORY OF MY MOTHER

FOREWORD

THE NINETEENTH CENTURY witnessed the passage of a unique person across the stage of Spanish American history. He never gained the stature of a true universal genius, nor could he be pointed to as a worldwide leader in any one field. But the diversity of his accomplishments, the success of his endeavors, the strength of his personality, and the literary style that expressed them combine to make him the most striking figure in the eventful Latin American historical drama.

The western frontier province of San Juan in Argentina founded its first school in 1815, and its teachers were soon surprised by the alertness and intelligence of one of its youngest pupils. Ten years later, the people of San Juan wondered at a young man of fifteen who neglected the serious pursuit of shopkeeping for the frivolities of reading. In the years that followed, many parts of America witnessed the activities of this young man. The miners of Copiapó, Chile, were amazed to see him laboriously translating Sir Walter Scott by the light of a lamp far beneath the earth's surface. The literary circles of cultured Santiago de Chile were startled at the appearance of a young writer with a new, fresh, and powerful style; and the politicians of that city were quick to seek his aid when they discovered the power of his pen. Europe, North Africa, and the United States caught a glimpse of a man of thirty-five as he traveled through the civilized world, learning from his observations what he could not learn from his books. Small local tyrants and the great dictator Rosas were sorely injured by the journalistic attacks of this man; and when the Argentine Republic finally freed itself from dictatorial bondage and set out to create for itself a constitutional government, he was a leader in the national organization.

The United States received from the Argentine Republic

a new minister plenipotentiary who proved to be one of the most potent instruments for friendship that those two countries had ever known. He returned to his own nation to assume the presidency, and his administration stands out as the most progressive period of the nineteenth-century history of that country. This man founded agrarian communities to settle the wild Argentine Pampa. He founded newspapers to inform the Argentine people. He founded schools to educate the Argentine youth. He offered his nation a new political system that he thought would solve its political problems, and he did much to make this system a reality.

The history of Spanish America is overloaded with the names of presidents, dictators, and men on horseback. Some were great, some mediocre. In their own nations they are studied by every schoolboy and debated by every historian; outside their own countries they are for the most part unknown. But one name stands out above this mass of historical figures. It is the name of a man whose life transcended the geographic limits and social categories that confine most of the leaders of the Ibero-American continent. Domingo Faustino Sarmiento cannot be enclosed within the borders of his Argentine homeland, for an entire continent was affected in one way or another by the fact that he lived. His personality cannot be confined in one category. He was a thinker, a writer, a diplomat, a journalist, a sociologist, an educator, and a politician who did much to change the history of Argentina.

Above all, Domingo Faustino Sarmiento was an immense personality. Born with nothing, he created his own life with the tools at hand. It is to this act of creation that this biography is dedicated.

My study of the life of Domingo Sarmiento was initiated in 1944. At that time my research was limited to published works in the United States, especially in Princeton and at the Pan American Union in Washington. In 1946 I was granted a State Department research fellowship to continue this work in South America. I worked in Buenos Aires in the Museo Histórico Sarmiento, where I discovered a wealth of untouched and unpublished material; at the Archivo General de la Nación; at the Biblioteca Nacional; and at other museums, libraries, and private collections. In Montevideo, Asunción (Paraguay), San Juan, and Santiago de Chile, I was able to continue my research in archives, libraries, and private homes. In 1948 I was granted a faculty research fellowship by Princeton University, and I returned to Buenos Aires to complete my work. Over this period of time I have been able to examine more than 15,000 unpublished letters relative to my subject, most of the published works related to the life and times of Sarmiento, and all of his published works.

I owe a great debt of gratitude to all those who have aided me in my work. The Department of State and Princeton University, through their generous grants, made my research possible.

To Professor Américo Castro I owe the major part of my inspiration and intellectual guidance. His encouragement, help, and direction were forever present in my work.

In Buenos Aires I received the warmest cooperation from all quarters. Señor Antonio P. Castro, then the Director of the Museo Histórico Sarmiento and now the sub-Secretario de Cultura, opened the doors of the Sarmiento Museum to me. He helped me in every possible manner, allowing me access to the unpublished archives and to all the facilities of the museum.

Such renowned Sarmientistas as Alberto Palcos, Antonio Bucich, Augusto G. Rodríguez, Juan Rómulo Fernández, Rosauro Pérez Aubone, and all the members of the distinguished Sarmiento Society extended to me their encouragement and aid. I am particularly indebted to Don Alberto Palcos, not only for his warm personal friendship but also for the brilliant interpretation and insight into the character of Sarmiento that he offered in his biography.

Other Argentine scholars and artists, such as Juan Carlos Rébora, Carlos Sánchez Viamonte, Enrique de Gandía, Leopoldo A. Kanner, Juan Mantovani, and Luis Perlotti were helpful in their respective fields.

My work in Buenos Aires would have been impossible

without the kindness and cooperation of Señor Manuel Mujica Láinez and his family and without the valued friendship of Señor Roberto Mujica Láinez. Mr. and Mrs. Charles Bartlett and Mr. and Mrs. Eugene Clarendon made the years that I spent in Argentina on this project among the happiest of my life.

In San Juan, I was received cordially and helped by all, but I should like to thank especially Señor Kurt Farwig and Señora Hilda Sarmiento de Farwig, descendants of Domingo Sarmiento.

I should like to thank Professor Dana G. Munro and Professor Robert R. Palmer of Princeton for their kindness in reading and correcting parts of the manuscript.

Finally, I should like to express my appreciation to all the others who have helped me and who have borne with me through many years of hearing the name of Sarmiento repeated and discussed and discussed again. I hope that this work will justify the aid and the patience that have been extended to me.

ALLISON WILLIAMS BUNKLEY

Princeton, N.J.
November 1949

Publisher's Statement: The manuscript of this book was delivered to the publishers by the author shortly before his death in 1949. Since he did not have the advantage of revising in the light of critical reading of the manuscript by others, various scholars, at Princeton and elsewhere, generously helped with such criticism and advice, and the manuscript was finally prepared for publication in the light of this criticism by E. Anderson-Imbert and Miriam Brokaw. They did not, however, make substantive changes except to correct occasional factual errors, their effort being to keep this Allison Bunkley's book, with only such alterations as they thought the author himself would have made.

CONTENTS

BOOK V. THE CONSTRUCTION

BOOK VI. THE CONSUMMATION

BOOK VII. THE COUNTERACTION

ILLUSTRATIONS

These illustrations are used here by the gracious permission of the Museo Historico Sarmiento in Buenos Aires.

BOOK I

The Raw Materials

Chapter 1. Hispanic Man in the Nineteenth Century

THE great Spanish writer and philosopher, Miguel de Unamuno, was reading to a blind friend. He read with great delight and enjoyment, for the book was by one of his favorite authors. He read for some time, but he did not tell his listener the name of the author. When he had finished one of the chapters, he stopped and asked the blind man what he thought of the book. "It is great," was the reply, "and it is so typically Spanish. The author criticizes Spain as only a Spaniard can." The book was called *El Facundo,* and its author was not a Spaniard but an Hispanic American. He was Domingo Faustino Sarmiento.

The difference between Hispanic American and Spanish culture is not as great as the nationalistic literary critics and historians have been wont to make it in the past half century. The assumption that in Hispanic America intellectual independence was coincidental with political independence is not warranted by the facts. Nineteenth-century Hispanic America was still well within the framework of the Spanish cultural tradition. In spite of all her attempts to adopt European or North American forms and institutions, her political, economic, and cultural way of life was still basically Spanish.

The Hispanic tradition is one of the essential elements in understanding the life of Domingo Sarmiento and the framework within which he lived and developed. It was the element that Sarmiento himself recognized in the last years of his life when he referred to his fellow Argentinians as the "Galicians over here" as opposed to the Spaniards who were the "Galicians over there."[1] It is an element without which it is im-

[1] "los gallegos de allende y los gallegos de aquende."

possible to understand his personality, his way of thought, and his later development.

In many important respects the Hispanic tradition stands apart from the mainstream of Western European culture. The Spanish nation has always been peculiarly aware of the reality of national characteristics and national individuality. Other nations have been highly critical of what they considered an exaggerated historical approach; but to understand a truly Hispanic figure we must take this attitude into account and understand the reasons for it. We must define those elements in the Hispanic tradition which distinguish it sharply from the Western European tradition. Only then can we think and talk about an Hispanic man in his terms rather than in ours.

Spanish history began to diverge sharply from the mainstream of European history early in the Middle Ages.[2] In 711 the Iberian Peninsula was invaded and almost completely occupied by a distinct and foreign civilization. For over seven hundred years Spain was divided between the Islamic world and the Christian world, between the Orient and the Occident. She absorbed a different way of life, a different way of thought, a hybrid cultural tradition that was to hold her apart from other nations of the Western tradition. She formed a national individuality, a national character, in the true sense of the word, and it is this which historians and philosophers have sensed and attempted to express. It is this which makes the Hispanic world impossible to understand in purely Western terms and which necessitates an attempt to understand it in its own terms.

Hispanic man has existed in a state of tension between the Orient and the Occident. He absorbed enough of the Islamic way of life to set him apart from other Western Europeans, but he never became an Oriental; he never adopted the way of life of the East. On the one hand there was the logical form of thought of the West: its clearcut categories of existence, its

[2] A complete discussion of the Islamic-Hispanic tradition can be found in Américo Castro, *España en su historia*, Buenos Aires, 1948. The ideas in this book are the basis for the discussion that follows. (Translated into English by Edmund L. King and to be published by Princeton University Press.)

interest in the relationship between man and objective reality, and its ability to think in terms of abstract and objective values. On the other hand there was the impressionistic thought process of the East: its inability to approach reality in terms of anything but an integral existence, its picture of a subjective world in which the object is illusory and ungraspable, and its inability to separate thought from the spontaneous vital process sufficiently to make it possible to think in terms of objective rather than personal values.

The state of tension between these two ways of life has made the existence of Hispanic man forever agonized. He has tried to be a part of Western civilization; he has been unable to and has cursed himself for his failure. Although he has tried to think in terms of the abstractions of the Occident, he has never been able to remove his personality from his thought. Although his philosophy and theology have attempted to categorize existence in European terms, he has always thought in terms of an integral reality. Although he has sought to approach life rationally and logically, he has approached it spontaneously and vitally. The egocentricity, personalism, and integralism of Hispanic man have made possible his great art and his genial self-expression, but they have kept him from perfecting the political, social, and economic institutions of the modern world. They have created for him a history of Persons rather than of Ideas or Things.

A panoramic view of Spain's history makes this personalistic character immediately evident. She produced no great Things. Her science was negligible. Her industry and commerce were backward. She produced no great Ideas. Her constitutions were borrowed. Her philosophy was either European or North American. She left no milestones of material or intellectual progress. But she produced great men and great personalities. Her history can be told either in terms of the success of her personal efforts or in terms of the failures of her material and intellectual efforts.

Hispanic history has never been able to remove the human being from the center of the stage. As the human being became less important in the mechanized, industrial, scientific world of western Europe, Spain strayed farther and farther from the mainstream of European thought. As the world progressed materially, Spain did not follow.

Prior to the so-called modern era of history, such a form of life as the Spanish could successfully compete with the other cultures of Europe. The Renaissance saw the Spanish Empire build itself into the greatest political force of the Western world, and the century that followed this political success saw Spanish art and letters produce a crop of geniuses and works that rivaled those of any other nation of the time. This golden age of Spanish history led, however, into a period of national decline that continued, for the three centuries that followed, to reduce Spain to a third-rate military and political power and a nonproductive and imitative culture. The reason for this change cannot be attributed solely to a decadence inherent in the Spanish people of the period. It must be seen fundamentally in terms of a split between the values and the form of life of Spain and the values and form of life of the rest of the Western world.

The modern era of Western civilization was ushered in by Newtonian science and the Cartesian rationalism of the seventeenth century. The new science pictured a world that was no longer the biocentric, teleological world of medieval science, but one in which the individual was but an infinitesimal speck in an infinitely large and alien universe. The philosophic and vital problem presented by such a world-view was how to know and perhaps control this overpowering objective world. The civilization of the Enlightenment, which followed in the eighteenth century, was based on a belief in the reality of the Idea and the value of the Rational. It sought to mold the institutions and the thought of mankind in terms of the dictates of Reason. Reason became *the* absolute value, and it reigned supreme in the fields of literature, art, and thought.

The Hispanic tradition did not react favorably to the civilization of the Enlightenment, to the Age of Reason. Its way of thought and its way of life were fundamentally opposed to the world-view and to the basic absolute values of that historical period. Western Europe had turned to a civilization of Ideas and Things. This was in contrast to the Hispanic tradition of Persons. As Don Quixote had said of the inventor of firearms, "I am persuaded he is in Hell receiving the reward of his diabolical invention by which he made it easy for a base and cowardly hand to take the life of a gallant gentleman." The firearm, and other Things; the constitution, and other Ideas, were destroying the position of the Person in life, and the Hispanic world did not join in this destruction. "As opposed to the rest of Western culture, the Hispanic world, on both sides of the sea, followed the opposite course. One constant in our history is that the attempt to twist the habits of our people to make them fit in any system of ordered discretion, submitted to rational laws and founded on hierarchies based on internal values, has ended in tragedy."[3]

While the rest of Western European civilization surged ahead in the fields of enlightened economics (laissez faire), enlightened politics (the enlightened despots, and later constitutionalism), enlightened industry (mechanization and systematization of production), and enlightened science (the understanding and control of natural phenomena), the Hispanic world remained "benighted." The Hispanic world which had led Western civilization during the late Renaissance—whose personalities such as Cortés, Pizarro, and Charles V had led the Spanish Empire to political predominance in the sixteenth century; whose artistic personalities such as Don Quixote, Don Juan, and the figures of El Greco had led Spain to artistic predominance in the seventeenth century—fell into a period of political, economic, and artistic decadence during the eighteenth century. Her politics and economics, which were basically dynastic, fell behind in a world of new objective political forms and new economic principles that conformed to abstract economic laws. Spain was unable to produce an industry, a science, or even an art to match her national rivals. By the end of the eighteenth century she had fallen to the position of a second- or even third-rate power.

During the Age of the Enlightenment, Spanish history

[3] Américo Castro, *La peculiaridad lingüística rioplatense y su sentido histórico.* Buenos Aires, 1941, p. 59.

manifested two important trends. The first of these was the artificial attempt to "twist the habits of the people" to fit the civilization of the time. The new Bourbon royal family and its court attempted to introduce certain French customs, political reforms, and economic reforms to the Hispanic world. Spanish thinkers and artists turned to French, German, and English models. They wrote neo-Classic literature, and they painted neo-Classic paintings. They compiled encyclopedic knowledge, and worked within a framework of a rationalistic philosophy. But in none of these fields did they excel. They produced nothing great and nothing original, and Spain gave the world no universal figure during the Enlightenment.

The second trend was one of bitter self-criticism. Seeing the wide gap between the Spanish way of life and the way of life that was bringing Western civilization to new heights of political and economic achievement, Spanish writers and thinkers violently attacked their own tradition and asked why it was unable to measure up to that of its neighbors and rivals. Hispanic man was agonized by his failure. In the seventeenth century, Diego de Saavedra Fajardo had asked, "To what causes can we attribute the decadence of our land?"[4] And his answer had been that Spain lacked the important attributes that had made the rest of Europe advance. She was not mechanical. Her commerce was backward. "There is lacking the cultivation of the fields, the exercise of the mechanical arts, trade and commerce, to which this nation does not apply itself." Spaniards must go abroad and learn the way of other nations to avoid "that coarseness and natural awkwardness, that stupid and inhuman pride that ordinarily is born and remains in those who have not dealt with other nations."[5] A century later, at the height of the Age of Reason, José Cadalso wrote that in Spain "the sciences are decaying more and more every day. . . . Everyone knows that to give one's life to science is to starve to death."[6] He and his con-

[4] Diego de Saavedra Fajardo, *Empresas políticas* in "Autores españoles" series, XXV.

[5] *Ibid.*

[6] José Cadalso, *Cartas marruecas* in "Autores españoles" series, XIII.

temporaries compared their nation's sad backwardness to the progress of eighteenth-century Europe, and they could only regret the differences they saw.

Toward the end of the eighteenth century, it appeared that the Age of Reason was triumphing in the Western world. The French Revolution brought the Goddess of Reason to the revolutionary temple of Paris. It sought to impose the idealism of constitutionalism and the rational reforms of the Enlightenment *philosophes*. In the material realm, the Industrial Revolution revealed the gains that could be made by the application of science and the rationalization of methods of production. The Age of Reason in politics and in economics seemed to be on its way, but in the very movements which heralded the supremacy of Reason were the seeds of its decay as an absolute, governing value. The chaos and disruption brought on by the French Revolutionary and Napoleonic Wars and the social dislocation caused by the Industrial Revolution made it increasingly difficult for the individual man of flesh and bone to solve his personal problems and plot his personal life in terms of his reason.

The enigma created by the dichotomy between the way the world *should be* and the way the world *was* induced new human solutions that manifested themselves in art, literature, and history to create a new era to replace the Age of the Enlightenment. This period has been termed by its own and later generations the Romantic Revolt. It expressed itself in several distinct manners. Some, seeing the contrast between the absolute values of rationalism and the irrational world, sought to reform the world to make it fit the ideal pattern. This might be called "the way of reform."[7] Others abandoned the values of eighteenth-century idealism and sought a new, more valid reality. More and more their personal experience led them to sense that the ultimate reality could not be found in their minds, and hence the highest value did not reside in their reason. These persons began to turn to their emotions or their wills as the human faculties in which the ultimate reality could be found and known. The emphasis on emotion

[7] J. Huizinga applied this term to a similar reaction in another age, *The Waning of the Middle Ages*, London, 1937.

produced the art and literature of the early Romantic Period and the nationalistic political theories which replaced the idealist constitutionalism. The value of the will produced literary and philosophic titanism and voluntarism and the modern politics of the will.

Spanish man had been conscious of the enormous gap between Hispanic reality and the Enlightenment ideal. The Romantic Revolt was quickly understood by him, and he joined in the nineteenth-century European movements which sought to bridge the gap. Part of the Hispanic world reacted against the eighteenth-century way of life by turning to Romanticism in art and literature and relativism and personalism in politics. The Romantic movement in literature and art, which turned to the emotions and to the titanic will, was taken up by the Spanish artistic world. There was a cultural revival that contrasted sharply with the sterility of eighteenth-century art, and Romanticism spread throughout the Hispanic world from Andalusia in Spain to Chile in South America.

Another part of the Hispanic world sought to reform its tradition, to adapt it to the ideals of a rationally ordered universe, to give to it the new institutions, the new Ideas and Things of Europe. The same frame of mind that had prompted Saavedra Fajardo and Cadalso to criticize the Spanish way of life in the seventeenth and eighteenth centuries and try to change it to better conform to the cultural, political, and economic ideals of the rest of Europe formed the basis of an important sector of Hispanic thought at the beginning of the nineteenth century. Young thinkers throughout Spain and Spanish America were reading the works of Rousseau, Paine, and Montesquieu. They were seeing the sharp contrast between the world in which they lived and the framework within which these writers wrote. "The encyclopedism, the rationalism of the Social Contract, the call of the Revolution of eighty-nine" were heard throughout the Hispanic world.[8]

In the southern part of South America, in the area where

[8] Alberto Zum Felde, *El problema de la cultura americana*, Buenos Aires, 1948, p. 124.

Domingo Sarmiento was born at the beginning of the nineteenth century, the leading young thinkers were basing their solution of the problems that faced their country on the way of reform. Studying in France, England, or at the more advanced universities in the Hispanic world, they developed theories of how to reshape the political, economic, and social life of the viceroyalty of the River Plate[9] to fit a rational pattern. Mariano Moreno and Bernardino Rivadavia sought to impose a rational abstract structure of law on the political life of the area.[10] Manuel Belgrano wrote a tract advocating free trade and seeking to base the economic life of the area on the abstract "natural laws" of the new economic science. It was into this world that Domingo Faustino Sarmiento was born.

Chapter 2. Personalism versus Nomocracy: The Hispanic Political Conflict

THE political drama into which Domingo Sarmiento was thrown was a confusing one. His nation was less than a year older than he, and it was still in the throes of the most painful growing pains. The May Revolution of 1810 was a dividing point between past and present, and Argentina was at a crossroads in its history. An understanding of the problems of the young nation is necessary for an understanding of the problems of the young man.

The River Plate area had held a peculiar place among the Spanish lands of America, for it was one of the few areas which did not have gold or silver or Indians capable of heavy

[9] The political division of the Spanish Empire that included the area now comprising the Republics of Argentina, Uruguay, and Paraguay.

[10] See Alberto Palcos, *La visión de Rivadavia*, Buenos Aires, 1936.

labor. These were the elements that the Spanish conqueror sought first, and he paid little attention to the areas that lacked them. As a result, the small colonial town of Buenos Aires stood in sharp contrast to the glittering cities of Mexico and Lima.[1] It is little wonder that it did not reach the rank of a viceroyalty until the end of the eighteenth century, and it is not surprising that its population was drawn, not from the adventurous nobility of Spain, but from the lower *hidalgo* class which came to America for entirely different reasons from those of their neighbors in Perú, Chile, and Mexico. The fact that the Argentine people started from the same social level and grew together as a nation gives her a place apart from the rest of Latin America. It relieved her of that eternal struggle which existed in her sister countries between the nobility and the common people. The Argentine people were able to develop with more unity, more like a nation, than any of their neighbors. This situation had another effect: it created in Argentina what was in a sense a democratic spirit. It was not the democratic spirit of the eighteenth century, or of France, or of North America. It was more a feeling of social equality and tolerance that arose as a result of the common needs of the entire population.

Until 1776, the River Plate region was but a captaincy. It held a very inferior place in the hierarchy of Spanish dominion, and was allowed to struggle along, pretty much on its own, with little attention or interference from the Crown. In Buenos Aires, unlike the rest of South America, the King did not even bother to send "corregidores"; he let the governor appoint his deputies from among the creoles. The lack of royal interest in the territory allowed it to grow more freely and with a feeling of unity. As early as 1671, the governor of Buenos Aires addressed his municipal officers as "criollos e hijos de esta tierra."[2] This would have been unthinkable in the viceroyalties of Perú or Mexico, where the feeling between the "peninsulares" (continental Spaniards) and the "criollos" was so strong.

[1] See Américo Castro, *La peculiaridad lingüística rioplatense, op.cit.*

[2] "Creoles and sons of this land," Kirkpatrick, *The Argentine Republic,* p. 22.

During the seventeenth and eighteenth centuries, Argentina grew as a nation. It had to face its own problems, unheeded by Madrid. Its unimportant position made it a mere sideline for Spanish trade. Because of the rigid commercial system, all goods coming from Spain to Buenos Aires had to be shipped from Europe to Lima and then across three thousand miles of rough and dangerous land to Buenos Aires. This inaccessibility made the prices on merchandise practically prohibitive and forced the people of Buenos Aires to resort to their own means, illegal or legal, of getting goods. In a similar way, with little help from the mother country, the people of Argentina faced alone the long struggle with the Indians of the pampas, the intermittent fights with the Portuguese in the north, and the occasional clashes with the English.[3]

Argentina became a self-assured nation, with a feeling of national unity, but like all of the Spanish world she was by tradition still tied strongly to one center, the King. She developed individually and perhaps differently from the rest of Latin America, but she was as strongly bound by the ties to the Crown as any of her neighbors, and she was as much a part of Spain as Catalonia or Andalusia. As early as 1595, González Fernando de Oviedo had written that the only unifying force in Spain and in the Spanish Empire was the fact that all the people were "vasallos de la corona de España."[4] It was this same almost mystic tie that throughout the following centuries held Argentina and her sister nations bound to the European motherland. It was the breaking of this tie that set them all free.

Historians usually list a series of reasons for Argentine independence: (1) the fight between the creoles and peninsulares; (2) the self-confidence generated by the successful repulsion of the English Invasion of 1806-1807; (3) a new contact with the outside world and the introduction of eight-

[3] As early as 1762 the British with three frigates, one "snow," five store ships, and 1,050 men attempted the invasion of the River Plate. Expecting to base at Colonia, they were surprised to find it had fallen from Portuguese hands and was in the hands of the Spanish. In the fight that ensued, the British flagship *Clive* exploded, and the fleet turned back.

[4] "Vassals of the crown of Spain."

eenth-century ideas of "democracy" and "freedom"; (4) the fall of the monarchy. All of these were undoubtedly contributing factors towards the establishment of Argentine independence, but the utmost care must be taken in weighing the relative importance of each. Without the fall of the monarchy, all the rest would have had little effect. Without the destruction of that transcendent personal tie, it is very doubtful if Argentina would have broken with Spain. The other factors, once the royal bond had been broken, stimulated the move for complete independence and directed its course, but they were not the prime moving influences.

The entire Spanish Empire collapsed within one decade. The reason why the collapse came at that particular time and why it was almost simultaneous throughout the Empire is extremely important. The conflict between peninsulares and creoles had existed throughout the colonial period. In the years before independence, however, the situation had eased. In the River Plate region, an increasing number of creoles were holding important positions and guiding their own destinies. This conflict certainly could not have been the factor that set off the explosion which brought with it the destruction of the Empire. The self-confidence generated by the successful repulsion of the English invasions might have been a factor in the River Plate region. The people there, seeing their ability successfully to defend themselves without the help of Spain against two strong expeditions of the English army and navy, might have acquired a self-assured attitude of independence toward the mother country. But these invasions were limited to the area in and immediately surrounding the cities of Buenos Aires and Montevideo, and they do not explain the simultaneous movement for independence that struck the Spanish American Empire from Mexico to Patagonia. The ideas of the French and North American Revolutions, the ideas of constitutionalism and economic reform, might well have thrown into relief the contrast between the Spanish Empire and the changing world around it, but, again, such a factor does not explain the precise time and manner in which the final break came. As early as 1600 the works of Copernicus, Erasmus, the classical

Greeks, European physicists, and modern mathematicians had been shipped to America.[5] In the eighteenth century, too, Spanish America could read, with or without Inquisitional permission, the works of the most advanced thinkers. It was not that the new thought was just beginning to reach Buenos Aires at the beginning of the nineteenth century. It was rather that it had never been able to take hold before. It had never been any more than an undercurrent while the old imperial structure stood, but when the Empire collapsed, the new ideas became important. Their role in nineteenth-century Spanish American history was more the result of the collapse of the Empire than its cause.

The disintegration and the atomization of the Hispanic world came with the collapse of the Spanish monarchy. Spain had held her colonies together "thus far, not so much by her strength as by their traditional loyalty."[6] As the Argentine patriot, Mariano Moreno, later expressed it, "In the constitution of the Spanish monarchy, the King was the sole link which bound together the various estates."[7] This constitution fell apart when its "sole link" was destroyed. In 1808 the Napoleonic armies invaded and occupied Spain. Charles IV and later his son, Ferdinand VII, abdicated their rights to the throne, and were replaced by Joseph Napoleon, brother of the French Emperor. Suddenly the strong personalistic ties that had held the Spanish Empire together were broken. The Spaniard, from Chile to Catalonia, had had no political loyalty other than his fealty to his king. The old Spanish political motto had been, "Del rey abajo ninguno" (Below the King, no one). The Spanish political system had not been one of a hierarchy of loyalties. Each individual of the Empire had been held within it politically by one bond and one bond alone—his own personal loyalty to the person of the monarch. Below the King, there was no one to whom he was tied. The nobility was considered the useless and parasitic

[5] Otis H. Green and Irving A. Leonard, "On the Mexican Booktrade in 1600, a Chapter in Cultural History," *Hispanic Review*, January 1947. Irving A. Leonard, *Books of the Brave*, Cambridge, 1949.

[6] Dana Gardner Munro, *The Latin American Republics. A History*, New York, 1942, p. 148.

[7] F. A. Kirkpatrick, *History of Argentina*, Cambridge, 1931, p. 62.

estate. The bureaucracy was looked upon as the corrupt and harmful estate. Each subject of the Empire was a republic unto himself, held within one "confederation" by the direct tie with the person of the monarch. When that person disappeared from the political scene in 1808 as the Bourbon royal family retired to exile in Bayonne and was replaced by another sovereign to whom no one felt linked or even loyal, the millions of little "republics" split apart. The Empire was atomized. Each was his own law, his own political structure, and each individual now had to seek a new loyalty.

At first the Hispanic world would not accept the disappearance of its sole link. The people of Spain formed in "juntas" to preserve the royal authority until the return of "the king they longed for."[8] The City Council of Mexico declared: "We shall not recognize the puppet Napoleon. The king (whom God preserve!) is in the enemy's hands. The *audiencia* and the viceroy have, therefore, no source of authority since their authority comes from the King. Let us follow the example of the cities of Spain and set up a provisional junta of municipalities to hold the country until the King is restored." "Below the King, no one": once the person of the King had disappeared, the viceroy and the colonial government were meaningless. The basic structure of the Empire had collapsed and something new had to be found to replace it.

In the River Plate region, every subsequent ship that arrived from Europe made the situation less understandable. First came the news of the abdication of Charles IV, then of Ferdinand VII. A new viceroy arrived with authority from the Central Junta of Cadiz, the depository of royal power and authority. Finally, on May 13, 1810, news arrived of the fall of Seville and the dissolution of the Junta of Cadiz. The final link had been broken. The people of Buenos Aires met in an open meeing (*cabildo abierto*) and discussed their political future. On May 25th[9] they invaded the palace of the viceroy and demanded the formation of a new junta as the local governing body.

[8] Joseph McCabe, *Spain in Revolt, 1814-1931*, New York, 1932.
[9] Celebrated as Argentine Independence Day.

At first, the Spanish Americas looked upon the situation as a temporary one. Authority and power were being maintained until the return of Ferdinand VII. The Buenos Aires junta pledged itself to "observe the laws of the kingdom and to preserve this part of America for our august sovereign Ferdinand VII."[10] The loyal subjects of the Empire believed that their monarch would soon return to power. But as the years passed and the "Intruder King" remained in Madrid, the loyalty between subject and monarch cooled. Thought and ideas and circumstances changed, until, when the King finally returned, his subjects throughout the Hispanic world had found new loyalties and refused to return to the old relationship. In European Spain, Ferdinand ruled by force, but in the Americas he was never able to reestablish his authority and his power.

With the disintegration of the Spanish monarchical constitution between 1808 and 1812, the Hispanic world was left without political ties. A vacuum was created. The millions of individual republics splintered off on their own courses and chaos threatened. A new loyalty was needed to fill the vacuum, and there were three courses open to the ruptured Spanish world. It could turn to a new monarch, and thus accomplish a natural transference of loyalties within the same general framework of political thought. It could transfer its loyalties to a constitution, to a framework of abstract laws, rights, and freedoms. It could find a new personal loyalty, other than a monarchical one.

In different parts of the Hispanic world, each of the three solutions was tried, and each failed. In Mexico, General Iturbide declared himself Emperor of Mexico, but his royal line was far from any claim to legitimacy, and his attempt soon developed into a farce. In the southern part of the hemisphere, the great liberator and hero, San Martín, along with other leaders of the River Plate area, negotiated with members of the Portuguese royal family, but they were unable to secure sufficient support. In most of the Hispanic American world, the tendency was to transfer political loyalty to the personality of a local strong man. This solution was

[10] Kirkpatrick, *History of Argentina, op.cit.*, p. 72.

still within the framework of personal political ties, but it lacked the traditional sanction of the legitimate monarch. The hero of national independence, Simón Bolívar, established the Bolivarian Republic of the northwestern section of South America on a basis of personal dictatorial power and personal loyalty.

In the River Plate, there was an experiment with the third of these possible solutions. When the news of the fall of the Central Junta, the last remnant of the monarchical power, arrived in Buenos Aires, there was but one group ready to assume leadership and capable of offering a positive program. This was the small minority of intellectuals who had studied the European writers of the Enlightenment and who wanted to apply the French Revolutionary political and economic ideas to their own land. These men, like Mariano Moreno, Bernadino Rivadavia, and Manuel Belgrano, who had studied in France and Europe and had been saturated with the ideas of Rousseau, Paine, and Montesquieu, now had "the utopic idea that they could create an independent Hispanic America, united and in accordance with the democratic dreams of the eighteenth century."[11] These men wanted to fit the River Platanese political reality into the rational pattern created by the minds of the eighteenth-century idealists. They had no intention of trying to adapt the ideas, principles, and forms to their own environment and their own conditions. They wanted to lift them in toto from the French writers and politicians, and superimpose them upon their own country and people. When Rivadavia reached the presidency more than a decade later, he even dressed like the members of the French Directory and the Napoleonic era. No superficial detail was too unimportant to copy, for he intended to superimpose the total political pattern. As an English traveler described him, "His whole appearance is not very unlike the caricature portraits of Napoleon: indeed, it is said, he is very fond of imitating that once great personage in such things as are within his reach."[12]

[11] Américo Castro, *Iberoamérica, su presente y su pasado*, revised edition, New York, 1946, p. 136.

[12] J. A. B. Beaumont, *Travels in Buenos Aires and the Adjacent Provinces of*

The decade from 1810 to 1820—the years that saw the birth and early childhood of Sarmiento in San Juan—was divided between two main trends. The most important of these was the War of Independence. The forces of the River Plate region, under the leadership of José de San Martín, ousted the Spanish first from their own area, then from Chile and later from Perú. Independence was the great goal towards which the activities of the time were directed, the great unifying force for the various personalities and individuals of the Spanish American world. But underneath this main directive effort, the small group of thinkers and politicians was trying to organize the politics of the country according to the patterns that they had borrowed from abroad. For a decade the intellectuals of Argentina held sway over the nation's politics. From 1810 to the Constitution of 1819, these men tried to create a government based on law, a nomocracy,[13] a political form in which the personality was fitted into a pattern of political behavior created by an abstract system of law. These leaders chose conventions. They elected representatives. They promulgated constitutions. They passed, amended, and repealed laws. They dissolved assemblies, and they originated new ones. With great persistence, they continued to seek a formula from the French Revolution that would suit their circumstances. In vain they tried one solution after another. Mariano Moreno translated Jean Jacques Rousseau's *Social Contract*.[14] This was his Bible, and through it he saw the answer for Argentina's troubles. "They sought then to legislate according to the principles of the *Social Contract*

the Rio de la Plata, London, 1828, pp. 138-159; see also Rafael Alberto Arrieta, *Centuria porteña*, Buenos Aires, 1944, p. 120.

[13] This seems to be the best word to apply to the form of government in which an abstract system of law is above and beyond the personality. To this system, whether it be constitutional or traditional, the personality owes its loyalty. It limits and directs the political life of the individual. This word applies to the political trend that we are describing in Hispanic America better than does the word "democracy," which refers more specifically to "government by the people." The ideas of Moreno and Rivadavia did not center around *who* ruled but on *how* they ruled. An intellectual minority might rule, but they must do so within the framework and according to the forms of a system of abstract laws, rights, and freedoms.

[14] Santos P. Amadeo, *Argentine Constitutional Law*, New York, 1943, Chapter 1.

and thus to erect insurmountable barriers to the national illiteracy, to the incapacity of the half-breed and the Indian to deal with representative government, to the barbarity of gauchocracy."[15]

But as years passed, it became increasingly evident that the political forms of nomocracy were not claiming the loyalty or the adherence of the great masses of the population. There were two main factors that stood in the way. The vast frontier pampa environment would have made a nomocratic experiment difficult at best. The very physical scene upon which the eighteenth-century ideas and institutions were being imposed did not lend itself readily to the forms that had been better adapted to the closely-knit, well integrated French countryside. A contemporary traveler wrote: "Although immense regions of rich land lay uncultivated and unowned, yet something had been done. Small towns and establishments, five hundred and seven miles distant from one another, were thinly scattered over this vast extent of country; and thus a *skeleton map* of civilization had been traced. . . ."[16] The inhabitants of the region were not factory workers or even the small-farm peasants of western Europe. They were the wild and untamed gauchos of the pampa. They were men who lived on horseback, alone, unhampered by any law or any restriction. Their battle was for their life against the unfriendly elements, and they cared little for the niceties of a constitution or for the promises of natural rights. From their childhood they learned to fight and survive, and their lives depended upon their own abilities and their own power. Their personalities and their power to survive decided their fate, and they owed allegiance only to other personalities who commanded their respect.[17] As Sir Walter Scott described them: "The vast plains of Buenos Aires are populated by a race of savage Christians, known as gauchos, whose principal

[15] "Gauchocracy" is a convenient word to apply to the personalistic government of the Argentine gaucho who ruled locally throughout early Argentine history. Lucas Ayarragaray, *La anarquía argentina y el caudillismo*, Buenos Aires, 1926, p. 218.

[16] Sir Francis Bond Head, *Rough Notes Taken during Some Rapid Journeys across the Pampas and among the Andes*, Boston, 1827, p. 20.

[17] Mark Jefferson, *Peopling the Argentine Pampa*, New York, 1926, p. 24.

furnishings consist of the skulls of horses, whose food is raw meat, and water, and whose favorite pastime is to race horses. Unfortunately they prefer their national independence to our cottons and textiles."[18] And they preferred their personal independence to the nomocracy of Western civilization. They understood little of the constitutions and assemblies of Moreno, Rivadavia, and the intellectual minority in Buenos Aires.

But more important in the defeat of nomocracy in Argentina than the physical environment and its wild inhabitants was the very Spanish way of life that we have described. Its biocentric character, its personalism and relativism—all of these elements were alien to any rationalistic system of politics. Just as the Hispanic world had never entered into the civilization of the Enlightenment, so it was ill-adapted to a nomocratic form of government. As the Wars for Independence drew to a close, it became increasingly clear that the political structure of the Spanish world was split between the nomocratic ideas borrowed from France and North America and the personalistic tradition of the Spanish heritage and the gaucho-pampa environment. It was a "conflict between ideas come from abroad and the Spanish tradition. That struggle began in Spain at the same time as in America, and it has not yet stopped."[19] This fundamental clash between personalism and nomocracy has been the basic conflict of Hispanic and Hispanic American history during the nineteenth century. It was one of the most important elements of Sarmiento's life.

"With Moreno, the Argentine intellectual minority began its first rebellion against gauchocracy which was later to enthrone itself due to the fact that on its side were the historical and social traditions of the people. In this original clash, the *caudillo* was naturally triumphant over the intellectual, the general over the scholar, arbitrary politics over rational politics."[20] Soon the nomocratic forces were divided and fighting among themselves. Their minds favored a government by

[18] Quoted by D. F. Sarmiento, *Facundo*, p. 41.
[19] Américo Castro, *Iberoamérica, op.cit.*, p. 137.
[20] Ayarragaray, *La anarquía Argentina, op.cit.*, pp. 205-206.

law, according to rational patterns, but their own tradition led them to emphasize personalities. The intellectual minority itself began to divide over personalities. "For the partisans of Moreno, Saavedra was a tyrant; for the partisans of Saavedra, Moreno was a rebel."[21] Government followed government. "Saavedra succeeded Moreno, Pueyrredón succeeded Alvear, Martin Rodríguez succeeded Dorrego, Rosas succeeded Rivadavia."[22] Divided within, the nomocrats were unable to withstand the opposition of personalism from without. They had the decade from 1810 to 1820 for their experiment, and they failed to adapt the French rationalist political ideas to their own environment. They were unable to unite themselves. They were unable to claim the loyalty of the gaucho of the pampa or the inheritor of the Hispanic personalist tradition.

The experiment of the 1810's was followed by the chaos of the 1820's. The local personalist leaders who had been gaining power throughout the interior while the nomocrats had attempted to work out a government by law in Buenos Aires began to undermine the political forms set up by the Constitution of 1819. They rose up in opposition to this constitution and splintered the unity of the nation. Governments could stand no longer than a few months in Buenos Aires. Local boss fought local boss in the provinces. Chaos reigned. This was the beginning of the basic conflict that was to mark the entire history of the new Argentine Republic. Argentina was torn between the nomocratic ideas borrowed from abroad and the personalistic tradition of Hispanic history. As Alberto Zum Felde expressed it, France was her teacher, but Spain was her mother.[23] Sarmiento, growing up at this time, reflected this split. As he became conscious of his nation's politics, he was forced to choose his side.

[21] *Ibid.*, p. 210.

[22] José Ingenieros, *Evolución de las ideas argentinas*: Ezequiel Martínez Estrada, *Sarmiento*, Buenos Aires, 1946, p. 147.

[23] Zum Felde, *El problema*, *op.cit.*, p. 128.

Chapter 3. The Childhood

DOMINGO FAUSTINO SARMIENTO was born into a family that combined in it the various traditions that went to create his historical circumstances. His father's family was an integral part of the history of the Spanish conquest and settlement of this region of the new world. The Quiroga Sarmientos had figured in the conquest of Chile. Rodrigo Quiroga had been one of the first settlers of that region, and one of his descendants, Jacinto de Quiroga Mallea, appeared in the very earliest days of the history of San Juan and married a Micaela Sarmiento. The third generation of their descendants included many of the outstanding and distinguished figures of early Argentine and Chilean history. One of the more obscure of these was one José Clemente Sarmiento Funes.

It is sometimes claimed that the maternal side of Domingo Sarmiento's heritage traces back to a Moorish family of the twelfth century, Al Ben Razin. But this is to take seriously what Sarmiento himself said with tongue in cheek: "In fact, it flatters and amuses me—this ancestry which makes me apparent heir of Mohammed."[1] This family became Christianized and assumed the name of Albarracín. Many centuries later, in the New World, the Albarracín family assumed a position of prominence. Bernardino Albarracín was a mayor of San Juan in its later colonial period, and his son Cornelio Albarracín Balmaceda owned half of the Zonda Valley, the richest land in the vicinity. The latter's daughter, Paula Albarracín, was a capable and promising young girl, and would in all probability have married one of the most prominent men of the province had not her father suffered a twelve-year sickness that incapacitated him during the last

[1] D. F. Sarmiento, *Obras*, III, "Recuerdos de provincia," 60. After this, any reference to Sarmiento's *Complete Works* (*Obras*) will be abbreviated to *Obras*. See the Bibliography, p. 521, for a complete listing of the individual volumes of the *Obras*.

years of his life, and thus caused him to lose his fortune and the greater part of his lands. Paula therefore became not one of the most distinguished members of the family but the "poor cousin" whose eligibility was reduced and who had to use all of her promising talents in the difficult struggle for existence.

In 1801, when Paula was twenty-three years of age, her invalid father died. During his illness, his sons had worked his lands, but they had been forced to sell piece by piece. When the father died, he left only bare fields of little value. Paula, who had been raised in the traditional manner of a young lady of the Spanish world and who had never even thought of doing manual labor, decided to work. She was a young woman of strong will and she was determined that circumstances would not overcome her. She wanted to build a house, even if it was but a one-room cottage, and she began to weave and sell her weaving to enable her to accomplish this ambition. "With this, and two slaves belonging to her Irrazábal aunts, she laid the foundations of the house that she was to occupy when she should set up a family of her own. As her meager resources were insufficient for such an expensive undertaking, she set up her loom under one of the fig trees that she had inherited with the place and from there, with her shuttle flying back and forth, supervised her foreman and laborers as they built the house, and on Saturdays, having sold the cloth that she had woven during the week, she paid the workmen with the income from her own labors. . . . My mother wove twelve yards a week, enough for a friar's habit, and received six pesos every Saturday, not however without working into the night, reeling onto her bobbins the thread that was to be taken off the next day."[2] It took a year to complete the modest dwelling that she had planned, but when it was complete, Paula felt the security that she had sought. She thought it possible to marry and have children. On November 21, 1801, Paula Albarracín married José Clemente Sarmiento Funes. In the years that followed they had fifteen

[2] *A Sarmiento Anthology*, translated by Stuart E. Grummon and edited by Allison W. Bunkley, Princeton University Press, 1948, pp. 63-64. After this, the work will be referred to as *Anthology*.

IMMEDIATE FAMILY OF DOMINGO FAUSTINO SARMIENTO
THE SARMIENTOS AND THE ALBARRACÍNS

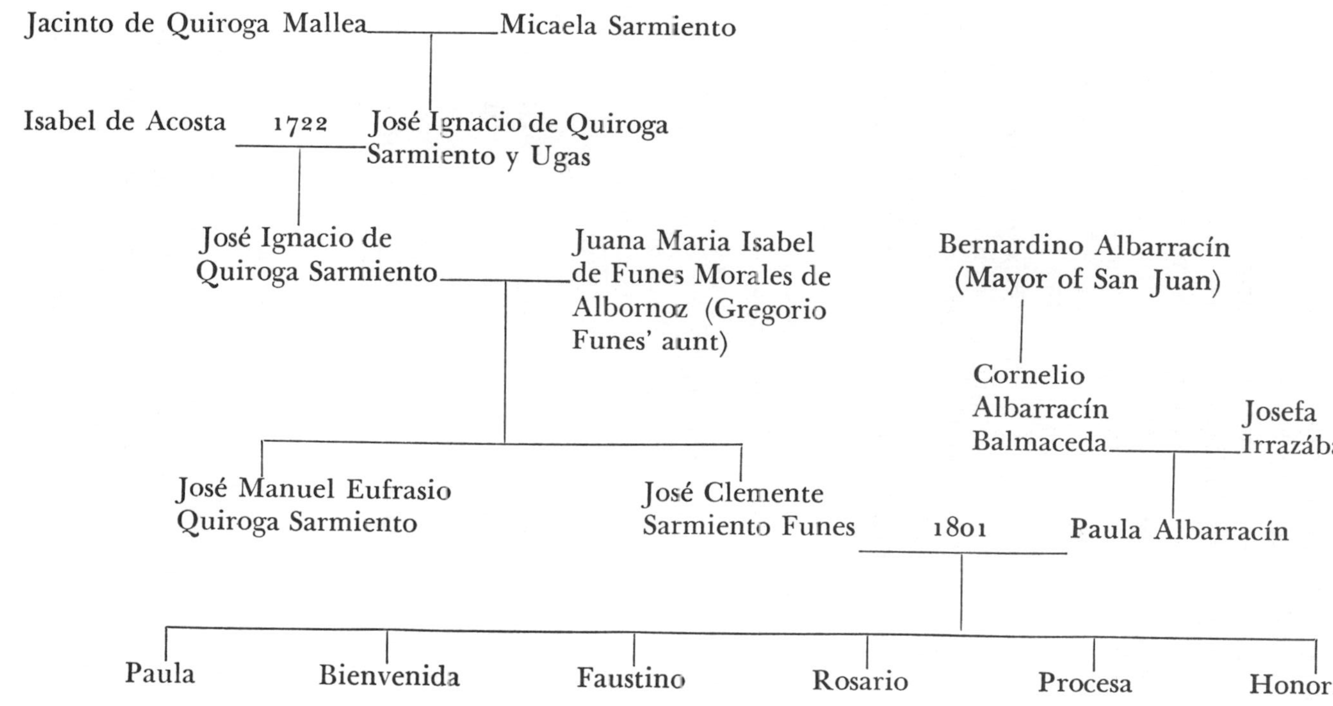

children, nine of whom died in childbirth. One of those who lived was Domingo Faustino.

The Sarmiento and Albarracín families were important elements in the history of colonial San Juan, and any member of the family could not but be conscious of his heritage.[3] In the very lifetime of Domingo Sarmiento, the family boasted members of distinction and importance, and some of these, though young Domingo knew them but slightly or not at all, had a profound effect in bringing him into contact with the principal currents of his time. His uncle, Domingo de Oro, was one of the outstanding figures in the history of the young Argentine Republic. He represented in this period the traditional Hispanic distrust for the democratic political forms being imported from abroad, and "this man who was so splendidly gifted opened the way for [the dictator] Don Juan Manuel Rosas."[4] Although the ideas that were forming in the intellect of young Domingo were diametrically opposed to his uncle's political actions, this disagreement did not keep him from studying what he believed to be his uncle's best features. Domingo de Oro was a great orator and a great scholar, and, whatever his beliefs, he came to stand for intellectual honesty and integrity. His power of expression and persuasion when speaking was a weapon that young Domingo saw as a valuable one. "I studied his inimitable example; I followed the thread of his speech, discovered the structure of his sentence, the machinery of that magical fascination of his word."[5] In later life, Domingo Sarmiento became as famous for his oratory as had been his famous uncle.

Gregorio Funes, Dean of the University of Córdoba, was a distant relative, perhaps a cousin, of Domingo Sarmiento. They did not have direct contact with one another, for Sarmiento was a boy of eighteen when Dean Funes died, but Domingo was always conscious of the relationship and an admirer of his famous relative. Funes had been one of the foremost students in the River Plate area during the late colonial period. He had studied in Europe, and had been an important instrument in introducing the ideas of the Enlightenment into "the very heart of the colonies."[6] In the

[3] *Obras*, III, 60ff. [4] *Ibid.*, p. 91. [5] *Ibid.*, p. 89ff. [6] *Ibid.*, p. 111.

years of nomocratic experiments in the Argentine government, Funes became a distinguished national figure. He tried to apply his ideas to the fields of economics, and politics; and he became one of the foremost examples of the attempt to superimpose a rationalistic pattern of behavior upon the political, economic, and human reality of the area. He read Voltaire, D'Alembert, Diderot, and Rousseau;[7] and believed that it was necessary only to overcome the ignorance of the populace in order to make their ideas successful in his Argentine environment.[8] Domingo Sarmiento grew with the consciousness of his relationship to Dean Funes, and he found in the educator's rational patterns of the Enlightenment and his applications of those patterns and hopes for the future both an inspiration and a guide for the solution of the intellectual problems that faced him as he grew and learned in San Juan.

Thus Domingo Sarmiento was born into a family that established relationships between him and the main historical currents of his age. "If we take the Albarracín family, it includes the following: the convent, theology, the inquisition, trips to Spain, the Declaration of Independence, Bolívar who finished it, the Civil War, the caudillos, Rosas, and exile. Three generations have been sufficient to consummate these happenings, three individuals have reflected them by acts and signs."[9] Through men like Funes and Oro, he was related to the abstraction we have called the Hispanic man in the nineteenth century, and became involved in his problems and his solutions. Sarmiento's family also gave him a background of genius and of insanity.[10] It was a family, not of normal, average people, but of eccentricity.

On February 15, 1811, Doña Paula Albarracín de Sarmiento traveled by horseback to the house of her friend Doña Fran-

[7] *Ibid.*, p. 117.

[8] *Ibid.*, p. 125. Cfr. Sesiones del Congreso de 1819, Archivo Nacional, Buenos Aires.

[9] *Ibid.*, p. 110.

[10] There was insanity in the Albarracín family. One member was an imbecile. Miguel was definitely eccentric. Fermín Mallea, Domingo's aunt, went insane in 1848. There were a number of abnormal members of the Oro family. (Manuel Gálvez, *Vida de Sarmiento*, Buenos Aires, 1945. After this, the work will be referred to as Gálvez.)

cisca B. de Oros, who lived quite a distance outside the town of San Juan. That day left a lasting impression in the mind of her daughter, Bienvenida, and some seventy-eight years later she described it from memory: "Being there, she became sick, for she was very pregnant, and as there were few coaches at that time, my father brought her back to town on horseback behind him; when her sickness increased, they would stop until it passed a little, and then they would go on."[11] Bienvenida and her sister, Paula, went ahead to prepare the bed in their home. Doña Paula barely reached the edge of her bed "and there the child wished to see light, without awaiting anyone." By the time the midwife arrived, the child had been born, and both mother and baby were out of danger. The child was a boy and he was baptized by the name of Faustino Valentín Sarmiento.[12] In history, the child is known by the name he assumed from the family saint, Saint Dominic, Domingo Faustino Sarmiento.

As for all infants and young children, the years that followed were for Domingo Sarmiento years of absorption and of aimless childhood pursuits. As might be expected, the two most important influences during these earliest years were his mother and father. They taught him an attitude towards life by their actions and by their examples rather than by any consciously didactic effort. When Sarmiento was but three years old, he was carried about literally tied to his mother's apron strings, "and there he humbly remained until they let him loose."[13] He would remain there saying with his newly found yet imperfected vocabulary, "yo soy el peyo, yo soy el peyo de la casa" (I am the doggy, I am the doggy of the house). He never remembered seeing his mother idle during

[11] Manuscript written by Bienvenida Sarmiento in May 1889, dated San Juan. This is to be found in the Museo Histórico Sarmiento in Buenos Aires.

[12] The baptismal certificate seems to contradict the traditional date of February 15: "In the year of Our Lord eighteen hundred and eleven, on the fifteenth of the month of February, in this Matriz Church of San Juan de la Frontera, the parish of San José, I, the assistant priest, put oil and chrism on Faustino Valentín, one day old, legitimate son of José Clemente Sarmiento and Doña Paula Albarracín. The other assistant Friar Francisco Albarracín baptized him. Godparents Don José Tomás Albarracín and Doña Paula Oro, whom I charged with his spiritual guidance and in evidence of which we sign. —José María de Castro."

[13] *Recuerdos.*

his early days. Many years later, when he was thirty-one years old, he commented that it was the first time that his mother had been able to sit down "with nothing to keep her hands busy."[14] As Doña Paula had built her humble little house, literally with the labor of her hands, so she supported her evergrowing family with her industry and diligence. "She made silk suspenders, scarfs of *vicuña* wool to send as curiosities to Spain, and cravats and ponchos of the same soft material. In addition to the weaving of these clothes, she made openwork for albs as well as laces, crinolines, jerseys, and a variety of needlework used to trim women's clothes and sacred vestments. My mother also knew every kind of knitting, and she was such an expert in the difficult art of dyeing that she had been consulted recently on how to dye a scarlet cloth blue and how to produce many of the softer tones that please European taste."[14]

Don Clemente aided little in the support of his large family, but his wife was determined that they should not want for the basic necessities of life. Doña Paula had had little time for schooling or learning. She had been forced to apply herself to the practical tasks of making a livelihood for herself and her children, but this near illiteracy did not detract from her character. A woman with the determination and the spirit to carry on and overcome the difficulties that she faced was indeed a wonderful example to any young child. As Domingo said in later life, "Notwithstanding her lack of mental training, her soul and her conscience had been better educated than they could have been by the greatest learning. I have watched her act under the impact of varied and repeated difficulties, and never once have I seen her untrue to herself. Never has she weakened or temporized even under conditions which would have made concessions to life excusable. I must here trace the development of the high moral ideas that formed my growing years."[15] As he later concluded, "Blessed are the poor who have had such a mother!"[16]

Domingo Sarmiento's environment was not a particularly promising one. "I was born in an ignorant and backward province. . . . I was born into a family that had lived for

[14] *Anthology*, p. 64. [15] *Ibid.*, p. 57. [16] *Ibid.*, p. 68.

many years in a state of mediocrity very close to indigence. . . ."[17] It was his mother, Doña Paula, who was the most important factor in overcoming these forces which were lined up against him. She taught him industry. He learned never to be idle, to take advantage of every moment to learn and act. She taught him a strength of character, a determination and a will, that he demonstrated in his actions throughout his life. She taught him a truly comforting religion, a belief in the ultimate solution of all problems by a kind Providence.[18] Domingo, when he was too old and too big to be tied to his mother's apron strings, never forgot her. "His mother, lost in the distant and almost forgotten San Juan community, was always with him in Spirit."[19] Wherever he was, from Naples to New York to Buenos Aires, her living example and lesson were always with him, an integral part of his behavior. His firm belief in the "physical transmissibility of moral aptitudes"—whether the belief was well-founded or not—helped to weave many of the mother's characteristics into the personality of the young boy.

Domingo did not find as much to learn from the example of his father as he had from his mother. When Doña Paula married Don José Clemente Sarmiento, he was "an elegant youth, of a family declining like her own, to whom she brought as a dowry the chain of privations and miseries in which long years of her life had been spent."[20] Doña Paula seems to have realized the failings of her husband even before she married him, but, as in so many other cases in her life, she let no obstacle stand in the way of the realization of her will. She knew that Don José Clemente was lazy and impractical. She waited until she had finished the building of her house before she married him. She had a home for her family, and she had learned skills that would insure her a livelihood in spite of any contingencies.

From his father, Domingo received a heritage of both poverty and untruthfulness.[21] Don José Clemente was never able to settle down to any steady life or any permanent pur-

[17] *Obras*, III, 6.

[18] *Ibid.*, p. 141-142.

[19] *Anthology*, pp. 55-56.

[20] *Ibid.*, p. 64.

[21] Gálvez, pp. 12, 13.

suit. At times he worked as a laborer or peon on nearby farms. At other times he was a muleteer and was absent from his home for many months on long journeys across the Andes to Chile. He seldom returned with any cash or any contribution to the support of his family, for what he had earned he spent carelessly before arriving in San Juan.

But like many such men who are unable to find themselves in normal everyday life, Don José Clemente found a way to express his more positive virtues in times of crisis. In spite of his shortcomings, he was a romantic idealist, and he found in the slogans of the revolution for independence the meaning for his life. "Once, in 1812, seeing the misery of Belgrano's army at Tucumán, he returned to San Juan and took up a collection for 'the mother country,' as he called our native land. The collection proved to be a large one and was denounced to the municipality by the loyalists as an act of despoilment. The authorities, however, having investigated the affair, were so pleased that Father was himself deputized to take the patriotic offering to the army, and from that time was given the sobriquet of 'Mother Country.' . . ."[22] General Belgrano himself was so touched upon the arrival of the aid, that he commented upon the arrival of the gifts, "Only a son of the homeland could have had such an inspiration."[23]

Five years later, at the famous battle of Chacabuco, after General San Martín had decisively defeated the Spanish in Chile, it was Don José Sarmiento who was entrusted with returning the prisoners of war to custody in San Juan.[24] This increased his prestige and reputation as a patriot, but when the wars were over his record helped him little. He spent much of his time in later life recounting his exploits during the wars for independence. Young Domingo listened, fascinated, to these tales, and from them he learned the same patriotism and devotion to the service of his country as his father.

Throughout his life, Domingo never spoke of his father

[22] *Anthology*, p. 65.

[23] Juan Rómulo Fernández, *Sarmiento*, Buenos Aires, 1938, p. 16.

[24] Many years later, when Sarmiento interviewed San Martín in France (1847), the old hero remembered this incident and remembered Don José Clemente. *Obras*, XLIX, 19-20.

except in terms of the most genuine admiration. "My father is a good man who has nothing more notable in his life than having given some service in a subordinate capacity in the wars of independence."[25] As is often true in such instances, the son was devoted to his idealistic, impractical father and saw only his best features. And, conversely, the father, who saw the aimlessness and lack of value in his own life, put a great deal of hope and love in his dreams for the future of his young son who seemed at a very early age to show unusual promise. José Clemente taught young Domingo to read all that he could obtain, and in the years that followed he spared no effort in trying to secure for his son the best education obtainable in the circumstances in which they found themselves.

The vivid memory of the home that his mother had built remained with Domingo throughout later life. He lived here with his five sisters and his mother. His father was often away, and he seldom associated him with his home. His only brother, Honorio, died at the age of eleven, leaving Domingo alone in a house of women. Domingo always remembered his home and the women in it with loving affection. Among the most beautiful pages of his prose writings are those on his "Home" in his "Provincial Recollections":

"My mother's house, the product of her own industry, the mud bricks and walls of which could be computed as so many yards of linen woven by her hands, has had some additions during the last few years, which in my opinion now give it a certain appearance of mediocrity. Its original form is the one to which the poetry of my heart clings, the indelible picture that always comes to my mind when I recall my childhood pleasures and amusements, my hours of play after returning from school, the secluded spots where I spent hours and weeks on end in utter happiness, making clay saints to set up and worship or armies of soldiers of the same material, that made me swell with pride at my exercise of so much power.

"On the southern part of our lot, thirty yards wide by forty deep, stood the single unit of our house, divided into two rooms, one serving as our parents' bedroom and the other

[25] *Obras*, III, 6.

and larger one as the living room, with its high couch and cushions, a relic of the traditions of the Arab divan still retained by the Spanish peoples. Two indestructible tables of algarrobo wood—which had been handed down from the time when the only lumber in San Juan came from the algarrobos in the fields—and a few chairs of various styles flanked the room. Two large oil paintings of St. Dominic and St. Vicente Ferrer—by an execrable brush, but sacred and inherited because of their Dominican habits—adorned the smooth walls. A short distance from the front door, the matriarchal fig tree raised its dark branches which, during my childhood, still shaded my mother's loom, the clatter from whose spindles, pedals, and shuttle awakened us before sunrise to announce that a new day had begun and with it the need to cope with its problems. Some of the fig tree's branches had grown until they reached the walls of the house and there, warmed by the reflected heat from the sun, their fruit ripened before the rest, offering their contribution of mellow fruit as early as November 23, my father's birthday, to heighten the family festivities.

"Other means of sustenance were to be found on the remainder of the lot, scarcely twenty yards deep. Three orange trees yielded fruit in autumn as well as shade throughout the year. Under a voluminous peach tree there was a small pool of water for the enjoyment of three or four ducks, whose offspring contributed to the complicated but meager system of income in kind upon which the family's livelihood depended. Since all of these resources were still insufficient, we kept a vegetable garden no larger than a scapulary, enclosed in order to protect it from the appetites of our chickens. This garden produced every vegetable used in South American cooking, and was brightened and cheered by beds of common flowers, a red rosebush and various kinds of flowering shrubs. Thus, in our home in the Spanish colonies, we duplicated the intensive type of cultivation practiced by the European peasant, which yielded us similarly inexhaustible products. The chicken droppings and the dung from the horse that my father rode were utilized every day to give new vigor to that piece of land which never tired of producing flourishing and varied crops. Once, when I attempted to suggest to my mother some ideas of rural economy casually picked up from books, I earned a merited reputation for pedantry in view of the scientific cultivation that had been the favorite hobby and occupation of her long life. Today, at seventy-six, she still slips out to the garden where we are sure to find her hilling up the lettuce, and she replies promptly to our chiding by saying that it would do her more harm to leave them without proper attention.

"There was still a little corner in that Noah's Ark where colors were steeped in alum or prepared for dyeing cloth, as well as a fermenting vat for bran, from which a quantity of exquisite white starch was produced every week. In prosperous times, there was also a shop where candles were moulded by hand. An attempt was made at plaster mixing, which always ended badly, and a thousand other operations were undertaken which it would be superfluous to enumerate. Such varied occupations did not prevent their being attended to in proper rotation, the morning beginning with the feeding of the chickens and the weeding of the vegetable beds before the sun heated them; then my mother immediately took her place behind the loom which for long years had been her principal means of support. I still have in my possession the shuttle of algarrobo wood, shiny and blackened by use, which she had inherited from her mother, who in turn had received it from my great-grandmother—this humble relic of colonial life spanning a period of nearly two centuries during which noble hands have tossed it back and forth almost unceasingly. Although one of my sisters inherited my mother's habit and need to weave, my covetousness prevailed and I have become the depository of that family jewel. It is a pity that I shall never be either sufficiently wealthy or powerful to imitate the Persian king who, lest he become arrogant and scornful of poverty, caused himself to be served in his palace from the clay vessels which he had used as an infant.

"Such was the home in which I was raised. It could not help leaving on the souls of its inmates—unless they were very recalcitrant—indelible impressions of morality, industry, and virtue, learned in the sublime school in which the greatest industry, the purest morality, dignity maintained in the midst of poverty, constancy, and resignation shared every moment of the day."[26]

At a very early age, Domingo showed signs of precocity.[27] In 1814, his father left town for one of his frequent trips, and Domingo was taken in by his uncle, José Eufrasio de Quiroga Sarmiento. He was a man of exceptional virtues and outstanding talents, and in later years became Bishop of Cuyo. At this time he was forty years old, and his young nephew was four, but he saw in the young child a promise of future value and greatness. He took him in and taught him to read. The little boy was the priest's acolyte, and he spent long hours at his side, learning the rudiments of reading and writing, two instruments that were to serve him well in the years to come.[28]

The next year, Domingo started to school. This was the year of the Congress of Tucumán and the declaration of the independence of the United Provinces of the River Plate from the Spanish Empire. The years between 1816 and 1820 were years of political peace and stability for the little town of San Juan. In nearby Mendoza, General San Martín was organizing and training his famous Army of the Andes for his campaigns in Chile and Perú which finally defeated the main centers of Spanish power in the Americas. San Martín left as his representative and governor in San Juan, José Ignacio de la Roza, a man of capabilities as a governor and as an administrator.

In 1816 the Buenos Aires governor sent two brothers to San Juan with the mission of starting the first school in the history of that town. Ignacio[29] and José Jenaro Rodríguez

[26] This passage, though long, I feel worthy of quotation in full. It is excellently translated by Mr. Grummon in *Anthology*, pp. 68-73.

[27] His sisters denied this, attributing to him the development of a normal, intelligent boy. The references to his precocity may have been apocryphal. They were all written either by Sarmiento or by others after he had become famous.

[28] *Obras*, III, 135.

[29] See Porfirio Fariña Núñez, *El maestro de Sarmiento. Ignacio Fermín Rodríguez*, Buenos Aires, 1931. He was born in Buenos Aires on July 7, 1790, opened the Escuela de la Patria on April 22, 1816, moved to Mendoza in July 1825, and died in Mendoza in August 1856. Pp. 4, 20.

came to the little provincial hamlet with the latest ideas on educational practice, and they came with the zeal and ambition of crusaders. They founded the little Escuela de la Patria (School of the Homeland) and here the five-year-old Sarmiento enrolled as one of the first students. In later years, after exhaustive studies of the latest theories of education, Domingo looked back upon his first school with approval and praise. "When I read the works of M. Cousin, I saw in my school a model of perfection. . . . They taught me to read very well, to write, arithmetic, algebra, and the rudiments of religion. . . . My father and my teachers stimulated me from my early youth in reading."[30]

The Rodríguez brothers, coming from the excited revolutionary atmosphere of Buenos Aires, brought with them the enthusiasm and idealism of this early period of republicanism. They sought a feeling of democracy and equality among the students, and they insisted that every pupil be called by the title of "señor," irrespective of his family or social standing. They taught standards of high morality and good taste. None of these very basic lessons was lost on their most apt young pupil, Domingo Sarmiento.

Domingo loved his school and the vistas that it opened before his provincial eyes. Between 1816 and 1824 he never missed a day of attendance, and though his interest lagged in later years because of the repetition of subjects that he had previously studied, he always proved himself a good and receptive student. The teachers built a special high seat at the front of the classroom for the best pupil, and it was "Señor" Sarmiento who was first asked to occupy it. He was the "Primer Ciudadano" (First Citizen) of the school, and this was an honor that he never forgot in future years. He was fortunate in having such outstanding teachers as the Rodríguez brothers, and they taught him not only the fundamental intellectual tools that he was to use in his later life, but also some very valuable lessons on the art and techniques of education. They taught him to detest the educational methods that had been carried on from the colonial period and they taught him to experiment and learn new methods

[30] *Obras*, III, 7.

and new theories.[31] Domingo became a great favorite with his teachers, and even when he was disobedient or when he had not studied his lessons they found it impossible to bring themselves to punish him. One day Don Ignacio Rodríguez came to see Doña Paula. At that time, Domingo had become bored with his work and had been inattentive to his lessons. "Every day," said Don Ignacio, "I get ready to punish that boy for laziness, and he always disarms me."[32]

During the summer of 1816-1817, General San Martín crossed the Andes Mountains to attack the Spanish in Chile. With his army went José Clemente Sarmiento. His family waited expectantly for the results of the campaign. Even his five-year-old son was conscious of its importance. On February 12, 1817, the Battle of Chacabuco was fought, and Spanish power was permanently broken in the southern part of the South American continent. The man chosen to return with the news and with the prisoners of war to San Juan was José Clemente Sarmiento. He was met with a popular demonstration and he proceeded immediately to make his report to Governor de la Roza. Among the crowd that gathered to witness the arrival was a young boy who was almost six years old. He saw his father in his proudest moment, and, unable to retain his own pride another moment, he scooted beneath the legs of the horses of the mounted guard and ran up to Don José Clemente and the governor. De la Roza was amused by the incident, and he lifted the young boy to his knee and held him there throughout the interview.

Domingo's mother had planned for Sarmiento to be a priest. He spent an entire year reading and learning the Bible. He seems to have had a religious vocation in mind, for many of his childhood activities pointed in this direction. He did not occupy himself with the usual boyhood pursuits. "I never knew how to spin a top, bounce a ball, fly a kite, nor to play any of the infantile games to which I was never attracted during my childhood."[33] He spent much of his time helping his uncle Quiroga Sarmiento with his church services. He was

[31] Ezequiel Martínez Estrada, *Sarmiento*, Buenos Aires, 1946, p. 19.

[32] MSS of Bienvenida Sarmiento, *op.cit.*

[33] Alberto Palcos, *Sarmiento*, Buenos Aires, 1938, p. 22.

fond of making clay figures of saints and he became so skilled at this art that his mother was sufficiently proud of the results to show them off to her neighbors and friends. On Sundays, Domingo would play with a group of his friends, pretending to be a priest and to hold mass. He and his companions would go through the whole service, and it seemed to his family that Domingo was preparing himself well and at a young age for his future vocation.

But as time went on, the religious interests dropped from Domingo's life. They became less and less important, and even his school began to bore him. Nine years is, after all, a long time to spend in elementary school, and as the years went by, Domingo turned to less profitable pursuits to occupy his time. He joined a gang of local ruffians, and it seemed for a short period as if he would be drawn into a kind of youthful underworld. In later life, he looked back upon these pursuits with a kind of pride at his manly exploits. A "half dozen urchins" formed his "imperial bodyguard," and he and his gang picked fights with other groups of boys from the other side of San Juan. He recalled one day when the opposing gang had challenged him and his group to a Sunday battle. They awaited the conflict, but only seven of his most faithful followers appeared. The opposing boys came at them in great number. The scene that followed allowed Domingo to demonstrate for the first time in his life not only his powers of leadership but the great courage that he was going to show in later years:

"Disconcerted, crestfallen, and almost ready to take to our heels, we seven took the cross street that leads to the Torres mill. In front of the bridge across the sluice gate, north of the mill, there was a smooth, solid, chalky strip of ground and, around the bridge itself, an enormous quantity of stones that had been removed from the ditch. An idea came to me which Napoleon would have applauded and Horatius Cocles would have claimed as his own. It occurred to me that if the seven of us took our stand on the narrow bridge, with that heaven-sent supply of stones at hand, we could hold it against the allied armies of Colonia and Valdivia. I halted my lads, explained the situation to them, harangued them, and ended by getting their firm and enthusiastic 'All right.' They promised me blind obedience. I took the center of the bridge with Riberos and Barrilito, stationing two more boys on either side of the trench formed by the mill-race. We all labored feverishly to gather piles of stones so as to make up for our numbers by the rapidity of our fire. Meanwhile, the crowd of boys had sighted us, and the air shook with their shouts as they rushed at us. My plan was not to throw a stone until we had them within range. The mob approached and suddenly we threw such a hail of stones that the urchins in the crowd who had been hit gave loud proof that our fire had been effective. The disordered rabble fled and my boys were about to rush pell-mell after them, but their general, who had calculated everything, realized that our only possible safety lay in holding the bridge.

"When I said that I had calculated everything, I was forgetting the most important thing which had not occurred to me: that was that the stones which we had thrown could be thrown back at us and that at their rear the immense mob had San Augustin Street, which was full of stones of the size that bruise horses' hoofs. The aggressors, having in fact recovered from their fear and sending boys by the hundreds to carry back stones in their ponchos, the bitterest fight ensued ever chronicled in the annals of vagabond urchins.

"A boy named Pedro Frías approached the trench that I was defending, to parley, and proposed that we fight with swords. Seven against five hundred! Having duly considered the proposal, I definitely rejected it and a moment later the air was so thick with stones flying in both directions that we almost swallowed some of them. Piojito's head was laid open and, dripping blood and tears and hurling obscenities, he flung stones by the hundred like an ancient catapult. Chuna had fallen fainting into the mill-race, in danger of drowning; we were all wounded and the fracas continued with increasing fury. The distance was now only four yards, but we at the bridge did not yield a step until Dionisio Navarro's Negro, Tomas, who was in the first line, cried out to his side, 'Hold your fire. Their general can't move his arms any more.' With this the firing ceased and the nearest boys quickly pressed silently around me, more pleased with me than with their own triumph. The fact was that in addition to the countless bruises that I had received on my body, so many stones had struck my arms that I could barely move them, and the stones that I still threw, out of sheer unwillingness to quit, fell spent a few paces away. Of my brave soldiers, two had weakened and fled. I shall not name them in order not to blacken their reputations, for equal courage is not vouchsafed to every man. Riberos was still at my side. Piojito continued to scream and curse and we dragged Chuna out of the mill-race so as to dress his wounds. Some heartless youngsters wanted to take me along, a prisoner. I resisted this with my last ounce of energy, my arms having fallen useless. The men in the crowd intervened in my favor, giving due merit and all the honors of the day to the vanquished. I retired, staggering home exhausted, where for a whole week I secretly wrung out cloths in brine and laid them on my black bruises which were so numerous that without my clothes on I looked like a piebald colt. Ah, comrades of glory on that memorable field! Alas! Piojito, if only you were still alive! Barrilito, Velita, Chuna, Riberos, and Capotito, I salute you even from my exile, as I do justice to the illustrious valor which you displayed! It is a pity that no monument has ever been erected at that bridge to perpetuate your memory. Leonidas with his three hundred Spartans did no more at renowned Thermopylae. Unhappy Acha did no less at the ditches of Angaco, laying low any imbecile incapable of appreciating the value of a ditch when a half dozen rascals stand their ground firmly on the other side!"[34]

At the age of ten, young Domingo Sarmiento was but one of a number of boys of his age studying and playing in San Juan. Some members of his family found him precocious and his teachers found him an apt but unruly pupil. He gave indications of an ability to lead others as he took command of his boyhood gangs, but he was still no more than a child, living from lesson to lesson and from game to game. The world outside of San Juan was but a vague reality. The existence and

[34] *Anthology*, pp. 86-88.

independence of his nation was but a chapter in his school text.

But at the age of ten, young Domingo's life reached a turning point. For the first time, he became conscious of the politics of his homeland, and for the first time these politics had an effect upon his own personal existence. In 1820 the Argentine Republic was thrown into an era of political chaos and civil war. Revolutionary armies marched and countermarched from the Andes to the pampa to Buenos Aires, and the little provincial town of San Juan could not escape the effects of these events. Argentina was at a crossroads of her history. A life-and-death struggle between two political forms, two political ideas, was ensuing; and the young boy who had spent his early years playing priest and soldier, learning the elements of study at the Escuela de la Patria, following the footsteps of his mother and admiring his father from a distance, suddenly found that even he was a part of his nation's conflict. Even his existence would be altered by it.

Chapter 4. The Education

THE politics of San Juan had been peaceful during the early years of Domingo Sarmiento's childhood. As a base for San Martín's Army of the Andes, San Juan devoted much of its efforts to the cause of national independence. Under the direction of Governor De la Roza, it followed the lead of Buenos Aires and the eastern provinces in attempting to set up a nomocratic or unitarist government, ruled by a constitution and law. The Congress of Tucumán met in 1816 and declared the independence of the United Provinces of the River Plate—later to become the Argentine Republic; and in 1819 a unitarist constitution was drawn up, modeled after the ideas and political forms of the French and American revolutions.

In 1820, however, the peaceful political situation that had reigned for the preceding five years degenerated into chaos. Buenos Aires was torn by revolution, and San Juan saw the peaceful government of De la Roza overthrown. Throughout the entire nation localism and personalism challenged the nomocratic experiment. The nomocratic leaders still struggled for power in Buenos Aires, but the nation as a whole divided into little separate units. Just as Santa Ana held sway over Mexico, O'Higgins over Chile, and Santa Cruz over Perú, so the Argentine Republic came under the control of *caudillo*[1] dictators. "One of the dominant—one might almost dare to say *the* dominant fact—in the political history of Hispanic America in this era has been the existence of the institution of 'caudillism,' based on the rule of the individuals commonly called 'caudillos.' "[2]

Hispanic American history can be told as the history of one personalist leader, one caudillo, after the other. It can be told as the history of Porfirism, Miguelism, Santanism, and Peronism. Throughout much of the nineteenth and twentieth centuries, the caudillo was the central political force. He may have appealed to the sentiment of patriotism. He may have used existing constitutions or created new ones, but primarily he was the government. "Under caudillos there was no hierarchy, no division of powers. They themselves were absolute. Their will was the law. Caudillism became the real constitution, despite imported 'fundamental documents.' "[3] The caudillos observed the constitutional forms when they were useful, but did not hesitate to change them when they were in the way. The abstractions of laws and constitutions and rights did not impede the will of the personality. Caudillism made "the country subservient to the individual rather

[1] Caudillo is the Spanish word for the personalist dictator. Caudillism has come to denote the political form in which the caudillo is the ruler. Note that General Francisco Franco in Spain uses the title "El Caudillo" just as Mussolini used "Il Duce" and Hitler used "Der Fuehrer."

[2] Charles E. Chapman, "The Age of the Caudillos: A Chapter in Hispanic American History," *The Hispanic American Historical Review,* XII, August 1932, p. 281.

[3] *Ibid.*, p. 293.

than the individuals to the country."[4] Principles and dogmas were unimportant. The personality was supreme.

The Argentine Republic of the 1820's refused to sacrifice its values for a "dogma." The "dogma" of the nomocrats was ignored. Political allegiance was shifted to the local caudillo. Thus the pendulum was swinging back once more from nomocracy to personalism.

Caudillism in the River Plate area passed through three important phases. The first of these was the period of gauchocracy, or government by local gaucho leaders. This was a time of decentralization in which the nation divided into many parts, each with its own leader and its own government. The second period was one of centralization. A strong caudillo replaced the many local gauchos and centralized the government of the nation. And, finally the last period of caudillism was one of adaptation. The caudillos adapted themselves to the political forms of their times: first to the outward forms of constitutionalism and democracy, and later to the newer twentieth-century political forms dominant in Europe and the rest of the world.

During the period of gauchocracy, the former United Provinces of the River Plate splintered into many small political units. In each area a different caudillo ruled. Political chaos predominated throughout the decade of the 1820's.[5] On January 9, 1820, Captain Mariano Mendizábal led his San Juan garrison in a revolt against the De la Roza government and established himself as the new governor. The year 1820 saw no less than five governors rule the province, and revolt followed revolt in rapid succession. "Mendizábal initiated his administration with terror, sack, and murder."[6] And this was the rule rather than the exception during this period. In August 1820, José Antonio Sánchez, a Chilean, came to power and initiated a government of relative stability that lasted for more than a year.

By 1821, the restlessness of the ten-year-old Domingo Sar-

[4] Salvador de Madariaga, *Englishmen, Frenchmen, Spaniards*, p. 250.

[5] Ricardo Levene, *La anarquía de 1820 en Buenos Aires*, Buenos Aires, 1930.

[6] Antonio Zinny, *Historia de los gobernadores de las provincias*, Buenos Aires, 1921, IV, p. 130.

miento was becoming apparent to his father, and he searched his mind for a way of putting the young boy back on the path that his ambitions had selected for him and taking him away from the environment of gang play and gang war. During the first months of the year Don José Clemente determined to take Domingo to Córdoba and enroll him there in the Seminario de Loreto (Loreto Seminary). But upon arrival in that city, which had become the educational center of the new republic, something happened to cause them to change their plans. It is not certain what was the exact cause, but Domingo and his father returned together to San Juan. Sarmiento later attributed this failure to start at a higher level of education to "sicknesses that attacked me."[7]

In January 1822, General José María Pérez de Urdininea led a new revolt in San Juan and overthrew the government of Governor Sánchez. This was a counterrevolution against the personalist trend. Urdininea brought with him a government of reform and progress. Two of his ministers, Narciso de Laprida and Salvador María del Carril, were Sanjuaninos[8] who had studied in Buenos Aires and who were seeking to apply the revolutionary doctrines of that metropolis to their own provincial town. They had learned the rational ideal pattern of human life that had been taught by the French eighteenth century, and they sought to impose that pattern on the reality that they governed. They were not men with selfish interests and egotistic aims but rather men with the "purest civic spirit and a decided desire to work for national organization and local improvements."[9] It was at this time that a similar nomocratic experiment was being carried on by the unitarist government in Buenos Aires. Martín Rodríguez had become governor following the period of chaos in 1820, and a powerful landowner, Juan Manuel de Rosas, had helped him to restore order and peace with his own private gaucho army. Rodríguez's minister of state, Bernardino Rivadavia, was carrying out many reforms from his ministerial position. He was attempting to impose a government by law on the Argentine Republic; and in order to prepare the Argentine

[7] *Obras*, III, 7.

[8] Natives of San Juan.

[9] Zinny, *Historia, op.cit.*, IV, p. 131.

people for such a way of life he was planning different ways of educating them.

On January 2, 1823, Rivadavia issued a proclamation. "The education, clothing, and maintenance of six young men from each one of the territories, that are now under independent government but were formerly part of the nation, will be paid for in schools of this country."[10] Each province was asked to supply a list of its best pupils. In San Juan, Domingo Sarmiento's name stood highest in the scholastic rating of the Escuela de la Patria. It looked as if his dreams, and the dreams of his father, for a higher and better education were about to be fulfilled. In Buenos Aires he would be able to absorb all the new ideas of the world. But fate was against young Domingo, and the authorities decided to draw lots to see which of the top ten students would go. Sarmiento's name was not drawn, and his chance was lost.

Domingo was discouraged by this setback, but his father never gave up. His fondest hope was to give his son a good education, and he could not endure seeing the chance slip away so easily. Don José Clemente addressed a plea to the governor of Buenos Aires. It was dated March 1823, and it read: "My project, sir, is great, perhaps even imprudent, but before the benevolence of Your Excellency, there disappears, in my way of thinking, all enormity, and any fear changes to a firm confidence that my petition will be received favorably. It is my desire for my son, in order that he may, if possible, be of service to America, and since my resources are on the threshold of beggary, that the kindness of Your Excellency should give him by an extraordinary favor a place in some school."[11] This petition was typical of Don José Clemente. He wanted his son to serve the ideals of America, and he expected the kindness of the governor to make this possible. The petition was received but never considered, and it is still filed in the archives of the Ministry of Government in Buenos Aires.

[10] J. Guillermo Guerra, *Sarmiento, su vida y sus obras*, Santiago de Chile, 1938, p. 20. After this, the work will be referred to as Guerra.

[11] This document was found by Damián Hudson and offered to Sarmiento in a letter published in *La Tribuna* on October 15, 1868. Published by Guerra, pp. 20-21.

In January 1823 Governor Urdininea resigned to take command of a military expedition against the Spanish in Perú. An election was held, which proved to be one of the first successful experiments in free elections held in Spanish America. "They took the most rigorous precautions to prevent intrigue. They assured the citizen his rights to elect freely the first magistrate. The election fell upon a young man of talent and patriotism."[12] This young man was Dr. Salvador María del Carril, who proved to be the most progressive governor that the young country had yet known. Del Carril was saturated with the ideas of the French and North American Revolutions, and he was determined to introduce them in his own government. His greatest mistake and the cause of his failure was his inability to see the great gap between the reality with which he was dealing and the ideals which he wished to apply to it. He failed to make any allowance for gradual change or adaptation. He granted complete freedom of speech and discussion. He reorganized the judiciary of the province in order to attain a more strict observance of the law. He published the famous Carta de Mayo (May Letter), which was the most advanced statement of the rights of the citizen and the individual that had yet been introduced in the River Plate region. San Juan lived under an extreme nomocratic experiment for more than two years.

One of the articles of the Carta de Mayo granted religious freedom and attempted to tear down the special privileges of the Church. This was perhaps the most abrupt and the most opposed reform that Del Carril introduced, and it proved to be one of the direct causes of his overthrow. On July 26, 1825, a revolt overthrew the Del Carril unitarist government. A proclamation in ridiculously ignorant and incorrect Spanish appeared on the door of the government house, warning the people that "the laws are operating against the Roman Catholic faith." A few days later, a crowd, which included Sarmiento's uncle, José de Oro, attacked the seat of government with shouts of denunciation for the Carta de Mayo. The governor fled into exile, and an interim government issued a proclamation announcing that "The Carta de Mayo will be

[12] Zinny, *Historia, op.cit.*, IV, p. 132.

publicly burned by the executioner, for it was introduced among us by the hand of the devil."[13]

The political situation in the months that followed was completely unstable. Del Carril escaped to Mendoza to seek aid, Plácido Fernández Maradona assumed the leadership of the revolutionary government, and the revolutionists prepared to defend their newly won position. During this time, Domingo found employment with Victor Barreau, a French engineer, who had been commissioned to draw a plan of the city of San Juan. Domingo became his assistant and apprentice, and in his work with Barreau he learned much about engineering and surveying.

On September 9, José Félix Aldao arrived from Mendoza with his gaucho army and overthrew the Maradona government. José de Navarro became the new governor, and he assumed dictatorial powers in order to restore order to the province. One of his first moves was to exile the outstanding leaders of the recent revolt. Among these were the Rodríguez brothers and Sarmiento's uncle, José de Oro. The Escuela de la Patria had to close. Even this rudimentary source of instruction and learning was now cut off from the ambitious young student.

José de Oro was a priest who was related to Domingo on both sides of his family. He had always been referred to in front of the boy as one of the most distinguished of his relatives. He had fought in the famous Battle of Chacabuco under San Martín, and had returned to San Juan to become one of the civic leaders of the province. During Del Carril's government he had served on the provincial junta, but had been alienated from the governor by what he looked upon as his anti-clerical measures. He "separated from the party of the men of progress," as his nephew later put it, to lead the overthrow that upset the unitarist government.

When José de Oro left San Juan for exile under the decree of the Navarro government, he asked his young nephew whether he would like to accompany him. Domingo was thrilled by the idea, and his family granted its permission. Together Don José and Domingo traveled across the moun-

[13] *Ibid.*, p. 134.

tains to the little hamlet of San Francisco del Monte in the province of San Luis. Here the young boy and his uncle lived for more than a year. Don José taught Domingo Latin, and he taught him in a very thorough manner the teachings of the Bible. They kept a notebook together that they called "Dialogue between a citizen and a peasant." Domingo was the citizen, and in the notebook he recorded the lessons that he was learning from his kindly uncle.

Life in San Francisco was a happy country one. Domingo and Don José loved to dance, and every Sunday they organized a party where all the local youths and girls gathered to dance. Young Domingo spent his time organizing a school. He taught all the young people from the surrounding countryside. Though he was only fifteen years old and many of his pupils were ten or fifteen years older, he was able to take this first step in what was to become a long life of teaching. The young "Dianas" that attended his school attracted the adolescent, and they must have awakened in him many emotions that had until then remained dormant, but he later solemnly affirmed that "no dishonest thought mixed with those innocent recreations."[14]

Domingo learned not only about books from Don José but about life. One evening they were alone in their little hut, and in the nearby church was the wake of a woman who had just died of dropsy. "Go," said Don José, "and bring me from the sacristy my Prayer Book, for I must see a *speibus* that there is against what Nebrija says."

"I had to enter through the door of the Church," recounts Domingo, "leave behind me the coffin that was surrounded by candles, take one for myself or resolve to engulf myself in the canyonlike darkness of the building and enter the sacristy. I was sweating seas of sweat at the door for a long time, advancing a step and then going back, until dissolving in fear I renounced my intentions of entering and returned with my tail between my legs to confess to my uncle that I was afraid of the dead. I was resolved to undergo this shame when I saw through a little window the placid, tranquil face of my uncle who was letting the smoke of a recent puff of cigar curl slowly

[14] *Obras*, III, 70.

upward. Upon seeing this face I believed myself to be vile, and turning on my trail I returned to the church, left the dead one behind, and on wings of the feeling of honor which had replaced fear, I took up the book and went out holding it up high as if to say to my teacher, 'Here is the proof that I am not afraid.' "[15] Don José never guessed the spiritual trial his nephew had undergone on such a simple mission.

During the time that they spent in San Francisco, Don José gave the people of the area his spiritual guidance. Together he and Domingo taught them, and also generally improved their lives. They introduced flowers and vegetable gardens that they cultivated and taught others to cultivate. They drew a map of the village, using the lessons that Domingo had learned from Barreau in San Juan. They took San Francisco as a little model and introduced many of the reforms that Sarmiento was later to turn to as the solutions for his entire nation.

They loved each other like father and son, and Sarmiento believed his uncle to be nearly a saint. Don José was the most important single teacher that Domingo had during his youth, and he did much to create the mind that was later to face the problems of his life. "My intelligence was molded beneath the impression of his. To him I owe the instincts for public life, my love of liberty and country, and my consecration to the study of the affairs of my nation, away from which neither poverty nor exile nor absence for many years could distract me."[16]

This happy, almost pastoral existence in San Francisco was interrupted toward the middle of 1827 by a message for Domingo to return to San Juan. The boy thought the matter over and wrote his mother that he preferred to stay with his uncle. A few weeks later, Don José Clemente arrived to get his son, and now there was no possibility of refusal. José Sánchez had returned to the government of San Juan, and José Clemente had persuaded him to send Domingo to Buenos Aires to study at the Colegio de Ciencias Morales (The College of Moral Sciences). Here was the event that father and son had long awaited, and José Clemente did not

[15] *Ibid.*, p. 72.

[16] *Ibid.*, p. 69.

propose allowing Domingo to pass it up. The boy parted sadly from his uncle and rode silently at his father's side down the mountain passes to the Tulum Valley and San Juan.

But again fate decreed that Domingo Sarmiento should not go on to higher formal education. The Sánchez government had been overthrown, and the hordes of Facundo Quiroga, the most terrible gaucho of them all, were in command of the political situation in all of San Juan. Throughout the nation gauchocracy was asserting itself as the dominant political form. Ibarra ruled in Santiago del Estero. Uruguay had been split off from Argentina by the actions of the gauchocrat Artigas. López ruled in Santa Fé. The Aldao brothers ruled in Mendoza. And it was Juan Facundo Quiroga who ruled in the western provinces and on the pampa.

Facundo was in many ways typical of the local leaders of this early period of caudillism. He was identified by his own violent and barbarous temperament and personality. His sole weapon was force; he held the admiration and respect of his followers by demonstrating the superiority of his own physical prowess. "Quiroga doesn't respect life or property," writes one of his biographers. "Death and the confiscation of property are his ideas and his works of government. He constructs nothing and devours all. He is not lacking in talent. All the caudillos have this. He lacks education and is incapable of acquiring it. He possesses the faculty of adaptation and assimilation to new environment. . . . Impetuous, audacious, astute, fast, timorous in action. . . . Of his courage legends are created and of his cruelty annals are formed. He attracts the multitudes who admire and fear him. He applies terror as a method of dominion."[17] Known as the "Tiger of the Plains," Facundo Quiroga was typical of the gaucho caudillo of the early period of Argentine history. It was under his dominion that Domingo Sarmiento received his first bitter lessons of politics.

When he returned home to complete his studies, young Domingo found Manuel Gregorio Quiroga, one of Facundo's underlings, as governor of San Juan. The boy's heart was

[17] Ramón J. Cárcano, *Juan Facundo Quiroga*, Buenos Aires, 1931, p. 26; see also Carlos M. Urien, *Quiroga*, Buenos Aires, 1907.

heavy with disappointment. There was seemingly no future for him in his home town. There was no school. There was no peaceful life. There was only war and chaos. He looked around to choose a pursuit in life. His Aunt Ángela Salcedo had a small country store, and she needed someone to manage it. Domingo Sarmiento chose this job as his first course in life. He must construct his own existence with the tools at hand.

BOOK II

The Commencement

Chapter 5. The Shopkeeper

IN 1827 San Juan was but a small provincial town, isolated from the rest of the world on the one side by the vast pampa, and on the other by the imposing Andes. Founded nearly three centuries before, it was just as its founders had laid it out.[1] Its area covered only a few city blocks. Its center was the traditional Spanish *plaza* or square, and out from that *plaza* branched the streets, carefully planned in parallel and perpendicular lines.

The population of San Juan numbered little over three thousand. It had no industries save the manufacturing in homes of *ponchos* and clothing worn by the Argentine plainsmen and soldiers.[2] The buildings were almost all of adobe, some with roofs of mud, others thatched. The streets were unpaved, and the dust blew in clouds through the town as the intermittent winds whipped down through the valleys of the Andes.

San Juan was the home of a poor, proud, and rugged people. Its climate was cold in the winter and hot in the summer, ranging from several degrees below freezing to nearly one hundred degrees. The soil was rich in the Tulum Valley, but the valley's very isolation limited the distribution of much of its produce to the region itself. "Poverty, ignorance, filth, boredom: this was life in San Juan de la Frontera at the beginning of the nineteenth century."[3]

[1] For a history of San Juan, see Antonio Pérez Valiente de Moctezuma, "El general Juan Jufré fundador de San Juan," *La Tribuna*, San Juan, June 15, 1941; Dr. Octavio Gil, "La fundación de San Juan," *Boletín de la junta de historia de la provinca de San Juan*, San Juan, June 1945, IV, p. 46; José Torre Revello, "La fundación de San Juan," *La Prensa*, Buenos Aires, July 26, 1936; Alonso de Ovalle, *Histórica relación del reino de Chile*, Santiago de Chile, 1888; Diego Barros Arana, *Historia de América*, Santiago de Chile, 1908.

[2] Gálvez, p. 9.

[3] *Ibid.*; Martin de Moussy, *Description géografique et statistique de la confédération argentine*, Paris, 1861, I, p. 389.

Not far west of the Central Plaza, just beyond the military barracks of San Clemente, there was situated a small general store or *tienda*. In 1827 the manager of this establishment was a young man of sixteen. He was large for his age and for the stock usually found in the area. His shoulders were broad. His neck was thick and bull-like. His head was massive and firmly set on his shoulders and neck. The feature that was particularly striking about him was the bright and penetrating gleam of his eyes. These eyes betrayed the vitality of the spirit that was hidden behind the rough exterior.[4]

Domingo Sarmiento had begun to manage his aunt's *tienda* in January of 1827. It was not an occupation suited to his temperament nor to his abilities, but it was nominally his work. Most of his time was spent, not in inventories, planning to stock the store, or even in selling goods to reluctant customers, but sitting quietly on his hard, straight chair, poring over whatever book he could find in the benighted intellectual atmosphere of San Juan de la Frontera.

One day, a particularly highly respected matron of the austere society of the city, which still maintained the customs and the way of life of the Spanish colonial period, paused as she reached the *tienda*. She had passed the little country store every morning for months past, and had peered into it with curious eyes, always finding the same sight: there was the young man sitting absorbed by a book.

"That young man must be a wicked libertine," commented the good lady as she passed the familiar sight.

"But, why?"

"Because for a year now every day, no matter at what time I pass by here, he is always reading. If they were good books, he would not read them with such enjoyment."[5]

The good lady, whose sound philosophy was no doubt very convincing to whomever it was directed, did not realize the character of the youth about whom she was speaking. If she had glanced over the young man's shoulder, she would have found such titles as *The Autobiography of Benjamin Frank-*

[4] For a description of Sarmiento's appearance, see the quotation in Madaline W. Nichols, *Sarmiento, A Chronicle of Inter-American Friendship*, Washington, 1940, pp. 21-22.

[5] *Obras*, III, 9.

lin, Rousseau's *Social Contract,* Paley's *Evidence of Christianity,* and Middleton's *Life of Cicero.*

As young Domingo looked around him, he saw a political situation that lacked all rationality and all order. The young Argentine Republic of which his province was a nominal part was torn by revolution and civil war. The central government in Buenos Aires was in the hands of the unitarist party, but the rest of the nation had risen up to oppose the centralized control of the capital city and its liberal reforms. Local caudillos led their followers in petty wars against each other and against the central nomocratic or unitarist authority. These miscellaneous forces of opposition to unitarist control were all grouped under the general term of "federalist"; federalists advocated local autonomy, local rights, and a decentralized form of government.[6]

The year of 1827 was a particularly disturbed one. The central Argentine government was at war with the Brazilian Empire. The unitarist president, Bernardino Rivadavia, had controlled the convention, which had drawn up a new constitution on July 19, 1826, that was naturally patterned to fit his party's political views. He now controlled the national congress, which met in Buenos Aires and passed a law making the capital city a federal district, separate from the provinces and the head of a strongly centralized republic. Neither the constitution nor the laws passed by the unitarist congress were acceptable to the federalist forces of the interior and under their caudillo leaders they led an active and warlike opposi-

[6] The use of the words "federalist" and "unitarist" for the political parties of these times is often misleading. The only way to understand them is to realize that their names refer to the superficial aspects of the political split. The essential split was between those who wanted to establish a government by law, a nomocracy, and those who wanted to rule by personality. In the early stages of this conflict, the only manner in which a government by law could be imposed was by its establishment in the city of Buenos Aires and its imposition by way of a centralized government on the rest of the provinces. The nomocratic party therefore took on the name of unitarist. The personalistic gauchocrats, on the other hand, each controlled his own little area. They did not want to be brought within the framework of laws of the central Buenos Aires government and the unitarist constitutions of 1819 and 1826. If they were to maintain their personal rule, the government would have to be highly decentralized. They therefore came to be known as federalists.

tion which brought political chaos to the nation.[7] Torn by a foreign war and bitter domestic strife, the world that young Sarmiento saw around him appeared to lack order, direction, and rationality. He sought to find some explanation, some order, some philosophy, in reading.

Sarmiento's reading formed, as he later wrote, "such disorganized studies."[8] He read whatever he could find in the poverty-stricken intellectual atmosphere of San Juan. In the local hardware store, he found such treasures as the Abbé de Pradt, Ackermann, and Rousseau. At the shop of an Italian tinsmith, he found the *Teatro crítico* of Feijóo. Most of the writers that he read were thinkers and writers of the eighteenth-century Age of Reason. Middleton's *Life of Cicero*[9] described in clear and precise terms the well-ordered and rationally organized world of the Roman orator and leader. Paley's *Evidence of Christianity* and *Natural Theology* examined the religious problem in a rational manner. Sarmiento read of Tom Paine's idea of a rationally ordered constitutional political system. He read the leading Spanish writer of the Enlightenment, Father Feijóo, and his treatise on *The True Idea of the Holy See.*

Finally, Sarmiento found in Benjamin Franklin's *Autobiography* the pattern of behavior of a young man in a rationally ordered world. Here was the typical thinker of the eighteenth-century culture—the scientist, the inventor, the political reformer, the organizer of society who started, as Sarmiento put it, "without any assistance but his own reason."[10] As the young man sat in the back of the small store in San Juan and read the life of Franklin, he saw his ideal form before his eyes: "I felt as if I were Franklin; and why not? I was poor as he, studied as he, and managing to follow in his footsteps, I could someday succeed in being like him, becoming a doctor *ad honorem,* and making for myself a place in the letters and politics of America."[11]

And so the projects of the young man were formed. Thus

[7] Munro, *The Latin American Republics, op.cit.,* pp. 206-207.

[8] *Obras,* III, 9.

[9] Translated into Spanish in 1790 by José Nicolás de Azara.

[10] *Anthology,* p. 92.

[11] *Obras,* III, 176.

he answered the questions that he had asked himself. From his readings he obtained an idea of the rationally ordered and understandable universe that *should exist.* Around him he saw the chaos that *existed.* His intellectual growth was stimulated by this dichotomy—this split between what should be and what was.

Sarmiento's readings were not the only influence working upon the sixteen-year-old mind. His learning process was varied; it included many phases other than the books that he devoured as he sat in the back of the San Juan store. "My poor studies were disorganized and incomplete; but to this very disorganization I owe great advantages. From the lack of any teacher—or any guide more than my own judgment . . . was born the independence of my thought." He was not confined to one idea by a teacher or a school. His was an education of thought, not of ideas. His entire future life was signalized by this outstanding feature: it was a life of fluid, everchanging thinking, never a life of frozen, lifeless ideas.

For more than a year, Sarmiento made nightly visits to the home of his uncle Juan Pascual Albarracín, one of the best-known priests of San Juan. Every night, for a year and a half, "without the interruption of one day," they spent the evenings from nine to eleven discussing the entire Scriptures, "the dogma, the discipline, and religious morality."[12] Father Albarracín's religious instruction followed the general pattern of Sarmiento's readings. His uncle was known to be a liberal, a partisan of the unitarist government of Rivadavia, and receptive to the newest thinking of the liberal world.[13]

But simultaneously with the liberalized teachings of his uncle, Sarmiento came under the influence of the fiery priest, Ignacio Castro Barros. Barros was preaching in San Juan in 1827, and young Domingo assiduously attended his sermons. Castro Barros was a moving orator. He preached violently against the unitarist regime and the liberal reforms that it was instituting in Buenos Aires. Many of these reforms, borrowed from the doctrines of the French Revolution, were opposed by the Catholic Church, and Castro Barros con-

[12] *Ibid.*, p. 8.

[13] Guerra, p. 27.

demned the unitarists as heretics and enemies of the faith. For him, the struggle was nothing less than a religious crusade. His eloquent appeals could not but have had an effect on the unformed and impressionable mind of the adolescent Sarmiento. He "succeeded in awakening in my soul the rancorous fanaticism that flowed from his mouth, foaming with anger, against the impious and the heretics, whom he abused in the most ignoble terms."[14] In later life Sarmiento was to write that Castro Barros planted in his soul the first seeds of religious doubt and hatred of fanaticism and superstition,[15] but one of his biographers wisely points out that this statement was probably an afterthought.[16] It is quite understandable how a young man of his age could be taken in and intrigued by such a great and fiery orator. In later life Sarmiento referred to Castro Barros as his "confessor in youth," but he termed him "the most fanatical theologian" that he had ever personally known.[17]

Under these contrasting and conflicting forces, young Domingo Sarmiento, reading whenever he could in the country store, continued to seek the solution for the questions of the world around him. Perhaps a broader view of the world would help him. One day his aunt, Doña Ángela Salcedo, the owner of the store in which he worked, proposed a trip to Chile. She would give him four thousand pesos with which to buy materials in Chile, and with these he would return and stock the *tienda*.[18] Here was the opportunity to learn in a different way, to see other cities and other places.

We know little about this first trip that Domingo made to Chile. He went by way of the city of Mendoza, where he bought sugar for Doña Ángela's store.[19] From there, in the company of his good friend, Saturnino Laspiur, he crossed the Andes on muleback. To entertain themselves on the long and tedious journey, they "told stories, described battles, or

[14] *Obras*, III, 173. [15] *Ibid.*, p. 175. [16] Gálvez, p. 44.

[17] Written in 1880's, *Obras*, XLVIII, 102.

[18] "Algunos rasgos de la vida de Domingo F. Sarmiento, por su hermana Bienvenida como la mayor." San Juan, May 1889. Original manuscript in Museo Histórico Sarmiento. Edited and published by Antonio P. Castro, Museo Histórico Sarmiento, Series II, No. 14, p. 32.

[19] Gálvez, p. 46.

recited verses."[20] Laspiur was able to recite by heart entire scenes of the famous dramatist Moreto's *El desdén con el desdén.* Sarmiento was so intrigued by the recitation of his friend and by Moreto's verses that at one time he hurt his eye by riding blindly into the low-hanging limb of a tree.[21]

In Chile, young Domingo's time was not completely occupied by his commercial pursuits. He carried with him a letter of introduction to a relative there, Friar Justo de Santa María de Oro. The friar was a man of distinguished record in the public and economic affairs of the new republic of southern South America. He had been a signer of the Argentine Declaration of Independence in 1816. At the time he was friar of the Recoleta Domínico in Santiago de Chile, but he was soon to take an active part in the affairs of Sarmiento's own country as Bishop of San Juan. The illustrious friar was struck by the intelligence and good judgment of his sixteen-year-old relative. It is a telling commentary on the impression made by young Domingo that the churchman engaged him in serious conversation and discussed his hopes and projects in regard to San Juan.

Both the contacts with Saturnino, the young and dreamy intellectual whose fluency in the literature of the European Enlightenment was so intriguing to the young traveling storekeeper, and the contacts with the distinguished churchman and liberal whose past was so filled with ideas and projects to reform and change the unhappy world that he saw around him, were broadening influences upon the intellectual development of young Domingo Sarmiento. They served to give perspective to what had formerly been limited to knowledge thirstily gleaned from books. But they were all influences in the same general direction. They all offered a similar picture and a like solution. The readings all painted a picture of the world as it ought to be: a rational world in politics, industry, thought and life, a world in which the ideal man was Benjamin Franklin, the inventor, the diplomat, the author of the almanac, the rational philosopher. This world-picture was

[20] Letter from Sarmiento to Saturnino M. Laspiur, November 20, 1846, in Museo Histórico Sarmiento.

[21] Gálvez, p. 47.

augmented by his contacts with liberal and advanced thinkers such as Juan Pascual Albarracín and Friar Justo de Santa María de Oro and by the works of Moreto and others that were recited by Laspiur.

This world-picture which young Domingo was forming in his mind did not, however, have any vital connection with the reality around him. For this very reason his world-picture had an utopic and an uchronic character; it was out of place and out of time. It was dimensionless, existing only in the realm of the ideal. Young Sarmiento did not realize, nor would he have admitted, this fact. Perhaps the world of San Juan and Argentina did not fit into the world-picture that he had formed from his reading and his personal contacts. But that ideal had a reality, probably in the France of Rousseau or in the United States of Benjamin Franklin. It might not exist now in South America, but it had a time. Its time was the future.

Upon his return from Chile, young Domingo retired once more to his commercial and intellectual activities in Doña Ángela's store. He was becoming less satisfied with the materialistic ends of a storekeeper's life. He began to dream of the life of Franklin, "robbing the skies of their lightning and the tyrants of their scepters."[22] Political chaos had spread throughout the republic. 1827 saw the end of the Brazilian War, and the loss in the treaty of peace of the Banda Oriental (Uruguay), in spite of the overwhelming Argentine victory at Ituzaingó. By the end of June, Rivadavia had fallen from the presidency and with him went the fictitious unity created by the unitarist constitution. Each province recovered full autonomy, and Buenos Aires elected as governor the leader of the federalist party,[22] Manuel Dorrego. By the end of 1828, the unitarist general, Juan Lavalle, returning with his veteran troops from the Brazilian War, overthrew Dorrego, had the federalist leader shot, and set up a dictatorial rule over the province of Buenos Aires. Meanwhile, another unitarist general, José María Paz, in the fall of 1829, led his troops inland to capture

[22] Ricardo Levene, "Sarmiento, sociólogo de la realidad americana y argentina," in *Sarmiento, Homenaje de la facultad de humanidades y ciencias de la educación,* Universidad Nacional de la Plata, 1939, 2nd ed., p. 84.

the city of Córdoba. The provinces were aflame with civil war. San Juan was still ruled by Facundo Quiroga's puppet. Other provinces were under federalist domination. The interior prepared to meet the attack of the unitarist armies from Buenos Aires. It prepared to defend itself against Lavalle and Paz.

The young storekeeper with his books and his memories of ideals and reforms described by his older relatives and teachers could not escape being drawn into this vortex of civil war and destruction. His was not a temperament to escape a fight. He was confused and disorientated. The chaos and fighting did not seem to fit anywhere into the rational world about which he had read. But it was there and he could not escape it.

In 1828 Sarmiento happened to be reading about *Tom Paine and the Revolution of the United States* (*Tom Paine i la revolución de los Estados Unidos*). He was reading of "constitutional principles of government and the rights of the governed." As he later commented, "All of this was theoretical and had no application in my country."[23] It did, however, serve to do one thing in the life of the seventeen-year-old youth. He liked the picture that had been created in his mind. He was revolted by the picture that he saw around him. He had been living in an "enchanted atmosphere," out of which he was suddenly drawn.[24]

One day, he stood on the corner down the street from his store, watching the gaucho hordes of Facundo ride in. "It was enough to convulse the nerves to see parade by those hordes of dirty, shaggy savages, with their canvas rags for clothes, with their hair and beards disheveled and unshaven in a period when full beards were not worn. . . .

"It was all changed now. What I saw was simply detestable. I knew nothing else. Rivadavia had disappeared from the scene, and the opposition had no body, nor visible form, nor program."[25]

The youth had not as yet found concrete ideas. His positive

[23] *Obras*, III, 12.
[24] Palcos, *Sarmiento, op.cit.*, p. 27.
[25] *Obras*, XLIV, 29.

picture of an ideal world still existed as a vague shadow. He did, however, know what he opposed. The young shopkeeper knew that the world of Facundo Quiroga could never fit into the world picture that he was slowly forming.

Chapter 6. The Vortex

By the late 1820's, the chaos brought by the period of gauchocracy—the decentralization of political power under local gaucho leaders—had reached a crucial point. It became evident that unless complete political disintegration and instability were to occur, some form of central power would have to be inaugurated. In February 1826 Bernardino Rivadavia had been elected president of the United Provinces of the River Plate. In December of that same year a centralized constitution had been ratified and promulgated, and it was hoped that the necessary unity could be achieved under nomocratic forms. But the interior of the nation rejected the new constitution and the new government. The provinces, remaining in control of the personalistic gauchocrats, refused to recognize the central government. By 1827 Rivadavia's position had become untenable. Quiroga had formed his own government in the Andean region. Bustos declared the independence of Córdoba. On June 27 Rivadavia resigned, still within the framework of thought of the rationalist eighteenth century, still believing in the ultimate progress towards reason, and appealing to the verdict of posterity: "I count at least on the justice of posterity, of history."[1]

Confusion followed the dissolution of the Rivadavia government, and it looked as if the "United" Provinces were

[1] Quoted in Ismael Bucich Escobar, *Los presidentes argentinos,* Buenos Aires, 1934, p. 37.

crumbling in a manner similar to the Bolivarian Republics of Central America. It was not a constitution nor a dogma that brought unity and order to the Argentine Republic. It was a personality. Juan Manuel Rosas first stepped onto the national political scene in 1828, and between then and 1835 he maneuvered himself into absolute control of the politics of Argentina. He either destroyed the opposition of local gauchocrats or he won their adherence. He gained dictatorial powers in the Buenos Aires government, and he held complete practical control over the fate of the entire territory of Argentina.[2] He held power with the strong hand of the tyrant, and he overcame by terror and despotism the chaos and disorganization that he encountered in the public life of his nation. His secret society, the Mazorca, roamed the streets of Buenos Aires, silently executing all opposition. Rosas' power extended to the most remote provinces, and where reason and law had failed to bring order and unity, fear and force succeeded.

Juan Manuel Rosas was a man of titanic energies and capacities, and it was he alone who forged the unity of the Argentine Republic during these years. "For thirty years, he strove to maintain the Argentine Confederation as a political entity in the face of continuous foreign and domestic strife."[3] He was faced with the opposition of both the nomocratic idealists and ambitious rival caudillos on the domestic front, and he was faced with wars against the Peruvian-Bolivian Confederation, against Uruguay, and against England and France abroad. He was a tireless worker. He held all the details of his administration in his own hands, entrusting them to no one, and in this singlehanded manner he carried the nation through crisis after crisis. He was the outstanding example of the caudillo during the period of unification and

[2] The House of Representatives of Buenos Aires Province decreed on March 7, 1835, "Brigadier General Rosas is appointed Governor and Captain General of the Province for the term of five years. The entire sum of public power is deposited in his hands. . . ." William MacCann, *Two Thousand Miles' Ride through the Argentine Provinces*, London, 1853, p. 178.

[3] Gilbert Bell Becker, *Rosas of Argentina; Patriot and Dictator. An Interpretation in the Light of New Evidence.* Doctor of Philosophy Dissertation, University of California, Berkeley, California, 1941, p. ii.

centralization of caudillos. "His government was so personal that he did not delegate to anyone the editing of the innumerable letters that he had to write every day."[4] His person was the center of loyalty and the center of power of the Argentine Confederation, and his personality accomplished the transition from chaos and disunity to order and unity.

When caudillism entered its second period of unification and consolidation under Rosas, its purpose became that of unifying the nation under one central authority. The petty caudillos were subjugated or won over. Political power was unified in the dictator. Although Rosas and his followers continued to call themselves federalists, they became the first really unifying forces that Argentina had ever known. Their names stood for decentralization, but their practical accomplishments were complete centralization. Meanwhile, the nomocrats came to see the dangers of such concentration of power, and they came to favor a doctrine of states rights and federalism. Still using the name of unitarist, they stood for a federalist doctrine. Thus, by the decades of the 1840's and 1850's the names of the two Argentine political parties were anachronistic. They were exactly contrary to what the parties really stood for. Whether the parties favored decentralization or centralization was a matter of expediency. The real conflict was between the newly acquired ideas of government by law and the traditional ideas of government by personality.

It was during the period of gauchocracy that Domingo Sarmiento grew to maturity, and it was during the dictatorship of Rosas that he entered into the politics of his nation. It was impossible for the young storekeeper of San Juan to remain isolated for long from the political struggle that was raging around him. The provincial governor, Gregorio Quiroga, docile instrument of the gaucho leader Facundo, had separated his provinces from the central unitarist government in Buenos Aires and had signed an alliance with the neighboring federalist provinces of San Juan and Mendoza.[5] Together these provinces were preparing for the imminent

[4] Carlos Ibarguren, *Juan Manuel de Rosas*, Buenos Aires, 1933, pp. 345-346.

[5] Ricardo Levene, *Historia de la nación Argentina*, Buenos Aires, 1941-—, p. 218.

attack from the unitarist forces of the east. Domingo Sarmiento still did not understand clearly the situation in which he found himself. "I heard the 'unitarists' and the 'federalists discussed, but what did those words mean?"[6]

In late August 1828, a few months before the December Revolution that brought the overthrow and death of Dorrego in Buenos Aires, and that ignited the spark of general civil war, Sarmiento was forced by circumstances to choose sides and set his future political course. His decision was brought about by events beyond his control, but the course that he chose was based on the values that he had acquired from the world-view and the ideals formed from his readings, his teachers, and his experiences.

By a decree of June 10th of that year, Governor Quiroga, in dire need of recruits for the defense of his government, named Domingo Faustino Sarmiento sub-lieutenant of a battalion of provincial militia.[7] Domingo had not asked for this commission, and he found that the duties it entailed interfered seriously with his job in his aunt's store. The need to continue employment in the *tienda* made him take his first step on what was to develop into his political career. When the time for his third guard duty arose, he offered his resignation, refused his assignments, and addressed a petition to the governor, referring to the personal inconvenience arising from his being drafted for military service. Under the conditions of emergency then existing, such conduct could not go unnoticed. The young officer was placed under arrest and brought for a hearing before the governor.

It was a warm and sunny day. The governor was seated in the patio of the government house, basking in the spring sun. His hat was on his head, and he looked up with a lack of concern and interest as this seemingly routine case was brought before him. The fiery young "Argentine Franklin" took immediate offense at the governor's attitude. His long meditations over the problems that faced him had magnified

[6] Ricardo Rojas, *El profeta de la pampa*, Buenos Aires, 1945, p. 72. After this, the work will be referred to as Rojas.

[7] Sarmiento's military record and his original commission were consulted by the author. They are to be found on exhibit at the Museo Histórico Sarmiento in Buenos Aires.

them to proportions of great importance in his own mind, and he was hurt by the governor's obvious indifference to the situation. As he started to remove his hat in the presence of his superior, he noticed that Quiroga had left his on. The over-sensitive sub-lieutenant quickly withdrew his hand and faced his governor with head covered and in a challenging attitude. "It was the first time that I had presented myself before an authority. I was young, ignorant of life, and haughty by education, and perhaps by my daily contacts with Caesar, Cicero, and my favorite characters."

"Is this your signature?" asked the governor, holding up the petition that Sarmiento had written. Quiroga was already annoyed by the attitude of his subordinate.

The harsh tone of voice and unexpected brusqueness of the governor startled the young man. He quickly removed his hat, obviously unsettled by the question. Then, gathering his wits once more, he calmed his nerves and answered in a resolute tone, "Yes, sir, it is."

No more words were spoken for a moment. There was a duel of stares that would have amazed an unexpected witness of the scene, for it left in doubt who was the commander and who the subordinate. The governor tried resolutely to outstare the young officer. Anger appeared and flashed in his eyes. But young Sarmiento's gaze remained firm and unyielding. Finally, Quiroga's eyes were lowered, and the duel was ended. In a fit of temper, the governor summoned his aide and ordered sub-lieutenant Sarmiento jailed on charges of insubordination.[8]

In jail, young Domingo was visited by his family and

[8] This incident is recounted in *Recuerdos de provincia*, p. 179, and in Bonifacio del Carril, *La vida sanjuanina de Sarmiento*, Buenos Aires, 1938, p. 22. The psychiatrist, Doctor Nerio Rojas, and the novelist, Manuel Gálvez, hold that this incident is probably a product of the overinflated ego and the overactive imagination of Sarmiento. They doubt if it occurred thus, and they hold that such insubordination would not have been taken so lightly by Governor Quiroga and that the young officer would have probably paid with his life for it. I recount it as it appears in Sarmiento's Autobiography and in countless biographies of the Argentine leader, for if it is not literally true, it is just as valuable as a symbolic explanation of how events forced the young man to a crucial decision, and how circumstances had a great influence on that decision.

friends. All were unanimous in their condemnation of his hasty and thoughtless action. Laspiur, his traveling companion to Chile, came to comfort him. Sarmiento's father arrived, and scolded him severely. "You have been very foolish, but now it is done. You must suffer the consequences without weakness."[9]

While in jail the young officer began to think over his situation. Many years later he found a Biblical parallel for this experience, and he called it his "Vision on the Road to Damascus." It is interesting to see how Sarmiento later interpreted the incident:

"All great ideas that change the face of nations have their vision on the Road to Damascus. . . .

"I was a businessman, and I was standing at the door of my store . . . seeing arrive six hundred men with the triumphal ostentation of dust and drunkenness. What a spectacle! The spirited horses, perhaps tamer than their riders, shied at the strange noises. . . . We saw advance a cloud of dense dust, filled with rumblings, with shouts, with blasphemies and outbursts of laughter, with dust-covered faces appearing now and then.

"This was my vision on the Road to Damascus, of liberty, of civilization. All of the ills of my country suddenly revealed themselves, barbarians!

"I had been educated in a family that sympathized with the federation. I suddenly disowned it, and two years later I turned in the key to the store and unsheathed my sword against Quiroga, the Aldaos, and Rosas: in my hours of rest which were to occur in exile, I opened schools and taught the masses to read."[10]

A tremendous change evidently occurred in Sarmiento's thinking while he was in jail. Finally he was brought to trial before a court martial, but the arrogant attitude he had shown in his interview with the governor was unchanged. He was asked if he had heard others complain of the present government. Yes, he had. There was a surprised silence in the court. Who? He would not divulge names. The court threatened to cut out his tongue, but his silence was maintained. Exas-

[9] *Obras*, III, 183.

[10] *Obras*, XXII, 244.

perated, with more important matters to attend to, the court dismissed the case.[11]

Meanwhile, Sarmiento had taken a more humble attitude toward Governor Quiroga. In a letter to his superior, he had acknowledged the hastiness of his action which "he regretted to the highest degree," and he excused himself by pleading his ignorance as to how "a subordinate should oppose his complaints to the higher government." He ended by asking the governor's pardon in the case.[12]

A few days later the young man was released. When he left the prison, he had chosen his political course. He had been caught in the vortex of his nation's politics. "At the age of sixteen I entered jail; and I came out with political opinions."[13] Sarmiento went in as a member of a family of federalists and he came out as a unitarist.[14] His party had not been chosen for its program. External circumstances, combined with a vague idea arising from the values he had received from his self-education, led him into a fight against the federalists, a fight against the barbarism that he had seen in his "Vision on the Road to Damascus." "It was not difficult to choose among the parties. I saw in the one the old reactionaries, the old Goths [derogatory term for Spanish heritage], and the ignorant gauchos. . . . Nourished on the books I had read, preoccupied by the fate of liberty which the history of Rome and Greece had taught me to live, without understanding the ways of realizing this beautiful ideal, I threw myself into the partisan struggle with enthusiasm and abnegation."[15] Sarmiento's political course was still a negative one. What he was fighting *against* was concrete and negative. What he was fighting *for* was vague and abstract. Sarmiento's program was simple: fight the caudillo—educate the masses.

[11] *Obras*, III, 183.

[12] Archivo Administrativo e Histórico de San Juan. Folio 189, Book 113. Year 1828.

[13] *Obras*, III, 182.

[14] Del Carril, *La vida sanjuanino, op.cit.*

[15] *Obras*, III, 12-13.

Chapter 7. The Revolutionist and Soldier

THE death of Manuel Dorrego, the federalist governor of Buenos Aires, brought a new wave of action on the part of the provinces against the unitarist government of Lavalle. Juan Manuel de Rosas, along with the caudillo leader of the province of Entre Riós, Estanislao López, led the federalist armies against the city of Buenos Aires. On April 26th, 1829, they defeated Lavalle's forces outside the city at Márquez Bridge, and the unitarists retired to the capital. López returned to his home province, and Rosas persuaded Lavalle to abandon the Buenos Aires government and retire across the river to Montevideo. Juan José Viamonte replaced Lavalle with a federalist government.[1]

With this important victory, there remained only one major unitarist leader to threaten the power of the federalist governors of the provinces. General José María Paz, the greatest tactician of his nation in that period, had seized the city of Córdoba and had defended it with his veterans of the Brazilian War. At the moment, General Paz was no threat to López or Rosas, and these leaders had entered into negotiations with him in hopes of avoiding a conflict. The caudillos of the western provinces, however, saw the unitarist forces across their supply line in Córdoba as a great danger, and they prepared to march against him.[2]

General Juan Facundo Quiroga was gathering forces from the surrounding provinces to lead against Córdoba. He had gained the support of the caudillo governor of Mendoza, Friar Félix Aldao, and he had demanded aid from Governor Quiroga Carril of San Juan. Quiroga Carril assumed personal command of the forces to join Facundo's expedition against

[1] Ismael Bucich Escobar, *Historia de los presidentes argentinos,* Buenos Aires, 1934.

[2] Gálvez, p. 51.

Paz, and another puppet of the gaucho leader, José María Echegaray Toranzo, was left as governor of the province.

Facundo assembled his expedition at Renca in San Luis Province. There he awaited the arrival of his San Juan contingent, but it failed to arrive. Unable to delay his advance any longer, Facundo led his gaucho forces across the border of Córdoba against the unitarist armies of Paz. One of the officers of his army was José Clemente Sarmiento, father of the young storekeeper who had now returned to his commercial pursuits after his unfortunate encounter with the federalist government of San Juan.

Facundo initiated his attack before learning of what had delayed the forces from San Juan under Quiroga. Actually, it was more than a delay. The unitarist underground in that region, led by Dr. Francisco Narciso de Laprida, former president of the Congress of Tucumán and framer of the Declaration of Independence in 1816, had intrigued with the sergeants in Quiroga's army and won them to his side. Thus when the forces reached a point near the San Juan frontier known as Las Quijadas, the soldiers had revolted. They had overthrown Quiroga Carril and returned to the city of San Juan on June 6. Governor Echegaray had fled to Mendoza for aid, and the unitarist government that had thus established itself put Major Nicolás Vega in command of its troops and at the head of the government.

Overnight the situation had changed. The young storekeeper, whose hatred for federalist rule had grown day by day as he was faced with the barbaric attitude of the government, now saw his opportunity to act. He had long since reached the conclusion that he would have to oppose force with force.[3] He still had no clear idea of his positive goal. He only knew what he opposed, but this, he concluded, must be opposed with force.[4]

Young Domingo Sarmiento put his beloved books on their shelves, put his papers in order, locked the store, and took

[3] Augusto G. Rodríguez, *Sarmiento militar,* Museo Histórico Sarmiento, Series II, No. 10, Buenos Aires, 1943, p. 16.

[4] Julia Beatriz Bosch Vinelli, *Sarmiento y Urquiza, del unitarismo al federalismo,* Paraná, 1938.

The cottage in San Francisco del Monte, San Luis, where Sarmiento lived for a while with his uncle Don José de Oro. From a watercolor by his granddaughter, Eugenia Belín Sarmiento

Daguerreotype of Sarmiento as a soldier in 1852

EL ZONDA

[PERIODICO SEMANAL.] [PRECIO, UN REAL

NUM. 1º SAN JUAN, SABADO 20 DE JULIO DE 1839. [Año 1º de su publicacion.]

SANTA LIBERATA VIRGEN Y MARTIR. Y SAN ELIAS PROFETA.

Nos hemos propuesto escribir un periódico, y por rudo que sea el lector no dejará de suponer que contamos con todas las cualidades necesarias para desempeñarnos con acierto. Vasto caudal de luces, literatura, sana critica, miras elevadas, acendrado patriotismo, juicio recto, prudencia &. & &. y algunos ecsigiran tambien proteccion, ó al ménos tolerancia de las autoridades, de todo lo que les daremos repetidas, é incontrovertibles muestras en nuestras páginas.

Pero ántes de que se convenzan de nuestra idoneidad para el fin propuesto, creémos indispensable instruir á nuestros futuros lectores de los motivos que nos arrastran á escribir y de nuestros designios ulteriores, que son sin duda grandes, como el movil que nos compele á abrazar la no muy segura carrera de EE. PP.

Como nuestros lectores habrán de principiar naturalmente á leer nuestro periódico por el titulo, era muy consiguiente que es lo hiciésemos previamente, como es de uso y costumbre, las razones que nos inducen á preferirlo á cualquiera otro; pero como nosotros nos ocuparemos con preferencia en el discurso de nuestras publicaciones, de nuestro gusto mas bien que del de nuestros lectores, hemos creido oportuno revelarles primero nuestro objeto, y despues nos ocuparemos del titulo que es un órden secundario.

Cualquiera que haya leido diarios ó periódicos nuevos, recordará cuanto en su prógrama, dicen los EE. sobre desinteres, patriotismo, amor al órden, deseos ardientes de promover el bien público y otras mil bellezas, que no siempre justifican los resultados.

Mas nosotros aleccionados por la esperiencia, el conocimiento pleno que tenemos de nosotros mismos, y temerosos de desmentirnos en la segunda publicacion si aventurasemos aserciones tan positivas y halagueñas, hemos tomado un rumbo enteramente nuevo. Nada de promesas, nada de protestas: la verdad pura y limpia; y aunque esta verdad es un poco embarazosa y dificil de decirse, nosotros nos hemos resignado á confesarla sin rodeos.

Nadie ignora el estado de penuria y miseria á que han reducido á esta provincia digna de mejor suerte los pasados trastornos politicos, los estragos causados por los desbordamientos del rio, y otras irrupciones y plagas no ménos funestas. Separados sus habitantes por largas distancias, ó por penosas y dilatadas cordilleras de los focos del comercio estrangero, condenados á buscar en su propio seno los escasos medios que pueden proporcionarse para su subsistencia. Sin fortunas, sin capitales que fomenten las empresas mercantiles, espuestos á las depredaciones de los barbaros en su larga travecia á Bs. As.; recargadas sus producciones agricolas ó industriales de onerosos y tiránicos derechos en todas ó la mayor parte de las otras provincias, carecen de los medios de rehacerse rapidamente de sus pasados quebrantos.

Y si por desgracia entre los tales habitantes hay algunos (como nosotros por egemplo) que sin aptitudes para el trabajo penoso y arduo á que se ven condenados los otros, se sienten dominados por la fuerte tendencia al placer y folganza, á que por nuestra malaventura es tan propensa la flaca naturaleza, su posicion llegaria á hacerse desesperante, si una esperanza reanimadora, si un proyecto vital de industria y ganancia no viniese á sacarlos de la inaccion y letargo á que su miseria les ha reducido.

La causa, pues, que reunió á los hombres en sociedad, formó las costumbres, dictó las leyes, crió los Gobiernos: la causa poderosa que hizo nacer las artes, la ciencia y produjo siempre asombrosos resultados, es la que nos ha reunido á emitir nuestros pensamientos é ideas ....La necesidad!!!

La necesidad de vivir de algo, sin robar, ni matar, ni cometer otros pecados es, pues, la unica causa que nos mueve á esta empresa.

Si alguno de nuestros lectores ha calculado una vez en su vida, una especulacion, juzgará si hemos acertado en la nuestra. En primer lugar, nos hemos dicho, no hay periódicos en la provincia, y ya se deja ver, que haremos un horrible monopolio de la prensa; y no hay mal negocio cuando se monopoliza. En segundo lugar, si descendemos á la parte demostrable, aquella que se puede comprobar con la pluma en la mano, lo que hace la parte sólida del cálculo se verá que, segun se nos antoja creer, se nos antoja decirnos, por que en 30 años de libertad é independencia, no ha habido tiempo ni ocasion de hacer un padron, la poblacion asciende á 30000 habitantes por lo ménos. De estos los 25000, no saben leer: corriente, quedan 5000. De estos, 4000 se les ha olvidado por falta de egercicio, ó lo que es lo mismo, por que no se habia publicado nuestro periódico. De los mil que quedan, á 600 no les importa nada lo que nosotros escribamos. Pero aun quedan 400. De estos que nos quiten 200, aquellos que quieran reducir al ultimo apuro nuestro cálculo, entre viejos que no gustan de papeluchos y bagatelas ó no alcanzan á ver la letra: las señoritas, que seria una impropiedad querer que lean periódicos, como los hombres: los jóvenes que tienen su cafe ó sus amorios y visitas en que entretener sus ocios; en fin los artesanos, sus oficiales y otros muchos, siempre quedan á nuestro favor 200 personas que puedan leer. Ahora les damos de barato 150 que pedirán prestado el periódico, porque no vale lo que cuesta, y por que no sirve sino para el momento en que se lee por primera vez, siempre nos quedarán, quieran que no quieran, 50 lectores escogidos, que valen tanto como 50 reales de plata acuñada por semana, que son 200 reales al mes, 100 pesetas, 50 cuatro bolivianos ó 25 pesos fuertes al mes; y con 25 ps. fuertes al mes hay ya sobre que caerse muertos dos, tres y aun cuatro Editores de periódicos, pues por lo demas, Dios no falta habiendo, segun dice el proverbio.

Esto solo es para los principios, que despues los avisos, los comunicados, suscripciones de afuera y otros gajes, y lo que es mas, el egercicio de leer que rehabilitará á aquellos 4000 que calculamos se les habia olvidado, les tentará la curiosidad á aquellos otros 600, que no se curan por ahora de nuestras publicaciones: de los 200 agregados despues se mueren los unos, empiezan las otras á hallar menos impropio el leer, y ultimamente crecen en todo este tiempo los niños de la escuela, con cuya aficion á la lectura y demas medios que llevamos apuntados, sube á tal número el de nuestros lectores futuros, que nos llena de orgullo y de gusto desde ahora, imaginarnoslos á todos engolfados en la lectura del ZONDA. Para entonces se ha acreditado el periódico, subimos su precio á dos reales por numero, y henos aquí con un poco de paciencia y maña, rellenos de plata, consideracion, y lo demas que se deriba de la adquisicion de la *non numerata!*

El Zonda, a newspaper founded by Sarmiento in 1839

One of Goya's etchings, "Tampoco," from *The Disasters of the War*, in which he depicts the horror of the French Revolution and Napoleonic invasion

Sarmiento's sketch, "El Ahorcado" (The Hanged Man), which crudely portrays a similar scene

the keys to his aunt. "Doña Ángela," he said, "here is the key. I am going to join the army." That is all there was to it. He gave no explanation, even to his parents. He took with him his father's sword, and he left to join the unitarist forces at their camp in Pocito, just outside San Juan. There he was received enthusiastically, and he was put into the squadron of Commander Javier Ángulo with the rank of lieutenant. The young man's fighting spirit was now aroused, and he was spoiling for a fight. His wishes were not long in their fulfillment.

Colonel Vega moved his forces away from San Juan. Some fifty leagues from that city, he established his camp at Jachal. He was stalling for time, for the time necessary to train an effective force to meet the expected federalist counterattack. Governor Echegaray had reached Mendoza and was returning with a force under General Francisco Aldao. The federalists advanced cautiously on San Juan, but when they found themselves unopposed, they entered the city, reestablished Echegaray as governor, and then set out to find the unitarist revolutionaries. The encounter was not long in taking place, and the two forces met at Niquivil, some forty-five leagues to the north of San Juan.

At the Battle of Niquivil, Lieutenant Sarmiento went through his baptism of fire. Here he became a soldier as well as a student, and his conduct on that day became for him a source of pride for the remainder of his life. Sarmiento had been made aide to Commander Ángulo. On June 10, 1829, the line of cavalry was drawn up at Niquivil, but the fighting began with guerrilla and sniper action. These preliminaries were still taking place when Lieutenant Sarmiento approached Commander Ángulo to report. Colonel Vega, who was at the time conferring with Ángulo, took advantage of the young officer's presence to send him on a special mission. In the official military record of General Vega, the young lieutenant's action was mentioned. "On this brilliant day, two men distinguished themselves: Don Domingo Reaña, Lieutenant Colonel of the eleventh and commander of the Patagones during the Brazilian War, and Don Domingo Faustino Sarmiento, who was one of General Vega's aides de camp [sic].

Sarmiento crossed the enemy's fire to carry to Major Julián Castro Albarracín the general's order to turn the enemy's right flank. This movement, carried out with precision, brought about the enemy's complete defeat."[5]

In his *Memoires* Sarmiento clarified one mistake in this official report. He pointed out that he had not been the aide to General Vega, but to Major Ángulo.[6] But aside from this minor point of fact, the report was accurate, and young Lieutenant Sarmiento had won his spurs in action.

The fighting was hard and bloody, typical of the barbaric aspects of the gaucho tradition. Sarmiento saw one rider, swinging his sword wildly above his head, draw up to the side of an enemy rider and strike him with such a blow that the "crown of his skull, like a piece of watermelon, flew off, spinning around and around, until it fell on the ground."[7] Back and forth amid confusion and blood they rode, but the fate of the battle had been decided by General Vega's important maneuver.

The military situation in the nation as a whole was, however, in such a completely fluid state that no victory seemed final and no move decisive. When Francisco Aldao in San Juan heard of the defeat of his forces, he sent a more numerous army under his brother José to an encounter with the unitarists. General Vega received news of this latest move, and instead of waiting to meet the superior foe he marched his troops around the mountain range and suddenly appeared in the now unguarded city of San Juan. News had arrived of the defeat of Facundo Quiroga's gaucho hordes in their advance to the east, and the position of the unitarists appeared now in a far different and improved light.

This appearance proved, however, to be illusory. While Lieutenant Sarmiento, in command of a company and as a part of Major Javier Ángulo's squadron, was carrying out orders to seize a federalist supply depot near the city, the main unitarist forces of General Vega had met the returning army of José Aldao and had been defeated in the Battle of

[5] *Biografía del general argentino don Nicolás Vega*, Buenos Aires, 1876.
[6] *Obras*, XLIX, 34. See also Rodríguez, *Sarmiento militar, op.cit.*, p. 18.
[7] *Obras*, XLIX, 34.

Tafin, just outside San Juan. Sarmiento and his men heard of this defeat, and as they rode back to join their army they encountered on the road some "insects with little green ponchos."[8]

"Halt there! Who goes?"

"The Second Flankers," came the reply.

Sarmiento and his companions did not wait for any more. These were the federalists. They had cut the lines to their main unitarist army. Sarmiento spurred his horse, and he led his handful of men to escape across the countryside.

This was actually a fortunate turn of events for the young soldier, for the part of General Vega's army which had remained in San Juan and met Aldao's troops had now been taken prisoner. San Juan was again in the hands of the federalists, and unitarist power seemed to be broken in the west.

There was no road that young Domingo could take. Facundo Quiroga and his defeated army were returning from their disastrous defeat in the east, thus killing any hopes of escape in that direction; and the principal cities of the west were in enemy hands. Again, however, the fluidity of the situation made the scene change overnight. The Aldao brothers, returning with their victorious troop to Mendoza, had no sooner reached that city than their soldiers, the very ones who had been successful at Tafin, revolted, overthrew the governor, imprisoned Francisco Aldao, and pronounced themselves in favor of the unitarists.

Here was the desired haven, the center to reorganize resistance. Sarmiento and Major Ángulo lost no time. The young soldier was now accompanied by his father, who had just returned from Facundo Quiroga's expedition and who cared little on which side he fought. They rode silently over the sandy desert that separated Tulum Valley from Mendoza. Sarmiento respected his father and admired many of his qualities, but intellectually they found they had little in common. They could not even discuss the political situation in the same terms. For Don Clemente Sarmiento, fighting was a vocation, a life that he had known since the early years of

[8] Rojas, p. 88.

the revolution, a life to which he had grown accustomed. To his young and enthusiastic son, it was a romantic adventure, but it was also an ideal, a means to an end.

Riding along the road under the sun that even in the winter grew warm when reflected by the sands of the valley, the group of riders met with another distinguished traveler who was headed in the same direction, the famous Dr. Francisco Laprida, signer of the Declaration of Independence, and President of the Historic Congress of Tucumán. Here was a companion with whom Sarmiento could talk. Here was a man who thought in the same terms as he. Sarmiento listened in admiration to the conversation of this national hero and was impressed by the fact that even a distinguished leader such as this felt disoriented and confused by the chaos into which the national political life had degenerated.

The little town of Mendoza, snuggled up against the foot of the imposing Andes, was a welcome sight to the travelers. It was welcome as a contrast to the arid country that they had crossed. And it was welcome to the young soldier as a haven of fellow fighters, a unitarist oasis in the now federalist west.[9]

When Sarmiento and his companions arrived in Mendoza, the commanding general, José Rudecindo Alvarado, was seeking aides for his staff. On the basis of his intellectual attainments and his recent military experience, young Domingo was chosen to be one of these. As he later said of himself, "the adults accepted him in the society of men, thanks to the exceptional education that had developed his intelligence and formed his character at such an early age."[10]

But Sarmiento's new position was not as satisfying as it had promised to be. His principal duty was to do nothing. Alvarado, "respectable and elegant with the airs of a lord," remained in the "regal quarters that had been prepared for him."[11] Meanwhile, the federalists reestablished their position in the surrounding countryside. Friar Félix Aldao, the third and most important of the three famous brothers, returned

[9] José L. Calle, *Memoria sobre los acontecimentos más notables de la provincia de Mendoza a 1829 y 1830.*

[10] Gálvez, p. 55.

[11] *Ibid.*

with his army from the province of San Luis. His agents helped his brother, Francisco, to escape from prison in Mendoza, and Alvarado, still hoping to avoid another open conflict, tried to come to terms with the federalist caudillos by naming the Friar chief of the Southern Frontier. This arrangement was not, however, agreeable to the more sincere unitarists. One group attacked a detachment of Aldao's troops as they headed south. Others attacked distinguished federalists in the city of Mendoza. Finally, Aldao, seeing that the truce was but a sham, recommenced hostilities on the fourth of September, after but a few weeks of peace.

General Alvarado realized that if he was to hope to maintain his position he would have to act. He would have to avoid a juncture between Aldao's troops and those from La Rioja and San Juan under General Benito Villafañe. He led his army out of Mendoza to prevent such an eventuality, but during the night of September 13 the enemy infiltrated right through his lines. There was nothing for the unitarists to do but retire to Mendoza and prepare for a siege.

A little after dawn the next day, a ten-day siege began. Sarmiento was bored with his position on General Alvarado's staff, and for a little diversion he often joined the guerrilla fighters on the outskirts of town. On one of these occasions he was about to be cut off from his outposts when his father, whose main task at this time seems to have been to keep his inexperienced son alive, appeared to guide Sarmiento back to his lines. A few days later, found missing from his post on the staff, he was ordered, upon his return, to turn in his rifle. Afterwards, Sarmiento always believed that his father had been responsible for this order.

This adolescent boredom was not to continue for long, however. One afternoon, Sarmiento heard shots, shouts, and hoofbeats in the city. A general exodus had begun, and confusion had replaced order. General Alvarado had capitulated. Lieutenant Sarmiento, refusing to accept the surrender, abandoned his post with the general and joined the San Juan detachment that was leaving the city to join the main unitarist army under General Paz.

On September twenty-first, they halted at a waterhole

known as Pilar. While resting there, they were surrounded by the federalist forces. There was nothing to do but dig in and defend themselves as the enemy prepared for attack. As usual, the impatient young lieutenant was anxious for action. He "borrowed" a force of twenty men from a Lieutenant Gutiérrez and set out to skirmish with the enemy's outposts. He was not long in finding a federalist detachment, but unlike himself, the soldiers on both sides, almost all militiamen, had no interest in firing at each other and killing their countrymen. Sarmiento wanted to test the spirit of the enemy soldiers, so he ordered a volley. He then advanced ahead of his own men and tried to provoke the enemy commander by calling him an ostrich and a bandit. The enemy commander ordered three or four of his men to fire on the overeager young unitarist, but the shots failed to reach their mark, and Sarmiento retired to where his soldiers were "in the most decent way I could in order not to go on serving as a target, after having drawn fifteen shots at twenty-five paces."[12] Luck was still with the foolhardy young lieutenant. He ordered a charge. Both sides stood looking at each other for a few moments; then, both detachments retreated, each towards its own camp. The eager young revolutionist could not incite a battle.

But on the way back, Sarmiento's soldiers noticed a man they did not recognize following directly behind the lieutenant. Sarmiento had noticed nothing unusual, for he was not well acquainted with his borrowed soldiers. A federalist soldier, separated from his own forces, fearing to make a run for it, had judged that the safest place was close to the commanding officer. The soldiers recognized the impostor and started after him. Here were odds that they did not mind fighting under. Young Domingo, more conscious of fair play, tried to save the unhappy federalist. He stepped in front to protect him, but it was of no avail. Panic-stricken, the soldier made a break for it. Domingo, with a blow of his sword, knocked him from his horse into a swift-moving stream that carried under his unconscious form.[13]

The next day the firing became more intense than young

[12] *Obras,* III, 185.

[13] Belín Sarmiento, *Sarmiento anecdótico,* Saint Cloud, 1929, pp. 9-10.

Domingo had ever seen it. Bullets fell everywhere in the unitarist camp, and the unitarists themselves used twenty thousand bullets and one hundred cannon balls in one day of fighting.[14] The inhabitants of Mendoza heard the firing in the distance and sent a commission of elders and priests to separate the combatants. At four in the afternoon, without having reached an agreement,[15] Francisco Aldao arrived in the unitarist camp to discuss terms. A conference ensued with the commanding general and a few officers, among them young Domingo. Unusual movements in the enemy camp were noted. A cannon was shot. The unitarist commander protested such action during a truce. More cannon shots. An officer exclaimed, "Treason!" The federalist cavalry advanced. Francisco Aldao, unable to explain what was happening, was shot by a unitarist officer.

"Everyone knows the origin of the shameful catastrophe at Pilar. Friar Aldao, drunk,[16] shot six culverins at the group of sixty officers around Francisco Aldao. . . . The disorder among our troops, dispersed due to the peace that had been signed, was converted immediately into defeat, in spite of useless efforts to reestablish our positions. Never has human nature seemed to me more unworthy. . . . I was confused, blind with contempt; my father came to take me from the battlefield, and I had the cruelty to force him to flee alone."[17]

Sarmiento stayed long enough to see Doctor Laprida, whom he so respected, go off to his death. Another aide died at his side, and he began to fight his way out of the disaster. An enemy lancer blocked his way. Sarmiento wounded him with his sword before a fellow unitarist cleared the way with a death blow. He went from street to street through Pilar; in some he was among his own men, in others in the midst of the enemy. "Over there were two Rosas brothers, from the opposing parties, fighting over a horse; further on I joined Joaquín Villanueva, who was later lanced; I joined his

[14] Gálvez, p. 57.

[15] Sarmiento says an agreement had been reached, but Manuel Gálvez denies this.

[16] Both Jorge Calle and Manuel Gálvez hold that Aldao was not drunk.

[17] *Obras*, III, 186-187.

brother, José María, who had his throat cut three days later."[18] Suddenly Domingo was recognized by a federalist soldier. He was a young Sanjuanino whom Sarmiento had once caned, and as he unsheathed his sword he reminded the young lieutenant of that event. Domingo's gaze was steady as he replied. He remembered the soldier as the former servant of some friends of his family. "If I ever command you again, I will beat you again." The soldier hesitated. He seemed to see in this young opponent the bearing of a master, and, forgetting his advantage, he spurred his horse and fled.[19]

The scene in which Sarmiento found himself soon degenerated into one of complete confusion. He made his way through the "labyrinth of dead men," but as he was leaving the city he was taken by a company of federalists on their way to sack the town. They disarmed him and turned him over to their commander, José Santos Ramírez, who took him in custody back to Mendoza.

The federalist victory brought with it the usual butchery of the frontier civil wars. An order was issued to shoot all the captured Sanjuanino youths. But again, luck intervened in favor of young Domingo. While many of his friends were being executed, his captor, José Santos Ramírez, intervened in his favor. "This young man is a guest in my house, and you will reach him only over my dead body." And thus he remained—a captive and a guest, enjoying the humanitarian protection and the hospitality of his captor.

One day an unexpected order for the federalist commanding general, Benito Villafañe, set the young unitarist prisoner free. It is not certain who requested his pardon. Most of Sarmiento's relatives were federalists. They were convinced that Domingo had perished at the Battle of Pilar, and one member of the family set out for Mendoza in search of the body.[20] Finding him still alive and in safe hands, they took him back home to San Juan.

Meanwhile, his father, Don Clemente, had followed the

[18] *Ibid.*, p. 187. [19] Gálvez, p. 59.

[20] All the early biographers, from Guerra to Gálvez, identify this relative as his Uncle Ignacio Sarmiento. Ricardo Rojas says it was another uncle, Domingo de Oro.

federalist army, thinking that it held his son prisoner. He carried on a single-handed guerrilla action until he finally fell into the hands of the outposts and was brought before Facundo Quiroga as a prisoner. The general gave him two hours to prepare himself for execution. At the end of this period, the federalist leader asked about the prisoner and was told that he had bought some wine and a little food, eaten heartily, and fallen into an untroubled sleep. The cold-blooded nerve of this attitude struck a responsive chord in the heart of the barbaric gaucho leader, and he ordered the prisoner freed.[21] A few days later, father and son were reunited at home, both having escaped death through a most generous fortune.

In San Juan, Domingo was temporarily out of the civil wars in which he had been so long involved. To prevent the young man's straying again into the opposition camp, his family agreed that he should remain at home. Between October 1829 and March 1830, Sarmiento was a virtual prisoner in his own house. As was typical of his ever-curious genius, these months were not wasted. "I took up the study of French as a pastime. I had thought of studying it with a Frenchman, a soldier of Napoleon, who knew neither Spanish nor his own grammar, but having been fired with enthusiasm at the sight of a French library belonging to Don José Ignacio de la Rosa, with the help of a borrowed grammar and dictionary, I translated twelve volumes, including the *Memoirs of Josephine*, one month and eleven days after I had begun my solitary apprenticeship. I can cite a convincing instance of my devotion to that task. I kept my books on the dining-room table, merely pushing them aside for breakfast to be served, again for luncheon and, at night, for supper. My candle went out at two o'clock in the morning, but, when absorbed in my reading, I have spent as much as three days at a stretch, thumbing the dictionary. It took me fourteen years after that to learn how to pronounce French, which I did not really speak until 1846 after I had reached France."[22]

The political situation did not remain stable for long. Soon the ceaseless fighting between the unitarists and the federal-

[21] Belín Sarmiento, *Sarmiento anecdótico, op.cit.*, p. 2.
[22] *Anthology*, p. 93.

ists was resumed, and in March, Sarmiento, along with a group of young unitarists, thought it best to flee once more from San Juan. They climbed the Andes and crossed the border into safety in Chile.

Meanwhile events were moving at a rapid pace throughout the nation. The federalist leader, Don Juan Manuel de Rosas, had been elected governor of Buenos Aires with extensive powers, and he had begun what was to prove to be a dictatorship that lasted, except for a few breaks in the early years, almost a quarter of a century. But two and a half months later, in late February 1830, one of Rosas' chief supporters, General Juan Facundo Quiroga, had been defeated by the unitarist General Paz, in the Battle of Oncativo, and federalist power in the interior had been broken.

On April 5 San Juan revolted against federalist rule and a new unitarist governor, Colonel Juan Aguilar, was raised to power. Sarmiento and ten or twelve friends had been living in a house in Santiago, gathering arms and munitions for an expedition. Under Major Hipólito Pastoriza they recrossed the Andes just in time to receive news of the April 3rd unitarist revolution in San Juan, and they marched to join their compatriots in their home city.

Young Domingo Sarmiento returned to San Juan as an experienced fighter and an experienced soldier. During the past years he had matured in a life of many tests and many hardships. He had entered the melee with the attitude of a romantic young man. He had been a revolutionist against the political beliefs of his family and the predominant political forces of his region. He had attacked them with the idealism of a young man who had read about a beautiful and rational world and who wanted to make the world around him fit the pattern of his reading. Fighting "was for me at that time poetry, idealization, the realization of what I had read. A youth of eighteen years, beardless, unknown by all, I lived in a permanent ecstasy of enthusiasm."[23] Sarmiento had come into this civil war green, enthusiastic, the reality of the situation often beclouded by dreams. Now, in early 1830, as he marched back to a unitarist San Juan, he was an experi-

[23] *Obras*, III, 184.

enced soldier of proved bravery. He had discovered the reality of the barbarous war in which he found himself, and he knew how to use that knowledge.

"The Governor and Captain General of the Province of San Juan, recognizing the qualities and aptitudes that combined in the person of Lieutenant Don Domingo Sarmiento have conferred upon him the position of Adjutant of the Squadron of Escort Dragoons, conceding to him the courtesies, exemptions, and privileges that correspond to that rank. I therefore command that he be found, held, and recognized as such Adjutant of the cited Squadron, and for which is issued this dispatch, signed, and sealed accordingly, and of which the principal paymaster will take note.—Given in the city of San Juan, the 13th of April of 1830—Juan Aguilar.—Nicolás Vega."[24]

Sarmiento's former commander, General Vega, had been made minister of the provincial government by Governor Aguilar. He personally requested his former subordinate to accept the commission as Adjutant of the Squadron of Escort Dragoons. The young man did not realize the full implications of the request when he accepted the offer.

The commander of the Squadron, Major Bárcena, was an officer of black reputation. A member of a distinguished family in Córdoba, he had come to be looked upon as one of the most barbarous caudillo leaders. "One-Eyed" Bárcena, as he was called, remained in a state of constant drunkenness, and his record of executions and throat cuttings ranks with those of such human butchers as Facundo Quiroga and Friar Félix Aldao. Sarmiento's service under Bárcena was to teach him that there were barbarians among the unitarists as well as among the federalists, and this lesson was to confuse rather than clarify the political picture in the young man's mind.

The armies of the Argentine civil wars were informal organizations with little more routine than a roll call and occasional guard duty. The youthful Sarmiento had formed ideas of what an army *should* be. He had read of the armies of Napoleon and of antiquity, armies of tactical and adminis-

[24] Original in Museo Histórico Sarmiento; *Obras*, XLIX, 38.

trative organization. He taught his fellow officers what he had learned from his experience and his studies, and he drilled them in the practical application of tactical theories in hypothetical problems. He organized the administrative machinery of the Squadron, regulating the rationing of supplies and the bookkeeping and accounting of the various companies.

One of Lieutenant Sarmiento's tasks was to direct the punishments by whipping. Once Major Bárcena was present at the execution of a sentence of this kind. Domingo stood behind the executioner, sword in hand to strike him if his blows were either too hard or too soft. He had already hit him several times for not administering the whipping with sufficient vigor. Bárcena noted this, and unfastening his belt, struck the victim with it several times. Then, angered by the violent reaction of the soldier to this attack, he stabbed him with his sword. The blow was not sufficiently strong and did not penetrate the clothing. In a temper, Bárcena struck again and again. Sarmiento intervened between the soldier and the officer. "Control yourself, my Commander; this is not your duty, it is mine." Bárcena, ashamed of his bad showing, threw down his sword and left.[25]

A few weeks later, Colonel Santiago Albarracín arrived from Mendoza as the special envoy of the unitarist leader, General Paz. He commanded a squadron of regulars and a company of negro veterans. Two weeks later, Bárcena and his troops received orders to join Albarracín's troops in nearby Pocito. The march was made under a hot sun, and upon arrival Sarmiento fell asleep in the dried-up bed of a small stream.

He was awakened with orders to report to the commanding officer. A little surprised and displeased at having his much-needed sleep disturbed, Sarmiento appeared before Colonel Albarracín, who received him warmly. The commander was seeking an officer upon whose judgment he could rely, and the young student-soldier seemed to be his most likely candidate. He questioned him on his political beliefs, his family, and his education; once satisfied by this information, he relied

[25] Gálvez, p. 65.

upon the nineteen-year-old officer for his information about the San Juan troops.

Two hours after this conversation, the bugles blew "To horse!" and the troops assembled. Albarracín incorporated San Juan militiamen in his squadron of regulars, and took with him two of the militia officers. One of these was Lieutenant Sarmiento. As they rode back to San Clemente Barracks, just down the street from the young officer's former store, Domingo felt a new pride and a new assurance in his position. He was now a member of the regular army.

The duties of his new post were more exacting than his former ones. His troops were veterans of the War of Independence and the Brazilian War. Most were negroes, and their discipline, morality, and experience were in sharp contrast to the men with whom Sarmiento was accustomed to fighting. The new officer, already considered "a kind of man of letters," was given all the tasks that required any intellectual capabilities. He acted as prosecutor in all courts martial. He studied army regulations and articles of war until he knew them by heart. He taught recruits, and his success at the Academy of Tactics soon brought him the position of second in command of that organization. This position brought him a commission.

The youthful spirit in Domingo was, however, still evident. Every night at eight o'clock he was supposed to make a report to an English major. It was always the same: "All quiet." Bored with this routine, he once arrived an hour late, having used the additional time to decorate the "sacred phrase" with "an arch of triumph," laurel wreaths, a Greek temple front, and other designs. Another time, he substituted the English "all right" for the usual report. The Englishman laughed good-naturedly.[26]

By the end of 1830, the political scene in San Juan was again disturbed. During the months that followed, the political changes were almost impossible to follow. In June, Governor Aguilar was overthrown by his former minister, Jerónimo de la Roza. De la Roza governed for eight days, offering the post of Assistant Minister of Government to Sarmiento, who

[26] *Ibid.*, p. 67.

refused it. General Gregorio Aráoz de Lamadrid arrived to overthrow De la Roza, but he departed after a few weeks, leaving Aguilar again in power and Jerónimo de la Roza as his minister. In December, the resignation of Aguilar brought Lieutenant-colonel Hipólito Pastoriza to the government.

Meanwhile Sarmiento's military career had progressed. He had been promoted to a captaincy, and he had been given the task of training the news corps of militiamen. He carried out this assignment with particular speed and efficiency, and his trainees returned from their camp outside San Juan to be incorporated in the unitarist army gathered in the city.

On November 7th, a group of sixty prisoners, headed by a negro named Panta, revolted in San Juan. The incident was not very important, and the revolt was overcome by seven regular soldiers. Domingo Sarmiento was, years later, to be accused of taking part in the bloody suppression of this revolt. The historian, Damián Hudson,[27] named him as one of the two officers who led in the overcoming of the revolt. But Sarmiento himself denied any part in it. According to his account, he took refuge in a nearby house, uncertain of the true proportions of the uprising.[28] The next day his executive officer notified him that the revolt had been suppressed. He rushed to headquarters, but he was too late to have any part in the measures taken against the prisoners.

By the first months of 1831, the political situation throughout the nation had reached a point of crisis. General Paz and his unitarist government, with headquarters in Córdoba, dominated nine provinces. The federalists were gathering their forces under Estainslao López, Juan Manuel de Rosas, and Facundo Quiroga in preparation for an attack. In the first days of February, war broke out and Facundo's forces stormed across the Córdoba countryside. Victory followed victory for the federalists, while the unitarists suffered a decisive defeat in the battle of Chacón on March 28th.

San Juan and its unitarist government listened grimly to the news of the enemy's victories in the east, and prepared to defend itself from the inevitable invasion. Governor Pas-

[27] Damián Hudson, *Recuerdos históricos de la provincia de Cuyo*, Buenos Aires, 1898.

[28] *Obras*, III, 15.

toriza, in mid-March, led his troops out of the city to meet Facundo before he arrived, but on April 3rd, upon the arrival of the news of Chacón and of Facundo's entrance in Mendoza, the government of San Juan fell, and a federalist governor was elected.

Pastoriza called Sarmiento to inform him of the extreme gravity of the situation. Refugees were streaming out of San Juan. There was only one escape: Chile. So Sarmiento and Pastoriza began the long trek into Chile. Along with them were most of the leading unitarists of the western provinces. Captain Sarmiento was given command of the rear guard to cover the retreat. With a handful of soldiers he guarded the withdrawal of troops and civilians.

A few days later, Juan Facundo Quiroga, "The Tiger of the Plains," entered San Juan. He ordered Doña Paula Sarmiento, Domingo's mother, to present herself at headquarters. He informed her that if he ever caught her son he would shoot him. The old lady was then dismissed.

The twenty-year-old exile advanced toward Chile. He still had no positive ideas or philosophy. He was a unitarist "by sudden inspiration and a fighter by youthful zeal."[29] He was still painfully conscious of the inadequacy of his knowledge, the incompleteness of his ideas, and the negative character of his beliefs. His withdrawal into Chile was truly a retreat. He knew from what he was retreating. He did not know towards what he could advance.

Chapter 8. The Wanderer

It was probably towards the middle of April of 1831 that Sarmiento, his father, and an army of unitarist friends reached

[29] Rojas, p. 96.

the watershed of the Andes and began the descent into the valleys of Chile. This was the third time that the young exile had visited the neighboring republic, and the trail through the mountain passes was beginning to take on a familiar aspect. The twenty-year-old soldier could help guide and direct the rest of the group.

The emigrating unitarists passed through Los Patos Pass and shortly after crossing the Chilean frontier reached the border town of San Antonio de Putaendo. Domingo and his father were traveling together, and they knew well to whom they should direct themselves. One of Don Clemente's cousins by the name of Domingo Sarmiento was the local governor. Both father and son spent their visit in Putaendo at the home of this government official and welcome relative.[1] The political exiles were greeted with both sympathy and enthusiasm by their Chilean cousins, and they tasted for the first time the openhearted hospitality that Domingo was to receive from Chile for many years to come.

This period of Domingo's life is hard to follow in any detail. He seems to have remained a short time in Putaendo and then continued down to the larger city of Santa Rosa de Los Andes (commonly known as Los Andes). Here he and his father temporarily established their residency. Doubtless helped by letters of introduction from their cousin in Putaendo, they entered the social life of the city and were received in the best homes. Young Domingo had been in Los Andes during his previous visits to Chile, and in 1827 he had visited there in the role of a young merchant from his country store in San Juan. Nor was this the first visit for old Don Clemente. He had known the city during his campaigns in the War of Independence, and he remembered many of his old acquaintances there. The visit in Los Andes promised,

[1] In his *Memorias*, Sarmiento says he went to the town of Aconcagua to find his cousin, Domingo Sarmiento; but in *Recuerdos de provincia*, written much earlier while the memory would be seemingly more distinct, he says that he was a guest of a relative in Putaendo. Most authorities take this earlier statement as the more accurate and assume that the "relative" was Domingo Sarmiento, the governor. As Manuel Gálvez comments, "Preciseness was not one of Sarmiento's virtues," *op.cit.*, p. 73.

therefore, to be a pleasant one, and Domingo and his father settled down on a semipermanent basis.

They became well acquainted with the family of Don Pedro Bari, one of the local leaders of society. His home, an estate on the outskirts of town known as "the House of the Monkey" (La Casa del Mono), was an imposing one with a wide gate, iron grill work, a red brick patio, and cages of song birds in the gardens.[2] Young Domingo became a close friend of Bari, but he became particularly closely associated with his son, Ramón, who had studied at the Institute and whose learning and intelligence often amazed the young Argentine exile.[3] Ramón's three sisters, Agustina, Dolores, and Merceditas, were all charming, and Domingo often sat and chatted with them in their family home. At one time he asked for the hand in marriage of one of these young ladies, but he was refused. The girl thought that he was not only indigent, but also ugly.[4] This was a blow to the pride of the young man, but it did not disturb his friendly relations with the family. He continued to frequent their house and enjoy the family's friendship.[5]

Domingo and his friends spent the months that followed in the gay pursuits of youths of their age, free of the cares that had burdened the young man in his own country. On Christmas Eve of 1831, a large group of them celebrated late into the night. As the party lasted on through the early hours of the morning, they decided that instead of returning to their homes, they would climb to the top of the church steeple and see the midsummer sunrise. There, at this highest point in town, they watched the breathtaking sight of the first colors of the sunrise against the shadows of the imposing Andes. As they climbed down the stairs, still cloaked in the darkness of the very early morning, they guided themselves by the handrail. As they neared the bottom, their hands touched something soft and they realized that someone had spread dung on the railing in what they all considered an ill-guided attempt

[2] See description by Sady Zañartú. Rojas, p. 98.

[3] *Obras*, III, 9. [4] Rojas, p. 99.

[5] Many years later, when he became President of the Argentine Republic, Domingo Sarmiento invited one of the Bari family to Buenos Aires to visit him and reminisce.

at humor. It seemed impossible to find the culprit, but Sarmiento determined that he would seek his revenge.

Once back on the street, Domingo went separately to each of the persons in the party. "Well, who could have been the author of such an amusing prank? Did you see what a funny joke it was? I didn't touch it, for I came last, but that doesn't stop it from being amusing!" Finally one of the young people nervously bit his lip and leaning close to Domingo's ear, said, "It was I, but don't tell anyone."

"Why should I tell anyone?" Sarmiento exclaimed, carefully raising a hand still full of what he had gathered on the handrail and spreading it over his young friend's face, from his forehead to his beard. "Go wash yourself, you pig, and count on my silence; the handrails of the church stairs are sacred and should not be profaned." As, Sarmiento explained in later life, "It was my duty to give lessons of manners to those rustic boors."[6]

But Sarmiento's life in Los Andes was not entirely a life of friendships and parties. He had to seek employment in order to support himself. His father had never been a steady provider, and he certainly could not depend on any paternal support in exile. By a fortunate chance, the local school, the Escuela Municipal, was in need of a teacher. Domingo's self-education and slight teaching experience qualified him for this position.

The teaching vocation was not a particularly respected or honored one in Chile. The newspaper, *El Araucano*,[7] tells of a young Argentine exile who was caught stealing the silver candlesticks from a church and whose criminal sentence consisted of a term of three years of teaching Latin in a small country school. Domingo was painfully conscious of the unfavorable position of the teaching profession in the scale of values of his civilization, and he determined to give his vocation a new importance and gain for it a new respect. His job paid only the pitifully small sum of thirteen pesos per month. The school was but one room in a humble house on the main square of the town. It was limited to the teaching of reading,

[6] Belín Sarmiento, *Sarmiento anecdótico, op.cit.*, p. 24.

[7] November 5, 1831.

writing, and the most basic rules of arithmetic. But the active mind of young Domingo was not one to be limited to the usual routine of such a provincial school. He had read much about the new educational systems with which Europe was then experimenting. He adopted the new Lancasterian method of teaching. In teaching the pupils to read, he substituted the syllabic method for the old letter-for-letter spelling.[8] But his chief objection and his major innovation were centered around the textbooks in use. He objected to the books of religious fables and descriptions of hell that seemed to him to confuse and disturb the children's minds rather than clarify them and rationalize them.

"Article I: *The Earth is motionless in the center of the firmament.* . . . This is proved by the fact that many astronomical observations are not mistaken when they suppose the earth to be in the center of the firmament (et sic de coeteris)."[9] Texts containing such statements as these could not but startle the young student of Paley and Rousseau and the admirer and imitator of Benjamin Franklin. He proposed an immediate banning of such false information and the substitution for it of the latest of scientific and human thought.[10]

A few friends heartily applauded the progressive reforms that the young teacher was instituting in the provincial school, but at best, a small town is often not the ideal place for experiments and innovations. The local governor, Don José Tomás de la Fuente, was in disagreement with the changes in teaching method, and he particularly opposed the changes in texts, changes that he thought to be contrary to the teachings of religion. Soon the difference in opinion evolved into open disagreement. Sarmiento was called into the governor's office. He was given official orders to halt his program of reform. But, with the same independence of spirit and the same objection to arbitrary and irrational authority that he had shown when faced with the orders of the federalist

[8] Guerra, pp. 44-45.

[9] Some of these texts are still in existence at the Museo Histórico Sarmiento in Buenos Aires.

[10] Belín Sarmiento, *Sarmiento anecdótico*, *op.cit.*

governors of San Juan, the youthful teacher refused to back down. No room was left for compromise. He was dismissed, and there was nothing left for him to do but move on to another town and seek new employment. Disappointed in love and in his new career of teaching, he found little left to attract him in Los Andes.

The political situation in Argentina had not improved from Sarmiento's point of view. The unitarist leader, General Paz, had fallen prisoner to the federalists. Facundo Quiroga had returned to San Juan, instituted a federalist government there, and shot the three remaining unitarists in town. He had imposed heavy fines and exactions on the city, milking it dry of its resources. Sarmiento's mother, Doña Paula, had been fined six oxen. Finding it impossible to meet this demand, she had been saved only by the timely intervention of a relative who had supplied the necessary items. With a newly equipped and newly supplied army, Facundo had then left the impoverished town and marched north to meet and defeat the only remaining unitarist army under General Lamadrid at Ciudadela.

With Paz in the enemy's hands and Lamadrid fleeing into exile, Sarmiento had no hopes of returning to his own land in the immediate future; he therefore made his way on to another town in Chile. Early in 1832, he and his father arrived in Pocura, some two leagues to the south of Los Andes. Again, it was up to the young man to supply the livelihood. In this little town there was no school for the children of the local families. Once more young Sarmiento took advantage of this situation to find for himself a means of support. He started a small private school where he taught the children of the village at so much per head. As before, the money that he received from such an endeavor was pitifully small, and this time he decided to augment it by another enterprise. He started a cheap alehouse (*bodegón*) in the village, probably with the funds supplied by his financially hard-pressed mother in San Juan.[11] With the combination of these two endeavors, Sarmiento was able to support himself and his father in their new residence.

[11] He speaks of "a little capital my family had sent me." Gálvez, p. 76.

They stayed in Pocura the entire year of 1832, and the life of the young man could not but take on a varied character. His duties in his bar and in his school were necessarily in sharp contrast with one another. He was at the age in which he was first tasting the full enthusiasm and the richly varied desires of a newly matured young man, and his year was full of new experiences.

At his school, he taught not only the youths of Pocura but also young Pedro Bari and his relative, Domingo Soriano Sarmiento, who traveled from Los Andes to study under him. He had already grown used to teaching young men who were older than himself, but here in Pocura he began also to instruct young ladies of his own age and a little younger. This was not an opportunity that the twenty-year-old youth would miss. He brought color and life to his classes by describing his campaigns in San Juan, his arrogance and defiance before Governor Manuel Quiroga. The eloquence and the stories of the young exile shook the society of the small village from its apathy and routine, and in spite of his "indigence and ugliness" the young teacher captured the imaginations of his female students.

One girl in particular was attracted by the colorful young instructor. Her name remains a mystery. She may have come from one of the better families of the locality. Or she may have been one of the "charming farm girls" of whom Sarmiento later spoke. He was known to have frequented the home of the Del Cantos, one of the leading families of the town, and his mysterious friend may have been their daughter, María de Jesús del Canto. Whoever it was, a love affair blossomed, and the reality of the affair was documented by one inescapable fact. On July 18, 1832, Sarmiento's first daughter, Emilia Faustina, was born.[12] Faustina, as she came to be called, was sent to Sarmiento's mother in San Juan when she was old enough to make the trip, and she became in later life one of Domingo's greatest comforts and closest companions.

[12] Palcos, *Sarmiento, op.cit.*, p. 29. Emilia Faustina later said that her mother was María de Jesús del Canto. Guerra, *op.cit.*, says that young Domingo frequented the Del Canto home. No letters or documentary evidence are, however, in existence, so the identity of the child's mother remains unproved.

In late 1832 Domingo Sarmiento left Pocura and set out for the larger city, Valparaíso, Chile's chief seaport. The reasons for his sudden departure are not completely apparent, but it was probably a combination of a series of factors. His alehouse failed financially, and this cut off an important source of his income. His amorous adventures were becoming more complicated and increasingly serious in their results. The urging of the grandparents of the illegitimate Faustina, combined with the financial losses incurred in the bankruptcy of the bar, may have combined to encourage his immediate departure.

In 1833 we are able to pick up the trail of Sarmiento in Valparaíso. Whether his father was still with him or whether he was now traveling alone is not certain, but his first occupation seems to have been that of a store clerk. The atmosphere of the seaport town stimulated the young man's imagination and fired his ambition. It was the first time that he had seen the sea. His vision had always been limited by the rugged peaks of the Andes. Many a young man has experienced the first thrill of seeing the vast expanses of the ocean, and many a view of life has been altered and widened by such an experience. This was the case with young Domingo, and he determined to widen once more the intellectual horizons of his thought.

His clerk's salary was but an ounce of gold a month. This was hardly enough to support him in the growing city, but he divided it in two in order to continue his studies. One day, as he was walking along the cosmopolitan streets of downtown Valparaíso, he saw a sign advertising an English firm. He could not read what the sign said, and he determined to learn. He found an English teacher, and he paid him half of his salary for lessons. He also paid the night watchman of the neighborhood to awaken him at two o'clock every morning in order to study the language. Henry Richard, as the Englishman was called, worked diligently with his ardent young student. On Saturdays, Domingo stayed awake all night "to make it all of a piece with Sunday," always using his time to pursue this new goal of learning. After a month and a half, Richard pronounced the lessons a success, and told his student that all he needed was to perfect his pronunciation.[13] Actually, it was many years before Sarmiento was able to speak or write English either fluently or correctly, but his study in Valparaíso made one very important thing possible for him: he could now read English, and this opened for him a wealth of new literature and thought.

In 1832, silver deposits had been found in certain mines in the northern part of Chile. Many of the Argentine *émigrés* had gone to this region, and many were making their fortunes with the new discoveries of this mineral. In 1833 Sarmiento joined the rush and left Valparaíso for the north. He sailed from Valparaíso to Huasco, and from there he headed inland to the mining center of Copiapó. Sarmiento had relatives who had preceded him in this region, so his name was not unknown, and he undoubtedly had friends to receive him.[14] In nearby Chañarcillo, General Nicolás Vega, his former commander, had bought the El Colorado mine and was employing many unitarist exiles in its operation. It was here that Sarmiento first sought employment, and General Vega, remembering the young officer who had aided him in his victory at the Battle of Niquivil, gave him a position as a workman in the mine. Within two years, Domingo rose to the position of foreman.[15]

Domingo adapted himself rapidly to his new environment. He fitted into the life of the miner just as he had fitted into the part of the shopkeeper, soldier, bartender, and teacher. He dressed like a miner; he came to talk like a miner; he became an integral part of the life of Chañarcillo. But, as in the former stages of his life, he never lost sight of one basic pursuit, one fundamental question—the pursuit of learning, the question of understanding life and his place in it. He continued his readings and his studies, and he could now

[13] *Anthology*, p. 93.

[14] While examining some of the small local periodicals of the time, I found a letter to the editor of *La bandera tricolor* in nearby La Serena, March 25, 1831, No. 8, signed "Sarmiento." At first, this seemed to be D. F. Sarmiento, but the date does not coincide with the time when he was in this region, and the content of the letter rules him out as its author. It does, however, show that the Sarmiento family did exist in the area.

[15] *Obras*, x, 292.

make full use of his newly acquired reading knowledge of English.

For a little less than three years, Sarmiento continued in his occupation of miner in Chile. It was not an easy life, and as it turned out, it was not the rewarding life that he had expected. For lunch every day the miners were brought a ration of *porotos* (a kind of beans), which they scooped up in both hands and ate greedily as their only nourishment until evening. Sometimes General Vega was unable to pay the miners' salaries, but since they were all fellow unitarist exiles they did not complain of their former commander's bad luck. They went on working, and when the pay did come they were usually so starved for relaxation and diversion that they would spend all their earnings in a spree of gambling and drinking. Once, after a particularly long wait for his pay and after having received his back salary all at once, Domingo left for the seaport of Huasco, where he remained for eight days of gambling and fun-making,[16] returning to the exhausting task of the miner without a cent to show for his past months' efforts.

The life of a miner seemed to fit the temperament of the young Argentine exile. He liked the opportunity of expressing the two sides of his personality—the driving, brute energy and the intellectual curiosity. He enjoyed the amazement of those who saw these contrasts within him. He thought of himself as "the miner they always saw reading." "For economy, amusement, and mischief I had outfitted myself completely in the picturesque miner's garb, and people became accustomed to think of this disguise as my normal costume. I wore slippers with felt over-boots, blue breeches, and a striped shirt, setting off this background, in addition to the familiar red cap, by a broad sash from which hung a pouch large enough to hold an *arroba* of sugar. In this I always carried a couple of handfuls of Tarija tobacco."[17] But, in his miner's garb, well-dressed for the role that he was playing, working far down in the shafts of the mines, he continued to satisfy his intellectual curiosity. From a nearby English resident, Edward Abbott, Sarmiento borrowed copies of Sir Walter

[16] *Ibid.*, III, 174

[17] *Anthology*, pp. 93-94.

Scott. Translating the English into Spanish, 500 meters underground, he read by candlelight at the rate of a volume a day and quickly exhausted Mr. Abbott's collection of sixty volumes.[18] He found the romantic adventures of Scott's heroes attractive to his own nature and his own spirit. The emotions and the excitement that he found in this new type of literature contrasted sharply with the coldly rational character of his former readings, and he began to feel a strong attraction to it.

In Punta Brava, Sarmiento and the other miners would gather in their moments of leisure. There they would talk and amuse themselves by demonstrating to one another their particular talents. Sarmiento often made drawings of animals and birds for his companions. He gave French lessons to some of the younger miners. And he met a mine foreman "who had such an extraordinary faculty for retaining what he had read that he could recite whole books without omitting a comma."[19] "Afternoons, Don Manuel Carril came up from the Desempeño mine and we would walk together to the Manto de los Cobos, where a half dozen Argentine superintendents, mine owners, and laborers gathered in the kitchen to talk politics. There was also a young Parisian, who joined our grimy, talkative group, to whom we gave lessons in such pure Spanish that one day when he met some ladies, he offended their ears and confounded his teachers by the rapid progress he had made. We took good care to summon him afterward and explain all the Spanish sentences, words, and interjections that we had taught him, which did not have easy currency except in the society of the Manto de los Cobos' kitchen to which he belonged."[20]

It was during this period that Sarmiento wrote his first work. It was a pamphlet on a project to colonize the Valley of the Colorado River in Southern Chile with emigrants from San Juan and Mendoza. The river was a navigable waterway, the surrounding country was fertile, and because of these two features, Domingo thought that a group of emigrants could make their fortunes in the development of a rich agricultural region. For 80,000 pesos ($20,000) he proposed to

[18] *Obras*, III, 178. [19] *Anthology*, p. 95. [20] *Ibid.*, p. 94.

make it possible for a thousand "reliable youths" to colonize the region. He went into his scheme in some detail, writing over ten thousand words on the project. But, unable to secure a publisher, he read it aloud to his Sanjuanino friend, Manuel Carril. Carril received the idea enthusiastically and exclaimed, "I would sell my shirt to put your scheme into operation."[21] But Carril did not sell his shirt; nothing was done about the idea; and it was soon forgotten, the manuscript lost.

During his last year in Chile, 1835, Sarmiento frequented the home of a fellow emigrant, Major Mardones, who was judge of mines in Copiapó. "His wife's conversation, manner, and neatness and their modest furniture reconciled us to civilized life, and we fell into the habit of going down in the evenings to his house in the Placilla where we spent many very agreeable hours."[22] One night Domingo appeared in his usual miner's garb and found another guest at the Mardones home, "a certain Señor Codecido, a spruce, sybaritic citizen who complained about the discomforts and privations of traveling. Everyone greeted him courteously. I touched my cap modestly and took a corner seat to avoid the glances that my costume usually drew, letting him see, however, as I passed, my braided gaucho belt, the *pièce de résistance* of my outfit. As was natural, Codecido took no notice of me. I was merely a miner whose employers had allowed him to join their company, and had I been a little nearer to him he would undoubtedly have asked me to give him a light or to fetch something else for him. The conversation turned on various subjects and there was disagreement on a point of fact regarding modern European history and geographical names. Carril, Chenaut, and the others instinctively turned to me for the answer. Thus brought into the gentleman's conversation I answered the question, but so positively and in such detail that Codecido's mouth opened a palm's width at each page of book learning that fell from the lips of a man whom he had taken for a common miner. The cause of his misapprehension was cleared up amid general laughter and from that moment forward we were on excellent terms."[23]

Sarmiento soon held a position of distinction in the little

[21] *Obras*, III, p. 179. [22] *Anthology*, p. 94. [23] *Ibid.*, pp. 94-95.

mining community. His fellow workers looked up to him for his learning. His fellow emigrants admired and followed him in his clearly and eloquently expressed attacks upon the federalist regime of Rosas in Argentina. One emigrant, discussing the young man with Mariano Fragueiro, another future leader of the Argentine Republic, predicted clairvoyantly that the miner-student would someday be president of Argentina.[24] Such was the position of esteem that young Domingo gained for himself during his three years in the Chilean mining center.

Meanwhile the political situation in Argentina had changed considerably. The dictator, Juan Manuel de Rosas, had successfully entrenched himself in power in Buenos Aires. He had cleverly been able to bring the entire nation under his own rule, defeating some of the local caudillos, subjugating others, winning over others. The dreaded personal enemy of Domingo, Juan Facundo Quiroga, was murdered in 1835, perhaps at the orders of Rosas himself.[25] It was a dark period indeed for the unitarists. "The unitarists take refuge abroad to save their lives. In the country they abstain completely from politics and shout, 'Long live the federation!' The federalist sentiment has been unified, unanimity has been founded, and unanimity means tyranny. Powers of control and equilibrium do not exist. The legislatures, where they should function, are servile except for a little sporadic resistance. They obey the voice of the governing caudillism. . . . The courts are a parody. In the republic there dominates discretional and enslaving will."[26]

In San Juan, General Nazario Benavídez came to power on February 26, 1836. He contrasted greatly with his predecessor, Facundo Quiroga. He lacked Facundo's ferocity, but he

[24] Unpublished letter from Mariano Fragueiro to Domingo F. Sarmiento, September 8, 1868, in miscellaneous collection at Museo Histórico Sarmiento in Buenos Aires.

[25] It has never been determined categorically whether or not Rosas had any complicity in this deed. For the pro and the con of this argument, see Ibarguren, *Rosas, op.cit.*, p. 311, and Ramón J. Cárcano, *Juan Facundo Quiroga*, Buenos Aires, 1931, p. 358. Sarmiento charges Rosas with instigating this murder in his *Civilización i barbarie* (*El Facundo*).

[26] Cárcano, *Quiroga, op.cit.*, pp. 187-188.

also lacked the gaucho caudillo's independence. He was under the control of the central authority of Rosas, and he did not dare resist the general policy of the Buenos Aires dictator.

Late in 1835 or early in 1836,[27] Sarmiento was taken violently sick. The illness was diagnosed as typhoid fever. He had undoubtedly been in a rundown condition from overwork and overexertion, and the sickness struck him with particular ferocity. He passed through a crisis of melancholy, prostration, sadness, extreme weakness, and repeated deliriums.[28] The psychologist-historian, Nerio Rojas, attributes this state to a part of a regular cycle of elation and depression that he finds in the psychological pattern of Sarmiento.[29] It seems much more probable, however, that it was nothing more than the quite frequent result of typhoid fever. Whatever the causes, Sarmiento's friends looked with alarm upon the turn that the sickness had taken. Domingo grew more depressed, weaker, and more frequently delirious as time went on. His friends soon became convinced that he had little time to live. They requested permission from Governor Benavídez to allow the dying exile to return to his home in San Juan. This permission was granted by the new governor, and Sarmiento started through the passes of the Andes just before the first snows of late fall of 1836.[30]

Chapter 9. The New Start

Domingo Sarmiento returned to his home at the age of twenty-five, sick, penniless, and fully convinced that he was

[27] Gálvez sets the date as 1835. Almost all the other biographers of importance from Guerra to Rojas set it as 1836.

[28] This state was described by his grandson, Augusto Belín Sarmiento to Ricardo Rojas in an interview in 1911. Ricardo Rojas, p. 106.

[29] Nerio Rojas, *Neurosis de hombres célebres.*

[30] *Obras,* III, 18.

returning to his grave. He was received by the federalist governor, Nazario Benavídez, with "consideration." In spite of his violent opposition to the government in the past, he was allowed to return to his home in peace. For many years afterwards he wondered what was the cause of the change in heart that made his homecoming possible. It was probably a combination of factors. His grave illness was undoubtedly a decisive consideration. The federalist government could feel little fear of an enemy in such a condition, and simple humanitarian considerations would permit his return to his home and family for his last days. Furthermore, young Domingo, in spite of his unitarist preferences, still had many relatives in positions of importance in the federalist community in San Juan. His uncle Friar Justo de Santa María de Oro was now Bishop of Cuyo. His uncle José de Oro was a leading federalist; and another uncle, José Manuel Eufrasio de Quiroga Sarmiento, was a church leader and within four or five months was to be made bishop of the region. All of these men were particularly fond of Domingo's mother, Doña Paula, and their arguments were undoubtedly instrumental in making possible the return of the exile.

Even more important, however, in creating a changed condition in San Juan was the replacing of the dictatorship of Facundo Quiroga by Governor Benavídez. The latter's greatest ambition had been to attain the governorship of his province, and he spared no efforts to reach that position.[1] Once there, however, although he followed the policy of the dictator, Rosas, he mitigated its effects whenever possible by his own easygoing and humanitarian way of acting. The first minister whom he named in his government was Aman Rawson, a Boston doctor, who had married a girl from San Juan and settled down in the little provincial Argentine town. Brought up in the strictly puritanical tradition of New England, Rawson brought into the Benavídez government a new element, a rigid respect for law and morality. The temperament of Benavídez himself contrasted strongly with the barbaric and violent character of many of the other gaucho caudillo leaders. He was "phlegmatic by temperament, soft and

[1] Guerra, p. 49.

temperate of thought, indifferent and lazy in the administration of public affairs."[2] Sarmiento confirmed this view of the federalist governor. "He has an excellent heart, is tolerant, and envy has little place in his spirit."[3] He was willing to allow the young exile to return, exercise the unusual talents that had already been demonstrated in his career, and express his restless spirit—all of this, as long as he did not act against or plot against the existing government.

Once back in San Juan with his friends and his family, Domingo began to recover from the depression and melancholy that he had suffered during his last weeks in Copiapó. It was not long before he was restlessly looking around for something to occupy his active mind and his increasingly active body. For a time he taught drawing to some of the children of the town. Later he picked up some money defending lawsuits in the local courts. There were, however, only a few of these suits, and he lost two of them in spite of the fact that a good friend was the presiding judge.

Soon Sarmiento began to feel the urge to continue his studying and to express some of his ideas in writing. He became a close friend of Manuel Quiroga Rosas, who had just returned to San Juan full of the new ideas of the French literary and philosophical world. Rosas had brought with him to San Juan a library of the best of the contemporary European authors. Together he and Domingo read enthusiastically the works of Villemain and Schlegel in literature; Lerminier, Jouffroi, Guizot, and Cousin in philosophy and history; Pierre Leroux's political and social theories; and the *Revue encyclopédique*, which served as a kind of synthesis of the doctrines of the contemporary writers. "Charles Didier and a hundred other names previously unknown to me long continued to quench my thirst for knowledge."[4]

These writers and thinkers, predominantly French in origin, were a welcome supplement to the reading that young

[2] Hudson, *Recuerdos históricos, op.cit.*, II, p. 502.

[3] Antonio Bucich, *Luchas y rutas de Sarmiento*, Buenos Aires, 1942, p. 9. See also Benjamin Villafañe, "Reminiscencias históricas de un patriota," *Revista nacional*, 1888, XII, p. 128; Argentina, Senate, Sesión del Senado de la Nación, August 25, 1888.

[4] *Anthology*, p. 96.

Domingo had done prior to this time. While in San Juan a decade before, his scope had been limited to rationalist writers of the eighteenth-century Enlightenment. In Chile, he had read one Romantic novelist: Scott. The rationalists had painted an ideal world for him, a world ordered and understood by the infallible human reason. The adventures and emotions of Scott had intrigued him. Now this new school of social writers was offering him a new approach. They were suggesting to him how to analyze what was wrong with the society he saw around him and how he could hope to change it. Sarmiento wrote, perhaps a little overoptimistically, "I studied two years, of philosophy and history at that time with very good teachers, and when I had finished the course, I began to feel that my own thinking, which had hitherto merely reflected other people's opinions, was beginning to stir and to move forward. My ideas became clearly and distinctly fixed, the shadows and vacillations frequent in early youth disappeared and the gaps that twenty years of disordered reading had left were gradually filled in as I endeavored to apply my gleanings to real life, and to put the European mind into American terms, with such adaptations as were necessary in view of the difference in environment."[5]

Domingo soon began to find a common ground for discussion and interest in a group of young men who gathered at Quiroga Rosas' library. This group included Antonio Aberastain, a young Sanjuanino who had studied at the university in Buenos Aires during the Rivadavia regime, and who had returned to receive a judgeship in San Juan under Benavídez. There were also Indalecio Cortínez, William Rawson (the son of Aman Rawson), and young Dionisio Rodríguez. These men were all destined to play important roles in the future histories of their province and their nation. They had one important feature in common: they were all of curious and active minds and they explored with great delight the new ideas that they found in the rich library of Quiroga Rosas. They all experienced the strong conviction that the society in which they found themselves contrasted strongly with society as it should be. As a result, most of these young men

[5] *Ibid.*, pp. 96-97.

felt in varying degrees a definite opposition to the existing governmental system of Rosas and his satellite, Benavídez.[6]

The group had organized a theatrical society known as the Dramatic-Philharmonic Society of San Juan. Antonio Aberastain was president of the society and young Domingo was quickly taken in and made "first decorator of the theater and the ball room."[7] The youthful members cooperated to put on amateur performances of great dramas. They performed *The Mayor of Zalamea,* by the great Spanish dramatist, Lope de Vega, and plays of important eighteenth-century dramatists, such as Beaumarchais' *The Barber of Seville,* and Jovellanos' *The Honorable Delinquent.* They met together to discuss the latest ideas from the Quiroga Rosas library, and they held dances and soirées that became central events in the social life of San Juan.

Domingo soon felt the need to express himself in writing. Ideas, emotions, and reactions were welling up within his restless spirit, and they were bound to force themselves to the surface. "At this time, Don Domingo F. Sarmiento in his spare moments and for amusement, in conference with friends, edited newspapers, manuscripts, and wrote verses."[8] In 1837, Sarmiento wrote a satirical poem against the Treaty of Pancarpata between Chile and the Peruvian-Bolivian Confederation. He gave the manuscript to his friend Damián Hudson to take with him to Mendoza to be published in a newspaper of that city. The editor refused, however, to handle the poem for fear of "compromising the government of the province in the good relations it maintains with the president of the state of Chile."[9]

It was at this time that Sarmiento made his first and last serious attempt at writing verse. He was accustomed to make frequent excursions to the nearby Zonda Valley and Zonda Baths. In fact, he had organized a "Society of Bathers" for

[6] Quiroga Rosas was so strongly opposed to the way of life represented by such caudillos as Facundo Quiroga and Juan Manuel de Rosas that he changed his name to Quirogarosas, in order to avoid any suspicion that he was related to those two federalist leaders, Carlos María Onetti, *Cuatro clases sobre Sarmiento escritor,* Tucumán, 1939, p. 25.

[7] Hudson, *Recuerdos históricos, op.cit.,* II, p. 388.

[8] *Ibid.*

[9] *Ibid.,* p. 389.

the purpose of visiting those health-giving waters. During one of these trips he was filled with a consciousness of the extreme scenic beauty of the valley and the surrounding mountains. Strongly influenced by his readings of the latest Romantic writers of France, he sat down and wrote a descriptive poem, calling it *Canto a Zonda* (Song to Zonda). He signed it with the pseudonym of García Román, and on January 1, 1838 he mailed it to the already famous young Argentine writer, Juan Bautista Alberdi, who was at the time living in exile in Montevideo. "Although I do not have the honor of knowing you, the brilliance of the literary name that you have gained from the beautiful productions with which your poetic pen has honored the republic overcomes the timidity of a young man who wishes to hide his name and submit to your indulgent and illustrious criticism the enclosed composition."[10] Sarmiento explained the contents of the poem as an attempt to celebrate the "happiness of a friend, a country scene of his native land, and the recreations of the Baths which the valley contains." He asked that Alberdi criticize them frankly and return them annotated with his criticisms.

The original of the poem has been lost, so we know of it only from the letters that Domingo wrote to the Argentine writer in Montevideo. We can picture him waiting expectantly for the answer, finally receiving it, and suffering under the blow of harsh but probably deserved criticism. He received Alberdi's reply by the end of May, but it was not until July that he wrote once again to his adviser across the South American continent. "I consider your criticism just," he admitted, "but I would have liked nevertheless for you to have explained in more detail the reason for your criticism of certain verses." One of Sarmiento's close friends at the time wrote that Alberdi had criticized some fifteen or twenty verses, "praising some as good, others as sublime, and approving as good the rest."[11] We can see some samples of the poem which Sarmiento quotes in his second letter to Alberdi. His romantic subject matter and images recall such contemporary European writers as Lord Byron and Lamartine, the influence

[10] Juan Bautista Alberdi, *Obras póstumas*, xv.
[11] Hudson, *Recuerdos históricos*, *op.cit.*, II, p. 390.

of both of which he acknowledges in the letter. He speaks of the Andes,

> Cuyas nevadas cúpulas
> Osan penetrar el Cielo.
> (Whose snowy domes,
> Dare penetrate the Heavens.)

Alberdi, who had little sympathy with the exaggerated sentimentality of Romanticism, undoubtedly criticized many of the poetic images of the young Sanjuanino, and it was perhaps this criticism which influenced Sarmiento never again to attempt seriously to write poetry. Many of his later works in prose border on the poetic in their expression, but actual verses almost never appear in his later writings.[12]

Alberdi was not the only harsh critic of Sarmiento's early attempt at poetry. One day, at a gathering in the house of Damián Hudson, Domingo was told of a very severe criticism of his poetry that had been made by the young president of the Dramatic Philharmonic Society, Antonio Aberastain. Sarmiento was too sure of himself, however, to let this news upset him. "Remember this date and this place," he said. "Not many days will pass before Doctor Aberastain, who today criticizes and ridicules me, will be my greatest and most enthusiastic, my warm and decided panegyrist."[13] Domingo's self-assurance proved justified. Aberastain soon became his great friend and admirer, and they later became the best of friends.

By 1838, Domingo Sarmiento had become a central figure in San Juan. He had returned from exile, recovered his health, and gained for himself a position of respect and admiration among his fellow Sanjuaninos. A history of San

[12] *Ibid.*

[13] See Alberto Palcos, "Sarmiento y la poesía," *La Prensa*, Buenos Aires, December 1, 1935. Rojas, *El profeta*, pp. 115-118, discusses the question of the authenticity of Sarmiento's authorship of the *Canto a Zonda* and reaches a positive verdict after a careful sifting of all evidence. Juan Antonio Solari, "Un poeta y su crítico," *La Prensa*, March 13, 1938. Rafael Alberto Arrieta, "Sarmiento y la poesía," *Sarmiento, homenaje de la facultad de humanidades y ciencias de la educación*. Universidad Nacional de la Plata, La Plata, 1939, pp. 35-45.

Juan during this period finds the young man important enough to devote an entire section to him.[14] He was continuing his studies and his reading. He learned Italian from young William Rawson in 1837. He was writing occasional bits here and there, but he was feeling an increasingly urgent need to express himself in a more positive form.

Chapter 10. The Newspaperman and Teacher

THE year 1839 marked an important turning point in the life of Domingo Sarmiento. It was at this time that he began in a positive and effective manner his career in two fields, the two fields that were to be his central instruments of expression and combat throughout his life. He started a school, and he started a newspaper.

Early in 1839, Sarmiento and his friends began to meet regularly for the specific purpose of discussing their readings and organizing their thoughts on political and public matters. They formed a literary society, and for two years Domingo attended its meetings without missing a single night. The young men met to "tell each other of the readings that we were doing and form a system of clear and fixed principles on literature, politics, and morals."[1] In these meetings confused and disorganized thoughts began to clarify and crystallize. The young men came to believe that through their studies and their self-education they had begun to realize what was wrong with the society in which they lived. It was barbaric. It was governed by force and by personalities. The

[14] *Ibid.*

[1] *Obras*, III, 9.

question for these young men was how to make the society of their time realize its own shortcomings. They had learned by educating themselves, by learning the truth through their reading and their study. Therefore, the rest of the people must also be educated. The "truth" must be passed down to all. The restless mind of young Domingo began to look about for a means of doing this.

For many months he had been thinking of founding a school in San Juan, but he had had neither the means nor the support for such a project. By chance, his uncle, Bishop Justo de Santa María de Oro, had had a similar plan of founding a school. He had thought of starting a religious school and had almost completed the building that was intended to house his project. Young Sarmiento had talked often with his uncle and discussed with him his educational ideas, and when the Bishop died before achieving his goal, Domingo took up the task of finishing the work. He convinced the new Bishop, Eufrasio de Quiroga Sarmiento, a paternal uncle, to allow him to take over the project. Domingo gained the support of the late Bishop Oro's sister, Doña Tránsito de Oro, for his plans, and on March 23, 1839, he published a fourteen-page pamphlet called *Prospectus for an Educational Establishment for Young Ladies to Be Directed by D. Domingo Faustino Sarmiento*.[2] This prospectus set forth the plans for the institution. He invited as its supporters "all the citizens who are lovers of civilization and the improvement of their country," and he promised that when the minimum of fifteen students was enrolled, the school would immediately be opened. It would be dedicated to the young ladies of the community, the future mothers and wives whom Sarmiento believed to be fundamental and decisive elements in society; the school was to prepare them as vanguards of a changed and better society. "Two transcendent ideas which were to orient Sarmiento throughout the rest of his life reveal themselves already in these projects of 1839: the reform of society through the school and the incorporation of the woman in such an enter-

[2] This was published in facsimile by Víctor M. Badano, Secretary of the Museo de Entre Ríos in 1942, Entre Ríos, 1942.

prise in order to unite the school, society, and the home in one single civilizing purpose."[3]

Sarmiento obtained the support of the most important persons in the little San Juan community. A Committee for the Protection of Education (Comisión Protectora de la Educación) was formed. It was presided over by the Bishop-elect, Quiroga Sarmiento, and it was composed of such civic leaders as Doctor Aberastain, Quiroga Rosas, and Doctor Cortínez. Sarmiento became director of the institution and he chose for his assistants his own sister, Bienvenida Sarmiento, and the sister of the deceased bishop, Doña Tránsito de Oro. Sarmiento's other sisters, Rosario and Tránsito, were instructors at the school.

The program of study and the constitution were drawn up by Domingo himself. The range of subjects and courses taught by the new school was as wide and as varied as the inquiring mind and knowledge of its director. The school taught the basic studies: writing, reading, arithmetic, accounting, grammar, spelling, geography, and drawing. But it taught each of these with an eye to their practical application. Correct pronunciation was stressed in the reading course. Mathematics was taught in terms of its practical application to domestic life and home economy. The teaching of drawing was centered around problems of design and home dressmaking. For the more advanced students, English, French, religion, and history were offered. The teaching of the piano, dancing, and parlor games was intended to round out the young ladies' education. Domingo spent long weeks in careful preparation of this advanced and varied program. There was nothing like it in the educational system of any South American country at the time. It was patterned carefully after the models that Domingo had studied in the latest educational works in Quiroga Rosas' library. The most advanced methods were used, and Sarmiento himself devoted his time to the teaching of a wide assortment of the courses.

The school was called the College of Santa Rosa of America, and its constitution was drawn up by Sarmiento well in

[3] Rojas, p. 125.

advance of its opening.[4] As he explained, an enterprise of this type "requires regularity, order, and method, and this cannot be secured without determined and permanent laws and statutes." He therefore set out to regulate every phase of the student's life. He provided a uniform for the young ladies. This was intended to foment the democratic attitude, the consciousness of equality among them. He edited a set of strict and all-embracing rules which included the prohibition of reading any book not specifically permitted by the Rectoress, of entering anyone's room without permission, of undressing in the presence of other students, or of spreading any gossip that might be harmful to the school. The young educator set up a system of punishments and rewards that were intended to obtain the best possible discipline. The fifth article of the constitution arranged for a series of prizes for achievement and good conduct "for if the fear of punishment has in effect a sterile and voluntary application, the hope of reward makes work sweet and stimulates extraordinary efforts." With similar theories of practical psychology, Sarmiento spaced the school's vacations in a manner that would, according to his beliefs, obtain the maximum amount of work from the girls when they were in the school. The vacations would be provided "in order that the students might enjoy the pleasures of the country, find distraction from their difficult tasks and acquire new strength and determination to start the next year."

On July 9, 1839, the anniversary of the Argentine Declaration of Independence, the leading citizens of San Juan gathered for the inauguration of the Colegio de Santa Rosa de América. It was a gala occasion, and an important event in the life of the young director. The meeting was opened by a few brief words by Sarmiento. He read the Declaration of Independence of 1816, and spoke modestly of his own small part in the founding of the school and of the important part played by the late Bishop Oro, the present Bishop, and

[4] I was able to examine the original of this constitution in the Museo Histórico Sarmiento in Buenos Aires. A facsimile copy was published by that institution in 1939 with an introduction by Ismael Bucich Escobar. *Constitución del colegio de señoritas de la advocación/ de Santa Rosa de América/ dirigido por/ Dn. Domingo F. Sarmiento/ en/ San Juan*, Buenos Aires, 1939.

Doña Tránsito de Oro. Beside the young director on the platform were Bishop Quiroga Sarmiento and Governor Benavídez. It was a day of excitement for the entire town, and most of its inhabitants had turned out for the event.[5]

The speech of the director was followed by a few words by Doña Tránsito de Oro and then an oratorical deluge by Sarmiento's many young friends who had followed with such interest and supported so loyally the development of the project. Dr. Quiroga Rosas made a scholarly dissertation on the problem of feminine education, but he did not fail to add a personal note of praise for young Domingo: "The young talent that has founded the Colegio de Pensionistas de Santa Rosa has made itself worthy of the recognition of its fellow citizens and of a reception in the ranks of these stoic spirits who never despair of the progressive march of the nation." Aberastain continued this train of thought: "But, gentlemen, the complete complacency with which I have heard the young man, who today raises one of the most glorious monuments of the homeland, does not impede me from rectifying the ideas which he has expressed. Modesty has caused him to minimize and almost annul his merit. Great enterprises generally give justly more glory to those who carry them out than to those who conceive them. He who executes a great idea is without a doubt he who has best conceived it. All of us know and approve of that which is good, we hope that it will be extended to society, but very rare are virtuous and strong young men who have sufficient valor and enough self-abnegation to sacrifice their pleasures, their rest, their tranquillity, and dedicate themselves to the overcoming of obstacles and the carrying on their shoulders of a great work. All the merit, then, of this grandiose project, this sublime thought, that today is realized, belongs to the virtuous young man, the founder of the School for Young Ladies."[6] Through the flowery rhetoric of these speeches a political note is discernible. The young men, the young students of San Juan, were expressing categorically their support of Domingo Sarmiento.

[5] The entire event is described in the newspaper *El Zonda*, No. 1, July 20, 1839.

[6] *El Zonda*, No. 2, July 27, 1839.

They were looking to him as a leader in the dark chaos of politics that they saw around them.

The school began under favorable conditions. Domingo had worked hard in preparing for the inauguration, but once begun, his duties were not as demanding as he had expected. The carefully-thought-out routine that he had planned flowed very smoothly. The young ladies arose at five in the morning, cleaned their rooms, made their beds, and dressed. At five thirty, they were due at the chapel for morning prayer. They then studied in their rooms until eight, when they breakfasted, and proceeded immediately to their lessons in sewing and in music. At noon, they had a rest and their mid-day meal, a short siesta until two, four hours of classes, another hour of rest, an hour of lectures, evening prayers, a late supper, and then a period of games and conversation. This was obviously a hard and dull schedule, but its very strictness and completeness lessened the duties of the director, who found himself occupied only with certain lessons and lectures.

The school was not enough to occupy the active mind of young Sarmiento. The man who had been able to combine the arduous life of a miner with intensive study and reading found a girl's school interesting and absorbing for a while, but he soon sought other more positive means of expressing his urge to improve his society.

Governor Benavídez still looked upon the activities of the group of young intellectuals, Sarmiento in particular, with amused benevolence. As long as they did not affect his political position, they had little interest for the political boss. His own government had steered away from its original liberal stand and closer to a typical personalism. Benavídez had dismissed Rawson as his minister of government and replaced him with a sure federalist, Timoteo Maradona. The position of his government seemed quite secure, and he had little to fear from a schoolteacher who read too many books from some distant, seemingly utopic country called France.

The good relations between Sarmiento and the Benavídez government at this time are attested to, not only by the governor's support of the new school and his attendance at the inauguration, but also by occasional appointments of

Domingo to small government jobs. An especially important one is recorded in a letter from Timoteo Maradona to Sarmiento on June 28, 1839. "To continue the repair and improvement of the provincial press, powerful for the advancement of civilization, precious and effective means of communication between the people and the government, His Excellency has decided to put at the head of such a useful establishment a citizen whose aptitudes join with a decided love and enthusiasm for those well-doing institutions that honor the country. . . . His Excellency for these reasons has decided upon you to occupy the administration of the provincial press. . . ."[7] Benavídez did not fear young Sarmiento, but he hoped that with such strategy as this he might buy the talents of such an unusual and energetic young man for his own ends.

It was not strange, therefore, that Sarmiento received no opposition from the government when he proposed to establish a newspaper of his own in San Juan. Here was another obvious manner in which to express his ideas and his projects. A newspaper could be an instrument of education for the entire population of the city. Since the original decree of unitarist Governor Del Carril in 1825, introducing the first printing press to the province of San Juan and authorizing responsible citizens to use it for the "public utility," no less than ten different newspapers had been founded and lived their short lives. Such names as *El Republicano* (The Republican), 1829, *El Constitucional* (The Constitution), 1835, and *El abogado federal* (The Federal Attorney), 1836, were still fresh in the memories of the local inhabitants.

In 1839, Sarmiento and Quiroga Rosas applied for permission to print a weekly paper, without political implications, at the provincial printing press. The costs would be covered by the sale of the journal. Governor Benavídez granted the necessary permission, and the first issue of the paper was printed on Saturday, July 20th. Sarmiento wrote most of the articles that appeared in his paper, but he gathered around him his friends and sympathizers, and men like Aberastain

[7] Archivo General de la Provincia de San Juan, copiador libro 1, caja 90, folio 185.

and Cortínez became his most important advisers as well as regular contributors. Their first problem was that of choosing a suitable name for the publication. They met in long meetings over this problem, but they were unable to reach any satisfactory decision. *The Argentine Patriot* was discarded as a title already discredited. *The Sanjuanino* "smelled of whiskey." *The Mercury* and *The Mercantile Gazette* seemed not to apply to a "country in which there were only pastures and ruined vineyards." Finally, someone suggested the name *El Zonda*, and Sarmiento broke into an eloquent praise of this suggestion—a praise that may have been but an echo of his former poetic endeavor, *The Song to Zonda.*

"Zonda is a delicious and happy valley surrounded by wild and monotonous hills. . . . Zonda is an embracing, impetuous wind that destroys all that is not firmly rooted, a wind whose strength shatters uselessly against the solid rocks and buildings; that parches the plants and tears off the branches of the robust trees. . . . It is heavy, bothersome, it weakens the fibres and produces strong headaches . . . it purifies the atmosphere and carries away with it the storms, it awakens other fresh winds that make one forget the vexations that it had caused. . . . Zonda is a cooling bath whose healthful waters alleviate a thousand pains, where youth enjoys the most varied pleasures, where pastimes, the graceful dance, the happy song, the merry revelry goes on uninterrupted for four months of the year, where etiquette is exiled, families are mixed, and social bonds are extended.

"A thousand bravos greeted the Zonda and it was resolved that the newspaper would be called here and everywhere *El Zonda* during the ten years of its proposed existence."[8]

The journalistic venture had a clear field. There were no other papers in the province,[9] and Sarmiento sarcastically estimated a minimum of fifty buyers for his paper. He estimated that out of the 30,000 inhabitants—25,000 never learned to read, 4,000 forgot how to read, 600 have no interest, 200 old people who can't see the print, young girls,

[8] *El Zonda*, July 20, 1839. Copies are in existence in Museo Histórico Sarmiento and in the Biblioteca Nacional in Buenos Aires.

[9] *Obras*, LII, 7.

and young gallants, 150 who will borrow the paper, 50 who will buy the paper.[10]

The license for the newspaper had been granted on the grounds that it would be apolitical, and the tone set in the first numbers stood by this provision. The editors promised to bring "the truth, pure and clean," but they held that their interest was in the social field and not in the political. "Some affect fears that our tendency will be to intervene in the politics of the country; and we repeat that *they affect them*, for there is nothing in our pages that could create any supposition of such a tendency. We are not men of prestige nor influence, nor wealth, nor do we count on anything but our own good desires and our own studies to carry out the enterprise. Our aims are not political: they are *social*: the little and big vices are the true obstacles to the happiness of the people; our aims are the little and big, or the biggest possible, remedies for these vices.

"We have nothing to say on any political matter. No factions exist here: here nobody opposes the elevated aims of the government nor the principles of the holy cause of the people."[11]

Sarcastically spoken, or truly felt, this was the program initially set down by the editors of *El Zonda*. They told the local news, and they filled their columns with articles on the mining industry, the possibilities of the cultivation of silk, and countless other "remedies little or big."

Domingo Sarmiento was now beginning his real vocation in his home town. He was directing his own school and his own newspaper. He had instruments of expression. The many ideas and programs that had been welling up within his mind could not be dammed up for long. They had to break out soon. Conflict was inevitable.

[10] *Ibid.*
[11] *El Zonda*, July 20, 1839; *El Zonda*, August 10, 1839.

Chapter 11. The New Fight

In 1839 the power of the dictator, Juan Manuel de Rosas, seemed to be at its height in Argentina. He was supported by Aldao and Benavídez in the west, by López in the central part of the nation, and by Ibarra in the northwest. There was little if any active opposition to his government, and the underground internal opposition seemed to have been negated or driven into exile by the bloodily effective secret police in Buenos Aires, known as the Mazorca. The popular name for this organization was the *Más horca* (more gallows), for the number of its executions was high, its sentences summary, and its efficiency deadly.

By the end of 1839, the stable political situation suffered a brutal upheaval. The dictator, who but a few months before had felt secure behind his gaucho armies and his secret police, was suddenly faced with opposition on all fronts. On March 23, 1838, after a series of diplomatic negotiations over the Argentine seizure and arrest of a French citizen, the French fleet under Admiral Le Blanc had begun a blockade of Buenos Aires. The French foreign office undoubtedly saw an opportunity of establishing a possible foothold in the southern American continent, and it took advantage of a minor incident to begin a controversy.[1] Although this action on the part of a foreign government succeeded in arousing a great deal of patriotic spirit to back the Rosas regime, many of the political exiles in Montevideo and in Chile refused to see the incident in nationalistic terms, and recognized in the French move an opportunity to challenge Rosas' army.

[1] Original orders from the French government to Admiral Le Blanc, now in archives of the Jockey Club in Buenos Aires, said, "You will seize all ships that are carrying cargo from that Republic, and you will have them taken to a place of safety to be held until further orders." One of Le Blanc's letters, also in the Jockey Club Archives, speaks of "establishing permanently in the River Plate the influence of France."

In 1839 the opposition to Rosas struck from every direction. The French blockade continued. In the southern part of the province of Buenos Aires, the *estancieros*, or ranchers, organized a revolt against the centralized power in the national capital. In the capital itself another plot was brewing. The Rosas government was still at war with Bolivia. The northeast was threatened by an invasion by the Uruguayan General Rivera. One of De Rosas' strongest supporters, Alejandro Heredia, was assassinated in Tucumán. His brother, Felipe, was overthrown in the province of Salta. And, finally, a strong unitarist army under General Lavalle invaded the northern part of the province of Buenos Aires.

This was the crucial test for Rosas' government, and a combination of luck and consummate military and political skill saved the day for him. He squelched the *estanciero* revolt in the south before it ever had a chance to begin. He signed the Treaty of Mackau with the French in October 1840 and thereby ended the long siege of his capital. Without French aid, Lavalle's army was easily turned back. And Rosas had only to worry about the trouble in the Tucumán and Salta area in the northeast. Here General Lamadrid had taken advantage of the revolt against the Rosas government and had led a unitarist army back from exile. He had gained the support of the provincial governors of Salta, Catamarca, and Jujuy; and he had joined with the caudillo leader of la Rioja, Tomás Brizuela, to prepare an invasion of Rosas' western provinces.

With the situation cleared on the eastern seaboard, the threat now came within the territory of Rosas' western lieutenants, Aldao and Benavídez. Brizuela and Lamadrid were organizing to the north of them and their own provinces of San Juan and Mendoza were threatened.

With the reawakened political situation, Sarmiento could not maintain his former neutrality and withdrawal from politics. He had two very powerful weapons, a school and a newspaper, and he found it difficult to restrain himself from making effective use of them. He and his young friends had been discussing their ideas for reform for several years; now they had a chance to see them put into operation. "When the revolution began to be organized, we young patriots left our costumes and our theatre, and we began to prepare ourselves for the fight that was about to begin."[2]

The principal intellectual opposition to the Rosas dictatorship had been organized by a group of young students, writers, and thinkers in Buenos Aires some years before. Esteban Echeverría, one of Argentina's greatest Romantic writers, returned from Europe in 1830 with the latest books and the latest theories, and soon assumed leadership of the group. In 1838 they formed an organization known as the Asociación de Mayo (The Association of May, i.e. the month of the Argentine Revolution for Independence). It had begun in the home of the young writer, Miguel Cané, as a literary and historical society. The historian, Vicente Fidel López; the philosopher, Juan Bautista Alberdi; the future political leader, Félix Frías; and the critic, Juan María Gutiérrez, were among the initial leaders of the movement. The young men studied the latest philosophical, literary, and political ideas from Europe, and they gathered to discuss them among themselves. The federalists soon came to recognize them as dangerous and brand their meetings as "an orgy of Sansimonian ideas and the stupidities of modern philosophy."[3] Soon they were forced to go underground and by 1839 most of the leaders of the group had fled into exile in either Montevideo or Chile.

"For the new rising generation, the gravest charge that could be made against the men of the Revolution of May and of unitarism consisted in their blindness to the economic and social problems of the country. They had thought that the importation of institutional formulae was enough to straighten out the national life; but the social reality, with its exuberant vitality, its urges and passions, had been stronger. Now there was no choice but to accept the consequences of the error and to prepare slowly what they called the regeneration of the country. . . .

[2] *Obras*, III, 18.

[3] Ibarguren, *Rosas, op.cit.*, p. 374. For a discussion of the intellectual opposition to the Rosas regime see José Manuel Estrada, *La politica liberal bajo la tiranía de Rosas*, Buenos Aires, 1942.

"To regenerate the country was, first of all, not to repeat the old mistakes. Their starting point was clear: neither the mere restoration of ideologies that had failed nor the exaggerated concessions to the rural masses; the task should be to secure the success of the ideals for progress by first transforming those masses. This principle led the political and social thought of the generation of 1837 and directed it toward success. . . .

"Surely the greatest achievement of this generation was the differentiation between the political and the social. Under the influence of the French thought—Saint Simon, Fourier, Leroux, Lamennais, Lerminier—and partly of the German thought—Hegel, Savigny—that reached them through some of this French group, the men of 1837 realized that the political solutions would be without foundation unless the social reality was thoroughly analyzed."[4]

The ideas and aims of the Asociación de Mayo had not been limited to Buenos Aires. The leaders had contacted young men throughout the provinces, and they in turn had organized related groups. Nicolás de Avellaneda was heading a group of young students and thinkers in the central city of Córdoba. The young men in San Juan who had formerly limited their discussions to philosophical and literary topics were now in contact with the Asociación de Mayo and were beginning to apply their ideas to the political field.

Echeverría, Alberdi, and their followers both in Buenos Aires and in the provinces had begun to formulate the ideals for which they were to fight. They saw the caudillo's personal or dynastic power as the power of the counter-revolution. Alberdi, the former critic of Sarmiento's early poetic endeavors, saw the situation thus: he could side with neither the unitarists nor the federalists, for both represented the tradition of personalist, dictatorial, or monarchical rule. What was needed, according to the doctrines of this new generation of intellectuals, was a democratic political form, based upon the European and North American doctrines. Only thus could the society of Hispanic America be compatible with

[4] José Luis Romero, *Las ideas políticas en Argentina,* Fondo de Cultura Económica, Mexico, 1946, pp. 131-132, 136, 144.

modern civilization.[5] "Right or wrong, with a borrowed philosophy, they pretended to solve the national problem."[6] Sarmiento was continuing to read the eighteenth-century rationalists with a sprinkling of the Romantic philosophers that he found in Quiroga Rosas' library. He refers to Descartes, Montesquieu, Rousseau, and Diderot.[7] These thinkers all set rational standards for the world, and they believed that once man was rationally and scientifically studied, his political, social, and moral problems would be solved. As John Locke explained it, "If we can find out these Measures, whereby a Rational creature, put in the state which Man is in this World, may and ought to govern his Opinions and Actions depending thereon, we need not be troubled that some other things escape our knowledge."[8] Sarmiento did not claim to know "those Measures, whereby a Rational creature . . . may and ought to govern his Opinions and Actions," but he thought that he was nearing a knowledge of them in their basic outlines. And above all, he knew that the world and society that he observed around him were far afield from any such "Measures."

The editor of *El Zonda* began to get farther and farther away from his original apolitical ends. He looked around himself and saw the political chaos of his nation. "Nobody ignores the state of penury and misery to which this province has been reduced, this province that is worthy of better fortune than the political upheavals, the havoc wrought by overflowing rivers, and the other eruptions and plagues no less devastating."[9] He contrasted this situation, the situation of the entire Hispanic world, with the rational-scientific-material civilization of the rest of the Western World. "The moderns turn to the customs of all of the civilized world. . . . They hold that the English, North Americans, and French are more moral than we."[10]

[5] Leopoldo Lugones, *Historia de Sarmiento,* Buenos Aires, 1945, pp. 128-129.

[6] Carlos María Onetti, *Cuatro clases sobre Sarmiento escritor,* Tucumán, 1939, p. 27.

[7] *El Zonda,* No. 6, August 25, 1839.

[8] R. G. Collingwood, "Human Nature and Human History," *Proceedings of the British Academy,* XXII, 1936, p. 99.

[9] *El Zonda,* No. 1, July 20, 1839.

[10] *El Zonda,* No. 5, August 17, 1839.

El Zonda began to speak of the ideals that were appearing in the thoughts and writings of the leaders of the Asociación de Mayo. It defined democracy as the "supremacy of *reason over matter*," and it called for adherence to such democratic ideals as charity, equality, the obligation of the governor to educate the people, judicial impartiality, and the free press.[11] And the next step, the obvious step, was to begin to apply these ideals as the "measure" to the society and the government of Argentina and San Juan.

Relations cooled between young Domingo Sarmiento and Governor Benavídez. Sarmiento's criticisms of the government were becoming too vocal and too obvious, and Benavídez began to realize that he would be unable to win the young editor over to his camp. He began to understand that there was an idea behind this man much more powerful than the individual personality.

Although *El Zonda* had proposed to operate for ten years, it lasted for only six weeks, from July 20 to August 25. Its financial position was far from secure. The sarcastic estimate of fifty subscribers had even been overoptimistic, and the total never reached above thirty-nine. Costs could not be met, and bankruptcy seemed inevitable. But financial failure was helped along considerably by the interference of the now dissatisfied government. Benavídez and Maradona began to snipe at *El Zonda's* policy and at its articles. The governor's wife, Doña Telésfora Borrego de Benavídez, was especially instrumental in bringing the newspaper into disfavor. The reasons for her attacks against it have never been clear, but the effect of these attacks upon the policy of the governor was obvious.[12] Finally, in the fifth issue of the paper, appearing on August 17th, there was a seemingly harmless article entitled "Be Careful of the Mad Dog." Its contents were allegorical, and it brought down the wrath of the government upon the newspaper and its editor.

"A little after its first appearance," began the article, "*El Zonda* was walking down the street, distracted and happy. . . . It was occupied with the task of editing an article that was

[11] *Ibid.*

[12] Hudson, *Recuerdos históricos, op.cit.*, II, pp. 402-403.

to be entitled 'The Education that a man should have in order to criticize the production of another,' when bow . . . wow . . . wow . . . a little Cuzcan bitch jumped out at it, seized it by the calf of the leg, shook it at will and sank its teeth into its flesh." A footnote referred to the "little Cuzcan bitch," saying, "*El Zonda* later learned that the masters of this little bitch called her Critiquilla and that they idolized her: she was the lap-dog of the house." The allusion was thus made perfectly obvious. The "Cuzcan bitch" was the governor's wife, and her attack upon the newspaper was being allegorized with the most bitter implications possible. The article went on to say "Forty-five days after that deplorable event, *El Zonda* began to have alarming symptoms." Rabies was setting in. She was meeting with "difficulty in the use of speech." Who was to blame? The Cuzcan bitch.[13]

The meaning behind the allegory was immediately obvious to all of San Juan, and the story of the Cuzcan bitch was soon on every tongue. The governor could not permit such an open challenge to his authority. *El Zonda* was sentenced to death. But Benavídez was far too clever a politician to think of a simple suppression of the newspaper after such a sensational attack. He had a much better plan than this, and he found it to be more effective. Referring back to an old law of the time of the unitarist government of Del Carril, he applied a heavy tax of twelve pesos a page on the paper. Sarmiento, already in financial difficulties, refused to pay it, and he was summoned to the government house.

Domingo remembered having been summoned once before by another governor to that same house and he remembered well the results. He faced Benavídez with the same pride and arrogance with which he had faced Quiroga.

"Have you paid for the last number of *El Zonda*?" asked the governor.

"Paid whom?" retorted Sarmiento.

"The Press."

"Why?"

"Because it has been ordered thus."

"Ordered by whom?" was the young editor's defiant reply.

[13] *El Zonda*, No. 5, August 17, 1839.

"The order has been communicated to you."

"To me? That is not true."

"Have Galaburri, the printer, come in."

(Galaburri enters.)

"Have you not communicated to the gentleman the order to pay twelve pesos per page for the printing of number 6 of *El Zonda*?"

"Yes, sir."

"How do you, Señor Sarmiento, say that he has not?"

"I repeat that I have received no order. Galaburri gave me a message from Don Nazario Benavídez; Galaburri is the same in this case as your Excellency's cook, who should not be made intermediary between the government and the citizens. As to the matter of the printing and of public affairs, the government makes itself heard through decrees and while the existent laws are not abolished by other laws that modify them, I have nothing to do with the rumors that Galaburri brings me of what the governor or his minister says."

"Where are the laws that you invoke?" asked the Minister Maradona.

"It is shameful that a minister should ask me that," Sarmiento replied. "He is the one who is charged with carrying out the laws. Go on, and search the archives."

"You will pay what has been ordered."

"Your Excellency will permit me to assure you that I will not."

"Señor Coquino, you will go at four this afternoon to the home of this gentleman to collect the amount owed."

"At four this afternoon Your Excellency will receive the same reply. It is not the small sum of money that I resist, but the manner of collecting it and the legality of the collection. I defend a principle. I will not submit to the arbitrariness of the government which has no extraordinary powers."[14]

Sarmiento returned to his home, where he was met by Quiroga Rosas, Cortínez, Aberastain, and other friends. They discussed the matter and its implications. The majority of them prevailed upon Sarmiento to give up the fight. If not,

[14] *Obras*, III, 190.

all would be lost. If he gave in, he could at least save the school.

Sarmiento paid the debt, but he did so under protest, and twelve years later he still referred to it as an illegal payment and held that Benavídez owed him that sum. The financial blow of the fine ended the short life of *El Zonda*, and the sixth number was the last in this initial attempt of Domingo in the field of journalism.

The sixth number of *El Zonda* appeared on August 25, and it started with the slogan, "Quod scriptum, scriptum" (What is written is written). The editors took back nothing that they had said. They wound up their journalistic career with a last attack upon the government. "The lack of a just administration of justice, individual liberty is imprisoned by arbitrariness." *El Zonda* left an eloquent last will and testament to the people of San Juan: "Item. I declare that although I am not married I recognize as my legitimate sons all country newspapers that might appear in the nation, for to me they owe their origin." "Item. I declare that my goods consist primarily of study and of the desire for the good and betterment of the country, which I leave to clear the darkness and haze, and I leave for this purpose my six published numbers and several manuscripts." "Item. I leave my heart to my country and my head to the land where it was raised." To the farmers and workers were left the articles on agriculture, new crops, the formation of an agricultural society, and new agricultural methods.[15]

Sarmiento continued to work through the summer with his school, and he continued to discuss and follow the political situation. He and his literary group who were now closely connected with the general oppositionist intellectual movement of the Asociación de Mayo had definitely fallen out of the good graces of the government after the *El Zonda* affair, and they were watched closely.

Early in 1840 an opportunity arose for Domingo to take a business trip to Chile, and he felt that his absence from the San Juan scene would be a desirable one from all points of view. He accompanied his uncle, the Bishop-elect, Quiroga

[15] *El Zonda*, No. 6, August 25, 1839.

Sarmiento, who was traveling to Santiago to be consecrated in his new position. On the 28th of January he had signed an oath of fealty to the federalist government, but this did not keep his nephew from remaining on good terms with him and joining him on his trip. On March 29th, the religious ceremony of consecration took place in the Cathedral of Santiago, but Sarmiento had not continued this far. He had stopped off at the little Andean town of San Felipe de Aconcagua just across the border in Chile.

Here he remained to complete the task for which he had come. He devoted himself to pursuits that would help him in his job as schoolteacher in San Juan and that would improve his Colegio de Santa Rosa. He visited all the schools in the area, especially the schools for girls, and he found many aspects of them superior to his own institution in Argentina. "I have seen surprising things in the embroidery and the drawing done by the students, and I promise to send my sister, Procesa, from San Juan to study in these subjects; as for the other aspects, they do not seem to be any better than our own school."[16] He bought books, drawing material and "a million other things for the School." He spent over two hundred pesos on his purchases, and he expected them to put his institution "at a high point of perfection."[16]

Sarmiento remained in San Felipe for several weeks. His reputation as schoolteacher and publisher had made many valuable connections for him in this neighboring nation. A number of distinguished Argentine exiles contacted him upon his arrival, and they "came to an agreement" in their common aims of opposition to the federalist regime in their homeland. Don José Calle of Santiago informed him that the newspaper of that city, *El Mercurio*, would be at his disposal for the publication of articles. Sarmiento communicated this offer to his friends in San Juan, and they probably made use of these facilities to express some of the new ideas brewing in their minds.[17]

The contrast between the progressive material life of Chile

[16] Unpublished letter from Sarmiento to Manuel José Quiroga Rosas. Dated April 9, 1840, San Felipe de Aconcagua. In the Archivo Nacional de Chile, Santiago de Chile, volume 253, pieza 12, No. 1.

[17] *Ibid.*

and the backward and chaotic situation in Argentina was a source of discouragement to the young man. "Friend," he wrote, "my ardour cools when I think that only I work *with the facts,* for so egotistical and so unimportant a homeland." He felt tempted to remain in Chile and move to Santiago, "where I count many possible friends who will offer me their aid. If I suffer a few more setbacks in San Juan in the next mountain range, I will come to this range where life is so positive and where there is room for material interests."[18]

After a few weeks in Chile, Sarmiento returned to Argentina with new information as to the exiled opposition to Rosas, with new equipment for his school, and with the assurance that in case of a crisis he would be able to seek refuge in Chile, among friends, and with an opportunity to continue his search for truth and his political crusade.

In the months that followed, Sarmiento devoted himself to winding up the first school year of his Colegio de Santa Rosa. He worked hard at the end to make the commencement a memorable one and an important occasion in the life of San Juan. The seventh, eighth, and ninth of July were set aside as the days of celebration and examinations for the school. Invitations were sent to the most important citizens of the town: "Be kind enough to attend the examinations of the students of Santa Rosa on the seventh, eighth, and ninth days of July; they will begin promptly at ten in the morning. Please notify your friends that this act being of public interest I do not feel it necessary to invite anybody especially, for all are and should be interested in attending it. I wish to *manifest to the public* the results of the teaching of this first year."[19] On those days, public examinations were held, and the people of the city could see the advances made by their children and their friends' children. The girls' knowledge of reading, writing, religion, and grammar was tested. They demonstrated in practical application their ability to use English and French, their drawings of flowers and local

[18] *Ibid.*

[19] Carmen Peñaloza de Varese, "Dos colegios de Santa Rosa," *Boletín de la junta de historia de la provincia de San Juan,* San Juan, 1945, pp. 67-68.

scenes, and their attainments in music and practical mathematics.

On July 9th, exactly one year after the inauguration of the school, a celebration took place. It was a great civic function attended by many. The school had undoubtedly demonstrated itself to be a great success. There was no other to equal it in Argentina in that period, and it certainly equaled any girls' school in the Americas at so early a date. That the desert, the Pampa, and the Andes which surrounded the little town of San Juan should be given such an oasis of enthusiasm and learning—all this was the first and one of the most lasting testimonies to the unusual character of the young man who had directed the enterprise.

But Domingo's life was not entirely absorbed in the intellectual phases of this pursuit. As had always been true and as always was to be true in his life, he was unable to separate one part of his living from another. What was basically an intellectual pursuit became involved in and complicated by other phases of his existence. One of the young girls who attended the school was the daughter of Doña Tránsito de Oro, the sister of the late Bishop Oro and one of the great supporters of Sarmiento's project of the school. Doña Tránsito had married Don José Genaro Rodríguez, and their daughter, Elena, attended the Colegio. Contemporaries attribute to her "great beauty and extraordinary intelligence," and she was undoubtedly the outstanding personality among the students of the institution. The young director fell in love with his student, and late in 1840 he was unable to contain and hide his feelings any longer. He wrote to Doña Tránsito of the "sadness and uncertainty that torments me." "To justify this pretension that you will label as daring, I have neither fortune to offer her nor anything that might satisfy the careful aspirations of a mother, but if the desire to create the happiness of this dear object of your tender interest and my own, together with an unsoiled record of behavior and the hopes of a young man, can in any way replace the gifts that nature and fortune have denied me, nobody could better me in these respects."[20]

[20] Albarracín, *Sarmiento, op.cit.*, pp. 12-13.

Doña Tránsito liked and respected the young man whom she had helped to sponsor, but she wanted something more secure for her daughter. She knew of the precarious political position that Sarmiento held in regard to the government. She was aware of his equally insecure financial situation. And she turned down the young lover's request, leaving him without any hopes for a future change in attitude.

This rejection marked a turning point in Domingo's fortune during this part of his life. Since he had returned from his first exile in Chile, he had built for himself a position of importance and promise. With this setback in his own personal projects and aspirations, there began an entire series of setbacks that traced the complete disintegration of his position.

The political situation was growing more grave in San Juan. As early as June 30th, Sarmiento was writing that "political affairs are every day taking on a darker and more menacing character. Everything is hidden by the heavy cover of mystery. We know nothing of Lavalle nor of Rosas."[21] Benavídez had just been reelected governor of the province with extraordinary powers, and it appeared that a showdown was about to occur in the western provinces. Unitarist armies under Lamadrid and Brizuela were attacking from the north. Brizuela had already invaded the province of San Luis, and Aldao had left Mendoza to meet him in battle. It was this grave military situation which had caused Benavídez to request extraordinary governmental powers, and it was this situation which made the governor fear the activities of that small group of oppositionist intellectuals which was beginning to center around the person of Domingo Sarmiento.

Sarmiento, Aberastain, Quiroga Rosas, Cortínez, and Rodríguez had formed a society known as the Group of Five. It was a carryover from the old dramatic and literary society that they had led, but it was more specifically directed towards a discussion of political and current problems. The group sometimes met at the Café of Commerce and at other times at the homes of the members. It followed the pattern set by

[21] Sarmiento to Quiroga Rosas, San Juan, June 30, 1840, Archivo Nacional de Chile, Santiago de Chile, volume 253, pieza 12, No. 2.

the Asociación de Mayo and planned moves against the government. It even went so far as to contact such unitarist leaders as Brizuela and discuss what could be done to aid the invading armies.

In November 1840, as the forces of Aldao and Brizuela were maneuvering in preparation for battle, a unitarist revolution in Mendoza overthrew Aldao's puppet governor, Correas, and elevated to power Don Pedro Molina, a unitarist leader. The Benavídez government was thrown into a panic. Fearing a spread of such a revolutionary spirit, the San Juan governor ordered the arrest of all unitarists in his province. Quiroga Rosas and Cortínez fled to Chile. Aberastain escaped to the Province of Salta, where the unitarists were in power. And out of the Group of Five, only Sarmiento remained to face the federalist wrath in San Juan.[22]

On Sunday, December 8, an order was issued for the arrest of Domingo Sarmiento, and he was brought to the private home of Governor Benavídez. Once more we find the conversation between these two men recorded in Sarmiento's writings:[23]

"I know that you are conspiring, Don Domingo," said the governor as he started the interview with a bald accusation.

"That is false," replied Domingo, "I am not conspiring."

"You go around influencing the Representatives."

"Ah! That is a different thing. Your Excellency sees that there is no conspiracy. I make use of my rights to direct myself to the magistrates, to the representatives of the people to prevent the calamities that Your Excellency is preparing for the country."

Governor Benavídez was becoming angered, but his young opponent continued in exactly the same vein. "Your Excel-

[22] Hudson, *Recuerdos históricos, op.cit.*, II, p. 402.

[23] Some writers have held that Sarmiento, in recording these conversations in later years, exaggerated the part that he played in them. Considering the extreme egotism that he later developed, this is possible. But several things point to the fact that these particular conversations are for the most part accurate. Sarmiento and Benavídez had been friends since their early childhood, when they went to school together. Moreover, Sarmiento published his account of the conversation while Benavídez was still alive and could have corrected any mistakes. The two actually met in 1855, years after the publication of the account.

lency is alone, isolated, determined to continue in his proposals, and I am interested that those who can and those who must should stop you in time."

"Don Domingo, you will force me to take measures."

"What difference does it make?"

"Severe measures!"

"And what difference?"[24]

"You do not understand what I mean."

"Yes, I understand. You want to shoot me. What difference does it make?"

Benavídez remained looking the prisoner straight in the eyes. Domingo did not flinch. As he later said, "I was seized at that moment by the spirit of God." He felt himself the representative of the rights of the people. He thought that he detected in the face of the governor signs of admiration, of compassion, and of respect.

"Sir," he said, "do not soil yourself. When you can tolerate me no more, exile me to Chile; meanwhile, Your Excellency may count on the fact that I must work to hold him back, if I can, from the path to which he is led by ambition and the loosening of his passions."[25]

At this, the young man was dismissed and he returned to his home. But, true to his promise, it was not the end of his activities. As he wrote to his friend, Quiroga Rosas, "After the exit of our friends from San Juan I remained in my post, the target for government attacks and federalist rancor, but I did not recant for a moment. I fulfilled my task with honor, if patriotism, if abnegation, and if sacrifice deserve to be honored." Domingo worked tirelessly, arguing with members of the government, protesting the official acts, and exposing what he considered the true evils that menaced the province and the true character of the struggle.[26] He continued to be in touch with the unitarist opposition in Chile as well as the military forces under Brizuela. A few days later he was again summoned to the governor's presence.

[24] Sarmiento's heroic stand might well have been exaggerated in this particular section, but the essential truth is undoubtedly there.

[25] *Obras*, III, 193.

[26] Sarmiento to Quiroga Rosas, Los Andes, December 15, 1840, Archivo Nacional de Chile, volume 253, pieza 12, No. 3.

"I have learned," started Benavídez, "that you have received papers from Salta and from the camp of Brizuela."

"Yes, sir," replied Sarmiento, "and I was preparing to bring them to you."

"I knew that the papers had reached you, but," he added slowly, "I didn't know that you wanted to show them to me."

"I had not finished the petition from myself that I wanted to accompany them. Here Your Excellency has both."

Benavídez examined them rapidly and then exclaimed, "These proclamations were printed here."

"You are mistaken, Sir, they were printed in Salta."

"Hum! You cannot fool me."

"I never deceive, Sir," said Domingo in a self-righteous tone. "I repeat that they are printed in Salta. The San Juan press does not have this small capital letter, this other type, that . . ."

Benavídez insisted on his point and had Galaburri, the printer, called in. Galaburri confirmed Sarmiento's assertion and convinced the governor of his error.

"Give me that manuscript," said Benavídez, pointing to the petition that Sarmiento had brought with him.

"I will read it, Sir, it is still in rough form."

"Then you read it." Sarmiento remained silent. "Read it."

"Your Excellency will have the chief of police leave the room. I have no desire to bring him into my confidence."[27]

The chief of police left the room, giving Sarmiento a glance that seemed to the young man to be filled with menace.[28] Domingo began to read the statement that he had prepared on the political situation and the ills of the federalist regime. He read with emphasis and emotion, emphasizing "those ideas I wanted to make penetrate further into his brain." He was caught by the spirit of his own reading, and when he reached the end he was filled with excitement and expectation. "I raised my eyes and read on the face of the caudillo . . . indifference. Not a single idea had taken hold of his soul. His will and his ambition were an armor that covered his heart and his spirit."[29] Again Sarmiento was dismissed from

[27] *Obras*, III, 193. [28] *Ibid.*

[29] *Ibid.* C. Galván Moreno, *Radiografía de Sarmiento*, Buenos Aires, 1938, p. 55.

the governor's presence. This time he was not free, but committed to prison on charges of conspiracy against the government. He was taken to the tower of the government house, overlooking the main square or plaza, where he was kept in custody. There he remained, not knowing whether to expect death, exile, or imprisonment, awaiting the will of the government which he had so long opposed and defied.

Aldao, upon hearing of the unitarist revolt in Mendoza, had turned back from his campaign in the north, returned to his capital city, and restored his puppet Governor Correas. Meanwhile, General Benavídez had also sent forces to assist the federalists in Mendoza. Once he was assured of the security of his position in San Juan, he had sent troops to the assistance of Aldao, but the San Juan division had gone only halfway on its journey when news reached it of the federalist restoration in Mendoza. The Sanjuaninos turned around and started back for their homes. On the night of November 16th, they had reached Pocito, on the outskirts of San Juan. Here they camped for the night, but many of the soldiers and officers received leave to go to the city to celebrate the federalist victory in Mendoza. As the night progressed, alcohol flowed freely and the spirit of the troops rose in direct proportion to their inebriation. By the early hours of the morning, the drunken troops were heading towards the central square and shouting for the blood of the unitarist prisoners there. They had learned of the imprisonment of Sarmiento and they called for his head.

About dawn on the 17th, Sarmiento was awakened by the sound of horses' hoofs and mass shouting in the Plaza. "Death to the savage unitarists" was the cry. This was the battle slogan that had reached the west from the Rosas mobs in Buenos Aires. The young man stumbled out of bed and listened to the cries. The gray light of dawn was already entering his cell, and the prisoner caught parts of sentences from down the corridor of the building. "The troops are coming to the Plaza." "Señor Sarmiento is . . ." "They are going to kill him."[30] A lynching mob was forming, and Domingo knew the consequences that such a move might

[30] Rojas, p. 152.

bring. The commander of the guard appeared suddenly at the door of the jail and ordered the prisoner to come with him.

"At whose order?" asked Sarmiento, stalling for time.

"At the order of Major Espinosa."

"I will not obey."

The guard went on to the next cell and took the prisoner out to show to the crowd, but the soldiers were not satisfied. "Not that one. We want Sarmiento!" Finally, realizing that he could no longer stall without endangering the safety of his fellow prisoners and making them suffer in his place, Sarmiento left his cell and appeared before the mob on the front porch of the government house. He was greeted with shouts of "Death to him!" "Send him down to us!" "Send him down!" "Down!" "Down!"

A voice commanded from below. "Officer of the Guard, make him come down. Use your sword."

"Get down," the officer ordered the prisoner, striking him with the broad of his sword.

"I will not go down," replied Sarmiento, grasping hold of the railing.

"Get down," the officer insisted, letting loose with some harder blows.

"I will not get down." Domingo's voice was still calm.

"Hit him with the blade," came the voice of Major Espinosa, who was below with the crowd. His tone was filled with anger. "If I come up there I will run him through. Officer of the guard! Make him come down!"

"For God's sake, please go down," the officer of the guard whispered between blows of his sword. "I am going to have to strike you next with the blade."

Sarmiento was still desperately stalling for time, and his maneuvres were successful. The noise created by the crowd had reached Benavídez's house only one hundred yards away. It had awakened most of the town, and Sarmiento's frantic mother had rushed to the governor's residence for aid. She broke into the quiet house and threw herself at the feet of the governor. The streets around were filled with voices and noises. "Sir, they are going to kill Domingo!" As Sarmiento later commented, "In vain, Benavídez had tried to wash his hands of such an anonymous crime." But he was brought into it by force, and he had to intervene. He sent his aid to control the situation.

Meanwhile, when the mob realized that they would be unable to persuade the prisoner to come down from his position, ten or twelve of the soldiers went up, seized him, and carried him down by his hands and feet. They reached the ground at the very moment that twelve sharpshooters Espinosa had sent for arrived. Before having him shot, Espinosa wanted to confront the prisoner face to face. He seized him and began to jab his sword into the young man's flesh. An actor whom Sarmiento had ridiculed on the stage and who had been made a captain in the federalist army also took advantage of the situation and sought his own revenge with jabs in his enemy's flesh.

Sarmiento continued to show no reaction to this treatment. He kept his face "stereotyped with the expression that my corpse should have." Espinosa became infuriated by the lack of any reaction. He jabbed harder, and finally he prepared to run the prisoner through. In one last desperate attempt to gain time, Sarmiento shouted, "Listen, major!" The officer stopped and turned to see what the prisoner was going to say. With a quick move, Domingo turned, jumped under the porch from which he had been brought down, and ran across to the other side. Once there, he was met with a "cloud of bayonets" and was seized by a sea of hands. At that moment, the governor's aid arrived and ordered the mob to desist. He allowed them to shave the prisoner and then return him to his cell.[31]

Governor Benavídez decided that if he was to avoid having the blood of the young editor-schoolteacher on his hands, he would have to exile him to Chile. The very next day, he gave orders to prepare Sarmiento for the trip. Back in his cell, Domingo looked out on his beloved San Juan for the last time for many years. Here he had been born, had been edu-

[31] This entire episode is told in detail by Sarmiento, *Obras*, III, 196-199. Incidentally, in the square where this episode took place, there is now a statue to Sarmiento.

cated, and had fought for his ideals. As he sat and thought of his situation, he composed a letter to Doña Tránsito de Oro, the mother of his beloved Elena. Doña Tránsito's decision on Sarmiento's suit already seemed justified. He was in jail, preparing for exile, penniless, seemingly without a future. Elena had already been engaged to marry another more stable if less talented man. "My good Doña Tránsito, finally (at two in the morning) this day ends. I am leaving for Zonda Valley now to get out of this anguish of worrying. After five days we shall be free. I entrust to you the school as long as it can exist. I also recommend to you Bienvenida [his sister] who I want to help little Elena as much as she can."[32]

The next day Sarmiento was visited by eight of the students from the Colegio. They promised to continue in their studies, and before leaving they sang their master's favorite song, the chorus from *Tancred*.[33] He was deeply touched by this show of affection and he remembered it with pleasure for many years to come.

On November 18, 1840, Domingo Sarmiento said goodby to his mother and sisters and, accompanied by his father and a few fellow unitarists, started the long journey across the Andes into exile. Escorted by a group of federalist soldiers, Sarmiento and his fellow-exiles moved slowly toward the Chilean border. As they passed a little hut that Domingo had built near the Zonda Baths, he stopped for a moment for a last look around. Within the shack, he had decorated the walls in bright colors, and he had painted the Argentine coat of arms, surrounding it with flags and banners. As the soldiers waited outside, Sarmiento entered his shack and, beneath the national coat of arms, wrote a quotation from one of the many French authors that he had been reading. The guards noticed what he was doing and demanded an explanation. They could not read the words of this strange foreign language. The expedition was delayed while an attempt was made to decipher what was believed to be a lewd quotation. They soon came to the conclusion that "this doesn't mean anything, the young man is insane."[34] The exiles continued

[32] Albarracín, *Sarmiento, op.cit*, p. 20.
[33] *Obras*, III, 88.
[34] Albarracín, *Sarmiento, op.cit.*, p. 22.

on their weary way, heartened by the message of the quotation. Sarmiento himself didn't remember the exact source of the words. He thought they were from the French writer Fortoul, but they might have been from any one of a number of French authors whom he was reading.[35]

The words were later engraved on a rock overlooking the Zonda Valley, and they remain as an inspiration for succeeding generations: "On ne tue point les idees." (Ideas cannot be killed.)[36]

[35] Antonio Bucich makes a good case for the fact that the quotation was from Volney. Bucich, *Luchas y rutas, op.cit.*, pp. 24-34.

[36] There has been considerable difference of opinion as to the exact place where Sarmiento wrote these words. Guillermo Guerra (*op.cit.*, p. 60) claims that they were written in charcoal on some rocks along the road. Adolfo Saldías holds that they were on the wall of a post station (Adolfo Saldías, *Páginas políticas*, Buenos Aires, 1912, p. 188). Secundino Navarro claims that he wrote them on the wall of his home (*Notas sobre la vida y escritos del Gral. Domingo Faustino Sarmiento publicados con motivo de la inauguración del monumento del prócer en San Juan el 17 de noviembre de 1901*, San Juan, 1938, p. 6). A commission appointed in October 1940 by the Junta de Estudios Históricos de San Juan made a report on "the place where Sarmiento wrote the apothegm of Fortoul when he left for exile in Chile." This commission concluded that Sarmiento had first drawn a coat of arms on a rock and then put the quotation beneath it. In the place chosen by the commission a plaque was placed containing the famous words, and in memory of Sarmiento's use of them. I found in the collection of unpublished letters from Sarmiento to Quiroga Rosas a letter dated Santiago, February 19, 1841. This was but a few weeks after the occurrence, and it would naturally still be vivid in the young exile's mind. He describes in detail the incident, and affirms that he wrote it on the wall of the shack that he had used at the Zonda Baths. My account was taken from this letter. (Sarmiento to Quiroga Rosas, Santiago, February 19, 1841, Archivo Nacional de Chile, volume 253, pieza 12, No. 13.)

BOOK III

The Conception

Chapter 12. The Exile

As Sarmiento stepped across the Chilean border in November 1840, he left the chaos of civil war behind him. He stepped across the border into a country that had enjoyed a relatively ordered civil life for the past decade. He stepped into a country that presented the individual with constitutional guarantees of his liberties and of his rights. He entered a country that was awakening to new ideas and new currents of thought, and he felt the thrill of a nation first experiencing the revolutionary changes brought about by nineteenth-century material progress. Chile, like Montevideo, was a haven for the exiles from the Rosas dictatorship. It was a country that presented them with a free press and individual freedom, that had established itself on a basis of order and law.

Politically, Chile was in the hands of the old "pelucón" or conservative party. This group had come to power in 1830 when a civil conflict that had been raging since the previous year was brought to an end by a military victory by the conservatives. The leader of the conservatives, Diego Portales, then took over and restored the country to order, albeit at the cost of many of the liberties that it had formerly enjoyed. Portales, a businessman who had undertaken to provide funds for the service of the government's foreign debt, assumed control of a provisional government. He did much that Rosas did in Argentina, but he avoided Rosas' bloodshed. He brought the army under control, suppressed banditry, and organized the economy of the government. Although the freedom of the press and free elections were done away with for several years, Portales turned the government over to one of his followers, General Joaquín Prieto, and little by little constitutional guarantees and individual liberties were restored. By 1841, the conservative government succeeded in bringing order to the country, in giving it a constitutional government, and in defeating a foreign invasion by General Santa Cruz, the protector of the Perú-Bolivian Confederation. The elections were still "rigged" by the government, and were to be for many years to come, but Sarmiento and his fellow *émigrés* found in Chile one of the freest and most nomocratic governments in Spanish America. The country was noted for its constitutional organization, its good public administration, and freedom to criticize the regime.[1] Sarmiento saw the effects of a decade of conservative government as salutary. He described it thus:

"The discrediting and disuse of revolutionary means of bettering or changing society. (Revolutions replaced by elections and discussions in the press.)

"Security of property, the continuation of order, and with both of these, the love of work and the spirit of enterprise that causes the development of wealth and prosperity."[2]

In Chile, Sarmiento's ideas took form and matured. He went into exile with ideas that he had received from his extensive but disorganized reading. These ideas he found inapplicable to the world in which he lived. Within five years, he had a definite philosophy, a world-view of his own. This is not to imply that Sarmiento's ideas did not change in later years. Many of his points of view were altered radically; many of his ideas were completely reversed. But the basis of his thinking was developed in this period. Between his arrival in Santiago in 1841 and his departure for Europe in 1845, he laid the foundations for his future thought.

Sarmiento did not abandon his idea that a rational order existed and that it was the key to human progress. He decided that the fault lay in the actual structure of society. Society must be reformed and made to fit into the rational order. Political, economic, and intellectual reform was necessary, and to this task he would dedicate himself. As his ideas clarified as to what changes and what reforms were necessary, Sarmiento developed his own methods of fighting for his

[1] Norberto Pinilla, *1842: Panorama y significación del movimiento literario*, Santiago de Chile, 1942, p. 7.

[2] "Los diez años precedentes," *El Nacional*, May 1, 1841. (From galley proofs of articles intended for *Obras* but for some reason never included. These galley proofs are collected in the Museo Histórico Sarmiento.)

ends. It was during these years that he proved himself an effective and powerful writer, a capable and far-thinking teacher, an important political force. Within four years he became one of Chile's outstanding journalists; he wrote one of South America's greatest books; he became a great pedagogue; and he gained the reputation of a relentless fighter and crusader. Once in Chile, he never rested, was never idle. Following his own belief that only indefatigable effort could bring success, he continued reading, writing, and experimenting. "From Chile we can give nothing to those who carry on the struggle under all the rigors of privation and with that destructive knife, like the sword of Damocles, at this moment hanging over their heads. We can give nothing—nothing but ideas, nothing but counsel, nothing but encouragement. We are given no arms to carry to the combatants save that of the Chilean free press which serves all men."[3]

Sarmiento and his father had crossed the Andes by the same route as during their previous visit in 1831. They passed through Putaenda and stopped in Los Andes in the Aconcagua Valley. Here they met a number of Argentine exiles who were following carefully the civil war across the border and doing everything in their power to fight from where they were the government of Rosas and his caudillos. They had an arsenal and were manufacturing arms and ammunition for future battle. They blocked the passage of those who were on their way to fight with the federalists in the western Argentine provinces, and they were carrying on an extensive propaganda campaign to gain the sympathy of important and influential Chileans for the unitarist cause.[4] Domingo saw that in this manner, even in exile, he would be able to fight against that which he believed to be evil in his country.

While Domingo and his father were in Los Andes, word came that the unitarist General Juan Lavalle had fought his way into Buenos Aires with 3,000 men and that Rosas had fled to the south with the remainder of his army, only some

[3] Bucich, *Luchas y rutas, op.cit.*, p. 62.

[4] Unpublished letter from Sarmiento to Manuel José Quirogarosas (Quiroga Rosas), Los Andes, December 15, 1840, Archivo Nacional, Santiago de Chile, volume 253, pieza 12, No. 3.

2,000 soldiers. This heartening news made the young *émigré* confident that the struggle was nearly over and that he would soon be returning home.[5] But disillusionment was not long in coming, for the news proved nothing more than an unfounded and false rumor.

Sarmiento decided to continue on to Santiago. He had made some contacts there during his earlier visit to the country, and had been assured that his writings could be accepted and used by the principal newspaper of the city, *El Mercurio.*[6] He arrived in Santiago in January 1841. For some reason, Don José Clemente had returned to San Juan, but this did not deter his son from pushing on to the Chilean capital. This time Sarmiento had no intention of working in the mines of Copiapó, nor did he wish to bury himself as a schoolteacher in a small provincial town. He sought the center of Chilean political and cultural life and the company of fellow Argentine exiles, men who were faced with the same problems of orientation as he. In Santiago, Sarmiento would be with his old friends Manuel Quiroga Rosas and Domingo de Oro. He had no immediate means of supporting himself, but that was a challenge he was determined to meet, for he had made up his mind.

When Sarmiento arrived in Santiago, it was a small town of 60,000 inhabitants. Life in the Chilean capital was not the life of a metropolis. It had none of the anonymity and objectivity of life in the big cities of today. The streets were mostly deserted during the day, but if one ventured to walk or ride along them, curious eyes would follow from behind half-drawn shades and cracked shutters. At dusk the inhabitants of the town began to appear. They gathered in groups before their houses and in the cafés, gossiping and discussing the events of the day. At night, there was often the theater, and there were always "tertulias," or conversational groups to discuss politics, literature, or the private affairs of fellow citizens.

In such a small-town atmosphere the new *émigré* from San

[5] *Ibid.*

[6] Sarmiento to Manuel José Quiroga Rosas, April 9, 1840, San Felipe de Aconcagua, Archivo Nacional de Chile, Santiago de Chile, volume 253, pieza 12, No. 1.

Juan could not go unnoticed. Although he was but thirty years old he looked much older, and he cut a rather extraordinary physical picture. His friend Joaquín Lastarria described him as appearing to be sixty, "with a high forehead and slightly bald, his cheeks fleshy, loose and shaven."[7] His shoulders were broad but bent. His frame was heavy, and his strong and massive head was set on a thick bull-like neck. His sparkling eyes when gazing intently seemed to penetrate wherever they were directed, and when angry they seemed to burn like a flame as a fair and sure warning of the blistering heat that would issue forth from his mouth.

Sarmiento's arrival in Chile was not a dramatic one. One of a number of political refugees, he was merely another "cuyano" seeking a livelihood. With little to offer but his persistence and his ambition, he was quickly absorbed into the life of his new homeland. His first few months in Santiago were lived in obscurity and poverty. He lived in a small third-story apartment in an outlying section of Santiago known as Sierra Bella (today Portal Fernández Concha). His apartment, situated on a corner of Ahumada Street, consisted of but one room. It was square, and its lack of furniture gave the impression of spaciousness. In the center of the room was a small table and a straw-backed chair, and in one corner stood a dilapidated little bed. The floor was without a rug, and piled on it were the volumes of the *Diccionario de la conversación*, the young *émigré's* most prized possession.[8] During the first month of his residence in Santiago, Domingo was forced to sell his beloved books which he had brought with him across the Andes. He sold them to his new friend Lastarria for four ounces of gold, and used the money to take care of his living expenses.[9]

It was not long before Sarmiento was meeting and attracting the attention of many of the interesting intellectual leaders of Chile of that time. He met Don José María Núñez, who introduced him to Joaquín Victorino Lastarria. He came

[7] J. V. Lastarria, *Recuerdos literarios*, quoted in Guerra, p. 64.

[8] Bernardo González Arrili, *Sarmiento*, 3rd edition, Buenos Aires, 1946, p. 19; Guerra, pp. 63-64.

[9] Armando Donoso, *Sarmiento en el destierro*, Buenos Aires, 1927, p. 13.

to know the famous Spanish writer, Rafael Minvielle, who, as Sarmiento recounts, "found me in a dismantled room with one chair and two empty boxes that I used as a bed."[10] These men recognized the spark of genius in their new acquaintance, and they planned to introduce him to the stage of Chilean politics and letters. Lastarria later wrote: "That embryo of a great man interested us greatly. He had the ability of embellishing with words his forms that were almost gaucho. We soon became intimate with him. Having suggested that he open a school to earn a living, we helped him to found it in that very solitary third-story apartment."[11] They decided to introduce him to Don Manuel Montt, one of the leaders of the conservative party; and they promised to aid him in entering the field of Chilean journalism.

With the help of these new friends and with a timely work of his own, Sarmiento made a dramatic entrance on the stage of Chilean public affairs on the eleventh of February 1841. One day early in the month he had read to some of his friends an article that he had written on the Battle of Chacabuco during the War of Independence. Lastarria and the others had liked it and they suggested that he send it to Rivadeneira, the editor and director of *El Mercurio*, the leading newspaper of Valparaíso. Sarmiento signed it anonymously as "a Lieutenant of Artillery at Chacabuco." It was dispatched by mail, and the young author waited expectantly.

"People who have received an orderly education, attended halls of learning, submitted to examinations, and felt strengthened by the acquisition of diplomas, cannot judge the emotions of novelty, fear, and hope that seized me when I sent my first article to the Chilean press. Had I asked myself then whether I knew anything about politics, literature, economics, or criticism I would frankly have answered, 'No.' As the solitary traveler approaching a great city sees from a distance only the cupolas, pinnacles, and towers of its tallest buildings, I saw no public in front of me, only names like Bello, Oro and Olaneta; and the schools, legislative chambers, and courts of justice, as so many centers of learning and

[10] *Ibid.*, p. 15.

[11] Lastarria, *Recuerdos literarios, op.cit.*

discrimination. My obscurity and isolation humbled me less than the novelty of the setting and the great mass of unknown men who, in my imagination, all seemed to be waiting for me to speak in order to judge me. Like a new playwright under the oppression of uncertainty, I waited for the arrival of *El Mercurio* of February 11, 1841. Only one friend was in on the secret. I kept to my house, hiding, because of fear. At eleven o'clock, they brought me good news: the article had been applauded by the Argentines! That was something. In the afternoon it was discussed by the cafe loungers, and at night in the theater. The next day I learned that Don Andrés Bello and Egaña had read it together and found it good. 'Thank God!' I said to myself. 'I am saved.' "[12]

That same day Sarmiento went to the house of an acquaintance. Present were a number of literary figures including Don Rafael Minvielle. Without admitting or even hinting at his authorship of the article, Sarmiento directed the conversation to that subject and listened hopefully. "The author couldn't be Argentine; the article even has Spanish provincialisms in it." Sarmiento suggested that it did not deserve the praise that it had received, but Minvielle indignantly countered this assertion. Sarmiento allowed himself to be forced to admit that the article was "irreproachable in style, pure in language, brilliant in its imagery, nourished with sane ideas, embellished by the soft varnish of sentiment."[13] The inner satisfaction of the young author is understandable: in later years he commented that this was one of the few times that Minvielle ever got the best of him in an argument.

The article was in many ways an outstanding one. We must discount as exaggerated some of Sarmiento's later accounts of his success. He stepped from obscurity into the limelight. He was no longer the unknown *émigré*, the unsuccessful poet, the small-town newspaper man and teacher. He was a man whose articles had been praised by the great Andrés Bello, patriarch of Chilean letters. He was a man whose style had captivated the reading public of Santiago and Valparaíso, a man sought after by both political parties, and a man praised by the stylist

[12] *Anthology*, p. 179.
[13] *Obras*, III, 200-201.

Minvielle. The success grew in his mind as time went on. When he wrote *Recuerdos de provincia* ten years later, the success was startling and dramatic, but his *Memorias* some forty years later painted the success as almost fantastic.

The article described the Battle of Chacabuco as one of the turning points of the revolution against Spain. It gave the Argentine General José de San Martín his rightful place as one of the great military leaders of the War of Independence. Partisan spirit, ambitions, and jealousy had beclouded the facts of history, and the anniversary of Chacabuco had ceased to be celebrated in Chile. San Martín had lost his position of a national hero. Sarmiento's article succeeded in righting this historical wrong. The following year, the Chilean Congress restored San Martín's name to the army register. "Free America was sown on the glorious fields of Chacabuco."[14] Chacabuco became a memorable date; San Martín became a heroic name.

Sarmiento also used this first article as his opening gun in his journalistic campaign against the tyranny of Rosas from whence he had fled. This propaganda battle, which he was destined to continue until the fall of the Argentine dictator, began with a plea to "save the homeland from an horrible tyrant . . . a despot who has sworn to exterminate all the soldiers of the War of Independence."[15] After showing the importance and greatness of the Army of Liberation and its defeat of the Spaniards, Sarmiento contrasted it with Rosas; he contrasted the ideas and ideals; he showed Rosas as an anti-revolutionary. Even in Sarmiento's overemphasis of the effect of the article in later years, the essence of truth remains: "In its time, it moved the spirits of Chileans and it launched the name of its author. . . . For public opinion the oration was the cry of its conscience, that had been held back by partisan spirit or international jealousy and that demanded reparation for an historical injustice."[16]

The article in *El Mercurio* seemed to open all doors for the young "Lieutenant of Artillery." Rivadeneira wrote to Lastarria, commissioning him to offer the author thirty pesos for

[14] *Obras*, I, 7; "12 de Febrero de 1817," *El Mercurio*, February 11, 1841.
[15] *Ibid.*
[16] *Obras*, XLIX, 98-99.

three or four articles per month. General Las Heras, one of the leaders of the liberal party, came to ask for Sarmiento's support. Don Manuel Montt, minister of education and leader of the conservative party, invited him for an interview. "For the liberal party, of which Vicuña and Las Heras were expressions, there were hopes of having found a champion worthy of its cause; for the government, the article revealed the existence of a political thinker placed above the pettiness of parties and whose thought might blaze new trails. . . ."[17] "The statesmen who directed politics in Chile . . . saw in the still unknown author a politician of importance, and they hastened to find from whence came the article and to call the author, even though they supposed him to be a foreigner, or to direct and express the politics of the government in the press."[18]

The years between 1841 and 1845 were spent in the heat of conflicts of thought and politics in Chile. Sarmiento never ceased to be an Argentine and to fight for his beliefs in his own country, but he also threw himself wholeheartedly into the battles of his adopted country. In spite of his multiple activities, however, we must take this period as fundamentally one of thought and development of ideas. To understand the Sarmiento of later years, the politician, educator, diplomat, and president, we must get at the essence of his ideas in this period. This can best be done by using as often as possible his own words, and then trying to understand their importance. Sarmiento's first month in Santiago had brought him into a position in Chilean public life that made the development of his ideas in the press, in the schools, and in politics possible. The "Lieutenant of Artillery" had been the key that opened the door. "Fifteen days later [after the appearance of the article] the Argentine *émigré* had two newspapers at his disposal and was in charge of the political direction of the press."[19] The door was open to the future. "Then, what is life? I cried."

Sarmiento was shrewd and sure enough of himself not to rush into anything overhastily. When Lastarria came to him with Rivadaneira's offer of an editorship on *El Mercurio* of

[17] *Ibid.*, p. 99. [18] *Ibid.*, p. 104. [19] *Ibid.*

Valparaíso, he asked for a few days to think it over. *El Mercurio* was at the time the only daily paper in Chile, and it was considered by many as the dean of Spanish American journals.[20] It had been founded in 1827, and in later years, since it had needed a government subsidy to exist, it had become a semi-official organ. After his consideration of the offer, Sarmiento gladly accepted the honored position.

Manuel Rivadeneira had bought *El Mercurio* in October 1841. He had brought to it long years of study and experience in the technical improvements of printing and publishing, and when he assumed the management, he "presented a completely new and absolutely modern newspaper."[21] He found in the young Argentine *émigré* who submitted to him the brilliant article on the Battle of Chacabuco the man who he thought could translate into the editorial field the newness and change that he had introduced in the journalistic technique. Together they became the "pathfinders" of a new age of Chilean journalism.[22] On March 5th, Sarmiento's first article appeared. It dealt with the subject of public education, a subject close to the Argentine *émigré's* heart. From that date until August 1842, *El Mercurio* was destined to become a steady vehicle for the developing ideas of Don Domingo. It brought him prominence and a position of influence in all phases of Chilean public life. "*El Mercurio* has brought me a great reputation among illustrious people."[23] It was the vehicle that was to carry him into the struggles of Chilean political life.

But Sarmiento's decision on the political offers that were made to him as a result of his successful newspaper article was more difficult to make. When General Las Heras asked him for his support of the liberal candidate in the forthcoming presidential elections, Sarmiento asked for eight days to think it over. It was a difficult choice. He was naturally con-

[20] Guerra, p. 65.

[21] José Peláez y Tapia, *Historia del diario "El Mercurio,"* Santiago de Chile, 1927, p. 39.

[22] *Ibid.*

[23] Unpublished letter, Sarmiento to Quiroga Rosas, Santiago, March 15, 1841, Archivo Nacional de Chile, Santiago de Chile, volume 253, pieza 12, No. 5.

sidered by all to be ideologically akin to the Chilean liberals. He was the *émigré* who had escaped the tyranny of Rosas. He was the avowed enemy of the Argentine dictator and the self-proclaimed champion of democracy for his country and for the Spanish world. His choice had to be based upon two considerations. Ideologically, what did the two Chilean political parties stand for? Practically, the support of which party would put him into a position to carry on his crusade against Rosas and to continue the clarification and development of his own ideas and ideals?

On March 15th he wrote to his friend Quiroga Rosas and explained his position. He had to take a stand in the politics of the country to which he had been exiled, but the political fight in his own country was still foremost in his interest. The question was which party could help him and his cause the most. "The damned elections prejudice us much and absorb all spirits. What can you find out where you are? Who do you think will be the president? Bulnes suits us. He hates Rosas to death."[24]

Before the eight days were up Sarmiento had made his decision. He called his friends and his fellow *émigrés* together and explained his reasons. "We were accused by the tyrant of our own country of being disturbers of the peace, agitators, and anarchists; and in Chile we could be taken as such if we were seen to be always in opposition to the government. We needed, on the other hand, to prove to America that we were not seeking utopias, but that given the imperfection of American governments, we were ready to accept them . . . and to infuse in them ideas of progress. . . . It would be fatal to our cause if we had excited the ill-feeling of the party that governed at that moment, if it triumphed, as I felt sure it would, in the forthcoming elections."[25] Sarmiento's friends agreed with his decision. Oro, who had been jailed for his opposition to the government, saw the reasonableness of his arguments, and he supported the stand before the other Argentines present. This was Sarmiento's answer to the prac-

[24] Sarmiento to Quiroga Rosas, Santiago de Chile, March 15, 1841, Archivo Nacional de Chile, Santiago de Chile, volume 253, pieza 12, No. 5.

[25] *Obras*, III, 202.

tical side of the question: he would have a chance to develop his beliefs and fight for them if he supported the winning side. This judgment was justified by the events that followed.

The practical consideration was perhaps the most influential in determining Sarmiento's course at the time, but the ideological or theoretical consideration and Sarmiento's conclusion drawn therefrom are interesting to investigate. Many writers have accused Sarmiento of abandoning his ideals and his principles in order to play on the winning side of Chilean politics. Is this true, or did he have theoretical reasons to justify his choice? In answering this question, we must keep in mind that Sarmiento did not yet have any definite political philosophy. He knew what he disliked; he knew what he opposed. But his reasons for that opposition were still vague. The actual study of the Chilean political scene helped in the development of his ideas, but his theoretical choice was based on negative rather than positive reasons.

When Sarmiento arrived upon the political scene, the president of Chile was General Prieto. Portales, the man who had brought him to power and organized the conservative regime, had been killed by mutinous troops during the war with the Perú-Bolivian Confederation, so the leadership of the party had passed on to other hands. General Manuel Bulnes, the victor of the Battle of Yungay, which had terminated the recent war, was the conservative candidate for the presidency in 1841. The liberals opposed him violently. They charged Prieto's government with "tyranny" and they even founded a propaganda sheet called *La guerra a la tiranía* (War Against Tyranny). The liberal leader was General Francisco Antonio Pinto, and he and his supporters were carrying on a heated campaign against the government. But in March 1841 the two opposing parties agreed that the winning party, whichever it might be, would carry out a conciliatory policy towards its erstwhile enemies after the elections.

Sarmiento had to evaluate the situation in Chile realistically and judge the validity of the accusations. "Despotism and anarchy are the two extremes that we must avoid," he explained.[26] What type of man would be best for the job

[26] "Chile i la América del Sur," *El Nacional*, May 8, 1841.

before him in leading Chile? "He who, without attachment for the ideas of the past, without vengefulness against those who have been considered enemies of the present regime, can form a government that is not exclusively of one party and does not propose a definite course for the future but allows public opinion to fortify itself and discuss its own interests—a man who avoids reaction to the past but maintains order in the present."[27] These criteria upon which Sarmiento based his political choice at this time are most revealing in regard to the stage of development of his political philosophy. He knew what he did not want: anarchy and despotism. What he did want was no definite program; it was merely order and freedom to develop a definite program in the future. These were Sarmiento's aims in 1841, and he decided that the conservatives were the best to provide them.

He did not think that the conservatives had a perfect record nor a perfect program. "We are far from being absolute panegyrists for the past administration; we are on the other hand persuaded that in the infancy of peoples, in the fight among parties and opinions, many injustices are committed. . . ."[28] But with all its faults the conservative government in Chile seemed to supply the law and order and freedom that was necessary if one hoped for a progressive future. The liberal party, on the other hand, presented a history of revolutions, the "revolutionary habit."[29] Sarmiento called it the party of "pseudo-liberals, who, invoking principles that they do not understand or advocating maxims that they do not practice, work only for their personal gain—they will convert themselves later into ferocious tyrants who dictate laws against the defeated—they will be the victors who execute their vengeance without respect for justice nor its forms."[30]

When Sarmiento was taken by Minvielle to meet Don Manuel Montt, the Minister of Interior, his impressions of the conservative leader confirmed his former speculations. An immediate and lifelong friendship began at that moment.

[27] *Ibid.*

[28] "Liberalismo del elector chileno," *El Mercurio*, April 20, 1841.

[29] *Obras*, XLIX, 13.

[30] "Gobiernos fuertes," *El Mercurio*, November 17, 1841; *Obras*, IX, 49.

Sarmiento saw in Montt a man of progressive ideas and aims, a man whose reforms in the field of education and administration would do more to move Chile in the direction of a democratic government than any of the cries and slogans of the liberals. Montt saw in Sarmiento a spark of genius, an ally and aid for his future projects. Sarmiento remembered always the words of Montt that won him over so completely: "Ideas, sir, have no homeland."[31] From then on, the Argentine and the Chilean worked and fought together for the ideas that they had and were to conceive in common.

In later years, as Sarmiento wrote an article on the death of Montt, he had no reason to regret his decision to join the conservatives in 1841. They had met his expectation. Montt left "a country as free as one of our countries could be."[32] Given the practical difficulties that Sarmiento sensed in the Chilean political scene, the governments of Bulnes and Montt after him gave Chile a "liberal" government. There was freedom of the press and individual freedom. There was material progress unequaled in the rest of Spanish America. Chile gained the reputation throughout the world as the great democratic country of Spanish America.[33]

After his interview with Montt, Sarmiento was given a post as political director of the administration press. He was to edit *El Nacional,* the paper founded to back the Bulnes candidacy, and he was to continue his articles in *El Mercurio.* The usual crop of new journals and newspapers had appeared in 1841 in order to carry on the election campaign. *El elector chileno, El verdadero liberal,* and *La guerra a la tiranía* were the most important opposition papers to come out. They all folded up after the elections had passed. Meanwhile, it was Sarmiento's job, at a salary of one hundred pesos, to meet their arguments and accusations with counter-arguments and counter-accusations in *El Nacional* and at times in his edi-

[31] Palcos, *Sarmiento, op.cit.,* p. 38.

[32] *Juicios de la prensa sobre Don Manuel Montt,* Santiago de Chile, 1893, p. 46.

[33] For an evaluation of Chilean history at this time see: Diego Barros Arana, *Un decenio de la historia de Chile,* Santiago, 1928; Sotomayor Valdes, *Historia de Chile durante los 40 años transcurridos desde 1831 a 1871,* Santiago, 1875; Augustín Edwards, *Cuatro presidentes chilenos,* Valparaiso, 1932.

torials in *El Mercurio*. Only nine numbers of the former paper appeared (between April 14 and July 7), but they were influential in the successful press campaign for Bulnes.

Chapter 13. The Struggle

ALTHOUGH his exile in Chile allowed Domingo Sarmiento to stand apart from the bitter political struggle in his own nation and contemplate it with more objectivity, his years abroad were not periods of quiet. Sarmiento was a man who could not exist without a struggle. "He fed on conflict, took strength from it. He lived, suffered, and enjoyed battle without respite."[1] Because of his relation to *El Nacional* and *El Mercurio* he held a position of importance in the presidential campaigns of 1841, and his activity brought him irrevocably into the conflicts of Chilean public life during his years in that nation.

The campaign was heated and extremely bitter, and the liberals never forgave the Argentine *émigré* for his opposition at this time. The elections were not free from illegal manipulations on either side. The last-minute maneuvering of the liberals was of no avail; General Bulnes and his party swept the elections and the conservatives remained in control of the government. Bulnes' administration was inaugurated on September 18, 1841. "The nation gave itself up to frank manifestations of happiness."[2] The poet Andrés Bello wrote an ode to the electoral victory, and a great inaugural feast was held at the government house. Amid 384 bottles of champagne and 88 bottles of cognac, to say nothing of beer and other beverages, Sarmiento celebrated with his newly

[1] Palcos, *Sarmiento, op.cit.*, p. 35.
[2] Augustín Edwards, *Cuatro presidentes de Chile*, Valparaiso, 1932, I, p. 9.

found friends the political success of their campaign. At last he was on the winning side, and he felt that his time had come to work more effectively for his ideas and beliefs.[3]

President Bulnes called Ramón Luis Irarrazábal to organize his first cabinet. Manuel Montt was chosen minister of justice and public education, and Manuel Rengifo was named minister of finance. These two statesmen were the dominant personalities in the Bulnes administration. Rengifo reestablished Chilean credit and restored his nation's finances to a healthy state. Montt inaugurated a life-long campaign to provide teachers, schools, and universities for Chile and thus to prepare her national psychology for a cooperative democratic government. Together Rengifo and Montt prepared Chile materially and intellectually for the years of peace and prosperity that lay ahead. Domingo Sarmiento became an important factor in the calculations of the new government. Montt saw in him his most valuable instrument in gaining his goals in national education and public instruction, and he was quick to enlist the young Argentinean's aid in his battle.

The government of Bulnes was essentially conservative. It looked back upon the period that preceded it and saw in it a fundamentally good government—one based on law and order, which had brought peace and prosperity to the nation. Bulnes and Montt wanted to *conserve* this structure of order and law and improve it. "The administration of General Bulnes, essentially and systematically, is openly conservative. Its program, announced from the beginning and observed until the end, consisted in conserving, strengthening and financing the consecrated institutions, maintaining the stability of peace and order as principles of life for Chile."[4] This for the Argentinean exile who had suffered the consequences of lawlessness and chaos in his own nation seemed a more real liberalism than any other known in the Spanish Americas. Progress and reform could be carried on within the framework of law and order. The ten years of Bulnes' government proved this estimate to be correct. They were years of

[3] For an account of the inauguration and subsequent celebration, see *ibid.*, II.

[4] Juan Bautista Alberdi, *Biografía del General Don Manuel Bulnes*, pp. 88-89.

advancement and improvement for Chile. "There was no branch of public service or national development that did not feel the reforming hand of the government; and these reforms, almost always discreet and always well intentioned, mark an immense progress in the history of our moral and material advancement."[5] It was within this framework of political life and in cooperation with this government that Sarmiento's positive ideas of life and politics were formed.

Within a week after the inauguration of General Bulnes, it appeared, however, that the political situation in Argentina was changing in such a way as to allow the exiles to return. For a few short weeks, Sarmiento had hopes of reentering his own country and his own political scene and fighting for his beliefs in a more effective manner. The Argentine exiles had never lost hope in their temporarily defeated struggle against Rosas and his caudillos. The Argentine commission in Chile was made up of a group of exiles who carried on propaganda and sent aid to any underground opposition across the border. During the first months of Sarmiento's stay in Santiago he was in close contact with this group, but they saw little hopes of extending their activities beyond the limited scope of propaganda and preparation. In July the commission met to discuss its accomplishments and, in view of the facts of the situation, to dissolve. It reduced itself to a skeleton administration of three members, General Las Heras, Zapata, and Sarmiento's uncle, Oro; these three men were to watch the situation carefully in preparation for a reorganization in case of a favorable turn of events in Argentina.[6]

Letters throughout the winter of 1841 indicate that the exiles were receiving little or no news from their homeland, but by the end of July rumors were heard of a new gathering of unitarist forces under General Lamadrid and a preparation for a decisive battle. With the conclusion of the presidential campaign in Chile, Sarmiento directed his attention more exclusively to the situation in his own nation, and it became

[5] Diego Barros Arana, *Juicio sobre el gobierno de Bulnes*, pp. 111-112; see also Munro, *The Latin American Republics*, *op.cit.*, p. 301.

[6] Sarmiento to Quiroga Rosas, Santiago, July 13, 1841, Archivo Nacional, Santiago de Chile, volume 253, pieza 12, No. 8.

increasingly evident that something was brewing across the border.[7]

The rumors that Sarmiento and his friends heard in Santiago were not unfounded. The political scene in Argentina had again burst into flames. General José María Paz had again appeared with a unitarist army in Corrientes, and General Gregorio de Lamadrid had formed a league of the north in which a number of the northwestern provinces joined together in opposition to Rosas.[8] A few days after the inauguration of the Bulnes administration, Sarmiento heard that Lamadrid had entered Mendoza and defeated the federalist forces in that area. "My resolution was made in an instant."[9] He would return to his own country and join in the active conflict under the command of the victorious unitarist general. With a warm interlined pea-jacket and leggings that covered his legs to the ankles, Sarmiento dressed in preparation for the cold weather of the early spring in the Andes.[10] On about September 20th, after a brief farewell at the home of Manuel Montt, he set out on the road across the Andes to Mendoza.

Sarmiento carried with him a letter of recommendation to General Lamadrid from the members of the Argentine commission in Chile. The letter spoke of the young patriot in glowing terms. "Adorned with patriotism and enthusiasm for liberty, his capacity is another claim that he be allowed to approach Your Excellency and that Your Excellency give him occasion to render as a demonstration whatever services he is able to. He had the confidence of his compatriots here and deserves the confidence of Your Excellency."[11] The note was signed by the outstanding Argentine leaders in Chile, General Gregorio de las Heras, Domingo de Oro, Gabriel Ocampo, and Martín Zapata.

On the afternoon of September 25th, Sarmiento reached the main range of the Andes. He was tired from a long day of walking, and he and his companions stopped briefly to rest and to enjoy the scenic beauty of the mountainous

[7] *Ibid.*

[8] Escobar, *Historia, op.cit.*

[9] *Obras*, XLIX, 113.

[10] *Ibid.*, p. 114.

[11] *Ibid.*, p. 115; *Recuerdos*, p. 208.

country. "One discovers towards the east chains of mountains that, while sketching a border on the horizon, dwarf it in comparison to their size. One discovers white valleys like ribbons that wind among the large black rocks that shine with the reflection of the sun. And below, at the foot of the incline, a pin point in the distance, was the little brick hut that serves as shelter and refuge for the traveler. 'We salute you, Argentine Republic,' we each exclaimed, pointing to the horizon and extending our arms towards it."[12] As the returning exiles stood there, excited by the sight of their homeland before them, someone looked carefully at the road below. On that narrow white ribbon he discerned groups of men on foot, and as he pointed them out to his companions, they instinctively felt alarmed at this unexpected appearance. They looked at each other without daring to communicate the fears in their hearts.[13]

When they reached the hut at the bottom of the hill, they found huddled within and around it the figures whom they had seen walking in the distance. Before they even reached the spot they heard the dread word "Derrota" (Defeat) and realized that they were faced with the remnants of Lamadrid's army fleeing into exile in Chile. On the previous day, September 24th, the army had been defeated at Rodeo del Medio by the federalist armies of the western provinces; during their retreat across into Chile they had been surprised, while in the midst of the mountains, by a violent snowstorm, and ice and cold for which they were not prepared. They had started out numbering several hundred,[14] but only the remains of the original group arrived at the little refuge hut, groaning with hunger and with sickness and with cold.

"It was necessary to act. I sent one of my men to Los Andes to send mules back up the mountains to us; and after speaking with the first refugees, we went back up the mountain that I thought I had left behind forever. Once in Los Andes, I established my office in the house of a friend; from one in the afternoon, I was an executive power with the authority

[12] *Obras*, XLIX, 115. [13] *Obras*, III, 208-209.

[14] Sarmiento puts this figure at one thousand, but Palcos, *Sarmiento, op.cit.*, p. 39, affirms that there were but a few hundred.

to help the unfortunate Argentineans who were threatened in the mountains."[15] Sarmiento's old friend, Pedro Bari, was his assistant, and together they worked feverishly to save the day for the freezing and starving remnants of the unitarist army. During the next twelve hours, Sarmiento demonstrated an initiative and a quality of leadership and organization that he had never before had the opportunity to reveal. In that short space of time, he and his aides found, contracted, and sent off twelve mountain muleteers to aid the refugees in their march; they bought and sent off six shipments of sheepskin to bind the cold and bare feet and legs of the soldiers. They sent coal, candles, tobacco, tea, sugar and countless other items that the refugees so badly needed. They sent word to the governor of San Felipe, notifying him of the disaster and asking aid and protection. Sarmiento talked to nearby Chileans, asking them to help with their donations, and he sent news to the Argentine commission so that it could go into action. He wrote to Montt asking the assistance of the government, and sent letters to many of the leading citizens of the nation, asking them to arouse the sentiments of charity in the Chilean public.

In the days that followed, the activities and accomplishments of Sarmiento gained the admiration and respect of both his compatriots in exile and the Chilean public. To him is largely due the saving of the lives of many of the Argentine soldiers. During the first weeks of October, he published three articles in *El Mercurio* describing the horrors of the unitarist disaster, the heroism of the soldiers, and the difficulties that they had faced and were still facing. He told of the men who had been wounded and who had contracted gangrene. He described in detail the horrors of their sufferings. He told of the soldiers sacrificing their lives for their comrades, and he told of the blizzards, the freezing temperatures, and the lack of clothing that they were faced with. This propaganda was effective, and money and supplies poured in as contributions from a friendly people. Sarmiento praised the "philanthropy and humanity that honors the Chilean character," and thanked the government for fulfilling "the duties that hu-

[15] *Obras,* III, 209.

manity and civilization impose upon it."[16] In response to a letter from Sarmiento, the Chilean General José Francisco Gana raised a subscription to aid "the unfortunate victims of the cause of civilization . . ." and he added in a letter to the young Argentinean exile, "I have never wished so much as now, at this moment, to be a man of influence and fortune."[17] Sarmiento returned to Santiago as a hero in the eyes of his fellow exiles, but he realized that there was now little hope of returning to his home for many years to come.

"A little later I returned to take over once again the editorship of *El Mercurio*, and from that time there begins one of the most active, most agitated, and most fruitful phases of my life."[18] Sarmiento entered the center of the stage of Chilean letters at a time when the cultural life of that nation was undergoing a marked awakening. With this awakening came an increased consciousness of nationality and even a cultural nationalism. That one of the leaders on the journalistic and literary scenc was a stranger was resented by many of the young Chilean intellectuals, and the new ideas that he discussed and for which he argued were automatically opposed by many. The small but vocal group of Argentine exiles were taken for ignorant and presumptuous heretics in literature, politics, and religion. "Sarmiento enflamed his enemies. One might say that he enjoyed fomenting tempests in order to feel himself living beneath the blowing hurricane."[19] Within a few months, and for the rest of his stay in Chile, Sarmiento was the center of raging conflicts on the Chilean political and intellectual stage. "Little by little I excited worries, rancor, hatred, and perhaps envy. . . ."[20]

During the last part of 1841 and the first part of 1842, Sarmiento remained as editor of *El Mercurio*. He and Rivadeneira continued to cooperate, and the newspaper continued to progress. Don Domingo saw in the newspaper his vehicle to power and fortune, and he fully expected someday to own

[16] *Obras*, VI, 9.

[17] José Francisco de Gana to Domingo F. Sarmiento, Santiago de Chile, October 1, 1841.

[18] *Obras*, III, 210-211.

[19] Palcos, *Sarmiento, op.cit.*, p. 40.

[20] *Obras*, III, 211.

it and wholly control it.[21] His hotheadedness caused many fights with Rivadeneira, but he always regretted what he had said and went to him to beg his pardon.[22]

It was during his editorship of *El Mercurio* that Sarmiento became involved in the first of the many conflicts for which he was destined to be famous during his stay in Chile. It was a polemic that raged in and excited the intellectual atmosphere of Santiago for several months during the winter of 1842. The cultural life of Chile was ruled by a small but closed group of intellectuals headed by the Venezuelan poet and grammarian, Andrés Bello. It was a group that adhered strictly to the clear-cut, rational, and formal style of the eighteenth-century neo-classic literature of the Enlightenment. Sarmiento represented for this group a movement of change. In his articles in *El Mercurio* he had demonstrated a style that was completely free from the bonds of neo-classic form and tending towards a naturalness that emphasized the content, the ideas, and the descriptions more than the structure and a strict adherence to rules.

In April 1842 a study appeared on "Popular Exercises in the Spanish Language," a collection of words that were incorrectly used in Chile. The author of the articles was a professor in the National Institute, Pedro Fernández Garfias. On April 27, Sarmiento published an editorial review of this work, in which he took the opportunity to attack the conventional literary theories in Chile at the time. He pointed out that it was the people and not the grammarians and writers who gave life to a language, and he held that the only function of grammarians or of academies was to codify in their dictionaries the new words and expressions that the people expressed.[23] This was the very type of heresy that Bello's disciples had suspected. They had devoted their efforts to an attempt to give form and order to the cultural life of Chile, and now this young *émigré* was denying their value. If

[21] In a letter to Quiroga Rosas, he states, "*El Mercurio* will be my property." July 31, 1841, Santiago de Chile, Archivo Nacional, Santiago, volume 253, pieza 12, No. 9.

[22] A letter to Quiroga Rosas, dated November 14 (probably 1842), tells of such a quarrel and Sarmiento's regret for what he had said. *Ibid.*, No. 11.

[23] *El Mercurio,* Santiago de Chile, April 27, 1842.

they allowed such a stand to go unchallenged, their position would be destroyed.

Under the pen name of *Un Quidam*, but in his own unmistakable style, Bello answered the editorial. He emphasized the need for an even closer study of the classics, and pointed to the desirability of adhering to the literary models of Spain's golden age. The increasing number of new words, especially French ones, that were appearing in the language alarmed him, and he saw the necessity of stopping such a trend.

With this answer, one of the most famous polemics in the history of Chilean literature had begun, and before it was through it had become a heated debate followed closely by most of the reading public of Santiago. Sarmiento advocated the freedom of literature. He criticized Chilean literature as being sterile, and he called for a new movement that would emphasize ideas and content over form. He asked for the exile of Bello "for being too learned."[24] The proud Venezuelan poet withdrew from the heated polemic, but one of his disciples, José María Núñez, carried it on under the pseudonym of *Otro Quidam*. Under the leadership of Núñez, the opposition to Sarmiento's new ideas became more bitter. He was called a foreigner and "ravenous for bread." The intellectual conflict was finally brought to an end by an article by Sarmiento that summarized the various arguments that he had been making. He published the article and allowed the public to digest it, and then he revealed that it was nothing more than a compiling of the thoughts of the great Spanish writer Mariano José de Larra. The revelation that this last article that Núñez and his group were preparing to attack was not by an illiterate Argentincan, but by the most influential of the Spanish writers of the time, took the wind out of their sails. The polemic ended with this successful blow by Sarmiento.

After September 1, 1842, when Don José Vicente Sánchez and Don Santos Tornero bought the newspaper from Rivadeneira, Sarmiento's position as editor does not seem to have been as satisfactory or secure. He wrote several articles and continued to edit the paper for several months after it changed

[24] *Obras*, I, 223-224.

hands, but he decided to leave it and initiate a periodical of his own.

On November 10, 1842, Don Domingo ceased writing for *El Mercurio* and inaugurated the publication of the first daily newspaper of Santiago, *El Progreso*. The new journal was greeted by an editorial in *El Mercurio* by Don Miguel Pinero, the editor-in-chief. He pointed to the successful sale of the first numbers and the valuable and serious character of the first articles as a good omen and an indication of the future success of the enterprise. "However, as always, there appears the doubt of whether this newspaper, and journalism in general which produces so many good results in all parts of the work, will be able to sustain itself and establish itself forever in our capital. . . . This is the problem that *El Progreso* must solve." The editorial ended on the assurance that although the new daily might become the newspaper of Santiago, *El Mercurio* would remain the newspaper of the nation.[25] With the aid of his fellow exile and friend, Vicente Fidel López, Don Domingo made a valiant effort to make a success of this first venture of daily journalism in Chile, but *El Progreso* was forced to close after eight months. During its existence it held a predominant position in Santiago journalism, and its pages contain some of the most important chapters in the ever-developing thought of Domingo Sarmiento.

The first polemic between Bello and Sarmiento over the importance of form and content in literature had not finished before the Argentinean exile was involved in another heated debate. García del Río, another of the intellectual leaders in the neo-classic tradition in Chile, initiated a new journal that he called *The Museum of the Two Americas* (Museo de ambas Américas). In it he advocated the propagation of "sane principles and conservative doctrines" in literature. Sarmiento and his friend, Vicente Fidel López, became the target of a new group of young students and writers who rose to García del Río's call, formed a literary society, and began to publish a new weekly known as *El Semanario*.

Sarmiento welcomed this new opponent with the spirit of a true fighter. *El Semanario* inaugurated the battle with a

[25] Tapía, *Historia, op.cit.*, pp. 215-216.

violent attack against Romanticism. Vicente López leaped to the defense with three brilliant articles in his newspaper *La gaceta del comercio*. He and Sarmiento, under continual attack from *El Semanario*, then proceeded to set forward their ideas on a literature that Sarmiento refused to call Romantic but that was fashioned after the romantic-socialist ideas of Pierre Leroux, Fortoul, and Saint Simon. The polemic became increasingly heated and personal as the youthful enthusiasm of both sides overcame the dictates of propriety. Sarmiento accused the young men of *El Semanario* of being conservatives and having hearts that were immune to the currents of the age. This brought a new element of pride into the struggle, and the Argentinean writers were termed fools and charlatans. The struggle would have degenerated into a bout of name-calling if it had not been for the timely intervention of Sarmiento's old friend, Lastarria, who was a more moderate member of the literary society. He persuaded Don Domingo to write a letter of peace to his attackers. Sarmiento did this, protesting the personal attacks that had been make against him, but asking for an end to the overheated debate. He ignored a last bitter article against him and allowed the fire of the polemic to die out and disappear.[26] *El Semanario* disappeared shortly afterwards, and its editors split up. Lastarria, already a friend of the Argentinean exiles, was won to their ideas and became one of their chief Chilean supporters.[27]

In late 1843 Sarmiento became involved in still another heated polemic with some of the leading thinkers of Chile. This time the discussion was set off by a paper that Don Domingo read to the newly founded University of Chile, in which he proposed a reform of the spelling of the Spanish language. He held that the spelling was often inconsistent and irrational. Democracy could not subsist in a nation that was ignorant and illiterate, and therefore all that was possible should be done to make it easier for the masses to learn to read and write and thus prepare themselves for self-government. He took this opportunity to point to the intellectual

[26] Lastarria, *Recuerdos literarios, op.cit.*, p. 169.
[27] Donoso, *Sarmiento, op.cit.*, p. 26.

backwardness of Spain, and it was this point which aroused the opposition of some Chilean thinkers.

Rafael Minvielle, formerly an ardent supporter of Sarmiento's views, felt that his anti-Spanish attacks were unpatriotic. He opposed the French ideas of his erstwhile colleague and asked why he did not call himself Sarmintier, thus clearly signifying his French adherence. The polemic raged between Minvielle and Sarmiento in the periodical press of Santiago, and, like the former controversies over Romanticism, it attracted the attention of the entire Chilean reading public.

Towards the end of 1842 Don Domingo became involved in a conflict that was of a far more personal and unfortunate character than his intellectual polemics. In a newspaper article he had made a chance remark about a currently known scandal involving a certain nun named Zañartú. One of the nun's relatives, a Don Domingo Santiago Godoy, felt injured by the allusion and immediately set out to discredit the Argentinean exile. His brother, Colonel Pedro Godoy, had been Chilean consul in both Mendoza and San Juan, and he claimed to know well Sarmiento's past. In especially printed leaflets he attacked Sarmiento as a murderer and a thief. He claimed that Don Domingo had been implicated in the mass slaughter of prisoners during the revolt by the federalist prisoner of war, Panta, in 1830.[28] He further charged a misappropriation of funds by Sarmiento during the relief of the refugees of the Lamadrid army in 1842. Both of these charges have been proved to be unfounded, but they called for a strong and definite defense on the part of the *émigré*, whose past was so unknown by his Chilean friends.

On January 25, 1843, Sarmiento brought suit against Godoy for criminal libel, charging "That for nearly two years now this man without provocation on my part has taken upon himself the ignoble task of discrediting me on all occasions and with all kinds of people . . . even to the extreme of announcing me not just once but constantly as an assassin."

[28] This was the incident that Sarmiento slept through and, hearing about it, went into hiding until all danger had passed. He later condemned the conduct of the soldiers who put down so brutally the revolt. See p. 86.

He submitted evidence to the court to refute Godoy's charges, and he asked the imprisonment and confiscation of goods of the defendant.[29] On January 10th, Sarmiento addressed a leaflet to the public defending himself against Godoy's calumnies. "For two years Domingo Santiago Godoi [note reformed spelling] has repeated in Santiago that I have committed I do not know what kind of crimes in my own country. Domingo Godoi lies like a miserable creature that he is."[30]

In the months that followed, the bitter personal conflict raged on. Godoy even went so far as to publish a newspaper, *El Desenmascarado,* whose sole purpose was to attack the person of Sarmiento. It had only one issue on February 7th and then closed.[31] At about the same time, Sarmiento published his first important book. It was a small pamphlet entitled *Mi Defensa* (My Defense), an autobiographical summary, phrased in a dignified and calm style and intended to answer Godoy's charges about his past in San Juan. A court order of January 31, 1843, ordered the imprisonment of Don Domingo Santiago Godoy,[32] but this decision was appealed and the suit went on until March 8th. Sarmiento was ultimately exonerated in the eyes of the public by *Mi Defensa,* and Godoy was finally punished by the law for his criminal libel.

The parliamentary elections of 1844 brought Domingo Sarmiento once again into the forefront of Chilean national politics. His newspaper, *El Progreso,* defended the government party, its administration, and its program, against such oppositionist periodicals as *El Telégrafo* of Concepción, the *Gaceta del comercio,* and *El Siglo.* Don Domingo held that the record of the conservative Bulnes regime was essentially a liberal one. "After the triumph in the presidential elections, the government began to incline towards the course of the defeated liberal party. . . . The most outstanding features of the liberal program were little by little incorporated into the national administration, a government that might be called a

[29] Domingo F. Sarmiento vs. Domingo Santiago Godoy. Archivo Nacional. Santiago de Chile, Archivo Varios, No. 318. pieza 3A.

[30] *Al Público,* Santiago de Chile, January 10, 1843.

[31] Gálvez, p. 128.

[32] Domingo F. Sarmiento vs. Domingo Santiago Godoy, *op.cit.*

'coalition.' "[33] The oppositionist press charged the Bulnes regime with a centralized dictatorial executive and with undemocratic control of elections. Sarmiento, in his role of semiofficial propaganda leader, attempted to defend the government on these points. He referred to the fact that even in the United States the administration always influenced the elections. The spoils system, which had been recently initiated in the Northern Republic, served such a purpose. Sarmiento held that he was not justifying such activity on the part of the government; he was only pointing out that it was always present.[34] He defended the Bulnes regime against charges of "despotism" and "tyranny" by arguing that a ministerial government was typical of a constitutional monarchy and that in republics, such as the United States, the executive controlled the cabinet and usually the legislature, thus setting the governmental policy during the presidential term of office.

The conflict between *El Progreso* and *El Siglo*, like so many of Sarmiento's other polemics, took on a definitely personal character. The editor of the oppositionist newspaper, Don Juan Nepomuceno Espejo, was a young man of little tact and strong passions. He attacked Sarmiento and his defense of the Bulnes government without mercy. He allowed Colonel Pedro Godoy, Sarmiento's old enemy, to attack the editor of *El Progreso* in the columns of *El Siglo*, and the personal character of the attacks soon brought a strong response from Don Domingo. One of the editors and the owner of *El Siglo* was Sarmiento's old friend Lastarria, and his connection with the bitter attacks created in the Argentinean exile a strong bitterness towards him. He wrote: "This letter is to warn you that all harmony and communication between the two of us has ceased, and I do not wish to be the plaything of you and your organs." Lastarria replied to this with a short and curt note: "Señor Sarmiento: I am in receipt of the declaration of war that you make against me, and I warn you that I will suffer from you no offense to my honor. Lastarria."[35] The polemic between *El Siglo* and *El Progreso* continued until

[33] "Las elecciones actuales," *El Progreso*, June 8, 1844.

[34] *El Progreso*, July 20, 1844.

[35] Donoso, *Sarmiento, op.cit.*, p. 38.

after the conservative victory in the parliamentary elections. When the fight was over, a neutral observer stepped into the fight and tried to separate the two contenders. He succeeded in securing the promise of *El Siglo* to cease all personal attacks against Sarmiento, and in this way he brought the two bitter opponents together in a truce. In later years the friendship of Lastarria and Sarmiento was renewed and became warmer and more genuine than ever after this bitter fight over the Chilean political battle of 1844.

The intensity of the fights and polemics into which Sarmiento entered during these years was such that he could not but become embittered. He went through periods of deep depression when a decided persecution complex showed itself and he felt himself despised by all Chileans. In his *Provincial Recollections* he tells of one such incident. "One day my exasperation reached a point of delirium. I was frantic, insane, and I conceived the sublime idea of a disastrous mistake, of punishing all of Chile, declaring her ungrateful, vile, and infamous. I wrote I do not know what kind of a diatribe; I put my name at the end, and I took it to the printer of *El Progreso*, putting it directly in the hands of the compositors. This done, I retired to my house in silence, loaded my pistols, and waited for the explosion of the mine that would explode me with it. But I would be avenged and satisfied of having done a great act of justice. I complained of the president, of Montt, of the Viales, in order that nobody should escape my justice. I complained of the writers and the public in mass. . . .

"The kindness of Don Antonio Jacobo Vial saved me from this certain danger. The frightened compositors showed him the manuscript, and he came to my house, sad, and talked to me in the sweet, compassionate tone with which one speaks to the sick. No sign of anger or resentment could be seen in his face."

" 'Don Domingo,' said Vial, 'the printers have shown me the article for tomorrow.'

" 'I am sorry,' replied Sarmiento.

" 'Have you calculated the consequences?'

" 'Perfectly.' Don Domingo pointed with his eyes at the loaded pistols.

" 'That is useless.'
" 'I know; leave me in peace.'
" 'Has López [Vicente Fidel] seen it?'
" 'No.' "

Don Antonio took his hat and went to see López and Montt. Vicente López hurried over to see his friend. He told him that he disapproved completely of the article. He pointed out the weakness of some of the expressions. And he suggested that Sarmiento take a rest, and go on a trip to Valparaiso. The psychological approach was perfect: first, the open attack, then pointing out the weaknesses, then offering a road of escape. Don Domingo still resisted the arguments, but his determination was weakened when he went to bed that night.

The next morning he was called to the office of Manuel Montt. Again a friend proved useful in this crisis. He started talking of other things, of the normal school, of current events. Then, carefully and with tact, he approached the subject. He pointed out how many people in Chile respected and admired Sarmiento. He played on the exile's deflated ego; he overcame the feeling of persecution. Montt allowed Sarmiento to talk and get his complaints off his chest. When the interview was over, Don Domingo left with a new outlook on the situation. "Thus this Chile which I had wanted to damn, showed me in that moment virtues worthy of respect. It showed delicacy and infinite tolerance and signs of sympathy and admiration, which made unjustifiable the suicide that I had prepared for myself."[36]

Sarmiento's polemics in the Santiago press on subjects ranging from spelling to political theory were trying for him, but they had a salutary effect upon the infant journalism of that nation. From 1841 the Chilean press was gaining a great reputation on the Pacific Coast, and much of its fame came from the lively polemics and discussions that it carried on. *El Mercurio* became a distinguished name throughout the Spanish world, and though *El Progreso, El Siglo,* and *La Gaceta* were short-lived the fame of their battles and their crusade spread far beyond the Chilean borders.

The years from 1841 to 1845 were years of struggle for

[36] *Obras,* III, 215.

Sarmiento. In *Mi Defensa*, he summarized well his activities at this time. "I threw myself suddenly into the press, fighting boldly two parties and defending another, establishing new principles for some, creating antipathies on the one side and attracting affections on the other, appeasing at times, clashing at others, and not seldom uniting all in one single chorus of approval and vituperations; preaching good constantly and working for evil at times; attacking the generally accepted ideas on literature; trying out all types; infringing through ignorance and by system the rules; driving on youth, brusquely pushing society, irritating national susceptibilities; falling like a tiger into a polemic, and at every moment moving all of society, and always using frank language even to the point of being discourteous and without consideration; telling bitter truths without any other right than the belief that they are useful; employed by the government, hired and placed at the front of a new enterprise that demands given aptitudes . . . enjoying in all a social position that seems advantageous and full of a future. . . ."[37] It was a period of conflict and struggle for Domingo Sarmiento, and in these struggles he conceived his ideas of life.

Chapter 14. The Program

DURING the five years between 1841 and 1845, the philosophy of Domingo Faustino Sarmiento was formed in the heat of conflict and polemic. There were three stages through which his thought passed in these five years. The first of these stages was a negative one. It was a period in which he defined more clearly what he was opposing. The second stage witnessed the formation of a generalized and abstract idea of his positive

[37] *Obras*, III, 2.

goal, what he was fighting *for*. The third stage included the formulation of methods to gain these ends.

When Sarmiento arrived in Chile he was conscious of what he opposed. He knew that he had fought and wanted to go on fighting Rosas and all that he stood for. In the back of his mind, there was an irreconcilable clash between the ideal rational world about which he had read and the irrational real world of the Rosas regime. While in Argentina, there had been no urgent need to define this target clearly for he had been able to fight it openly. But in Chile, such a need immediately arose. His only weapon there was the weapon of propaganda in the Chilean press, and if this propaganda was to be effective, he would have to have a clear idea of what he was opposing and be able to elaborate that idea in order to give more impact to his arguments.

First, it was necessary to describe the Rosas regime. A bare description was enough to show that it was undesirable. "A black and frightful chain of crimes has linked the acts of our hangman [Rosas], and after the years, the story still has not reached the ears of the government and the peoples of the other American nations.

"The consuls in Buenos Aires witness daily the barbaric acts that humiliate and degrade the citizen; they have seen the Minister Maza die within the sanctuary of law.[1] They see now the sidewalks sprinkled with the blood of the old and the young spilled by the fury of the mob which like a pack of dogs our hangman excites and incites. They know that these are not the acts of a popular irritation of the moment, but of an organized system of government."[2]

The most salient feature that Don Domingo found in this "organized system of government" was its personalistic character. Rosas relied on no ministers, entrusted no power to subordinates, recognized no higher law, and was immune to any abstract moral or ethical code. The personality of Rosas was the political common denominator, and the will of Rosas the political motive force. His instruments were arbitrary

[1] This is a reference to the assassination of one of Rosas' ministers, Maza, in the legislature in Buenos Aires.

[2] "El Emigrado," *El Mercurio*, March 17, 1841; *Obras*, I, 22.

force and terror, and with these his personality and will had a free reign. "The traditions of all forms of trial have been lost; throat cutting has been substituted for the course of justice."[3] These were the features of the regime that the young exile opposed. They were not, however, merely features of a particular government at a particular time. They appeared to be symptoms of a deeper political reality. If Rosas did not exist, another would be in power, and the same features would be evident.[4]

Like so many other thinkers of the Spanish world, Sarmiento broadened his attack upon Rosas and his personalistic dictatorship into an attack upon Spain and the Spanish way of life. The trouble arose from the fact that the Spanish world had reverted to the traditional Spanish way of life instead of following the ideas that had been offered to it by France and the eighteenth-century age of reason. "The revolution that the philosophers of the eighteenth century worked in America, the example of North America and France, an example that the Spaniards there and we here once followed, that revolution that promised so many benefits, was destroyed by a barbarian educated by his barbaric stepmother and who wants to realize in the Argentine Republic what Philip II realized in Spain."[5]

Unlike many of his nationalistic contemporaries in Spanish America, Sarmiento did not see the problems and destiny of each separate country as distinct and independent. He saw a basic similarity in the histories of all segments of the Spanish world in the nineteenth century, and the only explanation that he could find for such a fact was a common Spanish heritage.[6] The Americas revolted against the mother country and attempted an experiment in constitutional government. Simultaneously, Spain underwent a movement for constitutional reform. "It is a fact worthy of notice that Spain and her colonies in America began to move at the same time, one to

[3] "Conducta de Rosas i sus ajentes con el gobierno de Chile," *El Mercurio*, April 19, 1842; *Obras*, VI, 25.

[4] "El Jeneral Frai Félix Aldao, gobernador de Mendoza," *Obras*, VII, 244.

[5] "Quinta carta a Don Rafael Minvielle," *Gaceta del comercio*, October 28, 1843.

[6] *Obras*, VI, 3.

improve its institutions, the other to free itself from the foreign yoke, and if any difference is noted between the two it is due to their relative positions."[7] Both failed in their constitutional experiments, and a period of political chaos followed throughout the entire Spanish world. This could be attributable only to the common Spanish heritage; "the Spanish race condemned to consume itself in civil war and soil itself with all kinds of crimes and offer a depopulated and exhausted country as easy prey to new European colonization."[8] "Any form of government is impossible in South America, considering the fact that the Spanish race inhabits the continent."[9]

Sarmiento's opposition to Rosas could in this manner be objectified and explained by finding the roots of the Argentine dictatorship in the Spanish tradition and in the Spanish way of life. In article after article, Sarmiento attacked the Spanish heritage. "Liberty of the press, liberty of writing, liberty to deliberate on community matters, were things that Spain had only heard of and that she only began to enjoy at the time of our Revolution while Ferdinand VII was in the captivity to which the ambition of Napoleon had condemned him. . . . To appreciate the evils that Spain has left us it is sufficient to know that she herself is suffering even today as a consequence of the backward state in which she has remained in contrast to the movement and development that the other nations of Europe have worked in all phases of their life."[10] Sarmiento wrote of the barbarity of Spanish life and Spanish history. He told of the horrors of the Spanish Inquisition, and he described such atrocities as the burning alive of a Spanish general and the eating of his still quivering flesh even by the ladies of a Spanish town.[11]

[7] "Vindicación de la república Argentina en su revolución y en sus guerras civiles," *El Mercurio*, June 7, 1841.

[8] Originally published in *El Nacional* in early 1841; *Recuerdos*, p. 219.

[9] "Chile y la America del sur," *El Nacional*, April 14, 1841.

[10] "La América del sur y del norte," *El Nacional*, April 24, 1841; for other attacks on the Spanish way of life see: "Sobre la lectura de periódicos," *El Mercurio*, July 4 and August 7, 1841; "Contestación a un quidam," *El Mercurio*, May 19, 1842; "La Colmena," *El Progreso*, December 17, 1842.

[11] "Quinta carta a Don Rafael Minvielle," *Gaceta del comercio*, October 28, 1843.

It was to this common Spanish heritage that all the evils and ills of Hispanic America could be traced. The civil conflicts and hatreds that were "tearing out her entrails,"[12] the lack of original culture or learning,[13] the attachment to tradition and blindness to progress,[14] the social control by clerical superstition rather than reason,[15] and the complete lack of any original thought[16]—these were all the features that Sarmiento found to be common to the life of the Hispanic world, and he attributed each to the Spanish heritage and the Spanish way of life.

With this diagnosis of the ills of the Hispanic world completed, the line of propaganda for Sarmiento to take against Rosas immediately became evident. "Who do you think Rosas is? Rosas is the political inquisition of old Spain personified. He was nursed on the milk of despotism, the hatred for civilization and the liberty that he saw born in his homeland. . . . In Spain, thought has been prohibited for three centuries, and there has been a tribunal to persecute and to burn alive those who speak against, write against, or even those who are suspected of disloyalty to the king and to the dominant ideas; Rosas has created that same tribunal in his one person, to drown all murmur of disapproval, to suffocate all seed of liberty. Freedom of the press was unknown to Spain until 1833; Rosas has destroyed the liberty that we enjoyed since 1810. Spain has known no constitutional powers during the past centuries; Rosas hates even the name of constitution. Despotic, cruel, enemy of all that is national, that is to say, barbarian, Spanish—he has trampled all under foot, he has destroyed all; and he has finally realized after sacrificing twenty thousand victims the old Spanish government, which is his model, which is his type."[17]

This was the first plank in the platform of ideas that Sarmiento was forming during his years of exile in Chile: He was

[12] "Es julio, pascua del pueblo," *El Mercurio*, August 1, 1841; *Obras*, I, 98.
[13] *Obras*, IV, 36.
[14] "Las obras de Larra," *El Mercurio*, August 31, 1841.
[15] "La compañía de Jesús," *El Mercurio*, May 19, 1842.
[16] "Contestación a un quidam," *El Mercurio*, May 19, 1842.
[17] "Quinta carta a Don Rafael Minvielle," *Gaceta del comercio*, October 28, 1843.

against the regime of Rosas. Don Domingo was convinced that his primary objective and duty was the continued struggle against the dictator of his own nation. He felt that exiles, wherever they might be, could carry on an effective opposition. "The Argentineans emigrated, but they emigrate with their liberal principles and their love of civilization and liberty." Wherever the exiles were they used the local press to press their claims and to air their propaganda. In Montevideo, in Bolivia, in Chile, there were strong nuclei of exiles carrying on a successful sniping operation against Rosas.[18]

El Mercurio was Sarmiento's first important weapon in Chile, and he used it to expose the horrors of the Rosas regime and his arguments against it. "Sarmiento makes it [*El Mercurio*] shout against the tyranny of Rosas, and sometimes its cries become roars."[19] On December 23, 1842, Sarmiento and Vicente López inaugurated *El heraldo argentino* with the express purpose of carrying on a sustained propaganda attack against the Rosas regime. In its first issue, they set forward its program: "The soil of our Republic has been covered by blood. . . . A frightful and unparalleled disorganization has taken place in the extensive districts that carry the name of the River Plate. A wise and evil man has put into play all the springs of a Machiavellian political program, to make for himself a patrimony of a bloody soil, covered by thousands of corpses and by rubbish. But he has not yet achieved this, Argentineans. Let us not forget that he has not yet achieved it!"[20] The editors of *El heraldo argentino* were determined to do all in their power to keep him from achieving it.

But the opposition of the exiled Sarmiento to the Rosas regime was not confined to his propaganda efforts in the Chilean press. He also pressed for more tangible gains, and he urged the friendly Chilean regime to take direct action against its tyrannical neighbor. He talked with Manuel Montt at length about the possibilities of a war against Rosas, and he prepared to "educate the opinion of the government it-

[18] "Segundo comunicado," *El Progreso*, December 10, 1842; *Obras*, II, 60.
[19] José Peláez y Tapia, *op.cit.*, p. 91.
[20] "Prospecto," *El heraldo argentino*, Santiago de Chile, December 23, 1842.

self"[21] in order to persuade it of the advisability of such a move.

In early January 1843, when the third number of *El heraldo argentino* was about to be published, news arrived in Chile of the decisive defeat of the main unitarist armies by Rosas at Arroyo Grande. The *émigrés* saw in this news the end of their hopes for the fall of the dictator. The newspaper was closed in despair, and Sarmiento gave up hope of ever accomplishing the overthrow of his old enemy. "Now there is no other homeland than Chile," he wrote on January 11, "we must live only for Chile."[22] He now called himself an "ex-Argentinean."

With all hopes of successful opposition seemingly gone, this first phase of the development of Sarmiento's thought necessarily came to an end. Until now he had been defining and attacking that which he was against—Rosas. Now, when that attack seemed useless, it was necessary to think further along more positive lines. It was necessary for him to define that which he was fighting *for*.

The political thinkers of the eighteenth century had claimed that there were ideal principles and laws existing apart from and above the personality. The time for decision had come for Domingo Sarmiento, and he saw as his aim the creation of a form of government that clearly defined the rational principles of political behavior and made them predominant over the personalistic will of the individual. "There has arrived for South America the moment of crisis in which will be decided for many of the States that occupy it, if there will be constitutional, republican, democratic governments, or if power will remain deposited in the hands of a perpetual, perhaps in some way, hereditary, chief, without any more impediments to his will than the considerations required by the circumstances of the moment."[23]

This was the question for Sarmiento—the conflict between personalism and nomocracy; and the problem of the moment

[21] *Obras*, III, 203.

[22] "Despedida del heraldo argentino," *El Progreso*, January 11, 1843.

[23] "Política americana," *El Mercurio*, August 10, 1841.

was to formulate in his own mind his idea of the abstract principles and laws that exist outside of and control the human personality. He was interested in achieving a political system in which such abstractions as constitutions, laws, rights, and freedoms existed as factors dominant over the activity of the personality. This emphasis of form in the development of Sarmiento's thought is well illustrated in his polemic with Alberdi in 1844. Simón Bolívar had proposed many years earlier the calling of a congress of South American Republics, and a memorandum of the Ministry of Interior of Chile had finally suggested the fulfillment of this proposal. In spite of his friendship for Montt and his support of Bulnes, Sarmiento opposed such a congress. He agreed with its purpose—the political and economic cooperation of South America—but he did not believe it could be called until all the member nations had constitutional governments. Some were torn by anarchy and others were controlled by tyranny. In this way, he saw the *form* of the government as more important than the *results* of a congress. The congress might call for a laudable end; it would seek peace and order throughout the continent. Rosas could bring order, but the means by which he would bring it would be wrong, and they would not be justified, no matter how praiseworthy the end. It was this framework of thought that was typical of the philosophy and politics of the Enlightenment and that made possible the political form of nomocracy.[24]

This emphasis of form dominated Sarmiento's political aims and principles during this stage of the development of his thought. The form should be a rational one, and it could be found in the doctrines of the rationalists of the past century. A nation should have a "national reason," a rational pattern of political behavior. Political parties should not represent a personality or even a will; they should represent ideas. They should therefore not follow the "national will," as the traditional parties of Hispanic America of that time tended to do, but they should adhere to the "national reason."[25]

[24] See "Un congreso americano en 1844" in *El Progreso*, October 10, 1844; *Obras*, XXXIV, 7-11.

[25] "Las elecciones actuales," *El Progreso*, June 8, 1844.

The pursuit of the "national reason" should be carried on within a nomocratic framework of rights and principles. One of these principles was the equality of all men. Sarmiento did not think of this equality as an end—that is, economic equality, social equality, or any form of practical equality—but as a means. "The equality that our institutions proclaim does not consist, as some absurdly imagine, in the chimeric equality of learning and ability nor in the equal distribution of property; it consists only in the fact that the law establishes no differences between men, leaving to nature and chance that task."[26] He thought of the principle of equality as a framework within which all persons must act. It gave to each an equal opportunity, but it provided no political goal. It was a means and not an end.

Of as great an importance as equality of opportunity in the creation of a framework of political action were the rights of the individual. These rights were natural and rational, and all civilized peoples should recognize them as binding.[27] Along with the institutions, laws, and customs that went to make up the remainder of the political framework, they created the political "machine, with strong springs and a solid movement."[28] Sarmiento was more interested in creating that "machine" than in what it would produce.

This was one of the principal reasons why Sarmiento adhered to the government and program of Bulnes and Montt, who represented to him the "elements of legitimacy and stability," government by law. They worked within the framework of political action that came to be Sarmiento's political goal.[29] Government "must be legal, whatever else it is, because arbitrary action is license—the antithesis of system, method, and government."[30] Government by law, government within the framework of the rational principles of equality, rights, and forms of the eighteenth century would have to replace the government by personality that was then dominant in much of the Spanish world.

[26] "Apertura de la escuela normal," *El Mercurio*, June 18, 1842.

[27] *Obras*, XXXIV, 43.

[28] "Strong Governments," *El Mercurio*, November 17, 1841; translated in *Anthology*, p. 305.

[29] *Obras*, III, 207.

[30] *Anthology*, p. 308.

Sarmiento now knew what he was against, and what he was for. The problem became one of *how* to replace that which he wanted to destroy with that which he wanted to create. His problem became one of method.

Sarmiento's solution of the dichotomy between the ideal and the real was the solution of so many contemporary thinkers in the Hispanic world and of one of the mainstreams of thought of the nineteenth century in the Western European Civilization. It was the way of reform.[31] He would reform the real world to fit the ideal. "Our institutions are until today but a program; we have stated this fact before, and we all feel its truth. We must effect a revolution in ideas and customs; we are faced with an abyss on both sides, despotism on one side and anarchy on the other. It is impossible to stop now."[32] Action was necessary to make the ideal a reality, to make the world fit into the ideal pattern. "Great reforms, those founded on immutable and recognized principles, are brought about by closing the eyes and putting the shoulder to the wheel. When the French Convention ordered the organization of the famous decimal system of weights and measures . . . it was not stopped by the difficulties with which it had to fight, but it carried out the project."[33]

To effect this change, to bring about this revolution with which Sarmiento hoped to reform the world to fit the ideal that was his goal, it was necessary to understand the problem and analyze the factors that needed change. It was necessary to understand *why* the world was as it was and *how* it could be reformed.

In the library of Quiroga Rosas in San Juan and in the libraries of his friends in Santiago, Sarmiento had access to many of the historicist writers of Europe. He saw in their solution to the intellectual problem of their age a solution that he could apply to the intellectual problem of his environment. The task for the American thinker was "the philosophi-

[31] See page 9.
[32] "Apertura de la escuela normal," *El Mercurio*, June 18, 1842.
[33] Address on "Ortografía americana" delivered to Facultad de Humanidades of the University of Chile on October 17, 1843; *Obras*, IV, 4.

cal explanation of causes and effects."[34] "Who was the author, the chief of the revolution of independence in the American continent? Nobody. It was the antecedents; it was the age. It was Rousseau, Reynal, Montesquieu, and all the works of the eighteenth century. It was the North American and French and finally the Spanish revolutions. Given these antecedents, the revolution of independence of Spanish America had to follow immediately, and it did, in fact, follow. And this which is said of social movements can be applied even to the great discoveries."[35] Every human event had its cause, and it was only a question of discovering that cause to correct the effect.

Sarmiento expressed in a very concise and complete manner his philosophy of history in a newspaper article in 1844. "Nothing happens by chance. Out of this truth was born the philosophy of history. For the philosophy of our age . . . the moral world as well as the physical world has its invariable way of proceeding; and as in the phenomena of nature, there is an order and a continuity in the reality of the intelligence. . . . A new idea is the son of others, and it would be bad to call the thought of any writer original rather than to find out the circumstances that have created it and the mother ideas that he has received from the very society in which he appears."[36]

Sarmiento called for a Spanish American sociology, a study of the causal relationships in Spanish American society, and an analysis of the reforms necessary to change the existing conditions: "An important work would be that which tried to discover the hidden causes that undermine the existence of American societies and tried to explain the events that we are witnessing. . . . This would be a great service to all the new states."[37] In this manner, Don Domingo became the father of Spanish American sociology. He was one of the first to apply a philosophy of history to the social problems of the

[34] "Historia física i política de Chile por Don Claudio Gay," *El Progreso*, August 20, 1844; *Obras*, II, 210.

[35] "La reforma ortográfica," *El Progreso*, February 17, 1844.

[36] *Obras*, IV, 133-134.

[37] "Vindicación de la república argentina en su revolución i en su guerras civiles," *El Mercurio*, June 7, 1841.

Hispanic world, and he thus fathered generations of thinkers and writers who followed him with the same method.[38]

After a careful study of the political social situation in Argentina and other Spanish nations, Sarmiento concluded that it was a result of causes deeper than the mere ambitions of some caudillo,[39] or the weakness of the Spanish tradition. It was, rather, caused by a fundamental conflict between the forces of "civilization" and "barbarism." These were the names that Sarmiento gave to his ideal rationally ordered society on the one hand and the actual real chaotic society on the other.[40] His aim was to discover the various causes of barbarism in order that they might be remedied. "Backward ideas and their consequences are fighting for the last time with the ideas of liberty, constitution and progress."[41]

The causes that Sarmiento found for the barbarism of the Spanish world were many, and each had to be remedied in its own way, but according to rational principles. The ideas of reform that he developed during this period ranged all the way from a change in the spelling of the Spanish language to a change in the racial composition of the nation. Sarmiento's proposals for reform between 1841 and 1845 included linguistics, spelling, religion, national intellect, the social structure, the economic system, and the racial composition of the Spanish American nations.

Examining the Spanish literary language, Sarmiento felt that it did not fit the changing world of his time. To serve its rightful purpose in society, language should express the thought and the reality of the human being. The outmoded academic dictionaries of the time did not seem to Sarmiento to fulfill this purpose, so he proposed that they be changed and that the language thus be reformed to fit the reality of the time.[42]

[38] José Ingenieros, *Sociologia argentina*, Buenos Aires, 1918, p. 389.

[39] *Obras,* IX, 6.

[40] *Ibid.*, VII, 251.

[41] "Política americana," *El Mercurio*, August 10, 1841; *Obras*, IX, 9.

[42] "Ejercicios populares de la lengua castellana," *El Mercurio*, April 27, 1842; Sarmiento was not the first to propose such linguistic reforms. Juan Bautista Alberdi wrote an article on the "Emancipación de la lengua" (The emancipation of the language), advocating the abandonment of the "puerile Spanish language" for the "virile" French. Carlos María Onetti, *Cuatro clases sobre Sarmiento escritor,* Tucumán, 1939, p. 80.

The most obviously academic element in the language was the spelling. It did not conform to the pronunciation, and the teaching of the time was attempting to change the pronunciation to make it fit the way the words were spelled. This to Sarmiento's mind was senseless. "There is anarchy in Spanish spelling because there is no *authority* that can create rules for it."[43] His solution was a simple one: "each letter should have its own sound; and each sound should have its own letter."[44] He proposed dropping the letters *h, v, z,* and *x*. The *h* had no sound, and the sound of each of the other three was already taken care of by one or more other letters. Similarly, the soft *c* would be dropped, for its sound was expressed by the *s*. The *y* when used as a vowel could be replaced by the *i*, and the *g* before a vowel could be taken care of by its equivalent in sound, the *j*.[45] In this way the traditional spelling of "Argentina" would become "Arjentina," and the word *y* (and) would be spelled *i*. Thus, there would be a different sound for every letter, and there would be a letter for every sound. The spelling could be made simple and uniform, and this simplicity and uniformity would have been achieved through common sense.

The University of Chile approved Sarmiento's plan, and it became the officially accepted rule of spelling in Chile for several years. In the letters and articles that Don Domingo wrote during the next few years, he used his reformed method of spelling, but after a few years the system was forgotten. Within a decade the university reversed its former ruling in favor of the reform, and the official spelling went back to the former usage. By 1852, Don Domingo's letters had also returned to the traditional spelling, and the movement for reform had been forgotten.

Of more far-reaching implications, however, than Sarmiento's attempts to change the Spanish language were his attempts to remedy the socio-political situation in which he found himself. He was living amidst a "barbarism" that he wished to change to "civilization." He found three causes of

[43] "Contestación a un profesor de gramática, IV," *El Progreso*, November 29, 1843; *Obras*, IV, 108.

[44] *Obras*, IV, 1-2.

[45] *Ibid.*, 29.

barbarism to be more important than any others. The first of these was the material environment. Spanish economic life must be made to fit the rationally evident natural laws. The second was race. The Spanish race was traditionally backward and unable to adapt itself to the reforms that Sarmiento proposed. Finally, the mind of the people must be made ready for these changes. An ignorant people could never understand and fit into the patterns that he proposed. The people must be educated.

Economic ills and disorder seemed to Don Domingo to be the causes of many far-reaching ills in the society of his time. "The gap between the misery of the masses and the opulence of the minority will someday be filled with something, and revolutions are a horrible mortar, composed of blood and debris, that can fill these spaces."[46] Some commentators have spoken of Sarmiento as a "socialist thinker." He called his own ideas socialistic, and these critics see in his preoccupation with the economic problem a socialistic preoccupation.[47] But such an assumption is far from the truth. Don Domingo used the word in the very loosest sense. He was interested in the fate of man, in the problems of society; so he assumed that he was a socialist. Socialism meant for him the desire for social welfare, not the later program of economic reform. He used the word before the classic meaning had become well established, especially in his part of the world. The very basis of his economic thought is contrary to the essence of socialist thought as we know it today.

In regard to the economic organization of society, he adopted the principles of classic liberalism, then a novelty in South America. He followed the "classical economists" in pointing to laws of wages, laws of prices, laws of population, and laws of supply and demand. The problem of economic reform could not be solved by a government control of the economy but by reforming the economic system in such a way that it would be free to follow the natural laws. In an article in 1849, Sarmiento stated in a definitive manner his

[46] *Ibid.*, x, 16.

[47] Palcos, *Sarmiento, op.cit.*; Orestes Ghioldi, "La clase obrera y Sarmiento," *Derechos del hombre*, Buenos Aires, September, 1938.

economic philosophy. "The wages and price of work of hand does not depend upon human will; it rises and falls undefined, according to invariable laws: the owners of tailor shops who conferred and agreed on a lowering of the wages of their laborers were doing something of at least doubtful usefulness and desirability." He illustrated his "law of wages" with a typical example. He told of a man who wanted to build in a remote spot. The materials were nearby, but there was no available labor. A workman happened by and offered to work for ten pesos. The builder was forced to pay this, even though the established price only a few miles off was but two pesos. Another workman happened along, and he followed the new price in this district and asked ten pesos. Ten workers were needed, and one by one they arrived and each demanded this same amount. Finally after the builder had hired all ten of the necessary men, still another came by looking for work. The builder offered him eight pesos. He accepted, and one of the earlier workmen was discharged. When others came along, they were offered six, then four pesos, and the established price was forced down. Finally, when labor became plentiful, the wages reached the point of two pesos, the standard price for the surrounding districts. This was the "law of wages" for Sarmiento. It is typical of the mainstream of "laissez faire" economic thought prevalent in much of the world in that day. It was a natural law. The task of economic reform was to change the economic reality to fit the various natural laws.[48]

To accomplish an economic reform of this type, Sarmiento saw several steps as absolutely necessary. Complete freedom should be given to economic development. With such freedom, economic life would automatically follow the natural laws. Freedom became in this way the basis of all economic development. Little Holland overcame the mighty Spanish Empire because she had a free economic life and Spain's economy was in chains. "It is worth noting that the most commercial city in the Spanish colonies of South America was the first to give the cry of liberty."[49] Governments should

[48] "El salario," *La Crónica*, February 25, 1849.

[49] "Un viaje a Valparaiso," *El Mercurio*, September 2, 1841; *Obras*, I, 131.

guarantee two things in the economic realm. First, all men should be given a free and equal economic opportunity. Governments should insure such freedom and equality or the economy of a country could not progress.[50] Secondly, governments should guarantee order. Without this order, freedom would again be impossible, and the natural laws of economics would become inoperative. The businessman and industrialist were interested in achieving such order, and out of this interest grew a new respect for law and government.[51]

The economic chaos that Sarmiento found to be caused in his country by a lack of economic freedom was in turn one of the causes for the barbarism that he wanted to combat. A reform, therefore, would not be merely an economic reform; it would have implications outside the realm of the material. Such reforms "promise to change the complexion of the country and promise to give a new and stronger impulse to the national wealth and the development of the mind. The European goods exhale an odor of civilization, which, scattering in the air, leaves its imprint on all activity and all movement."[52] Sarmiento often asserted that his ideal was half material and half intellectual. The two were inseparable in his mind.[53]

Another important cause for the barbarism that he wanted to correct, Sarmiento found in the Spanish heritage. The Hispanic world seemed unable to adapt itself to the progression of civilization. Rosas and his personalist political system were identified with the Spanish heritage, and the only way that Sarmiento could see to overcome this handicap was by the introduction of new elements in the racial composition of the Spanish American world.

Sarmiento looked to North America and to Europe, and he found there political, economic, and social models that fitted far more perfectly the ideal patterns of life that he had conceived. "North America is our model," he declared,[54] and she

[50] "El teatro como elemento de cultura," *El Mercurio,* June 20, 1842.

[51] *Obras,* I, 131-132.

[52] *Ibid.,* 130.

[53] "El museo de ambas Américas," *El Mercurio,* April 8, 1842; also in *El Progreso,* December 16, 1842; *El Mercurio,* April 28, 1842.

[54] *El Mercurio,* June 3, 1841.

must be studied and copied. "The people of North America have no literature," he affirmed, "but in the absence of literature, they have liberty, wealth, the most complete civilization, inventions, steamships, factories, shipping, and sixteen million men that know how to read and understand what they read; and they have fifteen hundred and fifty newspapers and rights and equality."[55] Here was the living proof that his ideal pattern could exist in the world and be successful. The essential difference between North and South America, however, was the difference in their heritages. North America had inherited her liberty, her laws, her institutions, her customs, her ideas, and her principles from England; South America had inherited the opposite from Spain. England had bequeathed civilization; Spain, barbarism. "In North America the revolution was the realization of an idea, here the revolution had to create that idea; there it was the effect, here the cause."[56]

The problem, therefore, became for Sarmiento one of North-Americanizing South America. The Hispanic American world would have to seek its ideas, institutions, industries, and civilization from Europe and North America.[57] Before it could achieve any progress it would have to break its ties with Spain.[58] Spain's greatest writer and thinker of the time, Mariano José de Larra, had been working along these same lines of thought. He had called for a "Europeanization" of Spain. He had attacked the institutions and the thought of his nation and advocated that they be patterned after those of Europe. Sarmiento found the writings of Larra highly congenial to his own thought, and he even used the Spanish author's very words to win his polemic with Bello and Núñez.[59] He called Larra the greatest writer of contemporary Spain, and he referred to him as "the Cervantes of the regenerated Spain."[60] Sarmiento matched Larra's Europeaniza-

[55] "Apertura de la escuela normal," *El Mercurio*, June 18, 1842.

[56] "La América del sur i del norte," *El Nacional*, April 24, 1841.

[57] *Obras*, IV, 13.

[58] "Tercera carta al señor Minvielle," *Gaceta del comercio*, October 26, 1843.

[59] "Los redactores al otro quidam," *El Mercurio*, June 5, 1842.

[60] "Las obras de Larra," *El Mercurio*, August 3, 1841; "La zamueca en el teatro!" *El Mercurio*, February 19, 1842; José A. Oria, "Sarmiento costumbrista," *Sarmiento, homenaje de la universidad de la plata*, p. 49.

tion of Spain with his own North-Americanization of Spanish America.

Through an extensive and planned immigration from non-Spanish nations, the Spanish heritage would be overcome. Europe was overcrowded, and South America needed men. Herein lay the solution. "European immigration is one of the elements of American wealth, power and industry. Europe has an excess of men and a scarcity of bread; America has an excess of land and a great scarcity of hands."[61] Europe would get rid of her population; Spanish America would get her labor, and Spanish barbarism would be overcome. In 1849, Sarmiento read of plans to bring German immigrants to Valdivia in southern Chile. He called for a systematization of this into a policy or program. "We need a law on colonization that would give guarantees to the immigrants and would create known agencies in Europe to attract them."[62]

For any idealist who seeks to facilitate the historical progress the most important element with which he is dealing is the human intellect. The mind must understand and accept progress. Ignorance was therefore one of the causes of barbarism, and education was the only instrument that could overcome it. No matter how free and rational the economic system, regardless of the race, an uneducated people would still be a barbarous people. "Peoples like individuals need long preparation for social life, and this preparation is the same in all times and in all phases of civilization. It was necessary to free the intelligence in order that the public reason, which was sovereign, might become the perfect reason."[63]

Political democracy or nomocracy could not exist without an educated people. Where the workmen and the peasants were illiterate, they were easily controlled by their employers and political bosses. Democracy became a meaningless phrase and was replaced by a governing oligarchy.[64] Only education could create a people capable of governing itself within a framework of law. Education would create a "youth that upon reaching manhood will find itself gifted with knowledge

[61] *Obras*, x, 17-18.
[62] "Movimiento," *La Crónica*, September 23, 1849.
[63] "Educación política," *El Mercurio*, June 22, 1841; *Obras*, ix, 39, 40.
[64] "La venta de zapatos," *El Mercurio*, April 21, 1841.

and ideas to carry out with glory the immense task of elevating its country and giving something to the ministries, to the courts, to the national representation, to the press and to the other means of influencing the opinion of individuals and the course of public affairs."[65] Education was "the basis of a democratic government, a society of intelligent beings capable of knowing their rights, sensing the value of these rights, and of causing them to be respected."[66] The Rosas government had suppressed all public education. The budget for the Department of Schools in Argentina had dropped from $58,580 in 1838 to $2,300 in 1840. The Rosas dictatorship was creating an ignorant people, and this ignorance was one of the causes of the existing barbarism.[67]

By the middle of 1841, Domingo Sarmiento had gained a position in the public life of Chile that gave him many important instruments with which to fight for the reforms that he sought. He continued his profession of teaching which he had initiated at the age of fifteen at San Francisco del Monte and continued at intervals ever since; and the positions that he gained in this line enabled him to attack the ignorance that he felt was such a potent cause of the Hispanic American barbarism.

In addition to being a teacher, however, Sarmiento also held, by the end of 1841, a position of importance in the Chilean press and a position of influence in regard to the Chilean government. Both gave him valuable instruments with which to pursue his aims. He used his teaching, his writing, and his official positions for this end: "To write for the sake of writing is the profession of conceited dilettantes—men without principles or any real patriotism. To write just for the sake of insulting is the work of rascals and fools. To write in order to regenerate is the duty of those who study the needs of their times."[68]

[65] "Repartición de premios en el Instituto Nacional," *El Mercurio*, March 9, 1842.

[66] *Obras*, IV, 248; see also "Cajas de ahorro," *El Mercurio*, July 16, 1842.

[67] Ricardo Levene, "Sarmiento, sociólogo de la realidad americana y argentina," *Homenaje de la facultad de humanidades y ciencias de la universidad de la plata*, Buenos Aires, 1938, p. 102.

[68] *Anthology*, p. 185; "Diálogo entre el editor i el redactor," *El Mercurio*, July 27, 1842.

When Sarmiento wrote articles of literary or theatrical criticism, his consideration of style or *genre* was always secondary. His first yardstick of judgment was based on the author's intention. He asked if he was attempting to "regenerate" society.[69] The theater, for him, represented "the social necessities of the age" and had "a visible tendency towards the regeneration of customs and ideas, which is its true claim to glory."[70] If a writer was to be considered good, he would have to fulfill this role and present the "social necessities of the age." Sarmiento always looked upon the Spanish dramatist, Breton de los Herreros, as the greatest contemporary playwright. He praised him because he did not write "a single work that did not proclaim a principle, that did not attack a problem." The theater should attack the problem of "class, of all tyranny, whether public or domestic, and should elevate in its place the freedom of the individual of both sexes."[71]

In a similar manner, other institutions of contemporary society should be at the service of social reform. Even religion and the Church did not escape this first basic duty. Religion should "prepare man for the duties of the world, inculcating in him the moral principles and beliefs that would insure his future."[72] One of the great missions of Christianity was the "civilization" of man, giving him principles and beliefs, improving his behavior, and overcoming his passions.[73]

Sarmiento's greatest single weapon for the expression and the struggle for his ideas was the press. Whether it was his theories of education or literature or politics, his articles in the newspapers of Chile always carried a message and were an integral part of his crusade. He never wrote without a purpose, and as he told Mrs. Horace Mann many years later, his pen was but his weapon "to clean the soil of tyrants and

[69] Juan Pablo Echagüe, *Hombres e ideas*, Buenos Aires, 1928, p. 61; *Sarmiento crítico teatral*, Buenos Aires, 1925, p. 113.

[70] "El teatro como elemento de cultura," *El Mercurio*, June 20, 1842.

[71] *Ibid.*

[72] "Las hermanas de la caridad," *El Mercurio*, February 21, 1842; "Del clero en la política," *El Nacional*, May 8, 1841.

[73] "Los mineros," *El Nacional*, April 14, 1841.

found the Republic on rational bases."[74] "The eye of the press should see all abuses and indicate all dangers."[75]

Sarmiento saw the press in modern life as a power, as a potential danger, but also a potential weapon for good. If badly used or ill conceived it could do great harm in sowing discontent and disharmony in a society. But if used to treat problems of economics, history, and literature, to raise the level of the culture of the masses, to attack the abuses of government, and to propose reform, it could be an instrument of progress.[76] "The intimate connection between periodical publications and the material progress of a people, of its civilization, of its liberty" seemed to Sarmiento to be an inescapable fact.[77]

The way to defeat the enemy and achieve the goal was to study the causes of the former and attack them. Sarmiento had done this; his program was now established. As an educator, as a writer, in all phases of his life, he concentrated his energies on his goal.

Chapter 15. The Teacher

"The slow progress of human society has recently created an institution unknown in previous centuries. Public instruction, whose purpose it is to prepare the new generations, *en masse*, for the use of individual intelligence by even a rudimentary knowledge of the sciences and facts necessary for the formation of reason, is a purely modern institution. It was born of the dissensions of Christianity, and converted into a

[74] Letter from Sarmiento to Mary Mann, Boletín de la Academia Argentina de Letras, IV, 314-315; José A. Oria, *op.cit.*, p. 51.

[75] "La crítica teatral," *El Mercurio*, November 8, 1841; see also *Recuerdos*, p. 220.

[76] "El diarismo," *El Nacional*, May 15, 1841; *Obras*, I, 59-63.

[77] "Sobre la lectura de periódicos," *El Mercurio*, July 4, 1841; *Obras*, I, 75.

a right by the democratic spirit of present-day society."[1] One of the basic measures in reform was an educated mind. From his earliest experiences with the small country school in San Francisco del Monte until he was an old man, Sarmiento devoted many of his activities to teaching.

His favorite and most apt pupil in his educational efforts was always himself. Sarmiento had received most of his instruction by his own efforts, and he continued his self-education throughout his entire life. This fact explains the ever-changing aspect of his thought. It is impossible to speak of "Sarmiento's thought" in an abstract sense. One must always speak of it in relation to a particular time and place in his life. His ideas in one decade often changed radically the next decade.[2] He continued reading; he continued teaching himself; and as he saw, or thought he saw, his former fallacies, he changed his ideas and turned to new ones.

In Chile he continued to read the latest writers from Europe. He read the Romantic dramatists and reviewed their plays. He read the French philosophers of history and applied their methods to his problems. He read the latest treatises on educational theory,[3] and he used the ideas that he derived from these for the educational experiments that he was instituting. When he later wrote about these days of intense intellectual activity in Chile, he described how he carried in his pocket the works of the sociologist, Pierre Leroux; of the political observer, De Tocqueville; and of the historian and statesman, Guizot.[4] He read the literary criticism of Blair, Villemain, and Schlegel; Thiers and other French historians who offered a new philosophy of history derived from Vico and Herder; the poetry of Byron, Lamartine, and Hugo; and the drama of Dumas, Delavigne, Ducange, and Scribe.[5] He continued his study of languages, and his reading in French

[1] *Anthology*, p. 291.

[2] This is the basic mistake in Ezequiel Martínez Estrada's otherwise acceptable little study of Sarmiento's thought. He makes a penetrating analysis of certain phases, but he fails to tie this analysis in with its context. What he saw about it was true at one point in his life; it was different at others.

[3] Juan E. Casani, "Doctrinas pedagógicas de Sarmiento," in Universidad de la Plata, p. 67.

[4] "Reminiscencias de la vida literaria," *Nueva revista de Buenos Aires*, 1881.

[5] "Contestación a un quidam," *El Mercurio*, May 19, 1842.

and English improved his knowledge of these languages but did not perfect it. He could still say "god demn" in English and "peples" for "peuples" in French.[6]

Sarmiento's own learning was but an instrument for his deeper goal of educating others in order to prepare them to meet and solve the problems that faced them. "Public instruction is the measure of a people's civilization."[7] The problem did not seem to him to be one of advanced education, of universities and specialization. It was a question of the basic education of *all* the people. It was a matter of training the reason of the masses in order that this reason, as the democratic sovereign, might best govern itself and choose its leaders. "Without civilization, without enlightenment, there is no possible government other than despotism; there is no public opinion, no liberty, no institutions, no industry nor wealth. And the civilization of a country is not in the colleges nor in the universities; it is in the primary schools, when they are based on a liberal, philosophical, and rationalized plan."[8] His task was, therefore, the creation of a system of public primary education for all and the training of teachers for these primary schools.

After General Bulnes was elected to the presidency of Chile, he named Manuel Montt as Minister of Public Education. Montt felt deeply indebted to Sarmiento for his aid during the electoral campaign, and he was aware of the keen interest in education that Don Domingo shared with him. In 1842, he charged Sarmiento with the composition of a decree creating a normal school for teachers.

"Write a rough draft of the decree of foundation," suggested the Minister.

"I? What do I know about decrees?" objected Don Domingo. "I don't understand a single word about official red tape. It would turn out to be a newspaper article."

"Never mind. Just go ahead and do it," Montt insisted.

Sarmiento did. The decree was edited and organized. It was

[6] *Obras*, I, 132, 224.

[7] "Análisis de las cartillas, silabarios y otros métodos de lectura conocidos y practicados en Chile, por el director de la escuela normal." Dated August 22, 1842.

[8] This article appears in *Obras*, IV, 245, and in XII, 149, under different titles.

signed, and the creation of the first normal school in South America, the second in the New World, became a law. Only two years before the first such institution of the Western Hemisphere had been founded in the United States.[9]

Don Domingo was named the first director of the Normal School for Teachers of Chile. He had an immense task cut out for him. The entire job of organization was thrown into his lap, and the greatest obstacle that he would have to overcome was the lack of respect that was present throughout all levels of the population for the profession of teacher. He himself had great faith in the mission that his new institution was fulfilling. "The formation of the normal school for primary instruction holds within it an immense future for the social improvement and intellectual culture of all classes of society."[10] He therefore entered his new project with a missionary fervor.

On January 18, 1842, Minister Montt's decree was published. On June 14, the school was opened without ceremony.[11] Only twenty-eight students were enrolled the first year, and most of them were badly prepared from a scholastic viewpoint. Some could hardly read or write and knew only the basic rules of arithmetic. Among these were those who had studied in religious schools and had learned to speak a rudimentary type of Latin, but were still ignorant of the more basic three R's.

The courses that Sarmiento planned at his new school included the basic subjects of reading, writing, arithmetic, grammar, spelling, and religion. He added to these more advanced courses in geography, lineal drawing, history, and educational methods. Don Domingo taught what he called the "scientific" courses, and his only assistant, Ignacio Acuña, taught the arts. From the very first day, Sarmiento kept a 'diary of the operations and progress of the teaching, for what value it might be to the future."[12] This document provides us with a blow-by-blow description of the young

[9] For an account of this incident, see Palcos, *Sarmiento, op.cit.*, p. 48.

[10] *Obras*, IV, 246.

[11] Ministerio de Educación Pública, *Sarmiento director de la escuela normal, 1842-1845*, Santiago de Chile, 1942, pp. 26-27.

[12] Archivo de la Escuela Normal de Preceptores de Santiago.

teacher's struggle to make his dream become a reality. Classes began at six a.m. and ended at three p.m., and during this time the instructor worked hard to overcome the obstacles in his way.

One day one of the pupils in a class of cosmography dealing with the movement of the planetary system interrupted the class and objected to the teacher's explanation.

"I don't believe what you are saying. Furthermore, I will not even admit it as an hypothesis."

Don Domingo was growing used to such incidents, and he had learned to hold his temper and remain calm. "Very well," he replied charitably. "Do you know how much space there is between the earth and the sun?"

"Yes, sir," answered the doubting student.

"And between the earth and the stars?"

"That's an immense distance."

"Think of a distance of millions and millions of miles. If the earth does not spin around the sun, the stars must spin in twenty-four hours around the earth. That distance is the radius of a circle; then, multiplying the diameter or the radius by six, you will obtain the approximate distance that you are making the stars cover by day, by hour, by minute, that is to say, many millions of leagues per minute; while the other theory makes the earth spin around the sun at 6½ leagues per minute, which is a speed, a proportion of which is made by railroads. Thus, the true system is believable, while your system is absurd and useless. How could they cover that inconceivable distance and go that almost infinitely fast speed around our earth every day?"[13]

The student reconsidered after such a practical explanation of what had formerly been to him an abstract, or even a theological, question.

For a reading text, Sarmiento used Ackermann, whose encyclopedic knowledge served to instruct in facts as well as teach to read. This, according to Don Domingo, was according to "contemporary pedagogy."[14] Except for four or five of them, the first-year students were the worst possible

[13] Belín Sarmiento, *Sarmiento anecdótico, op.cit.*, p. 42.

[14] Archivo de la Escuela Normal de Santiago, July 1, 1842.

material for the educational experiment. The bar flies and gamblers habitually left the school illegally for their illicit escapades. Don Domingo found that "one of the principal problems until now has been the introduction of order, discipline, and morality among the young students." But this was written on August 1, 1842; and he already felt that he had partially overcome this obstacle.[15] Of the first group of twenty-eight, only half graduated at the end of their course in 1845. Some had dropped out; many had failed the courses; a few had been dismissed for misconduct. But meanwhile, the school was gaining in size, in prestige, and in efficiency. By 1845 it had forty-two pupils. "The seed had been sown: it would bear fruit."[16] The director devoted a great proportion of his time during these three years to this pursuit. He went so far as giving his own clothes to poorly dressed students,[17] and he studied hard the methods of teaching and their possible improvements.

One of the fundamental pedagogical problems of the time was to find a method to teach students to read. In 1841, a Spaniard, Juan Manuel Bonifaz, had introduced his *Reading Method* into the schools of Uruguay. The very next year, Sarmiento ordered that the work of the Spanish pedagogue, Vicente Naharro, *Practical Method for Teaching to Read*, be reprinted in Chile, but this proved a difficult text for use by inexperienced teachers. He therefore turned to the Bonifaz method, and in a communication to the Ministry of Public Instruction and in newspaper articles advocated its adoption.[18] He went on to advocate early readers for elementary students that would develop the children's intelligence rather than foster a parrot-like repetition. He favored the replacement of the traditional rhymes and proverbs of Spaniards like Martínez de la Rosa by simple tales in suitable children's language, such as the English Reader of Miss Edgeworth.

This study of pedagogical methods on a very elementary

[15] *Ibid.*

[16] Palcos, *Sarmiento, op.cit.*, p. 48.

[17] José Bernardo Suárez, *Rasgos biográficos del señor don Domingo F. Sarmiento*, Santiago de Chile, December, 1863, p. 16. Suárez was one of the better of the original students at the school, and his book gives many interesting details of the first years.

[18] Manuel A. Ponce, "Prologue" to *Obras*, XXVIII.

level culminated in 1845, when the director of the normal school published his *Gradual Method of Teaching to Read Spanish* (*Método gradual de enseñar a leer el castellano*). This was a summary of the experience that he had gained in three years of study and practice, and it became the basis of many of the educational systems of the Hispanic world. Two million children learned to read from this best seller of Sarmiento's works. In 1864, at the American Congress of Lima, Manuel Montt challenged Don Domingo by saying: "The Argentine Minister does not know which is the most important of the many books that he has written. If he does, let him tell us!"

"Of course I know," was the instantaneous reply of Sarmiento, "*The Gradual Reading Method* was the most important."[19]

But texts for teaching pupils to read were not the only books lacking in the Chilean educational system. Sarmiento found most of the books for elementary teaching "not sufficiently intelligible."[20] He found it best to teach geography and to supplement the teaching of history with maps. He outlawed such books as *The Sufferings of Hell* and replaced them with his own translations of *The Conscience of a Child* and *The Life of Jesus Christ*. The latter were simple and beautiful presentations of the Christian religion, and they were in sharp contrast with the hell-and-brimstone type of text that had formerly been used.

The pedagogical activities of the ambitious and active Don Domingo during his years in Chile were not confined to his directorship of the normal school. He was also appointed a charter member of the Faculty of Philosophy and Humanities of the University of Chile and the foundation of that institution in 1843. This position gave him one more position of prestige in the intellectual world of Chile, and it served as a sounding board for many of his pedagogical ideas. His paper to that body in October 1843 proposed his famous program of spelling reform; and it was to this group that he first introduced his *Gradual Reading Method*.

[19] *Obras*, XL, 384.

[20] "Aritmética práctica i mental, por Roswell C. Smith," *El Mercurio*, March 5, 1841.

For more personal reasons Sarmiento branched out into even another educational field. In partnership with his fellow exile, Vicente Fidel López, he started in 1843 a private school for the children of the wealthier families of Santiago. At that time, he was financially embarrassed. His family had just arrived from San Juan and imposed a new burden upon him, and his many debts included one of 500 pesos to Manuel Montt.[21] He felt that the new Liceo, as the private school was called, would not only liquidate his debts, but would also give him valuable experience that might in the future be of service to his country.[22] The Liceo started out as a promising venture with a definite future. A contemporary observer wrote that there were "many probabilities that it would succeed."[23] But in 1844, Don Domingo, not able to resist a fight, joined in a notorious polemic that was raging in Santiago. He backed Francisco Bilbao, who was considered a liberal and even anti-clerical by many of the leading citizens of the city. The fathers of the seventy pupils of the Liceo withdrew their sons en masse. The Liceo was forced to close down, and Don Domingo, instead of improving his financial state, lost one thousand pesos in the venture.

Thus, between 1842 and 1845 Sarmiento's pedagogical activities were intense and varied. Based on the theory that only an adequate system of elementary public education would fit a people for democracy, his educational efforts extended from the teaching of elementary pupils in his own school, to the directorship of the normal school, to a chair on the faculty of the University of Chile. His activities at this time were mostly on an elementary level. They were groundwork for future educational efforts; but the results did not go unnoticed. His ideas became the basis of much of Chile's educational system; and in later years these same theories, conceived in Chile and slightly modified by future experience, were to become the basis of the Argentine public school system.

[21] Sarmiento to Manuel Quiroga Rosas, April 6, 1843, Santiago de Chile, Archivo Nacional de Chile, Santiago de Chile, volume 253, pieza 12, No. 10.

[22] *Ibid.*

[23] Unpublished letter from P. Ortiz to Manuel Quiroga Rosas. Santiago de Chile, August 29, 1843. Archivo Nacional de Chile, Santiago de Chile. Archivo varios, No. 253, pieza 11, No. 7.

Chapter 16. The Book: The Romantic

DOMINGO SARMIENTO never admitted that he was a Romanticist. He attacked what he called "romanticism" as much as he attacked "neo-classicism," and in a typical manner he found for himself a more original name. He defined his "socialism," as we have seen, in terms of the social function of literature. "We have always been and we will always be socialists, that is to say, synthesizing art, science and politics, that is, the feelings of the heart, the lights of the intelligence, and the activities of actions, for the establishment of a democratic government founded on a solid basis, on the triumph of liberty and all the liberal doctrines, on the realization of the holy aims of our revolution."[1] Any writing that did not fulfill its basically social function did not meet with the approval of Don Domingo, and his own writings were all designed along these "socialist" lines. He attacked neo-classicism as "mechanical imitation," and he defined Romanticism as "writing for the sake of writing."[2]

Such a definition of Romantic art was of course a limited one. And Sarmiento's own writings revealed definite Romantic tendencies. His writings were intended to reform the world, but his personality seemed to be drawn to "the way of the titan"—the tradition that he had inherited from his family and his history. This way of the titan was closely related to the main tendencies of Romanticism—emotionalism and voluntarism. The highest value ceased to be the objective, universal, absolute reason. The emotionalist replaced the eighteenth-century "I think; therefore I am" with "I feel; therefore I am." The voluntarist said "I will; therefore I am." We might divide Sarmiento's artistic endeavors into two parts: the intention and the intent. The intention

[1] *Obras,* I, 311.
[2] "Concluye el análisis del artículo Romanticismo," *El Mercurio,* July 29, 1842.

of a work of art arises out of the mind of the person. It is the result of a process of rationalization. The intent of a work of art often betrays another side of the artist—his emotional or irrational side, his "livingness"; and it is the result of an artistic expression of this "livingness."[3] Sarmiento's intention is one of reform. He intends to create a "socialist" literature, but he often reveals himself as a Romantic.

The Chilean intellectual scene of the 1840's was just becoming aware of the new Romantic movement in European art and literature. Sarmiento and López's polemics with the Bello school of neo-classics awakened Santiago to the existence of a literary type other than that to which they were accustomed. As time went on, men like Salvador Sanfuentes showed definite Romantic influences. Sanfuentes had been a disciple of Bello and had begun his literary career writing neo-classic poetry, but by 1846 he demonstrated greater stylistic freedom and the marked influence of writers like Hugo, De Musset, Zorrilla, Espronceda, and Rivas.[4] Although Sarmiento continued to define the Romantic movement in very limited terms and although he preferred to call himself a socialist rather than a Romantic, he could not escape the intellectual atmosphere in which he was living. He had read the writers of the Age of Reason during his youth, but now he was submerged in a *milieu* of Romantics. "Racine, Voltaire, Rousseau, Montesquieu, Diderot, Buffon and all that constellation of great men (of the Age of Reason), have come to appear ignorant in the presence of Chateaubriand, Lamartine, Cuvier, Arago, Jouffroy, Cousin, Villemain, Hugo, Dumas, Saint Hilaire and so many other great men, who tied by their knowledge to the former ones, continue the spasmodic task of civilizing the world."[5]

The intent of his own work at this time and for years after

[3] Augusto Centeno, "Introduction: The Intent of the Artist" in *The Intent of the Artist*, Princeton, 1941. Mr. Centeno's use of the terms "intention" and "intent" seems especially relevant to Sarmiento. "Livingness" is derived from the German "Das Erlebnis" and grows out of the whole school of thought of Wilhelm Dilthey and his disciples Eduard Spranger, Hans Freyer, and others.

[4] Norberto Pinilla, Manuel Rojas, Tomás Lago, *1842, Panorama y significación del movimiento literario*, Santiago de Chile, 1942, p. 24.

[5] *Obras*, IV, 41.

reveals many Romantic elements. It demonstrates that his "livingness" was choosing a Romantic solution, while his intellect was turning to the way of reform. The most important indications of his intent, his subject matter, his interests, his characters, his style, his ideas—all have strongly Romantic features.

One of the most telling clues to the true content of a literary work and to the "livingness" of its author is revealed in his subject matter. In the case of Sarmiento, his subjects and his interests show a definite leaning towards the Romantic solution. The writers that he read most and imitated most during his five years of exile in Chile were leaders of the Romantic school in Germany and North America. James Fenimore Cooper, the only North American Romantic who had gained international fame, became one of Don Domingo's favorite writers.[6] He referred to him often in his writings, and frequently imitated his style and subject matter.[7] The German, Herder, became one of his favorites, and his theory of the *volks-geist* (spirit of the people) as the basis of human history and human life was to become one of the cornerstones of Sarmiento's own thoughts on history. "The history of human affairs is . . . a biography, the biography of a society of a people."[8] He proclaimed the Herderian theory that the individual in history is but "the echo of the human conscience," the expression of the "spirit of the people."[9]

The neo-classicist was interested in universal types as the subjects of his artistic creations. He was interested in those characters who had generalized characteristics and universalized features. The "emotionalist" and the "voluntarist" of Romanticism, on the other hand, were interested in a different kind of person for subject matter. The "emotionalist" was interested in the unusual, individualistic, striking per-

[6] María Inés Cárdenas de Monner Sans, "Algunos aspectos literarios de *Facundo*," in Universidad de la Plata, *op.cit.*, p. 222.

[7] The reference to the "redmen who wandered through the primitive forests of the Michigan" ("Los diez i ocho días de Chile, desde la derrota de Cancha-Rayada hasta la victoria de Maipú," *El Mercurio*, April 4, 1841) is undoubtedly a reference to the works of Cooper.

[8] "Apertura de un curso de historia en el colejio de Santiago," *El Progreso*, April 10, 1843.

[9] *Obras*, XLIX, 111.

sonality who would excite an emotion rather than recall an abstract concept. The "voluntarist" was interested in the strong, willful, titanic personality, who carved his own destiny with his own will and his own power. Whereas neo-classicism had dealt with universal types, the Romantic movement introduced into literature for the first time in centuries the prostitute, the pirate, the thief, and the elements of society that were outside the rational pattern, that were misfits or titans.

Sarmiento's characters betray a Romantic interest. "The most outstanding characters of this positive society," he wrote, "are those who crash head-on against the ordinary laws."[10] He wrote of unusual frontier types, of outlaws, of social outcasts. He wrote of pathfinders, trackers, and hunters. He wrote of bad gauchos and murderers and thieves. While in Chile, he found the miner to be one of the most fascinating subjects for his literary efforts, and the reasons that he gives for this attraction betray a Romantic emotionalism. "There is in the bosom of the American societies an exceptional class of men with peculiar dress, occupation, ideas, and customs. The laws that regulate their lives form a code apart. . . ." The miner had a different morality, a different mentality, and a completely different life. Sarmiento, the former miner, found that this way of existence—the colorful, the exceptional—appealed strongly to his Romantic "livingness."

The Czechoslovakian writer, Vaclav Cerny, has pointed out that one of the most prominent features of the Romantic movement in literature and art is this interest in titanic figures.[11] The titan is a personality who breaks all the bonds of rational and social order. He is the character who ignores all rules, whose will is his yardstick to measure his ethics, his morality, and his aims. Such a character was Shelley's Prometheus, and such a personality was Lord Byron's Don Juan. It was these characters whom Sarmiento sought in contemporary literature and applauded when he found them. "Great virtues and strong and rebellious passions are necessary to

[10] "La nona sangrienta," *El Mercurio*, August 29, 1841.

[11] Vaclav Cerny, *Essai sur le titanisme dans la poésie romantique occidentale entre 1815 et 1850*, Prague, 1935.

move the spectator."[12] For his own solution, for his own struggle against Rosas, he saw as necessary an element other than that of rational reform. "Let us glory, then, in belonging to that race of titans who derive their strength from their defeats, and let us not despair for the future of our homeland."[13]

Another outstanding feature of the Romantic movement was its revolt against the artistic forms imposed by the seventeenth and eighteenth centuries. Neo-classicism had emphasized form to a point where it often overshadowed the importance of content. Form was determined by abstract rational laws, and the "three unities" held absolute sway over Enlightenment drama. As an eighteenth-century Spanish critic saw it, the passions and intuition of the author would have to be limited by his reason (the rules of form) before he could produce great art.

Sarmiento attacked the neo-classic formalism of contemporary Chile. He charged that the overemphasis on form was destroying the life of the art. *What* was said seemed to him to be more important than *how* it was said. Just as the Romantic titan had to destroy the bonds of the rational forms of morality, ethics, and values, so the Romantic writer sought to destroy the confining bonds of artistic form.[14]

Sarmiento's style, more than any other feature of his writing, betrays his Romantic tendency. His style is spontaneous. He wrote rapidly and without reading over the finished work. He was not interested in the confining rules of literary form. From these he wished to be free. He was interested in the ideas that were expressed, and he expressed them in the unrestrained style that was his natural gift. "We seldom read over what we have written, leaving grammatical errors, just so we will not have to correct a sentence."[15] His finished products are often filled with mistakes, and the structure is sometimes sloppy and confused, but these failings are compensated for by a power of expression that could not be

[12] "El mulato—drama de Alejandro Dumas," *El Mercurio*, July 15, 1842.

[13] "Prospecto del Heraldo Arjentino," Santiago, December 23, 1842.

[14] "El rei se divierte—drama de Victor Hugo," *El Progreso*, December 15, 1842.

[15] *Obras*, xxv, 369.

secured without the natural spontaneity and freshness he insisted upon.

Aesthetic perfection for the rational mind of the neo-classic was symmetry, likeness, and balance. The columns of the Greek classical temples were the model for eighteenth-century architecture. They fitted into the ideal rational pattern of architectual form. The Romantic, however, ignored such an ideal form. He depended less on likeness and symmetry, and derived his aesthetic pleasure from contrasts and irregularities that broke the classical patterns, highlighted the individual expressions of the titanic personality and excited the reader's emotions. The Romantic style is marked by its emphasis on contrasts, and Sarmiento relied on this stylistic feature to secure many of his effects. "His words fell upon this excited scene like a stain on a dress suit."[16] He relies here on the technique of contrasting a stain with a clean dress suit in order to gain his effect. "It was a beautiful afternoon in the month of March, beautiful as are wont to be the places and days in which occur the tragedies of great men."[17] Again the author is relying upon the Romantic stylistic technique of contrasts to secure his picture.

Many of Sarmiento's ideas in his writings are also part of the Romantic attitude toward life. His attitude toward nature and the place of the individual are examples. Romanticism made the individual person the center of the universe. Things existed in so far as they could be integrated into the individual being. The relativistic values of the emotionalist and the titan gave an object no reality other than that subjective reality which made the object a function of the person's experience. Nature, for the neo-classic, was something cold and objective. He saw only its rational side, the mathematical precision with which it functioned. He felt that all the secrets of nature could someday be revealed by rational science. Romanticism gave a new meaning to nature, interpreting it in terms of the individual's experience; to the Romantic, nature's importance lay in the meaning it had for the personality.

By making nature and other inanimate parts of life functions of personal experience, Romanticism gave to them a

[16] *Ibid.*, II, 46.

[17] *Ibid.*, I, 28.

new vitality. Zorrilla, the great Spanish Romantic, even described stones by making them vital and alive, by associating them with history and human life. The importance of these stones to Zorrilla was not their objective, scientific, and rational value, but their meaning as watchers of centuries of history, a silent audience to the drama of life. Sarmiento's artistic treatment of nature fits into this aspect of Romantic content. His natural objects are also animated and vitalized. For the writer of the Enlightenment, nature was precise, clear-cut, and defined by science and the human reason. For the Romantic, it was mysterious, vague, and enigmatic. Sarmiento's style in the description of nature reveals these Romantic features. "The more the eye penetrates that uncertain vaporous, indefined horizon, the more it flees, the more it confuses, the more it sinks from contemplation and doubt."[18]

A representative passage of Don Domingo's works during his years in Chile will illustrate the features pointing to a Romantic content in his work. In describing the beginning of an important battle in the War for Independence, he writes: "If the moon had thrown one of its uncertain and pale rays on this army, exhausted by fatigue, seated in line, with the death-dealing arms in hand, one could have made out on its sullen face the bitter smile of victory which was foretold by the insulting pride of the victor and the confidence that accompanies always youth and good fortune.

"A shot is heard at the advance post! It is doubtless a rifle that went off by mistake, or the sentinel shot at a shadow he did not see but claims to have seen in order to distract himself from the monotony of fatigue. Two shots! . . . It is something! A volley! 'To arms!' But too late: defeat was already upon them."[19]

The style in this passage and its attitude toward nature reveals the prominent features of a Romantic writer. The moon does not clarify the scene. It might throw "its uncertain and pale rays," but the scene remains beclouded and mysterious. It is a scene for the emotions—not for the mind. The

[18] María Inés Cárdenas, *op.cit.*, p. 223.

[19] "Los diez i ocho días de Chile, desde la derrota de Cancha-Rayada hasta la victoria de Maipú," *El Mercurio*, April 4, 1841.

principal climax of the story is not achieved by a logical narrative development, but rather by the technique of contrasts. The appearance of victory, the appearance of a chance shot is suddenly contrasted to the reality of a full-scale attack and an immediate defeat.

Sarmiento's thought has always been considered an enigma. On the one hand, he sought to reform the world in which he lived so that it would fit a rational pattern. On the other hand, his art dealt with those elements of life which broke the rational pattern. He sought to escape the stylized forms of rationalistic neo-classicism and find the freedom of spontaneous artistic expression typical of Romanticism. His thought was rational, but his literary techniques emphasized the methods of the Romantic revolt. This seeming contradiction does not present an enigma if we realize that Sarmiento the man, the total man, was facing the historical problem of his age. He was facing the problem created by the contrast between the ideal order proposed by the eighteenth-century Enlightenment, and a world that did not coincide with this order. The intellect of Sarmiento, the reason of the man, analyzed this situation rationally. He saw the contradiction, and he proposed to solve it by reforming the world to fit the ideal order. This was his rational intention. The "livingness" of Sarmiento, on the other hand, was not rational; and it turned to another solution. He sought to solve the problem by abandoning the absolute values and turning to a relativistic concept of life. He sensed reality through its emotions, and he sought to recreate those emotions artistically. He was interested in becoming a titan, and he was interested in writing about titans. This was his vital intent. The distinction between the intention and the intent in the writings of Sarmiento resolves the enigma of his thought.

Chapter 17. The Book: *El Facundo*

IN FEBRUARY 1845 there appeared in *El Progreso* a serial on the life of Friar Félix Aldao written by Domingo Sarmiento. It came directly after the death of the "butcher priest" of Mendoza, and in it was painted the bloodthirsty and dissipated life of the friar caudillo. The vigorous style and sensational subject matter made the serial immediately popular with the reading public of Santiago, and Don Domingo soon published it as a pamphlet. The book itself was short, but in it was the seed of a future work that was destined to become the young writer's masterpiece and claim to literary fame.

The success of this life of Aldao, both in the literary field and as an instrument of propaganda against the caudillo in his own nation, was undoubtedly an important influence upon Sarmiento in causing him to write a more complete companion work. Soon after its appearance, the author began to compile data for a more extensive study of the life of the familiar Juan Facundo Quiroga. On February 22, Sarmiento wrote to Anselmo Rojo, telling him that he expected "to collect data for the biography of Quiroga." He added modestly that it would be "a brilliant work" and that he would send it to the famous *Revue des deux mondes*.[1] He wrote his old friend Antonio Aberastain and asked him to gather testimony from persons who had known Facundo Quiroga in La Rioja, and he sought the information on the caudillo's youth from Don Amaranto Ocampo, notorious for his hatred of the federalists and his lack of objectivity towards them. Countless other friends within and without Argentina were contacted and asked for material to complete the projected biography. But the young author was too impatient to wait for replies to all of his inquiries. He began to write immediately.

[1] Gálvez, p. 150.

Since his arrival in Chile, Don Domingo had written many articles against the Rosas regime. Such titles as "The Conduct of Rosas," "Commentaries on News from Argentina," "The La Plata Question," "The Foreign Policy of Rosas," "What Rosas Is as a Man and as a Governor," "Our Right to Attack Rosas," "The System of Rosas," and many others of political flavor demonstrate clearly the continued and incessant fire that Sarmiento carried on against the dictator of his country. The Bulnes government, and even Don Domingo's friend, Manuel Montt, agreed with the exile's charges and with his ideals; but they did not want him to cause a war between Chile and Argentina. They therefore urged upon him the utmost caution and all the forbearance possible. They forbade him to take his attacks to the limits that he would have wished.

Sarmiento's violent hatred for Rosas and the system that he represented therefore did not have a full outlet during the first years that he spent in Chile. His newspaper articles acted as a safety valve, but there was welling up within him an immense amount of pressure that sought release. The event that seems to have touched off the explosion of this pressure was the arrival of Rosas' special ambassador to Chile, Baldomero García, in Santiago. He and a number of embassy officials arrived in the Chilean capital in April, but they did not present their credentials to President Bulnes until May 8. Meanwhile indignation at the existence in the same city of representatives of his archenemy infuriated Sarmiento. The federalist slogan that the new diplomats carried with them was intolerable to the hot-blooded exile: "Death to the savage unitarists." On April 24th, Don Domingo published an article entitled "The Red Ribbon [federalist badge] at the Argentine Embassy." A few days later a young exile, Elías Bedoya, attacked one of the embassy employees and tore the federalist insignia off him. Bedoya was tried for assault, but Sarmiento was held by the ambassador to be partly responsible for the act. Among his instructions was a request for the extradition of Domingo Sarmiento to Argentina.

The hatred that had been building up within Don Domingo for the past four years suddenly burst out. His life of

Aldao had been successful, and its propaganda had been effective. How would he meet the challenge of García? Answer him with a book! He would immediately publish his life of Facundo Quiroga, and he would use it as a vehicle for his most vehement attack against Rosas and his system of government. A letter dated May first and addressed to the editors of *El Progreso* requested space for the publication of a manuscript, and on May second the first installment of the work appeared in the newspaper. It continued to appear, with the exception of a day here and there, for three months. It was taken up and published by *El Mercurio,* and on July 28th it appeared in book form. The title of the work was: *Civilization and Barbarism, The Life of Juan Facundo Quiroga* (always referred to as *El Facundo*).

Don Domingo might have chosen any number of more important figures than Facundo as a means of telling the history of his country, of examining its problems, or of attacking the government of Rosas. But he chose Facundo with premeditation and foresight. Facundo best served his purpose. "I have tried to explain the Argentine revolution with the biography of Juan Facundo Quiroga because I believe that he sufficiently explains one of the tendencies, one of the two different phases that struggle in the breast of that unusual society."[2] He might have chosen the more important figures of San Martín, Rivadavia, Alvear, Artigas, or even Rosas himself; but they would not have been as effective for his purpose. Facundo had invaded Sarmiento's own province of San Juan. Don Domingo had had personal contact with the caudillo, and many of his friends had had personal experiences with him. His less important life would be easier to handle for the inexperienced writer, and the implied attack upon Rosas through Facundo might be more effective than a direct assault. Those were the *reasons* for the choice of Facundo as the subject.[3] But more important than these was the romantic

[2] D. F. Sarmiento, *Facundo,* "Clásicos argentinos," Buenos Aires, 1940, p. 14. After this the work will be referred to as *Facundo.* There is also a critical edition: *Facundo: edición crítica y documentada. Prólogo de Alberto Palcos.* Universidad Nacional de la Plata, 1938.

[3] José A. Oría, *op.cit.,* p. 59.

attraction that the titanic figure of the caudillo gaucho leader had for the young artist.

The work was written with the utmost rapidity. Sarmiento had probably conceived the project some time before, but the arrival of García and his belligerent attitude towards the Argentine exiles hastened the writing and the publication. As Don Domingo wrote in a letter accompanying the manuscript to the newspaper, "An interest of the moment, to my mind both urgent and troublesome, causes me to trace rapidly a picture that I had hoped to be able to present someday, as finished as possible. I have seen it necessary to heap on the paper whichever of my ideas have come to me, sacrificing all literary pretension to the necessity of ending an evil that might be of transcendent importance for all of us."[4] The biography was finished before it could be completely documented or fully revised. The result was a number of errors in fact and a carelessness of style.[5]

But despite the hurried termination of the work, *El Facundo* became one of the prose masterpieces of the Hispanic world. It was not recognized as such in the Chilean intellectual environment. *El Progreso* and *El Mercurio* published it more as a favor to its author than with any realization of its greatness. Sarmiento gave away a number of copies and tried to insure its infiltration into Argentina for its propaganda value, but its immediate sales were negligible. A copy reached Rosas, and he exclaimed, "This is the best thing that has been written against me; that is the way to attack someone, sir; you will see that no one will defend me so ably."[6] Governor Benavídez received one in San Juan, but he kept it hidden. The literary value of the work was first recognized abroad. The French literary critic, Charles de Mazade, reviewed the book in the *Revue des deux mondes* and proclaimed Sarmiento to be "the only Argentine Romantic who has been able to make for himself a name in Europe. . . . Señor Sarmiento has written and published this work, new and full of attraction, instructive as history, interesting

[4] *Obras*, VI, 149.

[5] Gálvez, pp. 155-157, compiles a complete account of the factual errors of the book.

[6] Gálvez, p. 159.

as a novel, brilliant with images and color."[7] Many years later, another European, this time a Spaniard, Miguel de Unamuno, referring to *El Facundo,* declared that Sarmiento "was the one who in the field of literature reached the greatest degree of genius. He is the American writer of the Spanish language who has until today revealed the most robust and powerful genius and the most fruitful originality."[8]

El Facundo is the culmination and the summary of Sarmiento's thought and artistry during his years of exile in Chile. It contains the conclusions of his analysis of the ills of his nation, and it reveals the Romantic technique already noted in the author. *El Facundo* is primarily an attack against Rosas and his regime, but to effect such an attack, the author must analyze the situation that he is opposing and at least hint at some solutions for it. The causes of the ills that gripped the nation must be studied in the perspective of history: "Only after the French Revolution of 1830 and its inconclusive results did the social sciences take on a new direction and begin to dispel illusions. From then on, we begin to receive books from Europe that demonstrate that Voltaire was not so right, that Rousseau was a sophist, that Mably and Raynal were anarchical, that there are no three powers, no social contract, et cetera. Since then, we have learned something about race, about tendencies, about national habits, about historical antecedents. Tocqueville reveals to us for the first time the secret of North America; Sismondi uncovers for us the emptiness of constitutions; Thierry, Michelet and Guizot reveal the spirit of history; the Revolution of 1830 discovers the deception of the constitutionalism of Benjamin Constant; the Spanish Revolution shows all that is incomplete and backward in our race."[9]

El Facundo became, then, a sociological analysis of the situation in Argentina. It sought the causes, and it sought them in the elements pointed to by the historicist school that Don Domingo had been reading. He sought them in the "national antecedents, the features of the soil, in the popular

[7] *Revue des deux mondes,* October 1, 1846.
[8] Miguel de Unamuno, *Ensayos,* VII, p. 104.
[9] *Facundo,* pp. 191-193.

customs and traditions."[10] Sarmiento's ideal would have been to do a complete sociological study of the factors that were causing the situation in his nation. He would have liked to have been the De Tocqueville of Hispanic America. "The obstinate struggle that tears apart that Republic could then have been explained; the opposing, invincible elements that clash would have been classified. We could have defined the part played by the configuration of the terrain and the habits that it engenders, the part played by the Spanish tradition and the iniquitous plebeian national conscience that the Inquisition and the Spanish absolutism have left, the part played by the opposing ideas that have twisted the political world, the part played by the indigenous barbarity, the part played by the European civilization." But Don Domingo did not feel himself equipped to complete such a conclusive study, so he concentrated his study upon one man, with the hope of being able to generalize the conclusions that he therein reached.[11]

The very title of Sarmiento's principal work of analysis reveals the essential split that he was studying. He called it *Civilization and Barbarism*, and he attempted to analyze the factors that caused what he considered to be the barbarism of his nation, and he sought to find the changes that would replace it with civilization. The concept of "civilization and barbarism" was not a new one for Don Domingo. It appeared earlier in his works. Barbarism he identified with the plains and with the country.[12] It was the heritage of "the spirit of the pastoral, Arab, Tartar force that will destroy the city."[13] Civilization, on the other hand, was identified with the city. It was the heritage of Europe. The problem that Sarmiento felt that his nation was facing had been created by the victory of the plain over the city, the victory of barbarism over civilization.[14]

Arsène Isabelle, a French traveler in Buenos Aires in 1835, had analyzed the situation in Argentina in similar terms: "La campagne, ayant triomphé du parti de la ville."[15] Isabelle

[10] *Ibid.*, p. 4. [11] *Ibid.*, pp. 5, 6. [12] *Ibid.*, p. 161.
[13] *Ibid.*, p. 208. [14] *Ibid.*, p. 380.
[15] Arsène Isabelle, *Voyage à Buenos Ayres et à Porto-Alegre*, Havre, 1835.

was probably not the author of such an idea. It was doubtless a common analysis among the foreign population of Buenos Aires at the time of his visit, and it had probably come to the attention of Sarmiento during the next decade. Domingo de Oro had used similar terms to explain the problem to his nephew in 1842, and he had seen the spirit of the gaucho of the plain as barbarism pitted against the spirit of civilization in Buenos Aires.[16] Sarmiento's readings of Sir Walter Scott had revealed to him the English author's ideas of the barbarism of the gaucho and the connection that he made between this and the "somewhat Oriental character of the Spaniard."[17]

Whatever the origin of the concept, the conflict between civilization and barbarism became the essential problem that Don Domingo was studying. His intention was primarily to analyze the elements, the causes of each, in order to find a means for the triumph of the city and civilization. Sarmiento divided his study into two parts. First, he studied the environment and the effects that it had upon the problem. Second, he studied the human elements, the actors within the drama.[18] Although the plan was carried out only in the most rudimentary form, it followed the general pattern that was later to become the basis of sociological analysis. Sarmiento did this some time before Taine had systematized the method, and he did it coincidentally with the innovations of Buckle and without previous knowledge of the Englishman's works. The originality of the method rather than the penetration of the study offers its most important claim to fame.

The two factors that appear to be more important in the analysis of Argentine barbarism in *El Facundo* are the material and the moral. Sarmiento paints a picture of the general geographic aspect of the Republic, describing its vast and almost unpopulated plains, the small, isolated hamlets separated by great distances and unconnected by the necessary communications. He paints the primitive life and lack of material ease within this environment, and he shows the

[16] *Obras*, III, 99-100.

[17] "Essay on Chivalry" in *The Miscellaneous Prose Works of Sir Walter Scott*, Edinburgh, 1841, I, p. 529.

[18] *Facundo*, p. 17.

complete destruction of what economic life there had been as a result of the devastations of the gaucho hordes of the caudillo leaders.[19] To add to these geographic and material causes of barbarism, Sarmiento analyzes the features of the Spanish character inherited by the people of his nation. "I not only see . . . Facundo in relation to the physiognomy of the grandiosely savage nature that prevails throughout the immense extension of the Argentine Republic, but Facundo as a true expression of a way of being of a people, of its interests and instincts."[20] The Spanish heritage was to blame for much of the material backwardness, for the inability to navigate the rivers profitably, for the inability to accept a democratic and nomocratic government.[21]

It was a simple task for Sarmiento to analyze the causes of barbarism. But for Sarmiento the reformer, it was necessary also to know how to replace the actual barbaric state with a civilized one. What would be the causes of civilization? He could not study the factors that contributed to it, for the civilization he aspired to did not exist. Since he had discarded *a priori* reasoning, this presented an interesting problem in method. Don Domingo resolved the difficulty by a negative analysis. He studied what was missing in the barbaric society. He reasoned that those factors missing in barbarism would be the factors that would cause civilization. The naïve character of this method illustrates well the rudimentary stage at which the sociology of Sarmiento found itself at this time.

Sarmiento studied the province of La Rioja, the native province of Facundo. He asked what it did not have that it had previously had during the early years of independence. The answers were obvious, and he was thus able to compile a list of the "causes of civilization": school, religion, houses, money, doctors, lawyers, and judges. The lack of lawyers and judges indicated a lack of law. Law was therefore a cause of civilization. A lack of money and houses indicated a material backwardness. Material improvement would consequently be a cause of civilization. A lack of schools and religion indicated a faulty moral and intellectual training. Education and morality would be causes of civilization. The population of

[19] *Ibid.*, p. 318. [20] *Ibid.*, p. 15. [21] *Ibid.*, pp. 6, 380.

the province had greatly decreased; an increased population would therefore indicate the road to civilization.[22]

Sarmiento devoted a great deal of his book to the discussion of the manifestation of the causes of barbarism in the human being. He described the human types that were found on the Pampa. The gaucho was of course the generic word for the man of the Argentine interior, and Sarmiento found in him not only features of the Spanish-Arabic heritage, but also features resulting from the material environment. "The life of the country has developed in the gaucho physical faculties, but it has left him without any intellectual ones."[23] Don Domingo painted such gaucho types as the pathfinder, the outlaw, the minstrel, and the tracker. He showed their character, their lives, their customs, and their habits. This part of *El Facundo* is one of the best existent pictures of the nineteenth-century Argentine inhabitant of the interior.

In the last two sections of the book, Sarmiento personified the elements of the barbaric civilization that he had been examining in two central characters. The first of these was the local caudillo leader, Juan Facundo Quiroga; and the second of these was the national caudillo leader, Juan Manuel de Rosas. Each of these was painted as the product of a gaucho society, as the symbol of the triumph of the country over the city. Each was seen as the effect of material and racial causes. Rosas was no more than the product of "the *cattle ranch* on which he spent his entire life and the *Inquisition*, in whose tradition he was educated":[24] environment and Spanish heritage. The sections on Facundo and Rosas were but the stories, often inaccurate, of the lives and politics of these two men; but they were used to concentrate what had been until then generalized studies and bring the results of the studies to bear as attacks on the author's hated political enemies.

Sarmiento's thought had already hit upon a number of methods for solving the problem posed by the dichotomy of civilization and barbarism. In his life he had turned to the solutions of education as an instrument for civilization. In his writings he had advocated immigration and economic and

[22] *Ibid.*, pp. 115-116.

[23] *Ibid.*, p. 57.

[24] *Ibid.*, p. 384.

political reform for this same purpose. In the way of solutions, he added very little in *El Facundo*. He again advocated European immigration. This promised to be "the principal element of order and morality."[25] In the economic realm, he favored free commerce[26] and the improvement of internal waterways in order to foster interprovincial trade and communications.[27]

The principal solution was, however, a political one. *El Facundo* was first and foremost an attack against the Rosas regime, and the most important lesson that Sarmiento drew from his studies was the necessity of overthrowing the dictator-tyrant of his nation. "The evil that must be removed is that which is born of a government that trembles in the presence of thinking and illustrious men and that in order to exist must exile or kill them. It is born of a system that concentrates all will and all action in *one single man* and in which good cannot be done, because this one man does not think of it, is unable to do it, or does not want to do it. . . . '*Every man for himself*; the whip and the hangman for all': this is the summary of the life and government of all enslaved peoples."[28] This is the system that is the target for the main attack of Sarmiento's masterpiece. The government of Rosas and his symbolic lieutenant, Facundo, was the worst expression of the barbarism of his country. It is this element which had to be destroyed. "Terrible shadow of Facundo, I call upon you to shake off the bloody dust that covers your ashes and rise up to explain to us the secret life and the internal convulsions that tear apart the entrails of a noble people. Facundo is not dead; he is alive in the popular traditions, in the politics and in the revolutions of Argentina; he is alive in Rosas his successor, his complement."[29]

Although *El Facundo* is a sociological study of the factors at work to create the existent barbarism in Argentina and the remedies necessary to replace it with a civilized society, the book is primarily a propaganda piece. It is primarily an attack against the Rosas regime, and it makes its sociological inductions as well as every stylistic device at the service of the

[25] *Ibid.*, p. 450. [26] *Ibid.*, p. 188. [27] *Ibid.*, p. 319.
[28] *Ibid.*, pp. 287-288. [29] *Ibid.*, p. 3.

author fulfill this primary task. As such, the book was effective. It was a powerful instrument of propaganda against the Rosas government at the time, and it has been an important factor in discrediting the dictator in the eyes of posterity. Historians have proved many of the facts and charges to be unfounded, but the basic impression of the tyrannical and barbaric features of the Rosas caudillocracy has remained in the mind of the world until today.

As in Sarmiento's other works at this time, the intent of *El Facundo* seemed to be in contradiction to the author's intention. Although it was intended to be a sociological analysis of the historical situation of Argentina in the time of Rosas, and although it intended to advocate the replacement of the irrational barbarism by a rationally civilized society, its intent betrayed the same Romantic leanings that have been noted in the author's lesser works.

The same dichotomy had appeared in the life of Aldao. Sarmiento had started with the intention of analyzing the same "struggle between the barbarism of the interior and the civilization of Buenos Aires, between arbitrariness and constitutional guarantees."[30] He had started with the intention of using the book for an attack against Aldao and the system for which he stood. But the actual intent of the work betrays an unwilling sympathy on the part of the author for the titanic figure of the "butcher priest." He describes one of Aldao's battles: "In the pursuit that followed the Battle of Maipú, a Spanish grenadier of gigantic stature broke through hundreds of his enemies who surrounded him on all sides. Every blow of his terrible sword threw a mutilated corpse to the ground. An empty circle around him showed well the terror that he inspired, and all of the victors who had tried to pass him had paid with their life for their temerity. The valiant Lavalle followed him at a short distance, and by his own confession, he felt his valor weaken every time the heat of pursuit caused him to approach too closely the grenadier. Lieutenant Aldao reached him, saw the terrible Spaniard, threw himself upon him, and when his companions expected to see him fall split through the middle, they saw him stop

[30] *Obras,* VII, 254.

the tremendous blow of the sword that the grenadier aimed at him, and immediately bury the same sword up to the hilt and turn it several times in the soldier's heart. A thousand *vivas* were the immediate reward for his courageous thrust."[31] Don Domingo's "livingness" could not but be attracted to the heroism of this person he was intending to attack.

Sarmiento's most understanding biographer, Alberto Palcos, calls *El Facundo* "the biography that conquered the biographer."[32] Vaclav Cerny, in his discussion of titanism in European Romantic poetry, discusses the titanic heroes of many of the writers of the first part of the nineteenth century. He finds the perfect titan to be one that is strong and indomitable physically, whose passions are great and overbearing, and whose will dominates his reason and his entire being.[33] He describes Count Cenci of Shelley's famous drama and Don Juan of Lord Byron. But none of the figures of European Romanticism compares with the titanic personality of Facundo, the "Tiger of the Plains." It is little wonder that he should appeal to the Romantic young exile. It is little wonder that, though he intended to attack and destroy him in the eyes of his contemporaries and of posterity, Sarmiento was often captivated by him and showed a hidden admiration for his titanic qualities. "Quiroga possessed the natural qualities that made the student at Brienne, the genius of France, and the obscure mameluke that fought the French at the Pyramids, the viceroy of Egypt."[34] "All of the public life of Quiroga seems to me summed up in these facts. I see in them the great man, the man of genius in spite of himself, without knowing it himself, the Caesar, the Tamerlaine, the Mohammed. He was born thus, and cannot help it; he will ascend the social ladder to command, to dominate. . . ."[35]

Sarmiento's interest in such Romantic types as the gaucho outlaw, the pathfinder, the tracker, and the troubadour reveals more than a purely sociological interest in social phenomena. There is a Romantic interest. These are the social misfits in

[31] *Obras*, VII, 244.

[32] Palcos, *Sarmiento, op.cit.*, p. 61; see also Palcos, *El Facundo*, Buenos Aires, 1945.

[33] Vaclav Cerny, *op.cit.* [34] *Facundo*, p. 131. [35] *Ibid.*, p. 145.

the society that he is painting. These are the highly individual types that fit into no social pattern. They are almost identical to the characters who served as subjects for the North American writer, James Fenimore Cooper, and their unusual, colorful, and individualistic aspects are as important for Sarmiento as their interest as sociological symptoms or examples: "The bad gaucho is a type peculiar to certain localities—a sort of outlaw, squatter, or misanthrope. He is Cooper's Hawkeye or trapper with all of his knowledge of the wilderness and all of his aversion for the white settlements, but lacking his natural morality and his friendly relations with the Indians. He is called the bad gaucho, but that epithet carries with it no opprobrium. The law has been on his trail for many years. His name is feared and mentioned with bated breath, but without hatred, almost with respect. He is a mysterious character. A plainsman with a hideout in the cactus wastes, he lives on partridges and armadillos. If he should take it into his head to regale himself on a delicacy, he lassos a cow, throws it alone, kills it, cuts out his favorite morsel, the tongue, and abandons the rest of the carcass to the scavenger birds."[36]

This is a definitely Romantic type of mysterious misfit who is in conflict with the social norms and laws, but who is looked upon "almost with respect." Sarmiento's interest in such characters and their lives makes him one of the first formal writers, and one of the most important writers, of that phase of Argentine literature which has revealed itself to be most genuine and most original, the so-called gaucho tradition. This tradition has later been recognized as the core of a national literature and has manifested itself in José Hernández' great poem *Martin Fierro* and many later novels and plays.[37]

The style of *El Facundo* identifies it more than any other one feature with the Romantic school of literature. It is a style whose beauty puts it at times in the category of prose-poetry. Sometimes it has a strong epic character in its descriptions; sometimes it demonstrates a marked lyricism. But throughout there are certain features that demonstrate its Romantic content. The spontaneous character of this "work

[36] *Anthology*, pp. 128-129.

[37] Palcos, *El Facundo*, 36ff.

done in a hurry"[38] shows an emphasis on content and disinterest in form that has already been noted in the writings of Don Domingo. His interest in typically Romantic scenes, such as the following, show the true content of the work:

"I once witnessed a rural scene worthy of a primitive age antedating the institution of the priesthood. I was in the Sierra de San Luis, staying with an *estanciero* whose favorite occupations were praying and gambling. He had built a chapel in which, as there was no priest and no mass had been celebrated for years, he said a rosary himself on Sunday afternoons. The picture was Homeric. The sun was declining in the west and the flocks were returning to the fold, filling the air with their confused bleatings. The owner of the house—a man of sixty with a noble face whose pure European blood was proclaimed by the whiteness of his skin, his blue eyes, and broad forehead—conducted service, while a dozen women and a few youths made the responses. The youths' horses, not yet completely broken, were picketed near the chapel door. When the rosary was ended, a fervent offertory was made. I have never heard a voice of deeper feeling, a purer fervor, a firmer faith, or a more beautiful or fitting prayer than his. He besought God to give rain to the fields, fertility to the cattle, peace to the Republic, security to wayfarers. . . . I am very emotionally inclined and on that occasion I wept until I sobbed. Religious feeling, as though for the first time, deeply moved my soul. I had never witnessed a more religious scene. I felt that in that man's presence I was back in the time of Abraham, of God, and of God-revealing nature. The voice of that simple, guileless old man made my every fiber tingle and penetrated to my very marrow."[38] Such stylistic features as the emotional effect of the service, the build-up to a Romantic climax, and the primitive simplicity of the scene, combined with the subject matter of an unusual and colorful occurrence, mark this passage of *El Facundo* as one of highly Romantic content and style.

Américo Castro has compared the style of Sarmiento and that of the great Romantic artist, Francisco Goya.[39] He has

[38] *Anthology*, p. 114.

[39] Américo Castro, "En torno al 'Facundo' de Sarmiento," *Sur*, Buenos Aires, August 1938, p. 34.

shown the similarity of their interest as demonstrated by the subjects treated in Goya's "Caprichos" and in Sarmiento's *El Facundo.* In the notebooks of Don Domingo are to be found a number of freehand sketches that he made while he was writing. They are rough and talentless from a technical point of view, but they are interesting because of the subjects that they treat and because of the interests of the author that they demonstrate. One of these, which he calls "El Ahorcado" (The Hanged Man), can be compared in a striking manner, from the point of view of content, to the famous Goya etching entitled "Tampoco." Goya paints the horror of the French Revolution and the Napoleonic invasions. He paints the disorder, chaos, and suffering that they incurred. The very grimness of the subjects attracts his Romantic "livingness." Like Goya, Sarmiento also paints horror in all of its negative greatness, and many of the scenes in *El Facundo* would have been excellent subject matter for the "Caprichos." Facundo Quiroga is introduced to the reader in a scene such as this. Its beauty and its greatness as one of the finest passages of Sarmiento's prose warrants its quotation at length:

"Between the cities of San Luis and San Juan lies a broad, arid desert known as the Crossing. This waste region presents a bleak and mournful aspect and travelers from the east never pass the last waterhole or reservoir without filling up their canteens. A strange incident once occurred along this Crossing. One of the stabbings which are so frequent among our gauchos had compelled its perpetrator to make a hasty departure from San Luis in order to escape the long arm of the law, and to make his way on foot across the desert, carrying his horse's trappings over his shoulder. Two of his comrades were to overtake him as soon as they had succeeded in stealing horses for all three of them.

"The dangers that confronted the gaucho in the desert at that particular time were not only hunger and thirst; a man-eating jaguar, whose predilection for human flesh had already procured him no less than eight victims, was then on the prowl for any chance traveler. In such regions, where man and beast dispute the control over nature with each other, it occasionally happens that it is the man who falls under the bloody claw of the beast, which thus acquires a taste for human flesh and turns into a man-eater. The district judge nearest to the scene of the jaguar's depredation then summons all able-bodied males for the hunt and under his leadership the man-eater is pursued and rarely escapes the death sentence pronounced upon him.

"When our gaucho refugee had traveled something like twenty-four miles, the distant roar of a jaguar made his flesh creep. The cry of a jaguar is like that of a boar, but shriller, more prolonged and strident, and even when one is safe from attack it produces an involuntary shudder, as if one's very flesh had a foretaste of death.

"Some minutes later, the roar sounded more distinct and nearer. The jaguar had already taken up the scent and the only possible place of refuge to be seen was a single small algarrobo tree far ahead. The gaucho had to press on and finally to break into a run as the roars became more frequent —each more distinct and vibrant than the last.

"Finally, throwing his accoutrements down by the roadside, the gaucho raced for the tree he had sighted, fortunately quite a tall one, and, despite its slender trunk, he was able to climb to the top and balance himself precariously, half hidden by the branches, as the tree swayed back and forth. From that point of vantage, he was able to survey the scene that was taking place on the road. The jaguar bounded toward him, sniffing at the ground and roaring more frequently as he realized that he was closing in on his prey. However, he overran the point where the gaucho had left the road, and lost the trail. Furiously he circled about until he caught sight of the horse's accoutrements, which he tore to shreds, scattering them in the air with one blow of his paw. At length he picked up the trail again, beside himself with rage because of the delay. Then, finding the right direction, he glanced up and at last caught sight of his intended victim, swaying back and forth in a little algarrobo tree like a bird perched on the tip of a fragile reed.

"Instantly the jaguar stopped roaring. He leaped forward and in a twinkling his powerful forepaws were clawing the slender trunk two yards from the ground. The convulsive trembling which he communicated to the tree worked on the nerves of the insecurely placed gaucho. In vain the beast attempted to reach him by jumping. Then he circled the tree —his inflamed, bloodthirsty eyes measuring its height—and at length, roaring with rage, lay down on the ground, switching his tail ceaselessly from side to side, his eyes fixed on his prey and his dry mouth half open. For two mortal hours this horrible scene lasted. The gaucho's uncomfortable position and the terrifying and irresistible fascination that the jaguar's unblinking, fiery gaze exercised over him, held the man's eyes and had begun to weaken his powers of resistance. He realized that the moment was fast approaching when his flagging body would fall into the animal's capacious maw, but suddenly the distant sound of galloping hoofs gave him hope of rescue."[40]

It is an easy matter to picture a Goya etching of Facundo treed by a jaguar, as in this scene. The setting, the style, the subject matter are all Romantic and Goyesque. Other scenes in *El Facundo,* such as those in which the caudillo runs one of his officers through with a lance or in which Facundo is murdered by Rosas' outlaw henchmen, would also have been typical subject matter for the Spanish Romantic artist's etchings and paintings.

El Facundo has come to be known as one of the masterpieces of Hispanic American literature. Miguel de Unamuno has acclaimed it as one of the great works of the Hispanic world of the nineteenth century. It has been used as an authoritative and accurate picture of the period,[41] and it has been translated into many languages. It has gone through thirty-four editions in Spanish, and is perhaps the best-known work of nineteenth-century Latin-American literature. As a sociological study it is of little value to us today. Its technique is rudimentary and often naïve, but as a forerunner of the later "social sciences" and their methods, created independently by a young Argentine exile in Santiago de Chile, it is an interesting historical document. As a force in the history of Argentina and in the overthrow of the dictator Rosas, it is of equal interest. Its propaganda value and effect were un-

[40] *Anthology,* pp. 153-155.

[41] Diego Barros Arana, "Historiadores argentinos," *Revista Chilena,* 1876.

doubtedly important in the creation of opposition to the dictator at that time and in the discrediting of the dictator for posterity.

But more important than these intentional aspects of *El Facundo* is its content. It was a great Romantic work. The titanic figures of Facundo Quiroga, Rosas, and their gauchos are literary characters to compare with many of the great titans of Romanticism. The color and the descriptions, the subject matter and the scenes all rank the book as one of the great works of the Romantic era in Hispanic America. *El Facundo* demonstrates within it two of the principal approaches to life of the nineteenth century, two of the most important solutions. Its intention is the way of reform; its intent is the way of the titan.

Chapter 18. The Exile of an Exile

BETWEEN 1841 and 1845, Domingo Sarmiento's ideas and personality changed from a predominantly negative to a predominantly positive character. This evolution is evident in the development of his thought, but it can also be detected in the very style of his writings. In his first newspaper article in Chile,[1] Don Domingo's style was fundamentally a negative one. His adjectives were mostly of negative value: cold, sordid, unfortunate, monotonous, and horrible. The nouns were of the same type: butchery, slave, and horrors. The verbs tended to express actions of negative value: to flee, to emigrate, and not to be. This was the period in which Sarmiento had formed no positive program of life. By 1842, his ideas were beginning to take form. An analysis of just the verbs in an article at the end of that year demonstrates the new positive character of

[1] "12 de febrero de 1817," *El Mercurio*, February 11, 1841.

his style. To be, to smile, to sit down, to dispute, to come, to adorn, to contribute, to form, to mix, to inhabit, to establish[2] —these are without an exception verbs of positive value, demonstrating a less negative element in the psychology of the writer. By 1845, the style had become a forceful and definitely positive one. *El Facundo* or any of the articles of that year demonstrated the terse, clear-cut style that was to make Sarmiento famous as a writer.

During this period of intellectual maturation, Don Domingo interested himself in all phases of life. He did not limit himself to the economic, literary, and political problems. His articles include such subjects as: roads, slaughter houses, markets, the merchant marine, copper mining, the recovery of land from the sea, kinds of wood, streets and sanitation, new theaters, and intuition as a means of knowing the truth. He entered into every phase of Chilean life, and he studied every contemporary problem of his world. His ideas and world-view became positive, and he applied them in a very positive manner to every phase of life that faced him.

His own personal life was no less active and no less impassionate than his intellectual and public endeavors. His affairs with the young ladies of Santiago were doubtless many and complicated. His love life was definitely fickle and inconstant. In 1843 he saw a great deal of the three Pastora sisters, Carmen, Emilia and Helena. They were attractive, and he enjoyed especially dancing with the beautiful Helena: "Helena was the best-looking at the dance. What a mouth! What a body! How she could waltz!"[3] "The bed? I cannot even answer that." One night he was dancing with Emilia. He whispered something in her ear that she did not like, and "now we do not speak." "My relations with the Pastoras has cooled a great deal, a very great deal. I have not seen them for twenty days."[4] Ten days later, however, he was tired of them. "I went to see them last night. We have changed roles; now I despise them and they adore me." The fickle young man has changed

[2] "Fisiología del Paquete," *El Progreso,* November 14, 1842.
[3] Sarmiento to Quiroga Rosas, November 14, 1841, No. 11.
[4] *Ibid.*

his mind. "Do not worry about this matter because it means nothing to me now."[5]

At the same time there seems to have been a love affair in Don Domingo's life with far more serious elements and more far-reaching results. Benita Martínez Pastoriza, a young Argentine girl from San Juan, had married an elderly Chilean, Don Domingo Castro y Calvo. Sarmiento had known Castro y Calvo many years back in Copiapó and perhaps even before that in Mendoza. The Chilean had been a friend of Don José Clemente, and Sarmiento had carried a letter to him on his visits to Chile. Castro y Calvo was old and sick in 1844, and his wife, Benita, was only twenty-two years old,[6] charming, distinguished. She had become quite an admirer of the young exiled writer and teacher. There is no definite evidence that there was an actual love affair between them, but it is known that Don Domingo frequented the Castro y Calvo home and saw a great deal of Benita. The old man had despaired of having a child by his young wife, due to his weakened condition and his advanced age, but in 1844 Benita became pregnant. Most authors have assumed that it was Sarmiento rather than Castro y Calvo who was responsible.[7] In January 1845 Don Domingo wrote to his friend José Posse of the "pregnancy of Señora Martínez. You can imagine how such an occurrence would fill with happiness a married couple with so few hopes of succession."[8] It is known that a son was born in April 1845, and baptized with the name of Domingo Fidel.[9] After Castro y Calvo's death, Sarmiento married Benita and adopted Domingo, giving him his own name of Sarmiento. These facts imply Don Domingo's parentage of the young boy who was destined to become his most cherished relation, the later Dominguito or Little Domingo. It is interesting to note that Dominguito was born in the same month as Sarmiento's great literary masterpiece, *El Facundo.*

In the latter part of 1845, Don Domingo's public as well as

[5] Sarmiento to Quiroga Rosas, November 24, 1843, No. 12.

[6] Gálvez, p. 141.

[7] *Ibid.*, p. 142.

[8] Sarmiento to José Posse, San Felipe, January 29, 1845, in archives of Museo Histórico Sarmiento.

[9] Sarmiento to José Posse, San Felipe, January 29, 1845, in archives of Museo Histórico Sarmiento.

private life in Chile was becoming increasingly complex and complicated. His great variety of activities, the belligerent character of his ideas, and his impassioned personality were creating a web of opposition and misunderstanding around his person. He was being attacked from every side; he was attacking in all directions. And the attacks on both ends were becoming more and more bitter. Don Pedro Godoy, brother of Sarmiento's bitter enemy, Domingo Santiago Godoy, took over the editorship of the opposition paper, *El Siglo,* and the most violent attacks were initiated against the Argentine exile. "They called me a Cuyan horse, a coward, and I know not what else. Instigated by López, I went to the printing office of *El Siglo* and demanded the offender. They gave me no explanation, so I spit in his face. After he had overcome his fright, he tried to do something to avenge the affront. He tried to grasp me; he grasped hold of my hair; I freed myself of him and overcame him. I expected him to retaliate with something more serious, an affair of gentlemen; but an half hour later Santiago was abuzz (they were dancing with pleasure!) from some lie invented from fantasy. It seems that they had given me a severe drubbing with their kicks, knocking out my eyes. Two weeks later the entire Republic was filled with the story that they had cut me open. Aconcagua toasted the event. The priests preached it."[10] Sarmiento was deeply hurt by the attacks against him as a foreigner. He felt that he had served Chile loyally. He was even more depressed by the solidarity of the opposition of Chilean public opinion to his case.

Simultaneous with the Chilean attacks upon him in the press was the arrival of Rosas' envoy, Baldomero García. "He is not a guest of the nation; he is the representative of an enemy of Chile; he is furthermore the representative of a government that has enchained the press, that shows off an immense power. . . . He is the representative of a terrorist government that has symbolized its terror with a red ribbon, which, contrary to diplomatic usage, its agent in Chile wears."[11] The violent attacks of Sarmiento upon García and

[10] *Ibid.*

[11] "Nuestro derecho de atacar a Rosas," *El Progreso,* April 28, 1845.

his mission only hastened and intensified the Ambassador's attempts to have the young exile silenced or extradited. Minister Montt began to worry about the effect of this battle of words upon the relations between Chile and Argentina. He was aware of Sarmiento's depression as a result of the violent attacks against him in the periodical press, and he was aware of the fact that Don Domingo was contemplating a trip to Bolivia to escape the heated atmosphere of the Santiago battles. From these facts Montt conceived a solution to his dilemma. He would take his loyal supporter out of the atmosphere of these continual and bitter attacks, and he would also remove a source of dangerous irritation in Argentine-Chilean relations.

On October 17, Montt called Sarmiento to his office, and proposed to him a government-sponsored trip to Europe and North America for the study of the state of elementary education in Europe and of the methods of colonization in Algiers. The ideas met with Don Domingo's most hearty approval. As he wrote to his friend Juan María Gutiérrez in Montevideo, "I am going to Europe, I am going! . . . I took this resolution after a conference with Montt last night. It is the only sure road that remains open to me; they offer me facilities for this purpose and no other. Montt is a good friend. He made me feel this last night."[12] Sarmiento's project was a trip of one year, but it was destined to last much longer.

On October 28, 1845, the sailing packet *Enriqueta* put out from Valparaíso en route to Montevideo. Aboard the ship was Domingo Sarmiento. He had written in his last article in the Chilean press, "Five years of work in the daily press of Chile, five newspapers, six hundred editorial articles, various university papers and works for the instruction of the people, and several books, ephemeral but full of the true love of liberty and civilization, must have left, if not for anyone else, at least for myself (that is enough) the conscience of the solidity of my convictions."[13] Don Domingo's ideas had ripened and matured during the past few years. His positive attitude towards life had been conceived. In the years to fol-

[12] Palcos, *El Facundo, op.cit.*, p. 114.
[13] *Ibid.*, p. 30.

low, his thought would evolve as his self-education progressed; but the foundations would remain. He was setting out on a great voyage through the world yet unknown to him, and this trip was to confirm many of his viewpoints. The basis for his future life struggle had been conceived. The rest of his days would be devoted more to action, to the realization of his ends, than to thought. As the ship sailed out through the breakwater of Valparaíso harbor, Don Domingo looked back upon the high and rugged mountains of Chile. The mountains seemed to symbolize his character, his strength, his passion, and his hopes. Now, he turned his gaze to the limitless Pacific, and new horizons were opened to his life.

BOOK IV
The Confirmation

Chapter 19. Outward Bound

As THE sailing ship *Enriqueta* pointed slowly out into the calm Pacific, the storm created by one of its passengers continued to rage in Santiago. Colonel Godoy's newspaper, *El Siglo,* had not relaxed its attacks. "Death to the Cuyans! Death to the Cuyan, Sarmiento! Death to Minister Montt!"[1] *El Progreso* editorialized: "We know that Señor Sarmiento is leaving not without a little bitterness at seeing himself reviled by a portion of the contemporary press instead of being praised and extolled as would be just."[2]

But Sarmiento was quickly forgetting his bitter struggles in Chile. The prospects for the future were too bright and too interesting for him to remain involved in his past. He was setting out for a trip that would broaden his entire view of the world and its problems. He had formed a philosophy of life and had located his goal, but now he was to have the chance to test his beliefs in a broader field and check them with a wider experience. He took with him his ideas, and he confirmed them with what he saw throughout the important nations of Western civilization.

Don Domingo was the last to leave the deck after departing from the harbor of Valparaíso. He watched the distant land for a while, and then he turned his gaze seaward and remained lost in his thoughts. The weather was calm, and the sailing ship moved slowly in the almost windless ocean. Sarmiento had hoped this first leg of the journey would be rapid, but alternatingly bad winds and becalmed seas made that a vain wish. Days passed without event, and the man whose life had been set at such a feverish pitch until now was forced to learn to relax and to be patient. "On the sea, and above all on sailing ships, one learns to resign oneself to destiny and wait calmly."[3] Such an attitude was a new thing for Sarmiento.

[1] Palcos, *Sarmiento, op.cit.,* p. 63. [2] *El Progreso,* October 11, 1845.

[3] *Viajes por Europa, Africa y América,* 3 volumes, "La Cultura Argentina": Buenos Aires, 1922, I, p. 37. After this, the work will be referred to as *Viajes.*

The days on shipboard were "days without emotion." Don Domingo would stand by the railing and look out on the calm sea. He would sometimes follow with his gaze the flight of the sea birds. The porpoises and flying fish would catch his attention, and once as he climbed to the bridge to observe the navigation of the ship he saw four huge whales close alongside. Then, one day, he heard the terrifying cry of "Man overboard!" and he rushed to the after-deck to see what had happened. A sailor had fallen into the sea. He made frantic efforts to hold his body above water and to signal to his companions in order that they might locate his position and return to save him. Don Domingo looked upon this tragic scene with the helpless eyes of a landsman faced with the power of the sea. He saw a great wave engulf the sailor, and "the black abyss claimed its victim." For days this incident played upon the active imagination of the young Romantic. "The plaintive whistling of the wind lost for me its mysterious melody, for it seemed to bring to my eyes confused and distant moans, like the sobs of a man, like shouts for help; at night the Southern Cross, Venus, Jupiter, Saturn and Mars no longer detained my idle glance, for I was directing it furtively along the wide trail left by the stern of the ship, in the hopes of discovering a black form, moving to attract our attention."[4]

A few days out of Valparaíso a southwesterly wind carried the ship outside the Juan Fernández Islands. There are three islands in this group. Más a Tierra was the first that the ship passed. It is the closest to the mainland, lying only some 360 nautical miles from Valparaíso. The next, and smallest, is Santa Clara. And the last is Más a Fuera (Further Away). Más a Tierra was the island made famous by the shipwreck of Alexander Selkirk, and it later became the setting for the famous Defoe novel, *Robinson Crusoe*. It was off Más a Fuera, however, that the *Enriqueta* became becalmed.[5] Around and around it drifted, seemingly unable to get away. Sarmiento wrote a letter to his friend Demetrio Peña: "Tired of having

[4] *Viajes*, I, 39.

[5] For a description of these islands, see Edward Albes, "The Island of Juan Fernández," *Bulletin of the Pan American Union*, Washington, 1914, XXXIX, p. 201.

the island always near us in some direction, according to where the wind was pleased to have us awaken each morning, we accepted with enthusiasm the idea of the pilot that we make an excursion to the island and spend a day on land."[6] An eight-hour boat trip brought Sarmiento and a small group of passengers and sailors ashore. Don Domingo was sure that this was the island of the Selkirk and Crusoe stories, and his imagination undoubtedly fashioned the events to fit into the pattern left in his mind by the Defoe novel. Not far from shore the explorers saw the light of a fire, but to their alarm it quickly went out. The boat approached the surf. The pistols brought for hunting wild dogs were loaded. A ration of rum was distributed for the courage of all present, and the group landed for a night of very strange adventure, a night enjoyed and undoubtedly exaggerated by the Romantic spirit of Domingo Sarmiento.

In his letter to Peña, Don Domingo described the scene: "Late at night we finally arrived at the foot of the mountain. The pilot, straightening up to his full height, uttered a shrill and prolonged shout to which only the hundred echoes of the mountain, one after another, answered. This was frightening, and even more so was the silence, pregnant with uncertainty, that followed when the last sound of the decrescendo expired in the distance. After a second and a third shout, we thought that we distinguished another voice that answered the call, and it will not be hard for you to imagine how the pleasure of meeting men made us forget our past fears. Immediately the pilot, in spite of speaking Spanish, addressed in English someone who was approaching. An Englishman at sea knows no other language—as if his was the command of the sea as in other times the Romans had command of the land; and as if to justify this pretension, they answered us in English from the shore."[7] The boat's pilot ordered it about to seek a better point to land. "Oh, no, señor. For God's sake . . . ," came the voice from the land, "don't go away. . . . It has been so long since we have talked with anyone." The group from the *Enriqueta* landed on the beach, sure that their hopes for adventure had been fulfilled. They found that the inhabitants

[6] *Viajes,* I, 40.

[7] *Ibid.,* pp. 41-42.

of the island were North Americans. One was a Kentuckian named Williams. They lived in the style of Robinson Crusoe; their houses, their weapons, their lives, improvised from what they had salvaged and from what they could find on the island. But they differed from the famous novelistic character in that they did not want to return; they did not want to leave their island. Some were undoubtedly fugitives who dared not return to civilization. Perhaps they were mutineers, pirates, or outlaws. Don Domingo never found out, but he greatly enjoyed his comparison of these men to their literary prototype, Robinson Crusoe.

Sarmiento observed their life and the facilities that they had made use of to improvise not only their necessities but also their luxuries. He talked with Williams in the broken English he had learned in Chile. And late that night they retired to sleep in the adventurous atmosphere of shipwrecked sailors. Don Domingo and a Bolivian diplomat, Solares, slept on a pile of two hundred and fifty goat skins spread out to make a comfortable bed.

Early the next morning the islanders and their visitors set out on an expedition to hunt the elusive mountain goat, Más a Fuera's most important product. With the first rays of the morning sun, they began to climb the mountain in quest of their quarry. They spotted a goat on the peak, and Williams explained that this peak was where the lookout was posted to warn the others of the approach of hunters or any other possible enemy. The group divided in two parts and set out to flank their prey. Don Domingo lost his way in the labyrinth of the rocks and chasms of the mountain. He wandered over the difficult terrain, only to orientate himself by the shouts and the shots of Williams. The Kentuckian surprised the Sanjuanino with his "infallible marksmanship" and his "feet of a Swiss," as he pursued his prey across the rocks and felled him with his faultless aim.

Don Domingo returned to the camp to study the life of these strange islanders. He learned how some had reached there. Two had prices on their heads. Some had been shipwrecked. One was merely determined to remain in this idyllic life, holding no envy for the "civilized life" of the rest of the world. Sarmiento studied the simple economy of the island. He saw the devices by which the islanders obtained their food, clothing, and even housing. He saw how simple and uncomplicated and natural was their life. He had often dreamed of such an existence. He had dreamed of it when he read Rousseau and again when he read Defoe. Here it was before him. He now thought of how this little world contrasted with the complicated life of the outer world. The thought of remaining there crossed his mind, but there was something in his being that was more attracted by the struggles and incongruities in life than by the peace and rationality of his intellectual ideal. He listened intrigued by the stories of Williams' adventures and to the late news from the United States. But when the boat prepared to leave, he had no idea of not being on it. He and his companions carved at the foot of a rock: "ad perpetuam rei memoriam,"[8]

HUELIN.
SOLARES.
SARMIENTO.
1845.

The rest of the voyage was a slow and uneventful one. It was late spring as the *Enriqueta* passed through the Straits of Magellan. The polar lights created a startling setting for Sarmiento's view of the southernmost tip of the continent. "With the setting of the sun, the light continues to travel around the horizon, without losing any of its pale splendor, until it announces the arrival of the rising sun."[9] An Antarctic current was about to drag them from their route, but sufficient wind allowed them to keep their course, and they sailed on their slow and uneventful journey northward to the River Plate.

Late in December 1845 the *Enriqueta* reached the muddy river that separates Montevideo from Buenos Aires. The clouds and the barometer forecast the coming of a *pampero*.[10]

[8] *Ibid.*, p. 55. [9] *Ibid.*, p. 38.

[10] A *pampero* is a sudden and violent storm that comes up with very little warning in the River Plate region. It comes in from the direction of the Pampa, hence its name. In the age of the sailing ship, this was one of the

The muddy waters were stirred by the threatening weather, and their reddish tint was more noticeable than usual. Sarmiento stood by the side of the ship's captain, who looked down at the waters and commented, half seriously and half in jest, "We are in the river," and pointing to the reddened waves, "that is made up of the blood of those whose throats are cut in Buenos Aires."[11] His comment pierced Don Domingo, and he looked down "silently, sad, pensive, humiliated by my homeland, as a son is ashamed of insults to his father."[12]

The *pampero* broke rapidly. The horizon in all directions became filled with storm-laden clouds. The lightning and thunder struck at the water of the muddy river. The electric storm had for Sarmiento "magic charms. . . . There was illumination in the skies that night. Our fragile ship had its masts dressed with St. Elmo's fire, and the rapid succession of solar light and dark night dazzled the eyes that were fixed on some point in the clouds hoping to surprise the sudden brilliant light." Don Domingo and a few of his hardy companions remained on deck late that night to view the magnificent spectacle; when they finally retired exhausted to their bunks, they were thrown to the deck by the striking of a nearby bolt of lightning. The little *Enriqueta* weathered the storm and steered her course on across the mouth of the river to Montevideo.[13]

The city of Montevideo was at this time besieged by the armies of Rosas under the command of General Oribe. Alexander Dumas called it the "New Troy," and Sarmiento wrote from the besieged city, speaking of it in the same terms. "I will tell you something of the internal life of this Troy, which is not, in faith, besieged by Greeks, although let it be said in honor of the contenders that many Achilles and Priams abound here. Heroism wanders through the streets and fields, as they say of *l'esprit* in Paris."[14] The city was defended by troops of all nationalities. There were Uruguayans, Argentines, Brazilians, English, Italians, Germans, Basques, and Negroes. Garibaldi, who was later to make his

great navigational hazards of the area. The history of the River Plate is spotted with tragedies that resulted from the *pampero*.

[11] *Viajes*, I, 57. [12] *Ibid.* [13] *Ibid.*, pp. 60-61.

[14] *Ibid.*, pp. 78-79.

place in history as the Italian national hero, was leading a troop of his countrymen.

Sarmiento first sighted the famous hill that gave the city its name. He next saw the groups of ships anchored in the protected harbor, and then, as the *Enriqueta* made its way by the defensive chain across the mouth of the channel, Don Domingo began to note the buildings, the dress, and the people along the docks and on the straight streets leading up from the port. He saw the white "morisco" architecture blended with the latest English-style designs. "To the emotions of the trip there succeeded those of the port, the scenery, the docks, the multitude of Latin sails with which the Italians have animated the movement of the roadstead, the Hill crowned with cannon, the far-off points occupied by the enemy, that darken the landscape in the distance and give to the spectacle a serious and menacing element."[15] The *Enriqueta* made fast at the docks, and Don Domingo went ashore in the New Troy.

Sarmiento had been preceded by *El Facundo*, so his name and his views were known by his compatriots in the besieged city. "When I arrived here," he wrote to Manuel Montt, "I realized the full importance of my trip to Europe. . . . *El Facundo* had given me much popularity here, even among important foreigners. Ousley and Deffandis, I understand, sent it to their governments."[16] The book served as the best possible letter of introduction to the acquaintance and confidence of many of the leading Argentine *émigrés* in the city. Young Bartolomé Mitre, who had come from his exile in Bolivia to take part in the battle for Montevideo, had been publishing *El Facundo* in serial form in his newspaper, *El Nacional*, since October 3rd. Sarmiento met the young soldier and publisher and was favorably impressed by him. He described his future friend as a "poet by vocation; gaucho of the pampa by the punishment imposed upon his intellectual instincts; artilleryman, no doubt because he was seeking the shortest route of return to his homeland; of facile spirit, always even character, and an excellent friend."[17]

[15] *Ibid.*, p. 62.

[16] Sarmiento to Manuel Montt, Montevideo, January 24, 1846.

[17] *Viajes*, I, 103.

But the two most important figures whom Sarmiento met during his two-month stay in the New Troy were Esteban Echeverría and Florencio Varela. Echeverría was the leader of the new generation of thinkers and writers who had formed the Asociación de Mayo as an expression of their ideas and in opposition to Rosas. He was a Romantic and a utopian reformer. Varela, on the other hand, represented the old unitarist group of Rivadavía's time. He believed in the imposition of the ideas and forms of the French Revolution upon the River Platenese reality. He saw no contradiction between the two. Where Echeverría was a Romantic in spirit and in his literary expression, Varela was a classicist. Where Echeverría saw the need of changing the factors "causing" the "barbarity" of his nation, Varela thought that a new way of life could be imposed, as Sarmiento later put it, "by decree." It is clear that Sarmiento was more sympathetic with Echeverría. Conversely, it is more than likely that the young poet should feel and express a definite admiration for *El Facundo*, a book whose content revealed definite Romantic tendencies.

Partly due to the affinity of their beliefs, partly because of Echeverría's praise of his book, Sarmiento took a great liking for the poet. "I found Echeverría as gentle a young man as he is an ardent and impassioned poet. . . . A soul so elevated for the contemplation of nature and the refractions of beauty, Echeverría is neither a soldier nor a newspaperman; he suffers physically and morally, and he waits in vain for affairs to reach a conclusion that would permit him to return to his homeland and apply his beautiful theories of liberty and justice."[18] Echeverría read to his young friend one of his latest unpublished poems, and Don Domingo was struck with admiration for the extremely Romantic work. They spent many hours together reading poetry, discussing political and social theories, and these visits remained one of the pleasant memories in Sarmiento's later life.

The meeting with Florencio Varela was not so happy. Varela was critical of *El Facundo*. He criticized its hurried style and loose form; he did not like its Romantic exaggerations. Sar-

[18] *Ibid.*, p. 100.

miento requested that excerpts from both *El Facundo* and *La vida de Aldao* be published in Varela's newspaper, *El comercio del plata*; but his request was turned down on the excuse that there was not enough space available.[19] The historian, Adolfo Saldías, was present at the first interview between Sarmiento and Varela, and he recorded for posterity its results. Don Domingo offered the possibility of a federalist solution to the political problems of Argentina. Varela countered with extreme praise of the unitarist constitution of 1826. Sarmiento lauded some Romantic works, but Varela came back with his violent criticism of *El Facundo*. Don Domingo muttered sarcastically under his breath, "That just proves your ability to judge."[20]

Sarmiento's description of besieged Montevideo in a letter to Vicente Fidel López (published in his *Viajes*) is perhaps the best existing description of the city at that time. He did not see it as a unitarist stronghold besieged by the federalists. He looked upon the gaucho leader of the defending forces, General Fructuoso Rivera, as being as "uncivilized" as the attacking general, Oribe.[21] Both were representative of the worst elements of the Argentine political scene. For the essence of the struggle, Sarmiento looked elsewhere. Montevideo, to him, was representative of the forces of civilization. The besieging armies represented "the reproduction of the old Spanish tradition, the immobility, the pride of the Arab."[22] Montevideo was the new. It was inhabited by persons of all nationalities. The English dominated the commerce. The Germans, English, and French executed the manual arts. The Basques supplied the untrained labor. Sarmiento studied the commerce of the city, and discovered its virility. This proved to him the progressive tendencies of the city. He analyzed the figures of foreign immigration, and the order in which he named the various nationalities, irrespective of their relative numbers, is an interesting revelation of his values. The English came first; the French, second; last were the Spaniards and Italians. Sarmiento was applying his theories of the causes of barbarism and of civilization to a new scene,

[19] Gálvez, p. 166. [20] *Ibid.* [21] Rojas, p. 241.
[22] *Viajes*, I, 73.

and the changes and progress of Montevideo seemed to confirm his ideas. He saw a city that had been transformed from a sleepy, non-productive town to a city of stores and commerce and free trade. He saw a city changed from tyranny and government control to internal freedom.[23] "In a word, there is in Buenos Aires only Spain; in Montevideo there is cosmopolitan North America."[24] What had made it thus? Immigration. Economic freedom. Education. Montevideo was to fulfill its destiny as the haven for defeated ideas and the cradle for new movements.

After two months, Don Domingo left Montevideo for Río de Janeiro. He had a last visit with Echeverría. And at eight o'clock on the morning of his departure, Varela came to say goodby. They remained talking until four in the afternoon, and as the "last of the Mohicans of the unitarists" departed, he exclaimed, "Now that I have heard you talk, I am so sorry that I did not have more discussions with you while you were here."[25] Neither Echeverría nor Varela was ever again to return to the beloved homeland. Echeverría died within a few years, and Varela was murdered by one of Rosas' agents before the tyrant was finally overthrown. Sarmiento always looked back upon these two men with great respect and as symbols of important trends in the history of his nation.

Don Domingo's trip to Río de Janeiro was uneventful, but his entrance into that beautiful harbor was an aesthetic experience that he was never to forget. His descriptions of this tropical metropolis and his reactions to it represent some of the best pages of his literary work and some of the most poetic of his prose. On February 20th he wrote to his friend Miguel Pinero. "It is hardly six in the morning, my dear friend, and I am already prostrate, exhausted, as our constitution remains when we have adventured beyond the limits permitted us to enjoy. The sun is already there, on the edge of the horizon, scrutinizing the most hidden recesses of this open crater in whose interior is founded Río de Janeiro. The sun frightens me here, and I can see how tropical peoples have adored it. I seem to see in it, when it appears on the

[23] *Ibid.*, pp. 69-70. [24] *Ibid.*, p. 69.
[25] Belín Sarmiento, *Sarmiento anecdótico, op.cit.*, p. 52.

celestial borders, that figure of Michaelangelo that presides over the last judgment, implacable in its gaze that dominates the earth, athletic in its form that reveals its incomparable power. It is a tyrant on whose face one dares not turn a furtive glance; its rays seem present at all times, sharp as arrows, as penetrating as a rain of needles.

"After twenty days of residence in this city I remain immobile, my arms outstretched, my fibres without elasticity, oppressed by the lethargic influence. Hardly does the dawn announce itself before the heat of the sun, still absent, puts in motion the vegetation, itself turbulent, as well as the swarms of golden insects that inhabit it. In the tropics, nature lives in a perennial orgy. Life stirs everywhere, except in man, who humbles himself, perhaps to keep an unknown equilibrium among the forces of production. The man who is born in these latitudes resists its instantaneous action; but, in the long run, he is seen in his habits, in his children, to weaken and lose the original energy of the race. . . .

"Today, finally, one of those sensations that excite the effervescence of the spirit and overcome the decay of the limbs brings my pen to my hand. When the sun raises its colossal disk on the horizon, he who sleeps in the separate and dark retreat of the interior of the buildings knows it. Sleeping, one feels the air move in lukewarm waves that push on one after another, the blood itch, the pores dilate in order to be converted into fountains from which flow seas; and to the crazy ideas that upset the imagination there succeed strange movements, like those of lights that are going out, like phantoms that flee or evaporate, like lights that accumulate on the limbs and obstruct movement, with a seeming drag of the fibres that appears each time greater, until the sensation of strength has been replaced by languor, the death in life of the body and the enervation of the spirit. This is awakening in the tropics."[26]

But the tropical climate did not deprive Sarmiento of all of his usual energy. His two months in Río were eventful and fruitful. He was amazed by the scenic beauty of the harbor and by the modern aspect of the city. He became acquainted with a German naturalist by the name of Konig, and together

[26] *Viajes*, I, 104-105.

they visited the famous Brazilian botanical garden. Konig guided him among the tropical plants and explained them to him. He told Sarmiento of the amazing history of the coffee plant, introduced only fifty years before and now the principal product of the country. The fertile mind of Don Domingo was struck by this fact, and he began to think about the possibilities of introducing new plants and new crops to enrich his own nation.

Sarmiento brought with him to Brazil letters of introduction to many interesting persons. He met Doctor Sigaud, the emperor's physician, who put him in contact with Doctor Chavannes, the promoter of the new silk industry in the country. He had letters to Mr. Hamilton, the English chargé d'affaires, the *chevalier* Saint Georges, who held a similar post with the French government. One night at a formal dinner in Hamilton's home Domingo met the former unitarist commander of Montevideo, General Fructuoso Rivera. Sarmiento had heard much about him, and had already formed a low opinion of the man, but this was the first time that he met him face to face. He was stupefied by the gaucho's unkempt aspect, his lack of good taste, and his complete ignorance of table manners. The soldier's egotism was surprising to the more cultured egotist, Don Domingo. Many things were discussed, and in every conversation Rivera would enter, introducing his remarks with a "Well, I . . ." At one time he informed the gathering that the Brazilian Emperor, Don Pedro, had offered him the hand of the present queen of Portugal, María de la Gloria. The table was shocked at the statement. Sarmiento, ashamed of his countryman, and feeling himself a man of the world with his learning and his knowledge of languages, leaned towards Saint Georges and whispered, "C'est un bavard." This seemed to him to create a bond between himself and the French diplomat.[27] Sarmiento wrote sarcastically to his newly found friend, Bartolomé Mitre, in Montevideo, "Met Don Frutos (Don Fruit)! It is a shame that men of such stature still have a future in our nation."[28]

[27] *Ibid.*, pp. 123-124.

[28] Letter from Sarmiento to Mitre, Río de Janeiro, February 19, 1846. Museo Mitre, *Sarmiento-Mitre, Correspondencia, 1846-1868*. Buenos Aires, 1911, p. 8.

What seemed to be Sarmiento's most exciting new acquaintance in Río was the Romantic poet, José Mármol. "I found a jewel in Río de Janeiro, Mármol, the young poet . . ."[29] As was the case with Echeverría, the attraction that the two young men found for each other arose from the likeness of their art and of their thought. As the young poet read Domingo his yet unpublished *El Peregrino,* Sarmiento saw in it much of the Romantic content found in his own works. "Exuberance of life, an imagination that overflows and sends waterfalls of fantasy one after the other, beauty of detail, and the soul folding back upon itself"—these were the elements that Don Domingo found in Mármol's writings, and although he was loath to apply to them the term Romantic, it is clearly to that literary movement that such features belonged. But like Sarmiento, Mármol believed that his poetry had a social purpose. His poems attacked the Rosas regime. His famous novel, *Amalia,* published in 1851, was to be a bitter blow to it. He "believed sincerely in the influence of poetry on the redemption of nations."[30] Don Domingo could appreciate his poetic productions, and he could agree with his thought. The two men found at the time a true community of interests and a real friendship.

Sarmiento enjoyed his stay in Río. He thought of staying longer.[31] The mystery and color of the tropics appealed to his Romantic spirit. "There are in tropical nature melodies that are imperceptible to our ears, but that move the fibres of the aborigines. They hear the vegetation whisper as it unfolds, and in the palm trees where we only hear the murmurs of the wind, the Africans distinguish melodious songs, rhythms that appear like theirs."[32] Near the beginning of April, Sarmiento left Río and finally departed for the first time from the New World. The Romantic poetry of Mármol and Echeverría still echoed in his mind. The strange tropical nation of Brazil was still a mystery to him. The people seemed primitive and uncivilized. Their culture was backward but colorful and

[29] *Viajes,* I, 124.

[30] Adolfo Mitre, "Introduction" to José Mármol's *Amalia,* Buenos Aires, 1944, I, ix-x.

[31] Letter from Sarmiento to Mitre, *op.cit.*

[32] *Viajes,* I, 109.

beautiful. They were trying to progress and reform their political system, but he considered this impossible at their stage of development. "I only understand the republic as the last expression of human intelligence."[33]

Sarmiento sailed for Le Havre on the "beautiful packet," *La Rose*. Aboard were men of many nationalities, forty-five passengers, including Spaniards, Frenchmen, Brazilians, and other South Americans. Don Domingo found a new cosmos. He wanted to cut himself off from all memories of the New World and throw himself wholeheartedly into "that world of strangers in which he had to live in the future."[34] This was a new world, and he would choose his friends and the life that he would live in it. He remained aloof for a while, quietly surveying the passengers, and then he chose the ones that would be his friends and carefully approached them. One was a German youth whom he had met in Río. Another was Commander Massin, a French corvette captain on his way back from Tahiti to France, to whom Sarmiento had been introduced by the *chevalier* Saint Georges. The third was a pale young man with an aquiline nose and a black beard whom he had noticed among the passengers on the ship. His name was Tandonnet, and he and Don Domingo turned out to be close friends. "I had, then, my world, my friends, and my circle in that trio so arduously formed."[35]

Together they talked and lived during the long transoceanic voyage. Massin had been in Tahiti for some time, and he had been a member of the French expedition that had tried to establish a colony on the Straits of Magellan on what was now Chilean territory. Sarmiento found the young naval officer's experiences of great interest. Tandonnet, he soon learned, was an admirer of Rosas, a man who had had dealings with both the tyrant and his famous daughter, Manuelita. He was also a disciple of the socialist, Fourier. He had with him many of the French thinker's books, and he was versed in his ideas. Sarmiento spent long hours convincing him of his errors in regard to Rosas, and Tandonnet devoted himself to winning another disciple for Fourier. Sarmiento thought the economic theories the product of the mind of a mad man, and

[33] *Ibid.*, p. 120. [34] *Ibid.*, p. 133. [35] *Ibid.*, p. 135.

he blamed these doctrines for the fact that his new friend was "indifferent to the havoc done by the stupid despotism in Buenos Aires and a friend and admirer of the kindheartedness of Don Juan Manuel [Rosas]."[36]

The coasts of France were finally discernible on the distant horizon. Domingo was approaching the land about which he had read so much. Here was the nation that represented to him the civilization that he opposed to his own land's barbarism. "My heart jumped as we approached land."[37] This was his first sight of a new continent.

Chapter 20. A Broken Idol: France

On May 6, 1846, *La Rose* entered the harbor of Le Havre. It made its way through the basins to the docks, tied up alongside, and lowered its gangplank. Immediately, the ship was swarming with a mob of elegantly dressed hotel employees. "They assaulted us, they shouted at us, they surrounded us like flies, they insinuated themselves in our hands and in our pockets to deposit a card with the name of the hotels that sent them. It was impossible to speak to them, injure them, frighten them with the hands, flee or hide."[1] This was the first impression for Don Domingo of the France of which he had dreamed. This was the civilization for which he had fought. As he wrote in a letter to Carlos Tejedor, "Ah, Europe! Strange mixture of greatness and abjection, of knowledge and stupidity at the same time, sublime and filthy receptacle of all that elevates man and all that holds him degraded, kings and lackeys, monuments and pesthouses, opulence and savage life."[2] Le Havre was old and dirty, and

[36] *Ibid.*, p. 145. [37] *Ibid.*

[1] *Viajes*, I, 146. [2] *Ibid.*

Sarmiento found it materialistic and commercial. He hurried to move on—to penetrate farther into this land of his ideals.

He left the seaport on the historic riverboat, *Normandie,* which had once carried the ashes of Napoleon to Paris. He was accompanied by his friend Tandonnet, who was to act as his guide in this new land. They sat on the deck of the ship and watched the scenery pass by. Hamlets, chapels, woods, and towns passed in rapid succession. A band of wandering minstrels animated the passing landscape with their music. It was early in May, and the beginnings of spring were giving to the vegetation the most vital colors and "new charms to that bewitched land." Hardly had one point on the landscape been located before another was reached. The young traveler experienced a sincere and deep thrill from the scenic beauty, and his Romantic senses were intrigued by the historic significance of all that he passed. He seemed to see unfold before his gaze the historic events of the Middle Ages. Like Sir Walter Scott, this period intrigued him, and he took great delight in recalling to mind the medieval legends of the area through which he was traveling.[3]

In Rouen Sarmiento was more favorably impressed than in Le Havre, but again he was not struck by the modern aspects of the town. Rather it was the old, historic, Romantic elements that held his attention. He found himself in the midst of the most noble Gothic monuments of any city in Europe. "The centuries have stopped over this city; and from the fifteenth on there is nothing of importance that is modern."[4] The living history, the richness of detail, the vitality of the architecture of the Rouen Cathedral fascinated the young man. He explored the city, and he climbed to the tower of the cathedral. Then, aboard the river boat once more, he continued his trip along the Seine to Paris.

Four days after his arrival in France Sarmiento reached Paris. Paris was at this time the cultural capital of Western civilization. It was the home of the arts and of politics. It was the cradle of the new democratic and liberal political forms. It was the birthplace of the most important artistic movements of the first half of the nineteenth century. During his

[3] *Ibid.*, p. 151.

[4] *Ibid.*, p. 155.

first weeks in the city, Sarmiento enjoyed the simple life of a curious wanderer. He was intrigued by the French verb, "flâner," for it seemed to express so well his own way of acting during this time. "The *flâneur* seeks, looks, examines, goes ahead, goes quietly, makes turns, walks, and finally arrives . . . at times at the banks of the Seine; he also pursues something, but he himself does not know what it is. *Flâner* is an art that only Parisians possess in all of its details; nevertheless, the foreigner begins his rough apprenticeship in the charmed life of Paris in order to try his clumsy fingers on that instrument from which only those outstanding artists draw unending harmonies."[5] Sarmiento wandered from place to place, from sight to sight. He visited the exposition of 1846 at the Louvre. He was thrilled by the two thousand four hundred objects of art that occupied a league and a half in the museum. He spent days observing them and enjoying them.

Don Domingo and Tandonnet visited the eating places of the city. The Frenchman wanted to show his South American friend restaurants of all types and all qualities. The carefully kept expense book in which Sarmiento recorded every cent of expense during his trip testifies to the uneven quality of his eating places.[6] They went to the *Freres* [*sic*] *Provencaux*, where they dined for sixty francs. Lunch at the Café de Paris cost them thirty francs. But the next day they dined for ten francs and lunched for three. Finally they reached the low point of their gastronomical tour when they ate at the Hôtel Anglais. Here they were served raw meat "of suspicious origin," hard beans, "infamous beer," all for a franc.[7]

As he came to know Paris and feel at home in it, Don Domingo's mind began to turn to more serious pursuits. He was here on a mission, and he devoted much of his time to the study of the system of primary education. These activities brought him into contact "with savants, employees, and

[5] *Ibid.*, pp. 164-165.

[6] The original of this expense book is in the Museo Histórico Sarmiento. I found, upon a careful examination, that it was doubly interesting in a study of Sarmiento. Its entries and dates reveal an accurate itinerary of the events of the travels, and the care with which the account is kept belies the usual assumption that Don Domingo was haphazard and careless in attending to the details in life. Even the price of a streetcar is included in the list.

[7] *Viajes*, I, 171.

professional men"[8] in the field of education, and he recorded his learnings from these sources for the benefit of the Chilean government. For his own education, he studied not only the art of the Louvre and the customs of the Parisians, but he also studied sericulture in the Bergeries de Senart under the direction of M. Camille Beauvais. He would travel to the suburb of Mainville and attend the classes of the famous botanist. He hoped that he could someday introduce the silk industry in Mendoza, San Juan, or Chile. He had seen its success in Brazil, and he looked forward to the day when it would bring a new prosperity to his own nation.

Among the friends that he made during these studies was Julio Belín, the son of a reputable printer in Paris. This young man was intrigued by Don Domingo's stories of the opportunities of the New World, and he was persuaded to go to Chile and install a press there. Two years later Belín traveled to South America, where he became Sarmiento's partner in business and later married his illegitimate daughter, Faustina.

Near Mainville, on the banks of the Seine, there lived one of the great figures of the history of Argentina. General José de San Martín had been living in Grand Bourg for many years after his voluntary withdrawal from the center of the historical scene of Hispanic America a quarter of a century earlier. Sarmiento was a lifelong admirer of the "Liberator." He had glorified him in his initial article in the Chilean press —the article that had brought him fame in the world of letters in that country—and he had written favorably of him many times since and was to continue to write admiringly of "the first and noblest of the exiles" for the rest of his days. On May 24th he visited the home of the national hero, carrying with him letters of introduction from many of San Martín's friends and fellow soldiers. The "Liberator" did not like to receive curious visitors, but the laudatory letter of General Las Heras prevailed upon him to talk with the young visitor.

"I passed with him sublime moments that will be forever

[8] *Ibid.*, p. 195.

engraved upon my spirit. Together for a whole day, touching with skill upon certain chords in his being, memories recalled by chance, a portrait of Bolívar that I saw by hap. And then, the conversation taking on life, I saw him transform himself, and I saw disappear before my eyes the *campagnard* of Grandbourg and materialize before me the young general, that appears over the peaks of the Andes, throwing inquisitive glances at the new horizon opened to his glory. His small eyes clouded by old age, opened for a moment, and they revealed to me those dominating, bright eyes of which all that knew him spoke; his back, curved by years, had straightened up, his chest expanded as that of a soldier of line of that day; his head had been thrown back. . . . Then the small room in which we were had expanded, converted into a country, into a nation; the Spaniards were there, the general headquarters here, such and such a city over there; a certain farm, witness of a scene, revealed its stables, its houses, its trees all around us. . . ."[9] San Martín recreated for the active imagination of Sarmiento the scenes of the Wars for Independence, the battles of the revolution; he told him of the famous but still mysterious interview between himself and Bolívar in Guayaquil, the interview that resulted in the retirement of San Martín from the stage of Hispanic American history. Sarmiento remembered the details of this account and made use of them at a later date.

Don Domingo was disillusioned by his hero's praises of Rosas. Only a few days before his first visit, San Martín had written to the dictator in Buenos Aires, congratulating him on his defense of his country against the intervention of the French and English and calling the event "of as great importance as our emancipation from Spain."[10] Sarmiento attributed this sympathy for Rosas to San Martín's old age. Domingo's illusions based on a transformation to the hero's youth and the scenes of his glory, were suddenly destroyed by this note of the present. "An illusion! A moment later all that phantasmagoria had disappeared; San Martín was a man and

[9] *Ibid.*, pp. 190-191.

[10] San Martín to Rosas, May 10, 1846, in Archivo del Museo San Martín in Buenos Aires.

an old man, with earthly weaknesses, with sicknesses of the spirit acquired from old age."[11]

Sarmiento visited San Martín a second time; this time there were others present at the interview, the hero's daughter, his two granddaughters, and an Argentine, Manuel Guerrico. The day was rainy. San Martín's daughter was sewing. The writer Pastor S. Obligado describes the scene, but he probably received his information secondhand from Guerrico. The "Liberator" saw the government of Rosas as the necessary remedy to the disorder that followed the War of Independence. "The majority is convinced," he asserted, "of the necessity of a strong government with a firm hand, in order that the humiliating scenes of 1820 shall not recur, and so that it is impossible for any battalion commander to revolt and have shot the governor of the State."[12] Rosas symbolized for San Martín both order and independence for Argentina, and he seemed the only means of reaching these ends. On this matter, San Martín and Sarmiento could never agree. San Martín's beliefs were based upon the spirit of nationalism. The most important consideration for him was the independence of his nation. Sarmiento's beliefs were based upon the faith in liberty for all peoples: personal liberty, individual rights, prosperity, and culture. A government of free men was most important for him.

After Don Domingo's departure, San Martín wrote to his old friend, General Las Heras, in Chile. He referred to the recent visit of his young countryman, and their differences of opinion regarding Rosas did not seem to have cooled his admiration for Sarmiento any more than they had cooled Sarmiento's admiration for the old patriot. He referred to the young writer and pedagogue as a man of intelligence and ability, and prophesied for him an important and fruitful role in the history of his nation.[13]

[11] *Viajes*, I, 191.

[12] Gálvez, p. 173.

[13] José de San Martín to General Gregorio de Las Heras, Grand Bourg, September 26, 1846; original to be found in National Archives in Buenos Aires in miscellaneous files; photostatic copy in possession of author. General San Martín says of Sarmiento: "la aplicación e instrucción de este apreciado compatriota lo hacen acredor a toda consideración, pudiendo asegurarse desde ahora tendrá un provenir distinguido."

As a means of entering the life of Paris, Sarmiento carried with him two keys. The first was his official letter of introduction from the Chilean government. This gave him access to the facilities necessary for completing his mission of pedagogical study. His second key was his *Facundo.* In this he had placed his greatest faith. But the famous book helped him little upon his arrival in France. He complained that Spanish was a dead language in the civilized world, and that no person of note had read his book.[14] He took it to the important reviews for comment, but he was put off by them week after week until it became apparent to him that his work had never even been read.

Finally Sarmiento took his manuscript to the editor of the famous *Revue des deux mondes.* M. Buloz was director of the Comic Opera as well as the *Revue.* He put off the young South American author as had the others. Don Domingo was told to come back the following Thursday. He returned timidly. "It has not yet been read; come back next Thursday." The weeks passed, and finally the manuscript was inspected. This time, when Sarmiento arrived he was met with a different greeting. The book was well liked; it was highly praised by M. Buloz. It would be reviewed favorably by the *Revue,* and the editor "begged humbly" that Sarmiento would undertake the writing of a series of articles on America. Sarmiento was thrilled by the new turn of events, but unfortunately the review of the book would not be out for two months, and this would be too late for it to be of use to him in Paris.

Meanwhile, Don Domingo was entering into the life of Paris in other manners. Commander Massin, his companion on shipboard, had spoken of him to the officials of the Ministry of the Navy. Sarmiento was painfully aware of the misinterpretation of the River Plate situation that was so widespread among the policymakers of Paris. He asked for an interview in order to present his ideas on the subject. M. Dessage, head of the political section of the Ministry of the Navy,

[14] This is not strictly accurate. Spanish was not a widely known language, but most of the contemporary writers and artists were acquainted with it and were finding the art of the Spanish Golden Age of great interest.

received him first, but little was gained from this visit. Dessage had a very simple key to the situation. He made a parallel between the elements in the Argentine and those in the French political scene. Rosas he compared to Louis Philippe. *La Mazorca* was comparable to the Moderates. The gauchos were to him nothing more than the *petite proprieté*. The unitarists were the national opposition. He compared Paz, Varela, and other leaders to Thiers, Rollin, and Barrot. Sarmiento listened in amazement to the ideas of Dessage, but there seemed no way to counter such an obviously simple explanation. His next interview was with the Minister of the Navy, Mackau. Mackau received him amiably, listened attentively, and met each one of Sarmiento's statements with a nod of the head. When the interview was over, Don Domingo realized that the official had understood nothing. "Baron Mackau has a collossal reputation in Paris for being an animal on two feet."[15]

Sarmiento's next important visit was with the leader of the parliamentary opposition, Guizot. Guizot had little interest in the River Plate situation. He saw no importance in it. He had an attitude similar to that of the King when Louis Philippe commented, "N'ayez pas peur, mes pantalons garance ne verront jamais cette rivière de la Plata."[16] The political leaders of France seemed to have no interest in or judgment about the moral implications of the South American struggle: which side was right and which side was wrong.

Sarmiento went to see the government leader, Thiers, and here he was received by a more attentive listener. In the garden of the famous orator's house on the Rue Neuve Saint-Georges, Domingo spent the afternoon explaining his view of the Rosas government and its significance. Thiers listened with great interest, and often took notes. When his visitor departed, he invited him to the parliamentary debate the next day. It was to be one of the famous duels of oratory between Guizot and Thiers. The entire policy of the government was to be attacked and defended. Don Domingo went with a spirit of curiosity and interest. He noticed present such notable figures as the Spanish ambassador, Martínez de la

[15] *Viajes*, I, 176. [16] Rojas, p. 267.

Rosa, the journalist, Émile Girardin, and the poet, Lamartine. He listened excitedly to the debates, but it soon became evident to him that the oratory was empty, that it was a duel of wits and not of ideas, that Thiers' interest in his explanation of the River Plate situation was not a genuine concern for the truth in that matter but rather an interest in gaining one more instrument for his battle of words in the parliament.

France, which had been Sarmiento's former idol, began to crumble around him. The so-called rational order of nomocratic government for which he had admired that nation seemed empty and formal. Its officials were "beasts with two legs"; its leaders were orators without ideas. France was still colorful and intriguing. It was still the cultural center of the world. It continued to be a source of admiration for Sarmiento. But it was no longer the ideal after which he wished to pattern his own world. It too needed to be reformed. The causes for its troubles had to be discovered and changed. Before leaving France, Sarmiento wrote out a prescription for its cure: electoral and parliamentary reform, the reorganization of the national guard, the revision of the September Laws, and many others.[17] He had to seek further in his journeys before he found a replacement for France as his ideal. "Sarmiento left France 'de-frenchified.' "[18]

Chapter 21. The Cradle of Barbarism: Spain and Africa

IN LATE September 1846, Domingo Sarmiento crossed the border from France into Spain. This was the nation that he had attacked so violently for so many years. "This *Aspaña* [jokingly pronouncing the word for Spain as the natives of

[17] *Viajes*, I, 187. [18] Rojas, p. 265.

that country did] that has displeased me so much is finally in the amphitheatre, under my hand." He had arrived in the cradle of that way of life that he had termed "barbaric," and he meant to continue his indictment. His eyes in Spain were governed by no objectivity. "I came to Spain with the holy aim of verbally putting it on trial to give foundation to an accusation. As an already well-known prosecutor I must do this before the tribunal of opinion in America."[1] He was here to find the sources of barbarism just as he had sought the origins of civilization in France.

Spain at this time was near the nadir of her history. Though nominally under the rule of the Bourbon monarchy, the nation was torn by civil war and controlled by military caudillos. There was little difference between the political system of General Narváez in Spain and Rosas in Argentina. There was little difference between the political battle of personalities in Hispanic America and the struggle raging beneath the unconcerned eye of the Crown. The royal family had reached a new low of degeneracy. Queen Isabel's loose morality was in sharp contrast with the behavior of her distinguished namesake at the end of the fifteenth century. Her lack of consideration for her impotent husband and her nymphomaniac affairs with courtiers and guardsmen of the palace were common knowledge. The battle for control of Spain was being waged by the diplomatic representatives of France and England, and the nation that had once ruled half the world had fallen to near the stature of a colony. Economically and materially, Spain was backward. Her roads were poor; her industry was almost nonexistent. Her literature and art were basically synthetic, imitating the forms and the latest styles of France. Goya with his magnificent paintings of Spanish suffering, and Larra with his agonized criticisms of his nation's backwardness, had been the only exceptions to this cultural decadence in the early nineteenth century. It was an easy task for Sarmiento to confirm his opinions of Spain. It was an easy job to find in the Iberian Peninsula and the adjacent African continent the cradle of the barbarism inherited by the Hispanic peoples of South America.

[1] *Viajes,* II, 7 and 8.

But Sarmiento approached the problem of Spain in a way reminiscent of his attack on Facundo. He analyzed its backwardness and barbarity. He sought the "causes" for its troubles. But his Romantic "livingness" could not but be attracted by the irrationality, the color, the very primitive aspects of the country. As in *El Facundo,* he was captivated by the object of his attacks. He traveled across the country in a coach pulled by a team of mules. He went first to Madrid. He visited Burgos, Aranjuez, Córdoba, and finally Barcelona. Everywhere he criticized, but everywhere he was captivated by the Romantic aspect of turbulent Spain.

The bull fight seemed to him, as it has to many, to symbolize the life and problems of that country. His long description of a *Corrida de toros* is one of the most beautiful passages of his prose. Sarmiento, the humanitarian, criticized the brutality of the fight and "the certain and ignoble death of the horses." Sarmiento, the artist, saw in the mortal struggle an essential element in life. In close parallel to Ernest Hemingway almost a century later, the Argentine traveler pointed out that "danger is the pabulum of life"; death is the supreme drama for the artist.

"I have seen the bulls and felt all of their sublime attraction. Barbarous spectacle, terrible, sanguinary, and nevertheless full of seduction and stimulation. It is impossible to separate the eyes for a moment from that beast, that with peristaltic movements is studying the means of thrusting his razor-sharp horns through the elegant bull fighter that he has before him. The foreign novice cannot make flow the blood that gathers in his heart while, with pale face, contracted and dry mouth and ecstatic eyes, he awaits the results of the fight before he breathes. . . . Oh, the emotions of the heart! The necessity of emotions that man feels, and that the bulls satisfy in a way unequaled by the theatre or any civilized spectacle."[2]

This was Spain. It repelled his intellect, but it excited his emotions. He visited the Madrid Museum, and was captivated by the art and the artists of Spain's Golden Age. "Lope de Vega, Calderón, Murillo, Cervantes can be compared only with Pythagoras, Sophocles, Archimedes, Euclides, each a

[2] *Ibid.,* p. 35.

creator of a branch of art or science."[3] Sarmiento traveled through Don Quixote's country of La Mancha, and he noted many of the landmarks that he recognized from the plot of Cervantes' famous novel. He passed the inn at Puerto Lapice, and many other points made familiar by fiction. He traveled to the old Moorish city of Córdoba and south into Andalusia. He was fascinated by the colors of the landscape and the spirit of the country. "What imagination, what richness of spirit! How happy is the joyful Andalusia!"[4]

The Spain of 1846 was, however, on trial before the young Argentine, and Don Domingo led a vigorous prosecution. What *had* been a great culture was dead. The nation that produced Lope de Vega and Calderón now produced nothing. "The Spaniards left nothing to their own country. The novel created by Cervantes was reproduced in France; the brush of Murillo flowered in the Low Countries. . . . Modern Spain has neither sacred nor profane painting."[5] Sarmiento went to visit the great Escorial palace built by the later Hapsburg kings of Spain, and for him this great architectural monument was symbolic of the cultural death of the nation. "It is still a fresh corpse, that stinks and inspires disgust," he wrote.[6]

But Sarmiento's most telling criticism dealt with the contrast between Spain and the rest of civilization. This was Don Domingo's intentional intellectual criticism of the country. He saw it out of step with the rest of Europe. Its thought was dead, and its backwardness was shameful. Spanish politics was an act of "disgovernment."[7] Sarmiento saw man as an animal that had to be tamed by civilization. He achieved his maximum of freedom within a framework of law. In Spain, he found civilization had not exerted its domesticating influence, and government by law was non-existent. He analyzed "Modern Spain" and reached only negative conclusions:

"Cádiz has half the population as it had before."

"No new city has been founded; no town has become a city."

"No industry has been introduced in three centuries, except for the manufacture of terrible little match sticks."

[3] *Ibid.*, p. 52. [4] *Ibid.*, p. 59. [5] *Ibid.*, p. 52. [6] *Ibid.*, p. 49.
[7] *Ibid.*, p. 19.

"There is no national navy."

"There are no roads except for two large highways."

"There is no public education. There are no colonies."

"Printing and engraving have decayed like the cities. There are no engravers."

"The inn as described by Don Quixote exists immaculate of all improvement."[8]

As an envoy of the Chilean government, Don Domingo felt it his duty to study the educational system. He renewed his old attack upon the outmoded Spanish orthography, and offered once more his proposed reforms. During his visit, he criticized Spain violently and often with little tact. It is no wonder that he aroused the ire of patriotic Spaniards. One day he was speaking with Ventura de la Vega, who had been born in Argentina, about his orthographic reforms. Vega commented that such changes would tend to cut the colonies off from their mother country. There would be no cultural link.

"That is no great difficulty," answered Sarmiento softly and with the greatest amount of composure, "since we read no Spanish books over there; since you have no authors, nor writers, nor scholars, nor economists, nor politicians, nor historians, nor anything worthwhile; since you here and we over there translate, it is a matter of complete indifference to us if you write that which is translated in one manner and we in another. We have seen over there but one Spanish book, and that is not a book, but the newspaper articles of Larra. I do not know whether you consider the writings of Martínez de la Rosa as books also. There they pass as anthologies, for extracts, it being possible to cite the pages of Blair, Boileau, Guizot, and twenty more, from which he has taken such a concept or the mother idea that has suggested to him another conclusion."[9]

It is little wonder that Sarmiento's visit to Spain was resented. His criticisms were too well founded to be appreciated, and he was attacked mercilessly by contemporary Spaniards. In 1853, the satirist, J. M. Villergas, wrote a reply to some of the attacks that Sarmiento had meanwhile pub-

[8] *Ibid.*, p. 61.

[9] *Ibid.*, pp. 8, 9.

lished in his *Viajes.* Villergas entitled his work, *Sarmenticidio, o a mal Sarmiento buena podadera* (There is a play of words in this title that is not translatable: Sarmenticide, or for a bad Sarmiento—which means literally a runner vine—a good pruning knife). In this work he defended Spain against the charges of the Argentine writer. He denied the fact that Spanish books were not read in America.

"Finally I have seen this man,
Who achieved with his dramas [sic] and novels
An enviable and deserved name,
Upon his return thread a thousand . . . bagatelles;
And making Spain the target of his wrath,
I will not say a thousand . . . nay a million lies!"[10]

In spite of his unfavorable impression upon the Spaniards and their counterattacks, Sarmiento continued his indictment of Spanish "barbarism." Nevertheless, before he left, he was made an honorary member of the Society of Professors, and in later generations, although the most violent elements of his attack were still resented, he was regarded by Spanish artists and thinkers as one of the Spanish world's most gifted writers.

Barcelona was the last city in Spain that he visited. Sarmiento did not consider this a part of the country. "As you know, we are Americans, and the Barcelonans are Catalonians."[11] Barcelona was more closely related to the civilization of Europe, and Sarmiento admired it for this. "The inhabitants are active, industrious by instinct and manufacturers by convenience. Here there are busses, gas, steam, insurance, weaving, printing, smoke, and noise. There is a European people."[12] In Barcelona, for Don Domingo, were the signposts of civilization. He came there with Juan Thompson, a fellow exile from the dictatorship of Rosas. He passed happy days in that city. It was here that he received the review of his book by Charles Mazade which had appeared in the *Revue des deux mondes* on October 1st. This became his passport throughout the intellectual world of Europe. The French

[10] J. M. Villergas, *Sarmenticidio, o a mal Sarmiento buena podadera,* Paris, 1892, p. 4.
[11] *Viajes,* II, 63. [12] *Ibid.*

Hispanist, Prosper Mérimée, had read *El Facundo,* and he came to congratulate him upon his achievement. Mérimée,[13] in turn, introduced Sarmiento to the French consul general, Ferdinand de Lesseps, who was later to achieve worldwide fame for his engineering achievement in the construction of the Suez Canal. De Lesseps made it possible for the traveler to meet the English political agitator, Richard Cobden, who was at the time in Barcelona.

It was Cobden who gave Don Domingo one of the great spiritual experiences of his trip. Sarmiento saw the English leader as representative of the best forces in modern politics. He was leading the fight for liberal rational reform in his own nation. He was attempting to tear down the barriers to free trade and democratic government. More important than this, he was a man whose oratory was strong enough to carry his ideas into action. He contrasted greatly with Thiers and Guizot. They were orators, but they lacked the ideas and the sincerity. "With Cobden there begins a new era for the world; the word becomes flesh once more, producing by itself the greatest events."[14] Sarmiento and Cobden talked late into the night, and the Englishman refired the zeal of the Argentine crusader. Don Domingo returned to his lodgings excited and inspired. "I did not sleep that night; I had fever; it seemed to me that war would come to be ridiculous, when that system of the aggregation of wills, the juxtaposition of masses, was generalized, was put into practice to destroy abuses, governments, institutions. What an easy matter! Today we are two, tomorrow four, next year a thousand, joined publicly for the same end. Will the government resist? It is just that we are not yet many; there are still many more who are in favor of the abuses. The preaching continues, and the leaflets, and the newspapers, and the Associations, and the League. Government and the Houses know the day and the hour when they are defeated and they surrender. Go plant such a beautiful system in America."[15]

From Barcelona, Sarmiento traveled by ship to the Mallorca Islands. He stayed in Palma for over a week, but during most

[13] Author of *Carmen,* etc.

[14] *Viajes,* II, 65.

[15] *Ibid.,* p. 66.

of the time he was unable to leave his room because of the terrible storms that were raging. When he did get out for a walk, he wandered through the city in search of its historical landmarks and monuments. Soon after, however, growing tired of Palma and bored with the quietness of his life, he decided to cross the rest of the Mediterranean in a small *laut*. This primitive sailing ship promised to inject more excitement into the voyage than there ordinarily would be. "A crossing in a *laut* must have its charms for a traveler from far-off lands who comes charged with historic notions, to seek in Europe like poetry the traces of ancient life."[16] The *laut* is a ship that remains unchanged since Roman times, and it was not until Don Domingo boarded it that he realized the full implications of his choice of such a conveyance. Two thirds of the deck was covered with thirty pigs, and in the rest of the space, accommodating themselves wherever possible amidst the cargo, were three women, four sailors, five passengers, two dogs, and dozens of turkeys and hens. Feeling sorry for these unfortunate creatures that had to travel in such discomfort, Sarmiento approached the captain to ask for his cabin.

"And where should I sleep?" he asked.

"Wherever you wish," answered the captain, indicating with a sweep of his hand the various layers of cargo that were still empty.

"But what happens if it rains?"

"It is only a one-night trip, sir."

"But will there be a bed?"

"Not unless you brought one."

Sarmiento picked a place as far away from the animals and the people as possible, wrapped himself in his poncho and gazed up at the sky in an attempt to go to sleep. The trip lasted more than the projected time, and Don Domingo spent day after day gazing at sea and sky, meditating on the "inconsistency and vicissitudes of human affairs." The sailors told stories of smugglers and pirates and the sea. Don Domingo scratched himself as the bugs from the nearby pigs reached him. He refused to eat for two days, for he was so repulsed by the odor. Sitting wrapped in his poncho on the

[16] *Ibid.*, p. 70.

deck, he wrote to his friend Joaquín Thompson: "There are horrors that can be described, but my feelings and my anguish, neither could you ever hear, nor could my mouth ever express them."[17]

On the third night the *laut* entered Algiers. There was a strong wind, and the small boat tossed on the waves, and after it had finally dropped its anchor to secure its position in the harbor, the weather would not let it rest. Around and around it was blown, and when the first lights of dawn appeared they were very welcome to Don Domingo. "The unusual aspect of the city appeared like an Arab's white cloak spread from the top to the bottom of the sharply inclined hill."[18] In Algiers Sarmiento came for the first time into contact with the Orient. He had studied the history of the East, and he had found many of the ills of his own culture as those received from the Moorish heritage of the Hispanic peoples. Now he was to come into contact with this other civilization, and again he was to confirm his views.

Sarmiento carried a letter of introduction to Marshall Bougueaud, duque d'Isly, from Monsieur de Lesseps in Barcelona. He lost no time in making use of such an *entrée* to French colonial officialdom, and he very promptly called on the famous military governor of the colony. Bougueaud had recently gained world-wide renown for his successful campaign against the Arabic leader, Abd-el-Kader. Don Domingo listened with interest and with sympathy to the old soldier's accounts of his campaigns. Here was a parallel to his own fight. He compared the French attempt to "civilize" North Africa to the unitarist attempts to "civilize" Argentina. He listened to Bougueaud's descriptions of his strategy and methods as a young student would listen to a wise teacher. He learned how the "Arabic gauchos" had been defeated, and many years later he referred to these military lessons as the bases for his claims to military leadership against the caudillos of his own nation. The Marshall was so impressed by the sympathetic audience that he received from his South American visitor that he asserted that he had finally found someone who understood him.[19]

[17] *Ibid.*, pp. 71, 72. [18] *Ibid.*, p. 73. [19] Gálvez, p. 179.

Don Domingo left Algiers on the steamboat, *L'Étât,* which touched at the ports of Cherchel, Tunez, Mostaganem, and Arsow. He landed at Mers-al-Kebir, and proceeded by land from there to Oran. Marshall Bougueaud had given his visitor a letter of introduction to the Governor of Oran, General Lamorcière, with instructions to allow Sarmiento to travel into the interior and study the life of the Arabic villages and the strategy of the French occupation armies. But General Lamorcière was not in the city upon the arrival of the South American traveler, and Don Domingo submitted the letters of introduction to the local district chief, who received the foreigner as a distinguished guest and afforded him all of the necessary facilities for his proposed journey. With a safe-conduct written in Arabic,[20] a servant who would serve as interpreter, two Arabic horsemen, and an Army officer of Turkish birth, Sarmiento set out to explore the desert regions of North Africa. This to him was the Pampa of the Old World.

In Sarmiento's observations of North Africa we find the same seemingly contradictory attitude that was apparent in his earlier life and thought. He looked at the scene around him with the eyes of a Romantic, and he criticized it with the mind of a reformer. "I cannot describe the mixed feeling of fear and admiration that is caused me by the sight of this Arabic nation."[21] He criticized it as he had criticized Facundo and Spain, but he was captivated by its artistic beauty. The artist looked at the scenic attractions. "The Atlas range is interrupted there to give way to crystalline streams that descend from its bowels, revealing in its bosom ravines soft and rich with vegetation."[22] The reformer looked at it with the eyes of a critic. "Not two months ago a town of eight hundred inhabitants was suddenly flooded; the waters rose in a few hours to the height of the roofs where the dwellers had taken refuge, until inhabitants and habitations had disappeared forever."[23] This was a view of an Africa that needed to be reformed.

As Don Domingo rode out into the desert, however, his

[20] *Obras,* XLIX, 140. [21] *Viajes,* II, 78. [22] *Ibid.,* p. 76.
[23] *Ibid.,* p. 76.

Romantic "livingness" came to the surface. "The gaucho instincts that lie dormant in all of us while we have at our disposal only carriages, trains, and steamships, had suddenly awakened at the sound of the hoof beats of a group of horses; and after leaving Oran, like a musician who runs over the keyboard before daring to execute some difficult variations, I applied the spurs to the horse, making him cut capers in order to discover *his play,* that is, all of his agility and skill. Immediately, wanting to assume the air of an Arabic *agah* or *tolba,* I studied slyly the way my companions wore their cloaks."[24] Sarmiento imitated the mannerisms, the habits, and the customs of the men of the desert. In a letter to Joaquín Thompson, he described the trip, and this description ranks among the most beautiful to be found in his works.

The group traveled to an Arabic village. Soon Sarmiento was not only riding like an Arab, but was swearing by Allah in his conversation. A *diffa,* or feast, was prepared for the guest, and the description of Don Domingo's part in this meal is one of the most humorous passages in Spanish prose. Sitting among the Arab dignitaries, Sarmiento felt himself compelled to receive the feast well and eat it in a spirit of true enjoyment. Fried pancakes were brought to the table, and over them was poured sour rancid butter. Sarmiento assumed the attitude of a martyr, and with what he considered true courage, he ate the course without resorting to "the subterfuges and deceptions that would in a similar case have served an ordinary epicure."[25]

The next course, however, brought on a crisis. It was a dish of the famed *cuscussu,* or flour, rolled by hand, without salt or flavoring, and then submerged in milk. When the plate appeared, Don Domingo broke out in a cold sweat at the thought of its taste. His body began to tremble from head to foot. His heart "beat like that of a child whom the teacher has just sent to stand in the corner." "At once, like one who on swimming in the sea, dives suddenly in head first after having vacillated a long time for fear of the cold, I buried my spoon to the sleeve, and taking it out full of *cuscussu* and milk I entombed it in my mouth. What happened within me

[24] *Ibid.,* pp. 94, 95.

[25] *Ibid.,* p. 99.

at that moment defies description. When I opened my eyes, I seemed to find myself in a new world. All of my tendons, contracted by the sublime effort of will that I had just made, loosened up little by little, and dispersed with the joy of soldiers that abandon formation after the dissipation of an alarm born of false news." He finished the dreaded *cuscussu*, and a barbecued lamb was brought before him. This dish brought memories of home to the traveling gaucho, and the meal ended on this note of enjoyment and gastronomical pleasure.[26]

The life of the nomadic village intrigued the artistic eye of the observant Sarmiento. He heard a murmur of voices in the background and noticed a group of people weeping pitifully. He found that they were bemoaning the loss of one of the younger men of the family who had been drafted to go to France and serve in the army. To these simple people such an occurrence was equivalent to death. Don Domingo asked his interpreter if it was frowned upon for him to observe more closely the women of the village. The chief replied that this could be arranged, but he would accompany the stranger. The young girls of the village gathered around the traveler and Don Domingo seemed to detect a sparkle of invitation in their black eyes until an elderly "old witch" called them to the more important task of praying. Sarmiento was able to gain the attention of one beautiful Arabic girl. He noticed her beauty and her unusual appearance, and knowing well the universal character of woman, the South American, instead of following her with his eyes, looked away and down to the ground. He suddenly looked up and caught her gazing upon him. Her beauty startled him. "Oh women, women, I seemed to say to her, looking at her smilingly, you are the same everywhere,—everywhere you are curious."[27]

The return trip was as picturesque and fascinating for Don Domingo as had been the first part. He passed camel caravans that moved slowly and silently across the desert, carrying with them dwarf donkeys, cows, and oxen. He saw the beautiful contrasts between the monotony of the desert sands and the beauty of the Atlas mountains. But before he returned to the

[26] *Ibid.*, pp. 99, 100.

[27] *Ibid.*, pp. 102, 103.

North African coast, the reformist intention of his spirit broke through the Romantic intent. He passed the village of Sig, which was at the time being built by the French in the same site as an ancient Roman city. The new buildings, the irrigation projects, the sanitation, and the experiments in manufacture that the French were instituting under their colonial policy in this area struck the reformer as the very elements necessary to change the causes of barbarism into the causes of civilization.

Sarmiento seemed to learn many lessons in North Africa. The trip confirmed his theory of the Spanish heritage of barbarity from its contact with the Moorish culture. He confirmed his comparison of the gaucho and the Arab horseman, and he found in the French solution of colonization and material reform a possible cure for the barbarism of the Arab lands that might be borrowed as a solution for the struggle on his own pampa.

Before he departed from Africa, Sarmiento's often prophetic vision combined the artistic imagination of the Romantic with the intention of the reformer to paint a picture of that land in the future. As he rode beneath the heat of the desert sun, his muscles relaxed, his mind reviewed what he had seen and done during his trip in the land of the Arab. As the scene passed before his mind's eye, the time shifted from past to present to future, and he began to see Algeria in the period when the French colonial policy had reached fruition. "Everywhere there hustled the European population devoted to the multiple operations of civilized life. The plains, now deserted, I saw covered with farmhouses, with gardens and with ripe wheat and grains, and those lakes, that from the heights of the mountains are seen shining here and there, like the dispersed fragments of a mirror, had taken regular forms in the Mitidja, Mascara and Eghress, their waters captured by ordered canalizations, opened into the center of the plains, as they had been in Roman times. The plans for towns and cities that I had only seen on paper, now multiplied infinitely, appeared suddenly, the plains and mountains suddenly bristling with theatres, temples, and palaces. . . .

"And suddenly, with the abrupt petulance of the imagination to transport itself from one place to another without rational transition, perhaps guided only by the analagous external appearance of the Sahara and the Pampa, I found myself in America, on this side of the Andes, where you and I were born, in the midst of those limitless plains on which the sun rises and sets without a human dwelling imposing itself between the eye of the traveler and the distant horizon. And so, I thought, it is going on four centuries that a Christian people has possessed undisputed that rich soil, equal in area and superior in fertility to all of Europe, and yet it does not count one million inhabitants. And I thought of the fact that there were no endemic diseases, as in Africa, to decimate the population. . . . There is no brutal religion, no rebellious language that delays there the advance of civilization."

Sarmiento saw, however, his nation torn by strife and struggle. He saw it without inhabitants and without progress. He dreamed of a change on the Pampa similar to the change being brought about by the French in North Africa. The civilization and industry, the European population and the material reforms were suddenly transferred to the Argentina of the future: "When my train of thought reached this point I shook my head to assure myself that I was awake, and spurring my horse, as if to leave behind the evil spirit that tormented me, I quickly joined my party."[28]

Sarmiento rode on with his group to Oran, remained there a very short time, and embarked to recross the Mediterranean.

Chapter 22. Italy, Switzerland, Germany

THE ship carrying Don Domingo Sarmiento sailed across the Mediterranean in mid-winter. The January crossing was

[28] *Ibid.*

rough, but the traveler had become accustomed to all types of weather at sea. He made friends with a bishop from India, a missionary from Oceania, and a French abbot. He picked these companions carefully, for from them he could prepare his way for a visit to Rome. He learned what to see and what to do in the capital of Roman Catholicism, and he made use of his acquaintances upon his arrival in that city.

The first port of call in Europe was Marseilles. The ship later put into Genoa and Pisa, and on February 8, 1847, Don Domingo disembarked at Civitavecchia and set out by land for Rome. The travels through Italy made a profound impression upon the artistic senses of the South American observer. Sarmiento was always disgusted by the backwardness and filth of the country, but this repugnance was never emphasized in his writings. Rather he pointed to the scenic beauty of the countryside. He was profoundly conscious of being in the midst of monuments of countless centuries of history, and he made a point of studying carefully the artistic wealth of the Italian cities.

The trip by coach from Civitavecchia to Rome was slow and dirty. Don Domingo was impressed by the misery of the country. Beggars along the way besieged the travelers with requests for *qualche cosa,* and shepherds dressed in goatskins revealed their poverty-stricken existence. Tired of the continued drain on their pocketbooks made by the multitude of beggars, the passengers of the coach refused to give any more. A quarrel with the postillion ensued, and while passing over the next bridge, whether by negligence or malice on the part of the driver, the vehicle struck against one of the posts, and a wheel was splintered into a thousand pieces. The coach, with fourteen passengers, balanced precariously for a moment on the side of the bridge. One of the horses collapsed from exhaustion, and the fate of the travelers seemed to depend on the absence of any slight movement that might jar the vehicle from its position. One by one the passengers crawled carefully out; but even after all were safe, their situation was still not a happy one. The next coach had no room. As the passengers carefully unloaded their baggage, it began to rain; and it was not until late in the night that they found an old cart on which to load their trunks and upon which some of the passengers could travel. Don Domingo and a French missionary gallantly offered to be the ones who continued on foot. Following the cart, losing it in the black darkness, finding it again, and continuing on their way, the strange entourage wound its way on to Rome.[1]

In the Italian capital, the French abbot whom Sarmiento had met aboard ship became his guide to the classical imperial city. He took him to Plaza Araceli, and both rented rooms at a boardinghouse that seemed to cater to churchmen visiting the Papal capital. Above the entrance to the house was an image of the Virgin Mary, and each of the rooms, instead of having a number to identify it, had the name of a saint. Sarmiento lived in one called "Mary conceived without sin."

Don Domingo had the happy way of entering into the spirit of the place that he visited. He became a devotee of religion and art while in Rome. He entered into the spirit of the place that he visited in a way that would allow him to enjoy it to the maximum.

The day of his arrival in Rome, the bells of the capital began to ring in double time just after mid-day. A general murmur greeted this outburst, and the famous Roman Carnival began, "like the voice of the angel of pleasure who calls the dead to feverish life."[2] Suddenly it seemed to Don Domingo that the city had come to life. The carnival was the signal for Rome to let loose with all its hidden energies and passions. For fifteen days from twelve to five in the afternoon a scene of carnival revelry was repeated to the great enjoyment of the visitor from the Andes. Each day the excitement became a little more intense, and Don Domingo's presence at this colorful and unusual event was one of the keystones of his visit to Rome.

There were certain other aspects of the imperial city, however, that Sarmiento could not and would not miss. The artistic monuments were something to be studied and analyzed by the traveler. He saw the effect of good art upon the human soul and upon the soul of a people or a civilization as of profound importance. The art of Rome had had an im-

[1] *Viajes*, II, 121-122.

[2] *Ibid.*, p. 126.

portant inspirational effect upon the development of Christianity. Michaelangelo, Rafael, Titian, and the other great names that brought splendor to the city were inseparable from Roman Catholicism and its effect in beautifying the spirit of man. Art "separates the savage from the civilized man."[3] The lack of good art in America seemed to Don Domingo to be one of the many factors creating the unhappy situation of that chaotic continent. He, as a future leader and teacher of America, devoted much of his time and effort to the study of Roman art, and a cultivation of a taste for the best in painting and sculpture. He accomplished his purpose of study, but he left Rome with a still sadly undeveloped taste. He visited all of the churches, museums, ruins, and catacombs. He studied the great works of the Renaissance, and he tried to investigate the works of contemporary artists in Europe. In his comments on what he observed, he demonstrated a typical mid-nineteenth-century bourgeois artistic taste. He admired the large paintings, those that answered "the necessities of modern society" by covering entire walls with historic scenes full of landscapes and actions. As a member of the civilization that was just discovering the value of mass production in bringing the material attributes of civilization to the masses, he saw the art of copying masterpieces as an equivalent accomplishment. "It is easy to understand," he wrote in a letter to the Bishop of Guyo, "what an advantage it would be to acquire copies of the works of the masters of Rome."[4] This taste, demonstrated in his approach to the fine arts in Rome, was an example of the bourgeois reformer and not of the sensitive artist who produced many magnificent pages in his own works. It was the reformer trying to analyze the social significance of art in civilization and formularizing a solution to the social problems of his country through its use. His excessive praise of such mediocre sculptors as Coghetti and Benzoni shows the same uncultivated artistic values as those that prompt the praise of "useful" large paintings and copies of masterpieces.

Even more important than the artistic monuments of Rome were the religious aspects of that city. Don Domingo visited

[3] *Ibid.*, p. 137.

[4] *Ibid.*, p. 141.

the church and the church dignitaries, but the high point of this phase of his "study" of the city was an audience with the Pope. Pope Pius IX had only recently ascended the pontifical throne. He was the successor to the tyrannical Gregory XVI, who had been one of the important instruments and supporters of political reaction during the period of the Holy Alliance in Europe, and who had fought bloodily against the revolutions of Pietro Renzi. Pius IX, the former Cardinal, and Count de Mastai-Ferretti had been elected after a bitter fight in the College of Cardinals. The Austrian forces of reaction that had been dominant under Gregory XVI were opposed by the more liberal forces appearing in the Church, as elsewhere, in this period. The liberals carried the victory, and their candidate Pius IX inaugurated one of the most important pontificates in the history of the period. He pardoned the thousands of political prisoners being held in Roman jails. He instituted many liberal economic and political reforms, and he became one of the idols of the people of Rome and the surrounding countryside, not only for what he was but also for what he did.

Father O'Brien, the papal correspondent for Sarmiento's uncle, the Bishop of San Juan, arranged an audience for the young South American traveler. Pius IX was the first Pope to hold that office who had visited America, and it so happened that he had traveled in the actual area of Don Domingo's birth and childhood. He had been in Buenos Aires and Mendoza, and he had crossed the Andes by mule, probably across the same passes that were so familiar to Sarmiento. With such circumstances to give a concrete interest to the interview, Don Domingo was received by the Holy Father.

"Señor Sarmiento, from what part of South America do you come?"

"From San Juan, in the Argentine Republic, Holy Father."

"Well. Is that San Juan of Cuyo, some three or four days north of Mendoza?"

"Not more than two."

"Yes, but you people live on horseback and gallop instead of walking. I walked through that country. I know Buenos Aires, Mendoza, Chile . . ."

"We know that, Holy Father, and the peoples of America who had the pleasure of receiving you must have received with enthusiasm the news of the ascent of Your Holiness to Pontifex Maximus. You are the first Pope who has visited America."

"Yes, that is true. . . . Tell me—Rivadavia—General Pinto. What news is there of them?"

"The former died not long ago in Cadiz, exiled and poverty-stricken. His administration fell in 1827 because of the resistance created by his political and religious reforms, and his followers have been exiled or exterminated."

"Oh!" exclaimed the Pope, with a tone of disgust, compassion and distaste.

"General Pinto," Sarmiento went on, "for similar reasons left the government in 1830, and, more fortunate than Rivadavia, was able to retire to private life where he remains respected and tranquil."[5]

Don Domingo found the Pope to be as ignorant of the political situation in America as had been the other European leaders whom he had met. But the Pope differed from the French politicians in that he wished to be informed of the truth.

"How are the present governments?" he asked; and such a question gave Sarmiento the very opportunity he was seeking. He launched into his attack against the Rosas dictatorship, his analysis of the reasons for his nation's barbarism, and his crusade for the civilization of his country. Pius IX listened patiently and with interest, and after he departed from the interview, Don Domingo thought of many other matters he would liked to have touched upon, but the hurried character of his trip made another audience out of the question.

Sarmiento was able to tie in the studies that he made in Rome with his overall world view that he had been forming in the past years. He studied the short reign of Pius IX, and he saw many familiar features that had to make it such a success. He analyzed the Pope's reforms and proposals for the modernization of Italian agriculture. Here was a parallel to the economic reform that Sarmiento had advocated for his

[5] *Ibid.*, pp. 144-146.

own nation. He read the Pope's decrees and proposals for widespread public education, and again these struck a sympathetic note in the South American's thought. Finally, the moves on the part of the Pope to end arbitrary political rule, free political prisoners, and institute a government of law and liberties seemed to Don Domingo to be the cornerstone for the successful Papal government that he observed.

From Rome, Don Domingo traveled to Naples, where he visited the ruins of Pompeii and climbed the mighty Vesuvius. Pompeii to him was a thrilling visit into the past. He studied the architecture and imagined the life of the ruined city, and then joining a party of sightseers being conducted by a professional guide, he made an excursion up the sides of Mount Vesuvius. Again the history of what he saw attracted his Romantic imagination, and the beauty and excitement of the climb inspired many striking descriptions in his letters and later works.

The volcano above presented a forbidding aspect, while the scene of the harbor and city below took on greater beauty as the height increased. As Don Domingo climbed, absorbed in his own thoughts, he heard the startled cry of the guide. "Le pietre! Le pietre!" And the Italian waved excitedly in the direction of the summit, where several large lava rocks were being belched forth from the volcano's mouth. Too frightened to gather his wits, Sarmiento could only lower his head, round his shoulders, hold his elbows behind him, and stretch his mouth into that tense shape that is typical of a man expecting a heavy blow. A mass of some six hundred pounds of lava landed within a yard of him and within a few feet of his guide. Four or five other fragments landed further away. Don Domingo's fright disappeared little by little, but it was replaced by wonder as he realized the closeness of his escape. Wide-eyed and open-mouthed, the South American traveler and the Italian guide looked at each other in silence.

But such an adventure did not deter Sarmiento from going on. An English sightseer suggested climbing to the mouth of the volcano. Only Don Domingo was willing to accompany him, and together they made the breathtaking ascent and observed the landscape from the best possible vantage point.

"The lapis lazuli sky of Italy was at that moment illuminated by the golden rays of the setting sun; in front there extended a cup full of quiet and smooth sea, decorated here and there by fishing boats, like the decoration of a Venetian mirror. Below, the slopes of Vesuvius covered with vineyards and gardens on whose background stand out like white objects spread over a rug, a thousand farmhouses. And following the coast of the most picturesque bay of the world, Resina could be made out linked to Naples by a thread of buildings extended along the beaches and rising into the hills until reaching the Santelmo which stands as a sentinel on the heights."[6]

From Naples, Sarmiento traveled north through the Italian peninsula. He felt the need of a companion on the trip "in order to unload in colloquies the excess of ideas and emotions that he was experiencing."[7] He traveled up the peninsula in a coach carrying twelve passengers, but he was so interested in seeing all that they passed that at first he paid little heed to his companions. "For a day I passed most of the time with my head out of the door watching pass the torn fields ripped by the volcanic eruptions."[8] Before reaching Bologna, however, Don Domingo had made friends with two young Frenchmen. These became his long-sought traveling companions, and finding common bonds of interest, the three became inseparable friends in the days that followed. In Bologna they saw the sights together, and in Florence they lodged together. "We discussed and adopted a campaign plan to visit monuments, libraries and museums, and we were already friends."[9] One of the Frenchmen Don Domingo found to be especially interesting. He was a young aristocrat by the name of Ange Champgobert; but in spite of his social and family position he was a Republican. To Sarmiento he was one of the few who had seen the light. He was a republican "by study, by profound conviction, *reasoned,* in spite of his family and the circle in which he lived."[10] He was a living example of the triumph of human reason over tradition, custom, or the irrational elements of man. Together, he and Don Domingo saw the ruins of old Europe. They saw the monuments of the

[6] *Ibid.*, p. 177, 178.
[7] *Ibid.*, p. 189. [8] *Ibid.*, p. 191. [9] *Ibid.*, p. 192. [10] *Ibid.*, p. 193.

past, but they discussed together the lessons that they could learn for the future.

Florence was one of the high spots of the journey for the South American. It surpassed all other cities that he had visited in its beauty. He went to see Santa Croce and Santa María dei Fiori, the Palacio Vecchio and the Campanile. He recalled the great figures of the city: Galileo, Amerigo Vespucci, Michaelangelo, and Machiavelli. His comments on the latter are typical of his mid-nineteenth century thought. His belief in the ultimate triumph of a rational order, an order in which man lived and acted beneath the framework of laws, principles, and rights, made the Renaissance political writer an evil figure in history. His political relativism, his "philosophized immorality" made him for Sarmiento the doctrinaire of caudillism. "Machiavelli wrote in *The Prince* what men . . . from the Grand Inquisitor of Spain to Pizarro . . . believed and practiced.[11] He might very well have added the names of Rosas and Facundo, but these men seemed remote from the ancient grandeur of Florence.

The three companions traveled across northern Italy together to Padua and Venice. Sarmiento was struck by the wealthy aspect of the land in this section as contrasted with the poverty of the South. Here was a "delicious garden," cultivated, irrigated and joined by water and land communications. He dreamed of the pampa of the future undergoing similar alterations and becoming the fertile garden of his own land.

Venice was sad and melancholy. Under the Austrian rule, the Venetians suffered the burdens of censorship and oppression. The city was poverty-stricken. The palaces were empty. The population was hungry. Don Domingo had brought with him some of the latest books of the contemporary European political thinkers. He was reading one on the train as it approached Venice when an Italian sitting near him noticed and exclaimed. "Ma, il Gioberti!" he said. "You will go directly to jail; Marucini has been incommunicado for six months for having been found with that book."

[11] *Ibid.*, p. 196.

"But I am a foreigner," protested Sarmiento. "I am an American."

"Perduto! Olvidatto!" exclaimed the Italian with pain. "Who then will bail you out?"

Don Domingo and his companions consulted on the matter, and hiding the forbidden books within the covers of Venetian guide books, they smuggled them through the unsuspecting customs. "And thanks to this, Gioberti, Lamartine, Michelet, and Louis Blanc made their triumphal entrance into Venice."[12]

From Venice, the three travelers went on to Milan, where they regretfully parted, each to go his own way. The Frenchmen were going on to Jerusalem and the Holy Land, and Don Domingo turned northward towards the Alps. His principal mission was to study European educational methods, and Prussia was the nation that offered the most profitable lessons. Italy had been a romantic interlude for Don Domingo. The historical color, the monuments, the climb up Vesuvius, a moonlit night in a Venetian gondola—here was the color and the beauty that the artist enjoyed and absorbed, but now he felt himself forced to turn back to the immediate problems of his trip, to "seek the thread that links the present with the past."[13]

As Sarmiento crossed into Switzerland and Germany, he changed from the Romantic to rationalist. He was still conscious of the natural beauty. He was awed by the Alpine scene and intrigued by the historical monuments in South Germany and along the Rhine. But his main interests now became the intellectual analysis of the factors present in modern Germany. "In Spain I had seen, in both Castile and La Mancha, a people that was ferocious, tattered and hardened in ignorance and laziness. The Arabs of Africa had become fanatical to the point of their own destruction. And the Italians of Naples had shown me the last degree to which can descend human dignity."[14] But he found Switzerland and Germany to contrast sharply with the other countries that he had visited. He went to Zurich and saw the peaceful operation of the Swiss democracy. He traveled to Munich, where

[12] *Ibid.*, pp. 204-205. [13] *Ibid.*, p. 213. [14] *Ibid.*, p. 220.

he watched the beer-drinking, polka-dancing, "peace-loving" Germans and commented upon their high degree of civilization. Continuing on to Dresden, Leipzig, and Berlin, he entered into the most progressive areas of central Europe. The system of public education in Prussia appeared to him to be the most advanced in Europe and seemed to explain in large part the progressive character of the nation. It certainly confirmed his own faith in the results of a good educational system. Sarmiento gathered all the data possible on the institutions that he inspected, and he later published the details in *El Comercio* of Valparaíso and in several subsequent books. Herr Eikhorn, the minister of public education, received Don Domingo as the official envoy of the Chilean government and afforded him every aid and facility. "Prussia, thanks to its intelligent educational system, is more prepared than even France for political life, and universal suffrage would not be an exaggeration in a place where all the classes of society have cultivated and have use of their reason."[15]

In Germany, Sarmiento was able to pursue the study of another of his principal interests—the problem of emigration to his country and the other nations of South America. Germany was one of the biggest sources of immigrants at this time, and Don Domingo considered the German the best possible material for the advancement of his land's civilization. He contacted Herr Dieterice, the chief of the Office of Statistics. He informed himself of the numbers of emigrants to the various American nations, and he studied the methods of attracting these immigrants. He found the statistics of the startling number that were emigrating to North America, and he attributed to this fact a large amount of the advancement of the northern portion of the Western Hemisphere. He became acquainted with a Professor Wappaus, a student of Spanish American history, and the author of a treatise on German emigration and colonization. Don Domingo became very friendly with the scholar and later had his book translated into Spanish. Before he departed from Germany, he had not only made a study of the educational systems of that

[15] *Ibid.*, p. 229.

country, but he also had formulated a plan for attracting and absorbing immigrants in Chile or Argentina.

Professor Wappaus took his South American visitor to see the university town of Gottingen. Here Sarmiento was received with warmth and with interest. He was bombarded with questions about his nation's history, geography, and customs; and he was shown around the historic university town. A Bible with the signature of Martin Luther was shown him, and he was accepted into an intimate discussion group of German scholars where he spent an interesting evening discussing the religious aspects of the Reformation. The next day he was given a place of honor on the platform with the faculty during the university's commencement exercises. "With seriousness and with imperturbable calm I listened from beginning to end, and without going to sleep, to an erudite speech in Latin."[16] While in Paris, he had locked himself up for a fortnight with a German dictionary and grammar, and he had learned enough of the language to get along in it during his trip, but his Latin was not adequate to cope with the scholarly oration. He could only preserve his dignity and "face" by a pretension of understanding.

From Gottingen, Don Domingo traveled down the Rhine to Holland and Belgium and then back to Paris. Here, he felt like a veteran traveler. The streets and monuments and houses looked familiar to him, and he was already acquainted with many of the important personages of the city. He arrived on June 13, 1847, and he remained there until July 31st. It was during this period that he was honored with his election as corresponding member of the French Institute of History. On July 1st he delivered a paper before the assembly of that organization, dealing with the relationship of the two great leaders of South American independence, San Martín and Bolívar. He based his facts upon the conversations he had had with the Argentine leader during his previous visit to Paris. In discussing the famous interview between the two leaders at Guayaquil, Don Domingo painted San Martín as the great and selfless patriot who sacrificed all ambitions and retired from the public scene at the insistence of a less disin-

[16] *Ibid.*, p. 239.

terested Bolívar, who believed that the continent was too small for both men.[17] San Martín was present at the session, and his tacit confirmation of the facts included has given to this paper a historical significance for any students of the lives and acts of the leaders of the War of Independence.[18] In the minutes of the Institute, the admission of Sarmiento was mentioned on July 7th and his approval by the Assembly on July 30th.[19] This was an honor of which Don Domingo was to be proud for the rest of his life. He sent a number of studies of Spanish American history to the Institute, and he supplied the French historians with documents and facts on the occurrences in his part of the Western Hemisphere for many years to come.[20]

On July 18th, Sarmiento visited General San Martín for the last time. At the famous leader's home in Grand Bourg, he met once more Mariano Balcarce, the hero's nephew, and the other members of his family. They had a cordial reunion, and when Don Domingo left they presented him with a sheet of paper with their autographs. The old General quoted a saying of De Weiss in French, "Un prejugé utile est plus

[17] *Obras*, XXI, 32; This was published in the *Journal de l'institut historique* under the title of "Étude politique sur San Martín et Bolívar." Also published by Sarmiento in Spanish as *Discurso presentado para su recepción en el Instituto Histórico de Francia por D. F. Sarmiento*, Valparaiso, 1848.

[18] Gálvez, p. 186, holds that Sarmiento did not deliver the paper in person and that San Martin could therefore not have been present. Vicente Lecuna in his *En defensa de Bolívar*, Caracas, 1941, refutes the facts in the Sarmiento paper. Antonio P. Castro in *San Martín y Sarmiento*, Buenos Aires, 1947, answers both of these attacks satisfactorily. He shows that although Sarmiento's admission had not been finally approved by the Assembly of the Institute, it was perfectly possible for him to have delivered the paper on July 1. Among a number of pieces of evidence that he cites is an unpublished letter from San Martín's nephew, Balcarce, to Alberdi, dated in 1847, referring to the fact that Sarmiento had delivered a paper to the Institute upon his admission as a corresponding member.

[19] Sarmiento's diploma as a member of the Institute is dated July 7, 1847. The original document is preserved in the Museo Histórico Sarmiento. In his expense book of his trip, Don Domingo notes under the date, July 24, 1847, the spending of 20 francs for his diploma and another 20 francs for his annual dues.

[20] One of his most important manuscripts presented to the Institute was his *Guerre de l'indépendence dans l'Amérique du sud*. In the minutes of a session of the Institute of October 6, 1847, the secretary began to read a manuscript of Sarmiento, but "the hour being advanced, the reading could not be finished." (*Journal de l'institut historique*, October 6, 1847.)

raisonnable que la verité que le detruit.."[21] On this enigmatic note they parted, but Don Domingo was never to forget these historic meetings, and he often wrote of the military leader in the years to come, always with sympathy and admiration.

As Sarmiento prepared for his departure from Paris he found that his funds were running very low. Only 600 pesos remained in his money belt, and as he figured his expenses it became obvious that such a situation seriously limited his future course. It would be just enough to get him back to Chile the way he had come. But he had seen that route, and he wanted to go across the Isthmus of Panama and down the East Coast of South America. The minimum cost of such a trip was 700 pesos. Don Domingo was puzzled as to what to do. He counted his money over and over again, but this did not help. It always came out 600 pesos. Finally he made his decision. This was his trip to see the world. This was his trip to study the civilization that his own nation needed. He dreamed of seeing England and its great financial and industrial centers, and he dreamed of seeing North America with its expanding energy, its public education system, and its democratic government. He made his usual decision. "I will go with my watch in one hand and my purse in the other, and where this torch goes out, I will be groping in the dark, and with cunning I will find my way back to Chile!"[22] He figured that once he reached Spanish-speaking countries he would be able to earn his way by giving lectures in such cities as Mexico, Havana, and Caracas. On July 31st, he set sail for England. He visited London, Richmond, Manchester, Birmingham, and Liverpool. He saw the accomplishments and the problems of the maturing of the great Industrial Revolution. He saw the land of Cobden, and he saw the ills that his friend was seeking to cure.

In Liverpool, fortune smiled upon him. He met Norberto de la Riestra, a young Argentine *émigré* who was working with a commercial firm in England. De la Riestra took Don Domingo to his own home to live, and he arranged passage

[21] The original manuscript exists in the Museo Histórico Sarmiento in Buenos Aires.

[22] Rojas, p. 304.

for him on the ship *Moctezuma* for New York. On August 17, Sarmiento set sail from Liverpool. He was aboard a ship full of immigrants. The lower decks were filled with poverty-stricken, illiterate, sick, and dirty passengers. Their misery touched Don Domingo deeply, but their hope and faith in the future was a source of comfort to him. He watched them sing their songs beneath the warm summer moon on the deck at night. He saw them die and be buried at sea and the songs and dancing go on as before. It was a scene of human suffering, drama, and hope.

One night Don Domingo was trying to open the door to his cabin but it seemed locked. Suddenly a voice from the adjoining cabin called out to him in Spanish, "Pull. It's open." Sarmiento turned in surprise only to find the voice to be that of a Mr. Ward, an English employee of the Huth Gruning firm of Valparaíso. Don Domingo told him of his own connection with Chile and his mission from the Chilean government, and they became close friends. Ward introduced the Argentine traveler to George Bliss, a politician from Massachusetts,[23] who was returning from England, and the latter opened to Sarmiento one of the most valuable doors in North America. He gave him a letter of introduction to the great pioneer of public education, Horace Mann. With his English and North American friends and his introduction to the intellectual centers of Boston and New England, Don Domingo again had chosen traveling companions that would be most helpful and most suitable in the next country that he was to visit.

[23] Sarmiento erroneously refers to him as a "Senator from Massachusetts." Bliss was the only politician from that state on the *Moctezuma*, see Justo Garate Arriola, "Novedades acerca de Sarmiento," *Nueva Era*, Tandil, Argentina, August 23, 1949.

Chapter 23. The Dream Materialized: The United States

On September 14, 1847,[1] the *Moctezuma* entered the outer approaches to New York Harbor, passed through the narrows, by Staten Island and Ellis Island, and up to the Battery. On deck, watching intently and with excitement, was a young man of thirty-six years, a man who was seeing for the first time the land of his dreams, the nation about which he had read and studied, the civilization that he had adopted as his ideal and model. The wooded Palisades on one bank of the Hudson and the orderly buildings, canals, and streets on the other bank were sights that the traveler was expecting. The size and contrasts of the city intrigued him.

Domingo Sarmiento wandered through the streets of New York enthralled by this New World metropolis. "Whole sections of the city contain narrow, dirty streets lined with mean-looking houses. Pigs are inevitable personages to be met with in the streets and dark corners, where no one disputes with them their rights to citizenship. Through the center of the most beautiful part of the city runs Broadway, a wide avenue, beginning at Garden Castle. Farther north on Broadway stands Trinity Church, a Gothic structure of beautiful architecture and some magnificence—a rare thing in the United States. It was built by subscription, like all great American undertakings. Along Broadway, too, there are handsome private residences, a white, marble market, believed to be unrivaled even in Europe, and a theater for Italian opera, still under construction. In one hour, I counted passing the windows of my boardinghouse on Broadway four hundred and eighty vehicles of all sorts, including omnibusses, carts, and carriages. 'Hernani' was being played that night in an im-

[1] This is the correct date according to contemporary newspapers. Sarmiento said he arrived on the thirteenth.

provised theater in Garden Castle. . . . New York is the chief city of the wealthiest state in America. The magnificence of its municipal structure would be comparable only with that of the Roman senate, if it were itself not composed of a senate and a house of representatives that legislates for the well-being of half a million inhabitants. . . ."[2]

It was an exciting new atmosphere in which Sarmiento suddenly found himself. He studied and saw everything that there was to study and see. He visited Brooklyn and the factories of that neighboring village. He went to see the great Greenwood Cemetery and was struck not only by its size but by its elaborate architecture. He visited the Croton Dam and waterworks, and he carefully studied the statistics of this great engineering feat. He seems to have carried with him Appleton's United States traveler's guide, for the statistics that he recorded are consistent with those to be found in that volume, and the passage in his *Viajes* in which he describes the size and appearance of the Croton Aqueduct is a direct translation from that work.[3] He noted its size, capacity, and its imposing aspect. He undoubtedly visited it personally, but for the sake of greater accuracy, he seems to have relied upon the guidebook for the statistical description.

The real Mecca of Don Domingo's United States tour was Boston, the home of Horace Mann and the center of North American culture and education. He therefore set out from New York for that New England center, but in a typically Sarmientan manner he traveled to Boston by way of Buffalo. He took the river day-boat from New York to Albany and made the trip of one hundred forty-five miles for one dollar.[4]

[2] *Anthology*, pp. 229-230.

[3] *Viajes*, III, 122-123; this is a direct translation of Wellington Williams, *Appleton's New and Complete United States Guide Book for Travelers*, New York, 1847, p. 131.

[4] This sounds like an unbelievably small price, but one traveler writes a year later, "For this purpose I left my kind host of the Croton Hotel, in Broadway, and repaired to the wharf at the foot of Cortland Street; and on my arrival was surprised to find that I could get passage on board a steamer for nothing, owing to the great opposition on the river; where one company would take a passenger on board their boat for no fee whatever, before they would suffer him to take passage on board a boat belonging to their opponents, which is a course pursued by one company for the purpose of breaking

"The Hudson River is poetically, historically, and commercially speaking the center of life in the United States—the road to Boston, Montreal, Quebec, Buffalo, Niagara Falls, and the Great Lakes and the principal artery that carries the produce of Canada, Vermont, Massachusetts, New Jersey, and New York. Its waters are always literally covered with shipping, sometimes to the point of obstructing traffic, as happens in crowded city streets. Steamboats shoot past each other like meteors, and tugboats tow a whole line of cargo boats whose prows raise a regular tide ahead of them. Fourteen laden boats precede and follow the tugboat, occupying a large part of the surface of the river. Cargo boats on American rivers are like two-story floating houses, with flat roofs and a lower deck.

"The sight of these floating hotels, grandiose in themselves, on account of their colossal size, is heightened by the cultured, well-groomed, and polite appearance of the passengers, for it is a general practice among American men and women to dress their best for railroad and boat trips, although the coldness of Yankee character and society gives these great crowds a certain appearance of aloofness that would be called aristocratic in Europe. Here, it is considered rustic by European visitors, although as a matter of fact it is merely desirable reserve. The ladies occupy the forward part of the great saloons and are the object of every official attention. The placing of the pilots and helmsmen in the bow of the ship, at a conspicuous height, sometimes covered by an elegant superstructure, gives more animation to these ships. Moreover, since the wheel is turned from that point of vantage, by chains attached to the rudder, the course can be kept constantly in view, as if the pilot and helmsman were really the head and soul of that machine. The bell is constantly tolling to announce the approach of a landing stage, so that people who are getting off will have time to make ready.

"From the top deck, dominating both banks of the river, the traveler watches pleasant villas and knolls crowned by trees and buildings slip past him, and, in the water, hundreds of boats of every description traveling in the opposite direc-

---

up the other." J. C. Myers, *Sketches on a Tour through the Northern and Eastern States, the Canadas and Nova Scotia*, Harrisonburg, 1849, pp. 82-83.

tion along that immense public thoroughfare as bright and smooth as a mirror. Similarly, when putting out to sea from New York, one reviews the moving panorama of ships, picturesque islands, straits, and canals of New York bay. Opposite the New York wharf lies Jersey City and near it Weehawken Rock, which rises abruptly from the water and serves as the base for a villa built on its crest—a picturesque advance guard at the entrance to the Palisades. The Palisades are a perpendicular wall of steep rocks, rising 415 feet from the surface of the water; they border the western bank of the river for a distance of 20 miles. This freak of nature lends indescribable grandeur to the landscape, while on the opposite shore, villas, cities, towns, hills and woods hold the traveler's attention and stir his curiosity. The heights are sometimes crowned with ruins, and the names of Hamilton and Washington are recalled by a few stones still standing of forts captured and destroyed during the Revolutionary War. A living monument, however, is West Point, the military academy at which 230 cadets permanently tend the sacred fires of military tradition and science. The Greek architecture of the orphan asylum, the insane asylum, and other public buildings adorns the heights overlooking the river, which rivals the Rhine in beauty and is itself unsurpassed, except in China, for the volume of its water traffic."[5]

By that evening the river boat had reached Albany. Don Domingo did not linger long in this political capital of the State of New York. Sarmiento's boat arrived only a few moments before the departure of the Buffalo train, so he went directly to the depot to buy his ticket and board the next vehicle of his journey. For twelve dollars he made the three hundred twenty-five mile trip across the northern part of New York to the Great Lakes,[6] and he began to realize that his limited funds would carry him a long distance in this new land of cheap transportation. Across the fertile valleys of

[5] *Anthology*, pp. 231-232.

[6] Sarmiento refers to the price of this trip as twelve pesos (*Viajes*, III, 125). This was translated into English as twelve dollars (*Anthology*, p. 230). According to the railroad price lists of the time, the one-way fare from Albany to Buffalo was $6.60 (W. Williams, *Guidebook, op.cit.*, p. 190). The price of twelve dollars might have been the round-trip fare.

northern New York, Sarmiento traveled and observed. He saw the farms whose houses were beautified and kept by their proud owners, whose fields were carefully cultivated by the latest methods.

Buffalo was a wealthy city of some thirty thousand inhabitants. Recent waves of German immigrants had brought it a new life and a new spirit of expansion. As Don Domingo walked down the wide Main Street and saw the stores and houses lining each side, he saw in this the model for an expanding New World town, rationally laid out, alive with the vital energy of an immigrant population, so placed as to be a trade center joining canals, rivers, and lakes.

"A swarm of steamboats belched forth a dense mass of smoke and sparks from their smokestacks. The unloading of buffalo hides and other products of the Indian trade interfered with the procession of passengers proceeding toward the port. Looking back at the city, one saw hundreds of men on top of the buildings busily engaged in new construction, hastily expanding the city to meet the needs of a population which increases annually by 20,000 souls. Buffalo, like all of the predestined centers of future trade in the Union, has a coal deposit within easy access, in the peninsula formed by Lake Michigan and Lake Huron."[7]

From Buffalo, Sarmiento traveled on into "the most beautiful portion of the earth." He followed the Niagara River away from Lake Erie. It was "gentle and glassy, reflecting on its surface the mixed stands of rhododendrons and oaks that form blue perspectives of primeval forest in the distance. Under their branches, the mysterious moccasin tracks of unconquered Indians can still be seen. The river divides at the point where Grand Island forms, after which it reunites to prepare the sublime water play that begins at the Rapids and ends in Niagara Falls."[8] He followed the increasingly swift-moving river down the rapids to the scenic wonder that even then was "swelled by throngs of sightseers." From the nearby town of Niagara Falls the great roar of the water could already be heard.

[7] *Anthology*, p. 233.
[8] *Ibid.*

"I considered myself a tolerably well-educated traveler in the matter of waterfalls. The sight of other falls has always made me smile with pleasure, but at Niagara I felt my legs tremble and noticed the same feverish sensation that one has when the blood recedes from one's face. As one arrives by way of Goat Island, which splits the river in two, one's spirits are properly prepared for the less tumultuous scene offered by the rapids, where the Niagara River drops fifty feet in one mile. The primitive forest that covers the island, concealing the neighboring city behind its foliage, and the upstream perspective of the winding river offer one of those charming, unspoiled views so common in the United States. The Canadian Falls are horseshoe-shaped and more than a half mile long, with no break, or other interruption. The American Falls, called the lesser falls, are 600[9] feet wide. In both, the water drops 165 feet and the receiving channel, hollowed out of the rock, is 100 yards deep and 130 yards wide. When we see these figures written down, which have been checked by actual measurement, we realize the inability of the human eye to grasp great size. St. Peter's in Rome looks like a building of normal dimensions and Niagara Falls shrinks, on actual sight, to our own diminutive stature."[10]

Don Domingo visited the caves at the foot of the Falls in order to receive an impression of their full magnificence. He put on a rubber cap, and holding tightly to the iron railing constructed to protect the sightseers, he descended to the bottom of the gallery. "Giddy and overwhelmed by the noise and drenched by heavy showers from the Falls," he saw the seemingly solid crystal wall of water before him. "Leaving that damp inferno and seeing the sun and sky once more, one can say that one's heart has experienced the sublime. A battle of two hundred thousand combatants would not cause deeper emotion."[11]

He left Niagara by railroad for Montreal and Quebec, but he was still thrilled by the sights that he had seen. He reviewed the experience as the railway coach made its way into Canada, and expressed his wonder and admiration to a North American who was traveling next to him.

[9] 1,400 feet wide. [10] *Anthology*, p. 234. [11] *Ibid.*

"Beautiful! Beautiful!" replied the North American, but his aesthetic values proved to be somewhat different from the Romantic emotions that Sarmiento had been experiencing. "These Falls are worth millions. Along the Rapids machinery has already been installed, which is turned by water diverted into cheaply constructed canals. When the population of the States increases in this region, the immense wealth of water in the American Falls can be broken up and carried by canals running along the upper level, to points of discharge in the lower bed of the Niagara, where textile and other factories will be built. Can you imagine," he said, "that turbines can be used, capable, if necessary, of generating 40,000 horsepower? Then Niagara will be a street flanked on both sides by seven miles of factories, each with its own fall of water of the proper volume for its machinery. Ships will tie up at the port and carry their merchandise down the St. Lawrence, Lake Champlain, or the Oswego canal to New York and Europe. Beautiful! Beautiful!"[12] This dialogue between Don Domingo and a North American is symbolic of the dialogue that was taking place within the being of Sarmiento throughout his travels. He admired with Romantic enthusiasm the scenic beauty of what he saw, but he described in statistical terms the material progress of the foreign lands, and he dreamed of a world of the future in which the aspects of "civilization" as he saw it would be extended from the Sahara to the Virgin forests of Northern New York and eventually even to his own Pampa.

He traveled on by rail to Queenstown and then by steamer down Lake Ontario into the Saint Lawrence River. He passed the Thousand Islands, whose landscape seemed to him "like a dream out of a fairy tale." His steamboat was carried by the rapid current of the St. Lawrence, and the gullible South American solemnly recorded the claim of the ship's pilot that the vessel was traveling at sixty miles an hour and compared the speed with the Manchester-Liverpool express. Don Domingo visited Montreal and its fur-trading centers and Quebec, where he examined a barrack which the British government had constructed for the reception of Irish immigration.

[12] *Ibid.*, p. 236.

He recrossed the St. Lawrence to La Prairie; and then crossing Lake Champlain to New York he traveled down the Erie Canal to Troy, where he took a train for Boston. His route from New York to Boston had certainly not been a direct one, but the low costs never ceased to amaze Don Domingo. The round-trip to Quebec cost only seven dollars, and the trip through the canal to Troy was only three dollars. He had seen one of the most scenic centers of the United States. He had seen it alive with commerce and trade by railroad, steamer, and canal boat. He had seen former frontier towns now growing with the pulsating life of the North European immigrant. He had been thrilled by the grandeur and beauty of Niagara Falls and the landscape of Cooper and the "Last of the Mohicans," and he had dreamed a dream of a mechanical future to be supplied by the natural energy of the area.

But Boston was his goal. It was the "Puritan city, the Memphis of Yankee civilization." It was the city that for him symbolized the ideal of public education and of representative government. As he wandered through its streets the first day, Sarmiento recalled the first compulsory public education law and the first "town meetings."

While in London, Don Domingo had read Horace Mann's *Seventh Annual Report* of the Board of Education, and he had been impressed by the North American's pedagogical theories.[13] So the day after his arrival, armed with the letter of introduction from the politician from Massachusetts whom he had met aboard the *Moctezuma*, he took the train for East Newton and called at the home of the distinguished educator. Mann was a tall, thin, frail man, of handsome countenance with "a noble brow over a kindly face."[14] He received his guest with warmth and enthusiasm. They discussed their labors in the education of their respective nations. Mann showed Sarmiento the training school for teachers that he had founded near his own home. Don Domingo saw the tuition-free students, men and women, working in mathematics,

[13] *Educación popular*, Buenos Aires, 1896, p. 25.

[14] Watt Stewart and William Mashall French, "The Influence of Horace Mann on the Educational Ideas of Domingo Faustino Sarmiento," *The Hispanic American Historical Review*, xx, 13; see also Mary Tyler Peabody Mann, *Life of Horace Mann*, Boston, 1888, p. vii.

chemistry, botany, and anatomy. When the two men met personally, they found that they had so much in common that their subjects of conversation and discussion were almost limitless. With the help of Mrs. Mann, who acted as interpreter, these conversations had a profound influence upon the future pedagogical ideas of the Argentine leader.[15]

Mr. Mann gave his South American visitor letters of introduction to many of the educational, intellectual, and political leaders of the country. Don Domingo met many of the leading figures of Boston. He visited the nearby manufacturing districts of Lowell. He studied the industrial methods and results. He visited the schools of the districts, and made careful notes for his report to the Chilean government.

Then, unable to remain any longer, he recommenced his journey across the United States. He returned first to New York, where he met a Chilean friend, Santiago Arcos. Together they discussed their financial resources. Fortunately for Sarmiento, they agreed upon a pooling of wealth and a joint continuance of their trips. The Chilean was evidently satisfied to pay part of Don Domingo's expenses in return for his lively and pleasant company. They agreed to separate while Sarmiento visited Baltimore and Washington and then to meet again in Philadelphia. From there they would travel together to Harrisburg, Pittsburgh, and down the Ohio and Mississippi Rivers to New Orleans.

Baltimore and Philadelphia were for Sarmiento cities of great interest and individuality. As in other places that he had visited, he inspected the schools, the public buildings, and the layout of the streets. The approach to Washington by the river was a beautiful one. Sarmiento watched historic Virginia pass to his left and thought of the birth of representative government in America in Jamestown in 1619. As his boat turned a bend in the Potomac, the public buildings of Washington came into view. The Washington Monument was

[15] Mary Tyler Peabody Mann was the second wife of Horace Mann. She was the daughter of a dentist and physician, Nathaniel Peabody. One of her sisters, Sophia, was Mrs. Nathaniel Hawthorne. "Mrs. Mann was her husband's active collaborator and influenced his life and thought profoundly." G. H. Genzmer, *The Dictionary of American Biography*, XII, p. 246.

almost completed. The Capitol itself stood out on the hill.[16] Don Domingo found more than usual to attract him to the capital city. The White House, Mount Vernon, the new Monument, and the many other buildings and places of interest were of deep interest for him. He wondered at the political situation of Washington. Here was a capital that was not a capital. It was merely the center of a federation. It held an independent, almost isolated status of its own. He saw for such a city a great future. It would be the cradle of a truly American art, an art already born with the architecture springing up on all sides. It would be the center of a great nation. There began to take form in Sarmiento's mind an idea that might be applied to his own nation. Here was a possible compromise between the centralized policy of the unitarists and the completely chaotic ideal of the federalists. Here was a city that was both the seat of government and the leader of sovereign states. Here was a city that was neither in one state nor another but whose government came directly under the national congress. Here was a city that was built from nothing. It was therefore all new; all that was created was created for the specific purpose which it would serve.

Don Domingo called upon the Chilean Envoy Extraordinary, Señor Carvallo, who insisted that Sarmiento stay with him during his visit to the capital. The secretary of the Chilean representative, Astaburuaga, was an old friend. Together the two young men wandered through the streets of the city. The Chilean, who had been there longer, was able to point out the sights to the Argentine traveler. "In this way he could show me on Pennsylvania Avenue which among the young girls that caught our attention were daughters of a senator, which were daughters of a banker, and which were simple dressmakers or other persons of lesser quality."[17] Astaburuaga took Don Domingo to visit a number of important political leaders in the capital. Sarmiento tried to get a view of the political situation at the time, but his limited knowledge of the background and his imperfect English made this

[16] William Q. Force, *Picture of the City of Washington and Its Vicinity*, Washington, 1850.

[17] *Viajes*, III, 162.

difficult. In rewriting his notes for *Viajes* only a few years later, he made the mistake of referring to the president at the time of his visit to Washington as Zachary Taylor instead of James K. Polk. He met a Mr. Johnson, whom he identifies as an editor of the *National Intelligencer* (he calls it the *Washington Intelligencer*) and a leading member of the Whig party.[18] Together they discussed the philosophical bases of democratic government. Johnson was pessimistic about the future of democratic forms. He held Vico's view of political cycles and saw democracy followed by liberty, liberty by license, and license by chaos. Don Domingo countered with one of the clearest expositions of his political thought to be found anywhere in his published works. He compared moral progress with physical and material progress. The latter had followed a varied but unbroken line upwards. The nineteenth century had brought the railway, the steamboat, factory production, and the expansion of the civilized world. In a similar way it would bring the abolition of aristocracy, of tyranny. It would bring "the nation, with equality of rights, with personal industry to live, with machines to help work, railroads, telegraphs, presses, primary schools, colleges, asylums, hospitals, penitentiaries."[19] Sarmiento's was a picture of progress and optimism. He and Johnson argued late into the night.

"Ah!" exclaimed Don Domingo, "if you only had, like us in South America, to fight with masses, in which the European element that you find so backward, is a precious and scarce element of civilization."[20] It surprised him that a member of a nation with so many gifts and so many elements of greatness could have such a dark view of the future.

Don Domingo's stay in Washington lasted a day longer than agreed upon with his friend Arcos, and when he arrived at their meeting place in Harrisburg he found that the Chilean had already left. Assuming that there was a United States hotel in every North American city, they had picked

[18] It is impossible to deduce from these two clues the definite identity of Mr. Johnson, but he might well have been Mr. Reverdy Johnson, later Postmaster General in the Cabinet of President Taylor.

[19] *Viajes*, III, 168.

[20] *Ibid.*, p. 169.

this for their rendezvous in the Pennsylvanian capital. "What was my surprise to learn that there was no hotel by that name in town!" From hotel to hotel Sarmiento rushed, trying to find his friend or some news from him. Finally at the Post House Hotel, he found Arcos' name in the register and after it these disheartening words, "Shall wait for you at Chambersburg."

"Considerably disgruntled and crestfallen at this contretemps, I started for Chambersburg, where, after visiting the inns with increasing alarm, I was able to get no information about Arcos. This was not surprising, as he spoke English with such rare perfection—putting on a nasal twang for fun when conversing with Americans—that nobody, not even those who had talked with him, recognized the young Spaniard for whom I was inquiring in my English, which shook the poor Yankees to their very core. I still cherished the hope that he was shooting somewhere in the neighborhood, because a camping expedition in the Allegheny Mountains had figured in our travel program. At length, I learned that he had left a note at the post office, repeating the Harrisburg message: 'Shall wait for you at Pittsburgh.' 'Malheureux!' I exclaimed, deeply distressed. One hundred and fifty miles from Chambersburg to Pittsburgh, with the Alleghenies between us, $10 for a seat in the stage coach, and I had only $4 in my pocket, barely enough to pay my hotel bill! After a careful investigation of the details of my elusive forerunner's indiscreet departure, I learned that as there had been no seat inside the stagecoach, Arcos had ensconced himself on a bag of hay carried on top to provide fodder for the horses, that he had had to travel two days and two nights to get there, and that I had been put to all this anguish because of the juvenile restlessness of a wretch unable to stay in one place for eight hours—the difference in time that separated us, between one railroad train and the next. There I was, therefore, in the heart of the United States, afoot in the wilderness, so to speak, without a sou, barely able to make myself understood and surrounded by those impassive, frozen American faces.

"What a fright and what tribulations I endured in Chambersburg! I called the hotel keeper and orally and in writing explained my situation to him: 'A young man, traveling ahead of me, has my money, not knowing that I do not have enough for my traveling expenses. I must pay $10 for a seat in the mail coach, but I have only $4 to pay my hotel bill. I have a few valuables in my suitcase, however, and I want to persuade the post office to retain them until my fare has been paid in Pittsburgh.' On hearing this lamentable story, the innkeeper's only reply was to shrug his shoulders. I related my trials to the postmaster, who stood looking at me as though I had not uttered a word. Two days of constant torment and despair had already passed and the worst of it was that there was not even a seat in the coach, as all had been engaged from Philadelphia to supplement the railroad accommodations which ended there. At length, they suggested that I telegraph to Arcos, which I did, sending forty words for the price of $1, and in the most feeling terms. Notwithstanding the necessity for telegraphic brevity, I started my message with: 'Don't be a swine,' and told him what had happened to me through his thoughtlessness. 'Where is the person to whom this is being sent?' 'At the United States Hotel,' I answered, beginning to wonder now whether there was any hotel by that name in Pittsburgh, and to spare myself any further disappointment I suggested that he be looked for in the principal hotels in that city."[21]

With impatience and in suspense, Don Domingo waited for a reply. He tormented the telegraph operator with his repeated questions. No answer came. Hours passed. Then came the message: "There is no such person!" Sarmiento was stunned by the news. He did not know in what direction to turn when a chance remark of the operator revealed that he had been in contact with Philadelphia instead of Pittsburgh. Don Domingo's bad English had created an added element of confusion, and before they could get through to the more western city the telegraph offices were closed and the attempt had to be put off until morning.

"Great mental stress can be relieved only in one's own language, and though English has a passable 'God damn,' for special cases I preferred Spanish, which is so round and

[21] *Anthology*, pp. 255-256.

sonorous for uttering roars of rage. Yankees are little accustomed to manifestations of Southern passion and the innkeeper, hearing me curse very excitedly in a foreign tongue, glanced at me, terrified. Waving his hand for me to stop a moment before biting them all or committing suicide, he rushed out into the street, doubtless looking for a constable to arrest me. That, thought I, would have been the last straw! The very idea of it suddenly restored the composure of which my troubles had momentarily deprived me. A few minutes later, he was back again, accompanied by a man with a pen stuck behind his ear. This person coldly asked me, first in English, then in French, and finally in halting Spanish, what was the cause of my excitement, about which the innkeeper had told him. I related in a few words what had happened, told him my place of origin and destination, and begged him to intercede with the postal authorities to accept my watch and other valuables as a pledge until I had repaid my fare in Pittsburgh. He listened to me without moving a muscle of his impassive face and when I had finished speaking he said in French: 'Sir, all I can do . . .' (what an opening remark! thought I to myself, swallowing hard) 'all I can do, is to pay your hotel bill and fare as far as Pittsburgh on condition that when you reach that city, you deposit at the Merchants Manufactory Bank, to the account of Lesley and Company of Chambersburg, whatever amount you think necessary for me to advance you here.' I had to draw a deep breath before answering him: 'But, my dear sir, thank you, but you don't know me, and can't I give you some guarantee?' 'It's not necessary sir. People in your position don't swindle.' So saying, he took leave of me until later. I immediately ate twenty-five cents' worth of apples, the series of emotions through which I had passed during the preceding three days having awakened my hunger. I spent the afternoon walking around the city and its environs, feeling the need to move about and stir my legs, in order to realize that I was once again my own master. In the early evening, my guardian angel reappeared, laden with books."[22]

Mr. Lesley brought with him copies of Quevedo, Tasso,

[22] *Ibid.*, pp. 257-258.

and a number of French authors for Sarmiento to read on his trip. He seemed pleased to have a chance to talk with a foreigner, and he boasted of his knowledge of Greek and Latin and other languages. The next day he returned with four five-dollar bills, and as he was about to leave, he turned again, blushing and said, "Excuse me, sir, but I've found another banknote in my pocket. Please take it too." Moved by the Mr. Lesley's generosity and kindness, with ten dollars more than he needed, Don Domingo departed by coach from Chambersburg, never to forget this amazing example of "Yankee hospitality."

On the trip Sarmiento had further occasion to enjoy American hospitality. On the stage coach there was a lady from New Orleans whose husband, he later learned, had died only six weeks before. She was on her way South to put his affairs in order. She had a little girl of nine years, and both mother and child were in deep mourning. As the coach bumped its way along the stage road, Don Domingo began to doze. He was awakened by a voice, in French.

"I believe that you have been in some difficulty, sir."

Don Domingo was indignant at this invasion of his private affairs. "Why, no, madam," he replied.

A silence ensued, as Sarmiento thought over the question and as the lady realized the way her question had been taken. "Forgive me, sir," she went on, visibly perturbed, "if I have asked an indiscreet question, but in Chambersburg this morning I happened to be in a room from which I could not help hearing what you were telling another gentleman."

"It is true, madam, but as you doubtless heard, everything has been taken care of." Sarmiento's tone was now a little less indignant.

"And what do you intend to do, sir, if you should be unable to find your friend in Pittsburgh?"

"Your question terrifies me, madam," replied Don Domingo, a trifle startled at the thought. "I have not even given it a thought, and I tremble to think that such a thing is possible. I would return to New York or to Washington, where I have friends."

"And why should you not continue on your journey?"

"How could I plunge into an unknown country, madam, without funds?"

"I mention it because my house is fifteen miles this side of New Orleans and I wanted to offer it to you. From there you could learn where your friend is, and if you should be unable to find him, you could write to your own country and wait until they sent you what you needed."

Sarmiento realized that Mr. Lesley's actions had not been an isolated example of Yankee generosity, and that there was much to be learned from his North American attitude of trust and kindness. In Pittsburgh, the lady's parting remark was an invitation to the traveler to visit her home in the South.[23]

Fortunately for Sarmiento, there was a United States Hotel in Pittsburgh, and there he found Arcos in the act of composing an advertisement for the newspaper to notify his lost companion of his whereabouts. Don Domingo was angry with the young Chilean, but Arcos' delight at seeing him softened his intentions to chastise him. And perhaps even more important, it was Arcos who had the money. They did not delay long in Pittsburgh. The *Martha Washington* was sailing immediately for Cincinnati, and the two travelers hurried to board it. In the main saloon, they found the kind lady from New Orleans waiting to hear how Sarmiento had fared. She crossed the room to greet him, and pretending to shake hands she handed him *sub rosa* a bag of gold. Don Domingo did not accept. Instead, he introduced Arcos and made it clear to the lady that all was well again. Sarmiento and his friend from New Orleans parted when they reached Cincinnati. Don Domingo never saw her again, and he could not even remember her name when he came to recount the story, but the incident always stood out in his mind as another example of the North American character.

The winding Ohio River between Pittsburgh and Cincinnati passed through the rolling countryside, and again Sarmiento was able to note not only the extent, but the fertility, of this North American continent. One day as he stood on the deck surveying the scene, the boat rounded another of the

[23] *Ibid.*, pp. 259, 260.

hundreds of bends that they had passed in the last days and suddenly there appeared before the South American's eyes a large city whose busy wharves jetted out into the water. Cincinnati was at the time the largest city inland from the Eastern seaboard. Known as the "Queen City of the West," it housed some 50,000 inhabitants, and it was one of the big commercial and industrial centers of the area.[24] The *Martha Washington* tied up at the public landing at the foot of Broadway and Main Street, and Sarmiento landed to explore a type of metropolis that they had not found in the East.

Cincinnati was the center of a vast system of communications that linked it with all parts of the country. Canals, roads, and rivers brought it into contact with centers in the North, Far West, and South. It was one of the focal points of the nation's trade. Its own economy was based upon the hog industry, "and there is a group of local society that has been dubbed the pork aristocracy, as its wealth is derived from raising swine." Two hundred thousand hogs were sold in Cincinnati every year, and merchants from all over the nation flocked there to buy their pork, sausage, bacon and ham.

But the feature of Cincinnati that most intrigued Don Domingo was the large number of literary, scientific, and philanthropic societies. He visited the College of Cincinnati, Woodward College, St. Xavier's College, the Ohio College of Medicine, the College of Jurisprudence, the Mechanics Institute, and the Western Academy of Natural Sciences. The Mercantile Library with its 200 volumes, the Catholic asylums, orphan asylum, and poor house—these were the many features of this frontier city that Sarmiento studied and visited and that made him compare his own San Juan so unfavorably with it. Here was the model of an inland, almost frontier, metropolis, a center of culture, civilization, and progress.

"Arcos and I spent four or five days in Cincinnati, carried away by the pleasure of wandering through its streets and suburbs at random, visiting its museum and enjoying the tourist's *dolce far niente*. It was in Cincinnati where Arcos, seeing a peaceful Yankee sitting reading his Bible before the

[24] W. Williams, *Appletons' Southern and Western Travellers' Guide*, New York, 1853, p. 18.

door of his shop, stopped in front of him, took the cigar that he was smoking out of his mouth, lighted his own, stuck the cigar back into the good man's mouth, and continued on his way without the Yankee's raising his eyes or making any movement other than to open his mouth for the cigar to be reinserted."[25]

Leaving Cincinnati by steamship for New Orleans, Sarmiento spent eleven days traveling down the Ohio and then the Mississippi Rivers. The boat stopped at Marietta, Louisville, Rome, and Cairo. The passengers watched the country change from the well-cultivated and settled areas of Ohio to the semi-savage wilderness farther south.

"My trip down the Mississippi is one of the most beautiful, calm, and lasting memories that I have. The river winds majestically along the floor of the greatest valley in the world. The scene changes at every turning and the moderate width of the greatest of rivers allows one's vision to follow both banks, to penetrate the shadowy vastnesses of the forests, and to wander over the plains and the clearings in the trees that occur from time to time. Meeting another steamboat is an eagerly awaited event, on account of the closeness and speed with which it passes. From the top decks of these floating palaces, one's eyes fall upon a fleet of barges full of coal floating down the river. Farther off, one sees a peddler traveling in his tiny sail vessel to retail his wares in the neighboring villages. To go ashore at the towns and hamlets where the boat called, to run through the streets, peep into a mine, examine everything, buy apples and cakes, all the time keeping our ears open for the bell that would announce our early departure, was a much appreciated relaxation, which we never failed to add to our experiences, just as we never failed to jump across a ditch for a short run in the forest while the boat was loading wood to stoke its furnaces. . . ."[26]

As the boat approached New Orleans the travelers began to note a change in architecture along the banks of the river. The large plantation houses with their colonial columns began to appear near the waterfront. The isolated rural populations disappeared, and the large single dwellings became

[25] *Anthology*, p. 264.

[26] *Ibid.*, pp. 264-265.

more frequent. "As the steamboat turned one of the semicircular curves described by that immense, smoothly flowing body of water," the travelers were suddenly shown an immense cupola "against the horizon—dominating steplike clumps of trees in every shade of autumn colors, below which spread the emerald lines of broad sugar plantations."[27] The dome reminded Don Domingo of St. Peter's in Rome, or a great cathedral or palace in some other part of Europe. But it was the St. Charles Hotel. In America, it was the common lodging that had the largest and most imposing structure, and as Sarmiento explored the architectural wonders and the comforts of this great hotel he became more and more amazed at the basic difference between the European and North American civilizations.

Yellow fever was raging in New Orleans, and the city appeared lifeless, empty. The travelers sought the first possible transportation away from the infected city and soon found themselves on a "wretched, pestiferous little sailing vessel . . ." headed for Havana. The visit to the United States was over. Domingo Sarmiento was on his way home. He stopped shortly in Cuba, where he bought 1,000 cigars, probably as a business venture to help pay his way home. He and Arcos crossed the Isthmus of Panama on horseback and sailed down the Pacific Coast to Lima, Arica, and finally to Valparaíso. On February 24, 1848, Domingo Sarmiento disembarked in the Chilean seaport after two years and four months of absence.

Chapter 24. A South American De Tocqueville

As Domingo Sarmiento sailed across the warm Gulf of Mexico in November 1847, he wrote to his friend Don

[27] *Ibid.*, p. 213.

Valentín Alsina. He was filled with the impressions of his trip through the United States.

"I am leaving the United States, my dear friend, in that state of excitement caused by viewing a new drama—planless and without unity, but full of incidents and bristling with crimes, whose sinister glare throws into relief acts of heroism and self-sacrifice. The stage scenery is fabulous and splendid, depicting century-old forests, flowery meadows, forbidding mountains, and peaceful human dwelling where innocence and virtue reign. I want to tell you that I am departing sad, thoughtful, pleased, and humbled, with half of my illusions damaged while others struggle against reason to reconstitute again that imagery with which we always clothe ideas not yet seen, just as we supply a face and a tone of voice for a friend whom we know only by correspondence. The United States is without precedent, a sort of extravaganza that at first sight shocks and disappoints one's expectations because it runs counter to preconceived ideas. Yet this inconceivable extravaganza is grand and noble, occasionally sublime, and always follows its genius. It has, moreover, such an appearance of permanence and organic strength that ridicule would ricochet from its surface like a spent bullet off the scaly hide of an alligator. That social body is no misshapen being, no monster of known species, but rather a new creature, the offspring of a political generation, as strange as the fossil monsters whose bones are still being uncovered. In order to learn how to observe it, therefore, it is essential first to educate one's own judgment to overlook its apparent organic defects in order to appreciate it in its true character. The risk must be run, however, that, having overcome one's first surprise, one may then become deeply attached to it, find it beautiful, and proclaim a new judgment about human affairs."[1]

Not many years before this, a young French aristocrat, Alexis de Tocqueville, had traveled through the new republic known as the United States of America. He too had been captivated by the bustling life of the nation and the spirit of the people. He too had left to write an enthusiastic eulogy of the young republic. But he had waited too long. He had be-

[1] *Anthology*, p. 193.

come disillusioned by the democratic institutions in his own nation. He had become embittered about the ability of the people to govern themselves, and his book, *Democracy in America,* turned out to be a negative treatment of the subject. He pointed to the dangers of democracy, the weaknesses of government by the people. "The sight of such universal uniformity saddens and chills me."[2] But Domingo Sarmiento did not delay the writing of his book on the United States. He wrote it when the memory was still fresh in his mind. What he had seen did not conform exactly to the ideal that he had formed in his mind, but he liked what he found, and he expressed a sympathetic understanding of it. The Frenchman criticized the republic as an abstraction. His was a rational, intellectual treatment. The Argentine described it as a part of his own vital experience. He described its faults, but he was captivated by its life and its spirit.

The Romantic "livingness" of Don Domingo was attracted to the grandeur and color of the yet untapped natural resources of the North American continent. The falls of the Niagara, the scenery along the Ohio and the Mississippi—these were as important elements of his treatment of the country as was his intellectual analysis. His interest in the "squatter" as an anti-social type, the forerunner of civilization,[3] his admiration of the "ancient heroic spirit,"[4] and his appraisal of James Fenimore Cooper as the outstanding writer of North America,[5] all betray the still Romantic interest of the writer.

But, as in his other works, the intention of his travel accounts differs sharply from his intent. His work was intended to be an analysis of the elements of North American civilization. He studied the political scene of the United States, and a superficial perusal seemed to make it coincide reasonably well with the ideal political pattern that he had formed in his mind. He saw the Republic as part of the political heritage of the Anglo-Saxon and English histories. He saw it based upon the Bill of Rights, the Declaration of Independence

[2] For an excellent treatment of this subject, see Wyndam Lewis, "De Tocqueville and Democracy," *The Sewanee Review*, LIV, 1946, pp. 557-575.

[3] *Viajes*, III, 52. [4] *Ibid.*, p. 54. [5] *Ibid.*, p. 57.

and the Constitution.[6] These elements created a government in which the personality operated within a framework of abstractions and laws.

With such a political basis, with such a framework within which to work, the United States had followed a course of continued progress and development. At every turn Don Domingo wondered at the amazing intellectual and material progress of the nation and its limitless possibilities for future development. The possibilities of harnessing the power of Niagara, the future of a harbor such as that of New York, a commercial center like Cincinnati, an industrial center such as Lowell, and an intellectual atmosphere such as that of Boston—all of these signified a history of progress to the mind of Sarmiento. The great educational system founded by men like Horace Mann, combined with the physical possibilities of the nation, created the formula that Sarmiento saw as the key to the future.

"God has at last permitted the concentration in a single nation of enough virgin territory to permit society to expand indefinitely without fear of poverty. He has given it iron to supplement human strength, coal to turn its machines, forests to provide material for naval construction, popular education to develop the productive capacity of every one of its citizens, religious freedom to attract hundreds of thousands of foreigners to its shores, and political liberty which views despotism and special privilege with abhorrence. It is the republic, in short—strong and ascendant like a new star in the firmament. All of these factors are interdependent: freedom and abundant land; iron and industrial genius; democracy and the superiority of American ships. Try as you will to disjoin them in theory, assert that liberty and popular education have nothing to do with this unexampled prosperity which is leading inexorably to undisputed supremacy, the fact will still remain that European monarchies are an amalgam of decrepitude, revolution, poverty, ignorance, barbarism, and the degradation of the majority."[7]

This was the product of Sarmiento the thinker. He had dreamed a dream in San Juan and in Chile, and now he

[6] *Ibid.*, pp. 80-81.

[7] *Anthology*, pp. 225-226.

seemed to see this dream materialize. He had seen an ideal of government by law progressing towards moral, intellectual, and material perfection. He had analyzed the factors that seemed to be necessary to fulfill such a dream, and now he seemed to see before him these very factors and the dream in the process of fulfillment. He criticized many aspects of the North American scene,[8] but his analysis was far more positive than negative. In this respect, he might be called "a positive De Tocqueville."

Don Domingo analyzed the United States at the high point of its possibilities. It was a period of expansion and vitality. The Industrial Revolution had reached the American shore, and had brought with it only its benefits and few of its evils. The frontier was being conquered, but there was still room for expansion. There was still almost limitless wealth to tap. It was a period of energy and optimism. It is little wonder that a traveler with a dream and only a few short months to see the country would leave starry-eyed and captivated. It is little wonder that he would see the positive elements and tend to gloss over the negative ones. What Sarmiento missed was what De Tocqueville saw. The Frenchman saw the underlying elements, those which were still under the surface, which would be future dangers in both the Democratic government and the Industrial Revolution. Sarmiento saw the optimism of the surface. De Tocqueville saw the pessimism of the undercurrent. Both are interesting to read as chronicles of an age. One is an inspiration. The other is a warning.

But the important fact for the Argentine leader's own life is not the accuracy or inaccuracy of his portrayal of the political and material factors of North American civilization but rather the fact that he did see what he saw, and that it had a lasting effect upon his future life. North America replaced France and Europe as his model for civilization. The United States became his idol. He had begun his travels with the picture in his mind of a mortal struggle between barbarism and civilization. His idea of the roots of barbarism was confirmed by his visit to Spain and North Africa. His idea of civilization suffered a sad disillusionment at the hands of

[8] See Gálvez, pp. 188-189.

Thiers, Guizot, and the France of Louis Philippe. Now that ideal was renovated by the United States. It was brought once more to life, and he had a living model in the Republic of the North.

If we are seeking, however, the element of accuracy and value in Sarmiento's treatment of the United States in the 1840's we will not find it in his analysis of North American politics or of the progressive aspect of its civilization. This analysis was admittedly superficial and, at times, blind to one entire side of the scene. But we must turn to Sarmiento's artistic understanding of the North American people. He painted a picture of the individual in the society of the United States that is sympathetic, accurate, and true even today. He may not have captured the intellectual phase of the North American, but he portrayed well the essential human element of the national character. He picked out those vital characteristics which only an artist can find, those characteristics which identified a people in 1847 and still identify it today. He chose for description a typical village of the United States, and his description of its physical appearance and its everyday life would hold true, with very slight modifications, at any period in the nation's history.

Sarmiento told of the North American as a type. He was a man who followed everything on his map. Move by move the Mexican War was recorded in every home and in every hamlet by the citizens of the United States. (What war in which the United States has participated has not been followed in a similar way by its citizens?) The North American's eating habits were a source of amazement to the South American. The "Yankee" ate in a few moments. He ate jellies with his meat, and he used tomato sauce irresponsibly with almost anything that was put before him. The United States was one of the few countries in the world where it was considered impolite for a person to start eating as soon as his food was put before him. He had to wait until all were served. The reason for this strange custom? If one was allowed to start before the others, there would be none left by the time the last was served. These descriptions of the "strange eating habits of the

Yankee" must strike a responsive note in any foreigner who visits the United States even today.

The North American was painted by Sarmiento as a man who loved to travel. "If God were suddenly to call the world to judgment He would surprise two-thirds of the American population on the road like ants."[9] "In the United States you will see constant indications of the religious veneration which the nation pays to the noble and worthy instruments of its wealth—its feet. While conversing with you, the Yankee of careful breeding will rest one foot on his knee, remove his shoe to rub his foot, and listen to whatever complaints his overworked toes may have to offer. Four persons seated about a marble-topped table will invariably rest their eight feet on it, unless they can find a seat upholstered in velvet, which, for softness, Yankees prefer to marble. In the Tremont Hotel in Boston, I once saw seven Yankee dandies in friendly discussion, seated as follows: two with their feet on the table, one with his feet resting on the cushion of a nearby chair, another with a leg hooked over the arm of his own chair, another with both heels on the edge of the cushion of his chair so as to prop his chin on his two knees, another embracing the back of his chair with his leg in the same way as we are accustomed to rest our arms. This posture, impossible for the rest of mankind to achieve, I have tried unsuccessfully, and I recommend it to you to give yourself cramps in punishment for some indiscretion. Another, finally—if those already mentioned do not add up to seven—in some equally absurd position. I do not recall ever having seen Americans sitting on the backs of their chairs, with their feet on the cushions. I am certain, however, that I never saw one who prided himself on courtesy, in the natural posture.

"Lying down is the height of elegance, and people in the know reserve this gesture of good breeding for times when ladies are present, or when a 'locofoco' is listening to a Whig speech. On reaching Washington, the secretary of the Chilean legation had some business to transact with a Mr. N., a member of Congress. He went to the Capitol during a session, asked for the Congressman's seat, and finally came upon Mr.

[9] *Viajes*, II, 22-23.

N., sprawling on his chair with both legs stretched out across his neighbor's seat and snoring soundly. He had to wake him up, and when their business was concluded, Congressman N. stretched himself out again on the other side, doubtless waiting for the end of an interminable speech by some orator of the opposition."[10]

Perhaps the most charming insight into North American character is Sarmiento's description of the American girl before and after marriage. As one of the high spots of his writings on the United States, it is worth quotation in full:

"The unmarried woman, or *man of feminine sex,* is as free as the butterflies until the moment she is shut up in the domestic cocoon to fulfill her social functions by marriage. Before that event she travels around alone, walks about the city streets, and carries on chaste and open love affairs under the indifferent eyes of her parents. She receives visits from people whom her family has never met and comes home from a dance at two o'clock in the morning, accompanied by her escort who has waltzed or danced polkas with her all evening. Her good Puritan parents sometimes poke fun at her young man, about whose love they have heard from public report. She enjoys skillfully parrying their conjectures and denying the evidence alleged.

"After two or three years of flirtation, dancing, walks, trips, and coquetry, the girl in the story reluctantly asks her parents at breakfast one day whether they recall a certain tall, blond, young man, a machinist by trade, who has been coming to see her every day for some time past. They have been waiting for a year for this announcement. The upshot of the matter is that a marriage has been agreed to, of which the parents were informed only when it was about to take place, but which they had already heard about from all the neighborhood gossips. As soon as the marriage knot is tied, the young couple take the next train to parade their happiness through woods, towns, cities, and hotels. In the coaches, these enchanting couples of twenty summers are to be seen in close embrace, reclining very affectionately against each other to the edification of all the travelers, with the result that even the crusty

[10] *Anthology*, pp. 219-220.

old bachelors immediately decide to get married. Propaganda for marriage could not be more effectively carried out than by such flaunting of matrimonial delights. For this reason no Yankee passes the age of twenty-five without having a large family, which is the only way that I can explain the astonishing propagation of the species in that happy land. . . .

"Returning then to the thousands of newly-wed couples that warm and electrify the atmosphere with their breath of spring, the steamboats on the Hudson and other popular rivers have special staterooms fitted out for them. They are called bridal suites! The discreet light that pervades them comes from colored glass that sheds all the soft hues of the rainbow. Rose-tinted lamps burn at night, and day and night the perfume of flowers and of burning aromatic essences sharpen the privileged tenants' appetite for pleasure. Paris factories have created no damasks or muslins too costly for the flowing folds hanging from gilded canopies, to veil the lawful saturnalia of the bridal suite. After viewing Niagara Falls, bathing in the hot springs at Saratoga, visiting a hundred cities and traveling three thousand miles in a fortnight, the couple returns, weak, dazzled, and happy, to the sanctified boredom of their home. The wife has said good-by forever to the world, whose pleasures she so long and so freely enjoyed; to the cool, verdant forests, witnesses of her love; to the waterfalls, roads, and rivers. Henceforth, for life, the closed domestic asylum is her prison; roast beef stares her constantly in the face; the teeming, blond, frolicsome children are her constant torment; and an uncivil but goodnatured husband, perspiring by day and snoring by night, her accomplice and solace."[11]

These are the insights into the United States that still hold charm for the reader after the passing of a hundred years. This was Sarmiento's true art. His sympathetic observation of the "Yankee," of the citizen of this nation of his ideals, produced a description of the North American character that could not be duplicated by the cold intellectual analysis of De Tocqueville or by any self-analysis of a North American.

[11] *Ibid.*, pp. 209-211.

Chapter 25. The Homecoming

WHEN Domingo Sarmiento returned to his foster home in Chile, he brought with him the memories and lessons of two crowded years of travels throughout the civilized world. He brought with him a wealth of impressions and a sometimes confused mass of ideas. His desire was now to relax, to be with his family, and to gather and organize his thoughts. His mother was at the time in Santiago, and Don Domingo rushed upon his arrival to greet her. His sisters and his illegitimate daughter, Faustina, were in San Juan; and he was equally anxious to see these beloved ones after such a long absence. He planned a trip to the watershed of the Andes, where he would meet them and visit there. Soon after his arrival in Chile, he traveled to Puente del Inca on the frontier of Mendoza, and there in a little Andean inn he enjoyed a reunion with the other members of his family. Together they talked and reminisced, and Faustina and her aunts heard of Sarmiento's many adventures on the four continents that he had visited.

That evening another traveler stopped at the same inn at Puente del Inca. Don Domingo judged that he must be a personage of importance, for he brought with him a military escort. But his identity remained a mystery, and the next day he left as quietly as he had come. Sarmiento and his family had a happy reunion and parted sadly, Sarmiento returning to Santiago, and the others to San Juan.

Upon his return to Santiago Don Domingo received a letter from his friend Mariano Sarratea: "You escaped with luck! The night or day that you left Puente del Inca, there arrived, crossing the Andes to return to this side,—can you imagine whom? I will give you ten guesses. It was Cuitiño, the executioner Cuitiño, with his escort of aides and assistants. . . . They are famous for their efficiency."[1] Ciriaco Cuitiño had a

[1] *Obras,* XLIX, 129.

bloody record as executioner of the terroristic society of Rosas, the Mazorca. He had left Buenos Aires sometime before with the ostensible purpose of taking health cures in the Mendoza River Baths,[2] but Sarmiento was convinced for the rest of his life that his true mission was a much bloodier one. Florencio Varela, the leading anti-Rosas propagandist in Montevideo, had recently been assassinated by the agents of the dictator. Don Domingo thought that the same fate was in store for him. But, as he wrote in later years, "Nothing happened, for the clocks of Providence and Destiny, that dispute the government of the world, were not in agreement."[3]

After his return to Chile, Don Domingo sought more than any other thing a chance to relax, gather his family around him, organize his thoughts, and put into writing what he had learned and what he had confirmed during his travels. In such a frame of mind he learned of the death of Domingo Castro y Calvo. His widow, Benita, was living at her country estate of Yungay with her son, Dominguito. Sarmiento went to call upon them, and whether the young boy was really his illegitimate son or not, Don Domingo took a great fancy to him. Doña Benita was not beautiful, but she had other attractions.[4] She was only twenty-six years old and of passionate temperament. She had been married to a man many years older than she and perhaps the only really passionate love she had ever known was that of the young Argentine *émigré*, Domingo Sarmiento. She was wealthy. She owned a country estate that would not only financially support Sarmiento and his family, but would also offer a peaceful retreat for him to continue his work. All this is not to say that Don Domingo was not in love with the young widow. If Dominguito was truly his son, there might well have existed a real and ardent love between the two. But, whatever the emotional truth involved, Sarmiento did not delay in asking Benita to marry him, and she was not long in agreeing to the arrangement. On May 19, 1848, not three months after his return to Chile, Domingo Faustino Sarmiento married Benita Martínez, widow of Don

[2] *La gaceta mercantil*, Buenos Aires, 1848, no. 7830.

[3] Quoted by Gálvez, p. 197.

[4] *Ibid.*

Domingo Castro y Calvo.[5] The bride and groom retired to the Castro y Calvo estate at Yungay for their honeymoon and for many months of peace and happiness.

From 1848 until 1851, Don Domingo remained at Yungay. He gathered around him here his family, and he produced a number of books to summarize and organize the material that he had absorbed during his travels. Doña Paula, his mother, lived with them on the country estate, and his daughter Ana Faustina came to Yungay, where she met and married Julio Belín, the young printer whom her father had met in Paris and had urged to come to America. Belín joined the growing family circle, and, founding a publishing firm in Santiago, he became one of Sarmiento's closest associates in the years to come.

The member of the family who brought Don Domingo the greatest pleasure, however, was Dominguito. At an early stage he showed signs of precocity, and his educator-father devoted much of his time to the cultivation of his young mind. "Only this precocious and sympathetic young boy allowed Sarmiento to enjoy days of tenderness and intimate hopes."[6] In later years he loved to recount incidents of Dominguito's childhood.

One day at luncheon, Dominguito overheard his father and Belín discussing a current electoral question in Chilean politics.

"Papa," asked Dominguito, "why can't I vote?"

"You can. You are a Chilean."

"Where do you vote?"

"You belong to the San Isidro district. The voting table is near here."

A short time passed. "Papa, how do you vote?"

"It is the simplest thing in the world," replied Sarmiento. "You take one of these tickets, you go to the table where there are many people; you say that you are going to vote; you present the vote; they receive it; and that is all there is to it."

[5] Marriage certificate quoted by Dr. Porfirio Fariña Núñez, *Los amores de Sarmiento*, p. 124.

[6] Edmundo Correas, "Centenario del Nacimiento de 'Dominguito,'" *Los Andes*, Mendoza, April 17, 1945.

They did not speak any more of the elections. The conversation went off on other subjects, but when the luncheon was finished, Dominguito had disappeared. Where was he?

"He must have gone to vote," said his father with a smile. They did not think any more about it, but they did not realize how close they were to the truth.

Dominguito had indeed gone to the voting table and announced, "A citizen wants to vote."

The electoral judges had maintained their seriousness. "Yes, sir, you may vote. From what district do you come?"

"The San Isidro District."

"Your name?"

"Domingo Sarmiento."

"No, sir, you may not vote. You must be the son of the Cuyan Sarmiento."

"I am a Chilean."

"Are you married?"

"No, sir." (General laughter.)

"For whom do you vote?"

"For Don Manuel Montt!"

"Ah, rascal, don't let him vote," cried a crowd of the opposition. "He is a supporter of the despotism."

Undisturbed by this turn of affairs, Dominguito rushed home to his father. "Papa, I voted." He was greeted with surprise and amused laughter.[7]

Aside from these short, happy interludes of family life, however, Sarmiento's days at Yungay were filled with more serious intellectual and artistic efforts. His first task was to make a report of his trip. In 1849 he published the first volume of his *Viajes en Europa, Africa y América.* In the form of a series of letters to his friends from different places that he visited during his travels, he attempted to present an account of what he saw and what he experienced during his years of absence from Chile. This was not a study of events of facts in foreign lands. Such a work was better done by scholars or by journals and newspapers. "If I had described all that I saw, like the Count of Maule, I would have repeated a work al-

[7] D. F. Sarmiento, *Vida de Dominguito,* Editorial Tor: Buenos Aires, 1945, pp. 21-22.

ready completed by a more competent and learned pen. If I had written my *impressions of travel* the task would have gotten out of hand. I have therefore written *what I have written*, for I would not know how to classify it in any other way, obeying instincts and impulses that came from within, and which at times my reason itself could not brake."[8] These *Viajes* turned out to be among the most charming literary productions of Domingo Sarmiento, and his impressions and observations of the countries that he visited are not only important for an understanding of his own personality and thought but are also valuable for a historian of those countries.

But more important results of the trip were his books on education. Such a study had, after all, been the purpose of Sarmiento's travels, and the pedagogical works that he published upon his return became "the matrix from which were born almost all the constructive ideas which he disseminated in the thirty successive years of his educational apostleship."[9] His book *Educación popular* (Public Education) was based on the official report that he made to the Chilean government upon his return, and it was published in early 1849. Later works such as *Memoria sobre educación común* (1856) (Memorial on Public Education) and *Las escuelas—base de la prosperidad i de la república en los Estados Unidos* (1866) (Schools—The Basis of the Prosperity and the Republic in the United States) were based fundamentally on this earlier work and on the lessons that the author had learned during his studies and travels through the principal countries of Europe and North America. "After 1849 Sarmiento insisted constantly on the cardinal ideas of this book. . . . This was the message of the civilizer to the barbarous native."[10]

Educación popular shows clearly the influence that the ideas of Horace Mann had had upon the thinking of Domingo Sarmiento.[11] He discussed the need of an independent revenue for the public schools, a revenue derived from a tax for

[8] *Viajes*, I, 29.

[9] Ricardo Rojas, "Introduction" to *Educación popular*, p. 14.

[10] *Ibid.*, pp. 16-17.

[11] Watt Stewart and William Mashall French, *op.cit.*, p. 22.

that specific purpose. He pointed to the great advantage of the new institutions of kindergartens that he had found in Europe and in North America, and he advised their adoption in the South. In a chapter on public schools he discussed in detail such varied factors as the size of classes, the size of buildings and rooms, and the competence of teachers. In all of these matters he drew from the knowledge and statistics that he had gathered during his travels.

Some of Sarmiento's own pet educational theories had been confirmed by his studies abroad. His contacts with the cultured and charming Mrs. Mann and her associates had fortified him in his belief in the civilizing effect of the education of women. Two thousand women were needed in Chile alone as teachers, and these women would have to be educated first.[12] He continued his old crusade to give more dignity to the teaching profession. Even at this period teaching was looked upon as a degraded vocation, and Sarmiento insisted now and throughout the rest of his life that it should be lifted to a position of importance. "The profession of teaching requires as much, or greater, preparation than any other."[13] He pointed to the good and even great teachers whom he had encountered abroad, and he showed not only their accomplishments but also their important contributions to society. He finally dealt with the old question of orthographic reform. He showed how a simplified and rationalized spelling would improve teaching methods and facilitate the task of the teacher. He again drew upon his new experiences, especially in Spain, to back and verify these assertions.

His later works on education follow along the same lines. *Memoria sobre educación común* showed the influence of primary instruction on all phases of life and then went on to point out the reforms needed to create an effective public education system. *Escuelas—base de la prosperidad* . . . merely served to illustrate these main points, using the United States and the success of that nation as an example. As Don Domingo wrote to Mrs. Mann many years later, "At the age of thirty I undertook from Chile the great crusade which you see me continuing at this time, and which after I had made use of

[12] *Educación popular*, p. 146. [13] *Ibid.*, p. 176.

my own lights and those I acquired in French books, was converted after 1847, into a prolongation to South America of the campaign so notably ended in the North by your worthy husband, Mr. Mann, whose path I have followed ever since."[14]

Returning from years of travel that had been packed with experience and learning, Domingo Sarmiento retired to a quiet married life with his wife and family in Yungay. Here he enjoyed for the only time in his life a few months of quiet and a relationship with his family that was rewarding and memorable. Here he had time to digest what he had learned; and, recording his travels in his *Viajes,* he organized in other books his pedagogical theories that were to be the basis of his educational activities throughout the rest of his life.

Chapter 26. Duel with Rosas

IN SPITE of his marriage and his family life and his withdrawal to Yungay, Don Domingo did not after his return to Chile leave the scene of active politics. On May 26, 1848, only seven days after his marriage to Benita, he wrote a letter to General José Santos Ramírez, the former federalist officer who had saved his life some nineteen years before. Sarmiento wrote to the general to recall the incident but also to urge him to join the forces of opposition to Rosas. He pointed out that the recent liberal revolutions throughout Europe had changed the entire political complexion of the world. An old order was disappearing, and with it would go Rosas and his tyranny. "Twenty years of sacrifice by you have had as their reward exile. You have grown old serving a sterile cause, which has

[14] Sarmiento to Mary Mann, Oscawana, New York, June 15, 1866. Original in Museo Histórico Sarmiento.

created only crimes, persecution and blood; and after twenty years we are as we were the first day."[1]

In the days that followed, Sarmiento missed no chance to contact the other military and civil leaders, both within and without Argentina, and to urge them to join in his humane crusade. In the eyes of the Argentine law he thereby became a traitor, and as the character of his activities became evident the official temper in Buenos Aires was aroused. Late in January 1849, Don Domingo began the publication of a new journal, *La Crónica.* The express purpose of this periodical was to attack Rosas and his government, and it let no opportunity go by to harm or vilify the Buenos Aires regime.

Perhaps the most famous campaign that Sarmiento carried on in *La Crónica* was that incited by the official claim of the Argentine government of sovereignty over the Straits of Magellan. Don Domingo had learned something about this situation through his acquaintanceship during his trip to France with the French naval officer who had commanded the expedition of that nation to establish a base in the area. The Chileans had, however, arrived there first. Since 1843 Chile had maintained a colony on the shores of the straits. On March 11, 1849, shortly after the Argentine foreign officer had officially brought up the question, Sarmiento published in *La Crónica* an article entitled "Cuestión Magallanes." This was the first in a series of articles that defended Chile's rights and attacked the Argentine claims.

Don Domingo's position in this matter was predominantly determined by his opposition to Rosas. Here was the first major issue that had arisen in which he could gain the popular sympathy of Chile against the tyrant of his own country. He did not look into the legal and nationalistic aspects of the question as much as he considered this very practical point. The Argentine government raised the cry of "treason" and branded the exile as a traitor to his country and to his country's interests. But Don Domingo continued with his articles. He cited the Law of the Indies of 1609 to demonstrate the fact that the Straits were historically the legal property of Chile. As for the *de facto* rights, the answer was obvious.

[1] Quoted by Gálvez, p. 199.

Carried away by his enthusiasm in condemning Rosas' "imperialism" and in gaining support for his attacks against the Argentine dictator, he went on to say, "It remains to be seen if the title for the creation of the Viceroyalty of Buenos Aires expresses that the lands to the south of Mendoza, and possessed even today by Chileans, entered within the borders of the viceroyalty. If they did not, it would be possible for Chile to reclaim all the territory that stretches between the Straits of Magellan and Cuyo."[2] In later years, Sarmiento's stand in this argument reacted against him. His political enemies later dug up these debates to prove his unpatriotic attitude. And when the question of Antarctic limits arose during Sarmiento's presidency, the Chileans often used his own words against him. It is evident, however, that the principal factor in his evaluation of the situation at this time was his desire to harm Rosas and his regime. In later years, when such factors as nationalism and the question of right and wrong became the basic factors in his evaluation, he held to his former stand of granting the Straits' settlements to the neighboring nation, but he backed down on a number of his more radical and less carefully considered statements, especially those which opened the possibility of a Chilean claim to Patagonia.[3]

In article after article, Don Domingo continued to attack every aspect of the Rosas government. The files of *La Crónica* are filled with studies of Argentine economic, political, and intellectual backwardness. On May 1, 1848, the first number of *La Tribuna* appeared in Santiago. Again, it was Don Domingo who was the principal editor, but this time it was his son-in-law, Julio Belín, who was the publisher. This periodical also had as its purpose the merciless attack on the government of Juan Manuel de Rosas.

The Argentine government in Buenos Aires was, in the meantime, beginning to realize that Sarmiento's propaganda was becoming a definite danger and threat. He was not only plotting with military leaders to instigate an insurrection

[2] *Ibid.*, p. 202.

[3] For the texts of Sarmiento's articles on this question, see *Obras*, XXV. See also Alberto Hidalgo, *Sarmiento y la cuestión de Patagonia*, Buenos Aires, 1945. For a general discussion on this subject, see also Rojas, Chapter XXVI.

within the borders of the Republic, but in Chile he was opposing the claims of the Buenos Aires government and attacking its policies. On April 11, 1849, the Argentine government officially requested the extradition of Domingo Faustino Sarmiento, to be brought to trial in his own country. The request was ignored.

On May 25th, the anniversary of Argentine independence, a group of leading exiles gathered at Yungay to celebrate the date. Among those present were Nicolás Rodríguez Peña, one of the leaders in the movement for independence; General Las Heras, a companion of San Martín in the Andean Campaign; Bartolomé Mitre, future president of the Republic; and many others who were distinguished leaders of the nation both before and after that date. Sarmiento had been undergoing a particularly strong attack in the recent weeks as a traitor to his nation. He had begun to doubt the support of his own countrymen. But these exiled leaders, conscious of his true motives in the quarrel, took this opportunity to demonstrate their loyalty and support. Among those present was Martín Zapata, who announced that he had an important document to read to the gathering. It was a letter from General Ramírez to Rosas, denouncing Sarmiento's attempt to arouse him against the federalist government. In the letter he referred to Don Domingo's "hallucinations and criminal plans against our Independence and our holy federal cause, which I have sworn to uphold." With such a letter, the Rosas government had proof of Sarmiento's "treachery." It would undoubtedly renew its requests for extradition. After Zapata had finished reading the letter there was a "pained silence." Someone arose and offered a resolution that "we sacrifice our fortunes and lives in defense of the person of Sarmiento, in case the good sense and the wisdom of the government are not enough defense."

Sarmiento paused and then answered the resolution. "In the midst of the emotions and the memories of the ancient glory of the homeland, in the family sanctuary improvised in exile, the fury of the tyrants reaches me. I accept, sirs, with immense gratitude the sacrifice that you offer me, less in honor of my person than of the principle attacked. Let us drink to the French revolution that came last year on this day to augment our enthusiasm, to the letter of Ramírez that I wrote the next day and that returns today to be present in this party, bringing me the curse of the tyrant to recall to me that I still have a homeland."[4] The group drank the toast with red Chilean wine, and other toasts were offered. Soon the party took on the carefree air of a patriotic rally. A group of young men from another dinner joined them later in the evening. There were speeches, harangues, and more toasts. As the evening drew to a close, Don Domingo arose once more: "Today is the most important day of my life. The memory of the 25th of May; the presence of the heroes of Independence; that of the exiles of our own period; that of you the representatives of the generation that approaches; the Argentine flag that the ladies of Montevideo put into the hands of the illustrious Lavalle; and the very unburdening of the fury of the tyrant of our country; three generations here present; liberty and despotism—all has passed this day through the portals of my dwelling."[5] The morale of the exiles had reawakened itself. The Argentine national anthem was sung, and all left with renewed fire to fight their battle against the dictator of their nation.

But Juan Manuel Rosas was fighting back. Whether the supposed plan to assassinate Sarmiento was fact or a figment of the latter's active imagination is a matter of conjecture, but the Argentine governor did use other means for a counterattack. In Mendoza near the Chilean border, a periodical was founded. Under the able direction of Juan Llerena and Bernardo de Irigoyen, *La Ilustración Argentina* carried on a continual political polemic with *La Crónica* and *La Tribuna.* It presented Rosas' arguments in the "Straits Question," and it presented rebuttals to Sarmiento's many other charges and attacks. Speaking of *La Crónica* it said, "It is today the most fanatical organ of the principles and tendencies of that band of ignorant dreamers; its editorship is trusted to the most furious and irresponsible utopian that the American soil has produced."[6] In subsequent numbers it attacked not only Sar-

[4] *Obras,* XIII, 273. [5] *Ibid.*, XLVI, 42.

[6] *La Ilustración Argentina,* May 1, 1849, Volume I, no. 1.

miento's ideas, but also his character, integrity, and morality.

Armed with the Ramírez denunciation, the Buenos Aires government also continued its attempts to bring legal action against the vociferous exile. On July 21, 1849, another note was presented to the Chilean government, requesting the extradition of Domingo Faustino Sarmiento. Again the request was denied by the Santiago administration. In December of that same year, Rosas dedicated eight pages of his annual message to the legislature of the province of Buenos Aires to an attack against Sarmiento. He discussed his activities in Chile. He charged him with all manner of crime. Referring to the "savage unitarist Domingo F. Sarmiento," "the rebel Sarmiento," "the hateful Sarmiento," "the traitor Sarmiento," and "the criminal conspirator Sarmiento," he again demanded that he "be brought to justice."[7] The Chilean government continued to insist, however, that the constitution guaranteed freedom of speech and freedom of the press. It suggested that a libel suit might be brought against the writer, but it warned that the courts would probably dismiss it.

Meanwhile, however, the political situation within the Argentine Republic was changing, and this change suggested an alteration of strategy on the part of Sarmiento. The position of Juan Manuel de Rosas, which had seemed too impregnable a few years before, was now rapidly deteriorating. Justo José de Urquiza, governor of the province of Entre Ríos, was beginning to oppose the Rosist centralization. There were no visible signs of the disintegration of the confederation, but there were elements of dissatisfaction and disaffection. Don Domingo saw the need for a more positive attack against the regime. His sniping at its policies through the press and through letters to people within the country was leading to no constructive end. It was only being met with counterattacks and counteraccusations from the official press and from the leaders of the Argentine government. Don Domingo had formed positive programs of political action during his years of residence in Chile, and his travels had confirmed them.

[7] *Mensaje*, pp. 117, 118, 120, 121, and 125.

On January 20, 1850, the publication of *La Crónica* was suspended. In March of that same year, Sarmiento published in Santiago a political treatise entitled *Argirópolis.* Adhering to the basic principle of nomocracy and democracy, he proposed a definite program of action in Argentina to replace the "confederation" of Rosas. The stated purpose of the book was to "end the war, construct the nation, and the animosities, conciliate interests that are divergent in themselves, conserve the actual authorities, lay the bases for the development of the wealth, and give to each province and to each state involved that which belongs to it. . . ."[8] Don Domingo dedicated the work to the one man who seemed to be in a position to instrument the ideas that it contained, General Justo José de Urquiza. History proved this to be a wise choice.

Sarmiento's basic thesis was one that he had held in his arguments with General San Martín in France. Independence was not a goal in itself; it was merely a method to reach a better political and social life.[9] The Rosas regime, although it maintained the liberty of the nation, brought with it all the features of the colonial period. The promises of independence had gone unfulfilled in the past two decades. Only a government by law, "a constitution that regulates the relations between states and guarantees the rights and liberties of the citizens" could end the hatred, the fratricide, and the chaos dominant under the existent personalism.[10] Sarmiento turned to many of his old theories to demonstrate how such a change could be brought about, how his nation could be reformed. First, a foreign population was needed. "It is necessary to attract a population from other nations to augment our number and wealth and introduce the knowledge of the arts and sciences that we lack."[11] Next, there was needed a rationally reformed economic system: free navigation, free trade, expansion of internal markets and improvement of internal communications.[12] "On this point, our interest is nearly the same as that of the European powers; and it would be sufficient to have a few intelligent and forward-looking laws that

[8] *Argirópolis,* Editorial Tor: Buenos Aires, 1938, p. 7.
[9] *Ibid.,* p. 174.
[10] *Ibid.,* p. 128.
[11] *Ibid.,* p. 179; see also pages 176 and 159.
[12] *Ibid.,* pp. 97 and 151.

would harmonize economic activity."[13] And, finally, a changed political system was needed to make these reforms possible.

In dealing with the alterations needed in the Argentine political structure, Sarmiento relied heavily upon the lessons that he had learned during his travels, especially in the United States. Throughout *Argirópolis,* there is a continued reference to the North American republic as an example and a model.[14] The most important feature of the book that derived from the lessons the author had learned in the United States was that dealing with the benefits of federalism. Don Domingo held that the Rosist government, although it called itself federalist, was in fact the last word in dictatorial centralization.[15] The federalism of the confederation was but a fiction. What was needed was a true federal system, one that was modeled after the structure of the United States. The very nature of Argentina seemed to prescribe such a solution. "The nature of the country and relative positions of the provinces indicate what should be their relationships. The national will, violence, facts have given to the state a federal form. . . . As to the federal mechanism, there is no other rule to follow for the present than the Constitution of the United States."[16]

Sarmiento proposed a federal system that would include the states of Argentina, Uruguay, and Paraguay. According to geography, heritage, and history, these three nations should be incorporated into one. None should be the master. All should have a share in the mutual federal system. The capital could not be in Buenos Aires, Asunción, or Montevideo, for such an arrangement would make one or the other of these cities dominant. As in the United States, a new capital should be founded and built for that specific purpose. Don Domingo proposed the Island of Martín García. Situated at the meeting place of the great rivers of the area, it would belong equally to Paraguay, Uruguay, and various provinces of Argentina, but it would be dominated by none of them. It would hold a favorable commercial position and therefore be economi-

[13] *Ibid.*, pp. 156-157.
[14] *Ibid.*, pp. 118 and 189.
[15] *Ibid.*, p. 166.
[16] *Ibid.*, pp. 201-202.

cally self-sufficient. It would be politically objective but in a situation of command.

Argirópolis was a book typical of Sarmiento's thought. It was a blueprint conceived wholly in the abstract. It was an intellectual ideal that was far removed from reality. Most of his compatriots ignored it. Many scoffed at it, looking at the mosquito-ridden Martín García and ridiculing it as the capital of an important nation. The man to whom it was dedicated was far too practical to give it much notice. When he finally met its author in person he did not even mention the work. The book was stored away and had no practical value. Its only importance was as an illustration of the thinking process that was still operating within the mind of Domingo Sarmiento.

In the same year of 1851, Don Domingo completed another work that would serve as an important weapon in his positive attacks against the dictator Rosas. This was his book *Recuerdos de provincia,* or *Provincial Recollections,* which was published in December of that year and has lived on as one of the great works of the Argentine writer. George Ticknor, the leading North American Hispanist, later proclaimed it as one of the great works of Spanish literature, containing pages unsurpassed in Spanish prose.[17] It has become one of the most widely read books of the nineteenth-century Hispanic world and one of the most beloved works in Argentine literature. It represents the maturing of Sarmiento's literary artistry.

Recuerdos de provincia had a far more personal aim than *Argirópolis.* "The desire of every honest man not to be looked down upon, and a patriot's eagerness to retain the respect of his fellow citizens, have led me to publish this little book which I entrust to its fate without any excuse other than innocence of intent. It is difficult, of course, to talk about one's self and to reveal one's good qualities without giving rise to scornful comment and drawing criticism upon one's self, sometimes legitimately. But it is even harder to sit silently by under dishonorable imputations, to swallow injuries, and allow modesty itself to conspire to one's own hurt. I have not

[17] Belín Sarmiento, *Sarmiento anecdótico, op.cit.,* p. 46.

hesitated for a moment in choosing between these alternatives. . . .

"My *Provincial Recollections* are merely what their title implies. I have searched my memory and have resurrected, so to speak, the recollections of some of my relatives who have deserved well of their country, risen in the church hierarchy, or honored American letters by their labors. I have deliberately restricted myself to my native province, to the humble home in which I was born—frail boards, no doubt, like those floating in the ocean at which shipwrecked mariners grasp to keep their heads above water, but they enable me to realize that if I enjoy discovering moral, noble, or delicate sentiments around me in my predecessors and in my mother, teachers, and friends, it is because I have some in me too. There is an imperishable, democratic nobility of patriotism and talent which can disadvantage no one."[18]

The continued attacks and calumnies by Rosas and his agents were having an effect upon Don Domingo's reputation. *Recuerdos de provincia* had, therefore, three principal purposes. It was to attack the personalist government of the caudillos as Sarmiento had seen it during his youth. It was to point to the positive reforms that he advocated in his other writings. But most important of all, it was to clear Don Domingo's good name. If Rosas was going to fall, and eventually he would have to, Sarmiento wanted to have before himself and the people of Argentina, not only a positive objective program, which he supplied in *Argirópolis,* but also a favorable subjective picture of himself. He planned to play a leading role in the reconstruction of his nation after the fall of the dictator. It was about this time that he was circulating pictures of himself signed by the "Future President of the Republic." The egotism of "Don Yo" (Mr. I, as his enemies called him) was well-known; Sarmiento was not reticent about the fact that he would be a good leader for his nation. He pointed to the role his ancestors had played in his nation's history. He recorded for himself a patriotic and spotless record. He submitted this "humbly" to the public for its perusal. It was an answer to Rosas, yes; but it was also his

[18] *Anthology,* p. 47.

passport to popular leadership in the reconstruction of his nation, whether along the lines that he had advocated in his book earlier that same year, or along lines yet to be proposed.

1850 was a year of comparative quiet and contemplation for Don Domingo. He composed two of his major works. He calmly thought out his political projects and plans. But in 1851 he threw himself once more into the heat of battle. On January 24th of that year he began the publication of another periodical, *Sud América*. This, like its forerunners, had as its principal purpose an attack against the Rosas government. In April he published the second edition of *El Facundo,* his most powerful propaganda work, a book that still carried a heavy blow against the political form that it attacked. Article followed article in the Chilean press, attacking every phase of the dominant Argentine regime.

1851 was also an important year in Chilean politics, and Sarmiento with his usual enthusiasm entered into the third major presidential battle in which he had participated in that nation. The conservative government of General Bulnes was just coming to the end of its second term, and it was not eligible for reelection. Don Domingo's old friend and associate, Manuel Montt, was the government candidate to succeed Bulnes, and Sarmiento offered his services in the campaign. He looked upon the accomplishments of the conservative government as important ones. The government was far from perfect in his eyes, but it contrasted favorably with the personalism and chaos in the other nations of Hispanic America. It had not offered complete political freedom to the country, but it had offered a government by law, with courts, with liberties, with rights. "Between 1846 and 1849 there are not only four years, there is an entire age that separates two governmental tendencies. Between the first and the second of these dates, there has occurred for Chile, that is to say for the thinking and governing part of society, an immense political revolution. . . . The republican spirit in Chile does not find itself today so disoriented."[19] There was a long way yet

[19] "Derogación de la ley de imprenta—Moción Lastarria," *La Crónica,* July 1, 1849.

to go, but the conservative government seemed to be on the right trail, and Don Domingo meant to support it.

At dawn on April 20, 1851, there broke out a military mutiny in Santiago. On hearing this news, Sarmiento mounted his horse in Yungay, armed himself well and rode to La Moneda, the government house, to help defend the government. He helped Minister Varas to edit a forceful edict against the rebellion. The mutiny was overcome, and the administration remained deeply grateful for this display of loyalty on the part of the Argentine exile. In September, Montt was elected to the presidency, and in the years that followed he was a valuable and sincere friend to Domingo Sarmiento.

Towards the middle of the winter of 1851 rumors began to reach Chile of an open quarrel between Rosas and Urquiza. In April there was talk of a circular letter from Urquiza to the provincial governors, inviting them to unite against the central government. In May there was news of a formal "pronouncement" against Rosas. The forces of rebellion were gathering in Urquiza's province of Entre Ríos. The Chilean electoral campaign was nearing its climax. The elections themselves would be in September, but Sarmiento suddenly lost interest in this question. He awaited every mail from across the Andes. He sensed the end of Rosas to be near. His chance to put his projects into operation was approaching. His opportunity was at hand to construct in his own nation the civilization of which he dreamed. Domingo Sarmiento awaited the opportunity to join the fight.

BOOK V
The Construction

Chapter 27. The Tyrant Falls

In 1848, on the last leg of his famous travels, Domingo Sarmiento had stopped at the seaport of Arica in northern Chile. Here he met his uncle, Domingo de Oro, and together they had discussed the political situation in their homeland. Before Sarmiento left, he had revealed his hope of returning to Buenos Aires and had predicted that he would be there in 1852.[1]

The events of the year 1851 seemed to bring this prediction closer and closer to fulfillment. On the surface, Rosas' power had reached its highest point. "In 1850 and 1851, popular and social adhesion to his government reached enthusiastic climax, and he reached the peak of his absolute power. He dominated without financial check and without responsibility. The liberating campaigns or crusades had failed one right after the other."[2] On September 26, 1851, the House of Representatives of the province of Buenos Aires declared to its governor and dictatorial ruler, "that all the funds of the province, the fortunes, lives, fame and future of its Representatives and of its constituents are without any limitation nor reservation whatsoever at the disposition of Your Excellency. . . ."[3]

Beneath the surface, however, the fall of the dictatorship

[1] This prediction is contained in a manuscript diary of Sarmiento which he entitled "Diario de la campaña del tente. Corl. D. F. Sarmiento en el ejército grande de Sud América." The original of this diary in Don Domingo's own handwriting is to be found in the Museo Histórico Sarmiento in Buenos Aires. It is a very valuable source of information on the campaign that led to the defeat of Rosas, for it was written on the spot. His later published work *Campaña del ejército grande* included many incidents taken from this diary, but it was written some time later and reflects the anti-Urquiza bias that he developed after the Battle of Caseros.

[2] Juan Antonio González Calderón, *El general Urquiza y la organización nacional*, Buenos Aires, 1940, p. 13.

[3] Pedro de Angelis, ed., *Recopilación de las leyes y decretos promulgados en Buenos Aires*, 1810-1858, Buenos Aires, 1836-1858, IV, 201.

was being prepared. The wealth of the capital city as compared to the increasing poverty of the provinces was beginning to appear as a factor working against the Buenos Aires government in the political thought of the interior.[4] The propaganda of exiles such as Sarmiento, from Chile, Montevideo, and all points bordering on the national territory, was beginning to take its toll upon the thinking of many formerly unconcerned or neutral persons. But most important of all was the growth to power of another personality, whose ability and prestige came to be recognized as a true threat to Juan Manuel de Rosas. General Justo José de Urquiza had in the past years been one of the dictator's chief supporters and most valuable military leaders. He had defeated the forces of Rivera in 1845. He had overcome a revolt in the province of Corrientes in 1846. And he had kept the peace in the northeastern portion of the nation ever since.

In 1845, when Urquiza was reelected to the governorship of the province of Entre Ríos, he was still on good terms with Rosas; but in the years that followed, this relationship degenerated. The provincial governor resented the increasing wealth of Buenos Aires. He objected to the economic advantages held by that city. As the absolutist character of the Rosist political domination became more accentuated, the caudillo from Entre Ríos showed even more resentment of his subordinate role in Argentine affairs.[5] When in 1851 Rosas repeated the periodical gesture of resigning his presidency of the Buenos Aires legislature and awaiting a new expression of allegiance from both his own government and the rulers of the provinces, Urquiza made his move. Feeling sure of the support of the provinces of Entre Ríos, Corrientes, and Santa Fé, and counting on the promised aid of Brazil and the unconditional support of the patriotic refugees in Montevideo, the caudillo pronounced himself in rebellion against the Rosas regime. He proclaimed Entre Ríos a sovereign federal province and withdrew the powers it had ceded to the Buenos Aires administration.

[4] Juan Antonio González Calderón, *op.cit.*, pp. 12, 13.

[5] For a detailed account of the disintegration of relations between Rosas and Urquiza, see Carlos Ibarguren, *Juan Manuel de Rosas, op.cit.*, pp. 423-428.

The news of Urquiza's pronouncement came as a thunderbolt to Domingo Sarmiento. In May 1851 Urquiza signed with Brazil and the Oriental Republic (Uruguay) an offensive and defensive alliance. Its immediate objective was to break the siege of Montevideo, but its ultimate end was the overthrow of Rosas. Entrerian forces invaded Uruguay in July, defeated Oribe in September, and triumphantly entered the city of Montevideo. In November, in view of the warlike preparations being carried on by Rosas in Buenos Aires, the three allies agreed that the Buenos Aires government was incompatible with their peace and security. General Urquiza took command of an army of 21,000 men, 4,000 of whom were Brazilians and Uruguayans; and he prepared to invade the territory of the long-dominant dictator.

As the weekly mails brought the news of these startling events across the Andes, Don Domingo did not remain idle. He conceived a daring plan. He would form in Chile some battalions of volunteers, fall upon the western provinces, and march across the pampa to join the armies of Urquiza. Sarmiento took his ideas to his fellow exiles, but he met with little enthusiasm. William Rawson called the project a "sublime insanity." Don Domingo was indignant. "Doctor," he retorted, "you have the intelligence of a German scholar; your heart is good; but your arms are broken."[6] The plan was abandoned, however, for lack of support.

As the uprising led by Urquiza grew in momentum, the exiles in Chile could stand idle no longer. On September 12, 1851, Sarmiento, Bartolomé Mitre, General Paunero, and General Aquino boarded the frigate *Medicis* for Montevideo. It was another long voyage aboard this sailing ship, and the patriots were chafing at the bit for some action. For forty days they sailed down the southern coast of Chile, through the Straits of Magellan and up the coast of Argentina. Finally, on November 1st they put into the long-besieged harbor of Montevideo. They had been many weeks without news, and they were anxious to hear of the latest events. It would be impossible to land until morning, so Don Domingo leaned over the rail and shouted to one of the passing boatmen.

[6] Palcos, *Sarmiento, op.cit.*, p. 93.

"Hello! Hey! Who is in command of the city?"

"The government."

"Oribe?"

"He is at his home."

"And Urquiza?"

"He embarked yesterday for Entre Ríos."

"And is the siege still going on?"

"It has already ended. Everyone surrendered. There is peace."[7]

Don Domingo's enthusiasm was even more kindled by the news.

The next morning a launch came to take the passengers of the *Medicis* ashore. Sarmiento and his companions, as they neared the docks, leaped ashore; and each went his own way. Don Domingo went up Ancha Street. He watched a parade of Italian, French, Basque, and Negro soldiers pass in full dress. It was a holiday for Montevideo. The long siege had been lifted.

Sarmiento did not, however, remain long in the city. He wanted to meet as soon as possible the military leader of the opposition to Rosas. Aboard the *Uruguay*, along with a division of troops, he set sail for Entre Ríos. General Urquiza had his headquarters at the village of Gualeguaychú, and here Don Domingo presented himself, in the uniform of a lieutenant-colonel, a rank which the commanding general was quick to recognize in reward for Sarmiento's campaigns "against the Aldaos and Quiroga."

The first interview between Sarmiento and Urquiza was a happy one. The general awaited his visitor at the so-called government house. Don Domingo entered, filled with emotion at the thought of meeting this historic personage. He was greeted as he entered by a growl from Urquiza's large dog, Purvis, named for the English representative who was most opposed to the politics of Rosas. Purvis (the dog) was famed for his vicious bite, and only the voice of his master could hold him in check. Urquiza called to him. Sarmiento watched nervously and then entered.

Each man used this occasion to estimate the other. Each was

[7] *Obras*, XIV, 97.

anxious to win the friendship of the other. Sarmiento saw in Urquiza the key man in the future of Argentine politics. Urquiza saw in Sarmiento a valuable friend and a dangerous foe. An acquaintanceship could not have been inaugurated under more favorable psychological circumstances, but the personalities of the two men clashed from the beginning. Each was vain and egotistical. Neither would make allowances for these features in the other. Urquiza did not mention *Argirópolis,* the book Don Domingo had dedicated to him, nor did he refer to any of the many letters that Sarmiento had written him during the past few years. Don Domingo, on the other hand, did not satisfy the caudillo's ego. He did not refer to the recent military successes. He did not lay enough emphasis upon the victories that Urquiza had already won. Before they parted, the Commander of the Grand Army appointed Sarmiento as the Chronicler of the Army. He would mount a printing press, and he would accompany the armies on their advances. He would combine the tasks of propagandist, reporter, and historian of the campaign. Don Domingo was disappointed with the assignment. He had dreams of military glory to augment his artistic and intellectual accomplishments. But he accepted the task in good humor and resolved to carry it out to the best of his ability.

During his stay in Gualeguaychú, Sarmiento had three more interviews with his commander. It was during this period that the first signs of a split between the two men began to appear. There were several points of possible conflict, and although both men attempted to maintain the best of relations with one another, these differences inevitably found their way to the surface. Urquiza was, in spite of his opposition to Rosas, a federalist. He looked upon Sarmiento as a unitarist. He was annoyed when the writer did not wear the red band, the symbol of federalism, that he had ordered; and his personal secretary and aide, Ángel Elías, pointed this fact out to Sarmiento time and again. Don Domingo consistently refused to give in on this point. He and Urquiza never brought the subject up in their interviews, but it was always present in the background. Another source of basic conflict was Urquiza's lack of respect for the part of the intellectual and the writer in the overthrow of Rosas. He recognized Sarmiento as an important force, but as the propagandist tried to make his importance more and more obvious, Urquiza became annoyed and tended to minimize the part Sarmiento had played and was playing in the struggle. Nothing could have had a more adverse effect upon an ego such as Sarmiento's.

Finally, the approach that the two men had to the political reality that they were facing was diametrically opposed. Urquiza saw a fight ahead. He saw a struggle, a series of battles and compromises, and the possibility of the unification and future prosperity of the country. Sarmiento saw no such picture. He would make no compromise. He wanted to impose his pattern and apply it, and if this were done he thought that the future of his country would be insured. Such a divergence in their approaches to the problem was the essential factor in the disintegration of the relations between the two leaders. Urquiza's practical approach seemed cynical to Sarmiento. Sarmiento's abstract approach seemed ridiculous and impractical to Urquiza.

Sarmiento did not delay long in Entre Ríos. He was impatient to get started on his new job. After six days in Gualeguaychú, he set sail once more for Montevideo. On this return trip his ship stopped at the island of Martín García, the spot that he had picked for the capital of his federal union of Argentina, Uruguay, and Paraguay. He disembarked here to see his "utopia" and he left the inscription "1850—Argiropolis—1851—Sarmiento."[8]

Montevideo was the site of great excitement when Don Domingo arrived. Battalions and armies were forming and leaving to join Urquiza's forces. Sarmiento joined the battalion of Colonel Lezica and trained with it for a few days. Then he received orders from the commander-in-chief to buy a printing press in the Uruguayan capital and proceed immediately with it to Entre Ríos to join the main force of the army. This was no easy assignment. A press was not easily found and bought in a city that had been so long cut off from regular communication with the rest of the world. But finally

[8] *Diario de la campaña . . .*, p. 8.

Don Domingo found one. It was a little too big for his purposes, but it had to do. He loaded it aboard the *Uruguay* and headed for the river port of Colonia. Here he encountered the Baron of Caxias and the Brazilian admiral in command of the allied fleets. These officials received Sarmiento cordially and offered him passage on their flagship the *Affonso*. Along with Mitre and General Paunero, Sarmiento was aboard the ship when it fought an artillery duel with the guns of General Lucio Mansilla at the Tonelero Pass. Mitre and Sarmiento leaned on the railing and counted the cannon balls flying by, while Paunero, more out of fear of the water than of the bullets, remained in a less vulnerable place.[9] Aboard the *Affonso*, Don Domingo jotted down notes: "I leave Montevideo for Paraná—impressions—appearance—islands [the word "manuscript" is crossed out]—coal—wood—rice—floods—ideas that this spectacle awakens."[10]

While in Montevideo, Don Domingo had bought a full European uniform and outfit. His view of the struggle in progress included the complete defeat of one way of life and its replacement by another. "The saddle, spurs, polished sword, buttoned coat, gloves, French kepi, and overcoat instead of a *poncho*, everything was a protest against the gauchesque spirit. . . . This seems like a small thing," explained Sarmiento, "but it was a part of my campaign against Rosas and the caudillos. . . . While the dress of the Argentine soldier does not change, there must still be caudillos. While the *chiripá*[11] exists, there will be no citizen."[12]

Upon Sarmiento's arrival at Urquiza's headquarters, the difference between the two men's approaches to reality became immediately evident. The caudillo, along with most of his army, saw Don Domingo's costume as ridiculous. He laughed at the affected European garb. Then, when Urquiza saw the press that his officer had bought, he reproached him for its large size. Sarmiento pointed out that he had had little choice.

[9] The three Argentine leaders were awarded the Order of the Rose for their "participation" in this naval engagement.

[10] *Diario de la campaña . . .*, p. 8.

[11] The *chiripá* is a kind of blanket that the Indian and gaucho wrap around themselves for covering from the belt down.

[12] D. F. Sarmiento, *Mi Vida*, Buenos Aires, 2nd ed., 1939, Vol. II.

"Yes," broke out the commanding general, "you people [meaning the unitarists] spend money without any care. That is why you have never accomplished anything."

Sarmiento was taken back by this outburst. He defended the value of his purchase. Urquiza, seeing the danger of a split, changed his tone. "I am not saying this about you." He claimed he referred to the unitarists in general, but the underlying connection that he was making in his mind between Sarmiento and the opposition party became increasingly evident as repeated slips were made.[13]

At the town of Diamante on the bank of the Paraná River, Domingo Sarmiento published the first bulletin of the campaign of the Grand Army. In the two subsequent months, he followed every move of the campaign with his press, loaded upon a cart, and his bulletins. The purposes of his publications were several, but primarily propaganda. They represented at the time the most advanced example of war propaganda to be used in modern times, and even today they stand out as models of that kind of writing. They attacked Rosas and his government mercilessly. They praised Urquiza and the Grand Army. Written in concise and powerful prose, they had an important effect upon not only the morale of Urquiza's army, but also upon the civilian population along the route of advance. Their second, and less important, purpose, was that of news and history. The publications reported the latest events of the campaign, and they preserved these notices for a permanent record of that important phase of history.

On December 24th, Urquiza's army began the crossing of the Paraná River at Diamante. This was a major operation and in his Bulletin 3, Don Domingo records the sight in some of the greatest pages of his prose work. "Yesterday's sun illuminated one of the greatest spectacles that nature and man can offer; the passage of a great river by a large army." Cannon and baggage were floated across on rafts. Horses and riders crossed swimming. Fifteen thousand soldiers made the crossing, and the scene was immortalized by the famous bulletin that is still read by every Argentine schoolchild.[14]

As they stood on the bank and watched the soldiers cross

[13] Gálvez, p. 234.

[14] *Obras*, XIV, 153.

the Paraná, Urquiza and Sarmiento spoke of the future. "When we arrive in Buenos Aires," said the general, "it will be necessary to hang many or else return home and let the people avenge themselves as they will."

"But, general," objected Don Domingo, "it will not have to be either one or the other. Let us not get ahead of events. I know the situation in the Republic and the spirit that dominates."

"You will see the resistance," insisted Urquiza.

"You are frightened, general! We will be victorious. Where will they oppose us? In the press, in the court, in the army? We will see."

"I, afraid, when I have challenged the power of Rosas?" retorted the commander.

"Fear of ghosts, general, That is how men are."[15]

The friction was beginning to show.

Once he was on the other side of the Paraná, Domingo Sarmiento had reached the true pampa for the first time. He ordered a horse to be saddled for him. "To reach land and mount a horse was but the work of a few minutes. On horseback on the bank of the Paraná, seeing the soft, but infinite waves of the pampa unfold before my eyes until being lost over the horizon, the pampa that I had described in *Facundo,* that I had felt, by intuition, now I saw for the first time in my life. I stopped for a time to contemplate it, and I would have taken off my cap to salute it had it not been necessary to conquer it first, to submit at the point of the sword that rebellious pampa, that has for forty years sent out horsemen to ride down beneath the hoofs of their horses the civilized institutions of the city. I began to gallop over it, like one who take possession and dominion. And I arrived very shortly at the camp of Colonel Basavilbaso to orientate myself and to ask for orders to unload my park of type, ink, and paper to make the word play. . . ."[16]

During the weeks that followed, the Grand Army advanced slowly but surely along the road to Buenos Aires. During the entire period, Domingo Sarmiento and his mobile press ac-

[15] Belín Sarmiento, *Sarmiento anecdótico,* p. 67.
[16] *Ibid.,* pp. 67, 68.

companied the troops. Bulletins were issued periodically, and their effect upon the troops and the civilians was startling, and important.

Meanwhile, however, the rift between Sarmiento and his commanding general widened. The very success of Don Domingo's venture accentuated the split. Everywhere he went, he was known and acclaimed; and the warm reception that he received belied the view that Urquiza had wanted to hold of the relative worthlessness of both his previous and his present propaganda endeavors.

As he was passing through the little town of Pergamino, Sarmiento was stopped by an old gaucho. They talked for a while, and then the old horseman asked, "And of what Sarmientos are you, sir?"

"I belong to the San Juan family, sir."

"Yes, but which one of them? I knew Tomás, José, and many others that must already be dead."

"I am the son of Clemente," answered Don Domingo.

"Clemente! Clemente, a tall man, who had a burn on his forehead? It's been years since he has traveled to Buenos Aires."

"He is dead."

"Poor Clemente!"

The two men were alone. The old one came closer, looked around him cautiously, and then speaking in a low tone, asked, "And what about the other one?"

"Which other one, sir?"

"The one in Chile."

"That is I, sir."

"The one that writes, the one that attacks Rosas . . ."

"Sir, it is I."

The old man drew back and gazed at Don Domingo. He looked at him in amazement and in admiration.[17] Such scenes as these brought home to Sarmiento and even to Urquiza the extent of the effect of Sarmiento's propaganda efforts upon public opinion.

When Urquiza's army was camped some three leagues outside of Rosario, Don Domingo rode into town and was put

[17] *Obras,* XIV, 213.

up in the house of a famous Rosist, Santa Coloma. Soon after his arrival, the entire population had heard of his presence. The whole neighborhood turned out to greet him. The judge, the priest, the city officials, soldiers, men, women, and children—all came to pay him tribute. With shouts they called him to the window and proclaimed him their liberator from the tyrant.

Don Domingo was afraid that news of such demonstrations would arouse Urquiza's ire. He did not know exactly what to do about it, but he hastened to write to his commander, and, referring to the incident, pointed out that the population had really been waiting for the general, but in his absence had cheered the first officer to arrive. Sarmiento had, however, correctly judged the effect of the news upon Urquiza. Don Domingo ended his letter by saying, "I am happy with the results of the Bulletin. It distracts the idleness of the country, puts in motion the population, animates the soldier, and frightens Rosas . . ." When he read this, Urquiza could stand it no longer. He dictated a letter to his secretary.

"My dear friend: His Excellency, the general, has read your letter of yesterday and charges me to tell you in regards to the feats that you say the press accomplishes in frightening the enemy that the presses have been shouting in Chile and other places for many years and until now Juan Manuel de Rosas has not been frightened. On the contrary, every day he grew stronger. (signed) Ángel Elías, secretary to General Urquiza."[18]

This letter made a profound impression upon Don Domingo. He was not again on a plane of confidence with Urquiza for many years to come. The two men's approaches to the problem confronting them were too divergent to allow them to meet on a common ground without a conscious effort. The two men's ambitions were at the moment too much at odds for either to make the effort to see the other's point of view. Until the end of the campaign they made repeated efforts to avoid an open break. Urquiza gave Sarmiento a free hand with his bulletins, interfering only now and then when

[18] Carlos Rodríguez Larreta, *Conferencia leída en el Rosario el 15 de Mayo de 1911*, Rosario, 1911, p. 5.

he was especially anxious that the propaganda line take some definite path.

On January 15th, the Grand Army reached the Medio Stream, which separates the province of Santa Fé from that of Buenos Aires. The official bulletin referred to this as the passing of the Rubicon. "Soldiers of the Grand Army! Beneath the torrents of rain and above the burning flames of the countryside, embraced by the January sun and challenging the tempest's lightning, 'To Palermo!' will be our war cry. Urquiza is on his way to Palermo."[19] On the 29th, the army reached Luján. On the 30th, it crossed the Márquez Bridge and defeated a strong detachment of 5,000 Rosists. On February 1st, the two armies faced each other near Morón. On the third, they began a historic battle.[20] Step by step, the campaign was recorded by Sarmiento in his bulletins, until at the Battle of Caseros, Don Domingo abandoned his press and entered into the fighting itself.

The Battle of Caseros ended the twenty-year-old dictatorship of Juan Manuel de Rosas, but it was not a battle of hard fighting or heavy casualties. The Rosists knew that they were defeated. "A bronze statue has its feet in the sand, and perhaps Rosas knew this."[21] The dictator left his brother-in-law, General Mansilla, in command of the city of Buenos Aires. General Pacheco was given command of the rear guard, and Rosas himself rode out to the town of Monte Caseros to meet the onslaught of Urquiza's forces. Before he left he had already arranged for his flight by boat from Buenos Aires harbor. Caseros was Rosas' first and last important battle. It did not last long, and he soon found himself at sea, embarked for England and a life of exile in Southhampton.

Don Domingo enjoyed a day as a soldier on February 3rd. He joined the Lezica battalion and advanced with the front-line troops. He attacked and took a farm house, served as General Virasoro's aide for a half hour, and acted as messenger and general handyman during the rest of the battle. Several

[19] Bulletin no. 14.

[20] For chronology, see Antonio P. Castro, *Vida y obra de Urquiza*, Buenos Aires, 1946, pp. 45-46.

[21] Rojas, p. 385.

weeks later, Mitre referred to his conduct by saying, "Our Sarmiento acquitted himself as a hero."[22] He had fought the tyrant with his pen in Chile, with his mobile press across the pampa, and now he fought him with his sword at Caseros.

The Battle of Caseros was signified in a celebration at Mendoza by the crossing of a sword and a pen. This was intended to symbolize the cooperation of the military under Urquiza and the intellectual under Sarmiento. In reality, it symbolized the reason why the two men could not get along. Neither was satisfied with his own weapon. Urquiza was jealous of the victories of Sarmiento's pen. Don Domingo wished to equal the feats of his general's sword.

Chapter 28. New Targets: Urquiza and Alberdi

On the afternoon of February 4, the day after the decisive Battle of Caseros, Domingo Sarmiento, now a member of the general staff, rode into Palermo, on the outskirts of Buenos Aires, and was one of the first of the invading army to enter Rosas' former mansion. Here he took great pleasure in addressing a number of letters to his friends in Chile and putting for the date line, "Palermo de San Benito, February 4, 1852." He found one of the famous Rosist banners proclaiming, "Death to the savage unitarists," and he took this with him as a souvenir of the momentous occasion.[1] It was a memorable day for Don Domingo, for it represented the fulfillment of the prediction that he had made to Domingo de Oro in Arica some four years before. It was 1852, Rosas had fallen, and Sarmiento was in Buenos Aires.

[22] *Obras,* XLIX, 204.

[1] This banner is on exhibit at the Museo Histórico Sarmiento in Buenos Aires.

In Palermo news began to reach Don Domingo of the occurrences in the provincial capital. The city was wild with happiness at its new freedom. Many leading federalists had escaped. Many others had been pardoned by Urquiza. A division of troops that had revolted a month before and murdered its commander, General Aquino, had been condemned to death by the conquering general. Don Vicente López y Planes, the author of the national anthem and the father of Sarmiento's young friend, Vicente Fidel López, had been appointed governor of Buenos Aires, and the unitarist, Valentín Alsina, had been designated his minister of government.

Don Domingo remained outside of Buenos Aires at the Holmberg estate until the 19th of February. He watched the events in the port city from this vantage point, but he did not take part in them. In spite of this aloofness, the growing differences between Sarmiento and Urquiza continued to increase. Sarmiento did not cease to be annoyed with Urquiza's conciliatory policy. He had looked forward to a clean sweep, a quick change from one form of government to another, but the "Victor of Caseros" made it clear that he believed this to be impossible. Don Domingo went to see the general to request an expedition to San Juan, but Urquiza was well aware of his need for men like Benavídez. To overthrow the provincial governors would not only mean arousing strong and determined forces which would be difficult to overcome, but it would also create a state of near chaos in the nation. After Sarmiento had left the room, Urquiza turned to his chief of police and said, "But don't you see that this Sarmiento wants me to make war on the governors? I have not yet come to that."[2]

Don Domingo saw in Urquiza's compromises a defeat for the very principles for which he and his fellow exiles had fought throughout the past decades. As he later explained to one of his friends: "There is nevertheless one point on which I have always been inflexible: I have held to principles and not to men, to the general interest rather than to my own personal interests.

"In 1852 I advised General Urquiza to serve such principles

[2] Gálvez, p. 245.

without compromising with those who had fought them. . . . He thought that he could act otherwise, and two years of wavering have shown that I was right."[3]

The continued insistence on the part of Urquiza that members of his government and of his army wear the traditional red ribbon of the federalists began to worry Don Domingo. For him and his fellow exiles, all those who had fought for twenty years against the Rosas regime, the red ribbon was one of the most definite symbols of the fallen dictator. Its adoption by Urquiza automatically signified in their minds that tyranny was returning. If Sarmiento had stopped to think this question over objectively, he would have seen that it had no practical importance. He would have seen that Urquiza needed the support of many former federalists if the civil wars were not to go on indefinitely, and the use of the red ribbon was among the most harmless methods of gaining that support.

Urquiza, however, was also to blame in allowing the split to widen between Sarmiento and himself. The same things that had annoyed him about the writer during the campaign continued to annoy him in Buenos Aires. Everyone who came to greet the victor of Caseros asked about Sarmiento. They were as anxious to meet the writer as they were to meet the soldier. Urquiza began to answer his visitors sarcastically, "Why I have done nothing! . . . I just came to meet the writers from Montevideo and Chile. They did it all." Mitre asked him one day if he was annoyed with him. "Not with you, but with that Sarmiento. He is pretentious, a madman, an intriguer, an anarchist." In a decree referring to the use of the red ribbons, Urquiza spoke of the "savage unitarists, who with unheard-of nerve claim the heritage of a revolution that does not belong to them, of a victory in which they did not take part, of a homeland whose peace they disturbed, whose independence they compromised and whose liberty they sacrificed to their ambition and to their anarchical conduct."[4]

[3] Unpublished letter from Sarmiento to Aniceto Sánchez, Santiago de Chile, December 17, 1854, Archivo General de la Nación, División Nacional, Sección Gobierno, Archivo del General Justo José de Urquiza, Legajo 67.

[4] Quoted in Gálvez, pp. 246, 249.

It soon became evident that the two leaders would not be able to reach a common ground of agreement in the near future. No overt act, no open break occurred; but Don Domingo decided to abandon his homeland once more for a voluntary exile. He left quietly, without telling anyone but his close friends, Mitre, Alsina, López, and Guerrico. He had secured permission from Urquiza more than a week earlier to return to Chile in order to arrange his affairs in that country. He left with Colonel Hornes a letter to General Urquiza:

"Having obtained from Your Excellency permission to return to Chile, after the completion of the commission you were kind enough to confer upon me in the army, I have resolved to take advantage of the early sailing of a ship for Río de Janeiro in order to take from there one of the many ships that sail for the Pacific.

"This resolution is accelerated by the purpose of the proclamation that you circulated yesterday, it being my decided intention not to subscribe to the menacing insinuation of wearing a red ribbon. Such a course is repugnant to my convictions and contrary to my honorable record.

"May God illuminate the way of Your Excellency along the difficult trail upon which you have set out. It is my profound conviction that you are straying from it, allowing to dissipate over a more or less long period of time, but no less fatal for its length, all the glory that for a moment you had gathered about your name.

"I take this opportunity to offer to Your Excellency the respects and consideration with which I subscribe as Your Excellency's true servant. D. F. Sarmiento."[5]

Before departing, Don Domingo forecast the defeat of Urquiza as he had predicted the defeat of Rosas. And when Mitre came down to the dock to see him off, he turned to his old friend with the prophetic words, "Mitre: You will be the first president of the Republic, but remember that I reserve for myself the second presidency."[6]

Sarmiento sailed for Río de Janeiro on the *Prince*. They put into Montevideo for a short time, long enough for Don Domingo to hear from Mitre that his letter had had an effect

[5] *Obras*, XLIX, 203.

[6] *Ibid.*, 213.

upon Urquiza. Because of it, the general "received nobody and awoke with a headache." Sarmiento protested that his letter "had the merit of moderation and biblical simplicity."

Aboard the *Prince* were many important federalists fleeing into exile after their defeat at Caseros. Juan Terrero, relative and friend of Rosas; Lucio Mansilla, Don Juan Manuel's brother-in-law; young Mansilla, the dictator's nephew; and many others were aboard. Sarmiento was still burning with his old hatred for Rosas and Rosism. He was still determined to destroy every vestige of the regime. "He can well save his body from the gallows that awaited him, but there remains to us his execrable name which like that of Quiroga we will carry on to posterity to be eternally damned."[7] But daily contact with the members of the Rosas family aboard the ship was inevitable. Don Domingo began to talk to them. He allowed his former hatred to die down, and in later years he regretted many of his excesses against Rosas' name.

In Río de Janeiro, Sarmiento began to organize an opposition to what he considered a new tyranny. He wrote to his friend, José Posse, and confided his plans. Urquiza would have to be overthrown, and he could see no one in the Republic capable of doing it. "Buenos Aires has nobody, nor is there any national figure, who can oppose Urquiza, except for General Paz and myself."[8] He therefore would have to assume the responsibility for such a task. The provinces would be his main support. He contacted Rawson and Aberastain in San Juan, Pedro León Zoloaga and Juan Godoy in Mendoza, Domingo García in La Rioja, Palacios and Labaysse in Santiago del Estero, and Manuel Tula in Salta. He outlined a set of principles for which they would fight: (1) the organization of national customs, (2) the abolition of internal frontiers and customs, (3) the creation of custom houses on rivers and frontiers, (4) the reunion of a congress in a place where it could not be intimidated by Urquiza or anyone else.

These were the principles for which Sarmiento proposed to fight. He hoped to gain the support of many of his distin-

[7] Belín Sarmiento, *Sarmiento anecdótico, op.cit.*, p. 98.

[8] Sarmiento to Posse, Rio de Janeiro, April 1, 1852, unpublished letters in the Museo Histórico Sarmiento. Now published in *Epistolario entre Sarmiento y Posse*, I, 29.

guished friends in the provinces. Meanwhile, their first target was the destruction of the Urquiza regime. He proposed a number of strategic moves towards this end. He suggested that the election of national deputies be delayed. He urged the support of friends, "who are full of our ideas," as deputies. And he proposed the support, or at least the absence of opposition, to Buenos Aires. "There, more than in the interior, I have an immense personal following. I only need the support of the provinces to convert this into a political party."[9]

Don Domingo's political ambitions, his objectives, and his plans were thus starkly revealed to his close friend and confidant, José Posse. As he wrote him, he planned to put himself in a position in which he would be supported by all parties. The slogan that was later to be famous as his political motto was beginning to form in his mind. "Present me always as the champion of the provinces in Buenos Aires. Present me as the provincial who is accepted in Buenos Aires as well as in the provinces, the only Argentine name accepted and esteemed by all: by the Chilean government, by the Brazilian government, by the provinces, by Buenos Aires, by the army, by the federalists, by the unitarists—as the founder of the policy of the fusion of parties as a result of all my writings."[10]

While in Brazil, Don Domingo was careful to make strong his ties with the Brazilian government. He spent twenty days with the emperor in the mountain capital of Petropolis. Pedro II was one of the most unusual rulers that Iberoamerica ever produced. He was a patron of the arts and sciences. He was a great admirer of the intellectual. "He gave titles and decorations to artists, scientists, and men of letters; he encouraged such men as Pasteur and Graham Bell."[11] It is little wonder that he was attracted to the figure of Sarmiento. Here was a man who combined so many of the artistic and literary qualities that he so admired. He was thrilled by the characters of Quiroga, Navarro, Oro, Barcala, and Aldao. He liked *El Facundo,* which he held to be "full of novelty." Before he

[9] *Ibid.*

[10] *Ibid.* This very valuable Sarmiento-Posse correspondence, which I was able to read at the Museo Histórico Sarmiento, reveals an intimate aspect of Sarmiento that was never captured in formal biographies.

[11] Erico Veríssimo, *Brazilian Literature,* New York, 1945, p. 56.

left Brazil, Sarmiento was decorated by the emperor, and was able to boast that his "situation here with the ministers could not be higher or more respectable."[12]

When Sarmiento left Río de Janeiro for Chile, his hopes for the future were high. He had a program. He thought that he was in a favorable position to carry it out. "If the plan is followed by my intimate friends with the perseverance with which I carried out my opposition to Rosas, we will triumph; for the elements on our side are immense. What we need is unity of action and a name that will unite all the wills. If not, we will have ten more years of caudillism."[13] He had the plan for unity. He had the name. In Chile he would pilot the overthrow of General Justo José de Urquiza.

Domingo Sarmiento's ambitions and plans for the future as he departed from Brazil were based on the fundamental premise that the new government of General Urquiza was destined to be a tyrannical personalism similar to that of Juan Manuel de Rosas. But such was not the case. On the contrary, General Urquiza's political views and political methods were quiet different from those of the former dictator. He was a promoter of public education; he fostered the development of the latest agricultural methods; he backed the economic development of the nation.[14] Furthermore, Urquiza devoted his efforts during the early months of his regime to the pacification, unification, and organization of the nation. These were facts that Sarmiento at this time could not see or refused to recognize.

"General Urquiza was anxious to hold a convention with the least possible delay for the purpose of framing a new constitution. He realized that the position of the province of Buenos Aires in the federation presented many and serious difficulties and he was determined to have the fundamental problems settled before the opposition had opportunity to become thoroughly organized."[15] Following a conciliatory

[12] Sarmiento to Posse, *loc.cit.*

[13] *Ibid.*

[14] Antonio P. Castro, *Nueva historia de Urquiza—industrial, comerciante, ganadero*, Buenos Aires, 1947. See also A. P. Castro, *Tres capítulos en la vida de Urquiza*, Concordia, Entre Ríos, 1945.

[15] L. S. Rowe, *The Federal System of the Argentine Republic*, Washington, 1921, p. 37.

policy towards all factions, he attempted to gain the support of the various contending elements. By his moderate attitude towards the federalists he gained the support of all the important provincial governments between February 16th and March 19th.[16] By the friendly gesture of appointing López y Planes and Alsina to govern Buenos Aires he sought to gain the support of that important sector. And by offers of trade privileges and protection, he hoped to win the friendship of foreign governments.[17]

On April 8th, General Urquiza took the first step towards the constitutional organization of the nation. He realized that he would have to gain the support of all the contending factions if such an organization was to be successful. On that day, he issued an invitation to the provincial governors to meet at San Nicolás de los Arroyos for discussions preliminary to a constitutional convention. Urquiza believed that if certain fundamental principles could be agreed upon, if certain necessary compromises could be made at such a time, the actual framing of a basic law for the nation would be a relatively simple one. Informal discussions were initiated on May 20, and the conference began on May 25. The result of the labor completed by the provincial governors during the days that followed was the famous Acuerdo de San Nicolás (The San Nicolás Agreement).

This agreement provided a seemingly satisfactory compromise for all interested parties. For the provincial interests it recognized the Federal Pact of 1831 as the "fundamental law of the Republic." For the constitutionalists, it set the calling of a constituent congress for the month of August of that same year. For the "liberals," it provided for the free passage of goods throughout the nation and the abolition of internal customs, the free election of deputies to the constituent con-

[16] Adherence of the provinces to Urquiza's program came in the following sequence: Entre Ríos (February 16, 1852), Santa Fé (February 23), Córdoba (February 27), Corrientes (March 5), Tucumán (March 12), Salta (March 14), and San Luis (March 19).

[17] Justo José de Urquiza to President of the United States, Paraná, March 31, 1854. National Archives, State Department Division, Argentine Republic, Incoming Correspondence, Volume 2, Notes.

gress, without limitations, and the inviolability of deputies after their election. For the unitarists, a clause was included attacking localism as an instrument of anarchy.[18] The agreement was a bid for cooperation and unity, and if it had succeeded the organization of the nation would have proceeded peacefully.

Thirteen of the fourteen provinces of the Republic ratified the agreement within a short time, but the last and most important, Buenos Aires, held it up, and destroyed its chances for success. The unitarists of Buenos Aires were still fearful of Urquiza's intentions. The commercial interests of the port city did not want to give up their favored position by entering into a federation of equal provinces. Buenos Aires held a position of economic and political predominance, and it was loath to give it up. Bartolomé Mitre, a deputy in the Buenos Aires legislature, opposed the agreement. A violent debate ensued. Governor López y Planes and his government resigned their posts. "The political situation thus took on a grave character. The government of the province of Buenos Aires was going to remain acephalous. The city, convulsed by the opposition press and the stand of the chamber, was a threat. . . . The fruits of victory might well degenerate into the chaos of national dissolution and civil war."[19]

The adamant attitude of Buenos Aires exhausted the patience of General Urquiza. He realized that all of the opposing interests would have to be satisfied and compromises reached, but he was exasperated at the thought that one of these interests could thus destroy all the work completed. In desperation he ordered the closing of the Buenos Aires legislative chamber and the calling of new elections. This was, however, to no avail. On October 30th, Valentín Alsina was elected governor of Buenos Aires. He represented the most extreme wing of the Buenos Aires party. Bartolomé Mitre was named minister of government. Urquiza despaired of bringing the major province of the nation into his confederation. On September 11, 1852, the city of Buenos Aires revolted

[18] Registro Nacional, Volume II, p. 279.
[19] Juan Antonio González Calderón, *op.cit.*, pp. 109, 110.

against the national government and declared that its ties with the Urquiza regime were ended.[20]

In the months that followed, General Urquiza's efforts were divided between two ends. He continued with his task of national organization, and he made repeated efforts to bring Buenos Aires into the national structure, both by conciliation and by the use of force. On November 20, 1852, the constitutional convention met in the city of Santa Fé. It assembled "under the most unfavorable circumstances. It is true that every province with the exception of Buenos Aires was represented, but it is important to bear in mind what the absence of this province signified. The prospect of forming a vigorous federation without Buenos Aires was not encouraging. With less than one-third of the population and about one-fourth of the wealth of the country, the thirteen provinces were certain to cut a rather sorry figure in their isolation."[21] But in spite of the disaffection of Buenos Aires, the constitutional convention proceeded to draw up a fundamental law for the nation. Based primarily upon the Constitution of the United States, but including most of the suggestions of Juan Bautista Alberdi for adapting the North American document to the South American reality, the constitution of 1853 continued down to 1949,[22] with no fundamental alterations, as the basis of the Argentine government.

Simultaneously with the drawing up of the constitution, Urquiza made repeated efforts to bring Buenos Aires to terms. General Hilario Lagos led a revolt against the Alsina government late in 1852. Some months after that he laid siege to the city. Early in 1853 Urquiza received authorization from the Congress to negotiate for a settlement with Buenos Aires, but after a short armistice this proved to be futile. In April 1853 a fleet of the confederation under the North American, John H. Coe, laid siege to the city from the sea, but two months

[20] For a different view on this period, see Ramón J. Cárcano, *De Caseros al 11 de Septiembre*, Buenos Aires, 1918; Juan Antonio González Calderón, *op.cit.*; and Ramón J. Cárcano, *Del sitio de Buenos Aires al campo de Cepeda*, Buenos Aires, 1921.

[21] L. S. Rowe, *The Federal System, op.cit.*, p. 41.

[22] It was not until the administration of the twentieth-century personalist dictator, Juan Domingo Perón, that this nomocratic document was changed.

later Coe sold out to Buenos Aires for 26,000 ounces of gold and turned his fleet over to the port city. The situation was chaotic during this period, and it is difficult to lay the blame for the chaos on one side or the other. Urquiza seemed to be making sincere efforts to conciliate all sides. He seemed genuinely anxious to establish a unified republic on a basis of constitutional law. But he never fully recognized the relative power of the province of Buenos Aires in the economic and political life of the nation, and he never provided her with a position to correspond to that power. Buenos Aires, on the other hand, refused to recognize the sincerity of Urquiza's efforts. It was distrustful and zealous of its own favored position and its own power. It refused to compromise to make a unified republic possible.

As Domingo Sarmiento surveyed this scene from his vantage point in Santiago de Chile, he was unable to see it through objective eyes. His ambitions and his plans had taken hold of him while he was in Río de Janeiro. He had caught the sight of power, and he was blinded by it. He saw Urquiza and his government as he wanted to see them. He saw the general as a tyrant and as a dictator. He recognized no sincerity. He identified the new caudillo with the "barbaric invasions" with which he had charged Rosas.[23] "No one is a sincere supporter of Urquiza," he wrote.[24] "Buenos Aires is and will be all. She will be the faithful depository of civilization and liberty; but the provinces are, as you have seen, powerful for the cause of evil."[25] Urquiza typified the barbarity of the provinces, and he would have to be opposed by all true lovers of freedom. In a letter to his friend Mariano Sarratea, Sarmiento urged him not to turn over the Argentine consulate in Chile to an Urquista. The celestial blue of the Argentine national flag, rather than the flag of Urquiza, should fly over the consulates in Chile.[26]

[23] Sarmiento to Mitre, Santiago, January 25, 1853, Museo Mitre, *Sarmiento-Mitre, Correspondencia 1846-1868*, Buenos Aires, 1911, p. 27.

[24] *Ibid.*, p. 44.

[25] *Ibid.*, p. 31.

[26] Sarmiento to Mariano E. de Sarratea, Santiago, November 1, 1852. Unpublished letters in Carpeta VII, no. 813, at Museo Histórico Sarmiento in Buenos Aires.

Sarmiento published his book, *Campaña en el ejército grande de Sud América* (Campaign in the Grand Army of South America), and in this he began his violent public attack against General Urquiza. He described his own participation in the recent Caseros campaign, "Campaigning at my own expense with my own arms and horses, like the ancient Spanish captains; leaving behind family and fortune, in search of a free and civilized homeland, I sailed the Atlantic and the Pacific, went up the majestic Uruguay and the life-giving Paraná; crossing the Argentine provinces of Entre Ríos and Santa Fé; visiting the capitals of Montevideo and Buenos Aires, fighting on land and sea; and traveling and fighting, supporting the difficult fatigues and enjoying profound emotions; observing what my eyes saw and what my ears heard; thinking and writing and living the easy life of the enthusiasm of battle." This was his contribution to a great crusade. But what were its results? Another tyranny. Another exile. He blamed it all on the new caudillo leader, Justo José de Urquiza,[27] and he devoted the major part of his nominally historical account of the campaign to a belittling of the commanding general and an attack upon his later actions.

Retired to his country estate at Yungay, Don Domingo began to realize that this was a historic moment for his nation. He read of the San Nicolás Agreement, the constitution, the break between Buenos Aires and the confederation, the siege of Buenos Aires, the wounding of Mitre during the siege, and many other events that were occurring. He realized that there was a struggle going on between the interests of the port city and the interests of the interior, a struggle far different from that which he had imagined between a tyrant and a liberty-loving opposition, between barbarity and civilization. He did not realize this truth immediately. But he began to sense a feeling of isolation from the scene of action, from the true reality. Mitre, López, Mármol, Gutiérrez, and Vélez, all of his old compatriots, were playing leading roles in the new fight, but he remained strangely isolated. This isolation, this lack of participation in the true struggle of selfish interests was both the weakness and the strength of Sarmiento during this

[27] *Obras*, xiv, 64.

period. It was his weakness, for it distorted his view of the situation. It made him oversimplify it in his own terms and attack the opposition unfairly. It was his strength, for it allowed him to remain aloof from the struggle of interests and assume a disinterested position as the defender of national unity and law irrespective of the particular interests of Buenos Aires or the provinces. This position, which he had told Posse would be his key to success, allowed him to adopt the motto: "A citizen of Buenos Aires in the provinces; a provincial in Buenos Aires." This slogan later gave him the stature of a true statesman when his turn at the leadership of his nation's affairs finally arrived.

On August 1, 1852, Sarmiento was elected by San Juan as deputy to the constituent congress at Paraná. He could not accept this post because of his views on the conduct of the government of the confederation. Meanwhile, his friend Mitre urged him to return to Buenos Aires and accept a post in the government of that province, but his attitude towards the need for national unity prohibited his accepting any such offer.

Don Domingo saw that he could enter into the political scene in the manner that was traditional to him. He could conduct a propaganda campaign against General Urquiza, the man whom he considered to be the reason for the chaotic situation of the nation. Soon after his arrival in Chile, Sarmiento had called upon his fellow writer and compatriot Juan Bautista Alberdi. He had immediately assumed that Alberdi would agree with him and support him in his attacks against the current ruler of the confederation. He spoke with Alberdi for some time. He predicted an armed combat between the confederation and Buenos Aires, and he proposed a personal alliance between himself and Alberdi in which they would remain neutral during the fratricidal combat, maintain their objectivity, and be ready to offer a positive course once the conflict was terminated. Alberdi was a man of temperament quite different from that of Don Domingo. He was cool and unemotional. He was silent and preferred to express himself in well-considered writings rather than in passionate polemic or speech. He listened without a word to

Sarmiento's exposition of the situation. Then, when Sarmiento entered into his violent attack against Urquiza, his methods and his motives, again Alberdi remained silent. He did not, however, agree with his more impetuous friend. Three factors of difference entered in to prevent the two men from seeing eye to eye on this matter. Alberdi did not have the ambitions that partly accounted for Sarmiento's hatred of Urquiza. He did not have a set formula of civilization versus barbarity into which he would have to fit the present conflict, thus distorting it. And, finally, his temperament allowed him to view the scene with more calm, with more objectivity, than the hotheaded publicist. When Don Domingo had finished talking, he paused. He was still confident that Alberdi was in complete agreement with him. When the latter expressed himself in opposition to some of the views on Urquiza, Sarmiento was furious. Why had he not spoken before? He had tricked him into exposing his views. He had made a fool of him.

This was the first friction between Sarmiento and Alberdi, but for some time after this, the two men attempted to maintain friendly and cordial relations. As in the case of the relationship between Sarmiento and Urquiza, however, a break eventually came. Again it was caused partly by divergent views on the situation, partly because at this particular period of transition and uncertainty in Don Domingo's life, he was blinded to true motives by his own subconscious plans.

In the meanwhile, Alberdi published his famous *Bases,* a book containing a proposed platform for the constitutional organization of the nation. Sarmiento was one of the first to praise this work, calling it the Argentine Decalogue, "the flag of all men of the heart." He even went so far as to organize a club of Argentine *émigrés* whose purpose was to propagandize and support the ideas contained in the *Bases.*

It was not on an ideological plane that the break came between Sarmiento and Alberdi. It was over the two men's evaluations of Urquiza. Sarmiento maintained his violent hostility towards the general. This was an uncompromising attitude, partly motivated by the many psychological factors already discussed. Alberdi, on the other hand, viewed the efforts of Urquiza sympathetically. He saw the leader as a man trying to bring about the unity and liberty of his nation by the most practical means possible, by compromise, cooperation, and tireless effort. To Alberdi, Sarmiento's attitude was merely an obstruction in the way of the efforts of Urquiza, and he would not be a party to it.

On October 13, 1852, as Urquiza was preparing for the constitutional convention at Paraná, Don Domingo addressed to him the famous letter that has come to be known as the "Carta de Yungay" (Letter from Yungay). In this work he referred to his points of difference with the general. He charged Urquiza, with his red ribbon and federalist support, with being a successor to the former tyranny of Rosas. "A Thermidorean like Tallien, he overcame his companion and accomplice, Rosas, the Robespierre of Argentina."[28] He attacked him for allowing Benavídez to remain in power. He attacked him for draining the resources of the nation by maintaining an army of seven thousand men. He attacked him for his policy towards Buenos Aires. "Your Excellency is a lost man, without the possibility of rehabilitation. He is, to my poor judgment, the last of the procession of victims that are sacrificed in revolutions."[29] Sarmiento proposed that the "lost man" redeem himself and save his country by appointing the nation's leading men to reorganize the political system. Among these suggested were Alberdi, Alsina, López, Mitre, Lagos, Vélez, Del Carril, Aberastain, Mármol, and, strangely enough, Sarmiento.

The "Carta de Yungay" was published for all to read, and the next month Don Domingo published his *Campaña en el ejército grande,* with its dedication to "my dear Alberdi," and with its attempt to blacken the name of General Urquiza. If these efforts were directed partly towards winning over Alberdi to join the opposition to the president of the confederation, they were badly judged. At that very moment in Paraná, the constitutional convention that had been called by Urquiza was drawing up a document based upon the ideas

[28] D. F. Sarmiento, *Las ciento y una,* Editorial Sopena: Buenos Aires, 1939, p. 52.

[29] *Ibid.,* p. 51.

proposed in the *Bases*. To Alberdi's way of thinking, Urquiza was still on the right track. He was still doing the best he could to complete a difficult task. Sarmiento was an annoying thorn in his side. In answer to Don Domingo's attacks, Juan Bautista Alberdi published early in 1853 a series of letters entitled *Cuatro cartas sobre la prensa y la política militante en la República Argentina*. These were written at Quillota and came to be known as the *Cartas Quillotanas*. Here Alberdi showed his impatience at Sarmiento's continued and intemperate attacks against Urquiza. He called Don Domingo a "caudillo of the pen," and he went on to define his character: "He detests all yokes, even that of logic, even that of authority. Free as the centaur of our pampa, he attacks the Spanish Academy with as much daring as he attacks the first authorities of the Republic."[30]

The break between the two exiles had occurred. There ensued one of the most bitter polemics ever to be carried on in the press of Chile. In a series of articles entitled *Ciento y una* (One hundred and one), Don Domingo attacked Alberdi's character, his motives, and his ideas. "You will note that there is a great difference between this brusque language of a soldier, improvised in the heat of indignation, and the mellifluous paraphrases and oblique attacks that you have meditated, corrected and soaked in the subtle and imperceptible prussic acid during sixty days of retirement and meditation at Quillota. But I have many pens in my inkwell. I have a terrible, justice-dealing one for the evil and the powerful, like Aldao, Quiroga, Rosas, and others. I have the complimentary one for honorable men like Funes, Balmaceda, Lamas, Alsina, Paz, and others; I have the severe, logical, circumspect one to argue with Bello, Pinero, Carril, and others. For the sophists, for the hypocrite, I have no pen; I have a whip, and I make use of it without pity, because for them there is no other brake than pain. They have no shame when they appeal to such means to harm others."[31]

Over a period of several months, a cruel and bitter exchange of verbal blows was carried on between the two men.

[30] Juan Bautista Alberdi, *Obras completas*, IV, 21.
[31] *Obras*, XV, 237.

The basic difference arose from their distinct ways of thinking. Both had the same end in view: the unity, the peace, and the constitutional organization of their nation. Alberdi, like Urquiza, believed that the means of achieving this end would have to be adapted to the circumstances. Sarmiento would allow no compromise in means. A clean sweep was necessary. Alberdi's compromising attitude seemed to Sarmiento a pure opportunism. He accused his opponent of sacrificing all to obtain a diplomatic post from Urquiza. Sarmiento's inability to adapt his means signified to Alberdi a lack of mental discipline, a mind that would not submit to any authority, a mind basically anarchical. These conclusions as to motives could lead only to the most bitter conflict.

In 1853, the Argentine constitution was finished. It was founded upon Alberdi's *Bases,* which Sarmiento had formerly praised, but accomplished by Urquiza's means. In his *Comentarios a la constitución de la confederación Argentina,* Sarmiento assumed the role of constitutional lawyer. He attacked the document in terms of the Constitution of the United States. Alberdi wisely answered these attacks by pointing to the difference between the two nations. What would be suitable for one would not work for the other. The history and the tradition of North America were to Alberdi's way of thinking sufficiently distinct from that of South America to require differences in the basic law and differences in the organization.

Throughout 1853 Sarmiento continued his attacks against Alberdi and Urquiza in periodicals and in pamphlets. In November he founded his former newspaper. "I founded once again my old *Crónica,*" he wrote to Mitre. "This serves me better than books or pamphlets."[32] Reports from Mendoza indicated that the recreation of the newspaper was having its former effect. "I hope to follow the march of events, and prepare public opinion, insofar as I can, for that which will develop later."[33]

By the end of the year, however, Sarmiento was beginning

[32] Sarmiento to Mitre, Santiago, November 2, 1853; Museo Mitre, *op.cit.,* p. 37.

[33] Sarmiento to Mitre, Santiago, November 29, 1853; *Museo Mitre, op.cit.,* p. 40.

to feel dissatisfied with his position in Chile. He did not like to be separated from the center of action in his own country. He no longer took part in Chilean affairs. He edited, at the request of President Montt, the educational periodical, *Monitor de las escuelas primarias* (Monitor of the Primary Schools), but this was the total extent of his Chilean activities. Meanwhile, he felt that his quarrels with Urquiza and Alberdi were putting him in an unfavorable position. He began to feel depressed. "My health is broken. . . . I have seldom suffered as I have at this time! I live alone, like a prisoner that Alberdi and his club stand guard over. I groan beneath his lash. They are the powerful ones of the earth."[34] Sarmiento wanted to get back into action. He wanted to get away from the bitterness of his verbal battles.

Chapter 29. The Road Back

EARLY in January 1854 Domingo Sarmiento left his home at Yungay and started the long trip across the Andes. With him were his wife, Benita; his son, Dominguito; two Frenchmen, Eugène Leloutre and Charles Polino; and three servants. Late in the afternoon they arrived in Los Andes, where they stayed at the home of Pedro Bari, resting the next day, and continuing early the second morning. They stopped at Las Cuevas to rest, and there they were met by a traveler who brought letters and news for Don Domingo from San Juan. At Uspallata, high up in the mountains, they met the famous international banker, Buschenthal, and a young Sanjuanino, Rafael Ruiz, who brought two fresh horses for Sarmiento. The next night they spent at Villavicencio, and at noon on the day after they arrived in Mendoza.[1]

[34] Sarmiento to Mitre, Santiago, October 19, 1853; Museo Mitre, *op.cit.*, p. 33.

[1] Edmundo Correas, "Sarmiento es preso y procesado en Mendoza," Los

Don Domingo was tired of his inactive life as an exile. He was determined to return to his own country and enter into the task of its reconstruction. As one of his friends expressed it in a letter, "The indefatigable and noble patriot Sarmiento finally resolved to move to his home in San Juan, to work there in the midst of danger for those principles whose triumph we all seek. . . . Sarmiento recognizes the risks that he must run, but he feels strong in his sane intentions, strong in his will."[2] He intended to settle on a semi-permanent basis in Cuyo, found a town in the Uspallata Valley, and establish an experimental farm near San Juan.[3] In the political field he had further plans to attempt to bring about a change in the existing provincial government. "He has hopes of convincing Benavídez and bringing him back on the path of his duties and of his interests; and if his noble efforts are successful, the nation will see of what he is capable."[4] Here Sarmiento saw an opportunity to return to the stage of national politics through the back door, by way of his own province. If he could accomplish something in this area, he would be forcibly brought to the attention of the public.

Don Domingo had notified the government of Mendoza some months before of his intentions of making such a trip. He had requested permission from the various provincial governments involved. He had received no objections, and he expected no trouble upon his arrival. But it soon became evident that his arrival had caused far more excitement than

---

Andes, Mendoza, 1945, September 9, 1945. Señor Correas had a detailed account of this trip, but he is mistaken on the dates. He places the incident in September 1854, but all letters and documents indicate that it was in January.

[2] Mariano de Sarratea to José Juan de Larramendi, Valparaiso, January 14, 1854; among unpublished archives of Museo Histórico Sarmiento, Carpeta VII, no. 814.

The reasons for Sarmiento's sudden trip at this time have long been a mystery to historians. His most recent biographer calls it "an incomprehensible thing at such a political moment." (Rojas, p. 398.) It is, however, possible to reconstruct a quite convincing motive from the unpublished letters and documents that I have had the opportunity to examine in Buenos Aires and elsewhere.

[3] This is according to the account of his grandson, Belín Sarmiento, *Sarmiento anecdótico, op.cit.*, p. 107.

[4] Sarratea to Larramendi, *op.cit.*

he had foreseen. He came to realize that his trip had more serious implications than he had suspected. "My aims were frustrated by the very surprise that my appearance in those places caused, the exaltation of my friends . . . the fear of my enemies."[5]

On the day of Sarmiento's arrival in Mendoza, he was lunching at the house of Jesús María Mayorga. In the midst of the meal, Doña Paula Rosas, the wife of a high official in the provincial government, arrived, out of breath, and in a state of excitement and confusion. "You sit there so calmly, Señor Sarmiento, they are on their way to arrest you, with orders to take you dead or alive."

Don Domingo laughed and asked, "But are we not in a free country that has just sanctioned its constitution?"

Doña Paula insisted. She had heard it from Juana Porven, who had it directly from the mouth of— "But look out the window. There they are. Now laugh!"

Don Domingo arose from his seat and went over to the window. A company of soldiers with fixed bayonets, led by an officer with his sword in his hand, was approaching the door. A servant opened it, and the officer entered.

"You are under arrest."

"Do you have a warrant?"

"I do not need one. I am the governor's aide."

"It is to guard against such orders that the guarantee was imposed requiring a warrant."

"I know my duty, sir."

"Very well, let me put on my cape." The officer and two soldiers with fixed bayonets followed Sarmiento into the bedroom. Two other soldiers seized some revolvers that were lying on the piano.

Sarmiento was amused with the precautions the officials took.

"Do you think, sir, that I and my family came to Mendoza to jump fences—at my age?"

"I only do my duty, and I don't have to answer anyone's questions."

The armed escort took Don Domingo through the streets

[5] Sarmiento to Mitre, Yungay, March 4, 1854; Museo Mitre, *op.cit.*, p. 44.

of Mendoza to jail. He was left in a cell with a guard in sight to avoid any possible slip. The prisoner asked for a blanket, and curling up in a corner he slept soundly until he was called at nightfall.[6]

Sarmiento was amazed and pleased at the great disturbance that his arrival had created. Several squadrons of cavalry were called to duty, guards were posted at the government house, and "for two days were ready and waiting for the battle with this imaginary enemy."[7]

While in jail, Don Domingo was held incommunicado, and when he was brought to trial he was charged with conspiracy against the government. The muleteers, servants, and the two Frenchmen who had come with him indicated the extent of his plans. A Kolton rifle and another weapon brought for personal use, along with their proper complement of bullets, served as exhibits for the prosecution. The most important evidence brought in the trial was a letter from Sarmiento to General Benavídez attempting to persuade the latter to join the forces of opposition to the Urquiza government. The court had in its possession only a copy of this letter. Don Domingo pointed out that a copy was without value unless properly authenticated by a notary public. This assertion stumped the prosecution, and the trial was halted. The suit was dropped, and within a few days Sarmiento was roaming the streets of Mendoza a free man.

Toward the middle of February, realizing that his excursion to Guyo had been a failure and fearing rumors that Urquiza had sent a detachment from Entre Ríos to seize him in Mendoza, Don Domingo set out again to make his oft-repeated crossing of the Andes. He returned once more to Chile, to his estate at Yungay, to the peace and frustration of a life of exile. But this time he knew that he would not stay in the neighboring nation. He had been made to realize his own importance in the politics of his nation. He was a force that the caudillos felt they would just have to cope with. In March he wrote to Mitre saying that he planned to go to Buenos Aires. "But I must cut loose from Chile, sell my lands,

[6] D. F. Sarmiento, *La vida de Dominguito, op.cit.*, pp. 44-46.

[7] Sarmiento to Mitre, Yungay, March 4, 1854; Museo Mitre, *op.cit.*, pp. 44-45.

leave the press, resign many sources of income; and to do all this without any urgent object in mind, it is necessary to take one's time. There is time to spare to watch the development of affairs that are now seen in the distant future."[8] So Don Domingo took his time. He continued to edit the *Monitor de las escuelas,* and he did a monumental job in this pedagogical effort. He carried on a campaign to increase the number of public libraries in Chile. He completed the translation of several books that were useful in primary school education. He published his *Educación común* (Common Education), and he continued his careful education and direction of Dominguito at Yungay.

In the meantime, opportunities were arising for him to enter into the politics of his nation, but the right time had not yet arrived. Tucumán elected him as deputy to the congress of the confederation. Sarmiento would have liked to accept, but he could not reconcile himself to working with the government of General Urquiza. At the end of April he was elected representative at the legislature of Buenos Aires, but he doubted his citizenship rights and he did not accept.

In 1855, Don Domingo began to wind up his business in Chile. He decided to abandon *La Crónica.* His trip to Mendoza had proved its inefficacy in Argentina. It sold only 187 copies in San Juan, "where it only uselessly arouses the spirits," 14 or 16 copies in Córdoba; and it arrived in Buenos Aires too late to be of any use.[9] He had no more ties in Chile, he wrote to Mitre, but he did not feel that it was yet time to go to Argentina. He suggested the idea of a trip to the United States, "to study there questions of administration, education, and the practice of federal and municipal institutions."[10] He hoped that the Chilean government might send him on another mission to study primary education. He suggested the possibility of a study of the records of the U.S. Patent Office in order to discover new methods of agriculture and industry. But such plans never materialized.

On March 11, 1855, Domingo Sarmiento set out again for

[8] Sarmiento to Mitre, Yungay, March 4, 1854; Museo Mitre, *op.cit.*, p. 47.
[9] *Ibid.*
[10] Sarmiento to Mitre, Yungay, April 8, 1854; Museo Mitre, *op.cit.*, pp. 50-51.

his homeland. This time he headed directly for San Juan. He had noted during his trip of the previous year that "the hatred for Benavídez is as universal as the desperation at ever being able to throw off his yoke."[11] Don Domingo set out with the somewhat impractical project of speaking with the old governor, convincing him of his errors, and persuading him to mend his ways. "In San Juan, I expect to make an effort to conciliate the two parties and see if I can make the government enter into a new order of things, without an uprising. . . . I will do nothing illegal."[12] He determined to use his rank as lieutenant colonel in the Army of Buenos Aires to claim protection under a treaty between the province and the confederation.

Upon his arrival in San Juan Sarmiento was met with an order to leave the territory of the province, but he still held his immunities as an elected deputy from San Juan. He continued on his way, and upon his arrival in the city, he directed himself to the house of William Rawson, a friend and collaborator of the governor, and requested an interview with Benavídez. This was granted, and Sarmiento entered the presence of his erstwhile enemy with the intention of making every effort to bring some solution to the political situation in San Juan. He talked at length with the governor. He offered his various projects and he made use of his eloquence. He advised him to join the other distinguished San Juan names and fight for national unity, to become a leader of the nation instead of the oppressor of women and children.[13] The aging Benavídez looked up at Sarmiento with an amused smile. "The same old Don Domingo! You have not changed at all."

Upon leaving the interview, Rawson expressed his horror at the daring that Sarmiento had shown. "How do you dare, Sarmiento?" he asked.

"Huh! Do you expect me to be afraid of him?"

That night a shot was fired through the window of Don Domingo's room. This was a warning. The crowds of Holy

[11] Museo Mitre, *op.cit.*, p. 46.
[12] Sarmiento to Mitre, Santiago, March 10, 1855; Museo Mitre, *op.cit.*, p. 101.
[13] *Obras*, XLIX, 213.

Week were beginning to enter the city. The streets were filled. The governor's advisers feared that Sarmiento would use the large concentration of people as a chance to strike a blow at the government. Don Domingo took heed of their none too subtle warning. The tension created by his very presence was too much for him. He left the next morning for Buenos Aires.[14] He *was* afraid of "him."

When Domingo Sarmiento arrived in Buenos Aires early in May in 1855, it was but an overgrown village. The urban district did not cover more than a few blocks. The dwellings consisted of low houses centered around the Plaza Mayor. Only a few blocks from the center of the town country life began. Livestock and cultivated fields appeared. There were no trolleys, railroads, or any internal communications. The port was small and primitive, and many of the ships were unloaded by taking large wheelcarts drawn by oxen out into the deep water alongside the vessels to carry both passengers and cargo to the shore. The principal buildings in the center of town were the Fort, the Cabildo, which was also the police station and the jail, the Legislature, the Cathedral, and the University.

For Don Domingo, his arrival in Buenos Aires was like arriving in a foreign land. He had visited the port city for a few days after the Battle of Caseros, but he had never come to know it. Yet this he knew would be the place where his destiny would be decided. This would be the city where he would or would not make his place in the history of his nation. Until now, all had been preparation. Now the real battle was to begin.

But Sarmiento's preparation had been far from useless. He knew what he wanted, and he knew the instruments that he would use in achieving his ends. As in Santiago de Chile some fifteen years before, he began to choose the weapons that he would use in his coming struggle. As during his exile, he knew that they would be centered around three primary instruments. He would use the newspaper and the school to "educate" opinion to his views. He would use the political institutions to put his ideas into action. With this in mind, it

[14] *Ibid.*, p. 219.

was not long before he had seized the instruments to power.

First, however, it was necessary for him to orientate himself in this new political scene. His two friends, Alsina, and Mitre, were in control of the Buenos Aires government, so he knew that he could count upon a friendly official attitude. The province was still separated from the confederation, but there were strong indications that a unification would be desirable for both sides. Don Domingo was careful to maintain his motto of "A citizen of Buenos Aires in the provinces, and a provincial in Buenos Aires." He was careful to maintain his position of objectivity, a position that would make him a key man when the time for unification came. "The Confederation without Buenos Aires is like that horseman who during the bombardment by the English, went on galloping and seemed to be brandishing his sword through the streets, long after a cannon ball had taken off his head. The State of Buenos Aires without the provinces is like the head of a man who has been guillotined but that goes on thinking and feeling for a long time."[15] The inability of the provinces to exist without Buenos Aires or of Buenos Aires to exist without the provinces was the basis of Sarmiento's platform. An increasing number of people in Argentina were beginning to agree with him.

Sarmiento did not move fast at the beginning. Doña Benita sold the property at Yungay, and with her son came to join her husband in Buenos Aires. Dominguito entered school and started the formal studies that his father had planned for him. Friendships were renewed, contacts were made. "One night we met Domingo Faustino Sarmiento in the house of Colonel Mitre. This chief dressed in a blue buttoned dress coat."[16] Sarmiento often wore his uniform of lieutenant colonel of which he was so proud. He became an intimate of the political and intellectual leaders of his new home town.

Before the end of 1855, he had gained positions of influence in all three of the main fields that he had chosen for his endeavors. A little over a month after his arrival, Bartolomé Mitre was made minister of war and the navy in the Buenos

[15] *Ibid.*, XVI, 128.

[16] Benjamín Vicuña Mackenna, *Obras Completas*, II, 402.

Aires government. The pressing duties of this new office forced him to give up his editorship of the newspaper *El Nacional*, and he appointed Don Domingo in his place. This was the very opening that Sarmiento needed in the world of journalism. Within two weeks he was named by Governor Obligado to a place on the consultative council of government. Here was an opening in the political field. Within the next year, he was appointed chief of the department of schools. Such a position gave him a decisive influence in the educational field. His instruments were in hand; the fight must now begin.

As time went by, the political situation in Buenos Aires appeared to be contrary to his liking, but Domingo Sarmiento was learning that he must adapt himself to circumstances. He was learning to fashion his means according to the situation at hand. Early in 1856 he looked favorably upon the political scene in Buenos Aires. "This country is now safe, prosperous; and our principles are triumphant."[17] But by the middle of that same year he had lost his enthusiasm. "I am disillusioned with it all," he wrote to his close friend, José Posse, "with Buenos Aires as much as with Paraná. Here there are ignorant egotists; there there are very wise badmen; here anarchy and disgovernment; there rule by a minority and exploitation."[18] In spite of this disillusionment, however, Don Domingo continued to build his political position.

The consultative council to which Sarmiento had been appointed the previous year was not an elective office. It seemed to fill no definite purpose in the government, and it soon became meaningless and without function, remaining an institution that was still-born. On March 2, 1856, however, Don Domingo acquired a more stable political post. He was elected by the Catedral al Norte District to the municipal council of the city of Buenos Aires. This was an organization with a very real function, and the forty-five-year-old patriot found in it an opportunity to demonstrate his administrative and political abilities. Among his fellow members on the council were

[17] Sarmiento to Julio Belín, Buenos Aires, February 3, 1856; unpublished letters in Museo Histórico Sarmiento, Carpeta XIII, no. 1681.

[18] Sarmiento to Posse, Buenos Aires, June 15, 1856, *op.cit.*

such distinguished names as Valentín Alsina and José Mármol. He found that these men were using the organization as a sounding board for their far-reaching projects and their flowery oratory. Sarmiento warned against this. The functions of the council were far more down to earth, and it was these functions that he meant to fulfill. "Here we are charged as municipal representatives with the sweeping of the streets and with the collection of garbage, and all these great and rhetorical amplifications are out of place."[19] On such a note, he became an important and respected leader of the city government. For two years he held his seat, and during that time he drew up a code of municipal regulations and an ordinance that provided for the widening of the city's streets. He fought the encroachment of the state government upon the jurisdiction of the municipal council, and he reestablished the power of the latter body which had been abolished during the long period of Rosas' dictatorship. All could see that Domingo Sarmiento was taking his political post seriously and fulfilling it well.

The following year Don Domingo was promoted to a more important position in the political scene of Buenos Aires. He was elected to the state senate from the tenth district around San Nicolás de Arroyo. Reelected in 1860, he maintained this position until 1861, and it was in this body that he performed his most important political roles during the period.

As a member of the senate committee on constitutional affairs, Sarmiento took a leading part in the debates on the trial of Rosas and the confiscation of his goods. He still held his burning hatred for the former dictator, and he refused to allow his name to be handed down to posterity without the curse of his accusations. "Leave him to me. I will take care of his memory. Poor thing!" He heartily backed the proposal to confiscate all of Rosas' goods, and he supported the right of the legislature to try the former dictator for the crime of *lesa patria*. Don Domingo read the report of the committee to the senate, and it was unanimously accepted.

In other legislative fields he was no less active. He fought for the adoption of the new commercial code of Vélez Sarsfield

[19] *Obras*, XXVI, 97.

and Acevedo. This was passed and later recognized as the law of the Republic. He proposed the introduction of the metric system of weights and measures, but this was not made into law, having to wait until Sarmiento's own presidency before it became effective. He backed a bill to institute the secret ballot. He fought a bill to pardon a woman who had been sentenced to death for the murder of her husband, and he combatted another proposal that foreigners be given the right to vote after two years of residence, without having first to secure their citizenship. The records of Don Domingo's debates in the senate during these years include such diverse questions as the publication of judicial decisions, military service, the state of siege, the foundation of cities, the colonization of fiscal lands, the ports in the southern part of the nation, asylums, churches, schools, public health, charity, treaties, and emphyteusis.

Don Domingo used the senate at this time as an instrument for his old solution to the problems of the world: reform. He sought to reform everything from the weights and measures to the electoral system and the economic organization of the nation. It was his same struggle to fit the world, little by little, into his ideal pattern. But more important than this, Sarmiento demonstrated through his activities in the Buenos Aires senate that he was a political leader of the future. He showed himself an orator of force and eloquence and a statesman of vision. On July 20, 1857, he faced the famed orator and poet, José Mármol, in a debate over Mármol's proposal for a constitutional amendment. Before a crowd of one thousand spectators, Don Domingo showed his superiority. Mármol had the advantage of parliamentary experience. Sarmiento started his speech with a shaky voice, but it grew in sureness and conviction. When the debate was over the motion was defeated, and the new senator had won his spurs in the field of parliamentary oratory.[20]

At a somewhat later date, Don Domingo took part in another debate that revealed him as a statesman of vision. The

[20] This event is described in a letter from Sarmiento to Sarratea, Buenos Aires, June 22, 1857; Unpublished Archives of Museo Histórico Sarmiento, Carpeta VII, no. 821.

subject was an appropriation of 800,000 pesos for the construction of the San Fernando Railroad. Such an amount seemed excessive to Sarmiento's fellow senators. They opposed the appropriation. Don Domingo arose from his chair to say that such a sum was nothing. Before he died he expected to see eight hundred million pesos spent on railroads. Such was the kind of life that the nation was entering. A roar of laughter by the senators greeted this assertion. They looked upon the sum as that of either a maniac or a utopian.

Sarmiento turned around abruptly upon hearing the laughter. He was crimson with rage as he turned to the stenographer and commanded that he record the hilarity. "I want the coming generations to know that to aid the progress of my country I had to have unbending confidence in its future. I want them to record those laughs in order that the future shall know with what kind of fools I have had to contend."[21]

At the same time as his parliamentary campaigns for reform, Don Domingo made good use of his journalistic weapon to support and further his projects. *El Nacional* was during this period a propaganda instrument of great value. "From the time of his arrival in Buenos Aires, he wrote feverishly in *El Nacional* to propagate his ideas, as he had done formerly in Chile, and to oppose the political situation, this time the confederation, and in service of his party."[22] The files of his newspaper between 1855 and 1861 tell the story of Sarmiento's battle, chapter by chapter.

This was a period in Don Domingo's life of many projects for improvement and reform. Each one of these was backed by a newspaper campaign to prepare the opinion of the public. In August 1855 he proposed in the columns of *El Nacional* the passage of a law to create a model agricultural community around the town of Chivilcoy. Here, hundreds of farmers lacked deeds to give them possession of the land that they worked. Others paid rent in goods to absentee landlords. Sarmiento proposed the awarding of definite titles to the workers of the soil, the division and sale of the lands at a low price, and aid in the organization and improvement of

[21] Belín Sarmiento, *Sarmiento anecdótico, op.cit.*, pp. 118-119.
[22] Rojas, p. 411.

the community. The proposal was accepted, and within eight years Chivilcoy had become one of the richest and most productive districts in the province. The principles of land sale and distribution used here became the bases of Sarmiento's later programs of colonization and agrarian reform.

Similar to this journalistic campaign were those carried on by Don Domingo in the columns of *El Nacional* in regards to the delta of the Paraná River and the valley of the Río Negro. The former district was near Buenos Aires. It was an expanse of unused, fertile lands, mostly islands, covering the area that comprised the delta of the great Paraná River. Sarmiento discovered that these wild, unpopulated lands, overrun by wild cats and dangerous beasts, could be converted into a beautiful center of recreation and cultivation. He himself set the example by occupying the Island of Carapachay and building a summer retreat there, and in later years this district became the resort center for vacationers from Buenos Aires.[23] The Río Negro was, on the other hand, a different problem. Situated on the southern frontier facing the Indian territory of Patagonia, it had recently been settled by a colony of French immigrants. Sarmiento foresaw a future value for this area, and he proposed a government campaign to drive back the Indian and establish strong frontier settlements.[24]

The pages of *El Nacional* during these years carried all phases of the rapidly evolving thought of Domingo Sarmiento. He expressed his approval of the installation of gas lines in the city of Buenos Aires in 1855. He advocated the formation of political parties based on ideologies rather than personalities. He fought for electoral reform and freedom, and he revealed and attacked mercilessly the irregularities in the voting system. Speaking of the elections of 1856, he said: "Thus is falsified the public conscience. Thus are engendered crimes. If you approve these elections, if you declare that fraud and violence have been practiced at all times and will be practiced in the future, the heads of your sons will pay tomorrow for the political crime committed by the immorality of their fathers."[25]

[23] *Obras*, XXVI, 16-45. [24] *Ibid.*, p. 305.

[25] Belín Sarmiento, *Sarmiento anecdótico*, *op.cit.*, p. 120.

From the columns of *El Nacional* Sarmiento continued his attacks against Urquiza and his government in Paraná. Following the course that he had set in Chile, he attacked the president of the confederation and the men that he had around him. Don Nicolás Calvo, in his newspaper, *La reforma pacífica,* took the other side of this political battle. He defended General Urquiza, and he termed the Buenos Aires group—Vélez Sarsfield, Mitre, Sarmiento, and many others—the "gang." He sought a fight with Sarmiento, but Don Domingo would give him no satisfaction. Finally, one day he challenged the editor of *El Nacional* to a duel. He published the challenge in his newspaper and asked Don Domingo to choose his seconds. Sarmiento answered in *El Nacional*: "I accept the duel. Hour: twelve noon. Place: the 25th of May Square. Seconds: the chief of police and the archbishop. Don't be a fool!"[26]

Calvo continued, however, to attack the ideas and the person of Sarmiento. He finally went so far as to accuse him of having poisoned the husband of Doña Benita. This was easily disproved, since Sarmiento was abroad at the time of Castro y Calvo's death. Don Domingo therefore took the rival editor into court on charges of slander and won his case.[27] Calvo finally had to leave the country.

Francisco Bilbao, the Chilean editor of *El Orden,* also carried on a violent personal polemic with Don Domingo. And Juan José Soto, another editor of *La reforma pacífica,* entered into such a bitter journalistic quarrel with Sarmiento that they ended in a fist fight on Rivadavia Street in downtown Buenos Aires. Both were taken to the police station and booked on charges of disturbing the peace. Tradition has it that Mitre happened to pass at that particular time, and, seeing his friend in trouble, intervened with the chief of police, one of his political appointees, to have Don Domingo released.[28]

Domingo Sarmiento had learned the very important lesson that the changes he wanted to bring about in his country

[26] *Ibid.,* p. 134. [27] *Obras,* LII, 157.

[28] This is the version told in the historical moving picture on Sarmiento, *Su mejor alumno,* Buenos Aires, 1945.

could not be brought about overnight, or even in a few years. He learned that he would have to compromise with situations and circumstances. He therefore set out to gain for himself a position in the press and in the politics of Buenos Aires. He was soon disillusioned with what seemed to him the weak government of Alsina and later Mitre, but his power in *El Nacional* and in Buenos Aires' politics depended on these men, so he continued to attack Urquiza and praise Mitre. Meanwhile he began to put into effect his positive program. Step by step he began to institute his reforms.

Augusto Belín Sarmiento summarized the activities of his grandfather during this period as follows: "He wanted to solve for the future the fearful social problem of the distribution of wealth—fence in rural property—plant forests to change the climate and create wealth—widen the streets of Buenos Aires in preparation for the future metropolis—create an educational system with independent income—solve the frontier question—separate the rural and civil police from the political power—the municipal regime—improvement of livestock—exportation of meat and animals on the hoof—agricultural and machine expositions—ports in the south—the development of the Paraná Islands—decimal system—liberty of the press—electoral laws—roads and railroads—the abolition of the passport—nationalization of foreigners. . . . It was necessary to show with acts of civilization that the fight against Rosas was not just to substitute one arbitrariness for another."[29]

Chapter 30. Campaign in Education

AFTER the fall of Juan Manuel de Rosas at the Battle of Caseros in 1852, one of the first acts of the new government

[29] Belín Sarmiento, *Sarmiento anecdótico, op.cit.*, pp. 82-83.

had been to nullify the decrees of the former regime in the field of public education. Valentín Alsina, then minister of government, restored the principle of free education that the tyrant had destroyed, and made education one of the items in the governmental budget. In the three years that followed, much was done towards the restoration of a working system of public education, but the efforts lacked coordination, and their most obvious result was the creation of a situation of conflicting jurisdictions and confusion of policy.

The organization of the educational system of the province of Buenos Aires was begun by the decree of April 5, 1852, which put under the Ministry of Public Instruction "the inspection and direct supervision of all that concerns schools and houses of education."[1] Sarmiento's old friend and fellow exile, Vicente Fidel López, was made minister of public instruction, and he initiated the task of recreating the school system. He tried to reorganize the University of Buenos Aires and found a normal school and a commercial school. But López had neither the force nor the burning missionary zeal that would have been necessary to do a really effective job, and his successes were few.

In the months that followed, subsequent decrees only went to confuse the jurisdiction and powers in the educational realm. A decree of May 16, 1852 reestablished the *Sociedad de Beneficencia* (Charity Society), which had been founded many years earlier by President Bernardino Rivadavia, and which was charged with the direction and supervision of feminine education. The society claimed a position of independence that complicated the problem of authority. On October 26 of that same year, a decree put all schools for boys under the Department of Primary Letters, headed by the Rector of the University of Buenos Aires. After the reestablishment of the municipal government of the city of Buenos Aires in 1854 and the creation by the body of a Comision de Educacion the situation had become hopelessly confused. There were now three entirely different and distinct authorities over the schools of Buenos Aires. Where the jurisdiction

[1] José Salvador Campobassi, *La educación primaria desde 1810 hasta la sanción de la ley 1420*, Buenos Aires, 1942, p. 189.

of one began and the other ended was a question that nobody could definitely answer.

When Domingo Sarmiento arrived in Buenos Aires in 1855, he was convinced that he could offer his greatest services in the field of education. He maintained his old belief that if a government by law and by the people was to be established, the people would have to be educated. Just prior to his departure from Chile for Buenos Aires he had published his *Plan combinado de educación común en el estado de Buenos Aires* (Combined Plan of Public Education in the State of Buenos Aires). This work contained a general program for the educational development of that province. The central theme of the book was to combine public education with agricultural pursuits. The solution of the agrarian problem was seen in the division of farm lands and the education of the farmer. Don Domingo wanted to give the land to those who cultivated it, and in every area of two and one half leagues he proposed the setting aside of enough land to support a school. On this land, aside from the school itself, there would be built a model establishment for the experimental cultivation of plants, a dairy, a library, a chapel, and a vaccination center. The teacher was to augment his pedagogical activities by being an agricultural expert and have some rudimentary knowledge of medicine.

Don Domingo brought with him to Buenos Aires his *Plan combinado*, and this along with his educational record in San Juan and in Chile was sufficient recommendation to give him a position of respect and importance in this field. As *El Nacional* wrote upon his arrival, "We can be sure, without fear of error, that the present intervention of the illustrious publicist in the realm of primary education will cause it to advance a century beyond the generation that is forming under the system followed until the present."[2]

On August 27, 1855, Sarmiento was appointed professor of constitutional law at the University of Buenos Aires. This was an honor that was particularly pleasing to the self-edu-

[2] Antonino Salvadores, "Sarmiento y la reorganización de la instrucción pública" in Universidad de La Plata. *Sarmiento. Homenaje de humanidades y ciencias de la educación,* La Plata, 1939, p. 159.

cated patriot. He always had an inferiority complex because of his lack of formal education, and any time that his learning was recognized in spite of his having obtained no degrees he felt gratified.

In February of 1855, the government of the State of Buenos Aires organized by decree the Council of Public Instruction, which assumed the direction of primary and university teaching. The council could not, however, control either the schools of the municipality of Buenos Aires or those of the Society of Charity. The result, therefore, was the same chaotic position that had existed previously.

The next year the state government seemed to complicate the situation even further by the creation of a general department of schools. On June 7, Don Domingo was appointed to head this organization; and from this vantage point, and with the use of his journalistic and political instruments of power, he did much to organize and reform the educational system of Buenos Aires. He was in continual conflict with the municipal government and with the Society of Charity. In official memorandum after official memorandum he urged the abolition of the complicated system and the creation of a unified authority. This unification was never brought about, but in the years that followed it was his organization that made the only advances and improvements of importance in the field of education.

In the press Sarmiento continued his campaign to convince the public of the value of public education. He continued to persuade the people "that all of its political, economic, and social problems were problems derived from their lack of education."[3] In 1858 he founded the pedagogical periodical, *Anales de la educación común* (Annals of Common Education). "The special object of this publication is to keep the public up to date on the efforts that are being made to introduce, organize, and generalize a vast system of education. Reforms of such radical nature and of such beneficial consequences are not initiated in the schools but in public opinion. It is not the teacher but the legislator who produces them, and the law will be a dead letter if the father of the family does not

[3] Antonino Salvadores, *op.cit.*, p. 160.

lend for its execution the heat of his sympathies."[4] In another issue, Sarmiento insisted that the magazine should be of interest not only to educators, but also to politicians and fathers. In each number, he published information, statistics, excerpts from his messages and memoranda, translated articles, and legislative projects.

Meanwhile in the senate of the State of Buenos Aires Don Domingo carried on an equally active campaign for educational advancement and reform. In 1857 he sponsored three very important legislative acts. The first of these provided that the money from the sale of municipal property should go for the creation of schools. This was passed by the legislature. The second proposal offered a number of means for the acquisition of funds for education. High fines, taxes on inheritances, the income from goods confiscated by the state, a part of the lottery, and the liquid income of the Banco de la Provincia (Provincial Bank) should all be devoted to such an end. He also backed a proposal for a retirement fund for teachers who had completed from twenty to forty years of service. Both of the latter proposals were defeated in the senate and did not become law.

During the remainder of his terms in the senate, however, he remained the legislative champion of the educational cause, and his accomplishments were many. As he said in a speech to that body in 1858, "As for me, I enjoy the satisfaction of having finally found a government that lets me do what I wish, and a people that understands what is demonstrated to it. The superior school that I have founded has produced a revolution. Believe me that in Europe such schools are unknown. . . . I hope to realize the greatest task in America and perhaps present a model for other peoples to follow. In Chile it is impossible to overcome the resistance of public opinion on the one hand and the system of government that concentrates all powers on the other. Within ten years Buenos Aires will have the entire North American system with all of its advantages."[5]

[4] José Salvador Campobassi, *op.cit.*, p. 250.

[5] Quoted by Sarmiento in a letter to Sarratea, Buenos Aires, October 18, 1858; Unpublished Archives of the Museo Histórico Sarmiento, Carpeta VII, No. 827.

From his post as chief of the department of schools, Domingo Sarmiento carried out a series of educational projects that completely transformed the system of schools and the methods of instruction in the nation. Between 1856 and 1861, he founded thirty-six new schools.[6] He caused the latest and best texts on religious doctrine, spelling, grammar, arithmetic, and many other subjects to be translated. He initiated the teaching of foreign languages—French, English, German, and Latin—as well as music and singing in the public schools of the state. He increased the number of women teachers. He wrote the law of August 31, 1858, for the building of new schools. This specified the proportion that each district should contribute to the purpose, and later a decree provided for state funds to those districts which could not raise the necessary amount. During his period of scholastic rule, the public school system of Buenos Aires became one of the best in the Americas.

As the most active and productive of the three existing educational authorities in Buenos Aires, the jurisdiction of the department of schools could not but conflict with that of the municipality and the Society of Charity. From the very beginning, Sarmiento carried on a struggle with the city government. Before either could found a new school, it would have to consult with the other. A jurisdictional dispute was always the result, and the two organizations existed in a continual state of mutual antagonism. In regard to the Society of Charity, Don Domingo looked upon its control over the education of girls as a deterrent to the advancement of public instruction. He did not consider that the normal school of the Society of Charity sufficiently prepared its candidates for teaching positions, and he did not believe that the schools it maintained did an adequate job in the education of the young girls of the community. In the columns of *El Nacional*, Sarmiento carried on a polemic in regard to the Society of Charity that threatened to develop into another example of his bitter personal feuds. He considered the society the seat

[6] Archivo Histórico de la Provincia de Buenos Aires, *Fundación de escuelas públicas en la provincia de Buenos Aires durante el gobierno escolar de Sarmiento*, La Plata, 1939, vii.

of an entrenched feminine aristocracy and a hotbed of snobbery. When Senator Eduardo Costa asserted publicly that he believed that the society should be independent of any government control, Don Domingo answered him heatedly. He considered the law that created the society and held it under the control of the municipal government to have been very well advised. To give the organization independence would be, according to Sarmiento, to create two municipalities, one for women and one for men.

Don Domingo's major clash with the Society of Charity came, however, on the question of the foundation of coeducational schools. The society considered this to be an infringement upon its field of feminine education, and it opposed any such move. A long and energetic debate ensued, but Sarmiento won his point. On April 15, 1859, he wrote to the president of the society: "The undersigned, authorized by the executive power to open an auxiliary school for the Monserrat District, has decided to call it the *Primary School Number 1*, entrusting its direction to Señora Doña Juana Manso de Noronha, and another or other assistants of her same sex. They are to admit boys or girls indiscriminately. . . . The undersigned proposes to create, in so far as necessity indicates, schools of this type in all districts and confide their direction to women teachers; for I am convinced of the advantages and conveniences of entrusting to women the rudimentary teaching that is so similar to maternal education. . . . Although boys will attend School Number One, I hope that such a fact will not exclude the beneficial influence that the institution of the Society of Charity is called upon to exercise in the education of our youth."[7]

On July 18, 1860, Domingo Sarmiento was present at the inauguration of the Model School of Catedral al Sud. This was the first result of his law of school construction. It had been built at a cost of 800,000 pesos, and represented the culmination of Don Domingo's many efforts in the field of education during the previous four years. It had the choice teachers of the public school system. It had the latest equipment and the latest texts. It had an independent budget. It

[7] Archivo Histórico de la Provincia de Buenos Aires, *op.cit.*, pp. 57-58.

had been built in spite of conflicting jurisdictions. Sarmiento was as proud of this accomplishment as he was of any other during his years of political activity in the State of Buenos Aires. Here was a concrete move in his campaign to educate the people.

Chapter 31. The Battle

IN AUGUST of 1858 Domingo Sarmiento resigned his editorship of *El Nacional* in order to devote his time more exclusively to his political and pedagogical pursuits. The next month he was named chief of staff of the reserve army of the province of Buenos Aires. The division between Buenos Aires and the confederation was becoming more acute, and it seemed as if a conflict were drawing near.

It was an event in Sarmiento's native province of San Juan that supplied the spark which set off the political explosion. Don Manuel José Gómez had finally ended the power of Nazario Benavídez and replaced him as governor. He inaugurated a progressive and liberal regime that began to remedy much of the backwardness that had become apparent during the long Benavídez administration. Fearing an attempt on the part of the old caudillo to return to power, Gómez had him jailed in the same prison that had once held Sarmiento. On the night of October 23, 1858, a group of federalists attacked the prison in an attempt to free their former leader. The attempt was frustrated by the resistance of the guards and the calling of the police forces. Once the attack had been repelled, the commander of the prison, Major Rodríguez, cold-bloodedly murdered his prisoner. The effect of this cowardly act was to electrify public opinion. The provinces were especially impressed by such a recurrence of the old violent methods. Sarmiento was among the very few who from the columns of a newspaper justified the occurrence as a just punishment for the former dictator.

The government of the confederation was indignant at the illegal action and felt that it indicated the inability of the provincial government to maintain order. On such a premise, acting under the provisions of the Constitution of 1853, it declared a national intervention in the province.[1] Santiago Derqui and Baldomero García were sent by the Paraná government to "guarantee the republican form of government" in San Juan. With the support of the armed forces under General José Miguel Galán, they met and defeated the San Juan army at Pocito, and installed as military governor of the province the famous authoritarian Colonel José Antonio Virasoro. Virasoro ruled with blood and fire. San Juan, under Gómez, had been the one important province that had supported the policies of Buenos Aires. The new government put it back into the ranks of the firm supporters of Urquiza and the confederation.

Such a turn of events brought a time of decision for the government of Buenos Aires. A friendly province had been attacked and its government had been "intervened." The tension had been mounting for some months. It was not that there were any basic differences that could not be settled, but the longer the split existed the more difficult it seemed for the two parties to get together. At the end of 1859, the government of Buenos Aires and that of the confederation resolved to settle their differences by armed conflict. Both mobilized their armies, and on October 23, exactly a year after Benavídez' death, the Battle of Cepeda took place in the province of Santa Fé. General Urquiza commanded the armies of the confederation, and General Mitre commanded the armies of Buenos Aires. The battle ended with the decisive defeat of Mitre's forces and his rapid retirement towards his capital city.

[1] Article IV of the constitution reads as follows: "The federal government shall have the right to intervene in the territory of the provinces in order to guarantee the republican form of government, or to repel foreign invasion; and, when requested by the constituted authorities to maintain them in power, or to reestablish them if they shall have been deposed by sedition or by invasion from another province."

Buenos Aires, left undefended by the defeat of its armies, was gripped with terror at the thought of an invasion by Urquiza's army. On October 29th, Domingo Sarmiento was appointed second in command of the lines of fortification outside the capital city. But it turned out that the fears and the preparation were not needed. General Urquiza, fearing that he would not be able to keep his own men in check if he invaded Buenos Aires, and aware of the permanently harmful effects of a possible sack, refused to move any further.[2] He saw that the opportunity had finally arrived for a possible conciliation and unification. He would not sacrifice such a chance to any feeling of revenge or anger. He demanded the resignation of Governor Valentín Alsina, who had been one of the leaders of the forces that opposed unification, and then he accepted the intervention and mediation of the dictator of Paraguay, General Francisco Solano López. On November 11, the Pact of San José de Flores was signed between Buenos Aires and the confederation. This provided for the incorporation of the seaboard province in the larger national unit, reserving for Buenos Aires the right to offer any amendments to the constitution that it deemed advisable.

The presidential term of General Urquiza was drawing to a close. The president was in a perfect position to maintain himself in power if he had been the personalist dictator that Sarmiento had believed him to be. But such was not the case. Urquiza called national elections and did not put himself up as a candidate. He did not wish to lose contact with the political scene at such a crucial period, so he did back a candidate whom he thought he could easily influence if not control, Santiago Derqui. Opposed to Derqui was Sarmiento's old friend, Mariano Fragueiro. As is so often the case in young and inexperienced experiments in representative government, the official candidate won the victory, and Derqui was elected the second president of the confederation. Urquiza's personal party remained in power.

Meanwhile, the province of Buenos Aires was also holding important elections. It was choosing representatives to a con-

[2] See a letter from Urquiza to Juan M. Aguirre published in *La Tribuna*, April 17, 1868.

vention that would discuss and suggest the amendments to the Constitution of 1853 that would be prerequisite to the incorporation of the province in the confederation. Domingo Sarmiento was among the many distinguished names elected as deputies.

The task of the Buenos Aires convention was not an easy one. The many delegates had in mind countless proposals for constitutional reform. Each had his pet project. Each had his own idea. The leaders realized, however, that the only way a successful unification could be brought about was through moderation. Buenos Aires would have to be moderate in her requests for reform. The Paraná government would have to be tolerant in receiving such requests.

For Don Domingo the important thing was to unify the nation. He had changed radically from the uncompromising attitude with which he had faced Alberdi and Urquiza not ten years before. He now saw as the basic necessity the unity of the nation under one government. If a few minor sacrifices of principles were necessary, he could see his way clear to accept them. During one of the first sessions of the assembly, Sarmiento proposed that it declare itself immediately in committee and turn to the important question at hand. He wanted to avoid the danger of being bogged down in details. His proposal was, however, defeated by a narrow margin, and a long period of discussion began. A committee consisting of Mitre, Sarmiento, Vélez Sarsfield, Mármol, Obligado, Domínguez, and Barros Pazos was appointed to study the various proposals for amendments. A report was drawn up by this group, and Vélez submitted it to the assembly.

The main line of action taken by the committee was towards the strengthening of the federalist aspects of the Constitution. Sarmiento followed the arguments to which he had adhered in his *Commentaries on the Constitution,* and he attempted to adopt wherever possible the spirit, if not the actual text, of the basic law of the United States. He opposed the choice of Buenos Aires as the capital. He proposed extending personal guarantees and the freedom of the press. He defeated the provision allowing the president to declare a state of siege even when the congress was in session, and he took an active part in the debates on all of the principal amendments offered.

During the entire period of these discussions there was one group of delegates, led by Félix Frías, that remained silent and took no part in the proceedings. Finally, as the sessions grew to a close, Frías proposed the one amendment, for which he had been holding his strength throughout the debates. He suggested an article that would declare the Roman Apostolic Catholic religion the official religion of the Argentine Republic. It would be backed and defended by the government.

The training and education of Domingo Sarmiento returned to him suddenly as he heard this proposal. All of his masters from Benjamin Franklin to Paley spoke to him once more. In a speech no less sincere than that of Frías he defended the principal of freedom of religion. This, he said, was one of the guarantees that the Constitution of 1853 had established. It was one that should be conserved.

"The member of the convention speaks to us of religion, of its virtues and of its morality. He speaks of it as if it were a seed brought from France or some other country to be planted for the first time on American soil. And in America, has it not had three centuries of religion, of its morality and of its virtue? Who kept it from producing such beautiful results here?

"If you believe that religion is the cause of such results, why did it not make of those countries a model which we would like to follow today? Why do those nations not prosper if the basis of liberty and progress is the exclusive predominance of one religion? Was not the Catholic religion then the religion of the state? Herein lay the error of those old governments. . . . What we have wanted to avoid in constitutions is that religions be allowed to have arms in their hands. . . . What we have wanted to guard against was that Catholicism be armed as it was in the beginning in America, with a torch to persecute or kill thought. Liberty of the peoples will not be found through persecution but through tolerance and liberty of conscience.

"Why did not religion, during the eighteen centuries that it was in possession of the earth, educate the world?

"Where there is no freedom of conscience, Mr. President, where religion has been a tyrant as in Spain and here, then the priest says: it is useless for the children to study their own religion, for the children are born and die Catholics. If not, they are burned alive."[3]

The eloquence of this heated exchange between Sarmiento and Frías was one of the oratorical high points of the convention. The proposal of the Catholic leader was put to a vote and was defeated. Once more, Don Domingo had carried the day.

On May 11, 1860, the convention finished its work and adjourned. The honor of the closing speech fell to the deputy, Domingo Sarmiento, and he filled his role admirably. He took this opportunity to express a plea for national unity and to suggest a name for the unified nation.

"We want to give the name United Provinces of the River Plate to our common homeland. This is the name left to us by our forefathers, those who framed the Declaration of Independence in 1816.

"I put the words United Provinces of the River Plate in front of the constitution in order to join with my enemies, forget our old dissensions, and embrace one another like brothers who return to see each other after long years of separation."

Sarmiento wound up his speech by saying, "We started this debate that was so difficult on the most bitter terms and with our hearts filled with ice, but a debate, with reason, with truth, always produces what it has produced here. We have all done ourselves justice."

"Then all arise," he concluded, turning to the benches of the opposition and involuntarily standing up, "and exclaim with us: We want to unite; we want to be once more the United Provinces of the River Plate."

At that moment, Frías, the leader of the Buenos Aires opposition, and Sarmiento, the provincial leader, embraced each other in a symbolic gesture. The convention arose en masse. The president and the secretaries got up from their seats, and all of the delegates, shaking hands with one another warmly,

[3] *Obras*, XIX, 135.

began to shout "Long live the United Provinces of the River Plate! Long live the Convention of Buenos Aires! Long live Sarmiento." The proposal was declared passed amid a general uproar, and the convention dissolved itself.[4]

The successful conclusion of the Buenos Aires convention seemed to give every promise of a peaceful and successful unification of the nation, and the events that had transpired while the convention was in session forecast for Domingo Sarmiento a position of power and distinction in the unified nation. He had been reelected to the Buenos Aires legislature on March 25. His friend, Bartolomé Mitre had been elected to the governorship of the province, and he had promptly appointed Don Domingo his Minister of State.

Sarmiento wrote to Dr. Juan Pujol, the Minister of Interior of the confederation, expressing his faith in the new move towards national unity. "The result of the work of the Buenos Aires convention," he wrote, "quieting the spirits, smoothing over past political passions, inspiring limitless confidence, and awakening a lively nationalist feeling in all of the inhabitants of this state, leads us to hope that if we follow the same path we will achieve fruitful results for the peoples of the confederation, and that the unrest of half a century of our history will come to a glorious and permanent end during the administrations of His Excellency the present president of the confederation and His Excellency the governor of Buenos Aires. . . ."[5]

Meanwhile Buenos Aires and the confederation were drawing closer and closer together. A treaty of free trade was passed. A national constituent convention was called to incorporate the suggestions of Buenos Aires in the constitution. Derqui and Urquiza visited Buenos Aires and were received warmly by both the government and the people. The old enmity seemed to have disappeared. In September, the national convention met, and once again Sarmiento was a delegate and played a distinguished role. He and Vélez were

[4] *Ibid.*, pp. 142-145.

[5] Unpublished letter from Sarmiento to El Señor Ministro del Interior de la Confederación Argentina, Dr. Juan Pujol, Buenos Aires, May 22, 1860, Archivo General de la Nación, División Nacional, Sección Gobierno, Archivo del General Justo José de Urquiza, Legajo 67.

determined to finish the business at hand in the shortest possible time. They refused to take part in any discussion of detail. They fought all moves to bring up minor points. The sessions lasted only a short time. A special committee approved the amendments. The convention accepted unanimously the recommendations of the committee, and on October 1, President Derqui promulgated the new document. Soon after, the province of Buenos Aires swore its allegiance to the constitution, and it seemed as if the long-awaited national unity had been achieved. In November, Mitre returned the call of Derqui and Urquiza by visiting Paraná. Derqui nationalized his cabinet by appointing a citizen of Buenos Aires, De la Riestra, as minister of the treasury; and he went further along these same lines by appointing Domingo Faustino Sarmiento as minister to the United States.

At this time, when all seemed to be going so well, when the policy of conciliation and cooperation seemed on the road to success, it was again the province of San Juan that caused a new break, an explosion that changed the picture overnight.

General Virasoro, the national representative sent by Urquiza after the death of Benavídez, was still in power in the Andean province. He had been denounced repeatedly by Sarmiento and other liberal Sanjuaninos as a despot and as a tyrant. In early November, Don Domingo recognized the inflammatory character of the situation. He pointed out that the province had been governed without ministers since September, that there were no law courts, that it was the personalist rule of a caudillo tyrant.[6] He warned Governor Mitre that in times like these when the entire nation was conscious that it was living in a period of change and reform, the liberal and progressive elements in San Juan would not live quietly under such domination. On November 12 he wrote to Mitre suggesting a joint letter from the governor of Buenos Aires, Urquiza, and Derqui offering Virasoro some other position in return for his governorship of San Juan.[7]

Governor Mitre was at the time of his reception of Sar-

[6] Sarmiento to Mitre, Buenos Aires, November 11, 1860; Museo Mitre, *op.cit.*, p. 103.

[7] Sarmiento to Mitre, Buenos Aires, November 12, 1860; Museo Mitre, *op.cit.*

miento's letter visiting Derqui and Urquiza in Paraná. They accepted Sarmiento's proposal, and on November 16 they jointly composed a dispatch to Virasoro, asking for his resignation and offering him a commission as general in exchange.

On November 16, the very day that this letter was composed, however, the situation exploded in San Juan. Virasoro was assassinated and the government was taken over by a group of Sanjuaninos led by Antonio Aberastain, Sarmiento's former close friend and associate. Upon hearing of this revolt, Don Domingo suggested that Colonel Mitre be dispatched immediately with armed forces to restore order, and that he, Sarmiento, be sent as national commissioner to investigate the situation.[8] Such a solution might have brought the unfortunate incident to a happy conclusion, but the leaders of the national government did not heed Don Domingo's suggestion. Instead of Mitre, they sent Colonel Juan Sáa, a military leader famed for his bloodthirsty and violent methods.

In a letter to General Urquiza in which he accepted his appointment by the government of the confederation as minister to the United States, Sarmiento warned the old caudillo of the danger of such a move. He pointed out that Sáa was taking an army with him to a city that was "awaiting him with open arms." "Why the army?" he asked. "With this the disasters will begin. Mendoza and San Juan live from their crops, and this disturbance means that those crops must be left untended. A million pesos lost in honor of José Virasoro. The army will go to San Juan, and without anybody being able to avoid it perhaps, it will sack the province.

"Then what will happen? Will another satrap be imposed on San Juan by Sáa? Will he judge the accused? Who will judge them under the influence of a conquering army? Who are the accused? Are Videla, Nazar, Sáa the jurisconsults, the constitutionalists who will settle these affairs?"[9]

Sarmiento's predictions of disaster were not unfounded. The army of Sáa was met with resistance. The revolutionaries

[8] Sarmiento to Mitre, Buenos Aires, November 18, 1860; Museo Mitre, *op.cit.*

[9] Sarmiento to Urquiza, no date (sometime between intervention of Sáa and death of Aberastain), no place (probably Buenos Aires), Archivo General de la Nación, División Nacional, Sección Gobierno, Archivo del General Justo José de Urquiza, Legajo 67.

in San Juan refused to receive such an envoy, and they resisted him at Pocito and were defeated. Aberastain was taken prisoner, and Sáa acted in character by ordering him shot the following day. Sarmiento's old childhood friend and compatriot in arms was executed along with other prisoners on the battlefield outside of San Juan.

This new development in the situation changed the crisis from a difficult one to an unsolvable one. The nation was shocked by the brutality of Sáa's action and the lack of foresight in the government's policy. Sarmiento, who had always felt particularly close to Aberastain, was deeply moved by the occurrence, and he dramatically swore vengeance for the act.

On January 31, 1861, Sarmiento resigned his post as minister of government in Buenos Aires. He felt that his emotions in regards to the San Juan incident would prejudice his correct conduct of public affairs. He turned down President Derqui's appointment as minister to the United States and he returned the 14,000 pesos he had received for his trip and expenses to New York. He began a violent press campaign against the national government and in condemnation of its policy in San Juan. He published a short life of Antonio Aberastain, in which he portrayed him as a high idealist, an incorruptible public servant, and a person of strict moral and ethical principles.[10] "This work was tender at times, impassioned at others, but always human."[11] Almost at the same time, he published another pamphlet on José Virasoro. This was a work of entirely different character. It was a violent diatribe, a bitter condemnation of the murdered governor.

The temper of the public and the atmosphere of public affairs grew increasingly tense. Mitre protested the assassination of Aberastain, and Paz, the governor of Córdoba, did the same. Meanwhile, in Paraná, it was Sarmiento who was under attack. He had borne the brunt of public indignation at the death of Virasoro and subsequent events.

Under such circumstances, the expected cooperation of Buenos Aires and the national government did not continue

[10] *Obras*, XLV, 23-78.

[11] Palcos, *Sarmiento, op.cit.*, p. 142.

as peacefully as might have been hoped. The province proceeded to elect its senators and deputies to the national congress. They were dispatched in due course to Paraná to take their seats, but the emotional tension that was being felt throughout the entire nation was reflected in the psychology of the members of the congress. The senators from Buenos Aires were allowed to take their places, but the deputies were not seated. The chamber charged that they had been elected under a provincial rather than a national election law. Their elections were therefore illegal, and they could not be accepted into the national congress. Derqui favored their admission, but the congressional majority under the influence of Urquiza carried the motion. Sarmiento took advantage of this latest turn of events to stir up public opinion to an even greater extent. He charged the legislative body with being servile, and he called upon the provincial government to end its national ties, ties that were no longer binding in the light of recent events.

Both sides began to arm by June 1861. Communications were broken between Buenos Aires and the Derqui government, and the national senate authorized the chief executive "to intervene in the Province of Buenos Aires in order to restore the legal order." The national army was mobilized,[12] and on August 10th General Urquiza was named commander-in-chief of the armed forces of the confederation. On September 17th, General Mitre with some 15,000 more men than Urquiza met the national army at the Battle of Pavón. The results of the conflict were indecisive, but it was Urquiza who retired first from the field and left the victory to the army of Buenos Aires. Whether the general's withdrawal was due to his dissatisfaction with the course of the government and the independence of President Derqui, or whether he saw in such a move the only hope of restoring peace and harmony, Urquiza lost the most decisive battle of his career without ever allowing it to reach its point of crisis.

With the defeat of its armed forces at Pavón, the Derqui

[12] *Documentos relativos a la organización constitucional de la republica Argentina*, Buenos Aires, 1911, pp. 251-253.

government was forced to resign. The center of national power was suddenly shifted from Paraná to Buenos Aires, and Bartolomé Mitre found himself president of the nation. He assumed the executive power of a provisional government and called for the election of a new congress.

The Provinces of Mendoza, San Juan, and San Luis did not join the general movement to shift allegiance from the Paraná government to the Mitre regime in Buenos Aires. Colonel Sáa remained in control in San Luis, and equally ardent Urquistas held the executive powers of the other two western provinces. It was therefore decided to dispatch a military expedition immediately to the interior to subjugate these rebellious sectors. General Paunero was appointed to head such a force, and Lieutenant Colonel Domingo Faustino Sarmiento was assigned the post of judge advocate of the army. "I must go to the provinces," he had written to Mitre, and the latter had responded with his appointment to that position.

The march through the interior was more of an excursion than an expedition. Little resistance was met. All three governors fled before the arrival of the troops, and there were usually few Urquistas of importance left by the time the army reached a town. Under the title of *Itinerary,* Don Domingo recorded the incidents of this trip. "The army marches for two hours and then camps on a mountain ridge under the impression of the most intense cold, without tents and without fire."[13] They departed from Buenos Aires in November. On the 20th of December, they reached Villanueva in the province of Córdoba. From here Colonel Rivas was sent by General Paunero to continue on to Cuyo and organize friendly governments in the western provinces. Sarmiento accompanied him. They reached San Luis, but Sáa had fled. They arrived in Mendoza on New Year's Day and found it in complete ruins as the result of a devastating earthquake. "I arrive on the first day of the year to these ruins, where I find the remains of a town, surviving a catastrophe only to be held prisoner still by the barbarity of its governors."[14] Again the

[13] The account of this trip is to be found in *Obras,* XLV, 122-176.

[14] Sarmiento to Sarratea, Mendoza (in ruins), January 1, 1862; Unpublished Archivos of Museo Histórico Sarmiento, Carpeta VII, No. 828.

governor had fled, and a new government had to be organized by the occupying forces. As soon as this task was completed, Don Domingo set out with a small detachment of soldiers under Colonel Rivas for his home town, and on January 9, 1862, he arrived in San Juan, a conquering hero.

BOOK VI

The Consummation

Chapter 32. The People's Choice

SARMIENTO's entry into San Juan was not as happy a one as it might have been. He passed through Pocito, the place where his close friend, Aberastain, had been murdered. He entered the town and went directly to his family home, but his homecoming was not joyful. On November 21st his beloved mother, Doña Paula, had died at the age of ninety-one. She had been living for the day of her son's return, and Don Domingo felt especially saddened that she had not survived to witness his moment of triumph. When he reached his house, the crowd of friends and relatives knew his sorrow and were respectfully silent as he entered the front door, wandered through the patio, ran his hand over his mother's old spinning wheel, and finally visited the old lady's room.

During his first day in his home town, crowds gathered to watch the mythical Don Domingo pass. There were cheers. Young men of the new generation pointed him out to one another. "Sarmiento was the man of the day, the tutelary genius of his province, sent providentially to lead it along the road to happiness. All sought a smile from that extraordinary man, even a glance to honor and fill with legitimate pride him who received it."[1] San Juan was little more than the dusty little village that Sarmiento had known in his childhood. But the now famous Don Domingo had changed. He had traveled throughout the world. He had pitted his strength against the great dictator Rosas. He had opposed the government of Urquiza and the intellect of Alberdi. He was a national figure, and now he had returned to San Juan. The town expressed its admiration and its pride.

The president of the provincial legislature and one of the supporters of Antonio Aberastain was Don Ruperto Godoy Cruz. On the very day of Sarmiento's arrival in San Juan,

[1] Nicanor Larrain, *El país de Cuyo*, Buenos Aires, 1906, p. 282.

Godoy appeared at his home to turn over the governorship of the province. He informed Don Domingo of the fact that he had just been named by the chamber of representatives as the interim governor and that he was expected to take over command immediately. "Don Domingo, you are going to be our governor. We have sacrificed ourselves many years for your ideas. The least sacrifice that you can make is to govern us."[2] Sarmiento called general elections, and on February 16, 1862 he was chosen legal and constitutional governor of the province of San Juan. "After the twenty years of absence of a young man, San Juan received in the midst of manifestations of jubilation an old man whose spirit, whether in the press, in the tribunal or in war, had never left the narrow, dark, and poor inclosure of his own province."[3]

For the first time in his life, Domingo Sarmiento had the power to put his ideas and his projects into practice. He was the actual governor of a small portion of his nation. He had a field of power of his own, and he could use that power to institute the changes that he had planned. "For twenty years I have fulfilled a role that was contrary to nature, writing, speaking, but unable to act—existing in the midst of resistances. At last I have the power to act, on a small scale it is true, but act; and in three years of government I will show them the fists that God has given me. You will see if I do not do what I say."[4]

Don Domingo's greatest mistake during his years of governorship of San Juan was that he did not allow for the limited scope of the territory and people with which he was dealing. He had formed a grandiose plan for the reform of the world and the improvement of the lot of mankind. He thought that this plan would be applicable anywhere. He thought that it could be applied to San Juan. But the little Andean province was poor, backward, and ignorant. It was not ready for many of the changes that he brought about. It was not capable of supporting others. Sarmiento's years of governorship were

[2] *Ibid.*

[3] Belín Sarmiento, *Sarmiento anecdótico, op.cit.*, p. 170.

[4] Sarmiento to Posse, San Juan, March 24, 1862; Unpublished Archives of Museo Histórico Sarmiento, *Epistolario Sarmiento-Posse.*

years of great energy. "I am sounding out the terrain, weighing the facts. San Juan needs everything, all at once; it is necessary to repair the wounds of so many sacks and disasters and open the road to improvements. I will begin now to govern, and devote myself to all that is purely internal, municipal."[5] He worked hard and did much. They were years of experiment. But they ended in disappointment, for the plan did not fit the place to which it was applied.

Don Domingo began immediately to work on his favorite and what he considered his most vital project. He began the task of educating the people of San Juan. He ordered a printing press brought from Chile and once again he founded his old newspaper, *El Zonda*. He then turned his attention to the public school system, and attempted to reform the educational process in San Juan as he had done in Buenos Aires. He gave to "public instruction an impulse until then unknown. With him there began an era of true flowering for public education in San Juan."[6] On April 2nd, the legislature passed a law authorizing the executive to codify and reform the laws of the province on public education. Don Domingo augmented the usual sources of income for the support of the primary education system with the revenues from fines and confiscations made by the courts. He decreed that all departments of the province would be obligated to pay for and maintain one or more primary schools in their district; and on November 12, 1863 a decree was published making primary education obligatory, thus giving "nerve and life" to a law of 1856 that had never been put into effect. "All fathers of families are obligated to send their children to school." If the parent did not comply, the justice of peace was ordered to notify the police.

On July 10th, work was begun on the educational project in San Juan that was closest to Don Domingo's own heart. When the news of the Pact of June 6 had arrived in the provincial capital, it had been received with great joy and celebration. It seemed to bring peace and harmony to the

[5] Sarmiento to Posse, San Juan, January 22, 1862; *Epistolario Sarmiento-Posse, ibid.*

[6] Nicanor Larrain, *op.cit.*, p. 355.

country. The Chilean consul in San Juan, Antero Barriga, had taken this occasion to raise a popular subscription that would be directed towards the erection of a school that would carry Sarmiento's name. When Don Domingo came to power in the provincial government, he gathered the funds that had been raised, and, augmenting them with government appropriations, ordered work to be begun on the projects. "I am erecting a great school," he wrote, "capable of teaching eight hundred children."[7] The school would be housed in what had at one time been the San Clemente Church and later a military barrack. This building would be renovated and converted into a lasting monument and a model school, incorporating all of the latest methods, equipment, and theory. The construction of this school went on during the entire length of Sarmiento's governorship, but the school was not inaugurated until after his departure from San Juan.

Sarmiento's primary preoccupation was always the preparation of the human being for the new age of civilization that he was ushering in. Education and information came first. But in addition to reforms, Don Domingo devoted much effort during his governorship of San Juan to the molding of that province into a model district. He left the personnel of the government exactly the same as the martyred Aberastain had formed it. "I found things thus, and I accepted them with all my heart, excluding nobody and changing no ministers."[8] But he did set out to reform radically the actual administrative machinery of the government. He created new offices such as those of the justice of the peace, the defender of minors, and the district attorney. He combined and consolidated government departments, and he created new ones. The topographical department under the German engineer, Gustav Grothe, was instituted. It drew up the first map of the province and the first important plan of the city and its contiguous agricultural lands. The national guard was reorganized, and

[7] Letter from Sarmiento to Manuel Passos, San Juan, July 19, 1862; Unpublished Private Archives of Señor Carlos Sánchez Viamonte in Buenos Aires. I would like to take this opportunity to thank Señor Sánchez Viamonte for his kindness in giving me access to his private archives.

[8] *Sarmiento-Mitre correspondencia*, p. 271.

both the infantry and the cavalry were trained in the latest military methods.

Sarmiento created an office of statistics, founded agricultural communities, organized rural and urban police, built schools, paved streets, increased municipal services, laid sidewalks, put name signs on the city streets, constructed hundreds of bridges, built houses for the legislature and the courts, organized regular mails to Mendoza and San Luis, founded public baths, instituted a house of correction for women, raised funds for hospitals, inaugurated a preparatory school for the university, planted model gardens, erected benches in the public parks, widened and lighted the streets, passed a printing law, founded a completely civil cemetery, opened rural roads, instituted a patent office, and inaugurated a system of agricultural inspection.[9] In a period of a little over two years Sarmiento attempted to make over the entire province.

It soon became evident that the poverty-stricken province would not be able to support financially all of the projects that its new governor was putting into operation. "It was necessary to invest large sums of money, and the people, who had to meet the high budget, began to realize the enormous and heavy burden that was being imposed upon them by the taxes."[10] By 1863 the financial situation was serious. The paper money issued by the national treasury in Buenos Aires lacked the confidence of the people, and the beginnings of an inflation were under way. The budget of San Juan for that year exceeded 132,000 pesos; and the resources, including the debt of the national government, were not enough to support the public administration.

Don Domingo realized the heavy burden that his reforms were imposing, but he calculated that his improvements would eventually pay for themselves. He had two projects in particular that he believed would in the long run go far toward the economic betterment of the province and the financial support of his "program of civilization." The first of these was his plan for the improvement and extension of

[9] Belín Sarmiento, *Sarmiento anecdótico, op.cit.*, p. 176.
[10] Nicanor Larrain, *op.cit.*, p. 284.

agricultural lands. In late 1862 he founded a Quinta Normal de Agricultura (Normal Farm for Agricultural Experimentation) with the end in view of improving and perfecting agricultural techniques and methods.[11] He went on to institute an extensive program of irrigation and flood control to better and extend the cultivable farm lands. In his message to the provincial legislature in June of 1862 he offered a number of projects in this general field. "Irrigation," he pointed out, "is for San Juan what blood is for the body. On it depends the subsistence of all, and the disorders in its equal distribution produce ills like those created in politics by anarchy and in health by excesses."[12] He proposed a system of irrigation canals and dams to control the rivers and streams in the seasons of melting snow. With the use of irrigation, he opened up lands that had never before been used productively, and he sponsored laws to found agricultural colonies populated by foreign immigrants. According to a law of December 1, 1862, the executive was authorized to make contracts with immigration companies, bring immigrants to new colonies, and construct canals to irrigate the areas.[13]

As a more immediate source of income and provincial wealth, Don Domingo turned to the development of what he considered a very promising mining industry in the mountains surrounding his capital city. "My platform is the mines. If they produce the results that they promise, all that I do will become a reality. If not, it will be best to de-populate this province. It has neither means of living nor an object in life."[14] "I hope," he wrote to President Mitre, "to create with the mines an industrious and sane political situation. . . . Help me in this and you will have satisfied my ambition to have power in order to create, transform, realize."[15] To fulfill this plan of mineral exploitation, Sarmiento called upon the aid

[11] *El Zonda*, in 1865, after Sarmiento's departure from San Juan, hailed the results of the Quinta Normal and praised Don Domingo's perseverance in founding and maintaining it. (*El Zonda*, v, No. 404, April 19, 1865, p. 2.)

[12] Agusto Landa, *Irrigación y vialidad en la provincia de San Juan durante el gobierno de Domingo F. Sarmiento*, San Juan, 1938, 11.

[13] *Ibid.*, p. 17.

[14] Sarmiento to Posse, San Juan, October 13, 1862; Unpublished Archives of Museo Histórico Sarmiento; Carpeta Sarmiento-Posse.

[15] *Sarmiento-Mitre correspondencia*, p. 154.

of an English engineer by the name of Rickard. Rickard explored the region and made a very favorable report on its possibilities. He published an announcement of his findings in the *English Mining Journal,* and Sarmiento hoped that the promising prospects would draw many engineers from abroad.[16]

Sarmiento's administration did all that was possible to foster the new mining industry. A deputation of mines was created. Rules were put into effect governing mineral deposits, prospectors' claims, and mineral rights. The office of inspector general of mines was instituted, and sites were expropriated for the benefit of the mines.[17] Sarmiento and Rickard organized a mining corporation, and the Englishman was sent to Buenos Aires to secure equipment and to float a stock issue to support the venture financially.[18] At first the stock was difficult to sell. Attempts were made in San Juan, Buenos Aires, and Chile and met with only lukewarm success, but within the year the necessary funds began to accumulate.[19] "The mining society has found all of its capital in Buenos Aires. With this I think that in the coming year we will be producing metals."[20] Sarmiento's enthusiasm about the project increased as time went on. He invested his own money in the project, and he held shares in the three richest mines.[21] By the first month of 1863 he was so optimistic about the produce of the mines that he predicted they would be making large amounts of money within the next half year.[22]

If Don Domingo had had a decade of government in San Juan, and if he had not been impeded by circumstances and opposed by hostile forces, his reforms might have taken effect, and the entire province might have been transformed according to his blueprints. But such was not the case. During 1863

[16] Sarmiento to Mitre, San Juan, June 3, 1862; Museo Mitre, *op.cit.*, p. 139.
[17] Nicanor Larrain, *op.cit.*, p. 282.
[18] Sarmiento to Sarratea, San Juan, October 3, 1862; Unpublished Archives of Museo Histórico Sarmiento, Carpeta VII, No. 836.
[19] Sarmiento to Sarratea, San Juan, September 26, 1862; Carpeta VII, No. 835.
[20] Sarmiento to Posse, San Juan, December 5, 1862; Carpeta Sarmiento-Posse.
[21] Sarmiento to Sarratea, San Juan, January 26, 1864; Carpeta VII, No. 854.
[22] Sarmiento to Posse, San Juan, February 14, 1863; Carpeta Sarmiento-Posse.

events seemed to turn against him, and his plans seemed to go sour. The financial burden was heavy, and such long-range remedies as the development of the farming and mining industries could show no positive and noticeable results for several decades. He was having personal difficulties: strained relations with his family, scandals. And as a final blow, his government was faced with bloody rebellion. The treasury was drained by military expenses. Public opinion was divided over crucial issues. And the land that he had tried to improve and reform was overrun by contending armies.

At the end of the first year opposition was already beginning to show itself. "This great movement of institutions and transcendent reforms carried the province with such rapid progress in a year of honorable and laborious administration, to an unexpected and surprising height. . . . Nevertheless there began to be noted general discontent and the effect of attack and bitter criticism began to be felt."[23] Landowners were beginning to complain of the financial burden that the reforms imposed upon them. As so often happens when a man ahead of his time attempts to impose sudden change, the common people did not understand either Sarmiento's methods or his ends. Don Domingo had not learned the lesson he should have learned from the Salvador del Carril government in San Juan during his youth. Del Carril also tried to bring change too quickly, and he was not careful to avoid conflicts with the traditions and beliefs close to the hearts of the common people. Del Carril fell to the prejudice and superstition of the crowd and the force of Facundo. Sarmiento made the same mistake. He chose for the place of his Escuela Sarmiento the Convent of San Clemente. Although this had not been a religious establishment for many years—in fact it had been a military headquarters—the religious element of the population was stirred. A later law that gave the income from confiscated ecclesiastical funds to public works, education, and the normal experimental farm put Sarmiento, in the eyes of many, in the category of the atheistic liberal reformer.

The political opposition to the government was able to exploit this impression. It was pointed out that Don Domingo

[23] Nicanor Larrain, *op.cit.*, p. 284.

was a mason. Rumor had it that he met with his lodge brothers in an unfinished building and that they held conferences with a black mule. One priest made the charge from his pulpit that the governor was a mason and that all masons were disciples of the devil. He concluded that they must have tails like the devil.

One day Don Domingo met the priest on the street. Holding out his hand as if to greet him amiably, he seized the arm of the religious man and put his hand on that part of his body where a tail should be.

"Come, come, father," said the governor, "touch it and assure yourself well so that afterwards you will be able to preach a new gospel."

In such a way, Sarmiento passed the situation off as a joke, but the hidden opposition remained. And it was no joke. All this happened because he had "made a church into a school, an old chapel into an experimental farm, and had taken a few yards of land from a convent to widen a street."[24] "Here apathy, niggardliness, and true poverty unite as a party of resistance."[25]

Simultaneously with the appearance of opposition among elements of the population of San Juan, Don Domingo's own position was being undermined by the demoralizing effects of a domestic quarrel. When he came to his provincial home he arrived with a military expedition. He was of course without any members of his family. During his first year, however, he still did not bring his wife to San Juan. There were obviously strained relations between them. Dominguito came several times to visit him from his school in Buenos Aires, and Sarmiento always showed the boy off with great pride to the citizens of his native town. "Dominguito is with me in body and spirit. With the beautiful naturalness that you know in him, man and boy at the same time, he amuses himself with the affairs of San Juan and takes part in them with enthusiasm. At the same time, he studies mathematics, linear drawing and metallurgy."[26]

[24] Belín Sarmiento, *Sarmiento anecdótico, op.cit.*, p. 178.

[25] Sarmiento to Posse, San Juan, October 13, 1862; Sarmiento-Posse Carpeta.

[26] Sarmiento to Mitre, San Juan, July 31, 1862; Museo Mitre, *op.cit.*, p. 152.

But Sarmiento's relations with Doña Benita in the meanwhile were becoming strained to the breaking point. The reasons for the estrangement of the married couple are not clear. Some have attributed it to an affair that Sarmiento had while in Buenos Aires with Aurelia Vélez which aroused the jealousy of his wife.[27] Other evidence points to an affair on the part of Doña Benita. It may have been either, or it may have been both. The contents of two hitherto unpublished letters point, however, to the fact that Sarmiento at least considered the break to have been caused by an action on the part of his wife. It is true that Don Domingo's past history would not exclude the possibility of an affair on his part, but his wife's unfaithfulness, or alleged unfaithfulness, and his public charges seemed to have been the cause of the estrangement during his governorship.

Late in 1862, he wrote to his very close friend Mariano Sarratea. "As for the confirmation of your fears, what do you want me to say? Such things resist the pen. I was dishonored and I published my dishonor in order to make it return to its origin. The break is then without hopes of mending. I am alone in the world; old age approaches, and I have been received by my domestic and paternal home, where neither treachery nor deception dwells. I have sacrificed all, and I propose never to back down. It is finished business. I would like to take her away from Buenos Aires, a thing that I am afraid I shall not accomplish. I shall not return to that city while she is there."[28]

In that same year, President Mitre wrote to Sarmiento and touched upon this subject.[29] He indicated that the scandal was common knowledge in Buenos Aires, and a few references that he made might indicate that his Minister Rawson was the third party.[30] In speaking of Doña Benita, the president

[27] Rojas, p. 427.

[28] Sarmiento to Sarratea, San Juan, November 28, 1862; Carpeta VII, No. 840.

[29] Unfortunately, most of the letters dealing with this topic have been destroyed by members of the family. The story has to be pieced together from a very few pertinent ones that I found in unpublished archives.

[30] This is only a vague inference, but if it were true, it would explain a heated personal element in the Sarmiento-Rawson polemic that occurred the following year.

wrote, "As for her, and without going into an evaluation of what has happened (since there is no remedy for that), I will tell you that she is a very unfortunate woman, and if as you tell me (because I have not found out for myself), you have proof of her guilt, you are avenged and well avenged, for in any event, she will be more unhappy than you. . . ." The letter further implied that Sarmiento had been willing to give up his family and his career to bring the affair in the open, but that Doña Benita and the third party (Rawson?) had backed down. Mitre advised Don Domingo to remain in San Juan, but he reassured him that "the publicity of the affair has not been as widespread as you suppose."[31]

Doña Benita herself continued to protest her innocence, and what she wrote to her husband seems to indicate that she was still deeply in love with him. "I love you with all the timidity of a young girl and with all the passion of which a woman is capable. I love you as I have never loved before, as I did not think it possible to love. I have accepted your love because I am sure that I am worthy of it. I only have one fault in my life and that is my love for you. Will you be the one to punish that? I have told you the truth about everything. Will you pardon my silly timidity? Pardon me, my charm, I cannot live without your love. Write me, tell me that you love me, that you are not angry with your lover who loves you so. You will write me, won't you?"[32]

What Dominguito's attitude towards the affair was is uncertain, but he was aware of his mother's unhappiness, and he tried to persuade his father to relent. In some of his letters to Don Domingo he used extremely harsh language to condemn the governor's attitude towards his mother.[33] And during one of his visits to San Juan in July 1862, there occurred a scene between father and son. Dominguito pointed with regret to past years of conjugal happiness in Yungay, and in Buenos Aires. The moment took on dramatic aspects. Don Domingo,

[31] Mitre to Sarmiento, Buenos Aires, July 18, 1862; Unpublished Archives of Museo Histórico Sarmiento, Carpeta Mitre-Sarmiento.

[32] Quoted by Rojas, p. 428.

[33] There is a collection of these letters in the Museo Histórico Sarmiento. The character of their content is such as to cause them to be treated as confidential. Permission was therefore withheld for quoting them.

more upset about it than he had allowed himself to admit, began to cry. Dominguito in a scene of tenderness went over and put his hand on the governor's shoulder. "Don't cry," he said, "An old man like you. . . !"[34]

With such a problem facing him in his personal life, Don Domingo devoted his principal efforts to the accomplishment of the ends that he sought in his public life. The many difficulties obstructing his path, however, combined with the continual psychological depression that he was experiencing at this time to make his task as governor of San Juan a particularly difficult one. Finally, in 1863, an event occurred that negated all the progressive steps that he had taken and seemed to make useless the continuance of his program: a full-scale civil war broke out and engulfed San Juan as its center.

Don Domingo's reforms and improvements during his first year as governor were based upon the premise of peace, and were made possible by a state of peace. "There had been terror, a lack of confidence, and insecurity"; he wrote, "in a fortnight I changed this spirit, making them feel a sense of their own strength and giving them a self-confidence. Today the country is peaceful."[35] By late in that same year, however, Sarmiento was beginning to sense trouble. One of the last of the old caudillo leaders of the type of Juan Facundo Quiroga was still living in feudal power on the plains in the Province of La Rioja. Ángel Vicente Peñaloza, known commonly as El Chacho, had inherited the tradition of the gaucho: his independence, his reliance on force, his lack of respect for the law. El Chacho was neither a unitarist nor a federalist. At times he had fought on different sides. He was merely a personalist caudillo who fought more as a profession than for a purpose.[36] Towards the middle of 1862, Governor Sarmiento began to see signs of danger from the neighboring province. In July he wrote to Posse that he was wary of El Chacho and his *montonera* operating in Catamarca province. In that same

[34] *Obras*, XLV, 316.

[35] Sarmiento to Sarratea, San Juan, May 28, 1862; Carpeta VII, No. 832.

[36] For an excellent and sympathetic account of the life of El Chacho see the article by the famous poet, José Hernández "Rasgos biograficos del general Ángel V. Peñaloza," in *El Argentino*, Paraná, 1863; for the other side of the picture, see D. F. Sarmiento, *Vida del Chacho*.

month he wrote to President Mitre: "The news that parties of Peñaloza's men have been rustling cattle of Fertile Valley has alarmed us. We have also heard that he has called together his followers at his *estancia*."[37] Don Domingo was well aware of what would be the effect of a civil war upon his plans in San Juan. He tried every means of averting one. At the end of July, he wrote again to Mitre, "There is something more serious on the frontier. El Chacho is El Chacho. . . . I have sent Captain Fonsalida to Fertile Valley with orders to speak to Peñaloza when he is not drunk. Fonsalida is moderate, his relative and his friend; and he might well bring him around to reason."[38]

Such efforts as this averted any serious outbreak in 1862. There were a few border incidents. The town of Chilecito (Villa de Famatina) in La Rioja was sacked several times by the bandit hordes of El Chacho and finally appealed for police protection to the neighboring governor of San Juan.[39] Towards the end of the year, some of the bands entered San Juan territory, but the Sixth Battalion of the line was dispatched and quickly dispersed them.[40] Meanwhile, however, Peñaloza remained at his ranch in Guaja, La Rioja, and gathered men and arms. Then, in March 1863, he declared himself in rebellion, and in a manner reminiscent of Facundo his hordes began to overrun and terrorize the western provinces of the Republic.

On March 24th, Sarmiento wrote to President Mitre: "I think that the time has come to fix La Rioja, to ask satisfaction for all that has been tried, to punish Peñaloza. How? As you do anything; by doing it. War? Yes, war. If not, these peoples will succumb politically and commercially."[41] The question immediately arose as to who would lead a punitive expedition against the bandit caudillo leader. Sarmiento was the man who had been in closest contact with the situation. He was the man who had made himself famous for his opposi-

[37] Sarmiento to Mitre, San Juan, July 19, 1862; Museo Mitre, *op.cit.*, p. 146.

[38] Sarmiento to Mitre, San Juan, July 31, 1862; Museo Mitre, *op.cit.*, p. 151.

[39] Petition from Citizens of Villa de Famatina (Chilecito) to Domingo F. Sarmiento, October 23, 1862.

[40] Sarmiento to Posse, San Juan, December 5, 1862; Carpeta Sarmiento-Posse.

[41] Sarmiento to Mitre, San Juan, March 24, 1863; Museo Mitre, *op.cit.*, p. 177.

tion to lawlessness and caudillism. He was near at hand. On March 28th, the minister of war communicated the decision of the president, naming Sarmiento director of war against Peñaloza and putting at his disposal the national armed forces in San Juan and Mendoza. The next day, Mitre wrote a personal letter to Don Domingo. "My idea," he said, "can be summed up in two words: *I want the war in La Rioja to be a war of police action.* La Rioja is a cave of bandits which menaces its neighbors and where today there is not even a government to command the police of the province. Calling the *montoneros* robbers is not to do them the honor of considering them as a political party, nor elevating their depredations to the level of reaction."[42]

The next week an article by Governor Sarmiento appeared in *El Zonda*: "Fellow Citizens: Peñaloza has removed his disguise. . . . From his *estancia* at Guaja . . . he proposes to reconstruct the Republic that he had devised with the Plains as a model. . . . Under his direction and impulse these provinces will soon be as vast a desert where pillage, unbridled barbarity, and bandit hordes backed by the government will reign."[43]

With such a warning Sarmiento called the western provinces to arms to defend themselves. He contacted the national armies that had been put at his disposal, and he personally directed a campaign to defeat El Chacho. General Arredondo was chosen as the military leader of the campaign, and his minute reports to Governor Sarmiento demonstrated the close contact that Don Domingo maintained with the operation.[44] Such a war is a difficult one for a regular army. The *montonera* bands were small and dispersed. It was hard to bring them to battle. The government forces could only hold back and wait for them to organize and strike.

On September 6th, General Arrendondo warned Governor

[42] Mitre to Sarmiento, Buenos Aires, March 29, 1863; Unpublished Archives of the Museo Histórico Sarmiento; Carpeta Mitre-Sarmiento.

[43] *Obras*, VII, p. 337.

[44] Letters of April 28, 29, 30, and May 2, report such details as scouting operations, areas scouted, arrival of 120 horsemen, and the punishment of a deserter. Letters from José Arrendondo to Sarmiento in Unpublished Archives of Museo Histórico Sarmiento, Carpeta XV.

Sarmiento that a crisis was approaching. "Peñaloza, Pueblas, Carrizo and others, have a force of more than a thousand men."[45] This is what they had been waiting for. In October the rebel began to move. The Department of Caucete was overrun. On November 1st, word arrived that the bandit armies were only four leagues from the city of San Juan. Panic broke out in the city. Sarmiento remembered the assassination of the former governors: Benavídez, Virasoro, Aberastain. He ordered two cannon shots to be fired as a warning, and then he sent out rapid orders to his armies which were dispersed in all directions in search of El Chacho. The militia of San Juan and Mendoza went out to meet the enemy, and the governor sent orders to Major Pablo Irrazábal, who with the first cavalry and sixth infantry was in search of Peñaloza, to countermarch quickly to the place of the invasion.

This was the move that saved the day. With forced marches, Irrazábal arrived at Caucete and surprised El Chacho's men. Hemmed in on a street of the town, the bandit soldiers found themselves caught in a hand-to-hand fight with trained regular soldiers. Without their horses, the gauchos were soon dispersed. Many prisoners were taken, and many were killed. Peñaloza, however, escaped. Governor Sarmiento, fearing a recurrence of the war if El Chacho were allowed to make a getaway, sent Irrazábal with a fast mounted division in his pursuit. It was found that El Chacho was in the small town of Olta, and on November 12th the vanguard of the pursuing force under Major Ricardo Vera entered the village at a gallop, surrounded Peñaloza's house, and the famous El Chacho was forced to surrender. The bandit leader was held *imcommunicado* until the arrival of Irrazábal, who ordered his immediate execution. El Chacho's head was cut off and placed on the head of a lance as a warning to his followers. The entire nation was profoundly shocked at this new demonstration of official barbarism.

For years after this event, enemies of Sarmiento have accused him of the murder of Peñaloza. Such an accusation is unfounded. Don Domingo himself specifically stated that he

[45] Arrendondo to Sarmiento, La Rioja, September 6, 1863; Carpeta xv, No. 1893.

had issued no orders for El Chacho's execution, and this statement went undisputed.[46] To understand the true motives involved, however, it is necessary to examine the general atmosphere that prompted Irrazábal's actions.

Governor Sarmiento had refused to take President Mitre's advice and regard the Chacho uprising as an incident of banditry. Don Domingo insisted upon tying it up with the underlying social conflict between civilization and barbarism. He saw connections between Peñaloza's activities and a general movement of reaction inspired by General Urquiza.[47] With such serious implications read into the rebellion, Governor Sarmiento took radical measures. Three times he decreed a state of siege to exist, twice in San Juan and once in La Rioja; and under the special powers granted to the executive in such a state of emergency, he issued decrees of a very extreme nature. Two hundred lashes or six months at hard labor were decreed for those caught illegally in possession of weapons. Similarly brutal punishments were prescribed for other acts that might connect the culprit to the revolt.[48] Don Domingo had great dreams for San Juan and what he could do for the province during his governorship. The actions of El Chacho seemed to threaten them all. Barbarism was again rearing its head against the forces of civilization. Sarmiento had learned from General Bougueaud in North Africa that it was necessary "to fight barbarism with barbarism," and he spared no measures in doing so. It is extremely doubtful, however, if he would have ever assumed the responsibility before the judgment of history of ordering the execution of Peñaloza. His extreme measures and his enthusiastic conduct of the war undoubtedly created an atmosphere that would react upon an unthinking subordinate such as Irrazábal to cause him to behead the rebel, but Irrazábal's action implicated Don Domingo only indirectly for the bloody deed charged to him by posterity.

The extreme legal measures taken by Governor Sarmiento in meeting the threat of the El Chacho rebellion did, how-

[46] Dardo de la Vega Díaz, *Mitre y el Chacho*, p. 351.

[47] Sarmiento to Sarratea, San Juan, March 22, 1863; Carpeta VII, No. 843.

[48] Nicanor Larrain, *op.cit.*, pp. 286-287.

ever, have certain other far-reaching effects. In a circular of March 13, 1863, Guillermo Rawson, the minister of interior in Mitre's government, pointed to the fact that it was constitutionally irregular for a provincial governor to declare a state of siege. Sarmiento's actions in San Juan and La Rioja were therefore censured. On June 13th, Don Domingo replied to this note by asserting that he had made his declaration of a state of siege with full consciousness of his rights in the matter. Arguing along the lines that the nineteenth-century states' rights theorists were following in many republics, Sarmiento built a legal case for his actions. A long and bitter polemic between the minister of interior and the governor of San Juan ensued, and the relations between the national and provincial governments were sorely strained. Sarmiento, once in power in his province, had forgotten his earlier arguments in his *Comentarios.* He had forgotten his earlier warnings against the dangers of caudillism in an overly centralized republic.

Although most constitutionalists today agree that Sarmiento's stand was not tenable,[49] that the power to declare a state of siege is outside the scope of a provincial governor, evidence points to the fact that contemporary opinion was closer to Don Domingo. The famed and respected jurist, Vélez Sarsfield, wrote to Sarmiento in regard to the debate: "Your opinion and the foundations upon which rest the provincial right to declare a state of siege have been applauded here, and your writing, I will call it that, has been read by everyone. As for me, I am entirely of your opinion and I owe my reasons to you who have taught me much in a subject that was new and which had never been discussed. The originality of your thought was soon converted into the most common truth."[50] Precedent was certainly on the side of states' rights. Córdoba had declared a state of siege in 1818. Provincial constitutions prior to 1853 of Corrientes, La Rioja, Mendoza, and San Luis had provided for such a state. The

[49] See Héctor R. Baudon, *Estado de Sitio,* Buenos Aires, 1939; Carlos Sánchez Viamonte, *Ley marcial y estado de sitio en el derecho argentino,* Montevideo, 1931; and other works.

[50] Vélez Sarsfield to Sarmiento, Buenos Aires, August 24, 1863; Carpeta xv, No. 1906.

provision of the Constitution of 1853 had, as Vélez expressed it, never been discussed. It was open to interpretation from either of the two legitimate stands of the time: nationalism or states' rights.

Towards the end of 1863, Sarmiento was becoming depressed with his position in San Juan. The opposition to his program, the setback received by his plans by the Chacho rebellion, his cooled relations with the national government due to his polemic with Rawson, his domestic difficulties—all combined to create a psychology of defeat and a desire for change. His closest friend, José Posse, tried to interpret his depression: "I think that I have penetrated to the bottom of your moral feelings to see there the inferno of your entire life. Someone other than you would have fallen prostrate under the weight of the thousand contrasts of your existence. Your glories of today are not worth the secret pains that are tormenting your soul. I see the efforts of your government to make a world out of nothing and I understand the difficulties, always renascent, that poverty and the real way of life of the provincial peoples will put in your way."[51]

In December of 1863 President Mitre was conscious of the difficult position of his old friend and of Don Domingo's desire to escape gracefully from the duties of his office. By naming him envoy extraordinary and minister plenipotentiary to the United States, Mitre offered Sarmiento a way out. The governor of San Juan accepted with enthusiasm this new suggestion; and after delaying his departure for several months to wind up his affairs in San Juan, on April 7, 1864, he went before the provincial legislature and offered his resignation. The next month found Domingo Sarmiento following the familiar trail across the Andes to his second homeland in Chile.

[51] Posse to Sarmiento, Tucumán, November 2, 1862; Carpeta Posse-Sarmiento.

Chapter 33. The Disowned Diplomat

THE early fall weather made the crossing of the Andes an easy one. The trip was pleasant. Don Domingo and his party took it in easy steps, and when they reached the peak of the trail, the usually windy mountains were quiet and still. Sarmiento lit his pipe in the open, and there was not enough wind to blow out his flame.

It was the most beautiful time of year when they arrived in Santiago, and Sarmiento was thrilled to see it once again. He held a warm spot in his heart for Chile, and he was always happy to revisit it. "I have returned to my old Santiago," he wrote. "What a transformation! How many palaces! What architectural majesty and beauty! The two countries separated by the mountain ranges can be distinguished by real differences. Buenos Aires is more beautiful as a whole, happier, easier, more within the reach of all. Santiago with its public monuments, its *cañada*, today a real boulevard, decorated with statues, water fountains, gardens, and magnificent houses. The carriages are as many and relatively better than those of Paris or London."[1]

Before his departure from San Juan, Don Domingo's appointment as minister to the United States had been augmented by a supplementary assignment as minister plenipotentiary before the governments of Chile and Perú. He had been given certain special assignments in these two nations and was expected to complete these missions during his trip north.

An incident at this precise time, however, gave an added significance to his post. At about the time of his arrival in Chile, news reached that nation of the attack on the 14th of April by a Spanish fleet under Admiral Pinzón on the

[1] Sarmiento to Posse, Santiago, May 20, 1864; Unpublished Archives of Museo Histórico Sarmiento, Carpeta Sarmiento-Posse.

Chincha Islands off the coast of Perú. This was a clear violation of the sovereignty of Perú, and the nations of the Americas immediately protested the action. Chile, being one of the closest neighbors to the injured nation, and being the country that would suffer most from any possible extension of Spanish aggression in the area, protested most strongly. Public sentiment in Santiago ran high.

It was into such an atmosphere that Sarmiento arrived, and when he heard the news his feeling was particularly strong on the matter. Spain was his old enemy, his "cradle of barbarism." The thought of her reintroduction into the New World infuriated him. Just as El Chacho had symbolized the forces of reaction in the field of provincial life, Spain symbolized the forces of reaction in the field of inter-American life. In his new role as diplomat Sarmiento could not but oppose it. "I found my old enemy among that nation of barbarians; I found a Pizarro, as brutal as his model, to represent in truly animal acts a Queen Isabel the second."[2]

Don Domingo took the opportunity offered by his reception by President Joaquín Pérez to express his views on the Chincha affair. Before presenting his credentials, he made a short speech. "The public instinct had a presentiment that I would say something about the recent happenings, and a large audience filled the steps to the palace and invaded the stately reception chamber. Upon hearing my speech delivered without affectation but with a sure voice, the public repeated the saying of someone in the audience: we can recognize the old republic, and this is the Sarmiento that we used to know."[3] His speech was a short one, but his words were strong for diplomatic language. "An unexplainable provocation made upon the Republic of Perú by Spain will perhaps make it necessary for us to give value to our titles, to our existences as nations; and then the Argentine Republic would claim as an honor and as a duty the right to be at the side of the Republic of Chile in the upholding of the rights of Perú that are today

[2] Sarmiento to Julio Belín, Valparaíso, May 2, 1864; Unpublished Archives of the Museo Histórico Sarmiento, Carpeta XIII, No. 1692.

[3] Sarmiento-Posse, Santiago, May 20, 1864 (this part of the letter is a continuation of an early part and is dated May 30); *op.cit.*

unrecognized by Spain. . . . If the flag of Perú must wave in the struggle to which they are being provoked, the tradition of its glories would seek and find at its side the star of Chile and the sun of Argentina that have crossed together their seas and their lands, and would not need to ask today which is the road which would lead to victory against the common enemy."[4]

Language such as this could not go unnoticed. Domingo Sarmiento had, in a very real sense, commenced his diplomatic career in a startling manner. The speech was praised in all quarters in Chile. His old adversary, Andrés Bello, congratulated him for his "brilliant reception speech," and members of both parties received him cordially as a result of his startling move. But his own government in Buenos Aires was not so pleased by his action. He had clearly gone beyond any instructions that he had received, and both President Mitre and Foreign Minister Elizalde wrote to censure him for his unauthorized move.[5] Mitre in a private letter to his representative asserted that Sarmiento's speech had been stronger than the protests of the Peruvians themselves. Chile had not answered the Spanish action in the same tone, and the Argentine minister's words had left his own country "out on a limb and ridiculous." "I would have liked it better if you had not gone so far in words and if you had gone a little further in actions and deliberated proposals. Such is the policy and the rule of conduct of the Argentine government."[6]

Don Domingo paid little heed to the scoldings and warnings of his government. He was still angry about the Spanish action, and he was very anxious to go on to Perú, where an American congress was assembling and where the question would surely come up for Pan-American action. "I will not go to Perú without authorization," he wrote, "and I am very

[4] *Obras*, XXI, p. 177.

[5] Sarmiento's original instructions from the foreign ministry, dealing with certain treaty and border adjustments to be made with the Chilean government, can be found in the Archives of the Foreign Ministry in Buenos Aires, Box 22, No. 15. For an account of the reception of his speech in Valparaíso and the reaction of his own government, see letter from Sarmiento to Posse, Valparaíso, September 30, 1864; *op.cit.*

[6] Mitre to Sarmiento, Buenos Aires, July 14, 1864; Unpublished Archives of Museo Histórico Sarmiento; Carpeta Mitre-Sarmiento.

much afraid that they will not send it to me, precisely because I have asked for it with so much insistence."[7] But within a few days after he wrote these words, instructions did arrive from Buenos Aires for him to proceed immediately to Lima and take part in the congress there. In spite of the fact that the text of the instructions was very cautious and that it limited him to the task of exploring and reporting on the situation,[8] the inexperienced and perhaps overanxious minister interpreted his instructions broadly. He saw them as "orders to act, in the same way as I had already started out. . . . They urge that I learn the policy of Chile and associate myself with that."[9] Therefore, without further delay, Don Domingo prepared his departure. He called upon his old friend Manuel Montt, who had been appointed Chilean delegate to the American congress, and in a half hour of conversation they came to an understanding on the situation. Montt discussed the problems with the Chilean cabinet, and it was agreed that Sarmiento would work with Chile for a settlement in Perú.

From Santiago, Sarmiento proceeded to Valparaíso, where he picked up the various members of his embassy staff who would accompany him to the United States, and, taking the first possible packet, he sailed for Perú.

The American congress that met in Lima in 1864 and 1865 had a number of specified purposes. It was to declare the American nations as one family, united by common principles and common interests. It was to sign a convention to facilitate mail communications among the various nations, and it was to adopt measures to settle boundary disputes.[10] But by the time it met in November 1864, all delegates were conscious of the fact that the most important question that would arise was the Chincha affair. Present among representatives from the various nations of the continent were some of the most distinguished statesmen of the time. Expectations ran high as to what would be brought about by this historical meeting.

[7] Sarmiento to Sarratea, Santiago, August 28, 1864; Carpeta VII, No. 866.

[8] Archives of the Ministry of Foreign Affairs, Caja 22, No. 15, p. 90.

[9] Sarmiento to Sarratea, Santiago, September 14, 1864, Carpeta VII, No. 868.

[10] Miguel Vara Velásquez, "El congreso Americano celebrado en Lima en 1864," *Revista chilena de historia y geografía*, Santiago, 1921, XI, pp. 72-100.

Don Domingo arrived in Perú under the most auspicious circumstances. The reports of his speech in Santiago had preceded him, and his arrival was looked upon as a good sign by the Peruvians. "For the moment that I disembarked in Callo I was the object of all kinds of attention on the part of the authorities and on the part of a group of Argentines who were awaiting at the dock to escort me."[11] He was taken to the capital city of Lima, where he was shown every courtesy by the Peruvian government and by the Limenian Society. The president gave a large official tea at which Sarmiento was the guest of honor. Bishops, generals, senators, judges, and the entire diplomatic corps of Lima were present. The president and his family were dressed in white with belts of sky blue (the colors of the Argentina national flag) in order to honor the minister from Argentina.[12]

When the Escuela de Artes y Oficios (School of Arts and Trades) was opened on December 9th, Sarmiento was invited to be present as a special guest. "The scene was a splendid one!" The palace that was to house the school was the largest to be devoted to an educational institution anywhere in the Americas. Don Domingo took his place among the diplomatic corps, but he was asked to take a special chair with the members of the faculty. There were over two thousand persons present, and when the Argentine minister was asked to say a few words he did so with a voice that was strong and sure of itself and filled all of the vast chambers of the school. He was interrupted repeatedly by the applause of the audience. Don Domingo was a natural-born actor who loved to hold the center of the stage, and he loved especially to receive the applause of the public.[13]

For the next few days Sarmiento was showered with congratulations, and the praise of his speech was far greater than he had expected. "Yesterday and today they talk of nothing else in Lima, in conversations, in the hotels, in the families;

[11] Sarmiento to Faustina Sarmiento de Belín, Lima, October 20, 1864; Unpublished Archives of Museo Histórico Sarmiento, Carpeta XII, No. 1632.

[12] Sarmiento to Bienvenida Sarmiento, Lima, October 10, 1864; Unpublished Archives of Museo Histórico Sarmiento, Carpeta XIII, No. 1743.

[13] Sarmiento to Posse, Lima, October 10, 1864.

and congratulations have overwhelmed me at all hours. I read and reread the speech, and to tell the truth I do not understand what there is in it that excites so much interest."[14]

The answer to this was obvious. Lima was going all out in its campaign to win the heart of its diplomatic visitor. It was grateful for what Sarmiento had done in Santiago, and it was hopeful that he would do even more in the American congress. These efforts did not go for nought. Sarmiento, being the man that he was, could not help but be flattered and moved by the warmth of feeling in Perú. "I see these manifestations that are so spontaneous from a people that hardly knows me. . . ."[15] Such a "spontaneously" friendly people could not be left at the mercy of barbarism. The champion of civilization felt that he would truly be appreciated if he came to the rescue of such a people.

Domingo Sarmiento assumed a position of leadership in the sessions of the American congress. "Without trying to, and only by force of circumstances, I have acquired in the American congress that position that you saw me hold at the Santa Fé Convention, giving impulse to the point of exaggeration, and often serving as a common ground for the meeting of opposing ideas, often finding the right phrases to conciliate divergences."[16] He joined in a resolution of the congress that the various American governments protest to Spain with the warning that if they were not heard they might change their status from that of neutral to that of belligerent. He himself offered a resolution that the diplomatic corps send a joint note showing that harm to Perú would be harm to all of America.

Again, Don Domingo had gone far beyond the instructions handed him by his government. Again Mitre and Elizalde vigorously protested his actions. The president went so far as to attribute his minister's actions to his love for glory and his weakness for the praise of women.[17] He considered the Congress a powerless instrument. Many of the delegates held

[14] Sarmiento to Bienvenida, Lima, October 10, 1864; *loc.cit.*

[15] Sarmiento-Posse, Lima, December 10, 1864; *loc.cit.*

[16] Sarmiento-Posse, Lima, December 3, 1864; Carpeta Sarmiento-Posse.

[17] *Sarmiento-Mitre Correspondencia*, p. 339.

no power from their governments. Others had already declared their unwillingness to take any action. He felt that the Peruvian government and Peruvian public were making a fool out of Sarmiento.[18] Mitre went on to oppose any further participation in the congress. "You know that it is one of the fundamental bases of Argentine policy not to take part in an American congress." He ordered the minister to leave the congress, and the reasons that he gave for this action were based on two basic premises. He was opposed to the congress on an ideal plane, for it was contrary to his nationalistic principles. It might hurt the national fortunes of the Argentine Republic. He was opposed to it on a practical plane, for it could be of no practical value to Argentina.[19] Sarmiento opposed both of these views. Ideally he saw a more basic problem of right and wrong, a moral question rather than a nationalistic one. Practically, he saw the need for inter-American co-operation. He felt that the danger of European agression against one American nation implied the danger of similar action against another. This could be avoided only through cooperation. Don Domingo's ego was undoubtedly exploited for the benefit of Peruvian policy, but as we look at the question in retrospect, his attitude towards the problem seems to enclose more vision and more statesmanship than that of his government.

In April, Sarmiento abandoned his efforts at the congress and departed from Perú. His stay there had been a pleasant one, but domestic unrest during the last weeks had made him impatient to leave. He traveled by ship to Panamá, crossed the Isthmus, and embarked once more for New York. The last leg of his journey was a bad one. The weather was rough. He had no private cabin, and he found himself sleeping with workmen from California amid bales of cargo.

[18] *Ibid.*, p. 347.

[19] Mitre to Sarmiento, Buenos Aires, March 24, 1865; Carpeta Mitre-Sarmiento.

Chapter 34. The Ambassador and His Ideal

On May 5, 1865, Domingo Faustino Sarmiento, envoy extraordinary and minister plenipotentiary, watched from the deck of his ship as it entered the harbor of New York. It was almost two decades since he had seen that city for the first time, since he had been thrilled by its size and dazzled by its glamor. Now, for the second time, he experienced that same sensation. "What a spectacle!" he exclaimed. "What a city, what civilization, what power!"[1]

"It would take a volume to tell you all my impressions after a two weeks' stay here. It is a whole year of life compressed into a few hours like a delirious fever. It is the temptation of Satan, displaying the kingdoms of the world from the high mountain.

"The changes since my first visit are so great that the most luxurious quarter of the city, where I am now living, did not even exist then. The magnificent avenues that divide this section are 40 yards wide, with streetcars in the middle and sidewalks 7 yards in width, lined with trees. The cross streets are only 20 yards wide with shady parks at short intervals. Broadway, 50 yards in width, is laid out for 7 miles, for more than 3 of which it is enclosed by marble, granite, freestone, or brick palaces. Palatial hotels for 1,000 guests, printing offices, banks, stores, clubs, and associations—today Broadway is unrivaled anywhere in the world for its architectural splendor and its crowds. It is there that the great fortunes are made, which will be spent on Fifth Avenue, another street of palaces like the famous one in Genoa. It is the Boulevard St. Germain of New York. . . .

"This spaciousness of the streets, the plantings of the trees, vines, and flowers, and the iron work, which instead of cover-

[1] Sarmiento to Bienvenida Sarmiento, New York, May 20, 1865; Carpeta XIII, No. 1749.

ing the stupendous buildings embellishes them, the confusion of coaches, omnibusses, streetcars, people, posters, and signs—make a strange impression on people who, like ourselves, have been accustomed to living in streets 12 yards wide, that shut out all our view."[2]

Don Domingo arrived at a crucial point in the history of the United States. The Civil War had just ended. President Lincoln had died of an assassin's bullet. The industry of the nation, stimulated by the impulse of war, was booming. All was optimism, action, and change. The new minister, in a typical manner, had lost his credentials on the trip north. It was impossible to present himself to the government in Washington without them, so he had to send for new copies and bide his time.[3] Sarmiento used the months in which he had to await the new documents from Buenos Aires to become acquainted once more with the nation that he had come to love during his previous visit eighteen years before.

He traveled to Washington to watch the review of the returning Army of the Potomac. Two hundred thousand men marched by. "A unique spectacle in history—a river of men, horses, cannons, and rifles that marched by in common company for two days. Constantly filing past came glorious chiefs and battalions with tattered, shapeless flags. The public, knowing their history, greeted them with frantic applause."[4] The Argentine minister was invited to occupy the official stand. Present were President Johnson, General Grant, General Sherman, and General Meade. Sarmiento was impressed by the armed might. He was impressed by his new position in a country that he had visited before in a state bordering on indigence.

The next day he attended the trial of Dr. Mudd and Mrs. Surrat for the murder of President Lincoln. "The English trial system is very impressive"; he wrote, "the defendants, who are present throughout the hearings, accompanied by their lawyers, hear the evidence of the witnesses and by cross-examination may question them in their turn. That day Negroes were witnesses, a novelty in this country, for pre-

[2] *Anthology*, pp. 269-270. [3] *Obras*, XXXIV, p. 185. [4] *Anthology*, p. 270.

viously they had not been permitted to testify. I was deeply moved by a mulatto woman who, when asked whether she had been a slave, replied with emotion, 'Yes, a slave! But now I am free!' "[5]

Don Domingo visited Richmond, where he visited by moonlight the ruins of the former Confederate capital that had been destroyed by fire. He went on to Petersburg, and there he inspected the fortifications and crossed over to the lines of General Grant's army. "In the space of half a block, which separates the two lines at this point, one cannot take a step without treading on a bomb fragment, a broken rifle, boots with legs in them, cartridge belts, heads, cannon balls, and tatters of uniforms—horrors!"[6] On his return he passed through Baltimore and Philadelphia. In the City of Brotherly Love he stayed at the Continental Hotel, the size and luxury of which amazed him. "I had to be guided three times before I could find my room, lost in the colossal labyrinth. Finally they showed me the furnished room that every five minutes goes up from the first to the seventh floor and down again, letting off the passengers, who sit on soft furniture, at the intervening floors. . . ."[7]

He returned to New York, where he sought lodging in a modest boarding house. The owner was a Methodist minister, but the landlady was cross and irritable and Don Domingo soon moved to other quarters. This was a period of extreme happiness in his life, extreme contentment with the world. "I shall tell you of my happiness, which for the moment is real. I rise at five o'clock in the morning. . . . I read little, because I would not know which to choose from the multitude of books, pamphlets, and newspapers that I am accumulating. I am writing, translating, compiling, and printing two books at once. I send off letters that are becoming more frequent and more full of interesting things each day. I am also publishing some articles in the daily press and when midnight arrives to my great regret, I find my 'downy couch' (because, speaking unpoetically, American beds are very good) the sleep that has eluded my eyelids for so many years."[8]

Finally, in November, the new credentials arrived from the

[5] *Ibid.*, pp. 270-271. [6] *Ibid.*, p. 271. [7] *Ibid.* [8] *Ibid.*, p. 273.

government in Buenos Aires, and Don Domingo traveled to Washington to present them. On November 9th, he was received by President Andrew Johnson, and in a short speech expressed his aims and his views of his diplomatic mission. He had come to study the model nation of the north. He had come to learn from its constitutionalists, its jurists, and its thinkers. And more than that, he had come to study its methods, its means of preparing its people for the political life that they led. "To the names of Washington, Franklin, and Lincoln is added today that of Horace Mann, both in the veneration of our peoples and in the purpose of taking advantage of the lessons that they have left to humanity."[9]

President Johnson responded in the same vein. "Believe me, sir, that it is a source of enduring gratification to the people of the United States, that they have framed for themselves a constitution for civil government, which so many of the new, enterprising, and enlightened states, which are growing up on this continent, have thought worthy to be adopted by them as a model. The fact, however, is one which had brought with it to us a great responsibility—the responsibility of conducting the administration of our cherished system in such a manner as to maintain, preserve and increase the confidence of mankind. . . ."[10]

Domingo Sarmiento had set for himself a task that was quite different from that of the ordinary diplomat. He did not establish his residence in Washington but in New York. He avoided the usual social life of the diplomat. He ignored receptions, teas, and meetings. His embassy was a center of study, and his object was to understand the nation to which he had been sent and to learn from its accomplishments lessons that might profitably be applied to his own land. "My desire was to realize an old idea of mine about embassies. I wanted to convert these havens for the lazy into offices of work, to send useful data, and establish relations, less with the government than with the people."[11] Don Domingo saw

[9] National Archives, State Department Division, Argentine Republic, Incoming Correspondence, Volume II, Notes, November 9, 1865.
[10] *Ibid.*
[11] *Sarmiento-Mitre Correspondencia*, p. 364.

his task as twofold. He divided his energies while in the United States between a sympathetic presentation of his own nation to the North American public, and a study of the institutions, in order to carry back with him to Argentina the valuable lessons that he might learn.

His first task—that of presenting his nation in sympathetic light to the United States public—was not an easy one. His mission in North America coincided with the period in which Argentina became enbroiled in her bloodiest war. It was a conflict that saw the sympathies of most of the governments and most of the peoples of the world lined up against Argentina, and Sarmiento found that his job was to alter those sympathies in the United States.

The disastrous Paraguayan War had begun with a civil struggle in Uruguay. General Venancio Flores revolted against the Montevideo government and threw the country into a bloody conflict. The fighting was localized at first, but before long Brazil had become involved by sending a division "to protect Brazilian interest" in the country. Brazil was known to be favorable to the revolutionary cause, and her action was taken by many as an act of intervention. Argentina immediately proclaimed her neutrality, but the little country of Paraguay did not hide her displeasure at the Brazilian move. General Francisco Solano López was the absolute dictator of Paraguay. He had lived many years in Europe, and he had become a great admirer and imitator of the military genius of Napoleon Bonaparte. Studying at the court of Napoleon III, he had learned the latest military methods and techniques, and at the death of his father, the former Dictator Carlos Antonio López, he had returned to Paraguay to take over the government of that nation. In the first years of his regime, he trained a small but highly equipped and highly specialized army. He devoted the major part of his attention to this task, and by 1865 he believed he had created for his nation the strongest army in South America. He was a man of fancy dreams of glory and of complete irresponsibility as to how such glory should be acquired. When the Brazilians refused to withdraw from Uruguay, Solano López mobilized his army, and within a month he had invaded without warning the Brazilian province of Matto Grosso and had opened the way to Rio Grande do Sul.

The territory between Paraguay and Brazil is an almost impenetrable jungle. There are no useful rivers. There are no roads. In 1865 there was no way that Solano López's crack troops could get to the main forces of the enemy. The only practical approach to the southern portion of Brazil or to Uruguay was to cross the Argentine province of Corrientes. Paraguay requested permission to do this, but the Mitre government, maintaining a strict neutrality and a sympathy for the Uruguayan rebels, refused. Without warning and without so much as a formal declaration of war, Marshal Solano López invaded Argentina with an army of 25,000 men. He seized two Argentine ships on the Paraguay River, and took the city of Corrientes. On May 3, 1865, the Argentine government received a laconic note from Asunción. "War is declared against the present government until it gives the guarantees and satisfaction due to the rights, honor, and dignity of Paraguay and its government."[12] President Mitre quickly contacted the Brazilian government and the government of General Flores in Uruguay, and the Triple Alliance was formed to oppose the Paraguayan attack.[13] In spite of the relative size of Brazil and Argentina as compared with Paraguay, they found it difficult to face the military might of Solano López. The Paraguayan dictator had 100,000 men under arms, and Mitre during the first months of the war found it hard to raise a force of 20,000.

When Don Domingo Sarmiento arrived in the United States, there was already much talk about the Paraguayan War. Opinion was already forming in opposition to the nations of the Triple Alliance. The Washington government looked with suspicion and distrust upon the new power of Brazil, the largest South American nation. It tended to see in a victory for the smaller nation a way of negating the growing strength of the two larger countries and thereby maintaining a kind of balance of power in the southeastern portion of the

[12] Ismael Bucich Escobar, *op.cit.*, p. 114.

[13] See H. G. Warren, *Paraguay: An Informal History*, Norman, Okla., 1949, pp. 217-244.

hemisphere. United States diplomatic agents, though maintaining a strict neutrality, were obviously sympathetic with the Solano López government throughout most of the conflict. The North American public, in a similar manner, felt an attraction for the Paraguayan cause. Public opinion began to build Marshal Solano López into a mythical hero. Here was a man, ruling one of the smallest nations in South America, who pitted his strength against the two largest nations combined. This was material for the newspapers. This was fuel for the imagination of the public.[14]

The Argentine minister immediately set out to counteract this atmosphere of opinion. He published articles in the *New York Tribune* and in the *Boston Daily Address* presenting his country's cause. He wrote of the history of Paraguay. He pointed to its Jesuit origins, its lack of any emphasis on the individual, and the communistic aspects of its way of life. Everything in Paraguay, from working to eating to praying, was done to a schedule, to the ringing of a bell. The nation had been ruled first by the absolute rule of the Society of Jesus and then by a sequence of three unchallenged dictators. The present ruler, according to Sarmiento, had prepared carefully for the present war against Brazil and Argentina.[15]

Don Domingo founded a newspaper of his own in New York. He called it *Ambas Américas* (Both Americas), and it was devoted to the exchange of information and ideas between the "two Americas." In the pages of this publication, too, he devoted articles to the clarifying and defending of his nation's position in the war.

At first, his propaganda had little effect. Sarmiento became exasperated at the persistently hostile attitude of the press, and he condemned its position as selfish and without foresight. "The newspapers find it useful, *sensational,*" he wrote, "to be

[14] For an excellent account of the events leading up to the Paraguayan War, see P. H. Box, *The Origins of the Paraguayan War*, Urbana, 1929. See also C. A. Washburn, *The History of Paraguay*, Boston, 1871. For a sympathetic treatment of the Paraguayan cause, Juan E. O'Leary, *El Mariscal Solano López*, Asuncion, 1926.

[15] These arguments are repeated in letter from Sarmiento to Mrs. Mann, New York, October 3, 1865; Academia Argentina de Letras, *Cartas de Sarmiento a la Señora María Mann*, Buenos Aires, 1936.

in favor of those savages. It is useless to show them the truth. The truth is unfortunate for them. It is necessary for the Guaraní [Indian] race to overcome the European, for the tyrant who was created by the Jesuits to dominate those of us who work towards becoming civilized."[16] He continued his campaign in person, by letter, and in the newspapers of the city.

Before he departed from the United States, however, the Argentine minister felt that he had accomplished in a respectable degree his purpose. He had defended his country's case in regard to the Paraguayan War, and he felt that he had presented his nation in a sympathetic light. He believed that he had brought Argentina and the United States a little closer together. "The Argentine Republic is beginning to be known, esteemed, not because it is worth in the public mind its true value, but because, as Suetonius or someone once said, it has someone who knows how to make it seem of value."[17]

The Paraguayan War struck home to Sarmiento in a very personal way while he was in the United States. On September 22, 1866, the Allied armies under the command of President General Mitre assaulted the Paraguayan fort of Curupaytí. The fortifications stood a little above the juncture of the Paraná and Paraguay Rivers, holding a commanding position over the two main approaches to the north. They were extremely strong emplacements, but due to a miscalculation of their strength, Mitre threw his armies against them in an all-out attack. The results were disastrous. The allies were thrown back, and the losses suffered by the assaulting forces were immense. Among those lost was Captain Domingo Fidel Sarmiento, Don Domingo's beloved Dominguito. It seemed like a needless death, due to what Posse called the "abominable error of Curupaytí, that defeat without any possible explanation."[18] The Argentine minister was deeply shattered by the news. He had placed his greatest hopes in his son.

[16] Sarmiento to Mary Mann, Washington, January 3, 1867; Academia Argentina de Letras, *op.cit.*, p. 21.

[17] Sarmiento to Posse, New York, February 27, 1866; Carpeta Sarmiento-Posse.

[18] Posse to Sarmiento, Tucumán, June 15, 1867.

With the deepest pride he had watched him grow and mature. An entire portion of the old fighter's future seemed to have been destroyed at Curupaytí.

In spite of this great personal disaster, Sarmiento pursued relentlessly the task that he had set before himself as the diplomatic representative of his country. In addition to the difficult job of presenting his own nation, he set out to complete the second phase of his mission: to know the country in which he was living.

The first phase of the North American scene that Sarmiento wished to penetrate was the human element. He wanted to get to know the people of the United States. Soon after his arrival in New York, he wrote to his old friend Mrs. Mary Mann, the widow of his schoolteacher idol, Horace Mann. He told her of his return to her country and his hopes of seeing her and his other friends in "New England, the homeland of my thoughts since I first was acquainted with it."[19] The results of this letter were what he had expected. Mrs. Mann invited him to visit her in Concord, and with great pleasure Don Domingo accepted the invitation. This was the very opportunity that he had sought. Here he would be in contact with the most stimulating minds of the country and the most influential intellects of the civilization that he so admired.[20]

Mary Mann received Don Domingo "like one of her family, with the true simplicity of New England, where all men are brothers, and with the affection and solicitude of an old friend." From that time until the end of their lives, Domingo Sarmiento and Mary Mann were the closest of friends. The New England widow translated into English the Argentinean's masterpiece *El Facundo* (Life in the Argentine Republic) and parts of his *Recuerdos de provincia.* She was his spiritual guide and his confidante during his stay in North

[19] Sarmiento to Mary Mann, New York, October 3, 1865; Academia Argentina de Letras, *op.cit.* The first two letters in this volume, dated March 6, 1865 and July 14, 1865, would seem to be, from internal evidence, of the years 1867 and 1868 respectively. The first date is impossible, since it is prior to Sarmiento's arrival in New York. The mention of the revolution in Corrientes and the presidential election campaign in Argentina would indicate that the second one was written later than 1865.

[20] He visited Concord in late October, not in May as stated by Rojas. See J. Garate Arrioles, *op.cit.*

America and for many years after. When Dominguito died on the battlefields of Paraguay, it was to Mrs. Mann that Sarmiento's sister and daughter addressed themselves. They knew that their brother "admires and loves you," and they begged her to comfort Don Domingo in his hour of distress "and use such other persuasion you may discern as conducive to appease his confused imagination."[21] For many years later, Mary Mann and Domingo Sarmiento carried on an extensive correspondence, the collection of which has proved one of the most revealing clues to Sarmiento's thought.

In Concord, Sarmiento had dinner with Emerson. Domingo had sent the North American philosopher a copy of *Facundo* and that work, as usual, served him as an introduction. "If to be a minister is not enough for everyone, to be an educator is already a great title to the friendly consideration of this nation of professors and schoolmasters, but I still keep *Facundo* up my sleeve. It is my Parrot cannon. Nothing stands up against it."[22]

Sarmiento visited George Ticknor, the foremost Hispanist in the English-speaking world, and one of his greatest admirers and most favorable commentators. Together they discussed *El Facundo* and *Recuerdos de provincia,* and Sarmiento was surprised that the New Englander considered the latter work to be his real masterpiece.

"From Mrs. Mann's house, they took me to Cambridge, the famous university, where I spent two days of continual banqueting, to be presented to all of the eminent sages who were gathered there. Longfellow, the great poet, who speaks perfect Spanish; Gould, the astronomer and friend of Humboldt; Agassiz (the younger), for whom they foretell a greater career than his father's; and Dr. Hill, the old president of the university."[23]

Sarmiento was taken to the Cambridge library, where he was asked to sign the visitor's book. The librarian handed him a pen that had been used by Jerome Bonaparte and U. S.

[21] Bienvenida Sarmiento and Faustina Sarmiento de Belín to Mary Mann, San Juan, October 21, 1866; photostatic copy of this letter in Unpublished Archives of Museo Histórico Sarmiento.

[22] *Anthology,* p. 275.

[23] *Ibid.,* p. 275.

Grant. "So you see, I am not such a nobody, even if I am the minister of the Argentine Republic and nobody knows where my country is."[24]

But knowing the people and the leaders of the United States was not Don Domingo's only interest. He wanted to know the country's institutions and its way of life. Above all, he wanted to study the way that its people were educated. From his arrival in New York in 1865 to his departure in 1868, he devoted himself to this purpose. His first means was to learn the language. He worked hard at this, but he never perfected it. In 1866, he was writing: "I had forgotten my first thought of commanding the Lincoln one; but no matter I accept at present the two. You can said no, to Mr. Gremnser. I shall not neither more rich nor more poor for the outlay of 600 dollars, and will get the likeness of the two men I love most."[25] However, Don Domingo learned enough of the language to get along, and he was very fortunate in having President Mitre's son, Bartolito Mitre, who spoke perfect English, as his secretary and constant companion.

In spite of his linguistic difficulties, Sarmiento took advantage of this opportunity to study all phases of the life of the northern republic. He collected an immense library on political science, law and education. He took back with him to Argentina such books as James P. Wickersham's *The Common School Laws of Pennsylvania,* and *The Code of Public Instruction in the State of New York.* After his controversy with Rawson over the right to declare a state of siege, he had determined to study that subject in the United States. "I hope to arrive in the United States," he had written to Nicolás Avellaneda, "and be able to by the practical study of those institutions, resolve the doubts that tend to obscure everything and confuse all the powers."[26] In North America, he purchased, read, and annotated such books as Thomas Hare's *The Election of Representatives,* Joseph Story's *Commen-*

[24] Sarmiento to Mrs. Mann, New York, May 12, 1866, marked "confidential"; Academia Argentina de Letras, *op.cit.*

[25] *Ibid.*

[26] Sarmiento to Avellaneda, Lima, April 26, 1865; in Unpublished Archives of the Museo Histórico Sarmiento. This collection is not yet organized or catalogued.

taries on the Constitution of the United States, Horace Burney's *The Privilege of the Writ of Habeas Corpus,* Alfred Conkling's *The Power of the Executive Department,* and Francis Lieber's *On Civil and Self Government.* In the last book, he marked many passages that agreed with his ideas. When Lieber referred to the fact that American liberty is a heritage from the Anglican tradition, Sarmiento made comments of agreement. Such statements as, "The supremacy of law is an elementary requisite of liberty," and "Education has been considered by many as the true basis of popular liberty," were marked by Don Domingo with heavy lines to show his interest and conformity.[27]

What he learned during his mission in North America, Domingo recorded for the use and the instruction of his compatriots in the South. He wrote for *El Zonda,* Vicuña Mackenna's *La voz de America,* which was published in New York, and many other South American journals. He published the first *Life of Abraham Lincoln* (*Vida de Lincoln*) in Spanish, composing it from excerpts from the existing biographies in English. He wrote his *Las escuelas base de la prosperidad y de la república en los Estados Unidos,* and included therein many of the observations he had made of the North American educational system. In 1867 he translated and edited a *Life of Horace Mann* and thus presented the great educational leader and his achievements to the Hispanic reading public.

Throughout his entire stay in the United States, Don Domingo took an active part in the pedagogical activities of that country. Soon after his arrival in 1865, he was invited by the Rhode Island Historical Society to deliver a paper before one of its general meetings. Sarmiento and President Mitre had been elected honorary members of the society in 1861, and this was the first chance that either had had to show his appreciation. Don Domingo accepted the invitation with pleasure, and on December 27, 1865, he addressed a special meeting. The society records state that "Señor Sarmiento

[27] The books collected by Sarmiento while he was in the United States are preserved in the Museo Histórico Sarmiento. They still have his comments and marks in his own handwriting, and they are invaluable comments on his thought and beliefs.

speaking English imperfectly, the paper was read by Reverend E. M. Stone."[28] The title of the discourse was *North and South America,* and its subject was dear to Don Domingo's heart. He compared the civilization of Anglo-Saxon North America with that of Iberic South America. He showed the strength of the former and the weakness of the latter. In analyzing the elements that were the basis of North American civilization, he resorted to all of his old theories: education, race, and economic progress. He pointed to the North Americans, especially the Rhode Islanders, who had aided Hispanic America in the past, and he called upon the United States again to assume the role of leadership, to send schoolteachers, inventions, new methods, and new products to bring a better civilization to its southern neighbors.[29]

The following year, the Argentine minister traveled to Indianapolis to attend a meeting of the National Teachers' Association. Mrs. Mann had given him a letter of introduction to the president of the Association, James Pyle Wickersham, who had just been appointed the Superintendent of Common Schools of the State of Pennsylvania.[30] "On the other side of the Allegheny Mountains the new world begins," wrote Don Domingo in an article for a South American Journal. "From Pittsburgh I continued on to Columbus, the capital of Ohio, and from Columbus to Indianapolis, capital of Indiana, the terminus of my excursion for the time. We speed on from capital to capital, the train swallowing up the intervening distances by the hour. I have an insatiable, inextinguishable curiosity. Probably nobody has seen more than I have, although many have traveled more. I can tell from the crowd traveling with me. They talk, read, and sleep. I am the one person with my eyes glued to the train window from dawn to dusk, looking, always looking, watching the

[28] I wish to thank Mr. Clarkson A. Collins, 3rd, Research Associate of the Rhode Island Historical Society for his aid in gathering this information.

[29] The Society voted to publish this paper. It was printed by Knowles Anthony & Co., at Providence, R.I., in 1866. A hundred copies of this 44-page booklet were released for sale. Spanish translation published in *Obras,* XXI, 195-236.

[30] Alexander Harris, *A Biographical History of Lancaster County,* Lancaster, 1872, pp. 618-620.

forests go by, and the corn and potato fields, the small houses, factories, estates, and waterfalls always looking out, happily, silently, and contemplatively. I have thus acquired the faculty of seeing, measuring, comparing, observing, reflecting, and recording.

"Every new tree attracts my attention, and if a small plant happens to be of the same species as one in my country, I greet it in passing as a friend. If I get lost, wandering through city streets, I have only to study the thousands of signs and printed notices. Then I recognize one on which, an hour before, I had noticed that the tip of an 'A' was missing; or a portrait of Lincoln or Grant placed on the right, which is enough to orient me, because I had examined everything closely—letters, prints, and architecture. . . .

"Twenty years ago Indianapolis was a mere cluster of Indian wigwams. Today it is a great city with its Broadway lined with palaces, stores, hotels, and clubs, and boasting thirty-yard-wide streets and urban street cars. I had come to Indianapolis to take part in an educational gathering which I had been invited to attend. . . ."[31]

During the course of the meetings, Sarmiento became intimate with the president of the association. As in the case of Mann twenty years earlier, Don Domingo found in Wickersham a kindred spirit. In the course of his introductory remarks, the president said, "The people are the primary source of all political power. Educational systems in this country should provide means of instruction for all."[32] In private conferences Wickersham pressed many more ideas with which Sarmiento so heartily agreed and which awakened the interest of the Argentine in this North American educator.

Don Domingo was invited to speak on the subject of "Education in Argentina," and he took this opportunity to expound his old theme of the need of intellectual cooperation between the Americas. "It is the province of the United

[31] *Anthology*, p. 277.

[32] *Proceedings and Lectures of the National Teachers' Association at Their Annual Meetings, Held in Indianapolis, Indiana, August, 1866, Albany, 1867*, pp. 25, 29.

States," he asserted, "the highest mission intrusted by Providence to a great people, that of conducting others through the new paths opened by mankind to advance firmly to their great destinies. . . . The republics of South America ought to be the first to avail themselves of the lessons given to them by the great republic of the north with such an enlightened exposition. But unfortunately it is not so. South America . . . is like a man who being sick refuses to take the simple remedies tendered him—common education—in order to be fit for liberty and republicanism. . . . I have witnessed in a South American legislature the sanction without opposition of the budget of war for four millions of dollars, and the bringing about of a stormy discussion over the amount of two thousand dollars, directed to support an educational paper like the *Massachusetts Teacher*."[33] North America's glorious mission, Sarmiento told the Teachers' Association as he had told the Rhode Island historians, was to lead the way for the other American nations in the field of education and civilization.

Towards the middle of 1867, Don Domingo left the United States for a brief period to visit the International Exposition in Paris. He sailed from New York on June 15th, and he sought in a long sea voyage rest from the arduous tasks that he was pursuing in his studies of the United States. He did not remain long in France. He visited the Exposition and had a brief interview with his old acquaintance Thiers.[34] He was feted by the Argentine residents in Paris, and then on July 23 he set sail once more for New York.

Upon his return to North America, the Argentine minister made another of his many excursions throughout the interior of the nation. Among his points of call was Harrisburg, Pennsylvania, where he visited his newly-made friend, Professor Wickersham. From there, he went on to Chicago to visit a close friend of Mary Mann, Kate Dogget. But it was during his stay in Harrisburg that there began one of the most romantic interludes of his life.

Through Professor Wickersham, Don Domingo met a certain Ida Wickersham who was visiting her relative. She offered to teach the Argentine English, and they spent much time

[33] *Ibid.*, pp. 77-79.

[34] *Obras*, XLIX, 263.

together during his brief stay in the Pennsylvania capital. Sarmiento seems to have had, in spite of his homely appearance, a mysterious but very strong attraction for women. From his early romances in San Juan through his passionate love affair with Doña Benita, this fact was quite obvious. Ida Wickersham was the young wife of a doctor in Chicago, a brother of Professor Wickersham. She had dark hair, and Sarmiento described her as "the most womanly woman I have ever known."[35] Don Domingo had been estranged from Doña Benita for some time. The implications seem obvious, to judge from what remains of the correspondence, that an affair developed between Don Domingo and Ida. Don Domingo, always weak in this respect, became infatuated with the young woman. Ida fell in love with the Argentine minister. There ensued a relationship and a lifelong correspondence which remains an outstanding chapter in Sarmiento's personal life. Ida Wickersham seems to have had no appreciation of the real importance of the public aspects of Sarmiento's life, but she had a real and lasting love for him. Only one side of this correspondence is still in existence—the letters from Ida to Sarmiento—but a few excerpts from them tell the story well.

On September 22, 1867, Ida wrote: "No letter from you since last Saturday and I am disappointed . . . you will not be able to tell me in so many words that *you still love me*, but I shall believe that you do. I have thought so many times since I came, of the days *we* passed here together. . . . But I suppose I must not say much about how much I miss you and would like to see you, for you will say 'mere words.' They *are not*, I am *true, and you*? . . . You may be with Mrs. Mann—then I am jealous. She cannot take my place. You will not let anyone do that—will you?"[36]

On December 12th, Don Domingo wrote to his daughter, Faustina, and spoke of a woman "so beautiful and so much in love that she would make me lose my head if she did not

[35] *Ibid.*, p. 297.

[36] Ida Wickersham-Sarmiento, Unpublished Archives of the Museo Histórico Sarmiento; this material is unorganized and unclassified. The excerpts quoted here from the correspondence are used by permission of Mrs. John Schlagle and Mrs. J. P. Wickersham Crawford.

live three hundred leagues away. Even that does not keep me from doing the most absurd things."[37]

Ida's other letters tell the remainder of a strange story. Their dramatic aspects and their worth as a sidelight on Sarmiento's personality warrant their quotation in part at this time.

On June 25, 1868, Ida wrote to thank Don Domingo for a necklace and some pearl earrings. "I should judge from what the doctor said he does not care what you send me. . . ."[38] On November 14, 1869, she wrote [Sarmiento is back in Buenos Aires]: "I hope you will have time to write me a long letter—and in *French* if you like—you can say what *you like* to me then—no one can read it in *this* family except myself."[39] Her attitude towards the importance of Sarmiento's public life is revealed in 1870: "I am so glad that the war in Paraguay is over, and that you have that much less to trouble you—perhaps you can write longer letters now."[40] Then, a disaster struck: "I write to you once more from Chicago, or what is left of that once large and beautiful city. One week ago today the most of the city was destroyed by fire, *the whole* of the great North side, *most* of the South side, and some of the West. At 12 p.m., we fled from the St. James and were all of that dreadful night until 9 the next day, on the ground, close to the lake in the track of the railroad on the breakwater, surrounded by flame except for that side and in a whirlwind of fine dust for hours. I fled at 9 a.m. the next day (Monday) to the railroad and ran up the track to escape being burned and with the danger constantly before me of being blown by the extraordinary wind into the Lake, but I live, thank Heaven! *You cannot imagine* the horrors we have passed through. . . ."[41]

And finally, the last act—a tragedy: 1882: "I fear that long ago you have forgotten me—for every year for five years past I have written to you—and still I receive no word from you and no sign of your existence ever.

[37] Sarmiento to Faustina Sarmiento de Belín, New York, December 12, 1867, Carpeta XII, No. 1641.

[38] Ida Wickersham-Sarmiento, Chicago, June 25, 1868.

[39] Ida Wickersham-Sarmiento, Chicago, November 14, 1869.

[40] Ida Wickersham-Sarmiento, Chicago, January 14, 1870.

[41] Ida Wickersham-Sarmiento, Chicago, October 18, 1871.

"You know that I got a *divorce* from the Doctor—and that I have been living in New York for the past four years and a half. They have been years of hard study and much trouble for me—as I wished to learn some art by which to earn my living. . . . I have studied Art—and make portraits in crayon, pastels and water colors—but I find it hard work for a woman to make her way in the world—especially one who has not been brought up to do so."[42]

This was a strange and romantic interlude in the life of Domingo Sarmiento.

In 1868 we find him entering into a completely new phase of his life. It was an election year for the Argentine Republic. Bartolomé Mitre's term was coming to an end, and according to the constitution he could not succeed himself. Towards the middle of 1867, there seemed to be three principal contenders for the presidency. General Urquiza, then the governor of Entre Ríos, was preparing to make a bid for a return to power. He hoped to gain the support of the provinces. Adolfo Alsina, the governor of Buenos Aires, had thrown his hat in the ring. He had been one of the leaders of the opposition to Urquiza, and he hoped to gain the support of Buenos Aires and whatever other provinces he could win over. Rufino de Elizalde, the minister of foreign affairs, was perhaps the most hopeful at this early date. He had the tacit support of President Mitre, and official backing very often meant election.

There had been some talk of Sarmiento's candidacy, but Don Domingo had not taken it very seriously. Since his break with Rawson over the Chacho question, and with Elizalde and Mitre over the American congress, he had felt that his chances had been killed. Sarmiento had written to Mrs. Mann in 1866 that the real reason for sending him to the United States was to have him out of the country until after the elections. "I did not wish to understand this, although others understood it, and the facts it manifests. Today everyone sees the *trick*."[43] Towards the end of 1867, however, Colonel Man-

[42] Ida Wickersham-Sarmiento, New York, April 23, 1882.

[43] Sarmiento to Mary Mann, New York, May 12, 1866, marked "confidential"; Academia Argentina de Letras, *op.cit.*, p. 13.

silla, from his headquarters at the front in Paraguay, launched Sarmiento's candidacy. It was immediately welcomed from many quarters, and by September of that same year, as he returned from his trip to Harrisburg, Don Domingo was calculating his chances of success. He could depend upon the province of Salta. Posse, his closest friend, could carry Tucumán for him. His supporters were disappearing in San Juan. Some influential leaders in Mendoza, backed by General Arrendondo, would be behind him. Vélez could control Córdoba. The big question mark was Buenos Aires and the attitude of Mitre.

President Mitre expressed his preferences from his headquarters in Tuyucué in Paraguay. In an open letter to Dr. José M. Gutiérrez, he made observations about the principal candidates. He discarded Urquiza and Alsina, and advised his adherents to back Elizalde or Sarmiento. He made certain reservations in regard to the latter, and it soon became obvious to Don Domingo's supporters that official support would go to the minister of foreign affairs.

Early in 1868, the situation broke wide open. President Mitre had been away from Buenos Aires at the front of the Paraguayan War for several years, and the powers of the presidency had been in the hands of the vice-president, Marcos Paz. In January, Paz died suddenly, and Mitre was forced to return to the political scene. On January 11, Sarmiento had been elected by the legislature of San Juan to the national senate. After the death of Paz, Mitre's cabinet, as a matter of course, offered its resignation. In an unexpected move Mitre accepted the resignation. He completely reorganized his government, reappointing Costa and Elizalde, but naming Domingo Sarmiento to the post of minister of the interior. Whether this was intended to put Sarmiento's candidacy on an even footing with that of Elizalde or, as the Sarmientistas believed, to embarrass the position of the Argentine minister to the United States, is not known. Mitre himself, in a private letter to his representative, protested the former motive. "For my own honor and for your honor I have been faced with the thankless necessity of proving that I have been serious, sincere, and friendly towards you."[44] Don Domingo, however, turned down the appointment.

At the beginning of 1868, it became increasingly clear that no one candidate would be able to win a majority. The leaders began to look around for combinations. For a while there was talk of cooperation between Elizalde and Urquiza, but neither wanted to play second fiddle to the other, and such a chance fell through.[45] Meanwhile, Sarmiento was gathering new strength in the provinces. Both Urquiza and Elizalde were feared, for they renewed memories of the old struggles between Buenos Aires and the confederation. General Emilio Mitre and Colonel Mansilla both carried large sections of the army in support of Sarmiento. General Arrendondo, another officer sympathetic to Don Domingo, had gained control in La Rioja.

Argentina had changed greatly since the early years of its existence. It was no longer controlled by the wild hordes of the pampas. Buenos Aires had grown into a large city whose power overshadowed the rest of the nation. The pampas had to a large extent been tamed and brought under the private ownership of powerful landowners. It was to the interest of the growing bourgeoisie of Buenos Aires and of the strong land-owning class of the interior to secure a peaceful settlement to the political squabbles of the country and insure a chance for the tranquil development of their respective interests.

Sarmiento represented the end of factional strife for these two powerful interests in Argentina. He opposed the provincialism and the caudillism of Urquiza as well as the narrow porteño aims of Elizalde. He represented the bourgeois way of thinking that would bring orderly and efficient government, material progress, and education for the nation. Sarmiento thought in a manner that was typical of the bourgeoisie of the nineteenth century. His outlook on history exemplified well this fact. His concept of the struggle between the progress and civilization of the city and the backwardness

[44] Mitre-Sarmiento, Buenos Aires, June 11, 1868; Unpublished Archives of Museo Histórico Sarmiento, Carpeta Mitre-Sarmiento.

[45] See article by Elizalde in *La Nación*, Buenos Aires, January 13, 1870.

and barbarity of the country appealed to the bourgeois mind. His respect for the moderates in the French Revolution and his distrust of the radicals and troublemakers such as Robespierre showed the landowners and the merchants alike that Sarmiento's attitude was closely akin to their own.

When the Club Libertad met in February to choose its candidate, both Alsina and Sarmiento held a great deal of strength. Their only weakness was the opposition of the government. The distrust of Alsina in the provinces hurt his chances considerably. As the Club Libertad met, Rufino Varela and Mansilla nominated Domingo Sarmiento. Alsina was proposed by Pastor Obligado. Then, the solution was offered. The long-awaited combination was found: Sarmiento for president; Alsina for vice-president. The formula was welcomed and approved.

In the United States, news of these events was arriving slowly and spasmodically. In May 1868 Don Domingo was pessimistic about his chances.[46] If he was elected, he wanted it to be by popular choice so that he would be free from ties and have the power "to *govern* and effect the ideas that I have emitted for thirty years."[47]

In June 1868 Sarmiento traveled west across the United States for the last time. He had been invited by Dr. Erastus Otis Haven, president of the University of Michigan, to attend the commencement exercises at that institution. Don Domingo took Bartolito Mitre along as his interpreter and adviser and they traveled across the mid-western states to Ann Arbor.

In later years, Bartolito looked back with pleasure upon the scene. "Ann Arbor! I still remember with pleasure its streets shaded by luxuriant trees, its houses surrounded by woods and gardens, with wide sidewalks to the street, its beautiful homes, models of tidiness and comfort—all of these things that contribute to making agreeable that very vast region of the American northwest. . . ."[48]

[46] Sarmiento-Mary Mann, New York, May 9, 1868; Photostatic copy in Museo Histórico Sarmiento.

[47] Sarmiento to Posse, New York, September 20, 1867.

[48] Edmundo Correas, "Michigan, la universidad de Sarmiento," *Los Andes*, Mendoza, 1945, February 11, 1945.

The morning of June 24th was sunny and bright. It was a day of activity for a college town at graduation time. Sarmiento paced the floor of his room. He wore his black gown which accentuated the size of his head and the large features of his face. He was nervous at this first attendance at a university graduation. He had always dreamed of a college education. It had been one of his unattainable ideals. At nine in the morning the voice of Bartolito called him. They must start for the university.

Don Domingo did not know it, but the day before the Board of Regents had voted him a degree of doctor *honoris causa.*[49] The Methodist-Episcopal Church of Ann Arbor had been chosen for the site of the commencement. Just before ten o'clock, President Haven entered. On his left was Sarmiento, and just beyond him was Bartolito. Also present were Professor Newton of Yale, Dr. Newman of New Orleans, Dr. May of Cincinnati, and Major General Pope. A soft light filtered in through the stained-glass windows. Don Domingo noticed the pretty girls in the audience of 1,500. At exactly ten o'clock the ceremony began. "Hail Columbia" was played by the military band of the 43rd Regiment. Twelve speeches were delivered, and then Dr. Haven arose to present the degree personally. Don Domingo and Bartolito were beginning to weary of the long ceremony. Lines of students received their diplomas. Sarmiento and his secretary began to whisper in Spanish. Then, with one last diploma on the table, the president called out in a loud voice, "Domingo Faustino Sarmiento." He spoke of the minister as a great schoolteacher who had devoted his life to the cause of education. He asked the entire audience to stand in his honor.[50]

Don Domingo was as surprised as he was moved. With eyes

[49] The Regents' Proceedings for June 23, 1868 read: "On motion of Regent Gilbert, the degree of Doctor of Law was conferred on Domingo F. Sarmiento, Envoy Extraordinary and Minister Plenipotentiary from the Argentine Republic." I would like to take this opportunity to thank Mr. Herbert G. Watkins, Secretary and Assistant Vice-President of the University of Michigan, for his aid in securing this information.

[50] See *The Michigan Argus,* June 23, June 24, 1868. See also Irving A. Leonard, "Sarmiento's visits to North America. A famous Argentine in the United States of the 1840's," in the *Michigan Alumnus Quarterly Review,* Vol. 49, July 24, 1943, No. 24, p. 324-330.

moist with tears, he leaned over to Bartolito. He wanted him to give the reply for him. He began to whisper excitedly into his secretary's ear what he wanted him to say. He was too confused to realize that Bartolito could not possibly remember it all.

The audience watched as the old man poured paragraph after paragraph into the ear of the young man beside him. Spanish, which few could understand, was rolled off in volumes, as the audience sat in amazement. At first, the public was confused. They could see the secretary objecting, trying to get away to say a few words. Then, the audience was uneasy. The old man was too carried away with emotion to realize what he was doing. Finally, the heart of the audience was won over by the sincerity and humanity of Don Domingo. Bartolito finally got away, advanced to the front of the platform, and repeated as best he could the words of the minister. The audience burst out in spontaneous applause.[51]

After the ceremony, Sarmiento retraced his steps along the long road back to New York. He passed many places that were now familiar to him. He was conscious that he was leaving for the last time this country that he loved so well. On July 23, 1868, he embarked on the steamship *Merrimac* for Buenos Aires. He still had not heard the results of the elections. He was pessimistic about his chances. But he was determined that, if elected, he would be beholden to nobody, that he would be free to transform his nation to fit the pattern of ideas that he had conceived over his long years of study, travel, and struggle.

[51] Edmundo Correas, "El doctor de Michigan," *Los Andes*, Mendoza, 1945, February 18, 1945.

Chapter 35. The President: a Program

On August 16, 1868, the National Congress declared Domingo Faustino Sarmiento President of the Republic of Argentina. He had received the votes of seventy-nine out of one hundred and thirty-one electors who voted.[1] Captain Richard F. Burton was present when the announcement of the results was made, and he described for posterity the reaction. "Rockets were being fired, *vivas* rang, and bells pealed; there changed hands in the 'camp' sheep and cows, and in the city hats and boxes of cigars, and the public expressed its great joy at the defeat of D. Rufino Elizalde, the chosen candidate and nominee of ex-President Mitre."[2]

Don Domingo knew nothing of all this, however. He was at sea, and his voyage from New York to Río de Janeiro was a memorable one for the aging patriot. It was a punctuation mark in his existence, and he was seized by that peaceful feeling of a man who has completed a task. As a result, he spent aboard the *Merrimac* some of the happiest days of his life. He described them in intimate detail in personal letters to Aurelia Vélez, the daughter of his close friend, Dalmacio Vélez Sarsfield. Don Domingo and Aurelia had been in love some eight years before in Buenos Aires. Their relationship was probably an important factor in the destruction of both of their homes, and when its full implication became obvious, they stoically resolved to break it off and remain on a plane of platonic friendship. Since that time they had carried on a close correspondence, reliving on paper their experiences.[3]

[1] There was a total of 156 electoral votes in the nation, but 25 were not cast. A few days prior to the counting, the Chamber of Deputies ruled that the election would be decided in favor of that man who received a majority of votes cast rather than a majority of the possible votes. As it turned out, this decision was not necessary for Sarmiento's 79 gave him a majority of the 156 total.

[2] Capt. R. F. Burton, *op.cit.*, p. 163.

[3] Rojas, p. 493.

"Farewell to the United States! I carry them with me as a memory and as a model. They are the Hudson River, Staten Island, Niagara Falls, and Chicago, as Nature. They are Mrs. Mann, Davidson, Emerson, Longfellow, and so many other noble characters, as human beings. The republic as an institution. The future of the world as a promise. Farewell! Farewell! Farewell!"[4]

The next day the ship was out of sight of land. The past was behind Don Domingo, and the future was not yet in sight. There was only the vastness of the waters and the warm breezes of the North Atlantic in summer. "I feel myself come to life. Now the horizon widens! Aboard ship, on a limitless sea, one ceases to be an individual, a people, the human race. In my home, on land, I am a planet. Here, God, the sea, thought."[5]

"The 25th—The devil pulled back the blanket. A strong wind on the bow; a fierce sea; waves athwart the ship and the steamer dancing and bouncing. It is the only bad habit that is carried over from the sailing ship. The passengers have disappeared. The women have been wiped out. There are only two or three of us Robinsons on this desert island. From time to time, from here and from there, escape the groans of those anguished souls. Purgatory. . . .

"The 27th—Blue sea of milk! Immense, serene plain. The wind blows hard enough to swell the sails.

"Happiness animates the faces again. I finally saw a woman. I am on a planet. Even the exactness of the movements of the steamer is planetary."

Then an interruption of this spiritual limbo. "I remembered my land today, and the thought of political matters and my future came back to me. I am sorry . . . I was so content to watch the waves, the clouds, the sunsets; yesterday's was glorious: a background of fire, cirrus clouds, mounted on two gates with golden crests. A rock of clouds was alone in front

[4] *Anthology*, p. 287.

[5] *Diario del Merrimac*. This manuscript diary is at present in the Museo Histórico Sarmiento. It was not intended for publication, so its contents reveal some particularly intimate aspects of Sarmiento's feelings and thoughts at this time. The following passages were found in that document.

of the sun, and it covered half of it as it set, so that it looked like a new moon. The sunsets are my loves. . . .

"The politics from over there return to me, like something indigestible. I arrive . . . great victories! I govern admirably one month, two . . . I present certain projects of law, and then the *fiesta* begins. A newspaper suggests an objection, the committee an amendment. Another project. . . . This Sarmiento, so imprudent; he does not take into consideration. . . ! This is the law . . . I can nourish myself on the spectacle of all of South America. Mexico in an orgy of banditry and civil war—Venezuela passing through our horrible year '40—Bolivia. . . ! Perú, bad of race, of antecedents, of impotence. . . .

"Are the waves green, black, blue? Problems to resolve in hours of contemplation, in years of traveling. But here on the high seas, beside the propeller of the steamship, there is discovered beneath the rising spray a seam, an abyss of sea blue, of cobalt blue, of a blue that is never seen anywhere else. It is an abyss of blue that covers the snowy foam that escapes from the propeller."

The sea voyage was a restful interlude for Don Domingo, an escape from pressing thought and action. Then on August 17th, the *Merrimac* entered the harbor of Bahia in Brazil. It passed near the United States frigate, *Warrior*, and the ship's band greeted it with a chorus of "Hail Columbia," and the guns of the ship sounded a salute of twenty-one guns. Domingo Sarmiento knew that he had been elected the next president of Argentina.

On the 19th, the *Merrimac* put into Río de Janeiro harbor. Here Don Domingo was transferred to the *Aunis*, which had been sent to meet him. He remained a few days in the Brazilian capital. The Argentine minister, Torrent, took him to call on the Emperor. The president-elect assured Don Pedro that the reports in the Montevideo newspaper, *El Siglo*, that he favored a separate peace with Paraguay were untrue. The Brazilian ruler's mind was put at ease, and he received his distinguished visitor with the same cordiality that he had shown him two decades before. Don Domingo asked to be called early in the morning so that he could once again visit the famous botanical gardens. For the second time he was thrilled by their tropical splendor and their scientific completeness. On the 23rd, Don Domingo departed from Río aboard the *Aunis* and headed directly for the River Plate.

The last lap of the journey from New York to Buenos Aires was not as pleasant and carefree as had been the first. Sarmiento's future had been decided for him by the Argentine electorate and he had to map his course along the lines that were specified. As he thought about his position, he realized that he was entering office under the best possible conditions. He remained uncommitted to anybody. When Colonel Lucio V. Mansilla had written him in New York the previous year asking for a program, he had tied himself down to nothing specific. "My program is in the atmosphere, in twenty years of life, actions, and writings: that is what is wanted; that is what it will be."[6] He had wanted to take office with no commitments and with a mandate from the people. If the government had not supported him, if he had not even been in the country to further his own candidacy, he must have been the choice of the people. It seemed that his conditions had been fully satisfied. As he planned his future aboard the *Aunis*, Domingo assured himself that he would be able to proceed with a free hand in putting into effect his program, the program that had been the basis of his life for many years.

Upon his arrival in Buenos Aires at the end of August, there was a popular demonstration at the docks. The crowds shouted as he appeared on deck. "Long live Sarmiento! Long live the homeland!" A lump caught in the old man's throat as he looked down upon the people. This seemed to be a reward for his efforts. "Educate the people," he had said, "and they will never elect a Rosas." Perhaps his prophecy had already begun to be realized. The next day he received another demonstration in his own house. This time it was the teachers and the students of the Buenos Aires school who came to greet him and cheer him, and again he was touched by the gesture and reassured that he held the support of the people and therefore their mandate to act.

Buenos Aires had grown a great deal in the seven years that Sarmiento had been absent. It had spread out many blocks in

[6] *Obras,* XLIX, 267.

every direction. Its life had taken on new color and new brilliance. The Colón Opera House was showing such works as "Mary Stuart" and "Francesca di Rimini." The youth of the city were seen more often, however, at the Alcázar, where French operettas and music-hall reviews were delighting the young gallants and worrying their more conservative parents. The writers of the city were beginning to produce important works once again. Gutiérrez's *Poetry,* Bilbao's *History of Rosas,* and Grimke's *The Nature and Tendency of Free Institutions* were on sale at the leading bookstores. Such periodicals as *La revista de Buenos Aires, La revista del archivo general,* and *Revista Argentina* represented the best in literary and historical journalism. There were eighteen newspapers in the city, Vélez Sarsfield's *El Nacional,* the Varela brothers' *La Tribuna,* and *La Patria,* being the most important ones to back the Sarmiento government.

The center of the city was very much as it had been. There was the government house on the corner of Bolívar and Moreno Streets, looking out over the harbor. Then there were the customs house and the imposing Congress. The Helvética Bar was on the corner of San Martin and Corrientes, where it can still be found over seventy-five years later. The colonial aspects of the city remained intact. Black and mulatto washerwomen washed and dried their clothes along the riverfront. The fishermen rode out into the river on horseback to set and take in their nets. And along the road that paralleled the river, the district was tough and dangerous. There were *boliches* frequented by sailors, loafers, and the underworld of the city. The police patrolled this area on horse rather than on foot.[7]

It gave Sarmiento a new sense of power and importance to wander through the streets of this growing city and to know that it was *his* capital. He had never before been particularly fond of Buenos Aires. San Juan had always been his home. But now he felt a possessiveness in regard to the city, a possessiveness that could not be denied.

[7] See Alfonso de Laferrere, "Nuesto país al aparecer 'La Nación' " and Manuel Mujica Láinez, "Fisionomía de Buenos Aires a lo largo de tres cuartos de siglo," both in *La Nación,* January 4, 1945.

On October 12th, Sarmiento was inaugurated president of Argentina. Prior to that date, he had begun to answer the big question in everyone's mind. What will your program be? When the schoolchildren came to pay homage at his home, he stepped out to speak to them, and he began to outline his projects. He promised to educate the people of Argentina. He would educate them in order to prepare them for democracy. "We are going to constitute a pure democracy," he declared, "and for that we cannot count on only the teachers but we must count on the entire youth that will form a generation to help me in my task. It is necessary to make the poor gaucho into a useful man in society. For that purpose we must make the entire Republic into a school."[8] This was the first plank in his platform: education and more education. This was nothing new for Don Domingo. Someone asked, "What will Sarmiento bring us from the United States? Schools, what else can he bring us?"[9]

But this was not all. A few weeks later Sarmiento was invited to speak in the town of Chivilcoy. This was the thriving agricultural center that was the product of his work in the senate several years before. It was the result of his land colonization, distribution, and cultivation plans; and it had been a great success. Here was the model for another plank in his platform. "But if success crowns my efforts, Chivilcoy will have an immense part in it, for it has been the pioneer that tried out with the best will the new land law and that has demonstrated in ten years that the pampa is not, as they would have us believe, condemned exclusively to giving pasture to animals, but in a few years, here as in the entire Argentine territory, it will be the seat of free, industrious, and happy peoples."[10] "I say then, to all of the Republic, that Chivilcoy is the program of President Don Domingo Faustino Sarmiento."[11]

Nor was this all. The school was to make the gaucho into a better citizen. Chivilcoy was to make the gaucho into a more productive citizen. It was all part of the overall program that had been forming in Sarmiento's mind over the past thirty years. He was going to make his nation fit into the pattern of

[8] *Obras,* XLIX, 276. [9] *Ibid.,* XXI, 244. [10] *Ibid.,* 263. [11] *Ibid.,* 266.

Sarmiento as governor of San Juan in 1862

Sarmiento as president of Argentina, 1868-1874

rational social behavior that he had conceived. It did not fit now, but with changes it would. If the people's minds were improved through education, if the people's economic life were rationalized, if the political life were brought under the constitutional forms, if more rational races were brought in through a more liberal immigration policy—if all this happened, the gaucho would be transformed—he would be rationalized; and Argentina would be fitted into the pattern in which its leader believed. Sarmiento was now in a position to make the changes he thought necessary. This was his program, and his dream. This was the intention of the president.

"Don Domingo has a stiff task before him. He has campaigned, but he is rather a civilian than a soldier. The later rule of Spain has familiarized, I have said, generations to the sway of generals, not doctors, and his only bourgeois predecessor, Dr. Derqui, lasted about a year. He is pledged by the promises of all his career to make sacrifices in the cause of the extended popular education. . . . He must honorably terminate the present state of things, and devote to European immigration the energies and expenditures lavished upon a disastrous war. He must reform his fleet, create an army, and repress the wild Indians."[12]

Sarmiento initiated a period of bourgeois domination in Argentina. His presidency marks the advent of the middle and landowning classes as the pivot of power in the nation. The age of the gaucho had ended; the age of the merchant and the cattleman had begun. The aim of this group was stability, order, and material progress. The program that Sarmiento offered to them fulfilled this bill. He had only to overcome the last vestiges of the old order to put his program into operation.

Don Domingo saw three general categories of opposition to the completion of his program. The first was the still present caudillo opposition. General Urquiza controlled most of the

[12] Captain Richard F. Burton, *op.cit.*, pp. 164-165; Sarmiento possessed a copy of this book, dedicated to "His Excellency Don Domingo Faustino Sarmiento, citizen of the United Provinces of the Rio de la Plata, alias the Argentine Republic, by one who admires his honesty of purpose and the homage which he pays to progress."

northeastern portion of the nation. The Taboada brothers controlled a part of the northwest. He knew that others would arise during his term of office, other Facundos, other Chachos. Secondly, he saw the material difficulties in the way of his administration. His nation was poor, its resources drained by war. As during his governorship of San Juan, it would be difficult to finance his reforms. Finally, his nation was embroiled in foreign disputes. The Paraguayan War was still raging. Weakened by this, Argentina was at the mercy of any aggressive designs on the part of her neighboring nation. The spirit of nineteenth-century nationalism was beginning to make itself obvious in the Spanish American nations, and with it came the dangers of conflict.

To overcome these sources of opposition, President Sarmiento needed a strong government. He chose his cabinet carefully and with an eye to the problems that it would have to face. Dalmacio Vélez Sarsfield was given the position of minister of the interior. He was the most distinguished jurist and constitutionalist that Argentina had yet produced. He would be a valuable instrument in the strengthening of the nomocratic forms. Nicolás Avellaneda was made minister of justice and public education. This young man was second only to the president himself in his enthusiasm for public education and its results, and he could be counted upon to carry forward with the utmost zeal Sarmiento's pedagogical program.[13] José Benjamín Gorostiaga, the minister of finance, Mariano Varela, the minister of foreign affairs, and Colonel Martín de Gainza, the minister of war and the navy, were all men well-suited for the roles that they would have to fulfill.

In the formation of Sarmiento's government, two unpleasant incidents occurred, however. His old supporter, and the original sponsor of his candidacy, Colonel Lucio V. Mansilla, asked the new president for the ministry of war.

"You, a minister! Sir, we need a very discreet and very calm minister to restrain me. They call us insane; they apply this

[13] See *Páginas de Avellaneda sobre educación*, Buenos Aires, 1937; Ministerio de Justicia e Instrucción Pública, *Páginas de Avellaneda sobre educación*, Buenos Aires, 1935; and Ministerio de Justicia e Instrucción Pública, *Pensamientos de Avellaneda*, Buenos Aires, 1937.

to you less than to me, perhaps because you have not yet deserved it as well. Together we would be unbearable."[14]

Instead, Sarmiento went to his old friend and former companion in arms, Bartolomé Mitre, and asked him to stay on as commander-in-chief of the allied armies in Paraguay and at the same time accept the ministry of war. The ex-president turned down both of these offers, and Don Domingo had to turn to Colonel Gainza to fill the post. These two incidents with Mansilla and Mitre were signs of the beginning of serious opposition. The president's treatment of his former supporter demonstrated his feeling that he had no commitments to anybody, that his actions were free, but the manner in which he handled the situation revealed the tactlessness that was to win him so many enemies during his presidency. Mitre's refusal to enter his government, even on the patriotic premise of winning the Paraguayan War, was an indication of a new attitude toward his former friend, an attitude which would soon become the focal point of the most ardent parliamentary opposition.

During the six years that Domingo Sarmiento was president of the Argentine Republic, he was successful in overcoming all of the principal sources of trouble that he had foreseen at the beginning of his administration. It was not an easy job. It took up much of his time and much of his energy. But it was completed satisfactorily. The old provincial caudillism was overcome. The material difficulties were gradually surmounted. The foreign problems were solved.

Soon after his return from the United States, Don Domingo had written to his old friend, José Posse, and expressed to him his fears of provincial opposition. Here was the home of the caudillism that he had always fought. Here was the seat of the barbarism which he sought to overcome. "Buenos Aires, the Buenos Aires that you think forms public opinion, is with me. The provincials which you will see in the majority are those who support all that might undermine the nation."[15] Imme-

[14] Belín Sarmiento, *Sarmiento anecdótico, op.cit.*, pp. 177-178.

[15] Sarmiento to Posse, Buenos Aires, August 20, 1869; Carpeta Sarmiento-Posse.

diately upon coming to power, he set out to conquer the provincial caudillism.

The Taboada brothers had controlled the province of Santiago del Estero for many years. Their influence extended throughout the northwest sector of the nation, affecting the provinces of Tucumán, Catamarca, Salta, and Jujuy. As long as they held power and as long as they maintained a hostile attitude towards Sarmiento, the activities of the administration would be greatly limited in an entire section of the country. Don Domingo tried first to overcome this center of caudillo power with conciliatory methods. He sent his old companion in exile, Régulo Martínez, as his special envoy to talk with and attempt to win over the Taboadas. This was, however, to no avail; and Sarmiento found it necessary to take stronger measures. He established an army corps under Colonel Ignacio Rivas in Tucumán to keep an eye on the caudillos' activities, and he dispatched a corps of cavalry under Major Julio Argentino Roca to Salta, where the Taboada forces were making trouble for the provincial governor. It was his capable performance in this assignment that first brought the future president, Roca, into the public eye of his nation.[16]

It was not, however, the Taboadas whom Sarmiento most feared as a source of personalist opposition to his government. The obvious center of provincial power, the man who, in the mind of Don Domingo, stood for the last remnants of caudillism was the governor of Entre Ríos, General Urquiza. While still aboard the *Merrimac*, Sarmiento had written in his diary that upon hearing of his electoral victory his blood froze at the thought of Urquiza. The caudillo had been defeated at the polls, but he still maintained a heavily armed private army and could count on extensive popular support.[17]

The new president's estimate of the victor of Caseros proved to be very faulty, however. Of all the early leaders of provincial politics, Urquiza was probably the least hostile to constitutional government, the most disinterested in personal gain, and the closest to the ideals and aims of Sarmiento. He

[16] *Obras*, LI, 378ff.

[17] *Obras*, XLIX, 322.

had made his province of Entre Ríos the center of public education and even advanced education in the interior. He had made it the most prosperous and modern sector outside of Buenos Aires. He had fought tirelessly for the unification of his nation and its foundation on a constitution. He had shown none of the traits of brutality and irresponsibility that had characterized men like Facundo and El Chacho. He had gracefully stepped out of power at the end of his presidential term and had with equal grace withdrawn from Pavón when there seemed to be no other way to achieve national unity. His differences with Sarmiento had arisen, as we have seen, from the inability of each man to see the virtues of the other, and the clashing of two nascent ambitions.

Upon the election of Don Domingo to the presidency, these conditions had changed. The new chief executive was anxious to win the support of his former adversary in a peaceful manner if possible and General Urquiza, now old and past the peak of his glories, wanted to contribute what he could to the harmony and unity of his nation.

General Urquiza made the first move. He wrote the new president a cordial letter of congratulation at his elevation to his high post. "Your Excellency can count on me as first among the servants of the nation who desires the opportunity to demonstrate his sincerity during your administration. If some resentment has put us in opposing ranks, the sole memory of having fought together for liberty beneath the shadow of the same flag and the interest that both of us have in the greatness and fortune of our homeland will unite us closely today, each in his own position, to seek what nobody has achieved, the destruction of partisanship, and reconstruction of one basis, that of the constitution. You at the head of the nation and I as governor of a rich, strong, and moralized province are in a position to realize that aspiration."[18]

Sarmiento was at first wary of Urquiza's true motives. He had opposed the old leader too long to be easily convinced of

[18] Urquiza-Sarmiento, San José, October 29, 1868; in Unpublished Archives of Museo Palacio San José in Entre Ríos. See also Enrique Moulía, "Las cartas de Urquiza a Sarmiento," *Aquí Está*, Buenos Aires, 1947, XII, April 14, 1947, pp. 20-21.

his sincerity. "My reply," he wrote to Mrs. Mann, "was as circumspect as was demanded by the liberty of action which I wished to reserve to myself. I said to him that the president of the Republic expected that he as well as others should accept the popular election, but that I could not, without compromising the dignity of the government, give my assurances or enter into any explanations of my policy."[19] This must have been an exasperating reply for Urquiza, but he merely bided his time, awaiting an opportunity to demonstrate his sincerity.

In 1869 this occasion presented itself. A revolution broke out in Corrientes. It threatened to prove serious, and the president feared that it would bring general disorder to the provinces. Colonel Mansilla called upon him and urged that he seek the aid of General Urquiza. "As the hero of Caseros and the author of the Constitution, nobody has as much interest as he in saving the institutions, and nobody has more power to arrest the pressure of Mitre and Mitrism."[20] Don Domingo was difficult to convince, but he finally agreed to send Vélez Sarsfield to talk with the governor of Entre Ríos. The minister of the interior found Urquiza very cordial and most anxious to cooperate to avoid a civil war. The meeting was a great success, and Dr. Vélez returned to Buenos Aires bearing friendly letters from the governor and a gift of a *robe de chambre* and a sleeping cap for the president.

From that time on there began a sincere friendship between the two former rivals. A correspondence was carried on in the most cordial terms.

Sarmiento came to see for the first time that he and Urquiza had a common aim and a common ideal, even though they had different ideas as to the means of achieving these. "You and I," he wrote, "approached along different roads the problem of forming a nation out of the disunited elements that thirty years of civil war had left. I think that I can say without offending you that you were the incarnation of the

[19] Sarmiento-Mary Mann, Buenos Aires, September 2, 1868; photostatic copy of original in Museo Histórico Sarmiento.

[20] Enrique Moulía, "El gorro de dormir de Sarmiento," *Atlántida*, Buenos Aires, 1947, XXX, April 1947, p. 38.

nation as it had been constituted by historical facts; at the same time I do not think it daring for me to say that I was its incarnation as the program of what it should be in order to enter into the regular conditions necessary to a civilized people.

"These two forces, the real and the possible, were bound to clash, and they did clash, until each one modified itself to conform to these absolute elements of each idea. We are finally in agreement, and if you attribute any importance to this judgment, you will believe that I sincerely count today on your support in order that we might constitute a republic in such a manner that our names, if they so deserve, will descend together to posterity. . . ."[21]

Don Domingo was always grateful and filled with admiration for the selfless attitude assumed by General Urquiza, and the Entrerian became his most powerful and also his most reliable support in the interior.[22]

Don Domingo summarized the entire matter to Mary Mann: "I found civil war in Corrientes threatening to bring on a conflict with Urquiza. You know my antecedent relations with that personage. He initiated a reconciliation in a direct way, and by direct agencies, and by means of decided cooperation I was able to bring the civil war to a close, disbanding the two bands in arms by a simple presidential order which sent them all to their homes. . . . This has given immense prestige to the government."[23]

On February 3, 1870, the president of the Republic made a visit to the governor of Entre Ríos at the latter's palace at San José. This move was intended to symbolize the national unity and the end of enmity between the two leaders. Don Domingo was received by four days of *fiestas* and the dances

[21] Sarmiento to General Justo José de Urquiza, July 17, 1869, Archivo General de la Nación, Division Nacional, Sección Gobierno, Archivo del General Justo José de Urquiza, Legajo 67.

[22] Letter from Urquiza to Sarmiento, San José, June 24, 1869, is among the many that exist among the Unpublished Archives of the Palacio San José and make up one side of this correspondence. Copies of many of Sarmiento's letters are to be found in Volume L of the *Obras*.

[23] Sarmiento-Mary Mann, Buenos Aires, November 12, 1868; Photostatic copies at Museo Histórico Sarmiento.

of which Urquiza was so fond. The Entrerian troops were formed in front of the palace for the president to review. They offered him their complete and loyal support. "Now I feel like a president," said Sarmiento.[24]

Chapter 36. The President: the Difficult Years

UNFORTUNATELY, this marriage of provincial and national governments, which promised to put an end to the most important threat of caudillism during Sarmiento's period of government, was brought to a sudden end by the assassination of Urquiza. The old leader's adherence to the new policy of national cooperation seemed to be an act of betrayal to many. He had been in power long, made many enemies, and excited many jealousies. On the afternoon of April 11, 1870, Ricardo López Jordán, a young officer who had been brought up under the tutelage and the protection of his old leader, led a revolt against the governor. The San José palace was invaded by a band of cutthroats, and Urquiza and his entire family were murdered.

The news electrified the nation. The president was infuriated. A meeting of the cabinet was called, and all of the distinguished patriots, supporters or opposers of the government were called to the government house. Bartolomé Mitre, Adolfo Alsina, Manuel Quintana, José Mármol, Carlos Tejedor, and many others were present. All were agreed that the act must be punished, that López Jordán must be brought to justice.

In a telegram to the commander of the army of observation

[24] Rojas, p. 539.

in Entre Ríos, Sarmiento said: "Urquiza assassinated in San José. His sons assassinated. Should the government ignore these acts and approve of such crimes? No! I shall descend from the position that I occupy if I cannot proclaim before the world that I cannot ignore anything. We have been in a four-hour session with our cabinet, and we have taken our decision."[1]

A proclamation was issued by the president:

"Compatriots:

"The national government has just been informed of an act sufficiently odious to cover the entire nation with shame.

"In the silence of night, in the bosom of his family, General Urquiza, governor of Entre Ríos, was assaulted and killed.

"Entrerians—Liberty does not use as an instrument the dagger.

"All Entrerians who are honorable, who are not in their hearts assassins, separate from those who have committed the crime.

"The national government will be among you with all of its power to keep the evil from growing worse. Put yourselves at the orders of the commander of the national forces; and days of calm and security will be your reward.

"Do not listen to the suggestions of obscure and ignorant ambitions, for whom hatred is a principle, crime a means.

"The peace of the Republic before all. Our glory and our interests demand it. Thus it is expected, thus it is ordered by your president.

D. F. Sarmiento."[2]

But the revolt soon had ramifications that Don Domingo had not expected. It spread to Corrientes and Santa Fé. Three days after the assassination, López Jordán was named by the provincial legislature as governor of Entre Ríos. President Sarmiento took immediate and energetic action. He declared Entre Ríos in a state of siege. He mobilized the militia of that province, Corrientes, Santa Fé, and Buenos Aires. He gave General Arrendondo command of the campaign, and he himself followed much of it in the field.

For five months there was comparatively little action. The

[1] *Obras*, L, 330.

[2] *Ibid.*, p. 324.

national armies pursued the rebels, but they did not seem to be able to come to any decisive action. By July, Sarmiento had 15,000 men in the field. In August, the United States minister in Buenos Aires, Robert C. Kirk, reported that "there has been no progress made by the national government in suppressing the rebellion in Entre Ríos, and it looks to me as if it is going to be very formidable, and will tax the best energies of the government to overcome it. Upon the success of the Argentine army," he added, "depends the usefulness of Sarmiento's administration."[3] A month later, there was still no progress.[4] Then, on October 12, 1870, the army of General Ignacio Rivas forced the rebels into the decisive Battle of Santa Rosa, which ended in López Jordán's complete defeat. In December, the rebel leader tried to negotiate a peace, but all attempts were turned down by the president.[5] It was too late for compromise. On January 26, 1871, the militia of Corrientes under Governor Bibiene defeated the remnants of the rebel army at Naembe, and the caudillo leader escaped across the border into the province of Rio Grande in Brazil.

This ended temporarily the opposition of personalist caudillism to Sarmiento's program of governmental action, but López Jordán was still alive, and he was still a threat to the nation. In Brazil and Uruguay, he began once more to gather his forces and to arm them for a return; two years after his first defeat, on May 1, 1873, he once more invaded the province of Entre Ríos. This time the revolt was even more threatening than before.[6] A large portion of the province was overrun and devastated, and many of the local and provincial officials adhered to the rebellion.

The national government had been forewarned of the plot,

[3] Kirk to Hamilton Fish, Buenos Aires, August 13, 1870; National Archives, State Department Division, Despatches, Argentine Republic, Volume XVIII, No. 64.

[4] *Ibid.*, September 13, 1870, No. 68. [5] *Ibid.*, December 14, 1870, No. 75.

[6] Julius White, the newly appointed United States minister in Argentina, in the inaccurate and uncomprehending manner which was to become typical of his reports, mentioned the new revolt in a dispatch but held that it was directed against "state rather than federal power" and was "not formidable." Julius White to Hamilton Fish, Buenos Aires, May 14, 1873; National Archives, State Department Division, Despatches, Argentine Republic, Volume XIX, No. 10.

and President Sarmiento immediately went into action. Again he declared the intervention of Entre Ríos. The congress approved this move and extended it to Santa Fé, where more trouble was brewing. Don Domingo suggested a reward of 100,000 pesos for the apprehension of the rebel leader, but this project was turned down by the legislative branch of the government. Colonel Gainza, the minister of war, went personally to Entre Ríos to direct operations.

Meanwhile, Sarmiento remained in Buenos Aires, attempting to carry through his governmental program in spite of the conflict in the interior. On the night of August 22, 1873, he was going by carriage from his home to the house of Vélez Sarsfield, when, on the corner of Maipú and Corrientes Streets, there was a sudden explosion that shook his carriage. The driver, fearful of what it might be, speeded along his way; but the president, already quite deaf, did not pay heed to it. The policemen on duty, however, did hear the explosion, and rushing to the scene of the noise they found two men, one with his hand badly injured, the other trying to help him. They were Francisco and Pedro Guerri, two Italians off a merchant ship then in the harbor. While in Montevideo they had been contacted by one Aquiles Sesatrugo, who had offered them 10,000 pesos for the assassination of President Sarmiento. The would-be assassins had never seen Don Domingo, and they had no personal grudge whatsoever against him, but they accepted the proposal and were given instructions as to how to proceed. Whoever it was that outlined the plan for them must have been well-acquainted with the habits and actions of the president, for their trap worked perfectly. They knew when the chief executive would pass, and the Guerri brothers were there awaiting him. One thing went wrong. They stuffed too much powder into the pistol, and it exploded in Francisco's hand, wounding him rather than killing the president. When the bullets were later examined in the police laboratories, it was found that they had been poisoned so that the slightest wound would have caused immediate death.[7]

[7] See Sarmiento's own account of incident in *El Nacional,* November 18, 1879.

That night, the United States minister to Argentina, Julius White, called upon President Sarmiento to congratulate him upon his fortunate escape. Don Domingo blamed the attempt on "anti-progesistas" (anti-progressives). He was sure that the plot had originated with López Jordán. He had been warned that "a meeting of Jordanistas had announced the violent death of the president as a project about to be carried out." The wife of one of the conspirators had let it be known that a Jordanista group in Montevideo was conspiring towards this end. The attempt represented a desperate, and what might have been a successful attempt on the part of the caudillo opposition to do away with the nomocratic president.[8] The Guerri brothers were sent to prison, but the police were never able to implicate any of the more responsible members of the conspiracy.

For the second time, the Entrerian revolt stretched out over a period of many months. In November, Don Domingo grew impatient and went personally to Paraná to direct operations. On December 9th, the caudillo was again forced into a decisive battle by the regular armies of the Republic. Led by Colonel Gainza, the government forces delivered a crushing blow to the rebels at Don Gonzalo. Once more, Ricardo López Jordán was forced to flee the country, this time into Uruguay. Once again, Sarmiento felt that he had rid his nation of the caudillo personalist opposition.

In addition to the caudillist opposition, President Sarmiento was aware upon assuming office that he would be faced with a serious material problem, the problem of a poverty-stricken and war-torn nation. Don Domingo had not, however, expected the large share of bad luck that plagued him during his administration. Nature seemed to have turned against him. No sooner had he entered office than a cholera epidemic, starting with the troops in Paraguay, swept and debilitated the nation. There were no means of defense against this tragedy, and the disease claimed many victims both in Buenos Aires and in the interior.

In 1871, however, Nature dealt an even meaner blow. Without warning, yellow fever struck the city of Buenos

[8] Julius White-Hamilton Fish, September 12, 1873, *op.cit.*, No. 29.

Aires. It, too, originated with the Paraguayan War, being carried by prisoners of war to Corrientes and then spreading to Buenos Aires. The first cases appeared in the San Telmo district of the capital in January, but there was no general alarm until the epidemic had claimed two hundred victims. In February the toll mounted to twenty deaths daily. The weather continued hot. Then the yearly carnival was celebrated. "The carnival was not brilliant, there being members of families who had already fled to the suburbs, but the theatres were, however, crowded."[9] On Ash Wednesday, the death roll had increased even more. A cordon was thrown around the San Telmo district. Fires were lighted in the streets, and carts with tar tried to disinfect them. But it was too late for such measures. On February 22, the first case outside the infected district appeared, and by the end of the month there were forty to fifty casualties per day.

By March the situation was extremely grave. There were 109 deaths in one day. The newspapers minimized the casualties in order to avoid a panic. Schools were closed. The police asked everyone to whitewash their houses. Then panic broke out in the city. The State Department in Washington received an undated communication:

"Yellow Fever in Bs. Ayres has numbered as many as two hundred deaths per day.

"People panic-stricken—

"Messages almost suspended.

"Mail delayed."[10]

The Italian immigrants were blamed for the epidemic. They were ousted from their jobs. They wandered along the streets, homeless; some even died on the pavements, where their bodies often remained for hours. There was a great rush for passages to Europe. The Genoese Company sold 5,200 tickets in a fortnight. "The people are panic-stricken, from thirty to forty thousand have left the city, the streets looked deserted, and of course business is almost suspended."[11] There were 4,800 deaths in March.

[9] T. E. Ash, *The Plague of 1871*, Buenos Aires, 1871, p. 8.

[10] Kirk-Hamilton Fish, *op.cit.*, No. 82.

[11] Kirk-Hamilton Fish, March 11, 1871, *op.cit.*, No. 82.

Then in April came Holy Week. "Gloom and desolation now reigned throughout the city. The streets were silent and deserted, except where a hearse appeared, followed by a solitary coach. From nearly every door a piece of crepe hung, the windows of the houses open, sometimes also the doors, but no signs of life within. The sun shone brightly, but the air was heavy with the odor of Death."[12] On April 10, 540 "tickets" for burial were issued. There were 7,500 deaths in April.

Then in May, the cold weather began to come, and the epidemic eased off. The city had taken on the appearance of a ghost town. "Today the city presents a deserted, desolate appearance, all faces show anxiety and sorrow. It is impossible to portray the true condition of affairs."[13] Don Domingo wrote to answer the worried inquiries of his sister, "Am I alive? You could have told that by the continued hostility of the press. . . . The political and social consequences of the fever are incalculable, and ten years hence we will be feeling them."[14] During the entire period of the plague, Sarmiento had worked tirelessly to defeat it. Sanitation measures were taken. Every effort was made to avert its spreading further. Don Domingo recognized the epidemic not only as a national calamity but as one more obstacle in the way of his projects.

During his entire administration, Sarmiento was faced with the basic problem of his nation's poverty. The need for heavy spending to crush internal disorders, to meet the expenses of the Paraguayan War, and to repair the havoc wrought by the yellow fever accentuated the material-economic obstacles that the president faced. Between 1869 and 1874, the import-export deficit of the nation increased considerably, and the difference between the revenue and the expenditure of the government grew.[15] It became increasingly difficult to finance

[12] Ash, *Plague, op.cit.*, p. 15.

[13] Kirk-Fish, May 12, 1871, *op.cit.*, No. 85.

[14] Sarmiento-Bienvenida, Buenos Aires, May 2, 1871; Carpeta XIII, No. 1767.

[15] The statistics on foreign commerce during this period are as follows (gold pesos):

Year	*Imports*	*Exports*	*Total*
1869	41,195,703	32,449,188	73,644,891
1870	49,124,613	30,423,984	79,347,697

the many projects of which Sarmiento had dreamed, and which were a part of his governmental program.

Don Domingo realized that the only effective way of remedying the financial-economic problem of his nation was by fomenting and stimulating new elements of the economy. Just as he had attempted to develop the mining industry and extend the cultivable lands in San Juan, he looked to new fields of economic endeavor for the nation. Soon after assuming office in 1868 he offered a prize for the person who discovered the best means of conserving fresh meat. He realized that the future economy of the nation could be revolutionized if the country could export the rich resources that it possessed both in cattle and sheep. He offered another prize to anyone who found a coal mine that could be exploited. He had learned during his visits to Pittsburgh what such a discovery would mean to the national economy. Late in 1873 he inaugurated a national bank that he hoped would help put the governmental financial system and monetary system on a sounder basis.

President Sarmiento never solved the economic and material problems that faced him. They were always present to deter his program. But he did try to meet them as they came. He survived the crisis of the plague, and he maintained a sufficiently sound economy to finance the reforms that he felt were necessary.

The third and last type of obstacle that Sarmiento was prepared to face during his presidency were the problems of

---

Year	*Imports*	*Exports*	*Total*
1871	45,629,166	26,996,801	72,695,967
1872	61,585,781	47,267,965	108,853,746
1873	73,434,038	47,398,291	120,832,321
1874	58,826,549	44,541,536	102,368,085

The revenues and expenditures of the government were as follows (in gold pesos):

Year	*Revenue*	*Expenditure*
1869	12,676,680	14,953,431
1870	14,833,904	19,439,976
1871	12,682,155	21,166,230
1872	18,172,380	26,462,786
1873	20,217,232	31,025,070
1874	15,974,042	29,784,096

international relations and frontier questions. The foremost of these was the Paraguayan War, which he inherited from Mitre, along with its high costs and its debilitating effect upon the population and the morale of the nation. The war was not a popular one in the interior, and as it dragged out year after year the unrest that it caused in the provinces was obvious. It was only General Urquiza's firm support that kept the more important provinces in line. In August 1869, the key fortress of Humaitá capitulated to the allies, and the armies of Brazil and Argentina advanced towards the Paraguayan capital. On January 5, Asunción was occupied, and Sarmiento believed the war to have ended.[16] The toll taken of the Paraguayan population was immense. An English doctor who had been in Asunción for fourteen years estimated that out of 500,000 inhabitants before the war, only 80,000 remained.[17] Over 150,000 male adults had perished.

The president's hope that the war was over in 1869 proved, however, to be overoptimistic. Solano López was desperate, but he would not surrender. With 20,000 men, he retreated into the mountains and awaited the onslaught there. Sarmiento hesitated as to whether to follow him. Argentina had already spent 50 million dollars and had 20,000 men in the war. Sarmiento thought seriously of withdrawing his troops from the pursuit.[18] Further thought, however, caused him to reconsider. He did not want the danger of the Paraguayan dictator hanging over his head. He wanted to punish the man whom he considered to be an international criminal. On March 1, 1870, with less than 500 men at his command, Solano López was surrounded by a large allied army at Cerro Cora. There he and most of his followers perished. The Paraguayan War was over but its drain on the human and material resources of Argentina would be felt for a long time to come.

No sooner had the Paraguayan War ended, however, before the victors began to quarrel over the spoils, and a new conflict

[16] Sarmiento-Mary Mann, Buenos Aires, January 12, 1869; Academia Argentina de Letras, *op.cit.*

[17] 221,079 persons were counted by the census of 1871. 28,746 of these were male adults.

[18] Kirk-Hamilton Fish, Buenos Aires, November 12, 1869, *op.cit.*, No. 28.

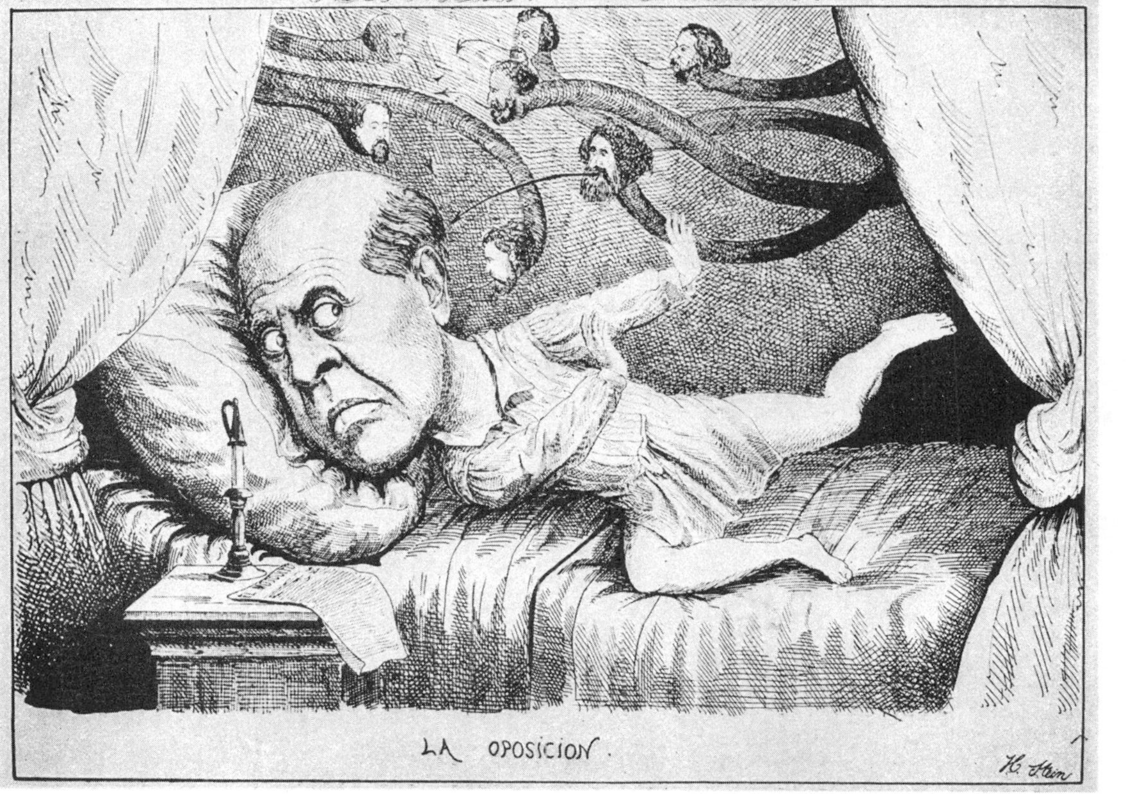

A cartoon of 1869, showing Sarmiento besieged in nightmares by the opposition

An attempt on Sarmiento's life on the night of August 22, 1873

loomed. A preliminary peace treaty was signed, but agreement on a final one was not reached until six years later. The little nation that had just been defeated by allied arms held a very valuable and strategic position between the two largest nations of South America. Both had sought throughout their histories to control it, but each had successfully blocked the encroachment of the other, thus making their rivalry the most effective guarantee of Paraguayan independence. With the termination of the war, Brazil demanded an immense indemnity, one that the United States minister to Buenos Aires, Dexter E. Clapp, described as nothing more than a "mortgage that can be foreclosed at any time." Argentina, on the other hand, laid claim to the southwestern area of Paraguay known as El Chaco. A railroad line was projected through this area to Bolivia, and Argentina wanted to control the territory.[19] Each of the two victor nations opposed the other's claims, and it appeared that war between them was near.[20] As a last resort, President Sarmiento appealed to Bartolomé Mitre to go as special envoy to Río de Janeiro and attempt to settle the problem amicably. Don Domingo was not particularly optimistic about the mission,[21] but Mitre's shrewd handling of the situation was crowned with success, and war between the two nations was averted.

Meanwhile, Argentine relations with her other neighbors were not faring any better. The various nations of South America were being reached for the first time by a wave of extreme nationalism, which was evident throughout western civilization at this time. A nationalistic spirit in the various Hispanic American nations could not help but be an artificial one. With common backgrounds, common heritages, common languages, a common religion, and a common culture, the nations, though they were divided into many small units, had a basic similarity. In an age of nationalism, where there was

[19] Dexter E. Clapp-William Hunter, Buenos Aires, June 12, 1872, National Archives, State Department Division, Despatches, Argentine Republic, Volume XVIII, No. 15.

[20] Sarmiento-Mary Mann, Buenos Aires, February 16, 1872 and May 7, 1872; photostatic copies in Museo Histórico Sarmiento.

[21] Sarmiento-Mary Mann, Buenos Aires, July 17, 1872; photostatic copies at Museo Histórico Sarmiento.

no natural basis for nationalistic spirit, an artificial nationalism was cultivated. Being artificial, it was extreme. School texts praised highly national heroes and condemned the leaders of neighboring nations. National boundary claims were made a point of honor, and national honor was sacred.

In such an atmosphere, and weakened by foreign war and internal strife, Argentina was at the mercy of her neighbors. In Uruguay, revolutionary armies, such as those of López Jordán, were allowed to organize and arm in peace. President Sarmiento protested this fact to the government in Montevideo, and relations between the two countries were cooled to a breaking point.

Chile renewed her claims to the southern portion of the continent. She wished to occupy the territory of Patagonia, and she referred to some of President Sarmiento's own statements during the "straits controversy" with Rosas to back up her claims. Don Domingo was in a very embarrassing position. The congressional opposition in his own country began to refer to his former stand as treacherous and unpatriotic. But the president maintained his position, refused to give in to the Patagonian claims, and as the Chilean government became more and more embroiled in a dispute with Perú and Bolivia in the north, the demands were dropped.

The frontier questions of Argentina at this time were not, however, confined to differences with foreign nations. There was also the internal frontier, the Indian frontier, which was still a problem for the government. In the north there were hostile Indians in the Chaco territory. In the south there were unfriendly Indians in Patagonia. It was during the presidency of Sarmiento that the internal frontiers were beginning to recede. Frontier army posts were maintained against Indian raids, and expeditions were dispatched to push the unconquered natives further and further back.[22] Don Domingo had no sympathy for the Indians' cause; for him they were impediments in the way of civilization, obstacles to his program of government.

One day an Indian chief by the name of Calfucurá came to

[22] The classic account of this period is to be found in José Hernández' epic poem "Martín Fierro."

Sarmiento's office in the government house in Buenos Aires. Sarmiento ordered that the windows be opened. The Indian said something to the interpreter, who turned to Don Domingo "Mr. President, the Chief asks why the windows have been opened."

"Tell him that Indians have a smell of ponies that is unbearable for Christians."

The interpreter conveyed the message, and heard the *cacique's* reply. He then turned again to the chief executive: "The Chief says that Christians smell like cows. The odor is disagreeable for Indians, and keep the windows open."[23]

Domingo Sarmiento's leading biographer, Ricardo Rojas, has referred to the period of his presidency as "six years of disorder, blood, and misery" that would have "broken any man who did not possess the courage of Sarmiento."[24] The difficulties and obstacles that he faced were indeed great. López Jordán, the Taboadas, and so many other elements of caudillism; the plague, the epidemics, and the economic difficulties; the Paraguayan War, the disputes with the neighboring nations, the internal frontier—all of these were problems that faced Sarmiento as president.

But in spite of everything Sarmiento went on with his program. He had to defeat caudillism, meet the economic and natural crises as they arose, and solve the foreign problems; but he still had the project of his life to complete. He still had to "civilize the gaucho." To do this he would educate the people. He would bring a new population and give it land on the pampa. He would reform the nation's economy.

In the six years of his presidency, the accomplishments in these fields were so numerous that a detailed account would be impossible. A mere summary of the projects that he realized is sufficient to indicate the extent of his activity. In the field of education, he went on with his lifelong task of educating the people. When he came to power there were 30,000 children being educated in Argentina. Six years later there were 100,000.[25] Aside from the mere increase in number,

[23] Belín Sarmiento, *Sarmiento anecdótico, op.cit.*, p. 277.

[24] Rojas, p. 517.

[25] Juan P. Ramos, *Historia de la instrucción primaria*, Buenos Aires, 1910.

he and his minister of education, Nicolás Avellaneda, had gone far in introducing the methods and reforms that Don Domingo had been advocating since his early articles in *El Mercurio* of Santiago. Sarmiento's administration backed the development of education in the provinces by subsidizing provincial schools. He created new national schools. He initiated a system of normal schools, and he brought teachers from the United States to run them.[26] He created the National Observatory in Córdoba and sent for his North American friend, Benjamin Gould, to direct it.[27] He founded the Faculty of Exact Sciences, the School of Mining and Agronomy, the Naval Academy, and the Military Academy. He extended and improved the system of public libraries, and he ordered many valuable books from Europe. He instituted schools for telegraph operators, night schools for adults, and an institute for deaf mutes. He founded physics laboratories, stenographic schools, and museums. He created mobile schools for the underpopulated regions of the interior. This was the chance about which he had dreamed for years, and he took the opportunity to put into operation all of the projects that he had formed during a lifetime of thought and planning about education.

Sarmiento's efforts in the educational field had a lasting effect. Today almost every child of school age in Argentina attends some institution of learning or another. Argentina can boast the best primary educational system in South America and one of the best in the world. "This wonderful structure is the result of the humble efforts of a single man."[28] That man was Domingo Faustino Sarmiento.

In the field of government, Don Domingo continued with his efforts to prepare his country for a government by law. He backed the adoption of the civil code drawn up by his

[26] Samuel Guy Inman, "Paraná, Exponent of North American Education," *Bulletin of the Pan American Union,* LIII, 1921, pp. 463-474.

[27] Félix Aguilar, "Sarmiento precursor de la astronomía en la República Argentina," in Universidad Nacional de La Plata, *Sarmiento. Homenaje de la facultad de humanidades y ciencias de la educación,* La Plata, 1939, pp. 213-220.

[28] C. E. Castañeda, "Latin America's First Great Educator," *The Current History Magazine,* XXII, 1925, pp. 223-225.

Minister Vélez Sarsfield. He revised the commercial code and reformed the military code. He modernized the plan of study for the law school at the University of Córdoba, and he backed a new citizenship law.

To overcome the racial features of his nation that he saw standing in the way of his program, President Sarmiento instituted a more liberal and more attractive immigration program. In 1868, only 34,000 immigrants entered Argentina each year. By 1874, this number had more than doubled. These immigrants were offered opportunities to acquire their own lands and to settle in the vast interior of the nation. The president sponsored the new Chubut Colony in the south. He advised provincial governors to divide up the land along the rivers, along the sea, and near the large concentrations of populations, and offer these lands to the new immigrants. He proposed a colonization law along these lines to the national congress, but it was rejected.

The administration of Domingo Sarmiento marks an especially important step in the material progress of the nation. The mileage of railroads was tripled. The lines from Rosario to Córdoba and from Córdoba to Tucumán were completed. Telegraph lines were introduced at the beginning of his administration, and during the next four years they were strung across the Andes to Chile and under the Atlantic to Europe. Communication by ship with the outside world was augmented greatly. In 1868, only four ships per month called at Buenos Aires. By 1874, there were nineteen. The amount of mail doubled during these years. The National Exposition that Sarmiento held in 1871 in Córdoba demonstrated to the world the strides that Argentina had made. It gave the people of the country a feeling of optimism and assurance in the future of the country. The first census of the nation in 1869 not only gave the nation a chance to take stock of itself, but it made possible the planning of many of the government's projects on a sounder factual basis.

By the end of his presidency in 1874, a great portion of what Domingo Sarmiento had set out to do had been completed. His was the most active and progressive administration in Argentine history. He had overcome the caudillo opposition. He had successfully faced the economic problems. He had solved the foreign questions. He had laid the foundations of an excellent educational system. He had modernized the communications and the economy of the country. He had brought into the nation hundreds of thousands of new immigrants. He had begun the colonization of the pampa as he had started it at Chivilcoy. He had improved the legal structure of the government. He had given his nation a few years of peace, and he had offered it prosperity for the future. It looked as if he were well on his way towards the goal of "civilization and modernization of the gaucho." But the year 1874 showed how little progress he had really made. Sarmiento was discouraged and confused. He faced the big question of the latter part of his life: *WHY*?

Chapter 37. The President: the New Caudillism

DOMINGO SARMIENTO's term in the presidency of the Argentine Republic was the culmination of a long life of action and thought. It was the climax of a process which had started sixty years before in the little Escuela de la Patria in San Juan, continued through the many civil conflicts of the 1820's, developed during his exile in Chile, and progressed through his travels and his struggle to power. It was the test of the concept of life that he had conceived and fought for—and something went wrong. Things did not work out the way they should have.

Sarmiento thought that he could "transform the gaucho." He thought that education, new economic institutions, and a little new blood would change the Argentinean, who had spent his history in conflict and civil war, into a peaceful citizen living within a framework of law and order. This was the *intention* of Don Domingo. But his basic fallacy arose from the fact that he did not take into consideration the *intent*: his intent and the intent of the people with whom he was working. In spite of his earnest intentions to transform his civilization and make it conform more closely to the civilization that he had observed and admired in Europe and especially in the United States, Sarmiento was still basically a Spaniard. He was still fundamentally a product of the Hispanic tradition. He instituted his government to transform the gaucho, but many elements of his governing reveal a gaucho intent. This was something for which he had not allowed in his calculations.

Similarly, he had not taken into consideration the vital reality of the people with whom he was dealing. He looked upon the features that he identified with the gaucho as something like a veneer that had been spread over his compatriots. Education, immigration, railroads, and telegraph lines would scrape that veneer off. Sarmiento did not realize that what he was attacking was the essence of his civilization, the basis of a long tradition, the very livingness of his people. He did not see that it was impossible to transform the gaucho overnight. Even if you put him in a school, gave him prosperity, mixed him with immigrants from Europe, he would still be a gaucho in different surroundings. What Sarmiento was fighting was something that could be changed only over a long period of time. He expected to spend six years in the presidency and leave his nation transformed. There was an element of magic in Sarmiento's method. The magic words (education, immigration, etc.) would be pronounced, and presto! the pumpkin would be turned into a carriage—the gaucho would be turned into a citizen, the Argentinean would be turned into a twin of his North American brother.

Such, however, was not the case; and the truth was a bitter blow for Sarmiento. During his presidency, he merely saw the ushering in of a new phase of the old caudillism. The gauchocracy of the twenties and thirties had been followed by the centralization of Rosas and Urquiza. Now the personalist politician found himself living in a constitutional government. He would have to adapt himself to the new forms. He would have to make use of the new institutions. But he was still a personalist. He himself was a modern caudillo.

Sarmiento himself, in spite of all his good intentions, was representative of this new caudillism. He was not an extreme case, for consciously he was always trying to institute a government by law, a government of freedom, a government by the people. It was more his methods of doing things than what he was doing that make it possible to put him into this category. From the very outset of his regime, it became apparent to the new president that the forces of opposition were great. He felt he would never be able to overcome these forces unless he used a strong hand. The government of Mitre had, to his mind, been too weak. Sarmiento was determined that this would not be true of his administration. He found that the provinces could not govern themselves,[1] that the López Jordán revolt would upset all his plans for transforming his nation,[2] that the opposition was blocking his every move. If, then, he expected to achieve ends, he would have to overcome these obstacles. To do this, he would have to concentrate power in his own hands.

Thus Don Domingo found himself in an illogical situation. His end: government by law to replace government by personality, the transformation of the gaucho. His means: to govern as a personalist. Thus he set himself up in direct contradiction to his goal. The situation was, of course, not quite as extreme as this. Sarmiento was always able to defend his method according to the best of theory. However, if we cut through his sometimes sophistic arguments to the essential truth, his methods often went beyond the strict limits of his ideal government and were often what he would have opposed had they been employed by someone else.

There are three elements of Sarmiento's governmental method that are open to question in this respect. The first of these was his conception of the strong position of the execu-

[1] Sarmiento-Bienvenida Sarmiento, October 30, 1868; Carpeta XIII, No. 1759.

[2] Sarmiento-Mary Mann, Buenos Aires, July 14, 1870; photostatic copies at Museo Histórico Sarmiento.

tive branch. The second was his use of interventions to overcome opposition in the interior. And the last was his use of the "state of siege" and the suspension of guarantees in order to suppress sedition or rebellion.

"No other portion of the Argentine political system has given rise to so much discussion as the position of the executive. This is due in part to the lack of clear and definite formulation of executive powers in the constitution and in part to the influence of deeply rooted political ideas and tendencies inherited from Spain."[3] Sarmiento did not hesitate to make full use of the constitutional provisions on executive powers to strengthen his own position whenever he deemed it necessary. His interest in receiving the mandate of the people was indicative of this trend in his thought. He ruled by decree as well as by law, and when a decree would be as effective as a legislative act, he would by-pass parliamentary opposition by resorting to this method. Sarmiento wanted to educate his people so that they would learn to live under a government of law, but he did not hesitate to found the schools and appoint the teachers by executive decree. He wanted to found agricultural colonies in order to replace the gaucho with a responsible citizen, but if he could have overcome congressional opposition by decreeing these colonies and their regulations, he would have done so.

In a similar manner, Sarmiento thought nothing of using his powers of intervention to overcome opposition to his government and his program in the provinces. Articles 5 and 6 of the Constitution of 1853, although modeled after Article IV, section 4, of the Constitution of the United States (guaranteeing a republican form of government), are much broader in their scope than their North American counterpart.[4] Sarmiento was quick to make use of these clauses whenever he

[3] L. S. Rowe, *op.cit.*, p. 91: see also Alexander W. Weddell, *A Comparison of the Executive and Judicial Powers Under the Constitutions of Argentina and the United States*, Williamsburg, Virginia, 1937.

[4] The articles of the Argentine Constitution read as follows: "Each province shall adopt its own constitution, which shall provide for the administration of justice in its own territory, its municipal system, and primary instruction, such constitution to be framed upon the republican representative plan, in harmony with the principles, declarations, and guarantees of the national

deemed it advisable. His presidency records five interventions, three by decree and two by law; and although this represents a smaller number than those of either of his predecessors in the office,[5] his attitude towards the use of this power is of interest in the light of his political philosophy. He was the man who would presumably oppose the use of this power. He was the man who would put it into an inoperative position, similar to that which it held in the United States. But such was not the case.

The most widely discussed example of President Sarmiento's use of the power of intervention occurred in San Juan in 1868 and 1869, soon after he had assumed the presidency. Manuel José Zavalla had been governor of the province since 1867. At the end of 1868, the provincial legislature was due to elect a senator to the national congress. In the legislature, there were two opposing forces equally balanced. The one was the government party, which backed the candidature of Sarmiento's old adversary, Guillermo Rawson. The other was the opposition force, led by Deputy Videla. Videla had been in contact with Sarmiento and had expressed his support of the new national government. His group was slightly outnumbered by the government faction. On October 28th, the last day of the legislative session, the Videlist group met and voted the deposition of the three of the opposing representatives and the incorporation of two of their own number whose credentials had not been approved by the plenary meetings of the legislature. The government faction complained to the

---

constitution. Upon these conditions, the federal government shall guarantee to each province the enjoyment and exercise of its institutions." Also, "The federal government shall have the right to intervene in the territory of the provinces in order to guarantee the republican form of government or to repel foreign invasion; and when requested by the constituted authorities, to maintain them in power, or to reestablish them if they shall have been deposed by sedition or by invasion from another province."

The corresponding article of the United States Constitution reads as follows: "The United States shall guarantee to every State in this Union a Republican form of government, and shall protect each of them against invasion, and, on application of the Legislature, or of the Executive (when the Legislature cannot be convened) against domestic violence."

[5] Urquiza intervened seven times (all by decree), Derqui nine times (seven by decree), and Mitre seven times (six by decree).

governor, and Zavalla replied by jailing the entire Videlist party. The Videlists, charging that this was a move to defeat their candidate for the senate, appealed under article 6 of the constitution for federal intervention. On December 3, 1868, President Sarmiento *decreed* the federal intervention in San Juan. Before the incident was over, Zavalla had been deposed and Videla was on his way to Buenos Aires as a national senator.[6] This was a very clear example of a case when a president with less extreme ideas on the power of the executive might have sent troops to maintain order in the province, but would have left the decision of the rights in the case up to the courts or up to the congress.

Sarmiento had not wanted to intervene. He had no sympathy for Videla's cause. "From all that they tell me," he wrote to his sister Bienvenida, "I gather that Videla and Gómez, to have themselves elected to the senate, have San Juan in revolt in order to put them in the majority in the senate. . . . People are already talking to me about the possibility of a revolution in San Juan to cause an intervention. No matter what happened it would cost San Juan or the nation a million pesos. . . . If I find myself forced to intervene, that troop of scoundrels might be sorry for many years to come that they wished for it." As he later expressed it to Mrs. Mann, he "had to intervene—against my own friends—who had imprisoned half of the legislature."[7] His intervention was not to help Videla. It was rather because he saw "that the provinces are incapable of governing themselves, and that they are condemned to ruin themselves in revolts, useless struggles, and interventions."[8] Sarmiento's lack of confidence in the very thing for which he was fighting—government by law and government by the people—caused him to take power into his own hands and defeat his ends.

The use of the state of siege and of martial law was even more widely disputed than Sarmiento's use of the power of

[6] See Narciso S. Mallea, *Intervenciones en San Juan—años 1868 y 1873—o Sarmiento presidente,* Buenos Aires, 1930.

[7] Sarmiento-Mary Mann, Buenos Aires, March 13, 1869; Academia Argentina de Letras, *op.cit.,* pp. 77, 78.

[8] Sarmiento-Bienvenida Sarmiento, Buenos Aires, October 30, 1868; Carpeta XIII, No. 1759.

intervention. Whereas other presidents before and after him had used intervention even more extensively than he, Sarmiento's proclamation of martial law in 1869 was the only example of this action on the part of a chief executive from the promulgation of the Constitution of 1853 until the Revolution of 1930. This incident was related to the intervention in San Juan previously discussed. In the course of the San Juan intervention, President Sarmiento decreed that: "All citizens who take up arms with the governor of San Juan to resist the national authorities shall be considered in rebellion against them, and will therefore be subject to the military laws that apply to the case."[9] Under this decree Zacarías Segura was condemned to death by the firing squad in the province of San Luis. Jurists then and since then have condemned this action as contrary to the basic law of the land. "The Argentine Constitution expressly excludes martial law and its extrajuridical consequences."[10] Bartolomé Mitre, speaking in the national senate, attacked it as "against the letter and the spirit of the Constitution."[11] This was another outstanding example of a case where President Sarmiento overstepped the bounds of his legal power in his anxiousness to overcome any opposition to a program intended to lead to a legal government.

Meanwhile, as this "new caudillism" was appearing in abbreviated and relatively suppressed form in the actual methods of President Sarmiento, it was becoming apparent with more serious implications in the camp of the opposition. Don Domingo was able to cope with the obstacles imposed by the old caudillism. He knew how to deal with the Taboadas and the López Jordáns. He had had his experience with Facundo, the Aldaos, and El Chacho. But he did not know how to cope with the new caudillism, for he did not understand it. His idea that a superimposed program would change the whole way of life immediately left him unprepared to find the same basic features of personalism in his new order. He suddenly found himself faced with a relentless personal

[9] Carlos Sánchez Viamonte, *Ley marcial y estado de sito en el derecho Argentino*, Montevideo, 1931, p. 106.

[10] *Ibid.*, p. 19.

[11] Diario de sesiones, June 19, 1869.

opposition, an opposition that worked within the framework of constitutional laws and republican institutions, but that obviously did not conform to the ideal pattern that he had conceived. Sarmiento could never effectively meet this opposition, for he never fully understood it.

"I begin to see a clearly defined, hostile, and impassioned opposition in the congress, with the confessed purpose of overthrowing the national government."[12] How the opposition came under the leadership of the former nomocratic president and Sarmiento's erstwhile compatriot, Bartolomé Mitre, is somewhat of a mystery. It was partly because the former chief executive felt a sincere horror for the strong-arm methods that the new president was employing in cases such as the San Juan intervention. It was partly because Mitre seems to have made up his mind that Sarmiento would not make a good president. The methods that Mitre used, the following that he gathered, all of which showed increasing signs of the methods and the elements of the new caudillism, were doubtless due to the fact that he, like Don Domingo, was unable to escape the Hispanic tradition that was inbred in his civilization. It was inevitable, under the circumstances, that the two men should come into conflict. Both had a conscious nomocratic intention. Both had a personalist intent, which demonstrated itself in a tendency towards direct personal action. The result was that each was righteously indignant (according to their conscious intention) at the other's methods and actions (which were expressions of their vital reality).

The initial break came after Sarmiento's intervention in San Juan. Mitre attacked this action on the part of the president and held that intervention was really the task of the legislative branch of the government, being assumed by the president only during a congressional recess. His faction later introduced a law that would have subjected executive interventions to legislative regulation. The bill was passed by both houses of congress only to be vetoed by the president.

From that time until the end of his term, the Mitrist faction

[12] Posse-Sarmiento, Tucumán, August 28, 1869; Carpeta Posse-Sarmiento.

in congress was a steady source of opposition to Sarmiento. Senators were elected for nine years, so there were many Mitrists left over when Don Domingo assumed power, and they maintained an effective majority during his entire regime. "You may imagine the influence of an ex-president launched anew into politics, and in a senate composed as to impede the progress of a new government which undertakes to correct the abuses of the past administration."[13] There was a continuous sniping at all of the administrative projects. When Sarmiento introduced a bill for the expansion of the Port of Buenos Aires, Mitre opposed it. Don Domingo held that the state of the harbor forced ships to anchor practically on the high seas, thus submitting them to undue danger. Six or seven millions of pesos would have been necessary to do an effective job of enlarging the port. Appealing to feelings of localism and provincialism, blinded to the real needs of the future, the Mitrists defeated the bill. "Calumny in the press, tumults in the chambers, insults against the ministers, the menace of civil war, and even anarchy—these are the means used, without reason, to make a *political* question out of one that is only of public interest."[14] This was but one of the many examples during President Sarmiento's administration of the seemingly pointless opposition to all phases of the governmental program by a parliamentary opposition centered around the personality of Bartolomé Mitre.

The most outstanding example during this period of the new caudillo, the personalist cloaked in constitutional garb and protected by republican institutions, was the senator from Santa Fé, Nicasio Oroño. Senator Oroño was a close friend and supporter of López Jordán. He had instigated an invasion of Santa Fé in 1872 that failed, and when he defended the Entrerian caudillo in the senate, President Sarmiento ordered the attorney general to gather evidence for his conviction for treason. A letter was revealed and its authorship acknowl-

[13] Sarmiento-Mary Mann, Buenos Aires, June 1, 1869; photostatic copies at Museo Histórico Sarmiento.

[14] Sarmiento-Mary Mann, Buenos Aires, October 21, 1869; Academia Argentina de Letras, *op.cit.*, p. 83.

edged by the senator, in which Oroño definitely implicated himself in a conspiracy against the government. The culprit escaped prosecution by appealing to his senatorial immunities, and a federal judge appealed to the senate to deprive him of this protection. A long debate ensued, and Senator Manuel Quintana declared: "The vote of this chamber should tell the president of the Republic and all good Argentines that it does not function to help with political or personal vengeance, but to defend the high interests of the people."[15] The senate rejected the court plea. The blow was a strong one dealt by the new caudillism to the president. Sarmiento defeated López Jordán, but he still did not know what to make of this kind of opposition.

As the presidential year of 1874 approached, the evidence of the new personalist elements in national politics became increasingly evident. As early as 1872, the lines of battle were drawn. In September, Sarmiento wrote to his friend Posse, "The presidential elections are now drawing near, and all the ambitions are already campaigning. My role will be to make them have their little party in peace. Will I succeed? I doubt it."[16] The minister of justice and public education, Nicolás Avellaneda, would be a candidate. The vice-president, Adolfo Alsina, would be another. And the former president, Bartolomé Mitre, would be the third. Where Don Domingo's sympathies would lie are obvious. He had been in a state of continual disagreement with Alsina ever since their government was inaugurated. Mitre was his arch rival. "My sympathies would be with Avellaneda, because he is one of my ministers, an intimate friend, and above all because he has forcefully seconded my efforts to diffuse and improve education."[17] Sarmiento did, however, try to maintain a strict neutrality, and "let them have their little party in peace."

In late 1873, Avellaneda resigned his cabinet post to devote himself to his campaign. He was replaced by Juan E. Albarrácin.

[15] Guerra, p. 245.

[16] Sarmiento-Posse, Buenos Aires, September 20, 1872; Carpeta Sarmiento-Posse.

[17] Sarmiento-Mary Mann, Buenos Aires, November, 1872; Academia Argentina de Letras, *op.cit.*, p. 89.

On February 1, 1874, congressional elections were held throughout the nation. The Avellanedistas triumphed without difficulty in most of the provinces. The Alsinistas won in Catamarca and La Rioja, the Mitrists in San Juan. The province of Buenos Aires was, however, still the key. The provincial authorities (Alsinists) attempted to intervene and influence the elections, but President Sarmiento brought up four battalions of the line to maintain order.[18] The Mitrists won all twelve seats from Buenos Aires. Then, in a desperate move, the supporters of Avellaneda and Alsina, who held a majority in the chamber, refused to seat the Mitrists, and accepted instead the Alsinist candidates who had been defeated at the polls.

Seeing his own lack of popular support in the February elections, Alsina withdrew from the race and threw his support behind Avellaneda, reserving the vice-presidential nomination for one of his own supporters, Mariano Acosta. When the elections were finally held, the situation was much as it had been in February. Avellaneda won eleven provinces. The Mitre-Torrent ticket carried only Buenos Aires, San Juan, and Santiago del Estero. This gave Avellaneda 146 votes to their opposers' 79.

No sooner had the votes been counted than there were cries of fraud from the Mitrist camp.[19] The losing party charged official interference at the polls similar to that which had taken place in February. It is impossible to determine the truth about such a controversy, but certain facts can be pointed out. The United States minister in Buenos Aires, Thomas Osborn, reported to the State Department that "It is claimed that frauds of the most serious character were practiced by the unsuccessful as well as by the successful party in the contest—but I learn from very good sources that the authorities have eliminated the frauds practiced by both parties, and the result is still in favor of the parties above

[18] Sarmiento-Augusto Belín, Buenos Aires, February 15, 1874; Carpeta XII, No. 1570.

[19] " 'La Nación' ante la politica interna del Pais." *La Nación,* January 4, 1945.

named."[20] On the other hand, a letter to Avellaneda from one of his supporters indicates bribery at least at some of the polls. The victorious candidate is told that he has already received eight thousand votes in that district without having one against him. His informant then adds that he is drawing one thousand pesos against Avellaneda's account to pay the "caudillos of the countryside."[21] Perhaps the most judicious appraisal of the situation was that which appeared in a pamphlet in 1875. It pointed out that "you can be sure that neither faction has a clean conscience." The Avellanedists made use of official pressure, but the Mitrists "made use of gold, which they distributed by the handful."[22] The president, as Osborn points out, probably did all that was possible to avoid fraud. The Avellanedists undoubtedly used whatever official pressure and financial help that they could get away with, while the Mitrists probably reciprocated in kind. Unlike the February elections, the Mitrists were allowed to hold what they won in Buenos Aires. They carried the other two provinces that they might have been expected to carry, San Juan and Santiago del Estro. The results were probably as close to being fair as could be expected.

Regardless of the truth of the charges of fraud, these same accusations led to a pronouncement of revolt against the government. Mitre was prevailed upon to lead the revolution; and on September 24, 1874, Erasmo Obligado, in command of the gunboat *Paraná*, joined the revolt and seized the gunboat *Uruguay*. General Ignacio Rivas, in command of the troops in southern Buenos Aires, declared himself in favor of Mitre. General Ivanowsky was treacherously murdered in San Luis, and General Arredondo took over his armies for the revolutionists. General Taboada pronounced himself in favor of the revolt in Santiago del Estero, and it seemed as if the nation were to be torn again by civil war. General Mitre

[20] Thomas O. Osborn-Hamilton Fish, Buenos Aires, June 13, 1874; National Archives, State Department Division—Despatches, Argentine Republic, Volume XIX, No. 11.

[21] Belindo Soaje-N. Avellaneda, Córdoba, April 20, 1874; Unpublished Archives of Museo Histórico Sarmiento. In collection under name of Avellaneda.

[22] *Datos interesantes de la revolución Argentina*, Buenos Aires, 1875, p. 12.

resigned his commission in the army and left Buenos Aires to put himself at the head of the revolution.

Sarmiento acted with energy and dispatch. He declared Buenos Aires, Santa Fé, Entre Ríos, and Corrientes in a state of siege. Shortly after, it was extended to the entire Republic. The forces of the interior were put under the command of Colonel Julio A. Roca, and the defenses of Buenos Aires were prepared hastily.

On September 26th, President Sarmiento delivered an address to Congress. "I have the honor to inform you that a revolution of which we had previous information broke out by the commander of one of our new gunboats seizing the commander of the other. . . . We can at once put 20,000 men under arms, without counting on the Upper Provinces. We consider it necessary to declare all the Republic in a state of siege, so that even in remote provinces the authorities may be able to crush any efforts towards prolonging a war begun in crime and treachery.

"Ten years' progress have been written on the face of the country in railways, telegraphs, home and foreign loans, joint-stock companies and enterprises that have brought hundreds of millions of dollars into play, while the credit of the Republic was on so solid a basis as to promise security and tranquility for the future.

"In three months not a stone will be left on another, of so splendid an edifice, raised and completed with such labor. In my idea the situation and cause are the same as the rebellion of the Confederate States of North America. There, as here, some individuals had been accustomed to govern the country, and regarded it as their exclusive right. When Lincoln was elected president, they refused to admit him, saying he was elected by the multitude and applying such coarse epithets as passion suggested. . . .

"Unhappy the Republic where any colonel in command of a battalion may assume to himself the right to say what authorities he is to obey."[23]

On October 12, 1874, Domingo Sarmiento turned over the presidency of the Argentine Republic to Nicolás Avellaneda.

[23] *The Buenos Aires Standard,* September 29, 1874.

He had done much in the past six years, but what he had done had not had the magical effect that he had expected in "transforming the gaucho." He left office with the country up in arms, torn by civil war, divided by personal ambitions and personal hatreds.

BOOK VII

The Counteraction

Chapter 38. The Decline

THE Mitrist revolution did not last long after the end of Sarmiento's government. Colonel Julio Argentino Roca defeated the revolutionists under General Arredondo of the interior at Santa Rosa in Mendoza; and Colonel Ayala defeated the forces of General Mitre in Buenos Aires at Verde. Mitre, Arredondo, and Rivas were all taken prisoners. The naval officer who had begun the revolt surrendered, and the nation was once again at peace. Thomas Osborn wrote to his government in Washington: "The Rail Road, the Telegraph (pushed forward under the administration of President Sarmiento), and the Remington Rifles (purchased in the United States) have triumphantly settled the question at last, I think, in this Republic of South America, that rebellion cannot succeed."[1]

In the meantime, Domingo Sarmiento had retired to private life, a tired and sick old man. During his presidency he had built himself a modest little home on one of the islands of the Delta of the Paraná. He had realized that after the end of his term of office he would be unable to afford a house in the city, so he prepared for his old age in the idyllic setting of his island. "The place is so beautiful that Englishmen and travelers believe it to be one of the most beautiful in the world."[2]

But Don Domingo could not be idle for long. In a short time he was rested and ready to throw himself once again into the main currents of life. President Avellaneda offered him a diplomatic mission to Brazil, but the old man had become quite deaf in the past year, and he was afraid that this handi-

[1] Thomas C. Osborn-Hamilton Fish, Buenos Aires, December 15, 1874; National Archives, State Department Division, Despatches, Argentine Republic, Volume XIX, No. 31.

[2] Sarmiento-Bienvenida Sarmiento, Buenos Aires, January 8, 1874; Carpeta XIII, No. 1777.

cap would impede him in fulfilling such a task to the best of his ability. Instead, he asked to be put in command of the Zarate Arsenal, which he founded during his presidency, and in charge of the Third of February Park, the construction of which he had begun while still in office but which had not yet been completed. Both of these posts were granted to him, and Don Domingo returned to Buenos Aires.

On October 26, 1875, he renewed his lifelong dedication to the cause of public education when the Alsinist government of the province of Buenos Aires named him director general of schools for the province. He immediately set to work along his old lines of endeavor, reforming the courses of study, building new schools, enlarging old ones. He founded a new pedagogical journal, *La educación común en la provincia de Buenos Aires,* and he began to contribute his ideas and his articles to it.

Early in 1875, the death of José María del Carril left vacant a seat in the senate from San Juan. Don Domingo's old friends and supporters in his native province put his name up for election and on March 9th the provincial legislature named him to represent it in the national congress. This was an honor that Sarmiento appreciated deeply. The title of senator pleased him greatly. It brought with it the prestige that he thought was due him as a former president of the republic. The senate at the time was filled with many distinguished names. This gave it a special distinction, and Sarmiento was honored to be a part of it.

In the congress, the sixty-four-year-old elder statesman entered into the thick of parliamentary questions. When he went onto the floor of the senate, he was never without a handful of books and papers. These were his notes and his references, and they served as the basis of some very famous addresses. "I never sing without my music!" he explained to a friend.[3] His grandson tells what he considers an apocryphal story of the old man's deafness at the time.

"And how do you manage, Señor Sarmiento, to hear in the senate?" someone once asked him.

[3] Belín Sarmiento, *Sarmiento anecdótico, op.cit.,* p. 297.

"I don't go to the senate to hear them but for them to hear me," was the reply.[4]

Soon after the opening of the congressional session, a bill came up to grant a general amnesty to all those who had been involved in the Mitrist revolution of the year before. Senator Sarmiento, reporting for the committee on constitutional affairs, proposed some modifications that would have completely altered the original bills. He supported his amendments in a memorable speech that pointed to the evils and dangers of rebellion and opposed the amnesty as a move that would tend to foster a repetition of the recent disorders.[5]

In other questions that arose during the session, Sarmiento took an equally active part. He was a member of the special committee to study a reform of the parliamentary rules of the congress. With a thorough knowledge of this subject from his studies in the United States, he finally drew up a report which completely reformed the old procedure and relied heavily upon O. M. Wilson's *Digest of Parliamentary Law*. His proposals were adopted and came to form the basis of congressional action. In May 1876, when a project was offered to indemnify the Society of Jesus for a church that had been burned by a mob the previous year, he opposed the proposal so effectively that it was dropped. During 1878 and 1879, when the senate was torn by debates over the border question with Chile, when a large sector of the congress favored the use of force, even to the extent of war, it was Sarmiento who led the heroic efforts for peace. Although he failed to secure the ratification of the Pierre-Sarratea Treaty of 1878, or the Balmaceda-Montes de Oca Pact of 1879, war between the two neighboring countries was averted.

The most important feature of Sarmiento's activity in the senate at this time was not, however, this positive one of legislative activity. It was rather a negative pursuit. He was out of power. He was beyond his peak of political life. He was no longer on the offensive. He had taken a defensive position. He spent much of his time defending his activities as president, defending his program and his methods of instituting that program. Between July 6 and 15, 1875, he became em-

[4] *Ibid.*, p. 302.

[5] *Obras*, XIX, 208-252.

broiled in a debate with his old adversary, Guillermo Rawson. Using the pretext of Senator Sarmiento's opposition to the Amnesty Law, Rawson took this opportunity to attack Don Domingo's "irregular actions" in the Chacho affair. Sarmiento's support of Avellaneda against the Buenos Aires candidate, Mitre, had lost him popularity with the people of Buenos Aires, and the galleries soon expressed themselves on Rawson's side. Don Domingo's deafness kept him from hearing the accusations. Each one had to be repeated to him. One day, Rawson began his most carefully planned attack. "Sarmiento is going to hear what he has never before in his life heard," he said as he entered the chamber.[6] He began with a long and elaborate praise of his opponent and his accomplishments. Then he set out to destroy this picture, step by step, coldly and methodically, until he had reached the point of the most violent insults. The discourse was repeated to Don Domingo. He was not hurt by it. He expected no more from his old rival. "That is the old custom of Sanjuaninos," he explained jokingly, "when they see each other after a long absence, they immediately get off some good insults."[7]

Rawson's speech had, however, so aroused the galleries that when Don Domingo reached the street he was greeted with shouts from a hostile crowd. "Crazy man! Assassin! Down with the roguish Sanjuanino! Down with the lame sow!" Rawson's speech had not hurt the old leader, but the attacks of the crowd wounded him deeply.

Two days later, when the debate began once again, Senator Sarmiento was given the floor. He began a speech in which he set forth his ideas on liberty, parliamentary government, and reform. He reviewed the Rosas tyranny and what it stood for, and he attacked it bitterly. This time he was greeted by applause from the galleries. They liked this side of Don Domingo which had not been seen for a long time. But the old senator waved down the applause and continued. He wanted to show the people of the new generation his true self, the old fighter. "Yes, I am the 'Don Yo,' as they call me, but this 'Don Yo' has fought hand to hand with Don Juan Manuel

[6] Belín Sarmiento, *Sarmiento anecdótico, op.cit.*, p. 295.
[7] *Ibid.*, p. 297.

de Rosas for twenty years and has crushed him beneath the sole of his foot, and he has been able to contain the disorders of Urquiza, fighting with him and dominating him; all of the caudillos carry my mark. I am not like the young whipper-snappers of today who have yet to beat me, in spite of my age. But within a few years nature will do that job."[8] The galleries again greeted him with applause.

"I wanted, Mr. President, the galleries to hear me once, to see all of the liberty of which I am capable. And it is a loss for the country that you chain, humiliate, scoff at this spirit that has lived for sixty years, lasting against all the difficulties of life; that has suffered the tyranny, the poverty that you do not know, and the afflictions that a man can feel who in school knew only how to read, and who since then has made his way with work, honor, and courage to challenge all difficulties."[9] The senate was silent. When Don Domingo left the chamber, the galleries were awaiting to applaud him as he went out into the street.

This was not the end of Sarmiento's efforts to defend himself. When a bill was proposed to give congress a check on the presidential power to declare a state of siege, it was Don Domingo who opposed the measure. His entire record and his seriously studied convictions caused him to see this power as an executive one. He defended it as such, and in this way he gave another of his old enemies, Senator Oróno, a perfect opportunity to attack his record. The senator from Sante Fé brought up the use of the state of siege by the former president to oppose the revolts of López Jordán and the cases of unrest in the interior. He referred to the "atrocities" committed in Sarmiento's name at these times, and he brought up once again the execution of Seguras in San Luis. Don Domingo did not answer these accusations. He merely pointed out that any such charges should have been made in the form of impeachment proceedings during his presidency and that once his term of office was over they were out of order.

As the election year of 1880 approached, the country was again split by its political passions, and again there was the

[8] *Obras*, XIX, 245-255.
[9] *Ibid.*, p. 264.

fear and threat of revolution. President Avellaneda had attempted a "policy of conciliation," but it had not been successful. Carlos Tejedor, the new governor of Buenos Aires and leader of its party, had taken an adamant stand on the independence of his province. He had held that the president and the national government were only in residence in the port city as the guests of the province. They had no rights there, and all local power was still in the hands of the Buenos Aires government. He held to the old states' rights argument that the national government held only delegated powers that could be taken from it at any time. The true deposits of power were the provinces. Avellaneda replied that "in the nation there is nothing superior to the nation."[10] The result of this controversy was a new and serious split between Buenos Aires and the interior, the arming of an independent militia in Buenos Aires, and the threat of conflict between the two factors in the coming elections.

In late 1878, Senator Sarmiento was beginning to analyze the possibilities of the coming elections. He thought that the "opinion without opinion" of Buenos Aires would gather around Governor Tejedor. He had heard rumors that Avellaneda would back a Quintina-Laspiur or a Rawson-Laspiur combination. He had also heard of an arrangement between some Mitrist and Laspiur.[11] By February 1878, however, the picture had changed. Laspiur seemed to have dropped out of the race, and there was growing talk in the provinces of General Julio Roca or Sarmiento. "Some believe that the latter predominates. . . ." But Don Domingo was not particularly optimistic about his possibility for he felt that he lacked the support of the "politicians."[12]

At about this time, Sarmiento resumed the editorship of his old newspaper, *El Nacional.* "It was my purpose to open a crusade against the revolutionary spirit or tendencies." This was a timely aim at such a crucial period in his nation's history, and within a few months he seemed satisfied with his progress. "*El Nacional* enjoys here great authority, disarming

[10] Felipe Yofre, *El congreso de Belgrano,* Buenos Aires, 1928, pp. 32-33.
[11] Sarmiento-Posse, Buenos Aires, December, 1878; Carpeta Sarmiento-Posse.
[12] Sarmiento-Posse, Buenos Aires, February 26, 1879.

antagonisms and penetrating into the impenetrable ranks of the Mitrists."[13]

As time passed and General Roca's chances for support in the provinces increased, Sarmiento forgot his brief hope for another try at the presidency. The contest was becoming narrowed down to two men. Tejedor would represent the forces of Buenos Aires and whatever provinces he could win, and Roca would represent the interior and its opposition to the large seaboard province. The division being so clear-cut and along the same lines that had been drawn in the disastrous confederation-Buenos Aires division three decades before, the dangers of an irreconcilable split and an open conflict increased. Governor Tejedor's "rifleros" (riflemen) constituted what was in truth a small provincial army, and they trained and drilled openly in preparation for the coming elections. The governor's continued insistence on states' rights increased the fears that he would not peacefully accept a defeat at the hands of the provinces. Towards the end of July 1879, Don Domingo wrote to his friend, Mariano Sarratea, "I have held myself until now outside the field of battle. . . . Until now all has been going well; but dangerous springs are being touched, among these the provincial jealousies. . . . This would still be a small thing if revolt and mutiny were not brought in as a last resort; and I have reason to believe that our parties will call upon them."[14]

As the danger of conflict came closer and seemed more obvious, President Avellaneda turned in this emergency to his old friend and leader, Domingo Sarmiento. On September 1, 1879, he offered him the post of minister of the interior and the head of his cabinet. Don Domingo resigned his seat in the senate and accepted the position. It was now his task to preserve peace and order until the elections had been held and the results ascertained. The new minister of the interior telegraphed his friend José Posse upon his appointment. "The colt throws his ears back. He will calm down, recognizing his old master. There will be government!"[15] In a calmer mood,

[13] *Ibid.*

[14] Sarmiento-Sarratea, Buenos Aires, July 29, 1879; Carpeta VII, no. 877.

[15] Telegram from Sarmiento to Posse, Buenos Aires, September 1, 1879; Carpeta Sarmiento-Posse.

after a fortnight had passed, he wrote to Sarratea: "I have the task of restoring the political morals, that have been depraved by the cursed policy of conciliation, which has created a terrible situation. . . . I fear for the public tranquillity; only a spark is needed for the fuel to burst into a conflagration. And nevertheless, the public confidence after my nomination as minister is such that gold is going down and would go down more if there was not produced every day, intentionally, a new incident to create unrest."[16]

Meanwhile, as the irreconcilability of the two opposing candidates and the danger inherent therein became more and more obvious, there was increasing talk of Sarmiento as a compromise candidate. Whether this was a factor in making him decide to accept the ministry of the interior[17] is open to question. In the light of his letters it seems doubtful. Nevertheless it was about the time of his appointment that Posse was writing to Uladislao Frías about the "serious works being done in Buenos Aires for the candidature of Sarmiento,"[18] and Don Domingo was beginning to show his opposition to both candidates, thus implying the need for a third, possibly his own. Tejedor "is a daring barbarian without reins. He would throw the republic into an abyss in an attempt to carry forward his caprice. The candidature of Roca is a pretext, although I believe that he is convinced that he is going to be imposed by the force of the governors."[19]

On October 6, Domingo Sarmiento resigned from the ministry of the interior. Ricardo Rojas holds that this action was taken when he learned that the support that he thought was his was really behind Roca.[20] Sarmiento himself gave a different reason to his friend Sarratea. "They asked me to give the government power and authority *and* truth in the elections, and I thought that this was an honest request. After a short time I was forced to realize that neither the one nor the other was in my hands, and I had to leave the post.

[16] Sarmiento-Sarratea, Buenos Aires, September 15, 1879; Carpeta VII, No. 872.

[17] Rojas, pp. 563-564.

[18] Posse-Uladislao Frías, Tucumán, September 16, 1879; Unpublished Archives, Museo Histórico Sarmiento, miscellaneous.

[19] Sarmiento-Sarratea, Buenos Aires, September 15, 1879; Carpeta VII, No. 872.

[20] Rojas, pp. 562-563.

"The intervention in Jujuy pulled back the curtain. Unwittingly and without any lack of confidence I came upon some coded telegrams, and I felt that they were burning.[21] More than the impression of having been betrayed, there came to me the idea of the responsibility of having been deceived into giving my name to serve guilty ends. I resigned then, not without protests against the abuse." This would imply that Don Domingo had accepted the post in the sincere belief that he would help his nation through a crisis by preserving order and insuring fair elections. He then discovered that Avellaneda was plotting to control the polls in certain areas, and he resigned his post. "Of the president it can be said without fear of being mistaken, that his conduct has not corresponded to the high duties of his position."[22] Immediately after presenting his resignation Sarmiento went to the senate chamber, where he delivered a famous oration: "The contemplations are over: *I hold my fist full of truths* which I will throw to the winds to dissipate the phantoms and the fog that frighten and blind public opinion."[23]

It was then that Sarmiento thought that he had cause for which to fight. After a short rest in the mountains of Córdoba he returned to Buenos Aires. On March 30, the Association of Youths for National Union proclaimed his candidacy for the presidency. "We want for our president during the next six years, the citizen with the most experience in public life, who will threaten less to divide the people within the country and who will aggravate less a war without the country."[24] A program of government was drawn up calling for the renovation of the power of the people through elections, the unity of the nation, the observance of the constitution and laws under all circumstances, the outlawing of civil war, and the predominance of the national power. Don Domingo answered with an inspiring address in which he pointed to the need of nomocracy before democracy. Without a government of law and rights and liberties the masses could be a danger rather than a benefit in political power. Representative gov-

[21] Idiomatic way of saying they were self-incriminating.
[22] Sarmiento-Sarratea, Buenos Aires, October 14, 1879; Carpeta VII, No. 873.
[23] *Obras*, XX, 393. My italics. [24] *Ibid.*, pp. 38-48.

ernment had been failing in Argentina, asserted the former president, because of the lack of the nomocratic spirit. It must not fail, however. They must fight for it. "Peace and national union forever."[25]

It was too late, however, for Sarmiento's candidacy to be an effective one. He had waited too long and had lost his chance. As Posse wrote to him in April, "Now I tell you that if you had presented your name at the right time, you would have had no opposition in any province of the Republic; now it is too late to turn back." Commitments were already made, deals completed, tickets drawn up.[26] The United States minister reported: "A few days previous to the election, the respective friends of ex-President Sarmiento and Dr. Irigoyen presented them as peace candidates, but did not put up any electoral tickets, and hence they are now considered as compromise candidates, in case a compromise should be effected between the parties.

"Fraud and force in the election are charged by both parties, and it is quite probable that both are correct.

"It is hoped by the foreign and business elements of the country, that the electors may be persuaded to ignore parties, and their candidates, and select a new man for presidential honors.

"Should this be the result, I am inclined to think that ex-President Sarmiento—whom everybody respects—will be the man, and peace and prosperity will be secured.

"But, if no compromise should be effected between the parties and the electors cannot be persuaded, for the sake of peace, to throw their votes for someone, other than Tejedor or Roca, then I believe there will be serious trouble."[27]

Mr. Osborn's guess was correct. No compromise was reached. Tejedor took the provinces of Buenos Aires and Corrientes, and Roca took the rest. General Julio Roca thereby became the president-elect of Argentina. In June the revolt broke out. The congress was forced to withdraw from Buenos

[25] A. Bel, *Reseña biográfica de Domingo F. Sarmiento*, Buenos Aires, 1880, p. 28.

[26] Posse-Sarmiento, Tucumán, April 1, 1880; Carpeta Posse-Sarmiento.

[27] Osborn to William M. Evarts, Buenos Aires, April 19, 1880; Volume XXIII.

Aires and take refuge in Belgrano, some miles from the city. Here, while the forces of General Roca were suffocating the revolt, the last phase of Argentine constitutional organization was completed. The city of Buenos Aires was declared separated from the province of Buenos Aires and made into a federal district, the permanent capital of the Republic. The long-irritating "capital question" was thus settled.[28] Sarmiento, who had long favored such a solution and who had vetoed during his presidency three attempts to put the capital in some other city, was far away from the scene of action when this historic event occurred. The lack of success of his candidacy, his bad timing in presenting it, all represented his last major move in national politics. He was no longer a power to be reckoned with. Sarmiento was a figure of the past.

Chapter 39. Twilight of an Idea

The major intellectual problem that faced Domingo Sarmiento during the last years of his life was: why had he failed? Why was Argentina not the twin brother of the United States? Why did Mitre revolt against his government? Why did Tejedor revolt against Avellaneda's government? Why were there no parties that stood for different political philosophies, instead of for personalism or geographic districts? Why had the educated Argentine voted for Roca instead of for him (when he was obviously the better candidate)? Why had a new caudillism replaced the old? In short, why had the gaucho, though brought to the city, educated and modernized, not been transformed?

This was not a problem that Sarmiento ever faced up to directly or even consciously in so many words, but it was

[28] See Felipe Yofre, *op.cit.*; and Museo Histórico Sarmiento, *Sarmiento y Avellaneda—el congreso de Belgrano*, Buenos Aires, 1939.

the problem that was at the base of his thought during his declining years. He answered it in two ways. First, he analyzed features of his various theories that had gone wrong. Second, he offered a modification of his old ideas.

Of all his old basic ideas—education, anti-Hispanism, immigration, and material modernization—he abandoned none. In his last years he reexamined specific phases of each. He pointed to certain weak spots and he filled in gaps.

In the field of education, he carried on his crusade. He held one position after another in the pedagogical field. He continued his campaign to increase the number of schools, improve the teaching staffs, and modernize the teaching methods. He carried on a violent fight against compulsory religious education in the public schools. He was not in favor of atheistic education, but he was in favor of lay education.[1] The national constitution was specific on this point, so he had only the clergy to oppose this idea. He carried on some very bitter polemics with the clergy on this subject, both in Buenos Aires and in Montevideo. He received the tag of "atheist" from many extreme Roman Catholics, and that label has stuck to him in the minds of many right down to this day.

Sarmiento gave a practical turn to his theory of de-Hispanizing South America's culture. From the time that he had declared that Spain had no culture worth knowing and no writers worth reading until the end of his life, Sarmiento had been convinced that his nation had nothing to learn from her mother country. He believed that she and her sister republics would do far better by learning from the active and productive cultures of Europe and of North America. In 1884, he undertook a project whose end it was to effect something positive along these lines. He asked President Roca to send him on a mission to the neighboring states to negotiate an international convention whose purpose it would be to work jointly in the translation of the leading works of western civilization.

He went first to Montevideo, where he received the support of the Uruguayan government for his project. He then trav-

[1] See Volume XLVIII of his *Obras*, entitled *La escuela ultra-pampeana*.

eled to Santiago, where he signed a convention with representatives of Chile, Uruguay, and Colombia. A thousand volumes were agreed upon for translation and publication. This was not as many as Sarmiento had hoped for, but it would be a good beginning. His nation's culture could be subtly turned toward the leading cultures of the age. His people would escape the barbaric and backward literature and arts of the Iberian Peninsula, and they would receive the stimulation of the latest movements of philosophy and literature from Germany, France, Italy, England, and the United States. Don Domingo's great disappointment in this affair came when his own nation's congress refused to ratify the convention. He had initiated the plan, talked the other nations into agreeing, and then his own people did not back him up. He was both disappointed and ashamed.

As Don Domingo surveyed the situation around him during the last years of his life, his hopes in the results of extensive European emigration to Argentina seemed to have been a grand illusion. He had hoped that new races would help to counteract some of the worst elements that his nation had inherited from Spain. He had hoped that the peopling of the pampa would bring a new economic prosperity to his country. Immigrants had entered by the hundreds of thousands, but neither of his goals had been accomplished. The immigrants had been drawn chiefly from the backward regions of southern Italy, rather than from Scandinavia, Germany, and England, as Sarmiento had hoped. They had congregated in the cities rather then spreading over the pampa. They had neither influenced nor been influenced by the way of thinking of their adopted country, for they remained apart and isolated from national life.

In the 1880's Sarmiento took up this problem and studied it. He blamed the failure to achieve results on the failure of the nation to absorb the newcomers. He remembered how the immigrants in New York had become "Yankees" in a very short time. They had been brought into their new cultures. Don Domingo campaigned during his last year for the incorporation of the foreigners into the Argentine nationality. He wanted to make them landowners, give them a stake in the country, before granting them citizenship. He wanted to do away with their isolated colonies and their national schools. He went to visit the Italian school in Buenos Aires. He found pictures of King Humberto and maps of Italy on the wall. He was surprised and angered at this,[2] and he devoted much time to attacking such practices. "And he reserved the most caustic sarcasm for the immigrants who enrich themselves in the country without becoming attached to it or its habits and its institutions."[3] His plans for the results of foreign immigration had not worked out as he had predicted, but he blamed their failure not on the basic theory but on the way it was executed.

One of Don Domingo's last books was the *Vida y escritos del coronel don Francisco J. Muñiz* (The Life and Writings of Colonel Don Francisco J. Muñiz), published in 1886. This was Don Domingo's tribute to a man he believed to be one of the great of his nation. Muñiz was Argentina's first naturalist, and he was one of the great scientists of the Hispanic world in the nineteenth century. Sarmiento took great pleasure in presenting this man to the reading public. Muñiz represented the material reform that the ex-president had sought so ardently for his nation. He represented the absorption of western scientific civilization by an Argentine. Muñiz was a man who had something to offer the world. He was not a politician unknown outside the country. He was not a farmer or trader producing for himself. He was a member of Western civilization.

In 1883, the seventy-two-year-old Sarmiento produced his last major work. It was the first volume of his *Conflictos y armonías de las razas en América* (Conflicts and Harmonies of the Races in America). This book was the continuation of his former lines of thought, with sufficient changes and modification to warrant terming it a new phase of his intellectual development. It was the culmination of his attempt to re-examine his old theories and determine why they had not worked as he had expected. He outlined the extensive efforts that he and his patriots had made during the past thirty years:

[2] Sarmiento-Augusto Belín, Asunción, June 27, 1888; Carpeta XII, No. 1605.
[3] Palcos, *Sarmiento, op.cit.*, pp. 231-32.

"Schools, colleges, universities, legal codes, literature, legislation, railroads, telegraph systems, freedom of thought, an active press, more newspapers than in North America, illustrious names. . . ."[4] These were the results of an entire generation of struggle, but something had gone wrong. The results were not what they should have been. Something had destroyed the labor.[5] What could it have been?

As he looked back upon the answer that he had given to his country's problems in *El Facundo,* Sarmiento began to see the shallowness of that book. But he also began to conceive a new point of view. "In *Civilization and Barbarism,*" he wrote to Mrs. Mann, "I limited my observations to my own country; but the persistence with which there reappeared the evils that we thought we had overcome by adopting the federal constitution and the university and the similarity of the happenings that occur in all of Spanish America, made me suspect that the root of the evil was in something deeper than the external accidents of the soil led one to believe."[6]

He analyzed the political evil that he was fighting as "military obedience and political indifference." This he opposed to "that disposition of the spirits of a country to adopt the written rules of a form of government."[7] He was merely contrasting what he termed personalism to what we have termed nomocracy. He found this evil of personalism recurring in his own nation at all times. In spite of constitutions, telegraphs, railroads, and schools, the same evil reappeared. In a similar manner, he found it in all parts of the Spanish world. He saw similar cases and parallel developments. These facts led him to his next conclusion.

"Starting with the fact that is evident to me, that *elections* are real in all other countries but those of South America, and that the governors have seized control of the vote, I tried to find out from whence arises the difference, and I have found

[4] D. F. Sarmiento, *Conflictos y armonías de las razas en América,* editorial Intermundo: Buenos Aires, 1946, p. 12.

[5] *Ibid.*

[6] *Obras,* XXXVII, 8.

[7] D. F. Sarmiento, "El constitucionalismo en la América de sur," *Revista de derecho, historia y letras,* Buenos Aires, 1898, I, p. 121. This was written in 1882, maybe for the second volume of *Conflictos y armonías,* or perhaps it was the germ of a new book. Published posthumously.

that the *voter* belongs to an Indian race. . . ."[8] Thus was born the beginning of the solution to the intellectual problem of his old age. His many reforms and changes had not "transformed the gaucho," not because there was anything wrong with them as theories and as reforms, but because of the inherent characteristics of the gaucho himself. This was an idea that had been present since his earliest writings, but now it was emphasized as of transcendent importance.

Don Domingo then began a careful analysis of the racial elements of Hispanic America. There was the Spanish, with its tradition of the Inquisition, the absolute monarchy, and its heritage from the Moors. There was the Indian, the quichua and guaraní in Argentina, with its tradition of subservience to a cacique or to an Inca, with its history of Jesuit domination during the colonial period, and finally with its record as an enslaved race under the Spaniard. Finally, there was the Negro, who had the worst heritage of all—barbaric Africa. Don Domingo expressed fear for the future of the new Republic of Liberia.

This racial mixture he found in South America contrasted strongly with the mixture in North America. Here it was almost exclusively white. The combination of the sober Puritanical tradition of New England and the aristocratic leadership tradition of Virginia created a mixture that was well suited for the society that was flourishing in the United States at that time.

"Is this evil without remedy?" asked the author of *Conflictos y armonías*. "No. In the city of Buenos Aires we have more white men than red; but the foreigner who has been brought here to augment our ranks has strayed as a result of our lack of planning.

"*Conflict* of the races—our civil wars—caudillos—electoral fraud—arbitrariness—they all come from the same source. . . . Harmony of the races—the Spanish Americans, with the European immigrant in large numbers: with the United States in principle of government . . . save ourselves from reconquest from without—from barbarity that already dominates all of America."[9]

[8] Sarmiento-Posse, Buenos Aires, August 22, 1882.

[9] *Ibid.*

Don Domingo's solution was not as clear as his diagnosis. The reason that he had been unable to "transform the gaucho" he attributed to the racial mixture within the gaucho. His solution he seemed to find in the creation of harmonic understanding and cooperation among the best racial elements.

There are actually two elements in his diagnosis that Sarmiento tends to confuse, but that must be separated. He refers at times to a racial, almost a biological, heritage.[10] At other times he refers to a traditional, a historical heritage.[11] He wrote this book at a time when a pseudo-science of hereditary influences was developing throughout the world. As a result of the stimulus given to the biological sciences by Darwinism, an attempt was being made to find the cause of more and more elements of life in heredity. Zola was popularizing this approach in his novels, and he was the leader of a large school of thinkers and writers. It is little wonder that Sarmiento, living at the time he did, and reading as extensively as he did, should have fallen into this vogue of pseudo-scientific study of heredity. Modern science has disproved the possibility of the inheritance by a race of such characteristics as those which Don Domingo treats.[12]

When he deals, however, with these characteristics as results of a historical tradition, not determined by biology but shaped by events, he is dealing with a very modern approach. His analysis of certain elements in Spanish and Indian history such as the Inquisition or the duty of the cacique is a definite beginning toward an understanding of the elements in the Spanish way of life that stood in the way of Sarmiento's reforms.

Don Domingo once called *Conflictos* his "*Facundo* grown old." However, there are important differences between the books. As Pedro Henriquez Ureña says: "When he wrote *Facundo* he clearly perceived and described the influences of geography and history upon the social and political life of Argentina—such facts as the vastness of the country and the

[10] *Conflictos,* p. 119. [11] *Ibid.*, p. 147.

[12] L. C. Dunn and Th. Dobzhansky, *Heredity, Race, and Society,* Pelican Books, New York, 1946, p. 11.

sparseness of the population, or the multitude of cattle and horses that made food and travel practically gratuitous. In the later work he wished to explain the history of Hispanic America from the point of view of race. But race explains nothing. And the method he adopted was an encumbrance for him—he read the latest books on ethnology and sociology, quoted authorities, gathered colonial documents. Evidently the process wearied him, for the book was never finished and even in the part he gave to the press the plan is not clearly discernible. In short, he succeeded in *Facundo* because he sought his explanation in culture; he failed in his last book because he sought his explanation in race."[13]

Chapter 40. The Fall

AFTER Don Domingo's resignation as minister of the interior in 1879, he had returned to his duties as director general of schools for the province of Buenos Aires. The events of 1880, however, which led to the federalization of the capital, created a completely new governmental organization and deprived him of the most important part of his jurisdiction. On February 1, 1881, the national government appointed him general superintendent of schools. He was to preside over a council of eight members, and together they would represent the executive power of the public-school system.

Not long after assuming this new office, friction between the authoritarian superintendent and his independent-minded council began to be evident. The question of religious and lay education arose, and the former president of the Republic clashed with some of the members of the council on this

[13] Pedro Henríquez Ureña, *Literary Currents in Hispanic America*, Cambridge, Mass., 1945, p. 252.

question. Don Domingo opposed pay for the members of the council, and this of course, affecting the pocketbooks of the men, created even more opposition. In November, the council was preparing to elect its vice-president. Sarmiento knew that his chief opponent in the council, Navarro Viola, was going to be chosen, so, to avoid a disagreeable encounter and seizing on the pretext of finding a hatchery for some carp that were arriving from Europe, he turned the meeting over to the secretary. He made the latter *ad hoc* president for the specific and limited task of presiding over the election of a new vice-president.

The hostile council immediately brought up the question of whether a secretary could preside over the meeting. The superintendent was accused of neglecting his duty, going to attend to some fish rather than being present at a distinguished meeting of the council. The secretary had in the meanwhile gone over to the side of the opposition to the superintendent, and he had, contrary to orders, allowed the meeting to go on after the election of the vice-president. Sarmiento, angered by these moves, asked the government to dismiss the secretary. Twice the government ignored his request, and finally Sarmiento resigned. Upon the acceptance of his resignation, an entire new council was named.

This was the second in a long line of defeats that had started for Sarmiento with the elections of 1880 and would continue until the end of his life. His battle with the council had been a bitter and well-publicized one. He had been called insane in so many words, and this and many other accusations had become common knowledge. With the acceptance of his resignation, he was angered and humiliated. He attacked the minister of public education, Didimo Pizarro, in the press. He drew him into a polemic, and the minister was finally forced to resign from the cabinet.

The following year, Sarmiento's name was put up for election to the municipal council of the federal capital. On April 22, 1883, his candidacy was defeated by a neighborhood pharmacist by the name of Otto Recke. The blows were falling from all sides.

During this entire period, Don Domingo was continuing to

edit his old newspaper, *El Nacional.* It was from its columns that he carried on his polemic with Pizarro. It was from its columns that he treated all the principal topics of the day. It was a political question that finally brought Don Domingo's separation from *El Nacional.* In 1883, there appeared a new figure on the scene of national politics, that of Miguel Juárez Celman. His name was soon mentioned as the official candidate to succeed President Roca. Sarmiento, in his usually belligerent manner, made some uncomplimentary remarks about Celman in a few of his articles. The publisher and owner of the newspaper was one of Celman's supporters, and he ordered the cessation of the attacks. Don Domingo was not the force that he once had been. He attributed the publisher's attitude to economic pressure. He did not feel equal to a fight. So he resigned his post from the newspaper and limited himself in the future to miscellaneous nonpolitical articles. "I am thinking of retiring from the periodical press," he wrote to his still close and loyal friend Posse. "My role is impossible in a world dominated by finances. My word is the voice in the desert."[1] And the once powerful, once influential, once indomitable crusader of the press stepped out of the journalistic scene that he had enlivened with his fights and with his projects for so many years.

In early 1884, Don Domingo traveled to Montevideo and then to Chile on his governmental mission to arrange international cooperation in the translation of famous books. In Uruguay he was received with a great ovation. "My presence in Montevideo has become a real public occasion. I have been and continue to be the object of the most general solicitude on the part of the entire city." President Máximo Santos called upon him at his hotel. The chief executive was followed by his cabinet and the most distinguished members of the diplomatic corps. Five banquets were given for him, and at all of them he was the subject of the most sincere and gratifying acclaim.

From Montevideo Sarmiento traveled to Chile. In both Valparaíso and Santiago he was given the reception of a conquering hero. He renewed old acquaintances and saw the old

[1] Sarmiento-Posse, Buenos Aires, August 26, 1883.

sights, and then he said goodby for the last time to the nation that had given him his first opportunities and that had taught him so much.

On his return trip to Buenos Aires, Sarmiento stopped off in Mendoza and in San Juan. As he was coming down the Andes into the Uspallata Valley, he was met by a municipal reception committee that had been sent from Mendoza to intercept him. "My reception here is a real occasion because of both its cordiality and its neutrality."[2] But his arrival in San Juan was the moment that he had really been awaiting.

Segundo Navarro described it in a telegraphic dispatch to Buenos Aires: "Yesterday at five in the afternoon General Sarmiento made his entrance into this city amidst a splendid ovation. . . . The general, followed by various carriages and a group of escorts on horseback, started for the city. Within a short distance he was met with two arches of triumph prepared spontaneously by schoolteachers in the district. The pupils were formed in line to receive him and one of them to offer him a bunch of flowers. She delivered a beautiful little speech. He continued on his way, being cheered everywhere and presented with flowers, until he arrived at the Retiro. Here fifty carriages with almost two hundred gentlemen awaited him." Among these were the governor and all the high officials of the town and the province. He was taken through roped-off streets lined with thousands of people. Everyone in town wanted to see their famous Don Domingo. "That's him! My father told me. . . . I have seen him!"[3] Through the cheering crowd of the main plaza that he remembered so well, Sarmiento made his way to the government house. By now, he was exhausted by the exertion. He appeared on the balcony for a moment to see the throng below. The students and teachers of his normal school arrived to offer him a new ovation and more flowers. Then they sang the national anthem, and "the general[4] was very satisfied with the spontaneous and enthusiastic reception of his fellow pro-

[2] Sarmiento to Augusto Belín, Mendoza, April 18, 1884; Carpeta XII, No. 1591.

[3] Telegram from Segundo Navarro to Augusto Belín, May 3, 1884; San Juan, Carpeta XII, No. 1592.

[4] Sarmiento had been made a general in 1877.

vincials." Late that afternoon he visited the tomb of his parents.

This triumphal tour to familiar places was particularly gratifying to Don Domingo in view of his diminishing power and importance on the public scene. Memories of past greatness returned. The siege of Montevideo, working in the department store in Valparaíso, his first article in Santiago, the siege of Mendoza, Facundo, El Chacho, the Escuela de la Patria—all of these memories must have passed before his eyes during the trip. He was not forgotten. His defeats in Buenos Aires in the present diminished before the realization of how his past lived in the minds of so many people in so many places. It was the triumphal march of a man who was coming to realize that he belonged to the past.

Upon his return to Buenos Aires, Sarmiento heard some more gratifying news. Congress had passed, and President Roca had signed, a law to publish the complete works of Domingo F. Sarmiento. Luis Montt, the son of his old Chilean friend and companion, was charged with editing them. Again this was a victory for the Sarmiento of the past and not for the Sarmiento of the present, but it pleased the old man greatly, and he took great joy in aiding in the project. When Montt wrote to ask which of the editorials in *El Mercurio* were his, he answered by telegram: "The good ones—those are mine."[5]

"In 1885 Sarmiento was the living symbol of three generations that had spent their lives to create the framework of the Republic."[6] He lived quietly in Buenos Aires, completely withdrawn from public life. One writer described him in the pages of *El Nacional*: "Domingo Faustino Sarmiento, general, writer, pedagogue, ex-minister, ex-diplomat, ex-conventionalist, ex-president, author of didactic books, of revolutionary pamphlets, of monumental speeches, of *El Facundo*, which is

[5] Belín Sarmiento, *Sarmiento anecdótico, op.cit.*, p. 300; his grandson holds that this telegram was misunderstood. Sarmiento did not mean to say that the best articles were his. All were written by him. He meant to tell Montt to pick the best of his editorials for publication.

[6] Carlos Heras, "La última campaña política de Sarmiento" in Universidad Nacional de La Plata, *Sarmiento. Homenaje de la facultad de humanidades y ciencias de la educación*, La Plata, 1939, p. 119.

like the *Quijote* of America. . . ."[7] Don Domingo seemed to have completely forgotten his old passion for the political battle. "I find two of your letters," he wrote to Posse, "asking for news and explanations of what is happening in politics. I do not even have that much interest, much less does such activity arouse me. I do not know what is happening."[8]

Toward the end of the year, however, Domingo Sarmiento was drawn again into the political arena, and he made his last attempt to return to a position of influence in the public life of his nation. The elections of 1886 were approaching, and the candidature of Miguel Juárez Celman had been proclaimed. He had been promised the backing of the government, and many thought that, in view of the candidate's obscurity and lack of popular support outside the province of Córdoba, where he had been governor, his election would be a farce and a mockery of the popular vote and the republican institutions of the nation. Don Domingo had been forced to resign from *El Nacional* for his previous opposition to Celman, but this did not deter him. In *El Debate* and *El Diario* he took up with renewed energy his attack on the proposed candidacy.

Of the other presidential hopefuls of the time, all but three had been eliminated. Dardo Rocha, backed by the "Great Argentine Committee," had the support of Buenos Aires. Bernardo de Irigoyen, the former minister of the interior, held the support of many influential men in the interior and the autonomist party in the federal capital. José Benjamín Gorostiaga was backed by the Catholic party. Celman held the support of Córdoba, and after conferences with the various provincial governors it was believed that he had come to an agreement with the political bosses of the interior. His most hopeful asset, however, was his support by President Roca. During 1885, Sarmiento supported none of these candidates, but he very decidedly opposed Celman. Mitre, after considerable wavering, threw his party behind Gorostiaga.[9]

Until the month of October, Sarmiento continued to pub-

[7] Sansón Carrasco, "Sarmiento en la brega," *El Nacional*, November 21, 1885.

[8] Sarmiento-Posse, Buenos Aires, April 26, 1885.

[9] Mitre to Bonifacio Lastra and Juan Carballido, May 5, 1885; published in *La Nación*, May 8.

lish in whatever newspapers were available repeated and heated attacks against Celman.[10] Then, an event occurred that galvanized Don Domingo into another field of action. Many of the leading generals of the time, including Lucio Mansilla, Napoleón Uriburu, Mitre, and Sarmiento himself, were taking active parts in the approaching political campaign. In Tucumán, however, a speech by a nonmilitary man, José Posse, proclaiming the candidacy of Rocha, was reported erroneously by *El Diario* to have been delivered by General Uriburu. The speech had many unfavorable references both to Celman and to President Roca. The chief executive, reacting against the reported version of this speech, issued an order that prohibited all military officers from publicly criticizing the acts of their superiors. Such an order had more far-reaching implications than the president had foreseen. It meant the silencing of such distinguished statesmen as the ex-presidents Mitre and Sarmiento, and their exclusion from any form of political partisanship. The decree infuriated the still fiery Don Domingo, and with a touch of his old enthusiasm he set out to deliberately defy it. On the thirtieth of October, in a letter to *El Diario*, he publicly announced his intention of continuing with his criticism of the government. "Having assured *El Diario* that General Sarmiento will let loose a cannonade from the press, the sergeant general at arms will proceed as is provided for in the final article of the general order."[11] Sarmiento defied them to arrest him.

As a fulfillment of his threat, Domingo Sarmiento founded on December 1 the newspaper *El Censor*, whose very title was a reference to the order. From the first issue, the prohibition was ignored. General Roca himself was sorely criticized for the very decree that was intended to outlaw such criticism. Celman continued under attack in the columns of the new journal as he was in the other papers for which Don Domingo had been writing.[12]

El Censor was welcomed warmly by the other opposition

[10] *Artículos publicados en El Nacional de Buenos Aires sobre Miguel Juárez Celman por Domingo Faustino Sarmiento,* Imprenta El Debate; Buenos Aires, 1885.

[11] *El Diario,* October 30, 1885.

[12] See *El Censor,* December 1, 1885; and succeeding issues during the campaign of 1886.

newspapers of Buenos Aires. *El Diario* commented: "If there remains in the people one spark of that fire that made the Argentine name Sarmiento great, it will be able to reawaken beneath the ashes that cover it."[13] Mitre's *La Nación* referred to the editor of the new journal: "The new newspaper is edited with the energy of virile age and the maturity of judgment of advanced age."[14]

In the months that followed, a violent battle of words was carried on between *El Censor* and the officialist paper, *La tribuna nacional.* Don Domingo's attacks were calmer and more mature than during his earlier polemics. He avoided personal arguments and maintained a strictly doctrinary approach. "Nothing lasting can come of Juárez (Celman). As a sworn enemy of revolutions, I will fight to carry politics to wider horizons."[15]

By the beginning of 1886, the candidates in opposition to Celman agreed to unite under the title of Partidos Unidos, or United Parties. At the beginning of February this group offered to Sarmiento the candidacy for the national chamber of deputies from San Juan. Don Domingo had no interest in such an offer, but, feeling that his support might help to defeat Celman, he answered by telegram: "D. F. Sarmiento accepts the candidature for deputy to congress for the province of San Juan, as a sacrifice, considering his age; as a duty in the hour of danger to the institutions that were conquered on February 3, 1852."[16] A few days later Sarmiento addressed a proclamation to the people of San Juan, appealing for the votes of "the generation that since 1860 has learned to read in the schools that I created as governor and supported later as president."[17] The old politician pretended to pay little attention to this contest, but deep down inside of him he must have realized that this was his last test, his last try. "Educate the people and it will never elect a Rosas," he had once said. Would the saying apply now?

[13] *El Diario,* December 2, 1885.
[14] *La Nación,* December 2, 1885.
[15] *Obras,* LII, 380.
[16] *El Censor,* February 3, 1886.
[17] *Ibid.,* February 6, 1886.

The candidate who opposed ex-President Sarmiento for the seat in the chamber of deputies was an obscure citizen by the name of Augustín Cabeza (literally translated Augustus Head). When the votes were counted, Cabeza had received 3,683; Sarmiento had received 2,037. As one writer put it, Cabeza "did not have the civilizing work of his illustrious adversary on his side, but he had been chief of police in San Juan."[18] It was a cruel blow to the old statesman. Sarmiento charged electoral fraud and took his evidence to the chamber of deputies, but Cabeza's credentials were accepted and he was seated. A few months later, in spite of the unification of Rocha, Irigoyen, and Gorostiaga behind the candidacy of Manuel Ocampo, the "league of governors" triumphed and Juárez Celman was elected to the presidency of the nation.

Sarmiento's efforts during the past year had broken his health completely. He was suffering from an acute psychological depression,[19] and he was physically weak and ill. He had reached the low point of his fortunes. He saw his life slowly expiring and his hopes and ambitions still far from realized. He had set out to change the world, and he had been unable to do it.

In June, he traveled west to regain his health and his spirits. He stopped in Córdoba and Tucumán and proceeded on to Rosario de la Frontera. At this time, he completed his life of Dominguito, a book that he had begun in a biographical sketch twenty years before in the United States.[20] The book reflected his mood. It was melancholy, reminiscent of happier days. It was romantic and sad. The life of his only son, Dominguito, was told from his birth in Yungay until his death at Curupaití. It was told with a gentleness and simplicity that has made the little book live on as one of the most beloved works of Don Domingo.

[18] Carlos Heras, *op.cit.*, p. 133.

[19] Guerra, *op.cit.*, p. 291.

[20] Sarmiento-Mary Mann, New York, September 27, 1867; Academia Argentina de Letras, *op.cit.*

Chapter 41. The End

DURING the last few days of his life, Domingo Sarmiento's popularity returned. He was no longer a threat to the ambitions of others. He was no longer a force to be feared. He was a symbol. He was a memory. He was a monument. Everywhere he went, he was greeted by friendly crowds. Everywhere he was received with the warmth and the enthusiasm given a father returning after a long absence to his children. On the fifteenth of February 1887, on his seventy-sixth birthday, Don Domingo was for the first time acclaimed and affectionately cheered by a group of students in Buenos Aires. It had been these young men of the port city who had shown him the greatest animosity during his declining years.

In September of 1886, an epidemic of cholera had broken out in the provinces. The former president, who had had such extensive though bitter experience with meeting such a crisis, was named president of the national commission of aid to the interior. In this role Sarmiento showed his usual energy and his usual effectiveness. But before he had fulfilled his duties, the strain had again affected his health, and his doctors advised him not to spend another winter in the damp and cold climate of Buenos Aires.

Don Domingo had been intermittently ill since 1876, when the doctors had diagnosed a swelling of his legs as hypertrophia of the heart. After that, periods of great strain had taken their toll on his health. 1880, 1886, and now the fight against cholera all left their effects.

In July 1887, as the weather in Buenos Aires was growing cold and threatening to the old man's well-being, he decided to make a trip to Paraguay for the winter. His doctors approved highly of this resolution, and Sarmiento proceeded to Asunción, where he spent the five worst months of the southern winter.

The Paraguayan capital is beautiful in the month of July. As you travel up the Paraná and Paraguay Rivers by steamboat, each day brings better weather. The fog and clouds of Buenos Aires are replaced by the sunny skies of the northern Argentine provinces. The bareness of winter disappears, and the luxuriant green of tropical growths takes its place. Asunción itself was little more than a small village. Its entire life was centered around a few blocks in the center of town. Its atmosphere was friendly and cordial, everyone knowing everyone else, stopping on the street to talk, entering the café for some coffee. The weather was warm and dry, and Don Domingo's health improved immensely during his stay.

The old warrior could never remain inactive. He spent his time reading and writing. He supplied material to newspapers in Buenos Aires and San Juan, and he became quite a regular contributor to *El Independiente* of Asunción. Paraguay was just entering into a new phase of her history. Directly after her independence from Spain, she fell beneath the rule of the dictator Dr. Gaspar Rodríguez de Francia. Though benevolent and paternal, he instituted the most completely isolated and most rigidly controlled dictatorship that had been known to the western world in modern times. Nobody left the country, few came in. Communications with the outside world were for all practical purposes cut. Dr. Francia was succeeded by another absolute ruler, Carlos Antonio López. Control seemed a little relaxed at this time, but only in contrast with the preceding regime. Finally there came Francisco Solano López, the South American Napoleon, with his beautiful Irish mistress, Madam Lynch. Together they continued the dictatorship, until the ruler threw his little nation into a bloody conflict with the largest nations of the continent and drained it of its resources and its manpower. Paraguay was attempting to recover from its disastrous past. It was in contact with the rest of the world. It was trying to introduce a way of life that would allow it to enter into the family of nineteenth-century nations. Sarmiento brought it many ideas, many suggestions, and many vistas. His wide experience in all phases of life was a very profitable lesson to the little Paraguayan nation that read what he said in the *Independiente*.

Then, on September 20, the anniversary of the death of Dr. Francia, Sarmiento wrote an article on that leader. He wrote exactly what he thought about him. A minister in the president's cabinet, who was a distant relative of the former dictator, resented what Don Domingo had to say. He challenged the Argentine leader to a duel, and in spite of his opposition to such a method of settling disputes, and in spite of his seventy-six years, Sarmiento accepted. The president quickly intervened before any such crime could be committed, and the minister resigned his post.

The people of Asunción in a gesture of friendship and appreciation presented Don Domingo with a plot of land in the town. He spent happy days here, thinking, working, dreaming. "Things are going very well for me here, for I am so much esteemed. I work so with my body and soul and I dream such possible dreams that I have no time for rest."[1]

Towards the end of the year, Sarmiento returned to Buenos Aires. He had a feeling that this would be his last visit to that city, so he wound up what business he could while he was there. He wrote farewell letters to his closest friends. He straightened out his economic affairs. "I feel," he wrote to David Peña, "that my strength is giving way, that my body is weak, and that I must begin another little journey very soon. But I am prepared, because little luggage is needed. . . . I carry the only passport that is admissible, for it is written in all languages: serve humanity."[2]

In May 1888, Don Domingo set out once again for the Paraguayan capital, this time accompanied by his daughter Faustina and his granddaughter María Luisa. As he sailed out of Buenos Aires harbor, he turned to his grandson, Augusto: "I will not get through this year, my son. . . . I am going to die." Then, squaring his shoulders and with a twinkle in his eye, he added: "Ah, if they had only made me president, I would have disappointed them by living another ten years."[3]

[1] Sarmiento-Augusto Belín, Asunción, September 20, 1887; Carpeta XII, No. 1601.

[2] Sarmiento-David Peña, January 1888, *Revista de derecho, historia y letras*, III, p. 489.

[3] Belín Sarmiento, *Sarmiento anecdótico, op.cit.*, p. 317.

His last words of bravado were directed at the city of Buenos Aires as it disappeared in the distance: "Morituri te salutant."

Sarmiento arrived in Asunción in June, and he stayed as before at the hotel known as La Cancha Sociedad. It had once been the residence of the notorious Madam Lynch. Don Domingo lived in a kind of shed with four rooms. He made them into two bedrooms, a dining room, and a study, and in the latter he spent much of his time working and writing and planning a future that he knew did not exist. In a letter to Augusto, he wrote of extensive plans for the schools of San Juan and Buenos Aires. "I will not have time to know whether they adopt them in whole or in part, but I would like to know what they are preparing there."[4]

Sarmiento spent much of his time outside in the warm Paraguayan sun. His lodging was near the river, and he enjoyed watching the boats pass and sitting on the bank to contemplate the scenery. He made friends with a Dr. Van Gulich and a group of German naturalists who were planning a trip into the unknown center of the continent. One day he went out with his friends in a boat, and they reached the mouth of the Pilcomayo River before they returned. They shot at the decoratively plumed "yacarés," and Don Domingo found the excursion great sport. Late in July, his health seemed to be better, and he seemed to be on his way to regaining his old strength.[5]

Soon after his arrival in Asunción for the second time, Sarmiento decided to build a house of his own on the plot of ground that had been presented to him. It would be especially designed, isothermal, and in the form of a chalet. His greatest problem was to dig a well to supply his projected dwelling with water. No matter where or how deep they dug, no water appeared. Don Domingo and the workmen alike were puzzled. During July and August, the old man spent most of his time overseeing the construction of his new house and wondering about the problem of his new well. Toward the beginning of August, a twenty-foot hole was dug, but still nothing happened.

[4] Sarmiento-Augusto Belín, Asunción, June 1888; Carpeta XII, No. 1603.
[5] Sarmiento-Augusto Belín, Asunción, July 30, 1888; Carpeta XII, No. 1609.

On September 6th, Sarmiento was notified that they had struck water on his land. "Hurrah, hurrah," he shouted excitedly, "stop work, bring beer for the workmen, put up the Argentine and Paraguayan flags."[6] Then he suddenly stopped and collapsed. He had suffered an attack of his old heart ailment. Dr. Andreussi was called, and he immediately saw that the old man's condition was serious. He notified the Argentine minister to Paraguay, Dr. Martín García Merou, who called in the best doctors of the country for consultation.

For the next few nights Don Domingo slept fitfully. He stayed awake in his bed or in the large mechanical chair that he had had constructed for his illness. On September 8th, he seemed to be better and he asked for a barber to shave him.

Then, on the afternoon of the 10th, eight doctors gathered in consultation. They advised Sarmiento not to move from his bed, and that night they issued a diagnosis, which was telegraphed to President Celman in Buenos Aires. The Argentine chief executive had asked to be kept in close touch with the situation. The bulletin read:

"Medical consultation held on the tenth day of September at three p.m. in Asunción del Paraguay. Diagnosis: organic lesion of the heart: Prognosis: very serious. (signed) Juan Borras; A. Calderon; David Lofruscio; S. Andreussi; Guillermo Hoskins; J. Vallory; Dr. E. Hassler; Francisco Morra."[7]

That night Don Domingo slept restlessly. He tossed and turned and muttered to himself. His face showed that he was in pain. He turned toward the wall. One hand was at his side. The other grasped his knees. The summer dawn was breaking.[8] He was heard to mutter: "I have written a book three times, and every time I have torn it up. It contained some very good things." It was two fifteen in the morning, Septem-

[6] For account of digging of well, see Palcos, *Sarmiento, op.cit.*, pp. 234-235.

[7] Rojas, p. 690.

[8] Tradition has it that before dawn, Don Domingo asked to be carried to his chair to watch the sun come up. This was done, and he died in the mechanical chair looking out at the sunrise. The story is symbolic and beautiful as an allegory, but statements by eyewitnesses and pictures of the body directly after his death (in existence at the Museo Histórico Sarmiento) indicate that he did not leave the bed while he was still alive.

ber 11, 1888. The pained body of Don Domingo was seized by a convulsion, and then it relaxed. Domingo Faustino Sarmiento was dead.

Almost three-quarters of a century after the death of Domingo Faustino Sarmiento, the struggle between personalism and nomocracy continues in the politics of Argentina. Sarmiento has been repudiated by the new personalism. His statues have been defaced by the "nationalist" followers of Perón. His pictures have been taken down from the walls of the schools that he founded. He has been painted in black terms by some of his latest biographers, and the historical revisionist school of scholars set out to destroy his reputation while whitewashing that of Rosas.

But despite this, Sarmiento lives on today. To realize the extent of that existence is to know much the difference between the Argentina of 1820 and the Argentina of a century later. The educational system that was founded by Don Domingo may not have changed the way of thought of a nation, but it remains today one of the best and most advanced in the entire world. It has educated millions of children; it has taught them the ethics, morality, aesthetics, and thought that is the heritage of humanity. The economic reforms instigated, or suggested, by Don Domingo did not make possible a nomocratic government, but they brought a material prosperity to Argentina that made her the wealthiest of Hispanic American nations, that gave her railroads, roads, ships, factories, and a prosperous agriculture. The racial reforms of Don Domingo brought no new love of law and democracy, but the masses of immigrants brought new hands to settle and work the great expanses of unsettled territory and an ambitious and vital population that created a nation with a future. Sarmiento's writings assumed a prominent position in the history of Hispanic literature. His *Facundo* led the vanguard of an Argentine literary *genre* that proved to be the most genuine and autonomous in the nation's history. *Provincial Recollections* contains pages proclaimed by George Ticknor to be unrivaled in Spanish prose, and Sarmiento's *Travels* still live as penetrating explorations into the ways of life of Europe, Africa, and North America in the nineteenth century. Such was the extent of the existence of Domingo Faustino Sarmiento—an Argentine Republic that was not transformed magically as he had expected, but that was irrevocably altered by his life.

Above all else, Sarmiento is a symbol. He is a symbol of the agony of the Hispanic world in the nineteenth century, a world that existed in one way but felt that it should be different.

Bibliography

A COMPLETE or even adequate bibliography for the study of the life of Domingo Faustino Sarmiento has never been compiled. Ricardo Rojas' *Bibliografía de Sarmiento* (Universidad Nacional de Le Plata, 1911) dealt mainly with the *Obras completas* (Complete Works). In the course of my work on Sarmiento's life, it was necessary to gather a detailed bibliography, although even the one I compiled cannot be considered complete.* For purposes of convenience, it is divided into the following categories:

I. The Published Works of Domingo Faustino Sarmiento
II. Published Archives, Manuscripts, and Collections of Letters
III. Unpublished Archives, Manuscripts, and Collections of Letters
IV. Books and Articles on the Life of Sarmiento
V. Books and Articles on Phases and Aspects of the Life of Sarmiento

I. THE PUBLISHED WORKS OF DOMINGO FAUSTINO SARMIENTO

The official collection of the "Complete Works" of Domingo F. Sarmiento includes fifty-two volumes of text and one volume of index. These *Obras completas* (53 volumes, Buenos Aires, 1884-1903) were compiled by Luis Montt and Augusto Belín Sarmiento. The *Obras completas* are divided as follows:

Volume 1. Artículos críticos i literarios
2. Artículos críticos i literarios

* The bibliography printed here is a selective bibliography from Mr. Bunkley's very extensive one.—THE PUBLISHERS.

3. Mi defensa. Recuerdos de provincia. Necrologías y biografías
4. Ortografía americana
5. Viajes por Europa, Africa, América
6. Política arjentina
7. Las vidas de Aldao, Quiroga, and El Chacho
8. Comentarios sobre la constitución
9. Instituciones sud-americanas
10. Legislación y progresos en Chile
11. Educación popular
12. Educación común
13. Argirópolis
14. Campaña en el ejército grande
15. Las ciento y una
16. Provinciano en Buenos Aires; porteño en las provincias
17. La unión nacional
18. Discursos
19. Discursos
20. Discursos
21. Discursos
22. Discursos
23. Immigración y colonización
24. Organización del estado de Buenos Aires
25. Política del estado de Buenos Aires
26. El camino del Lacio
27. Abraham Lincoln y Vélez Sarsfield
28. Ideas pedagógicas
29. Ambas Américas
30. Las escuelas, base de la prosperidad . . .
31. Práctica constitucional
32. Práctica constitucional
33. Práctica constitucional
34. Cuestiones americanas
35. Cuestiones americanas
36. Condición del estranjero en América
37. Conflictos y armonías de las razas en América
38. Conflictos y armonías de las razas en América
39. Las doctrinas revolucionarias

40. Los desfallecimientos
41. Progreso generales, vistas económicas
42. Costumbres, progresos
43. Francisco J. Muñiz y Horacio Mann
44. Informes sobre educación
45. Antonio Aberastain y Dominguito
46. Páginas literarias
47. Educar el soberano
48. La escuela ultra-pampeana
49. Memorias
50. Papeles del presidente
51. Papeles del presidente
52. Escritos diversos
53. Indices

Many of the more important of these books have gone through a number of popular editions, *Recuerdos de provincia, Conflictos y armonías de las razas en América, La vida de Dominguito,* and *El Facundo* are all examples, and it would be impossible to compile a complete bibliography of the many paper-bound, cheap editions of these works. There are two critical editions of *Facundo: Edición crítica y documentada,* Universidad Nacional de La Plata, Volumen I. Prólogo de Alberto Palcos, La Plata, 1938; and *Edición anotada por la Profesora Delia S. Etcheverry,* precedida de un estudio de la Señora Inés Cárdenas de Monner Sans, Editorial Estrada, Buenos Aires, 1940.

There are few English translations of the works of Sarmiento. Mary Mann's *Life in the Argentina Republic* (New York, 1868) is a translation of *El Facundo,* but it has long been out of print and difficult to secure. A section from *El Facundo* was translated under the title of "Argentine Tracker" in *Scholastic* (XLIX, November 26, 1945, p. 18). Stuart E. Grummon translated parts of *Recuerdos de provincia, El Facundo, Viajes por Europa, Africa, i América,* and miscellaneous articles in *A Sarmiento Anthology* (edited by A. W. Bunkley, Princeton University Press, 1948). But other than these selections, the works of Domingo Sarmiento are little known to the English-speaking world.

II. PUBLISHED ARCHIVES, MANUSCRIPTS, AND COLLECTIONS OF LETTERS

Academia Argentina de Letras. *Cartas de Sarmiento a la Señora María Mann,* Buenos Aires, 1936. Very important letters recording the intellectual relationship between Sarmiento and Mrs. Horace Mann.

Amigos de la verdad. *Cartas de Bilbao a Sarmiento,* Buenos Aires, 1875. Letters in the famous conflict between the Chilean and Argentine leaders.

Amunátegui Solar, Domingo. *Archivo epistolar de don Miguel Luis Amunátegui,* Santiago de Chile, 1942. A number of letters pertaining to Sarmiento.

Archivo Histórico de la Provincia de Buenos Aires. *Fundación de escuelas públicas en la provincia de Buenos Aires durante el gobierno escolar de Sarmiento,* La Plata, 1939. Contains records and laws pertaining to the establishment of new public schools under the direction of Sarmiento as director of schools in the province of Buenos Aires.

Argentine Republic. *Los mensajes. Historia del desenvolvimiento de la nación argentina . . . 1810-1910,* ed. by Heraclio Mabragana, 6 volumes, Buenos Aires, 1906. This series contains the presidential messages during the hundred years of Argentine history. It reveals the difference between the various presidents in regard to their political aims, methods, and philosophy. Sarmiento's messages are particularly interesting.

Argentine Republic. *Registro oficial de la república argentina que comprende los documentos expedidos desde 1810 hasta 1873,* 52 volumes, Buenos Aires, 1879-1906. An indispensable work, covering all fields of governmental activity. Volumes two to four were especially helpful for the study of Sarmiento's period.

Badano, Víctor M., editor. *Prospecto de un establecimiento de educación para señoritas, dirigido por d. Domingo Faustino Sarmiento,* Entre Ríos, 1942. A facsimile edition of the original manuscript of the prospectus of the Escuela de Santa Rosa in San Juan.

Barros Borgone, Luis. *Archivo Barros Arana. A través de una correspondencia Don Juan María Gutiérrez,* Santiago de

Chile, 1934. Letters relating to Sarmiento and his relations to Chile and his friends in Chile.

Brazil. *Actos diplomáticos do Brasil,* Río de Janeiro, 1912. Edited by José Manoel Cardoso de Oliverra, and containing material on Sarmiento's presidential regime and his visits to Brazil.

Bucich Escobar, Ismael, editor. *Constitución del Colegio de Señoritas de la Advocación de Santa Rosa de América,* Buenos Aires, 1939. A facsimile edition of Sarmiento's manuscript constitution of the Colegio de Santa Rosa. (Museo Histórico Sarmiento, Series IV, no. 1.)

Carranza, Naptali. *Oratoria argentina: recopilación cronológica de las proclamas, discursos, manifiestos, y documentos importantes, que legaron a la historia de su patria, argentinos célebres, desde el año 1810 hasta 1904,* 5 volumes, Buenos Aires, 1905. Some of Sarmiento's manuscripts when he was president and many of other statesmen during his lifetime.

Chile, Ministerio de Educación Pública. *Sarmiento director de la Escuela Normal, 1842-1845,* Santiago de Chile, 1942. The reports, letters, and decrees of Sarmiento and Montt concerning the normal school.

Epistolario entre Sarmiento y Posse, 2 volumes, Buenos Aires, 1946. A very valuable collection of intimate letters between Sarmiento and one of his closest friends. Edited by Antonio P. Castro. (Museo Histórico Sarmiento, Series V, no. 1.)

Echagüe, Juan Pablo, editor. *El Zonda de San Juan,* Buenos Aires, 1939. A facsimile reproduction of the first paper founded by Sarmiento.

García, Manuel Rafael. *Cartas confidenciales de Sarmiento,* Buenos Aires, 1917. A collection of miscellaneous hitherto unpublished letters of Sarmiento. Some of them extremely interesting.

Gez, J. W. "Sarmiento," *Revista nacional,* Buenos Aires, 1940. Includes letters from Sarmiento to J. A. Ortiz Estrada.

Museo Mitre. *Sarmiento-Mitre, Correspondencia, 1846-1869,* Buenos Aires, 1911. A great many of the very important letters in the Sarmiento-Mitre correspondence. All letters unfavorable to Mitre are omitted.

Ottolenghi, Julia. *Sarmiento a través de un epistolario,* Buenos Aires, 1940. A collection of letters made by Señorita Ottolenghi. They are chosen more for their color than for their serious implications, but they are of interest in a study of Sarmiento's personality and tastes.

III. UNPUBLISHED ARCHIVES, MANUSCRIPTS, AND COLLECTIONS OF LETTERS

In Argentina and Chile there are many sources of unpublished material that are extremely valuable for a study of Domingo Sarmiento. The most outstanding example of this is the Archives of the Museo Histórico Sarmiento (on the corner of Cuba and Juramento Streets in Buenos Aires). Here are collected a great wealth of personal items of Sarmiento, much of his library, and about 12,000 unpublished letters and manuscripts from or to him. Any study of the life of Sarmiento would have to be centered around the Museo.

In various private collections in Buenos Aires and in Chile there are to be found miscellaneous letters to and from Sarmiento. These are for the most part not particularly important. In the private collection of Señora de Gustavo Pueyrredón (Calle Quintana 557) and in the private collection of Señor Carlos Sánchez Viamonte, I found a number of interesting letters dealing with the period of Sarmiento's governorship of San Juan and presidency of the Argentine Republic.

Other important unpublished sources include:

Anales de la Universidad de Chile. The sections on the years 1843 and 1844 contain various documents pertaining to the period when Sarmiento was a member of the faculty of the University of Chile.

Argentine Republic. *Archivo general de la nación.* These national archives contain extensive material on the entire period and much specific material on Sarmiento. They are difficult to handle because they are completely unorganized.

Chile. *Archivo nacional de Chile.* These national archives in Chile contain a volume with very interesting letters from

Sarmiento to Manuel José Quiroga Rosas during the period from 1839 to 1845. Volume 318 contains the documents of the lawsuit between Sarmiento and Domingo Santiago Godoy.

United States. National Archives, State Department Division, *Argentine Republic.* Incoming Correspondence, Volume 2. Notes, February 1, 1854 to December 31, 1883. Notes from Sarmiento to the United States government both while he was minister to the United States and while he was president of Argentina. Outgoing correspondence, Volume VI, September 28, 1838 to October 31, 1896. This includes notes from the United States government to the Argentine government during the time that Sarmiento was minister in the United States and president of Argentina.

United States. National Archives, State Department Division, *Argentine Republic.* Despatches, Volume XVIII, July 21, 1869 to August 12, 1872; Volume XIX, August 22, 1872 to December 31, 1874; Volume XXIII, December 13, 1878 to July 1, 1881. These archives contain reports from United States diplomatic representatives prior to, during, and after Sarmiento's presidential administration. They contain interesting descriptions of Sarmiento and valuable accounts of the events of the time.

IV. BOOKS AND ARTICLES ON THE LIFE OF SARMIENTO

A. Books

There have been many biographies of Sarmiento published in Spanish and several in other European languages. Perhaps the most complete biography is Ricardo Rojas, *El profeta de la pampa* (Buenos Aires, 1945). The author did very little research in the unpublished material available at the Museo Sarmiento and confined himself almost exclusively to the *Obras completas* and a limited number of secondary sources.

The biography that has the most sympathetic approach to Sarmiento's life and the most living account of his personality is Alberto Palcos, *Sarmiento—la vida—la obra—las ideas—el genio* (3 editions, Buenos Aires, 1938). This work does not give a detailed account of its subject's life, but it is valuable for understanding Sarmiento's spirit. Palcos also failed to consult in any detail the unpublished archives in the Museo Sarmiento.

The work of José Guillermo Guerra, *Sarmiento, su vida y sus obras* (Santiago de Chile, 1938) was published for the first time in 1900. It remains until today one of the most valuable biographies of Sarmiento. Balancing the accurate account of his life that is found in Rojas with the understanding of his personality that is found in Palcos, Guerra produced a well-rounded work. It suffers from its early date of composition. At that date, the author did not even have the complete *Obras* to make use of, and he had no access to the many collections of letters that are today available.

Manuel Gálvez, *La vida de Sarmiento* (Buenos Aires, 1945) is an entertaining and detailed account of Sarmiento's life. While both the works of Palcos and those of Guerra show an excessive praise and admiration of their subject that detracts from their objectivity, Gálvez is obviously intending to attack Sarmiento violently. The most outstanding virtue of his work is his ability to weave the historical background into the narrative of the life in the most effective way possible. His style is lively and interesting, but the bias of the anti-Sarmiento view and the repetitious attacks on all phases of his personality and life become monotonous.

A short (175 page) biography by Juan Rómulo Fernández, *Sarmiento* (Buenos Aires, 1938) is an easily read, sympathetic account of the Argentine statesman's life and works. Leopoldo Lugones' *Historia de Sarmiento* (Buenos Aires, 1945), is a more critical and analytical account. Lugones attempts to define the elements of Sarmiento's thought and the "causes" of its development. He has some very penetrating observations in this respect. Other comments show a decided lack of understanding of the subject's personality.

There are several good works on Sarmiento's thought. Ezequiel Martínez Estrada, *Sarmiento* (Buenos Aires, 1946), is the most comprehensive study of Sarmiento's ideas. Raúl A. Orgaz, *Sarmiento y el naturalismo histórico* (Córdoba, 1940) is a very stimulating analysis of Sarmiento's thought, relating it to the main trends of European thought of his day. It suffers from the use of vaguely defined abstract terms. Aníbal Ponce, *Sarmiento, constructor de la nueva Argentina* (Buenos Aires, 1938) deals with Sarmiento's ideas as the basis of modern Argentina.

There are no important works on Sarmiento's life in English. Madaline Wallis Nicols' *Sarmiento, a Chronicle of Inter-American Friendship* (Washington, D.C., 1940) is but a pamphlet that does not pretend to do more than outline the outstanding aspects of its subject's life and show his interest in the United States. Allison W. Bunkley's "Introduction" to *A Sarmiento Anthology* (Princeton University Press, 1948) attempts to outline Sarmiento's life and integrate it with his artistic accomplishment and with his ideas.

Other books dealing with the life of Sarmiento are:

Albarracín, José Manuel H. *Sarmiento,* Buenos Aires, 1940. This is a brief and summary account by a descendant of Sarmiento's mother's family.

Amadeo, Octavio R. *Domingo Faustino Sarmiento,* Buenos Aires, 1939. A revised edition of a lecture on the life of Sarmiento given at the Jockey Club in Buenos Aires.

Argüello, Alfredo Federico. *Domingo Faustino Sarmiento,* Buenos Aires, 1938. A superficial account of his life.

Astolfi, José Carlos. *Domingo Faustino Sarmiento,* Buenos Aires, 1938. A superficial account that says nothing new.

Bel, A. *Reseña biográfica de Domingo F. Sarmiento,* Buenos Aires, 1880. By Sarmiento's grandson, Augusto Belín Sarmiento. A very useful short summary of the events of the subject's life before 1880.

Belín Sarmiento, Augusto. *Epistolario de Sarmiento,* Buenos Aires, 1925. An account of Sarmiento's life from a collection of letters.

Belín Sarmiento, Augusto. *Sarmiento anecdótico,* Saint Cloud, 1929. A collection of anecdotes about Sarmiento's life that is very amusing and extremely useful. Most of the incidents are taken from the *Obras,* but some are from the personal experience of the author.

Bosch Vinelli, Julia Beatriz. *Domingo F. Sarmiento,* Buenos Aires, 1938. A short account of his life.

Bustos Berrondo, Raúl. *Sarmiento,* Buenos Aires, 1938. A novelization of Sarmiento's life.

Castro, Isaac E. *Domingo Faustino Sarmiento,* Buenos Aires, 1938. A short account of his life with a definite anti-Sarmiento bias.

Díaz, Francisco Antonio. *Sarmiento,* no place, no date. Short pamphlet account of Sarmiento's life.

Duarte, Maria F. de. *Anecdotario Sarmiento,* Buenos Aires, 1927. A collection of 300 more or less amusing stories about incidents in the life of Sarmiento.

Fernández, Juan Rómulo. *Domingo Faustino Sarmiento,* San Juan, 1911. A short essay inspired by the new monument to Sarmiento in San Juan.

Franca, Acacio. *Em louver das Americas,* Río de Janeiro, 1944. A German account of Sarmiento's life.

Galván Moreno, C. *Radiografía de Sarmiento,* Buenos Aires, 1938. A fairly long (445 pages) study of Sarmiento's life and thought. It takes its material completely from published sources.

González-Arrili, Bernardo. *Sarmiento,* third edition, Buenos Aires, 1946. A readable, superficial work on Sarmiento's life used in primary schools as a text.

Holmberg, Eduardo H. *Sarmiento,* Buenos Aires, 1938. Short biography that adds nothing to other published material.

Larrain de Vere, A. *Sarmiento,* no place, no date. Pamphlet.

Lobo, Pedro. *Sarmiento, eminencia immortal,* no place, no date. Short panegyric of Sarmiento.

Mann, Mary (Mrs. Horace Mann). *Cenni biografici de Domingo F. Sarmiento.* Translated into Italian by Edoardo Calveri, Genoa, 1869. Mrs. Mann's biographical introduction to her translation of *El Facundo* as *Life in the Argentine Republic.* She received her material from Sarmiento himself.

Martínez Urrutia, Luis. *Sarmiento,* Buenos Aires, 1938. A brief and rather superficial account of Sarmiento's life.

Mendizábal, Ernesto de. *Domingo Faustino Sarmiento,* Buenos Aires, 1938. Pamphlet praising Sarmiento's life and works.

Navarro, Secundino J. *Notes sobre la vida y escritos del*

General Domingo Faustino Sarmiento publicadas con motivo de la inauguración del monumento del prócer en San Juan el 17 de noviembre le 1901, San Juan, 1938. Notes on the life and personality of Sarmiento by one of his contemporaries.

Oviedo, Gelanor M. *Sarmiento,* Buenos Aires, 1938. A brief and superficial account of his life.

Pico, Amelia. *Sarmiento-Síntesis cronológica de su vida,* Buenos Aires, no date. A pamphlet published by the Museo Histórico Sarmiento. A very useful summary of the important dates in Sarmiento's life.

Pico, Octavio S. *Domingo Faustino Sarmiento,* Buenos Aires, 1938. A pamphlet on the important events of Sarmiento's life.

Quesada, Vicente G. *Domingo Faustino Sarmiento,* Buenos Aires, 1904. This work deals pretty heavily with the diplomatic aspects of Sarmiento's regime.

Quintana, Carlos. *Domingo F. Sarmiento,* Buenos Aires, 1931. A brief account of his life.

Quintana, Carlos. *Une vie américaine; Sarmiento,* Paris, 1935. One of the few accounts of Sarmiento's life in French.

Quintana, Carlos. *Une vie américaine; Sarmiento,* Brussels, 1935. A lecture delivered in Brussels, similar to the pamphlet published in Paris, just above.

Suárez, José Bernardo. *Rasgos biográficos del señor don Domingo F. Sarmiento,* Santiago de Chile, 1863. An account of Sarmiento's life written by one of his students at the Escuela Normal in Santiago.

Valdés, Carmelo B. *Sarmiento y su obra,* Buenos Aires, 1913.

B. Commemorative Books

On different anniversaries of the birth and death of Sarmiento, books have been published to commemorate his life and works. Among these are:

Comisión Nacional de Homenaje a Sarmiento. *Sarmiento,* 5 volumes, Buenos Aires, 1938. On the fiftieth anniversary of his death, these five volumes included articles on different phases of his life, excerpts from his works, and speeches in praise of his accomplishments.

Comisión popular en el centenario de Sarmiento. *Homenaje de la comisión*, Buenos Aires, 1911. On the centenary of Sarmiento's birth, this book (254 pages) contained studies of Sarmiento's life and works.

Congreso Argentino de Educación. *Homenaje a Sarmiento*, Buenos Aires, 1938. Another collection of essays on his life and works.

Consejo Nacional de Educación. *Sarmiento*, Buenos Aires, 1889. A collection of the funeral orations after the death of Sarmiento.

Escuela "Juan José Paso," *Homenaje a Sarmiento*, Buenos Aires, 1938. The Juan José Paso School pays homage to Sarmiento on the fiftieth anniversary of his death.

Espinosa Bravo, C. A. "Ante el cincuentenario de . . . Sarmiento," *Universidad*, Mexico, November 1937, pp. 4-10. The Mexican universities pay homage to Sarmiento.

Ferreyra, J. Alfredo. *En el centenario de Sarmiento*, Buenos Aires, 1911. This discussion of the life and works of Sarmiento was written to commemorate the first centenary of his birth. It was also published in *La revista de derecho historia y letras*, Buenos Aires, XXIX, 415.

García, Jacinto Sixto. *Homenaje al ilustre educador argentino presidente Sarmiento en su centenario*, Mexico, 1911. Deals primarily with Sarmiento's efforts to promote Latin American culture.

Guerrero, Cesar H. *Sarmiento en el 50 aniversario de su muerte*, San Juan, 1938. A tribute by one of the historians of Sarmiento's birthplace.

Jofre, Elena. *Discurso en homenaje al centenario de Sarmiento*, La Plata, 1911. A speech in praise of Sarmiento's accomplishments.

Liga Patriótica Argentina, Biblioteca de la. *Homenaje a D. F. Sarmiento*, Buenos Aires, 1938.

Longhi de Bracaglia, Leopoldo. *Homenaje a Sarmiento en el Colegio de Buenos Aires*, Buenos Aires, 1938. This was published in *Archivos de la Universidad de Buenos Aires*, Buenos Aires, 1938, XIII, 336.

Melo, Leopoldo. *El centenario de Sarmiento en la facultad de derecho*, Buenos Aires, 1911. Articles by members of the faculty of law of the University of Buenos Aires on different phases of Sarmiento's work and life.

Mercade Vera, Evangelina E. M. de. *Homenaje a Sarmiento,* Buenos Aires, 1938. A collection of articles and poems by different authors. It also includes the plans for a course on Sarmiento.

Universidad Nacional de la Plata. *Sarmiento. Homenaje de la facultad de humanidades y ciencias de la educación,* La Plata, 1939. A collection of some very excellent articles on different phases of the life and thought of Sarmiento.

Universidad Nacional del Litoral. *Sarmiento,* Santa Fé, 1939. Articles of the same character as those in the preceding book.

Zubiarr, J. B. *Mi homenaje en el primer centenario de Sarmiento,* Buenos Aires, 1911. A laudatory study of Sarmiento's life.

C. Articles

Among the newspaper and magazine articles on the life of Sarmiento are:

Anonymous. "Educational Biography, Señor D. F. Sarmiento," *The American Journal of Education,* XVI, 1866, 593-598. This work talks of "Colonel Sarmiento," who was at that time Argentine minister in the United States. The source of the article is described as a "biography now in preparation, which the richness of the material has unexpectedly swelled from a brief memorial originally prepared for this article."

Barcos, Julio. "Sarmiento, a Type of the Complete Man," *Inter-America,* February 1920, p. 173ff.

Barroll, H. H. "Sketch of Domingo Faustino Sarmiento," *Education,* January 1901, XXI, 257-259. A brief and superficial account of Sarmiento's life.

Belín Sarmiento, Augusto. "Anécdotas de Sarmiento," *El monitor de la educación común,* Buenos Aires, April, 1931. A collection of unpublished anecdotes on Sarmiento's life.

Belín Sarmiento, Augusto. "Epistolario de Sarmiento," *Instituto de literatura argentina, sección de crítica,* Buenos Aires, 1925, pp. 131-144. Some of Sarmiento's hitherto unpublished letters.

Berrutti, Jose Je. "Sarmiento," *Bulletin of the Pan American Union,* LXXII, 1938, pp. 502-512. This article puts its emphasis on Sarmiento's literary work.

Blanco Fombona, Rufino. "Sarmiento" in his *Grandes escritores de América,* Madrid, 1917, pp. 77-171. A study of the life and thought of Sarmiento by the great Venezuelan historian and critic.

Calatroni, Ricardo. "Sarmiento," *Sarmiento, Homenaje en el cincuagésimo año de su muerte.* Universidad Nacional del Litoral, Santa Fé, 1938.

Cardarelli, Jose S. "Sarmiento," *Sarmiento, Homenaje en el cincuagésimo año de su muerte.* Universidad Nacional del Litoral, Santa Fé, 1939.

"Centennial Anniversary of the Birth of Sarmiento," *Bulletin of the Pan American Union,* September 1911, XXXIII, pp. 520-522.

"Cincuentenario de la muerte de D. F. Sarmiento," *Boletin del Museo Social Argentino,* Buenos Aires, September-October, 1938, pp. 245-255.

"Domingo F. Sarmiento, 50 anniversario de su muerte," *Norte,* Buenos Aires, October 1, 1938, p. 1.

"Domingo F. Sarmiento, socio honorario de la Sociedad Rural Argentina ye el Progreso Agropecuario Argentino," *Anales de la Sociedad Rural Argentina,* Buenos Aires, October 1938, pp. 921-924.

"En el cincuentenario de la muerte de Sarmiento," *Crónica educacional,* Buenos Aires, July-August, 1938, pp. 26-27.

Espinosa Bravo, C. A. "Ante el cincuentenario de . . . Sarmiento," *Mensaje,* Quito, October 1938, pp. 142-153.

Francioni, Isaac. "Sarmiento," *Sarmiento, Homenaje en el cincuagésimo año de su muerte,* Universidad Nacional del Litoral, Santa Fé, 1938.

Groussac, Paul. "Sarmiento," in his *Viaje sentimental,* Buenos Aires, 1923. An interesting interpretation of Sarmiento's life and thought.

Mazzoni, Eduardo D. "Sarmiento," *Sarmiento, Homenaje en el cincuagésimo año de su muerte.* Universidad Nacional del Litoral, Santa Fé, 1938.

Melo, Leopoldo. "El centenario de Sarmiento," *Revista de derecho historia y letras*, XXXIX, 222.

Nigro, Angel J. "Sarmiento," *Sarmiento, Homenaje en el cincuagésimo año de su muerte.* Universidad Nacional del Litoral, Santa Fé, 1938.

Orgaz, Arturo. "Domingo Faustino Sarmiento," *Derechos del hombre*, Buenos Aires, September, 1938.

"Portrait of Domingo Faustino Sarmiento," *Bulletin of the Pan American Union*, Washington, June 1941, LXXV, 341.

Rovertaccio, Ernesta C. "Sarmiento," *Sarmiento, Homenaje en el cincuagésimo año de su muerte.* Universidad Nacional del Litoral, Sante Fé, 1938.

Segovia, Eladio. "Sarmiento," *Sarmiento, Homenaje en el cincuagésimo año de su muerte.* Universidad Nacional del Litoral, Santa Fé, 1938.

V. BOOKS AND ARTICLES ON PHASES AND ASPECTS OF THE LIFE OF SARMIENTO

A. Books

There are literally hundreds of books and articles that deal specifically with Sarmiento but only with certain phases or aspects of his life or personality. These are all important in a study of his life as a whole. Among the books in this category are:

Aguiar, Henoch D. *Sarmiento: la lección de su infancia y juventud*, Córdoba, 1939. This book deals with Sarmiento's childhood and youth.

Alberdi, Juan Bautista. *Obras póstumas*, Buenos Aires, 1897. Volumes V and VI of these works contain material relative to Sarmiento; especially interesting is the correspondence regarding Sarmiento's early attempts at poetry.

Alcorta, Santiago. *Sarmiento y Tejedor*, Buenos Aires, 1889. A partisan account of the relationship of Sarmiento and his political enemy Tejedor.

Alvarez, Florencio. *Sarmiento agricultor*, Buenos Aires, 1945. A study of Sarmiento as a farmer and his aid to farmers.

Aubone, Guillermo, A. *Los eucaliptus, los mimbres y la*

higuera de Sarmiento, Museo Histórico Sarmiento, Series II, no. 7, Buenos Aires, 1942. An account of Sarmiento's efforts to introduce certain trees in Argentina.

Avellaneda, Nicolás. *Escritos y discursos,* Buenos Aires, 1910. Avellaneda was another contemporary of Sarmiento, and his observations and comments are of great interest. Volume I is of special importance in this respect.

Ayala, Eusebio. *Aspectos americanos de la personalidad de Sarmiento,* Museo Histórico Sarmiento, Series II, no. 4, Buenos Aires, 1939. A discussion of the Pan American spirit of Sarmiento.

Bosch Vinelli, Julia Beatriz. *Sarmiento y Urquiza; del unitarismo al federalismo,* Buenos Aires, 1938. An account of Sarmiento's relations with Urquiza and the former's swing from unitarism to federalism.

Bucich, Antonio J. *Luchas y rutas de Sarmiento,* Buenos Aires, 1942. This book contains chapters on different phases of Sarmiento's life. One deals with his phase "on ne tue point les idées." Another deals with his stay in Montevideo in 1846.

Bucich Escobar, Ismael. *Guia descriptiva del Museo Histórico,* Museo Histórico Sarmiento, Series I, no. 2, Buenos Aires, 1943. A descriptive guide of the contents of the Museo Histórico Sarmiento.

Bucich Escobar, Ismael. *Las reliquias de Sarmiento,* Museo Histórico Sarmiento, Series I, no. 1, Buenos Aires, 1940. A list of the personal items pertaining to the life of Sarmiento or belonging to Sarmiento that are now to be found in the Museo Sarmiento.

Canclini, Santiago. *Sarmiento defensor de la escuela laica,* Buenos Aires, 1946. This pamphlet contains excerpts from Sarmiento's works in which he defends lay education against religious education.

Canter, Juan. *Sarmiento, Groussac y Láinez,* Buenos Aires, 1928. Sarmiento is compared to the writer Groussac and the educator Lainez.

Castro, Antonio P. *El archivo del Museo Sarmiento. Epistolario entre Sarmiento y Posse,* Museo Histórico Sarmiento, Series II, no. 15, Buenos Aires, 1946. An account of the wealth of unpublished material pertaining to Sarmiento to be found in the Museo. Particular reference to the correspondence between Sarmiento and Posse.

Castro, Antonio P. *Las bibliotecas del Museo Sarmiento*, Museo Histórico Sarmiento, Series I, no. 3, Buenos Aires, 1946. A description of the libraries in the Museo Sarmiento.

Castro, Antonio P. *Rasgos de la vida de Domingo F. Sarmiento por su hermana Bienvenida*, Museo Histórico Sarmiento, Series II, no. 14, Buenos Aires, 1946. The publication of a hitherto unpublished manuscript by Bienvenida Sarmiento describing certain phases of her brother's life. Introduction and notes by Castro.

Castro, Antonio P. *Salas Belín Sarmiento*, Museo Histórico Sarmiento, Buenos Aires, 1946. A description of a new room in the Museo Sarmiento donated by Sarmiento's grandson, Augusto Belín Sarmiento.

Castro, Isaac E. *Sarmiento ante la montonera*, Buenos Aires. 1937. A critical discussion of Sarmiento's activities against El Chaco during his governorship of San Juan.

Círculo de la Prensa. *Sarmiento periodista*, Buenos Aires, 1938. A series of lectures on Sarmiento as a newspaperman.

Colmo, Alfredo. *Sarmiento y los Estados Unidos*, Buenos Aires, 1915. A lecture on Sarmiento and his ideas on the United States.

Correas, Edmundo. *Andanzas de un civilizador*, Mendoza, 1944. A pamphlet on Sarmiento's travels.

Correas, Edmundo. *Sarmiento y sus amigos*, San Juan, 1946. Sarmiento's friends and their influence upon his life.

Crespo, Eduardo. *Sarmiento y la ciudad de Buenos Aires*, Museo Histórico Sarmiento, Series II, no. 9, Buenos Aires, 1942. Sarmiento's relationship with the city of Buenos Aires.

Del Carril, Bonificio. *La vida sanjuanina de Sarmiento*, Buenos Aires, 1938. A superficial but handy account of Sarmiento's life in San Juan.

Doll, Ramón and Cano, Guillermo. *Las mentiras de Sarmiento*, Buenos Aires, 1939. A study dedicated to the untruths and contradictions in the works of Sarmiento.

Donoso, Armando. *Sarmiento en el destierro*, Buenos Aires, 1927. A very good account of Sarmiento in exile in Chile.

Durand, Luis. *Visión de Sarmiento; su inquietud fecunda*

y creadora, Santiago de Chile, 1938. A discussion of Sarmiento as a creator of the future.

Fain, Jordana. *El niño de Carrascal,* no place, no date. The childhood of Sarmiento.

Fernández, Germán M. *Sarmiento, rotariano,* Rosario, 1938. A discussion of Sarmiento as a Rotarian.

Fernández, Juan Rómulo. *Sarmiento escritor,* Buenos Aires, 1931. An analysis of Sarmiento as a writer and newspaperman.

Gallo, Vicente Carmelo. *Algunos aspectos de Sarmiento presidente,* Buenos Aires, 1937.

García, Germán. *Actualidad de Sarmiento,* Buenos Aires, 1938. Picturing Sarmiento as ahead of his time in ideas.

Goldstein, Mateo. *Domingo Faustino Sarmiento y la idea de la libertad,* Buenos Aires, 1938.

Heras, Carlos. *Sarmiento y sus recuerdos sobre los comienzos de la ciudad,* La Plata, 1939. Sarmiento and the history of the city of La Plata.

Hidalgo, Alberto. *Sarmiento y la cuestión de Patagonia,* Buenos Aires, 1945. This is the best account of Sarmiento's part in the dispute with Chile over the possession of Patagonia.

Landa, Augusto. *Irrigación y vialidad en la provincia de San Juan durante el gobierno de Domingo F. Sarmiento,* San Juan, 1938.

Larrea, Julio C. *Sarmiento educador,* Quito, 1938.

Lewin, Boleslao. *Sarmiento el paladín de la democracia,* Buenos Aires, 1938.

Mallea, Narciso, S. *Intervenciones en San Juan entre años 1868 y 1873 o Sarmiento presidente,* Buenos Aires, 1930. Criticism of Sarmiento's interventions in San Juan during his presidency.

Manito, Oscar. *Domingo Faustino Sarmiento pensador y maestro,* Buenos Aires, 1938.

Mantovani, Juan. *La pasión civilizadora de Sarmiento,* Santa Fé, 1938.

Martin, Percy Alvin. *Sarmiento and New England,* Chapel Hill, 1942.

Montt, Luis. *Noticias de las publicaciones hechas en Chile por don Domingo F. Sarmiento, 1841-1871,* Santiago de Chile,

1884. A bibliography of material published by Sarmiento in Chile between 1841 and 1871.

Mortillaro, Gaspar. *Esquema biográfico y anécdotas de Sarmiento,* Buenos Aires, 1938. An outline for a biography of Sarmiento and a collection of anecdotes on his life.

Moya, Ismael. *El americanismo en el teatro y la prédica de Sarmiento,* Buenos Aires, 1939.

Mullins, William G. *Sarmiento in the Periodical Press of the United States, 1866-1944,* unpublished thesis, New York University, 1947. A useful critical bibliography of all accounts of Sarmiento in the periodical press of the United States since the period when he was minister in this country.

Nelson, Ernesto. *Sarmiento y los Estados Unidos de Norteamérica,* Museo Histórico Sarmiento, Series II, no. 12. A superficial account of the influence of North America upon Sarmiento.

Nelson, Ernesto, *Sarmiento y el significado social de la escuela argentina,* Rosario, 1938. A discussion of Sarmiento's ideas on the social importance of public schools in the development of Argentine "civilization."

Onetti, Carlos María. *Cuatro clases sobre Sarmiento escritor,* Tucumán, 1939.

Osorio, Segundo V. *Glosando algunas ideas pedagógicas de Domingo F. Sarmiento,* Buenos Aires, 1938.

Otamendi, Belisario Jorge. *Sarmiento en la medalla,* Buenos *Aires,* 1939. The numismatics of Sarmiento.

Ox, Bachiller. *Sarmiento a la luz de la fisiología,* Buenos Aires, 1882. A pseudo-scientific attempt to interpret Sarmiento in terms of physiology.

Pagano, Jose León. *El problema estético en la psicología de Sarmiento,* Buenos Aires, 1940-1941. The aesthetics of Sarmiento.

Palcos, Alberto. *El panamericanismo de Sarmiento,* Museo Histórico Sarmiento, Series II, no. 6, Buenos Aires, 1941.

Palcos, Alberto. *El Facundo, Rasgos de Sarmiento,* Buenos Aires, 1945. The conception, the sources, and the writing of *El Facundo.* It also contains chapters on Sarmiento and poetry, Sarmiento and Manuel Montt, Sarmiento and the secret ballot, and Sarmiento as an orator.

Ponce, Manuel A. *Sarmiento en Chile,* Buenos Aires, 1899.

Ponce, Manuel A. *Sarmiento y sus doctrinas pedagógicas,* Valparaíso, 1890.

Quiroga, Mario E. *Sarmiento y sus viajes,* Buenos Aires, 1944.

Ríos Gallardo, Conrado. *Evocación de Sarmiento en Chile,* Santiago, 1926.

Ríos Gallardo, Conrado. *Evocación de Sarmiento en Chile,* Museo Histórico Sarmiento, Series II, no. 5, Buenos Aires, 1940.

Rivarola, Rodolfo. *Sarmiento vive,* Buenos Aires, 1939. A discussion of Sarmiento as the creator of modern Argentina.

Rodríguez, Etchart C. *Domingo Faustino Sarmiento,* Buenos Aires, 1913.

Rodríguez, Augusto G. *Sarmiento militar,* Museo Histórico Sarmiento, Series II, no. 10, Buenos Aires, 1943. Discussion of Sarmiento's military career.

Rodríguez Larreta, Carlos. *Conferencia,* Buenos Aires, 1939. A lecture delivered on Sarmiento.

Rodríguez Larreta, Carlos. *Conferencia leida en el 15 de mayo de 1911,* Rosario, 1911. Lecture on Sarmiento.

Rojas, A. Nerio. *La psicología de Sarmiento,* Buenos Aires, 1938.

Rossi, Angel F. *Sarmiento y la edificación escolar bonaerense,* Buenos Aires, 1937. An account of Sarmiento's activities in creating the Buenos Aires school system.

Saenz Hayes, Ricardo. *La polémica de Alberdi con Sarmiento,* Buenos Aires, 1926.

Sánchez, Luis Alberto. *Ideario de Domingo Faustino Sarmiento,* Santiago de Chile, 1943. A collection of Sarmiento's writings and sayings.

Santovenia, Emeterio. *Genio y acción—Sarmiento y Martí,* Havana, 1938. A comparative study of Sarmiento and Martí.

Sherril, Charles Hitchcock. *The Pan Americanism of Henry Clay, Sarmiento and Root,* Buenos Aires, 1909. The author sees these men as setting the standards for Pan American relations.

Sosa Loyola, Gilberto. *Sarmiento y San Luis,* San Luis, 1938.

Uzcátegui, Emilio. *Sarmiento, hombre de America,* Quito, 1941.

Villergas, J. M. *Sarmenticidio o a mal sarmiento buena podadera,* Paris, 1892. A violent attack on Sarmiento's criticism of Spain in his *Viajes.*

Wedell, Alexander Wilbourne. *In Honor of Domingo F. Sarmiento,* Buenos Aires, 1938. A very superficial discussion of Sarmiento's personality.

Wilgus, Curtis A. *Domingo Faustino Sarmiento: a Great South American Teacher Is Honored in Florida,* Washington, 1946. This pamphlet is on the dedication of a monument to Sarmiento at the "oldest wooden schoolhouse in the U.S.A." in Saint Augustine, Florida.

Zamorano Baier, Antonio. *Sarmiento el civilizador,* Buenos Aires, 1938.

B. Articles

Acosta, Alfredo. "En la tumba del Gral. Sarmiento," *El Progreso,* Santa Fé, 1889. A poem inspired when the author visited Sarmiento's tomb.

"Actuaciones en conmemoración del cincuentenario de la muerte de . . . Sarmiento," *Letras,* Lima, 3ª cuatrimestre, 1938, pp. 355-392. Contains speeches on Sarmiento by H. U. Urteaga, Pedro Dulanto, E. Colombes Marmol, Manuel Beltroy.

Agosti, Héctor P. "Sociología de 'Facundo,'" *Revista trimestral de cultura moderna. Universidad Nacional de Colombia,* Bogota, 1947, VIII, January, February, and March 1947.

Aguilar, Félix. "Sarmiento precursor de la astronomía en la república argentina," *Humanidades,* Universidad Nacional de La Plata, La Plata, 1938, XXVI.

Antille, Armando G. "Sarmiento político," *Sarmiento, Homenaje en el cincuagésimo año de su muerte,* Universidad Nacional del Litoral, Santa Fé, 1938.

Arrieta, Rafael Alberto. "García Román," *La Prensa,* October 16, 1938. This article deals with Sarmiento's early attempts at poetry.

Arrieta, Rafael Alberto. "Sarmiento y la poesía," *Humanidades,* XXVI, Universidad Nacional de la Plata, Buenos Aires, 1938.

Azzarini, Emilio. "La edición de 'Facundo,' de Sarmiento, hecha por la Universidad Nacional de la Plata," *Humani-*

dades, XXVI, Universidad Nacional de La Plata, Buenos Aires, 1939.

Barreiro, José P. "La Argentina que soñó Sarmiento," *Cursos y conferencias*, Buenos Aires, February, 1939, pp. 625-654.

Barroll, Henry H. "General Domingo Faustino Sarmiento," *Education*, XXI, 1901, pp. 257-259. The emphasis of this article is on Sarmiento's educational projects and accomplishments.

Beltrán, Oscar R. "Sarmiento, periodista enamorado de la libertad," *Aquí Está*, Buenos Aires, August 30, 1943, VIII, p. 6.

Bengoa, Juan León. "La vida gloriosa de Sarmiento, film del hombre que realizó su sueño," *Sociedad de amigos del libro rioplatense*, Buenos Aires, 1936, XXXI. This is in the form of a script for a movie on the life of Sarmiento.

Bielsa, Rafael. "La política jurídica de Sarmiento," *Sarmiento, Homenaje en el cincuagésimo año de su muerte*, Universidad Nacional del Litoral, Santa Fé, 1938.

Brumana, Herminia. "Sarmiento, Gaucho," *Derechos del hombre*, Buenos Aires, September 1938.

Calcagno, Alfredo D. "Sarmiento, el maestro de la patria," *Humanidades*, Universidad Nacional de la Plata, Buenos Aires, 1938, XXVI.

Candelon, Alejandro. "Sarmiento," *Revista de derecho, historia y letras*, XXXIX, 44.

Cané, Miguel. "Sarmiento," *La Biblioteca*, II, 517.

Carayon, Marcel. "Sarmiento et la formation de la conscience argentine," *La revue argentine*, Paris, 1938.

Cárcano, Miguel A. "Sarmiento et la France," *La revue argentine*, Paris, February 1939, pp. 3-8.

Cárdenas de Monner Sans, Maria Inés. "Algunos aspectos literarios de 'Facundo,'" *Humanidades*, Universidad Nacional de la Plata, Buenos Aires, 1938, XXVI.

Cardozo, Efraim. "Sarmiento y el Paraguay," *Sarmiento y Avellaneda—El congreso de Belgrano*, Museo Histórico Sarmiento, Series II, no. 2, Buenos Aires, 1939.

Cassani, Juan E. "Las doctrinas pedagógicas de Sarmiento," *Humanidades*, Universidad Nacional de la Plata, Buenos Aires, 1939, XXVI.

Castañeda, C. E. "Latin America's First Great Educator,"

The Current History Magazine, XXII, 1925, 223-225.

Castro, Américo. "En torno al 'Facundo' de Sarmiento," *Sur,* Buenos Aires, August 1938, pp. 26-34. This is a discussion of the Romantic elements in *El Facundo.* It makes a very interesting comparison of Goya and Sarmiento.

Castro y López, Manuel. "Sarmiento," *Revista de derecho, historia y letras,* XLVIII, 503.

Chapin, Clara Cutler. "Sarmiento the Teacher," *Bulletin of the Pan American Union,* Washington, September 1944, LXXVIII, 481-486.

Correas, Edmundo. "Centenario del nacimiento de 'Dominguito,'" *Los Andes,* Mendoza, April 17, 1945.

Correas, Edmundo. "El doctor de Michigan," *Los Andes,* Mendoza, February 18, 1945.

Correas, Edmundo. "En el centenario del 'Facundo,'" *Los Andes,* Mendoza, May 1, 1945.

Correas, Edmundo. "Michigan, la universidad de Sarmiento," *Los Andes,* Mendoza, February 11, 1945.

Correas, Edmundo, "Sarmiento es preso y procesado en Mendoza," *Los Andes,* Mendoza, September 9, 1945.

Correas, Edmundo. "Niños Cuyanos becados por Rivadavia," *Los Andes,* Mendoza, September 3, 1945.

Correas, Edmundo. "Sarmiento y el nacimiento intelectual de Chile," *Los Andes,* Mendoza, December 2, 1945.

Dana Montano, Salvador M. "Sarmiento constitucionalista," *Sarmiento, Homenaje en el cincuagésimo año de su muerte,* Universidad Nacional del Litoral, Santa Fé, 1938.

Daniels, Margarette. "Domingo F. Sarmiento," *Makers of South America,* New York, 1916. Deals with the missionary educational movement of the United States and Canada.

Doglioli, Rodolfo. "Sarmiento y la codificacion argentina," *Sarmiento, Homenaje en el cincuagésimo año de su muerte,* Universidad Nacional del Litoral, Santa Fé, 1938.

"Domingo F. Sarmiento, 'Facundo' y rasgos morales del gran americano," *La Cronica,* Lima, September 11, 1938.

Echagüe, Juan Pablo. "Sarmiento, critico teatral," *Instituto de literatura argentina, Sección de crítica,* Buenos Aires, 1925, I, no. 4, pp. 99-114.

Ewing, Enrique E. "Century of a Friendship, Sarmiento

and Horace Mann," *Bulletin of the Pan American Union*, Washington, December 1947, LXXXI, 664-667.

Fariña Núñez, Porfirio. "Los amores de Sarmiento," *Nosotros*, Buenos Aires, May 1933, pp. 50-64.

Figueroa, Andrés A. "Sarmiento y su propaganda en Chile contra Rosas," *Revista del archivo de Santiago del Estero*, Santiago del Estero, May-June, 1927, VI, no. 12.

Fonseca, Guillermo. "Sarmiento a través del Facundo," *Revista de la facultad de ciencias jurídicas y sociales*, Guatemala, September-October, 1938, pp. 182-193.

Galván, Moreno C. "Sarmiento, la mala prensa y la libertad de prensa," *Claridad*, Buenos Aires, September, 1938.

Gambino, Humberto C. "El carácter de Sarmiento," *Sarmiento, Homenaje en el cincuagésimo año de su muerte*, Universidad Nacional del Litoral, Santa Fé, 1938.

García Meron, Martin. "Sarmiento," *La Biblioteca*, II, 20.

Ghioldi, Orestes. "La clase obrera y Sarmiento," *Derechos del hombre*, Buenos Aires, September, 1938.

Giménez-Pastor, Arturo. "El 'Yo' de Sarmiento, *La Nacion*, Buenos Aires, May 15, 1911.

Gollán, Josué. "Significado del homenaje a Sarmiento," *Sarmiento, Homenaje en el cincuagésimo año de su muerte*, Universidad Nacional del Litoral, Santa Fé, 1938.

Gómez Haedo, Juan Carlos. "Sarmiento y el Uruguay," *Sarmiento y Avellaneda—el congreso de Belgrano*, Museo Histórico Sarmiento, Series II, no. 2, Buenos Aires, 1939.

González, Joaquín V. "Sarmiento," *Derechos del hombre*, Buenos Aires, September 1938.

Greca, Alcides. "Sarmiento periodista y maestro de la argentinidad," *Sarmiento, Homenaje en el cincuagésimo año de su muerte*," Santa Fé, 1938.

Hale, A. "Sarmiento and His Monument in Boston," *Bulletin of the Pan American Union*, Washington, 1914, XXXIX, 186-200. A discussion of Sarmiento's life, his works in the field of education, literature, and politics, and the proposed monument to him in Boston.

Heras, Carlos. "La última campaña política de Sarmiento," *Humanidades*, Universidad Nacional de la Plata, Buenos Aires, 1938, XXVI.

Howard, Jenni E. "La obra de las maestras norteamericanas," *El monitor de la educación común*, Buenos Aires, May 1931. This is an account of the work done by the North American teachers brought to Argentina by Sarmiento. The author is one of the more outstanding of them.

Ingenieros, José. "Las ideas sociológicas de Sarmiento," *Sociología argentina*, Buenos Aires, 1918.

Lavalle, E. Richard. "La juventud del prócer," *El Dia*, La Plata, September 11, 1944.

Leslie, J. K. "Problems Relating to Sarmiento's *Artículos críticos i literarios*," *Modern Language Notes*, LXI, 289-299, May 1946. This article discusses the accuracy of the editing of the first two volumes of the *Obras completas*. It deals with several articles that it holds were not Sarmiento's, and it points to mistakes and repetitions in the two volumes.

Levene, Ricardo. "Sarmiento, sociólogo de la realidad americana y argentina," *Humanidades*, Universidad Nacional de la Plata, Buenos Aires, 1938, XXVI.

Levene, Ricardo. "Significado del Museo Histórico Sarmiento," *Sarmiento y Avellaneda—el congreso de Belgrano*, Buenos Aires, 1939, pp. 11-16.

Márquez, Narciso. "La obsesión de Sarmiento," *Claridad*, Buenos Aires, September 1938, XVII, no. 329.

Marquez Miranda, Fernando. "Sarmiento y las "Ciencias del Hombre,'" *Humanidades*, Universidad Nacional de la Plata, Buenos Aires, 1938, XXVI.

Martínez, Teófilo. "Sarmiento," *Revista de derecho, historia y letras*, XXXI, 563.

Martínez Campos, Gabriel. "Sarmiento profeta," *Revista de derecho, historia ye letras*, XIII, 508.

Melfi, Domingo, "Montt y Sarmiento," *Atenea*, Concepción de Chile, 1937, XIV, 183-194.

Molina Téllez, Félix. "El fecundo temperamento de Sarmiento," *Claridad*, Buenos Aires, February 1938.

Moulia, Enrique. "El gorro de dormir de Sarmiento—un regalo significativo de Urquiza," *Atlántida*, Buenos Aires, April 1947, XXX, 38. This includes some Sarmiento-Urquiza correspondence that puts a new light on the relations between these two men when Sarmiento assumed the presidency.

Moulia, Enrique. "Las cartas de Urquiza a Sarmiento," *Aquí Está!* Buenos Aires, April 14, 1947, XII, 20-21. This also shows the attempt on the part of Urquiza to give his aid to the new presidential administration of Sarmiento.

Murua, P. Oscar. "Sarmiento: Ensayo de interpretación," *Sarmiento Homenaje en el cincuagésimo año de su muerte,* Santa Fé, 1938.

Muzzio, Enrique J. "Sarmiento y la Escuela Normal de Paraná," *Sarmiento, Homenaje en el cincuagésimo año de su muerte,* Santa Fé, 1938.

Nichols, Madaline Wallis. "A United States Tour by Sarmiento in 1847," *Hispanic American Historical Review,* Durham, May 1936, XVI, 190-212.

Noa, Frederic M. "Sarmiento: The Great South American Statesman and Educator," *The Arena,* Trenton, 1906, XXXVI, 390-395. Deals mainly with political activities.

Noé, Julio. "Sarmiento the traveler," *Inter-American,* English, IV, 1921, pp. 137-143. Hardly more than a review of the *Viajes.*

Normano, J. F. "Lost Monument: Sarmiento in Boston," *Hispanic American Historical Review,* Durham, May 1932, XII, 235-237. This article deals with the monument of Sarmiento that was proposed in Boston. The money was appropriated by the Argentine congress before World War I. The sculptor was chosen, but the monument was never completed.

Oría, José A. "Sarmiento costumbrista," *Humanidades,* Universidad Nacional de la Plata, Buenos Aires, 1938, XXVI.

Otero, José Pacífico. "Sarmiento," *Inter-America,* English: I, 1918. This article deals with such phases of Sarmiento's life as the political scene in Argentina just after the revolution. Otero describes the Rodin monument of Sarmiento in Buenos Aires.

Otero, José Pacifíco. "Sarmiento," *La reforma social,* X, 1918. Spanish version of article in *Inter-America.* Also appeared in *La revue de Paris* in February 1918.

Palcos, Alberto. "El epistolario inédito de Sarmiento," *La Prensa,* Buenos Aires, March 10, 1935. A discussion of the valuable unpublished letters of Sarmiento.

Palcos, Alberto. "La herencia de Sarmiento," *Humani-*

dades, Universidad Nacional de La Plata, Buenos Aires, 1938, XXVI.

Palcos, Alberto. "Sarmiento y la poesía," *La Prensa*, Buenos Aires, December 1, 1935.

Passadori, Josefina. "Creador de escuelas," *El Dia*, La Plata, September 11, 1938.

Peñaloza de Varese, Carmen. "Dos colegios de Santa Rosa," *Boletín de la Junta de Historia de la Provincia de San Juan*, San Juan, 1945, IV, no. 8, pp. 51-74. A description of the school founded by Sarmiento in 1839.

Pereira, Octavio Méndez. "Sarmiento y la educación popular," *Revista de las Indias*, Bogotá, November 1939, pp. 67-79.

Ramírez, Raúl. "Sarmiento y Chile," *Sarmiento y Avellaneda—el congreso de Belgrano*, Buenos Aires, 1939, pp. 23-38.

Rébora, Juan Carlos. "De Sarmiento a Horacio Mann," *El Dia*, La Plata, September 11, 1938.

Rébora, Juan Carlos. "Sarmiento, su figura de titán, a través de la doctrina del héroe civil y del genio constructor," *El Dia*, La Plata, February 15, 1911.

Reyes, César. "Sarmiento," *Revista de derecho, historia y letras*, LXIII, 333.

Salvadores, Antonino. "Sarmiento y la reorganización de la instrucción pública," *Humanidades*, Universidad Nacional de la Plata, Buenos Aires, 1938, XXVI.

Sánchez Viamonte, Carlos. "Sarmiento y la enseñanza laica," *Derechos del hombre*, Buenos Aires, September, 1938.

Solari, Juan Antonio. "Sarmiento, bandera de la civilidad argentina," *Derechos del hombre*, Buenos Aires, September, 1938.

Stewart, W., and French, W. M. "Influence of Horace Mann on the Educational Ideas of Domingo Faustino Sarmiento," *Hispanic American Historical Review*, Durham, February 1940, XX, 12-31.

"Teachers' Day Honors Sarmiento," *Education for Victory*, II, 26-27, April 20, 1944.

Towsend Ezcurra, Andrés. "Conducta americana de Sarmiento," *Claridad*, Buenos Aires, September 1938.

Tudela, Ricardo. "Meditaciones para un sentido integral

de Sarmiento," *Derechos del hombre,* Buenos Aires, September 1938.

Ucha, Antonio. "Sarmiento educator," *Sarmiento, Homenaje en el cincuagésimo año de su muerte,* Santa Fé, 1938.

Vedia y Mitre, M. de. "La figura de Sarmiento, *La Nación,* Buenos Aires, May 15, 1911.

Index

INDEX

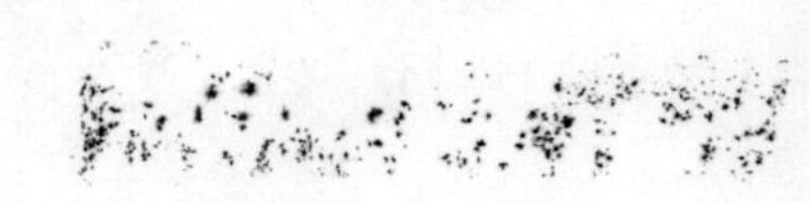